Given to Donald C. Sergee Ruth Thomson
by
Hubert Evans a dear friend
(and adapted brother) of our
(TOPLIS) family.
June 16, 1970

BIBLE TRUTH

By Oliver B. Greene

The Gospel Hour, Inc., Oliver B. Greene, Director
Box 2024, Greenville, South Carolina 29602

First Printing — April 1968 — 15,000
Second Printing — March 1969 — 15,000

$9.95

FOREWORD

In these days of confusion and uncertainty, when many have departed from the faith once delivered to the saints and much error is being taught in the name of "religion," the Lord has laid it on my heart to incorporate in brief outline the fundamental truths set forth in God's infallible Word as concerning the Holy Trinity and man's relationship to Father, Son, and Holy Spirit.

I say "brief" outline—for even in a volume of this size one could only touch the hem of the garment in setting forth *Bible Truth,* when all that *is,* all that has ever *been,* all that ever *will be* stands in relation *to* that truth.

It is my humble prayer that all who read this book may be led into closer communion with God, and into a better understanding of the meaning of "rightly dividing the Word of Truth."

—The Author

CONTENTS

BIBLE TRUTH

Chapter One

BIBLE TRUTH CONCERNING GOD

Before the first star traveled its course through the vastness of outer space, before the sun first threw its flood of light, energy, and warmth through space, before the great Milky Way appeared in the heavens, *God WAS!*

God is eternal—*without beginning.* He is above all course of time, He was (*and IS*) before all things. There has never *been* a time when God was not, there *will never BE* a time when God is not. God exists and works *in the eternal NOW:* "Lord, thou hast been our dwelling place in all generations. Before the mountains were brought forth, or ever thou hadst formed the earth and the world, even *from everlasting to everlasting, THOU ART GOD*" (Psalm 90:1,2).

God is infinite; man is finite. Therefore it is impossible for man to comprehend God—and I am exceedingly thankful for this great truth, for if man could understand God, then God would be no greater than man. I am so glad that the God whom I love and serve and in whom I trust is greater in power, love, and wisdom than any mortal!

God Is Spirit

"God is a Spirit: and they that worship Him must worship Him in spirit and in truth" (John 4:24).

9

In the Greek, the indefinite article *"a"* is not used. Therefore the verse simply reads, *"God is SPIRIT."* But what *is* "spirit"? We find the answer in the Gospel of Luke, where the risen Christ said to His disciples, "Behold my hands and my feet, that it is I myself: handle me, and see; *for a SPIRIT hath not flesh and bones,* as ye see me have" (Luke 24:39).

Jesus was in His resurrection body when He spoke these words. The disciples thought they were seeing His ghost; but He not only invited them to *touch* Him and be convinced that He was not a spirit—He also ate broiled fish and honeycomb in their presence (Luke 24:42,43).

To say that God is Spirit is to say that God is incorporeal and invisible. John tells us, *"No man* hath *seen* God at any time; the only begotten Son, which is in the bosom of the Father, *HE hath DECLARED Him"* (John 1:18). Jesus was God the Eternal Spirit *in flesh.* His Word plainly states "that *God was in Christ,* reconciling the world unto Himself" (II Cor. 5:19).

Note God's message to the children of Israel, given through Moses in Deuteronomy 4:15—18:

"Take ye therefore good heed unto yourselves; for *YE SAW NO MANNER OF SIMILITUDE on the day that the Lord spake unto you in Horeb out of the midst of the fire:* Lest ye corrupt yourselves, and make you a graven image, the similitude of any figure, the likeness of male or female, the likeness of any beast that is on the earth, the likeness of any winged fowl that flieth in the air, the likeness of any thing that creepeth on the ground, the likeness of any fish that is in the waters beneath the earth."

God *will not* tolerate idolatry. The first commandment thundered out on Mount Sinai was *"THOU SHALT HAVE NO OTHER GODS BEFORE ME! Thou shalt not make unto thee any graven image, or any likeness of any thing that is in heaven above, or that is in the earth beneath, or that is in the water under the earth. Thou shalt not bow down thyself to them, nor serve them: FOR I THE LORD THY GOD AM A JEALOUS GOD . . . !"* (Ex. 20:3—5).

Since *"God is Spirit,"* then in the light of Bible truth what is the meaning of Genesis 1:27? (*"So God created man in His own image, in the image of God created He him;* male and female created He them.") The Hebrew word translated *"image"* does not refer to *visible* (or bodily) *likeness,* but rather to intellectual and moral likeness—that is, in knowledge, in righteousness, in holiness.

In all of God's creation, *only* man is capable of having fellowship with God or living a righteous, holy life. Man is made in the image of God in that he is a trinity—body, soul, and spirit: "And the very God of peace *sanctify you WHOLLY;* and I pray God *your whole SPIRIT and SOUL and BODY be preserved blameless unto the coming of our Lord Jesus Christ"* (I Thess. 5:23).

The soul and spirit are not identical—they are divisible. In Hebrews 4:12 we read, ". . . *The Word of God is quick, and powerful, and sharper than any twoedged sword, piercing even to the DIVIDING ASUNDER OF SOUL AND SPIRIT, and of the joints and marrow, and is a discerner of the thoughts and intents of the heart."*

Man's soul and spirit are distinguished in the burial and resurrection of the body: "It is sown a *natural* body; it is raised a *spiritual* body" (I Cor. 15:44). To declare that there is no difference between the soul and spirit of man is to declare that there is no difference between the mortal body and the glorified body we will receive when we see Jesus: "Beloved, now are we the sons of God, and it doth not yet appear what we shall be: but *we know that, when He shall appear, WE SHALL BE LIKE HIM;* for we shall see Him as He is" (I John 3:2).

The spirit is the part of man which *knows:* "For what man knoweth the things of a man, save *the spirit of man* which is in him? even so the things of God knoweth no man, but *the Spirit of God*" (I Cor. 2:11). It is because of his spirit that man is capable of being God-conscious, and it is through his spirit that man can communicate with God: "There is a spirit in man: and the inspiration of the Almighty giveth them understanding" (Job 32:8).

The soul of man is the seat of man's emotions—affection, love, hate, etc. In the Garden of Gethsemane Jesus said, *"My SOUL is exceeding sorrowful, even unto death"* (Matt. 26:38). When He stood at the tomb of Lazarus, *"He groaned in the SPIRIT, and was TROUBLED"* (John 11:33). In Gethsemane, loving a world of sinners, He was facing demons and all the evil hell could hurl at Him as He fought the battle to overcome principalities and powers and purchase our redemption through His shed blood. Therefore He suffered not only in spirit, but *His soul* was about to die.

The soul of man is capable of loving God with deep affection—affection which will cause man to think on things above rather than on things of earth. The Apostle Paul counseled the Colossian believers, "If ye then be risen with Christ, seek those things which are above, where Christ sitteth on the right hand of God. Set your affection on things above, not on things on the earth" (Col. 3:1,2).

The *body* of man is the tabernacle (the house) in which the soul and spirit dwell: "For we know that if our earthly house of this tabernacle were dissolved, we have a building of God, an house not made with hands, eternal in the heavens. For in this we groan, earnestly desiring to be clothed upon with our house

EMOTION -controlled
By spirit which is
of God

which is from heaven: If so be that being clothed we shall not be found naked. For we that are in this tabernacle do groan, being burdened: not for that we would be unclothed, but clothed upon, that mortality might be swallowed up of life.

"Now He that hath wrought us for the selfsame thing is God, who also hath given unto us the earnest of the Spirit. Therefore we are always confident, knowing that, whilst we are at home in the body, we are absent from the Lord: (for we walk by faith, not by sight:) We are confident, I say, and willing rather to be absent from the body, and to be present with the Lord" (II Cor. 5:1—8).

God created Adam from *"the dust of the ground,"* and breathed into his nostrils the breath of life" (Gen. 2:7); but we also know that Adam was created in the image of God—body, soul, and spirit. There is a *possibility* that *in his innocent state* he resembled God in bodily stature, but if that be true he certainly lost that glorious appearance when he sinned! I personally believe that Adam and Eve, in their original state, were clothed in Shekinah glory; but when they sinned, the glory departed and they saw their nakedness. However, the deeper meaning of the statement that God created man *"in His own image"* does not have reference to *bodily* likeness, but to soul, spirit, and body—the ability to commune with God and fellowship with Him.

Several passages in the epistles of the Apostle Paul shed light on this subject:

In Colossians 1:15 he tells us that *Christ "is the image of the INVISIBLE GOD."*

In I Timothy 1:17 he wrote, "Now *unto the King eternal, immortal, INVISIBLE, the only wise God,* be honour and glory for ever and ever. Amen."

In Colossians 3:9, 10 he tells us that we have "put off the old man with his deeds; and have put on *the*

new man, which is renewed in knowledge AFTER
THE IMAGE of Him that created him."

In Ephesians 4:23, 24 we read, "Be renewed in the
spirit of your mind . . . that ye put on the new man,
which AFTER GOD IS CREATED in righteousness
and true holiness."

God is SPIRIT—but does that mean that He does
not have a body or that He has never been visible?
Again we will let the Word of God answer:

Concerning the baptism of Jesus, we read, "And
John bare record, saying, *I saw the Spirit descending
from heaven LIKE A DOVE, and it abode upon Him*"
(John 1:32).

Matthew testifies, "And Jesus, when He was baptized, went up straightway out of the water: and, lo,
the heavens were opened unto him, and *he saw the
Spirit of God descending LIKE A DOVE*, and lighting
upon Him: and lo a voice from heaven, saying, This
is my beloved Son, in whom I am well pleased" (Matt.
3:16, 17).

Then in Hebrews 1:7 we read, "And of the angels
He saith, *Who maketh His angels SPIRITS*, and His
ministers a flame of fire."

These passages tell us that the Spirit of God descended "like (or *in the form of*) a dove" and abode
on the Lord Jesus Christ when He was baptized. *Angels* are "ministering spirits" (Heb. 1:14), and certainly
angels have bodies. The Scriptures speak of God's
hands, His feet, His arms, His eyes. Yes indeed our
God has a body. He has manifested Himself *in visible
form:*

"Then went up Moses, and Aaron, Nadab, and
Abihu, and seventy of the elders of Israel: *and they
saw the God of Israel:* and there was under His feet
as it were a paved work of a sapphire stone, and as
it were the body of heaven in His clearness" (Ex.
24:9, 10).

Now what did Moses, Aaron, and the seventy elders *really see* when they "saw the God of Israel"? John 1:18 plainly declares, *"NO MAN hath seen God at any time;* the only begotten Son, which is in the bosom of the Father, He hath *declared* Him." Is there a contradiction here?

Also, in Exodus 33:18−23 we are told that Moses asked of God, "I beseech thee, *shew me thy glory."* But Jehovah replied, *"Thou canst not see MY FACE: for there shall no man see me, and live!"* God then told Moses, "Behold, there is a place by me, and thou shalt stand upon a rock: And it shall come to pass, while my glory passeth by, that I will put thee in a clift of the rock, *and will cover thee with my hand while I pass by: and I will take away mine hand, and thou shalt see my back parts: BUT MY FACE SHALL NOT BE SEEN!"*

This, too, seems like a contradiction to Exodus 24:9, 10−but not so. It is true that "no man hath seen God at any time," for *no mortal* could look into *the face of Jehovah God* and live! It is when we receive our glorified bodies in the resurrection morning that we will see God and dwell with Him forever. Moses, Aaron, and the elders did not see God Himself−that is, they did not see *God's invisible essence.* They saw a *manifestation* of God. 6 / 17 / 7?

JESUS *was God in flesh*−"the Word was made flesh, and dwelt among us" (John 1:14). Jesus was very man, made like unto His brethren in all things, sin apart; but He was also very God (II Cor. 5:19; John 10:30). So there is no contradiction between the Scriptures where Moses, Aaron and the elders saw the God of Israel and John's declaration that no man has seen God at any time.

Let us use a simple illustration: When we look into a mirror we see our likeness. Therefore it is true to say, *"I saw my face."* But it is equally true to

say, "I *did not* see my face," because what we see
in a mirror is only a *reflection*. Moses and the men
who were with him saw a *manifestation* of God, therefore it is true and correct to say that *they saw God*.
But it is also true and correct to say that *no man has
ever seen God* as He is in His invisible essence. The
statement of John the Beloved does not contradict the
statement from the Old Testament.

During the Old Testament era God appeared on
various occasions as *"the Angel of the Lord."* (There
is a definite distinction between *"AN* angel of the
Lord" and *"THE Angel of the Lord."*) In Genesis
16:7—10 we read, "And *THE Angel of the Lord* found
(Hagar) by a fountain of water in the wilderness, by
the fountain in the way to Shur. And He said, Hagar,
Sarai's maid, whence camest thou? and whither wilt
thou go? And she said, I flee from the face of my
mistress Sarai. And *THE Angel of the Lord* said unto
her, Return to thy mistress, and submit thyself under
hands. And *THE Angel of the Lord* said unto her, I
will multiply thy seed exceedingly, that it shall not
be numbered for multitude."

Then in verse 13 of that chapter we read, *"And
she called the name of THE LORD THAT SPAKE
UNTO HER, Thou God seest me:* for she said, Have
I also here looked after Him that seeth me?"

In this passage, verse 13 definitely identifies "the
Angel of God" with Jehovah. This is also true in
Genesis 21:17,18: "And God heard the voice of the
lad; and *THE Angel of God* called to Hagar out of
heaven, and said unto her, What aileth thee, Hagar?
fear not; for God hath heard the voice of the lad where
he is. Arise, lift up the lad, and hold him in thine
hand; for I will make him a great nation."

When Abraham would have offered Isaac in response to God's command, *"THE ANGEL OF THE
LORD called unto him out of heaven,* and said, Abra-

ham, Abraham: and he said, Here am I. And He said, Lay not thine hand upon the lad, neither do thou any thing unto him: for now I know that thou fearest GOD, seeing thou hast not withheld thy son, thine only son from ME" (Gen. 22:11, 12). In verse 12, "the Angel of the Lord" is definitely identified with Jehovah God. YEILDING CHILDREN TO GOD:

In Genesis chapter 18 we find a remarkable passage concerning God's appearing as "THE Angel of the Lord":

"And the Lord appeared unto (Abraham) in the plains of Mamre: and he sat in the tent door in the heat of the day; and he lift up his eyes, and looked, and, lo, three men stood by him: and when he saw them, he ran to meet them from the tent door, and bowed himself toward the ground, and said, *My Lord, if now I have found favour in thy sight, pass not away, I pray thee, from thy servant* . . . And they said unto him, Where is Sarah thy wife? And he said, Behold, in the tent. And He said, I will certainly return unto thee according to the time of life, and, lo, Sarah thy wife shall have a son. And Sarah heard it in the tent door, which was behind him. . . . And the Lord said unto Abraham, Wherefore did Sarah laugh, saying, Shall I of a surety bear a child, which am old?

"Is any thing too hard for the Lord? At the time appointed I will return unto thee, according to the time of life, and Sarah shall have a son. . . . And the men rose up from thence, and looked toward Sodom: and Abraham went with them to bring them on the way."

The passages just quoted are exerpts from Genesis 18:1—16. Three angelic beings appeared to Abraham, and *one* of the three clearly identified Himself with God. Then going on into Genesis 19:1 we read, *"And there came TWO angels to Sodom at even;* and Lot sat in the gate of Sodom: and Lot seeing them rose up to meet them; and he bowed himself with his face toward the ground." Notice that *only TWO angels* traveled to Sodom and appeared to Lot. *ONE remained behind,* and that one is identified in verses 17—22 of chapter 18:

"And *THE LORD said,* Shall I hide from Abraham that thing which I do; seeing that Abraham shall surely become a great and mighty nation, and all the nations of the earth shall be blessed in him? For I know him, that he will command his children and his household after him, and they shall keep the way of the Lord, to do justice and judgment; that the Lord may bring upon Abraham that which He hath spoken of him. *And THE LORD said,* Because the cry of Sodom and Gomorrah is great, and because their sin is very grievous; I will go down now, and see whether they have done altogether according to the cry of it, which is come unto me; and if not, I will know. And the men turned their faces from thence, and went toward Sodom: *but Abraham stood yet BEFORE THE LORD.*"

Yes, one of the three heavenly beings who appeared to Abraham was none other than Jehovah God manifested in the form of a man. This is further shown in verse 33 of chapter 18 where we read, "*And the LORD went His way,* as soon as He had left communing with Abraham . . . ."

"*THE Angel of the Lord*" was a visible manifestation of Jehovah God. In Judges 13:18 we read, "The Angel of the Lord said unto him, *Why askest thou thus after my name, seeing it is SECRET?*" The Hebrew word here translated "*secret*" could have been rendered "*WONDERFUL.*" The Amplified Bible translates it "Wonderful" and gives Isaiah 9:6 in connection with it: ". . . *His name shall be called WONDERFUL, Counsellor, The mighty God, The everlasting*

Father, The Prince of Peace."

Personally, I believe the Angel of the Lord in the Old Testament era was none other than the Son of God before His Incarnation. *"The Angel of the Lord"* does not appear in the Greek language in Scripture after the birth of the Lord Jesus Christ. It is true that the statement appears in the *Authorized Version* of the Bible, but it is not found in the *original* Greek after the Incarnation.

The Trinity

The Scriptures clearly teach the doctrine of the Trinity—not *three Gods*, but *ONE God manifested in THREE Persons:* Father, Son, and Holy Spirit. The unity of God is clearly taught throughout the Scriptures:

"Unto thee it was shewed, that thou mightest know that the Lord He is God; *there is none else beside Him"* (Deut. 4:35).

"Hear, O Israel: *The Lord our God is ONE Lord"* (Deut. 6:4).

"Ye are my witnesses, saith the Lord, and my servant whom I have chosen: that ye may know and believe me, and understand that I am He: *before me there was no God formed, neither shall there be after me"* (Isa. 43:10).

"Thus saith the Lord the King of Israel, and his Redeemer the Lord of hosts: *I am the first, and I am the last; AND BESIDE ME THERE IS NO GOD"* (Isa. 44:6).

"I am the Lord, and *there is none else, THERE IS NO GOD BESIDE ME . . .* For thus saith the Lord that created the heavens; God Himself that formed the earth and made it; He hath established it, He created it not in vain, He formed it to be inhabited: *I AM THE LORD; AND THERE IS NONE ELSE"* (Isa. 45:5, 18).

"Jesus said unto him, Why callest thou me good? *There is none good but ONE, that is, GOD*" (Mark 10:18).

"Jesus answered him, The first of all the commandments is, Hear, O Israel: *The Lord our God is ONE LORD*" (Mark 12:29).

The Hebrew word translated *"one"* denotes *compound unity*—for example, when God gave Eve to Adam to be his wife He said, "Therefore shall a man leave his father and his mother, and shall cleave unto his wife: *and THEY shall be ONE FLESH*" (Gen. 2:24). Adam and Eve were distinctly *two persons*, yet God declared them *"one flesh."* SEX - ACCEPTANCE

In Genesis 11:6 "the Lord said, *Behold, the people is ONE,* and they have all one language; and this they begin to do: and now nothing will be restrained from them, which they have imagined to do." In this instance there were thousands of people in the company of which God spoke, but *He declared them to be ONE*—one in language, one in thought, one in mission. Therefore God confused their tongues and scattered them across the face of the earth.

We find a similar word in the Greek language. Writing to the believers in Corinth the Apostle Paul said, "I have planted, Apollos watered; but God gave the increase. So then neither is he that planteth any thing, neither he that watereth; but God that giveth the increase. *Now he that planteth and he that watereth are ONE:* and every man shall receive his own reward according to his own labour" (I Cor. 3:6—8). Here under inspiration Paul declared that one person *plants the seed*, another person *waters* the planting, yet *both of those persons are ONE*—and this is true: *we are all ONE IN CHRIST.* For example, *I preach the Gospel*—by means of radio, in meetings, and through the printed page. Thousands of my listeners *support my ministry* with their gifts and by distributing

[handwritten: OBEYING GODS WILL EVEN WHEN WE DO NOT UNDERSTAND]

my literature. Thus, although we are literally *thousands* in number, *we are ONE in ministry.*

The Scripture further declares, *"For as the body is ONE, and hath many members, and all the members of that one body, being many, are ONE BODY: so also is Christ. For by ONE SPIRIT are we all baptized into ONE BODY,* whether we be Jews or Gentiles, whether we be bond or free; and have been all made to drink into *ONE Spirit"* (I Cor. 12:12, 13). Here the Holy Spirit is speaking of the New Testament Church, the body of Christ. *All members of that body are ONE.*

In Christ's prayer of intercession He prayed for believers, *"That they all may be ONE; as thou, Father, art in me, and I in thee, that they also may be ONE in us:* that the world may believe that thou hast sent me. And the glory which thou gavest me I have given them; *that they may be ONE, even as WE are ONE"* (John 17:21, 22). Notice the compound unity here in the words of Jesus: *". . . even as WE* (plural) *are ONE* (singular)."

To the Galatian Christians Paul wrote, "There is neither Jew nor Greek, there is neither bond nor free, there is neither male nor female: *for ye are all ONE IN CHRIST JESUS"* (Gal. 3:28).

In the Old Testament the word used most often for "God" is *plural,* and the very first sentence in Genesis declares both the unity and the Trinity of God. The *Trinity* is clearly set forth in the fact that the name *Elohim* (God) is plural. (In the Hebrew this word is at least threefold.)

The *unity* of God is suggested in the verb *"created"* (which in the Hebrew is singular). Thus it is definitely declared that God is both *three—and ONE.*

The same truth is seen in Genesis 1:26, 27: "And *God* (plural) said, Let *us* (plural) make man in *our* (plural) image . . . So *God* (plural) created man in

His (singular) own image, in the image of *God* (plural) created *He* (singular) him . . . ." In these two verses the Trinity is clearly taught—*ONE God, manifested in THREE Persons.*

Anyone who wants to know the truth about the Godhead can clearly *discover* that truth in the record of the *baptism* of Jesus, recorded in Matthew 3:13—17:

"Then cometh Jesus from Galilee to Jordan unto John, to be baptized of him. But John forbad Him, saying, I have need to be baptized of thee, and comest thou to me? And Jesus answering said unto him, Suffer it to be so now: for thus it becometh us to fulfil all righteousness. Then he suffered Him.

"*And JESUS, when He was baptized, went up straightway out of the water: and, lo, the heavens were opened unto him, and he saw the SPIRIT OF GOD descending like a dove, and lighting upon Him: and lo A VOICE FROM HEAVEN, saying, This is my beloved Son, in whom I am well pleased!*"

Beloved, here is the Trinity, *plainly declared*: Jesus standing in the waters of Jordan, *the Holy Spirit* descending like a dove and remaining upon Him, and *God the Father* speaking from heaven, declaring, "This is my beloved Son, in whom I am well pleased!" Yes, at the baptism of Jesus *the Godhead was present*—Father, Son, and Holy Spirit. There is but one God, but He makes Himself known to us as Father, Son, and Holy Spirit—three separate Personalities.

In *duration*, God is "*the EVERLASTING God*" (Gen. 21:33).

In *power*, He is "*the ALMIGHTY God*" (Gen. 17:1).

In *exclusiveness*, He is "*a CONSUMING FIRE*" (Deut. 4:24; Heb. 12:29).

In *pity*, He is "*a MERCIFUL God*" (Deut. 4:31).

In *fidelity*, He is "*the FAITHFUL God*" (Deut. 7:9).

In *vitality*, He is "*the LIVING God*" (Josh. 3:10).

In *greatness,* He is *"the GREAT AND TERRIBLE God"* (Neh. 1:5).

In tender *compassion,* He is *"a GRACIOUS God"* (Jonah 4:2).

In *independence,* He is *"I AM THAT I AM"* (Ex. 3:14).

It is interesting that in the Old Testament, *"Jehovah"* is usually printed *LORD* (in small capitals) and it occurs almost seven thousand times in Old Testament Scripture. The deep meaning of the Hebrew word translated "LORD" speaks of Him who *always WAS,* who *IS,* and who *ever SHALL BE.* In Revelation 1:4 John the Beloved wrote "to the seven churches which are in Asia: Grace be unto you, and peace, *from Him which IS, and which WAS, and which IS TO COME;* and from the seven Spirits which are before His throne."

In Malachi 3:6 God thundered out, *"I am the LORD* (Jehovah)!" Then He explained what *"Jehovah"* means: *"I change not."* Then He gave the application: *"Therefore* ye sons of Jacob *are not consumed!"*

Since Jehovah God is what He is, He cannot do other than He does. The nature and character of God make it impossible for Him to do wrong; all things performed by Him are righteous and right.

In the Psalms we read over and over again, *"Jehovah IS . . . ,"* and many times this is linked with the believer's faith:

He is *the ROCK* on which the believer rests (Psalm 18:2).

He is *the DEFENCE* in which the believer hides (Psalm 94:22).

He is *the KEEPER,* the *garrison* through which the believer is preserved (Psalm 121:5).

He is *the SHIELD* behind which the believer is protected (Psalm 28:7).

He is *the DELIVERANCE* by which the believer

WHICH IS   WHICH WAS   WHICH SHALL BE

is saved (Psalm 27:1).

He is *the SHADE* by which the believer is refreshed (Psalm 121:5).

Since our God is what He is and since He has done all that He has done for us, in the words of the Apostle Paul, *"What shall we then say to these things? IF GOD BE FOR US, WHO CAN BE AGAINST US?"* (Rom. 8:31). Then as believers we come to the conclusion of faith expressed by the Psalmist:

Trust in Jehovah (Psalm 37:3). He supplies all our needs.

Delight in Jehovah (Psalm 37:4). He is able to fulfill all our desires.

Commit thy way unto Jehovah (Psalm 37:5). He is able to accomplish exceeding and abundantly above anything we can think or ask.

Rest in Jehovah (Psalm 37:7). He takes care of His own, He is the Shepherd of the sheep, He will never leave us nor forsake us.

Wait on Jehovah (Psalm 37:34). He bestows all blessings. Every good and perfect gift comes from Him.

Jehovah rewards all who look to Him, all who trust in Him; but only as we trust in Him can we hope to become recipients of His saving grace and His keeping power. Study *all* of this wonderful thirty-seventh Psalm. The milk, bread, and meat of the Word found here will nourish and strengthen the inner man!

God Immutable

God is unchanging. His character, His purpose, and His counsel have always been the same and will be forever the same:

"For I am the Lord, *I change not . . ."* (Mal. 3:6).

"And also *the Strength of Israel will not lie nor repent:* for He is not a man, that He should repent"

(I Sam. 15:29).

"God is not a man, that He should lie; neither the son of man, that He should repent: Hath He *said,* and shall He not *do it?* or hath He *spoken,* and shall He not *make it good?"* (Num. 23:19).

"Wherein God, willing more abundantly to shew unto the heirs of promise *THE IMMUTABILITY of His counsel,* confirmed it by an oath" (Heb. 6:17).

"*Every good gift and every perfect gift is from above, and cometh down from the Father of lights, with whom is NO VARIABLENESS, NEITHER SHADOW OF TURNING"* (James 1:17).

Some people use Genesis 6:6 as a contradiction to these passages, but this is wrongly dividing the Word of God. It is true that the Scripture states, "It repented the Lord that He had made man on the earth, and it grieved Him at His heart," but that does not necessarily imply that God wished He had never created Adam! It simply means that *the wickedness of the SONS of Adam* grieved the heart of God—and rightly so because of God's character. Many times, little children do things that bring grief to the heart of their parents; but the *right kind* of parents do not want to *annihilate* their child because of the child's disobedience!

The wickedness of man in Noah's day was so great that God was grieved in His heart, and He turned from His creative dealings with man to sending destroying judgment upon him—which was necessary because of the very character of God. But *GOD did not change: MAN changed!* And man's sins demanded that the unchangeable, holy God *destroy man* from the face of the earth.

Enemies of the Bible also point to Jonah 3:10: "And God saw their works, that they turned from their evil way; and *God repented of the evil that He had said He would do unto them; and He did it not."* The

God - Creative dealing - "Christ in us the hope of glory!"

statement here that God "repented" does not mean
that He changed in character. God hates sin today
just as He has always hated sin—but this passage
from Jonah follows the declaration that the people of
Nineveh "believed God," they turned from their evil
ways, and because of the change in attitude of the
people, *God spared the city.*

Because of the character and nature of God, His
attitude toward sin and toward righteousness is unchangeable, but *when sinners repent of their sin* they
are no longer under the wrath of God and He saves
them for Jesus' sake. God's *dealings* with men change
as men change—that is, when a sinner sincerely re-
pents, God forgives the sinner, delivers him from "the
power of darkness," and translates him "into the
kingdom of His dear Son" (Col. 1:13).

The Personality of God

We have already discussed the fact that *God is
Spirit*—but He is also a *Person.* He is THE LIVING
GOD:

"The Lord is *the true God,* He is *the living God,*
and an everlasting King: at His wrath the earth shall
tremble, and the nations shall not be able to abide
His indignation. Thus shall ye say unto them, The
gods that have not made the heavens and the earth,
even they shall perish from the earth, and from under
these heavens.

"He hath made the earth by His power, He hath
established the world by His wisdom, and hath
stretched out the heavens by His discretion. When
He uttereth His voice, there is a multitude of waters
in the heavens, and He causeth the vapours to ascend
from the ends of the earth; He maketh lightnings with
rain, and bringeth forth the wind out of His treasures.

"Every man is brutish in his knowledge: every

founder is confounded by the graven image: for his molten image is falsehood, and there is no breath in them. They are vanity, and the work of errors: in the time of their visitation they shall perish. The portion of Jacob is not like them: for He is the former of all things; and Israel is the rod of His inheritance: *The Lord of hosts is His name"* (Jer. 10:10—16).

If you will read the first nine verses of this chapter from Jeremiah you will see that the prophet distinguishes between the one true God and idols. He makes it clear that idols are dead *things*—they are not personalities. They cannot move (v. 4); they cannot speak (v. 5); they must be carried about "because they cannot go." They cannot do evil—but neither can they do good (v. 5). They have done no creative work and "they shall perish from the earth" (v. 11).

But Jehovah is *"The TRUE God . . . The LIVING God . . . an Everlasting King."*

When Paul and Barnabas healed the impotent man at Lystra, the people cried out, "The gods are come down to us in the likeness of men!" and would have offered sacrifice to them. But Paul and Barnabas said, "Sirs, why do ye these things? We also are men of like passions with you, and *preach* unto you that ye should *turn from these vanities unto THE LIVING GOD, which made heaven, and earth, and the sea, and all things that are therein"* (Acts 14:8—15).

In I Thessalonians 1:9 the Apostle Paul speaks of the believers in Thessalonica having *"turned to God from idols to serve the LIVING and TRUE GOD."*

Psalm 94:9, 10 asks, "He that *planted the ear* shall He not *hear*? He that *formed the eye,* shall He not *see*? He that chastiseth the heathen, shall not He correct? He that teacheth man knowledge, shall not He *know*?"

Many, many other passages in the Word of God clearly teach that God is a *LIVING God*—He hears;

Created = Creative.   / GOD'S -EAR = OUR EAR
GODS - EYE   " EYE
GODS KNOWLEDGE - OUR KNOW.

He sees, He feels, He knows, He wills, He acts. God is a Person, He is eternal; and in the Word of God He is clearly distinguished from idols—dead things fashioned by the hands of man. They *hear not,* they *see* not, they *know* not, they *feel* not, and *they act not.*

In his epistles, the Apostle Paul describes God in various terms:

In Romans 1:23 He is "the *uncorruptible* God."

In Romans 16:26 He is "the *everlasting* God" in revelation.

In Colossians 1:15 He is "the *invisible* God" in the Person of Jesus Christ.

In I Thessalonians 1:9 He is "the *living* God" in power and "the *true* God" in manifestation.

In I Timothy 1:11 He is "the *blessed* God" in grace.

In Titus 2:13 He is "the *great* God" in splendor.

God is *all of these attributes* in character. *He IS a great God*—and certainly He is a very busy God; but He is not too great and He is never too busy to see and meet the need of one of His children! We see an example of this in the life of Daniel. Because Daniel purposed in his heart that he would not compromise with the gods of Babylon, he would not defile himself with the king's meat and wine, God delivered His prophet from harm when he was cast into the lions' den. So impressed was the king of Babylon with the testimony of Daniel that he then issued a decree:

"That in every dominion of my kingdom men tremble and fear before the God of Daniel: for *HE IS THE LIVING GOD, and stedfast for ever,* and His kingdom that which shall not be destroyed, and His dominion shall be even unto the end. He delivereth and rescueth, and He worketh signs and wonders in heaven and in earth, who hath delivered Daniel

from the power of the lions" (Dan. 6:26, 27). Read the
entire sixth chapter of Daniel for a complete account
of the prophet's steadfastness and deliverance.

The mercy of God rests upon all who trust in Him,
but His wrath abides on all who reject Him: *"He
that believeth on the Son hath everlasting life: and
he that BELIEVETH NOT THE SON shall not see
life; but the wrath of God abideth on him"* (John
3:36).

In Hebrews 10:28—31 we read of God's dealing with
those who reject His only begotten Son:

"He that despised *Moses' law* died *without mercy*
under two or three witnesses: *Of how MUCH SORER
PUNISHMENT, suppose ye, shall he be thought worthy, who hath trodden under foot THE SON OF GOD,*
and hath counted the blood of the covenant, wherewith
he was sanctified, an unholy thing, and hath done
despite unto the Spirit of grace?

"For we know Him that hath said, *VENGEANCE
BELONGETH UNTO ME, I WILL RECOMPENSE,
saith the Lord. And again, The Lord shall judge His
people. IT IS A FEARFUL THING TO FALL INTO
THE HANDS OF THE LIVING GOD!"*

God has a personal interest and an active hand in
all the affairs of men—"Behold, He that keepeth Israel
shall neither slumber nor sleep" (Psalm 121:4). God
sees all men, He knows the actions of all men. He
makes a path for His own and leads them in the path
of right living. He delivers those who trust Him, He
saves all who commit themselves to Him—*but He
punishes the wicked:*

"See now that *I, even I, am He, and there is no
god with me. I kill, and I make alive; I wound, and
I heal: neither is there any that can deliver out of
my hand.* For I lift up my hand to heaven, and say,
I LIVE FOR EVER. If I whet my glittering sword,
and mine hand take hold on judgment; *I will render*

*vengeance to mine enemies, and will reward them
that hate me!* I will make mine arrows drunk with
blood, and my sword shall devour flesh; and that with
the blood of the slain and of the captives, from the
beginning of revenges upon the enemy" (Deut. 32:
39—42).

These words were penned by Moses, under in-
spiration; and in the next verse he declared in simple,
understandable words, "Rejoice, O ye nations, with
His people: *FOR HE WILL AVENGE THE BLOOD
OF HIS SERVANTS, AND WILL RENL ER VENGE-
ANCE TO HIS ADVERSARIES, AND WILL BE MER-
CIFUL UNTO HIS LAND, AND TO HIS PEOPLE!"*

un LIMITED
POWER

God Is Omnipotent

ALL
POWERFUL

In Psalm 19 David wrote, "The heavens declare
the glory of God; and the firmament sheweth His
handywork. Day unto day uttereth speech, and night
unto night sheweth knowledge" (Psalm 19:1,2).

David also wrote that *only a fool would say,
"There IS no God!"* (Psalm 14:1; 53:1). Any person of
sound mentality, looking into the sky on a starry night,
must admit that this universe did not just "happen."
The earth—yea, *the entire universe—*is the product of
a Master mind, the result of the performance of One
who is all-powerful.

God is omnipotent—He can do all things. Nothing
is too hard for God.

In the first verse of Genesis we read, *"In the be-
ginning . . . GOD . . . ."* Beside this verse in my
Bible I have written, "I have no trouble believing any-
thing God has said." *I believe Genesis 1:1—*therefore
I have no difficulty believing anything else I find in
God's Word.

Job said to the Lord, *"I know that thou canst do
EVERY THING, and that no thought can be with-*

ALPHA-OMEGA

holden from thee" (Job 42:2).

When Jesus said to His disciples, "It is easier for a camel to go through the eye of a needle, than for a rich man to enter into the kingdom of God," the disciples asked Him, "Who then can be *saved?"* Jesus replied, "With men this is impossible; but *with God ALL THINGS are possible!"* (Matt. 19:24—26).

When God brought order out of chaos He said, *"Let there be light—AND THERE WAS LIGHT"* (Gen. 1:3). All God need do is speak—and whatever He speaks *happens.*

In Psalm 33:6—9 we read, *"By the WORD of the Lord were the heavens made; and all the host of them by the breath of His mouth.* He gathereth the waters of the sea together as an heap: He layeth up the depth in storehouses. Let all the earth fear the Lord: Let all the inhabitants of the world stand in awe of Him. *FOR HE SPAKE, AND IT WAS DONE; HE COMMANDED, AND IT STOOD FAST."*

John the Beloved wrote, *"In the beginning was the WORD, and the Word was with God, and the Word WAS GOD.* The same was in the beginning with God. *All things were MADE BY HIM;* and without Him was not any thing made that was made" (John 1:1—3). WE ARE NOTHING - OF OUR SELVES! AWESOME.

The Apostle Paul adds, "God, who at sundry times and in divers manners *spake* in time past unto the fathers *by the prophets,* hath in these last days *spoken unto us by His Son,* whom He hath appointed heir of all things, *BY WHOM ALSO HE MADE THE WORLDS:* who being the brightness of His glory, and the express image of His person, and *upholding all things BY THE WORD OF HIS POWER,* when He had by Himself purged our sins, sat down on the right hand of the Majesty on high" (Heb. 1:1—3).

In Psalm 107:25—29, David tells us that *God commands,* "and raiseth the stormy wind, which lifteth

ABSENT from self - Present WITH THE LORD.

up the waves thereof. They mount up to the heaven,
they go down again to the depths: their soul is melted
because of trouble. They reel to and fro, and stagger
like a drunken man, and are at their wit's end.

*"Then they cry unto the Lord in their trouble, and
He bringeth them out of their distresses. He maketh
the storm a calm, so that the waves thereof are still."*

The Prophet Nahum penned these enlightening
words concerning our God:

*"God is JEALOUS, and the Lord revengeth; the
Lord revengeth, and is furious; the Lord will take
vengeance on His adversaries, and He reserveth wrath
for His enemies.* The Lord is slow to anger, and great
in power, and will not at all acquit the wicked: the
Lord hath His way in the whirlwind and in the storm,
and the clouds are the dust of His feet. He rebuketh
the sea, and maketh it dry, and drieth up all the
rivers . . . The mountains quake at Him, and the hills
melt, and the earth is burned at His presence, yea,
the world, and all that dwell therein.

*"Who can stand before His indignation? and who
can abide in the fierceness of His anger? His fury is
poured out like fire, and the rocks are thrown down by
Him. The Lord is good, a strong hold in the day of
trouble; and He knoweth them that trust in Him. But
WITH AN OVERRUNNING FLOOD He will make
an utter end of the place thereof, and DARKNESS
SHALL PURSUE HIS ENEMIES"* (Nah. 1:2—8).

The character of God makes Him not only *"slow
to anger"* and *a "stronghold"* to those who trust Him,
but He also cannot—and *will not—"ACQUIT THE
WICKED."* God is just; and—through the finished
work of the Lord Jesus Christ—He is the Justifier of
all who *believe* in Jesus. He set forth His only begotten Son to be a propitiation for sin and to declare
God's righteousness, "that He might be just, and the
Justifier of him which believeth in Jesus" (Rom. 3:25,26).

Jesus came not to destroy the law, but to fulfill *every jot and tittle of the law* (Matt. 5:17, 18); and just before He went to the cross He declared to His heavenly Father, *"This is life eternal, that they might know thee the only TRUE GOD, and Jesus Christ, whom thou hast sent. I have glorified thee on the earth: I have finished the work which thou gavest me to do"* (John 17:3, 4). AM I ABLE TO SAY THIS?

James gives this solemn warning: *"There is one lawgiver, who is able to save and to destroy: who art thou that judgest another? Go to now, ye that say, To day or to morrow we will go into such a city, and continue there a year, and buy and sell, and get gain: Whereas ye know not what shall be on the morrow. For what is your life? It is even a vapour, that appeareth for a little time, and then vanisheth away. For that ye ought to say, IF THE LORD WILL, we shall live, and do this, or that"* (James 4:12—15). ARE YOU OH LORD! THE WILL

Everything that is necessary to life on this earth— even the air we breathe—comes to us as a gift from God, and every person *on* this earth (even the unbeliever) should bow his head and *thank God* for life! It is God who gives that which makes life possible, and He can *take away* life. His Word gives warning, *"Boast not thyself of to morrow; for thou knowest not what a day may bring forth"* (Prov. 27:1).

God is omnipotent, but His omnipotence is limited by His all-wise, holy, and loving will. *He can do ALL things—*or *anything;* but because of His character *He WILL NOT do anything that is not right.* Whatever He does *is righteous* and will bring glory and honor to His name throughout eternity.

God cannot acquit the wicked, but this fact does not limit His power: *"Behold, the Lord's hand is not shortened, that it cannot save; neither His ear heavy, that it cannot hear: BUT YOUR INIQUITIES HAVE SEPARATED BETWEEN YOU AND YOUR GOD,*

*AND YOUR SINS HAVE HID HIS FACE FROM
YOU, THAT HE WILL NOT HEAR"* (Isa. 59:1, 2).

The Lord is *able* to save, He is *powerful* to save;
but men who live in iniquity and ungodliness *separate
themselves* from God. Perfect harmony and gracious
fellowship existed between man and God until Adam
sinned—and even then, God did not hide from Adam;
it was *Adam* who hid from *God!* (Read Genesis chapter 3.)

While He tabernacled here on earth, Jesus longed
to save His own people, the Jews. He loved them, He
offered Himself to them, He had the power to save
them—but He did not save them because, in His own
words, *"Ye WILL NOT come to me,* that ye might
have life!"* (John 5:40).

On another occasion He said, "O Jerusalem, Jerusalem, which killest the prophets, and stonest them
that are sent unto thee; *how often would I have gathered thy children together, as a hen doth gather her
brood under her wings, and YE WOULD NOT!"* (Luke
13:34).

Some people ask, "If God is all-powerful, why does
He not destroy the devil?" God is all-wise, and knowing the end in the beginning, it would not be wise
for Him to destroy Satan just yet. But at the appointed time Jesus will personally put the devil into the
bottomless pit and seal him there:

"I saw an Angel come down from heaven, having
the key of the bottomless pit and a great chain in
His hand. And He laid hold on the dragon, that old
serpent, which is the Devil, and Satan, and bound
him a thousand years. And cast him into the bottomless pit, and shut him up, and set a seal upon him,
that he should deceive the nations no more, till the
thousand years should be fulfilled: and after that he
must be loosed a little season" (Rev. 20:1—3).

Why am I so sure that the "Angel" here is the

Lord Jesus Christ? Jude 9 tells us that Michael the
archangel, when contending with the devil about the
body of Moses, "durst not bring against him a railing
accusation, but said, *The LORD rebuke thee!*" If
Michael dared not rebuke the devil, then there *is* no
angel among *the host of angels* who could bind Satan
and put him in the pit—*except THE LORD JESUS
in angelic form.*

Then, in the final consummation of all things, the
devil will be "cast into the lake of fire and brimstone,
where the beast and the false prophet are, and shall
be tormented day and night for ever and ever" (Rev.
20:10).

UNIVERSAL
PRESENCE

God Is Omnipresent

STATE OF BEING
EVERY+WHERE
SAME TIME

The living God is everywhere all of the time, in
all parts of the universe. He is near each individual
and, in the Person of the Holy Spirit, He abides *in
the bosom* of every born again believer. In God "we
live, and move, and have our being" (Acts 17:28).

David cried out, "Whither shall I go from thy
Spirit? or whither shall I flee from thy presence? *If
I ascend up into heaven, THOU ART THERE: if I
make my bed in hell, behold, THOU ART THERE.* If
I take the wings of the morning, and dwell in the uttermost parts of the sea; even there shall thy hand
lead me, and thy right hand shall hold me" (Psalm
139:7—10).

Through Jeremiah God asked, "Am I a God at
hand, and not a God afar off? Can any hide himself
in secret places that I shall not see him? Do not I
fill heaven and earth?" (Jer. 23:23, 24).

In his sermon on Mars' Hill, the Apostle Paul
speaks of the omnipresence of the living God: "God
that made the world and all things therein, seeing
that He is Lord of heaven and earth, dwelleth not in
temples made with hands; neither is worshipped with

men's hands, as though He needed any thing, seeing
He giveth to all life, and breath, and all things; and
hath made of one blood all nations of men for to dwell
on all the face of the earth, and hath determined the
times before appointed, and the bounds of their habitation; *that they should seek the Lord, if haply they
might feel after Him, and find Him, THOUGH HE
BE NOT FAR FROM EVERY ONE OF US"* (Acts
17:24—27).

The Word of God clearly teaches that the living
God is in *some* places in a way He is not in *all* places.   Isaiah 66:1 declares, "Thus saith the Lord, *The
heaven is my throne, and the earth is my footstool:*
where is the house that ye build unto me? and where
is the place of my rest?"

At this present time, *heaven* is the place where the
presence and glory of God are visibly manifested in a
very special way. He was manifested *on earth* in the
Person of the Lord Jesus Christ: "No man hath ascended up to heaven, but He that came down from heaven,
even *the Son of man which is IN heaven"* (John 3:13).

God the Father sits on His throne in heaven, and
during this Dispensation of Grace Jesus the Son sits
at the Father's right hand. He is there to make intercession for believers: "For there is one God, and
one Mediator between God and men, the Man Christ
Jesus" (I Tim. 2:5).

Christ was the brightness of God's glory, "the express image of His person, and upholding all things
by the word of His power, when He had by Himself
purged our sins, (He) sat down on the right hand of
the Majesty on high" (Heb. 1:3).

Stephen was permitted a glimpse of heaven as the
enemies of the Gospel stoned him to death: "He,
being full of the Holy Ghost, looked up stedfastly into
heaven, *and saw the glory of God, and Jesus standing
on the right hand of God,* and said, Behold, *I see the*

heavens opened, and the Son of man standing on the right hand of God" (Acts 7:55, 56).

During this Church Age, God the Father sits on His throne, the Man Christ Jesus sits at the Father's right hand making intercession for His children, but *the Holy Spirit* is here on earth—He abides in the heart of every believer. He came, as promised, on the Day of Pentecost, and He will remain until the Rapture of the Church, at which time He will be caught out with the saints of God. This is clearly seen in Acts 2:1—13 (which records the coming of the Holy Spirit at Pentecost) and II Thessalonians 2:7, 8 where we read, "For the mystery of iniquity doth already work: only *He* (the Holy Spirit) *who now letteth will let, until He be taken out of the way. And then shall that Wicked* (the Antichrist) *be revealed,* whom the Lord shall consume with the spirit of His mouth, and shall destroy with the brightness of His coming."

Since the Holy Spirit dwells in the heart of the believer, it is also true that *IN the Person of the Spirit the FATHER and the SON* dwell in the heart of the believer:

Jesus said to His disciples, "I will pray the Father, and He shall give you another Comforter, *that He may abide with you for ever; even the Spirit of truth;* whom the world cannot receive, because it seeth Him not, neither knoweth Him: *but ye know Him; for HE DWELLETH WITH YOU, AND SHALL BE IN YOU. . . .* Yet a little while, and the world seeth me no more; but ye see me: *because I live, ye shall live also.* At that day ye shall know that *I am in my Father, AND YE IN ME, AND I IN YOU. . . . If a man love me,* he will keep my words: and *my Father will love him, and WE WILL COME UNTO HIM, AND MAKE OUR ABODE WITH HIM"* (John 14:16, 17, 19, 20, 23).

When Jesus gave His commission to His disciples

He said, "Go ye therefore, and teach all nations, baptizing them in the name of the Father, and of the Son, and of the Holy Ghost: Teaching them to observe all things whatsoever I have commanded you: and, lo, *I AM WITH YOU ALWAY, even unto the end of the world*" (Matt. 28:19, 20).

Christ in the believer is the hope of glory (Col. 1: 27). Believers are hid with Christ in God (Col. 3:3), and we "sit together in heavenly places in Christ Jesus" (Eph. 2:6).

God Is Omniscient

God knows all things: "For if our heart condemn us, God is greater than our heart, *and knoweth all things*" (I John 3:20).

God has *perfect* knowledge: "Dost thou know the balancings of the clouds, the wondrous works of Him which is *perfect in knowledge?*" (Job 37:16).

God has *infinite* understanding: "Great is our Lord, and of great power: *His understanding is infinite*" (Psalm 147:5).

God sees everything that happens — everywhere, every second of every hour of every day. He sees the evil and the good — nothing misses His eye. He also *knows* everything concerning nature and all creation.

God knows every star by name: "He telleth the number of stars; He calleth them all by their names" (Psalm 147:4).

He knows the number of sparrows that fly through the air: "Are not two sparrows sold for a farthing? and one of them shall not fall on the ground without your Father" (Matt. 10:29).

God sees every person on earth. David declared, "Thou knowest my downsitting and mine uprising, thou understandest my thought afar off. Thou compassest my path and my lying down, and art acquainted with all my ways. For there is not a word in my

tongue, but, lo, O Lord, thou knowest it altogether"
(Psalm 139:2—4).

God knows what each person is doing, He knows
their works and their ways: "The Lord looketh from
heaven; He beholdeth all the sons of men. From the
place of His habitation He looketh upon all the inhabitants of the earth. He fashioneth their hearts
alike; He considereth all their works" (Psalm 33:13—15).
"For the ways of man are before the eyes of the Lord,
and He pondereth all his goings" (Prov. 5:21).

In Exodus 3:7 we read, "The Lord said, I have
surely seen the affliction of my people which are in
Egypt, and have heard their cry by reason of their
taskmasters; *for I know their sorrows.*" God knows
when we are happy, He knows all of our sorrows. He
"searcheth all hearts, and understandeth all the imag-
inations of the thoughts" (I Chron. 28:9). He understands us much better than we understand ourselves,
"for He knoweth our frame; He remembereth that we
are dust" (Psalm 103:14). He is concerned about each
of us, and "if God be for us, who can be against
us?" (Rom. 8:31).

God cares for us as a father cares for his child,
providing for our every need: "He that spared not
His own Son, but delivered Him up for us all, *how
shall He not WITH HIM also freely give us ALL
things?"* (Rom. 8:32).

God cares for us as a mother cares for her baby:
"Can a woman forget her sucking child, that she
should not have compassion on the son of her womb?
Yea, *they* may forget, *YET WILL NOT I FORGET
THEE"* (Isa. 49:15).

God cares for us as a gardener cares for the plants
that grow in his garden: "I the Lord do keep it; I
will water it every moment: lest any hurt it, *I will
keep it night and day"* (Isa. 27:3).

He keeps us as the eyelid protects the eye—as a

very present help in time of trouble. He helps us *instantly:* "He found him in a desert land, and in the waste howling wilderness; He led him about, He instructed him, *He kept him as the apple of His eye*" (Deut. 32:10).

God cares for us as a friend: "*A friend loveth at all times,* and a brother is born for adversity" (Prov. 17:17).

He cares for us as a keeper cares for his charge— *watchfully.* He neither slumbers nor sleeps. "The Lord is thy keeper: the Lord is thy shade upon thy right hand. The sun shall not smite thee by day, nor the moon by night. The Lord shall preserve thee from all evil: He shall preserve thy soul. The Lord shall preserve thy going out and thy coming in from this time forth, and even for evermore" (Psalm 121:4—8).

God cares for us as a banker cares for the treasures deposited in his bank: "For ye are dead, and *your life is hid with Christ IN GOD*" (Col. 3:3).

The believer who looks up to God in prayer will always find Him looking down to provide the need which prompted the prayer. God is able to do exceeding and abundantly above anything we think, ask, or need—and because of His omniscience *He knows our need* before we ask. Because He is omnipotent, He is able to *provide* whatsoever we need: "Are not five sparrows sold for two farthings, and not one of them is forgotten before God? But even the very hairs of your head are all numbered. *Fear not therefore: YE ARE OF MORE VALUE THAN MANY SPARROWS*" (Luke 12:6, 7).

God knows each of His children by name: "To Him the porter openeth; and the sheep hear His voice: and *He calleth His own sheep BY NAME, and leadeth them out*" (John 10:3).

He counts our steps: "Doth not He see my ways, and count all my steps?" (Job 31:4).

He records our thoughts: "Then they that feared the Lord spake often one to another: and the Lord hearkened, and heard it, *and A BOOK OF REMEM-BRANCE WAS WRITTEN before Him for them that feared the Lord, and that THOUGHT UPON HIS NAME*" (Mal. 3:16).

He bottles every tear we shed: "Thou tellest my wanderings: *put thou my tears into thy bottle:* are they not in thy book?" (Psalm 56:8).

God holds our hand and leads us: "*I the Lord thy God will hold thy right hand,* saying unto thee, *FEAR NOT; I will help thee*" (Isa. 41:13).

He supplies our every need: "*My God shall supply ALL YOUR NEED according to His riches in glory by Christ Jesus*" (Phil. 4:19).

Beloved, if you have allowed the parasites of un-belief, doubt, and fear to rob you of your spiritual birthright of perfect peace and joy unspeakable, allow this defeat in your life no longer! "*Commit thy way unto the Lord; trust also in Him; and HE SHALL BRING IT TO PASS*" (Psalm 37:5). The person whose mind is stayed on Jesus will be kept in perfect peace (Isa. 26:3).

From the *beginning of eternity* God has known each and every detail of everything that will happen *throughout ALL eternity*. He is *the living God*. He has *always BEEN*, He always *will BE*. He has known all things, always. Even the plan of redemption was designed and perfected before creation began:

"Forasmuch as ye know that ye were not redeemed with corruptible things, as silver and gold, from your vain conversation received by tradition from your fa-thers, but with the precious blood of Christ, as of a lamb without blemish and without spot: *who verily was FOREORDAINED BEFORE THE FOUNDATION OF THE WORLD,* but was manifest in these last times for you" (I Pet. 1:18—20).

STANDING ALONE WITH GOD!

God the Son was fully aware of the purpose of His mission on earth, and just before His triumphal entry into the Holy City He said to His disciples, "Behold, we go up to Jerusalem; and *the Son of man shall be betrayed unto the chief priests and unto the scribes, and they shall condemn Him to death, and shall deliver Him to the Gentiles to mock, and to scourge, and to crucify Him: and the third day He shall rise again"* (Matt. 20:18, 19).

Everything that happened to Jesus while He tabernacled among men was foretold by the prophets as they penned down the things God spoke to them by the Spirit: *"But those things, which God before had shewed by the mouth of all His prophets, that Christ should suffer, HE HATH SO FULFILLED"* (Acts 3:18).

God knows everything we will face in the course of each and every day we live on this earth. Speaking to Moses concerning Pharaoh and the children of Israel He said, *"I am sure that THE KING OF EGYPT WILL NOT LET YOU GO, NO, NOT BY A MIGHTY HAND. And I will stretch out MY hand, and smite Egypt with all my wonders which I will do in the midst thereof: and after that HE WILL LET YOU GO"* (Ex. 3:19, 20).

God knew everything Pharaoh would do, He knew everything that would happen to the Israelites; and because of His perfect knowledge He could give Moses *perfect instruction.*

God knows everything that will happen in the life of each of His children. For example, *Elisha* declared:

"Thus saith the Lord: To morrow about this time shall a measure of fine flour be sold for a shekel, and two measures of barley for a shekel, in the gate of Samaria.

*"*Then a lord on whose hand the king leaned answered the man of God, and said, Behold, if the Lord

would make windows in heaven, might this thing be?
And he said, Behold, thou shalt see it with thine eyes,
but shalt not eat thereof. . . .

"And the people went out, and spoiled the tents
of the Syrians. *So a measure of fine flour was sold
for a shekel, and two measures of barley for a shekel,
ACCORDING TO THE WORD OF THE LORD.*
And the king appointed the lord on whose hand he
leaned to have charge of the gate: and the people
trode upon him in the gate, and he died, *AS THE
MAN OF GOD HAD SAID* . . ." (II Kings 7:1, 2, 16,
17).

Before *Saul of Tarsus* was born, God knew that
one day he would become the Apostle Paul, minister
to the Gentiles, and through him would be made
known the mystery of the body of Christ, the New
Testament Church. Concerning Paul, God said to
Ananias, *"He is a chosen vessel unto me*, to bear my
name before the Gentiles, and kings, and the children
of Israel: *for I will shew him how great things he
must suffer for my name's sake"* (Acts 9:15, 16).

Paul himself testified, "It pleased God, who sep-
urated me from my mother's womb, and called me by
His grace, to reveal His Son in me, that I might
preach Him among the heathen . . ." (Gal. 1:15, 16).

Peter acknowledged himself "an apostle of Jesus
Christ . . . *elect according to THE FOREKNOWL-
EDGE OF GOD THE FATHER,* through sanctification of the Spirit, unto obedience and sprinkling of
the blood of Jesus Christ" (I Pet. 1:1, 2).

However, the clearly proven fact that God is sovereign—omnipotent, omnipresent, and omniscient—does
not lessen the responsibility of each individual. It
is true that God knows His own, but each individual
becomes God's own through personal faith in the shed
blood of the Son of God. Throughout the Scriptures
we read such warnings as those contained in Proverbs

1:22—33:

"How long, ye simple ones, will ye love simplicity? and the scorners delight in their scorning, and fools hate knowledge? *Turn you at my reproof: behold, I will pour out my spirit unto you, I will make known my words unto you.*

"*Because I HAVE CALLED, and ye refused; I HAVE STRETCHED OUT MY HAND, and no man regarded; but ye have set at nought all my counsel, and would none of my reproof: I also will laugh at your calamity; I will mock when your fear cometh;* when your fear cometh as desolation, and your destruction cometh as a whirlwind; when distress and anguish cometh upon you.

"Then shall they call upon me, *but I will not answer*; they shall seek me early, *but they shall not find me:* for that they hated knowledge, and did not choose the fear of the Lord: *They would none of my counsel: they despised all my reproof. THEREFORE SHALL THEY EAT OF THE FRUIT OF THEIR OWN WAY, AND BE FILLED WITH THEIR OWN DEVICES.*

"For the turning away of the simple shall slay them, and the prosperity of fools shall destroy them. *But whoso hearkeneth unto me shall dwell safely, and shall be quiet from fear of evil.*"

This passage of Scripture plainly declares that *God calls many* who refuse to hear His call. *He stretches out His hand* to many who refuse His leading. *He offers counsel* to many who refuse to listen. And *because* they refuse to hear His call, be led by His hand, or obey His counsel, God warns that He will laugh at their calamity and mock when fear comes upon them! Oh yes—some of them will seek God, but they will not find Him. It will be too late, and He will not answer them. Why? *Because "they hated knowledge and did not CHOOSE the fear of the Lord."*

It is not God's will that any should perish; He

wants to save each and every one, *He would "that ALL should come to repentance"* (II Pet. 3:9). But not all will listen to His counsel, and those who *refuse* to hear Him *CHOOSE their own destiny.*

The plan of the ages and the part each individual will play in that plan has been known to God *from the beginning,* even in the eternities before creation began. The Apostle Paul speaks of God as "having made known unto us *the mystery of His will,* according to His good pleasure which He hath purposed in Himself: That in the dispensation of the fulness of times He might gather together in one all things in Christ, both which are in heaven, and which are on earth; even in Him: In whom also we have obtained an inheritance, *being PREDESTINATED ACCORDING TO THE PURPOSE OF HIM who worketh all things after the counsel of HIS OWN WILL:* That we should be to the praise of His glory, who first trusted in Christ" (Eph. 1:9–12).

In Ephesians 3:4—9 Paul wrote of how, *by revelation,* God made known to him *"the mystery . . .* whereby, when ye read, ye may understand my knowledge in *the mystery of Christ—which in other ages was not made known* unto the sons of men, as it is now revealed unto His holy apostles and prophets by the Spirit; that the Gentiles should be fellowheirs, and of the same body, and partakers of His promise in Christ by the Gospel: Whereof I was made a minister, according to the gift of the grace of God given unto me by the effectual working of His power. Unto me, who am less than the least of all saints, is this grace given, that I should preach among the Gentiles the unsearchable riches of Christ; and to make all men see what is the fellowship of the mystery, which FROM THE BEGINNING OF THE WORLD HATH BEEN HID IN GOD, who created all things by Jesus Christ."

Then in Colossians 1:25, 26 Paul speaks of "the

HIGHER-P LANE 6/19/70

Church, whereof I am made a minister, according to
the dispensation of God which is given to me for you,
to fulfil the Word of God; *even the mystery which
hath been HID FROM AGES AND FROM GENER-
ATIONS, but now is made manifest to His saints."*

Believers should never question God's dealings with
them, for *with HIM* there is no such thing as *"after-
thought."* No wonder the Apostle Paul cried out, *"O
the depth of the riches both of the WISDOM and
KNOWLEDGE of God! How UNSEARCHABLE are
His judgments, and HIS WAYS past finding out!"*
(Rom. 11:33).

God Is Holy

What is the *meaning* of "holiness" as having to
do with God? It means that God is absolutely pure—
free from any and all defilement. He cannot be tempted with evil (James 1:13).

In the book of Isaiah, God is called "the Holy
One of Israel" approximately thirty times. Jeremiah
and Ezekiel also call Him "the Holy One of Israel."

In I John 2:20 Jesus (God in flesh) is called "the
Holy One," and throughout the entire New Testament
the Holy Spirit, third Person of the Godhead, is spoken
of as "holy."

The *essential nature* of God is holiness. Isaiah
6:1—4 records that prophet's transforming vision:

"In the year that king Uzziah died I saw also the
Lord sitting upon a throne, high and lifted up, and
His train filled the temple. Above it stood the seraphims: each one had six wings; with twain he covered his face, and with twain he covered his feet, and
with twain he did fly. And one cried unto another,
and said, Holy, holy, holy, is the Lord of hosts: the
whole earth is full of His glory. And the posts of the
door moved at the voice of him that cried, and the
house was filled with smoke."

David also declared that God is holy. In Psalm 22:3 he wrote, "Thou art HOLY, O thou that inhabitest the praises of Israel." In Psalm 99:5, 9 he said, "Exalt ye the Lord our God, and worship at His footstool; *for HE IS HOLY. . . .* Exalt the Lord our God, and worship at His holy hill; *for THE LORD OUR GOD IS HOLY."*

While Jesus dwelt among men He declared the holiness of God: *". . . Holy Father,* keep through thine own name those whom thou hast given me, that they may be one, as we are" (John 17:11).

Peter testified to the absolute holiness of God: "As *He which hath called you is HOLY, so be YE holy* in all manner of conversation; because it is written, *Be ye holy, for I AM HOLY"* (I Pet. 1:15, 16).

Isaiah declared that *God's name* is holy: "For thus saith the high and lofty One that inhabiteth eternity, *whose name is HOLY:* I dwell in the high and holy place . . ." (Isa. 57:15).

That God is absolutely holy is the fundamental truth of the Word of God, both the Old and the New Testaments. *Only* a holy God could provide salvation for unholy sinners. The message of salvation is, *"GOD IS LIGHT, and in Him is NO DARKNESS AT ALL"* (I John 1:5). James 1:17 declares, "Every good gift and every perfect gift is from above, and cometh down from *THE FATHER OF LIGHTS, with whom is no variableness, neither shadow of turning."*

Because God is holy He cannot and will not look upon sin: "Thou art of purer eyes than to behold evil, and canst not look on iniquity . . ." (Hab. 1:13).

Wickedness is an abomination in the sight of God: ". . . all that do unrighteously are an abomination unto the Lord thy God" (Deut. 25:16).

"The way of the wicked is an abomination unto the Lord: but He loveth him that followeth after righteousness. . . . The thoughts of the wicked are an abomination to thè Lord: but the words of the pure are pleasant words" (Prov. 15:9, 26).

In Leviticus 20:26 God commanded, "Ye shall be holy unto me: *for I THE LORD AM HOLY . . . .*"

Hebrews 12:14 instructs us to "follow peace with all men, *and HOLINESS, without which no man shall see the Lord."*

God's holiness is manifested in that He hates sin and delights in righteousness and holiness. He can never do wickedly: "Therefore hearken unto me, ye men of understanding: far be it from God, that He should do wickedness; and from the Almighty, that He should commit iniquity" (Job 34:10).

It is *because* God is absolutely holy that the sinner is *separated from* God: "Behold, the Lord's hand is not shortened, that it cannot save; neither His ear heavy, that it cannot hear: *but YOUR INIQUITIES have separated between you and your God, and YOUR SINS have hid His face from you, that He will not hear"* (Isa. 59:1, 2).

Thus *the atonement* is a divine imperative, for the sinner could never approach God had not Christ atoned for our sins: *"But now IN CHRIST JESUS ye who sometimes were FAR OFF are made nigh by the blood of Christ"* (Eph. 2:13).

Jesus was made to be sin *for us*, "that we might be made the righteousness of God IN HIM" (II Cor. 5:21). He was made a curse *for us*. Paul said, "Christ hath redeemed us from the curse of the law, being made a curse for us: for it is written, Cursed is every one that hangeth on a tree" (Gal. 3:13).

It was *because* of the sin Christ bore for us that God of divine necessity turned His back on His beloved Son at Calvary. God cannot look on sin, and from the cross Jesus cried out, "My God! My God! Why hast thou forsaken me?"

Through faith in the shed blood and finished work

of Jesus, we are made nigh to God—yea, "hid with Christ in God" (Col. 3:3). We are *"sanctified through the offering of the body of Jesus Christ once for all"* (Heb. 10:10).

Man can approach God only through the Lord Jesus Christ. He declared, "I am the way, the truth, and the life: *no man* cometh unto the Father, *but by me"* (John 14:6). Our only claim to salvation is on the grounds of the shed blood of the Lamb, "and *without shedding of blood is no remission"* (Heb. 9:22).

Yes, thanks be unto God, *He is love* (I John 4:8)— but He is also *"a consuming fire"* (Heb. 12:29). We can never fully appreciate *the LOVE of God* until we realize His hatred of sin. Because God is *holy* He must punish the sinner. His very character *demands* judgment of sin, and His blazing wrath will be poured out upon the sinner just as fully and completely as His love was demonstrated on Calvary in His only begotten Son.

The love of God is not a *sentimental* love that overlooks sin, for sin cost Him His beloved Son. Sin cost Jesus His life, and God cannot deal with it lightly. *His wrath abides on every unbeliever:* "He that believeth on Him is not condemned: but He that believeth not is condemned already, because he hath not believed in the name of the only begotten Son of God. . . . He that believeth on the Son hath everlasting life: and he that believeth not the Son shall not see life; but the wrath of God abideth on him" (John 3:18, 36).

The pure blazing wrath of God's absolute holiness reveals the utter blackness of sin, and the blackness of sin demands that the wrath of God be poured out upon the one who chooses to *continue* in sin. For example, when Isaiah saw the glory of God he cried out, *"WOE IS ME! for I am undone; because I am a man of unclean lips, and I dwell in the midst of a*

people of unclean lips: *FOR MINE EYES HAVE
SEEN THE KING, THE LORD OF HOSTS"* (Isa.
6:5).

Job confessed, "I have heard of thee by the hearing
of the ear: but now mine eye seeth thee. *WHERE-
FORE I ABHOR MYSELF, and repent in dust and
ashes"* (Job 42:5, 6).

God Is Love

How wonderful that God—absolutely and infinitely
holy—could love such poor, sinful creatures as we are!
But love is the very essence of God's nature: He
does not simply "love"—*He IS love.* He is the *source*
of all love, and until we come into the right relationship with God we cannot know *perfect* love:

*"He that loveth not knoweth not God; for GOD
IS LOVE.* In this was manifested the love of God
toward us, because that God sent His only begotten
Son into the world, that we might live through Him.
. . . And we have known and believed the love that
God hath to us. God is love; and he that dwelleth
in love dwelleth in God, and God in him. . . . There
is no fear in love; but *perfect love casteth out fear:*
because fear hath torment. *He that feareth is not
made perfect in love. WE LOVE HIM, BECAUSE
HE FIRST LOVED US"* (I John 4:8—19 in part).

What IS love? Since God is love, the only place
to find the *true definition* of love is in God's Word:

In I John 3:16—18 we read: "Hereby perceive we
the love of God, because He laid down His life for
us: and we ought to lay down our lives for the brethren. But whoso hath this world's good, and seeth
his brother have need, and shutteth up his bowels of
compassion from him, how dwelleth the love of God
in him? My little children, let us not love in word,
neither in tongue; *but in deed and in truth."*

In Matthew 5:44, 45 Jesus said, *"Love your enemies,*

bless them that curse you, do good to them that hate you, and pray for them which despitefully use you, and persecute you; that ye may be the children of your Father which is in heaven: for He maketh His sun to rise on the evil and on the good, and sendeth rain on the just and on the unjust."

We see, then, that love is a deep desire for—and a sincere delight in—the welfare, happiness, security, and well-being of the one loved. God gave His only begotten Son to take our place and pay the sin-debt in our stead. *Surely* He did have a deep desire for our welfare and our security, and a sincere delight in our happiness and well-being! Christ is our sufficiency. All that we need we find in Him—*God's love-gift to man.*

God Loved the World

No one has ever loved as God loved. No mortal could ever be *capable* of loving as God loved. Yes, in spite of the blackness of sin, and while we were yet sinners, God loved the world and proved His love by giving His best for us:

"For God so loved the world, that He gave His only begotten Son, that whosoever believeth in Him should not perish, but have everlasting life. For God sent not His Son into the world to condemn the world; but that the world through Him might be saved" (John 3:16, 17).

However, the Lord Jesus Christ is the original and eternal *object* of God's love. He loved His Son before there was a world *to love. Before the foundation of the world* God had been in eternal, loving fellowship with His beloved Son; and when Jesus was baptized in Jordan God testified, *"This is my BELOVED Son, in whom I am WELL PLEASED"* (Matt. 3:17).

In Matthew 17:5, on the Mount of Transfiguration, God again testified, "This is *my BELOVED Son,* in whom I am *well pleased."*

God the Father has never made that statement
about any other being. No one else has ever *pleased*
God as Jesus pleased Him. The Son of God came
into the world to do the work and the will of the Father, and He did exactly that. When He came to the
end of His earthly ministry He could look into the
Father's face and say, *"I have glorified thee on the
earth: I HAVE FINISHED the work which thou
gavest me to do!"* (John 17:4).

Since God is *eternal,* He was "in the beginning";
and since *God is LOVE,* His love must of necessity
have *an eternal object;* and since *"in the beginning
GOD,"* there must also be a *multiplicity of Persons*
in the Godhead—Father, Son, and Holy Ghost. The
eternal object of the divine love of God is *the eternal
Son* who was in the beginning *with* the Father and
who in the fulness of time was born of the Virgin
Mary, and was named "JESUS: for He shall save
His people from their sins" (Matt. 1:21).

Jesus Himself declared the Father's eternal love
for Him. In John 17:24 He prayed, "Father, I will
that they also, whom thou hast given me, be with me
where I am; that they may behold my glory, which
thou hast given me: *for thou lovedst me BEFORE
THE FOUNDATION OF THE WORLD."*

God loves those who are in Christ by faith, and
all who *reject* God's beloved Son will be under His
eternal *wrath,* not His eternal love. Yes, God loves
the sinner and it is not His will that any should perish; but all who refuse to come to repentance, thus
refusing the love of God in Christ Jesus, must suffer
the wrath of God throughout all eternity. God loves
the world—but He has a singular and peculiar love
for those who believe on Jesus and accept Him as
Saviour:

Jesus declared, "He that hath my commandments,

and keepeth them, he it is that loveth me: and he that loveth me shall be loved of my Father, and I will love him, and will manifest myself to him. . . . If a man love me, he will keep my words: and my Father will love him, and we will come unto him, and make our abode with him" (John 14:21, 23).

In John 16:27 God's beloved Son tells us, "The Father Himself loveth you, because ye have loved me, and have believed that I came out from God."

Then in John 17:23 He said to the heavenly Father, "I in them (believers), and thou in me, that they may be made perfect in one; and that the world may know that thou hast sent me, and hast loved them, *as thou hast loved me.*"

God's love for *the sinner* manifests itself in the *salvation* of sinners when they believe on the Lord Jesus Christ. His Word plainly declares that *God has "no pleasure in the death of the wicked,"* but would "that the wicked turn from his way and live" (Ezek. 33:11). He loves the sinner to such degree that "when we were yet without strength, in due time *Christ died for the ungodly.* . . . God commendeth His love toward us, in that, *while we were yet sinners,* Christ died for us" (Rom. 5:6, 8).

Then in Ephesians 2:4, 5 we read, "But God, who is rich in mercy, for His great love wherewith He loved us, *even when we were dead in sins,* hath quickened us together with Christ, (by grace ye are saved)."

II Peter 3:9 declares, "The Lord is not slack concerning His promise, as some men count slackness; *but is longsuffering to us-ward, NOT WILLING THAT ANY SHOULD PERISH, but that ALL should come to repentance!*"

God's love toward the believer manifests itself in supplying the believer's every need, in protecting him, and in giving joy and peace. But His love toward His children is also manifested *in correction and chastening:*

"My son, despise not thou the chastening of the Lord, nor faint when thou art rebuked of Him: For whom the Lord loveth He chasteneth, and scourgeth every son whom He receiveth. If ye endure chastening, God dealeth with you as with sons; for what son is he whom the father chasteneth not? But if ye be without chastisement, whereof all are partakers, then are ye bastards, and not sons.

"Furthermore we have had fathers of our flesh which corrected us, and we gave them reverence: shall we not much rather be in subjection unto the Father of spirits, and live? For they verily for a few days chastened us after their own pleasure; but He for our profit, that we might be partakers of His holiness. Now no chastening for the present seemeth to be joyous, but grievous: nevertheless afterward it yieldeth the peaceable fruit of righteousness unto them which are exercised thereby" (Heb. 12:5—11).

God loves His own so deeply that when His children are afflicted He Himself is afflicted with them: "In all their affliction *He* was afflicted, and the angel of His presence saved them: In His love and in His pity He redeemed them; and He bare them, and carried them all the days of old" (Isa. 63:9).

It matters not how much *we* love our family and friends, we are finite and there are times when we become careless and forget—but God's love is manifested to His children in that He *never* forgets (Isa. 49:15, 16).

True love is measured by sacrifice. We are willing and anxious to sacrifice for those we love. God so loved the world that He sacrificed His best—He gave His only begotten Son in order to provide a Saviour for sinners. God spared Isaac when Abraham would have offered him in sacrifice in obedience to God's command (Gen. 22:1—13); but God could not spare

His own Son—His holy character would not allow it. The sacrifice of His only begotten Son was the only way redemption could be provided for a world of sinners.

God's love for us is measured by His sacrifice of Christ on the cross, and that love manifests itself in giving life to those who are dead in trespasses and sins. When they believe on the Lord Jesus Christ, God raises them *with* Christ, makes them sit with Him in heavenly places, "that in the ages to come He might shew the exceeding riches of His grace in His kindness toward us through Christ Jesus" (Eph. 2:4—7). *But that is just the beginning!* The fulness of God's love is yet to be manifested in that eternal home Jesus is preparing for His own:

"Beloved, NOW are we the sons of God, and it doth not yet appear what we shall be: but we know that, when He shall appear, we shall be like Him; for we shall see Him as He is" (I John 3:2).

"As it is written, *Eye hath not seen, nor ear heard, neither have entered into the heart of man, the things which God hath prepared for them that love Him*" (I Cor. 2:9).

Yes, God loves the sinner. He gave His only begotten Son to die for sinners, and He rejoices when an unbeliever is saved and becomes a member of the family of heaven:

"The Lord thy God in the midst of thee is mighty; He will save, He will rejoice over thee with joy; He will rest in His love, He will joy over thee with singing" (Zeph. 3:17).

"Bring hither the fatted calf, and kill it; and let us eat, and be merry: for this my son was dead, and is alive again; he was lost, and is found . . ." (Luke 15:23, 24).

"I say unto you, there is joy in the presence of the angels of God over one sinner that repenteth"

(Luke 15:10).

God Is Righteous and Just

Some people declare that they have always been mistreated, never having received justice in this life—and in some remote cases this might be true. But one thing is sure: *EVERY PERSON will receive justice at the hand of God! ALL will be dealt with justly and righteously:*

"For it is written, *As I live,* saith the Lord, *EVERY KNEE shall bow to me, and EVERY TONGUE shall confess to God.* So then every one of us shall give account of himself to God" (Rom. 14:11, 12).

Saint or sinner, when you stand before God you will receive exactly what is right. His character guarantees that He cannot judge wrongly. The believer will not be judged as to whether he is saved or lost—that must be decided in this life; but he will be judged for his stewardship. Many Scriptures in the New Testament declare that our reward will be according to our labors. If we have been faithful in all things, we will receive *a full reward.* According to the words of Jesus, *those who receive the Word will bear fruit*—some thirty, some sixty, and some *an hundredfold* (Matt. 13:23). God is glorified when we bring forth *much* fruit (John 15:8).

Sinners will be judged at the Great White Throne judgment and they, too, will be "judged out of those things which were written in the books, according to their works" (Rev. 20:11, 12). Souls are saved or lost in *this* life—there is no second chance after death. John 3:18 makes this fact very clear: "He that believeth on (Jesus) *is not condemned:* but he that *believeth not* is condemned *already,* because he hath not believed in the name of the only begotten Son of God."

Yes, every person—saint or sinner—will receive justice from God and will be judged in righteousness.

The Scriptures clearly testify to this fact:

"Let the heavens rejoice, and let the earth be glad; let the sea roar, and the fulness thereof. Let the field be joyful, and all that is therein: then shall all the trees of the wood rejoice before the Lord: for He cometh, *for He cometh to judge the earth: He shall judge the world with RIGHTEOUSNESS, and the people with HIS TRUTH*" (Psalm 96:11—13).

"*Gracious is the Lord, and RIGHTEOUS; yea, our God is merciful*" (Psalm 116:5).

"I will speak of *the glorious HONOUR of thy majesty,* and of thy wondrous works. . . . The eyes of all wait upon thee; and thou givest them their meat in due season. Thou openest thine hand, and satisfiest the desire of every living thing. *The Lord is RIGHTEOUS in ALL His ways, and HOLY in all His works. The Lord is nigh unto all them that call upon Him, to all that call upon Him in truth. He will fulfil the desire of them that fear Him: He also will hear their cry, and will save them. The Lord preserveth all them that love Him: but all the wicked will He destroy*" (Psalm 145:5, 15—20).

"Let him that glorieth glory in this, that he understandeth and knoweth me, that *I am the Lord which exercise lovingkindness, judgment, and RIGHTEOUSNESS in the earth:* for in these things I delight, saith the Lord" (Jer. 9:24).

"And they sing the song of Moses the servant of God, and the song of the Lamb, saying, *Great and marvellous are thy works, Lord God Almighty; JUST AND TRUE ARE THY WAYS, thou King of saints*" (Rev. 15:3).

God's judgment of sinners and the punishment meted out to them will be righteous and just. To the Christians at Thessalonica, Paul wrote:

"Seeing *it is a RIGHTEOUS thing with God to recompense tribulation to them that trouble you;* and

to you who are troubled rest with us, when the Lord
Jesus shall be revealed from heaven with His mighty
angels, in flaming fire taking vengeance on them that
know not God, and that obey not the Gospel of our
Lord Jesus Christ" (II Thess. 1:6—8).

In Revelation 16:4—7 we read, "And the third angel
poured out his vial upon the rivers and fountains of
waters; and they became blood. And I heard the angel
of the waters say, *Thou art RIGHTEOUS, O Lord,
which art, and wast, and shalt be, because thou hast
JUDGED THUS.* For they have shed the blood of
saints and prophets, and thou hast given them blood
to drink; for they are worthy. And I heard another out
of the altar say, *Even so, Lord God Almighty, TRUE
AND RIGHTEOUS ARE THY JUDGMENTS!"*

"And after these things I heard a great voice of
much people in heaven, saying, *Alleluia! Salvation,
and glory, and honour, and power, unto the Lord our
God: FOR TRUE AND RIGHTEOUS ARE HIS JUDG-
MENTS:* for He hath judged the great whore, which
did corrupt the earth with her fornication, and hath
avenged the blood of His servants at her hand" (Rev.
19:1, 2).

God's righteousness is manifested in His keeping
every promise He has ever made. Not one promise has
He ever broken—His character forbids it:

"Thou art the Lord the God, who didst choose
Abram, and broughtest him forth out of Ur of the
Chaldees, and gavest him the name of Abraham; and
foundest his heart faithful before thee, and madest a
covenant with him to give the land of the Canaanites,
the Hittites, the Amorites, and the Perizzites, and the
Jebusites, and the Girgashites, to give it, I say, to
his seed, and *hast performed thy words; FOR THOU
ART RIGHTEOUS"* (Neh. 9:7, 8).

God's righteousness is manifested in the fact that
He forgives the sinner when the sinner believes on the

Lord Jesus Christ and *confesses* his sins:

"If we confess our sins, *He is FAITHFUL AND JUST to forgive us our sins,* and to cleanse us from all unrighteousness" (I John 1:9).

"My little children, these things write I unto you, that ye sin not. And if any man sin, we have an Advocate with the Father, *Jesus Christ THE RIGHTEOUS:* and He is the propitiation for our sins: and not for our's only, but also for the sins of the whole world" (I John 2:1, 2).

God Is a God of Mercy

God's mercy is manifested toward all who love Him. His mercy is expended on all who serve Him and walk in His paths of righteousness:

"O Lord God of Israel, there is no God like thee in the heaven, nor in the earth; which keepest covenant, and *shewest mercy unto thy servants, that walk before thee with all their hearts*" (II Chron. 6:14).

"For as the heaven is high above the earth, so great is HIS MERCY toward them that fear Him. As far as the east is from the west, so far hath He removed our transgressions from us! Like as a father pitieth his children, so the Lord pitieth them that fear Him. For He knoweth our frame; He remembereth that we are dust.

"As for man, his days are as grass: as a flower of the field, so he flourisheth. For the wind passeth over it, and it is gone; and the place thereof shall know it no more. *BUT THE MERCY OF THE LORD IS FROM EVERLASTING TO EVERLASTING upon them that fear Him, and His RIGHTEOUSNESS unto children's children*" (Psalm 103:11—17).

"Many sorrows shall be to the wicked: *but he that trusteth in the Lord, MERCY SHALL COMPASS HIM ABOUT*" (Psalm 32:10).

"For thou, Lord, art good, and ready to forgive; *and plenteous in MERCY unto all them that call upon thee"* (Psalm 86:5).

"He that covereth his sins shall not prosper: *but whoso confesseth and forsaketh them shall have MER-CY"* (Prov. 28:13).

"And shewing MERCY unto thousands of them that love me, and keep my commandments" (Ex. 20:6).

God is merciful toward all who call upon His name—Jew or Gentile, rich or poor, bond or free: "For there is no difference between the Jew and the Greek: *for the same Lord over all is rich unto all that call upon Him.* For whosoever shall call upon the name of the Lord shall be saved" (Rom. 10:12, 13).

God's mercy is manifested in that He defends the believer in the day of trouble, He is a refuge for those who need shelter from the enemy or from the storms of life: "I will sing of thy power; yea, *I will sing aloud of thy mercy in the morning: for thou hast been my defence and refuge in the day of my trouble"* (Psalm 59:16).

Yes, our God is a God of mercy. He will be merciful to all who will call on the name of Jesus and put their trust in His shed blood and finished work.

God Is Faithful

In the Old Testament Scriptures, the Hebrew words translated "faithful" and "faithfulness" come from a root word which means "to support, prop, or stake." Therefore when those words have reference to a *person,* we know we may safely *lean upon* that person. Such is the character of God: He never varies, He is unchangeable: *With Him there is "no variableness, neither shadow of turning"* (James 1:17).

This is an age of unfaithfulness in almost every walk of life; *but the God in whom we trust is faithful!*

Paul wrote under inspiration, *"GOD IS FAITHFUL, by whom ye were called unto the fellowship of His Son Jesus Christ our Lord"* (I Cor. 1:9).

Paul also assures us, "There hath no temptation taken you but such as is common to man: *but GOD IS FAITHFUL, who will not suffer you to be tempted above that ye are able;* but will with the temptation also make a way to escape, that ye may be able to bear it" (I Cor. 10:13).

To the Thessalonians Paul wrote, *"FAITHFUL IS HE THAT CALLETH YOU, who also will do it"* (I Thess. 5:24). *"The Lord is FAITHFUL, who shall stablish you, and keep you from evil"* (II Thess. 3:3).

Writing to Timothy, his son in the ministry, Paul gives *"a faithful saying,* and worthy of all acceptation, that Christ Jesus came into the world to save sinners . . ." (I Tim. 1:15). *"If we believe not, yet HE ABIDETH FAITHFUL: He cannot deny Himself"* (II Tim. 2:13).

To the Hebrew believers Paul gave this assurance: "Let us hold fast the profession of our faith without wavering; *(for HE IS FAITHFUL that promised;) . . .* For ye have need of patience that, after ye have done the will of God, ye might *receive the promise.* For yet a little while, and He that shall come will come, and will not tarry" (Heb. 10:23, 36, 37).

God manifests His faithfulness to us in answering our prayers. David prayed, "Hear my prayer, O Lord, give ear to my supplications: *IN THY FAITHFUL-NESS answer me, and in thy RIGHTEOUSNESS"* (Psalm 143:1).

Before the World Was

Some people ask, "Since God is everlasting, what did He do *before the creation?"*

God the Eternal Spirit does not measure (or limit) time as "before" or "after." *He surveys ALL time at once.* To Him, the world in all of its extensions is already eternally present. I know we cannot understand all of this—that is why *God is GOD* and we are His created creatures. If man could *understand God* in all things, then man would *have* no God. We would be equal with God and He could not help us. But God is greater than man in love, in power, in wisdom, *in ALL things.*

God is love (I John 4:8). He has always *been* love because He does not change. Love is *the deepest element* of God, the innermost fountain from which God's nature eternally flows forth. Since God is love, there must of necessity be a *lover* and a *beloved*, for love proceeds from the lover and moves toward the beloved, intertwining lover and beloved together through the spirit of union.

The Eternal God is the Lover. Christ Jesus the Son is the Beloved. The Holy Spirit is the Spirit of love—*three* Divine Persons, *one God.* Mysteries upon mysteries! But we must remember, *"The SECRET things belong unto the Lord our God: but those things which are REVEALED belong unto us and to our children for ever . . ."* (Deut. 29:29).

What did God do before the world was? Before the foundation of the world was laid, God had been in eternal, loving fellowship and communion with His Beloved—Christ the Son, who was in the bosom of the Father "in the beginning":

"In the beginning was the WORD, and the Word was WITH God, and the Word WAS God. The same was in the beginning with God. . . . And *the Word was made flesh, and dwelt among us,* (and we beheld His glory, the glory as of the only begotten of the Father,) full of grace and truth. . . . No man hath seen God at any time; *the only begotten Son, which is in the bosom of the Father, He hath declared Him"* (John 1:1—18 in part). The Word which tabernacled

among men in Christ was in the beginning with God, eternally present with Him in mutual, responsive fellowship.

The Father loved the Son from all eternity. Jesus testified to this truth while He walked on earth. He prayed, "Father, I will that they also, whom thou hast given me, be with me where I am; that they may behold my glory, which thou hast given me: *FOR THOU LOVEDST ME BEFORE THE FOUNDATION OF THE WORLD*" (John 17:24).

Not only was Christ the *eternal Word* of God, He was also the eternal *wisdom* of God: *"The Lord possessed me IN THE BEGINNING of His way, before His works of old. I was set up FROM EVERLASTING, from the beginning, or ever the earth was"* (Prov. 8:22, 23).

Christ was the *eternally glorious One* with the Father: "And now, O Father, glorify thou me with thine own self *with the glory which I had with thee BEFORE THE WORLD WAS*" (John 17:5).

Also before the foundation of the world, God created the host of angels, and the stars. In Job 38:4—7 we read, "Where wast thou when I laid the foundations of the earth? declare, if thou hast understanding. Who hath laid the measures thereof, if thou knowest? or who hath stretched the line upon it? Whereupon are the foundations thereof fastened? or who laid the corner stone thereof; *when the morning stars sang together, and all the sons of God shouted for joy?*" We do not know just *when* God created the angels and the stars, but they were *before the world was created.*

Before the foundation of the world, God planned and settled the way of salvation for man. Before there was a sinner to save, God made *perfect provision* for the *redemption* of sinners:

"Forasmuch as ye know that ye were not redeemed

with corruptible things, as silver and gold . . . but
with the precious blood of Christ, as of a lamb without blemish and without spot: *Who verily was foreordained BEFORE THE FOUNDATION OF THE
WORLD,* but was manifest in these last times for
you.   Who by Him do believe in God, that raised
Him up from the dead, and gave Him glory; that your
faith and hope might be in God. . . . *Being born
again, not of corruptible seed, but of incorruptible,
by the Word of God, which liveth and abideth FOR
EVER"* (I Pet. 1:18—23 in part).

Yes, *prior to all creation* God had appointed believers in love unto sonship, righteousness, and holiness: "Blessed be the God and Father of our Lord
Jesus Christ, who hath blessed us with all spiritual
blessings in heavenly places in Christ: *according as
He hath chosen us in Him BEFORE THE FOUNDA-
TION OF THE WORLD, that we should be holy
and without blame before Him in love: having PRE-
DESTINATED us unto the adoption of children by
Jesus Christ to Himself, according to the good pleasure
of His will, to the praise of the glory of His grace,
wherein He hath made us accepted in the Beloved"*
(Eph. 1:3—6).

Before the foundation of the world, God promised
life eternal: "In hope of *eternal life, which God, that
cannot lie, promised BEFORE THE WORLD BE-
GAN"* (Tit. 1:2).

From the standpoint of God as being "in the beginning"—above time and before time—His grace is
given to us before the time of the ages: "Who hath
saved us, and called us with an holy calling, not according to our works, but *according to His own purpose and grace, which was given us in Christ Jesus
BEFORE THE WORLD BEGAN"* (II Tim. 1:9).

Although we are created beings, our Creator gave
us the privilege of choosing whom we will serve.   For

those who choose to serve God, He provided eternal life even before the world was. But all who choose to serve Satan must spend eternity with the one of their choosing: "Then shall He say also unto them on the left hand, *Depart from me, ye cursed, into everlasting FIRE, prepared for the devil and his angels*" (Matt. 25:41).

The New Testament Church is the body of Christ, made up of all born again believers in this Dispensation of Grace. *From eternity* that amazing body was determined, and its mystery was hidden in God—the mystery that those of all nations who trust in the shed blood of Jesus should be fellow-heirs with Christ and members of His body:

"For this cause I Paul, the prisoner of Jesus Christ for you Gentiles, if ye have heard of the dispensation of the grace of God which is given me to you-ward: How that *BY REVELATION He made known unto me the mystery;* (as I wrote afore in few words, whereby, when ye read, ye may understand my knowledge in the mystery of Christ) *which in other ages was not made known unto the sons of men, as it is now revealed unto His holy apostles and prophets by the Spirit;* that the Gentiles should be fellowheirs, and of the same body, and partakers of His promise in Christ by the Gospel: Whereof I was made a minister, according to the gift of the grace of God given unto me by the effectual working of His power.

"Unto me, who am less than the least of all saints, is this grace given, *that I should preach among the Gentiles the unsearchable riches of Christ; and to make all men see what is the fellowship of the mystery, which FROM THE BEGINNING OF THE WORLD HATH BEEN HID IN GOD, who created ALL things BY JESUS CHRIST*" (Eph. 3:1—9).

The *foundation of the Church* was laid before the world was, and *"other foundation can no man lay than that is laid, WHICH IS JESUS CHRIST"* (I Cor. 3:11).

Jesus Himself gave this same truth, in different words, in Matthew 16:13—18. He asked His disciples, "Whom do men say that I the Son of man am?" They gave various answers: "Some say that thou art John the Baptist: some, Elias; and others, Jeremias, or one of the prophets."

Then Jesus asked, *"But whom say YE that I am?"* and Simon Peter answered: *"Thou art the CHRIST, the Son of the living God!"*

Jesus then made this announcement: "Blessed art thou, Simon Bar-jona: for flesh and blood hath not revealed it unto thee, but my Father which is in heaven. And I say also unto thee, That thou art Peter, and upon this Rock *(CHRIST the Rock)* I will build my Church; and the gates of hell shall not prevail against it."

Before the world was, God planned, perfected, and prepared His eternal kingdom, where we will dwell in eternal glory with Him:

"Then shall the King say unto them on His right hand, Come, ye blessed of my Father, *inherit the kingdom prepared for you FROM THE FOUNDATION OF THE WORLD"* (Matt. 25:34).

To the believers in Corinth, Paul said, "We speak of the wisdom of God in a mystery, even the hidden wisdom, *which God ordained BEFORE THE WORLD unto our glory"* (I Cor. 2:7).

Before the world was, it was determined in the council of the Godhead that Christ Jesus the Lord would be the One to give His life's blood to save sinners, thus becoming the one Mediator between God and man: "For there is one God, and one Mediator between God and men, the man Christ Jesus" (I Tim. 2:5).

Not only was Christ the Mediator in *salvation,*

He was also the Mediator *of world creation:* "God, who at sundry times and in divers manners spake in time past unto the fathers by the prophets, hath in these last days spoken unto us *by His Son, whom He hath appointed heir of all things, BY WHOM ALSO HE MADE THE WORLDS"* (Heb. 1:1,2).

"For by Him (Christ) *were all things created, that are in heaven, and that are in earth, visible and invisible, whether they be thrones, or dominions, or principalities, or powers: ALL things were created BY HIM, and FOR HIM: and He is BEFORE ALL THINGS, and BY HIM ALL THINGS CONSIST"* (Col. 1:16,17).

"All things were made by Him; and *without* Him was not any thing made that was made" (John 1:3).

The Lord Jesus Christ was also the Mediator of the *preservation* of the world: *He upholds ALL THINGS "by the word of His power"* (Heb. 1:3). "And He is before all things, and *BY HIM all things CONSIST"* (Col. 1:17).

Christ was also the Mediator of *world redemption*— yes, even before there was a world to redeem: "For it pleased the Father that *in Him should all fulness dwell;* and, having made peace through the blood of His cross, by Him to reconcile *all things* unto Himself; by Him, I say, *whether they be THINGS IN EARTH, or THINGS IN HEAVEN"* (Col. 1:19,20).

"Blessed be the God and Father of our Lord Jesus Christ, who hath blessed us with all spiritual blessings in heavenly places in Christ: *According as He hath chosen us in Him before the foundation of the world, that we should be holy and without blame before Him in love"* (Eph. 1:3, 4).

"Forasmuch as ye know that *ye were not redeemed with corruptible things, as silver and gold,* from your vain conversation received by tradition from your fathers; *but with the precious blood of Christ, as of a*

*lamb without blemish and without spot: WHO VER-
ILY WAS FOREORDAINED BEFORE THE FOUN-
DATION OF THE WORLD,* but was manifest in
these last times for you" (I Pet. 1:18—20).

"For I reckon that the sufferings of this present
time are not worthy to be compared with the glory
which shall be revealed in us. For the earnest expectation of the creature waiteth for the manifestation
of the sons of God. For the creature was made subject to vanity, not willingly, but by reason of Him
who hath subjected the same in hope. Because the
creature itself also shall be delivered from the bondage
of corruption into the glorious liberty of the children
of God. *For we know that the WHOLE CREATION
groaneth and travaileth in pain together until now.
And not only they, but OURSELVES ALSO, which
have the firstfruits of the Spirit, even we ourselves
groan within ourselves, WAITING FOR THE ADOP-
TION, to wit, THE REDEMPTION OF OUR BODY"*
(Rom. 8:18—23).

It stands to reason that since God appointed Christ
Jesus to be *Mediator* of all these things, He also appointed Him to be *JUDGE of all things*—the One to
carry out world judgment: *"For the Father judgeth
no man, but hath committed ALL JUDGMENT unto
the Son"* (John 5:22).

What was God doing before creation? I think you
will agree that *since "the beginning"* there has been
much activity at God's house! There were no sur-
prises in the life of Jesus as He tabernacled among
men. Before the world was—from all eternity—He
knew exactly why He left the Father's bosom to be
born of the Virgin Mary, and He was willing to carry
out the work of redemption as agreed upon by the
Godhead before creation began. Therefore, Christ's
death on the cross was no surprise to Him, for although it was carried out *in time,* His death was an

act of *eternity.*

Eternal realities were settled before time began. Finally, endlessness flowed into time and God brought order out of chaos. He created Adam from the dust of the ground, breathed into his nostrils the breath of life, and man became a living soul. When God placed Adam in the Garden of Eden, He told him exactly what he was to do, and the one thing he was *not* to do. *God commanded*—and to show Adam that He meant business He clearly spelled out to him what the results would be *if he failed to obey that command.*

Adam sinned—but God in love and mercy promised the Saviour (Gen. 3:15). "When the fulness of the time was come," Jesus came as promised (Gal. 4:4,5). He died on the cross, He rose again, He conquered death, hell, and the grave. He ascended back to the Father, and today the Man Christ Jesus sits at the right hand of God, making intercession for those who have accepted Him as Saviour. He will continue there until the end of this Dispensation of Grace, at which time He will come to call His bride, the New Testament Church, to meet Him in the air.

Then after the Great Tribulation period, the battle of Armageddon, the Millennium, the battle of Gog and Magog, and the Great White Throne judgment, time will again flow into eternity and the ages of ages will roll on. God the Father, God the Son, God the Holy Spirit, the Church and *all creation, REDEEMED,* will share unending glory throughout eternity!

The eternal decree of redemption through the blood of the Lamb, conceived in God before the foundation of the world, became in time the covenant of God with mankind; and the ultimate goal of that covenant is *the EVERLASTING covenant* which Christ Jesus the Lord has dedicated through His blood:

"Now the God of peace, that brought again from

the dead our Lord Jesus, that great Shepherd of the sheep, *through THE BLOOD OF THE EVERLAST-ING COVENANT,* make you perfect in every good work to do His will, working in you that which is wellpleasing in His sight, through Jesus Christ; to whom be glory for ever and ever. Amen" (Heb. 13: 20, 21).

These great truths are recorded in the Word of God that we may know the vastness of His divine love. Even before the beginning of the ages God's highest concern and deepest desire was for our glory. Before ever the planets were hung in space or the stars began to run their courses; before the seas raged or the foundation of the world was laid, *God was thinking of you and of me!* Beloved, if that does not humble our hearts and cause us to cry out, "Woe is me! Lord, cleanse me and make me a vessel meet for your use," God pity us! The realization that before the ages began, the eternal God had His thoughts on us should cause us to present our bodies a living sacrifice and our members as instruments of holiness unto God.

As for me, I say with the Apostle Paul: "For this cause I bow my knees unto the Father of our Lord Jesus Christ," and pray that He will grant me, according to the riches of His glory, to be strengthened with might by His Spirit in the inner man; that Christ may dwell in my heart by faith, that I, being rooted and grounded in love, may be able to comprehend what is the breadth, and length, and depth, and height; and to know the love of Christ which passeth knowledge, that I may be filled with all the fulness of God (Eph. 3:14—19).

Since God Himself, by virtue of His deity, is the *highest,* the goal of His eternal will must always be that which lies within His own nature. Therefore, what God demanded, only God could provide. His work must be so ordered that all things *lead* to Him, all things must have their *end* in Him, and all things must be *to His glory.* Everything God has done from eternity, everything He will do *throughout* eternity, has Himself eternally as its goal. Regardless of what God does, it is done "for His name's sake" (Psalm 23:3).

Why did God the Father plan all this at the expense of the blood of His only begotten Son? He did it that He might present believers (the Church) to Himself—"*a glorious Church,* not having spot, or wrinkle, or any such thing; but that it should be holy and without blemish" (Eph. 5:27).

All things—in heaven and in earth—must climax *"to the praise of His glory"* (Eph. 1:12,14), *"THAT GOD MAY BE ALL IN ALL."* (I Cor. 15:28). Therefore the *purpose* of creation consists in the unfolding and the displaying of the glory of God—God *before* all things, God Himself the *beginning* of all things, the *center* of all things, and the *climax* of all things. But the greatest glory of all will be displayed in "the pearl of great price," the Lamb's wife, as the Church occupies the Pearly White City throughout the ages of ages:

"God, who is rich in mercy, for His great love wherewith He loved us, even when we were dead in sins, hath quickened us together with Christ, (by grace ye are saved;) and hath raised us up together, and made us sit together in heavenly places in Christ Jesus: THAT IN THE AGES TO COME HE MIGHT SHEW THE EXCEEDING RICHES OF HIS GRACE in His kindness toward us THROUGH CHRIST JESUS" (Eph. 2:4—7).

Jesus promised His disciples, "I go to prepare a place for you. And if I go and prepare a place for you, I will come again, and receive you unto myself; that where I am, there ye may be also" (John 14:2,3).

For more than nineteen hundred years our Lord has been preparing that city, the New Jerusalem. As John saw and described it in Revelation 21:9—27, it was filled with the glory of God. Its walls were of jasper, the twelve gates were of twelve pearls—each gate one magnificent pearl. The street of the city was of transparent gold. There was no temple there, for God and the Lamb were the temple of it. There was no need for sun or moon, "for the glory of God did lighten it, *and the Lamb is the light thereof.*"

The "saved nations" will occupy the new earth, and they will walk in the light of the Pearly White City—a fact which suggests that the city will be suspended between the third heaven and the new earth. Kings will bring their glory and honor into it. The gates will never be shut, because Satan will then be in the lake of fire and all wickedness will be forever banished. There will be no tempter—therefore no evil and no need to close the gates. Satan will never enter that city as he entered the Garden of Eden, for *"there shall IN NO WISE enter into it any thing that defileth, neither whatsoever worketh abomination, or maketh a lie: but they which are written in the Lamb's book of life"* (Rev. 21:27).

All creation will see the glory of God on display in the Pearly White City, the eternal home of the New Testament Church; and throughout the endless ages His glory will be seen as He abides in the presence of His redeemed people!

As we look around us today, it seems that Christianity is fighting a losing battle—but not so! Christians are in the minority, that is true—it has *always* been true. But one day we will be *the host of heaven* and we will abide with our God, our Saviour, the angels, and the host of the redeemed throughout eternity:

"But God commendeth His love toward us, in that,

while we were yet sinners, Christ died for us. *MUCH MORE then, being now justified by His blood, we shall be saved from wrath through Him. For if, when we were enemies, we were reconciled to God by the death of His Son, much more, being reconciled, we shall be saved by His life. And not only so, BUT WE ALSO JOY IN GOD through our Lord Jesus Christ, BY WHOM WE HAVE NOW RECEIVED THE ATONEMENT"* (Rom. 5:8—11).

Chapter Two

BIBLE TRUTH CONCERNING CHRIST

"Now the birth of Jesus Christ was on this wise: When as His mother Mary was espoused to Joseph, before they came together, she was found with child of the Holy Ghost. Then Joseph her husband, being a just man, and not willing to make her a publick example, was minded to put her away privily. But while he thought on these things, behold, the angel of the Lord appeared unto him in a dream, saying, Joseph, thou son of David, fear not to take unto thee Mary thy wife: for that which is conceived in her is of the Holy Ghost. And she shall bring forth a son, and thou shalt call His name JESUS: for He shall save His people from their sins.

"Now all this was done, that it might be fulfilled which was spoken of the Lord by the prophet, saying, Behold, a virgin shall be with child, and shall bring forth a son, and they shall call His name Emmanuel, which being interpreted is, God with us.

"Then Joseph being raised from sleep did as the angel of the Lord had bidden him, and took unto him his wife: and knew her not till she had brought forth her firstborn son: and called His name JESUS" (Matt. 1:18—25).

"In the sixth month the angel Gabriel was sent from God unto a city of Galilee, named Nazareth, to a virgin espoused to a man whose name was Joseph, of the house of David; and the virgin's name was Mary. And the angel came in unto her, and said, Hail, thou that art highly favoured, the Lord is with thee: blessed art thou among women.

"And when she saw him, she was troubled at his saying, and cast in her mind what manner of salutation this should be. And the angel said unto her, Fear not, Mary: for thou hast found favour with God. And, behold, thou shalt conceive in thy womb, and bring forth a son, and shalt call His name JESUS. He shall be great, and shall be called the Son of the Highest: and the Lord God shall give unto Him the throne of His father David: And He shall reign over the house of Jacob for ever; and of His kingdom there shall be no end.

"Then said Mary unto the angel, How shall this be, seeing I know not a man? And the angel answered and said unto her, The Holy Ghost shall come upon thee, and the power of the Highest shall overshadow thee: therefore also that holy thing which shall be born of thee shall be called the Son of God" (Luke 1:26—35).

"When Jesus came into the coasts of Caesarea Philippi, He asked His disciples, saying, Whom do men say that I the Son of man am? And they said, Some say that thou art John the Baptist: some, Elias; and others, Jeremias, or one of the prophets.

"He saith unto them, But whom say YE that I am? And Simon Peter answered and said, *THOU ART THE CHRIST, the Son of the living God.* And Jesus answered and said unto him, Blessed art thou, Simon Bar-jona: for *flesh and blood hath not revealed it unto thee, but MY FATHER which is in heaven*" (Matt. 16:13—17).

Men are still asking, *"Who IS Jesus?"* They are still trying, through their own wisdom, to discover the identity of this Man, born almost twenty centuries ago. Peter confessed, "Thou art the Christ, the Son of the living God." Jesus immediately declared him "blessed," and said, "Flesh and blood hath not revealed it unto thee, but my Father which is in heaven."

The same is true today. The only place to find Bible truth concerning Jesus is in *the Word of God.* Religions do not agree, educators do not agree, scientists do not agree; but from Genesis through Revelation the Scriptures are in perfect agreement concerning the identity of *Christ Jesus the Lord.*

"Now the birth of Jesus Christ was on this wise." Joseph was "espoused" (engaged) to Mary, but they had not yet come together as man and wife. When he discovered that she was "with child" he would have put her away because he knew what the law said concerning the birth of a child out of wedlock.

However, Joseph was "a just man," he undoubtedly loved Mary very deeply, and he was unwilling to make a public example of her. So he planned "to put her away privily." But God made known the truth about Mary's condition: *"The angel of the Lord"* appeared to Joseph in a dream and explained to him that Mary would be the mother of the Son of God, *JESUS the Saviour,* as prophesied by Isaiah.

"Then Joseph being raised from sleep did as the angel of the Lord had bidden him, and took unto him his wife: *And knew her not till she had brought forth her FIRSTBORN SON: and he called His name JESUS."*

This Scripture points out the Bible truth that *the MAN Jesus* was born in Bethlehem of Judaea about two thousand years ago, but *CHRIST the Son of God was "in the beginning WITH God."*

There are many Scriptures which definitely prove that Christ Jesus the Lord was very God in flesh, and "as the Father hath life in Himself, so hath He given

to the Son to have life in Himself" (John 5:26). *God*
had no beginning; *Christ* had no beginning. *THEY*
WERE before the ages began.

He who was born "Jesus of Nazareth" and grew
to manhood in the home of Joseph the carpenter was
none other than God in flesh, conceived of the Holy
Ghost, born of the Virgin Mary. He received His
flesh (His manhood) from Mary, but His inner life
(His blood) was from God.

The Apostle Paul, under inspiration of the Holy
Spirit, gave this statement to the elders in Ephesus:

"Take heed therefore unto yourselves, and to all
the flock, over the which the Holy Ghost hath made
you overseers, to feed *the Church of God, which He*
hath purchased with HIS OWN BLOOD" (Acts 20:28).
The New Testament Church was purchased with *the*
blood of GOD—the blood shed on Calvary's cross;
and that blood was *the blood of JESUS,* the Son of
God. Christ Jesus the Lord was God from all eternity.
He was wrapped in flesh, "made like unto His brethren," that He might pay the sin-debt and ransom
sinners—all who will believe in His shed blood and
finished work. He was God's Christ, very God, the
God who was "in the beginning":

"In the beginning was the Word, and the Word
was with God, *AND THE WORD WAS GOD.... And*
the Word was made flesh, and dwelt among us..."
(John 1:1, 14).

In II Corinthians 5:19 Paul declares "that *GOD*
was IN CHRIST, reconciling the world unto Himself
...."

Christ's Divinity

In the New Testament we find many *divine names*
applied to the Lord Jesus Christ. In Luke 22:70 we
we read, "Then said they all, Art thou then *the Son*
of God? And (Jesus) said unto them, Ye say that I

am."

Jesus — "the Son of God":

Forty times in the New Testament Jesus is called "the Son of God" — and if He had been called the Son of God but *once,* that would have been sufficient proof of His divinity, because God's Word needs no repetition to make it so!

In addition to being called *"the Son of God"* forty times, the New Testament refers to Jesus in many other *synonymous* expressions — such as "My Son... His Son . . . My beloved Son."

Jesus Himself declared His sonship: In John 5:17, 18 we read where He said to the Jews, *"My Father worketh hitherto, and I work."* This so angered the Jews that they "sought the more to kill Him, because He not only had broken the sabbath, but said also that God was His Father, making Himself *equal with God."*

Jesus — "the only begotten Son":

John the Beloved declared, "No man hath seen God at any time; *the ONLY BEGOTTEN SON, which is in the bosom of the Father, He hath declared Him"* (John 1:18). It is true that *all born again Christians* are sons of God, but *JESUS is the "only BEGOTTEN Son":*

"For God so loved the world, that He gave *His ONLY begotten Son,* that whosoever believeth in Him should not perish, but have everlasting life" (John 3:16).

In Mark 12:1—6 Jesus spoke of the Old Testament prophets as *servants* of God, but of Himself He said, *"Having yet therefore ONE Son, His wellbeloved,* He sent Him also last unto them, saying, They will reverence my Son." Jesus was *the ONE Son, wellbeloved and only begotten* Son of God — conceived of the Holy Ghost, born of the Virgin Mary, very God in flesh!

Jesus — "the first and the last":

John the Beloved was exiled to Patmos for his testimony, and of his experience there he testified, "I saw seven golden candlesticks, and in the midst of the seven candlesticks *One like unto the Son of man . . .* ," and the Voice that spoke to John declared, "I am Alpha and Omega—*the first and the last.*" (Please read Revelation 1:9—18.) If we can find this same term elsewhere in the Bible referring to *God,* we can know beyond any doubt that the One whom John saw in the midst of the golden candlesticks was the only begotten *Son of God,* Deity incarnate.

The Prophet Isaiah sheds light on "the first and the last": In Isaiah 41:4 we read, "Who hath wrought and done it, calling the generations from the beginning? I the Lord, *the first,* and with *the last;* I am He." Then in Isaiah 44:6 the prophet declares, "Thus saith the LORD the King of Israel, and His Redeemer the LORD of hosts: *I AM THE FIRST, and I AM THE LAST;* and beside me there is no God."

Jesus — "I AM":

In Exodus 3:1—12 we find recorded God's calling of Moses to lead the children of Israel out of Egyptian bondage, and the objections Moses offered in response to the call. Then in verses 13 and 14 we read, "And Moses said unto God, Behold, when I come unto the children of Israel, and shall say unto them, The God of your fathers hath sent me unto you; and they shall say to me, What is His name? What shall I say unto them?

"And God said unto Moses, *I AM THAT I AM:* and He said, *Thus shalt thou say unto the children of Israel, I AM hath sent me unto you!*"

Now let us compare these passages from the Old Testament with portions of John 18:1—8, where Judas led a band of men and officers into the Garden of Gethsemane to arrest Jesus:

"Jesus therefore, knowing all things that should come upon Him, went forth, and said unto them, *Whom seek ye?*" His enemies replied, "Jesus of Nazareth." Jesus then said to them, *"I AM He"*—and they "went backward, *and fell to the ground.*" Jesus then asked them again, "Whom seek ye?" and again they replied, "Jesus of Nazareth." He then said to them, "I have told you that *I AM He:* if therefore ye seek me, let these (the disciples) go their way."

In the Greek, the pronoun "he" is not in the original text. Therefore what Jesus said to His enemies was, "I AM!" In the passages from the Old Testament (Isaiah 41:4; 44:6; and Exodus 3:14), "I AM" refers to Jehovah God. In John 18:5,8, "I AM" refers to Jesus of Nazareth, the only begotten Son of God. Yes, the great "I AM" who declared Himself through Isaiah, the "I AM" who sent Moses to deliver the Israelites from Egypt, is one and the same with the "I AM" who stood in the Garden of Gethsemane and flattened His enemies to the ground with the power of His words!

In the Old Testament passages, Jehovah, God of the ages, is I AM—"the first and the last." In the New Testament, Jesus boldly declared, *"I AM Alpha and Omega, the first and the last. . . .* I am Alpha and Omega, *the beginning and the end, the first and the last"* (Rev. 1:11; 22:13).

Jesus—"the Holy One":

In Hosea 11:9 we read, "I will not execute the fierceness of mine anger, I will not return to destroy Ephraim: *for I AM GOD,* and not man; *the HOLY ONE* in the midst of thee: and I will not enter into the city."

Where else in our Scriptures do we find reference
to *"the Holy One"?* The answer is found in Acts
3:12—15:

Peter and John had just encountered the man who
had been lame since birth. Daily he sat at the gate
of the temple and begged alms. Peter said to the
man, "Silver and gold have I none; but such as I have
give I thee: *In the name of Jesus Christ of Nazareth*
rise up and walk!" (v. 6).

There was no denying the miracle that was wrought
on this man, for he stood, and leaped, and walked,
and "entered with them into the temple, walking, and
leaping, and praising God." The people who witnessed the miraculous healing ran to Peter and John
in great excitement, "wondering."

"And when Peter saw it, he answered unto the
people, Ye men of Israel, why marvel ye at this? or
why look ye so earnestly on us, as though by our own
power or holiness we had made this man to walk?
The God of Abraham, and of Isaac, and of Jacob, the
God of our fathers, hath glorified His Son Jesus; whom
ye delivered up, and denied Him in the presence of
Pilate, when he was determined to let Him go.

"But ye denied THE HOLY ONE and the JUST,
and desired a murderer to be granted unto you; and
killed the Prince of life, whom God hath raised from
the dead; whereof we are witnesses."

In the Old Testament passage from Hosea, *Jehovah*
God clearly declared Himself as "the HOLY ONE."
In Peter's sermon to the Jews after the healing of the
lame man, he just as clearly declared *JESUS* as *"the*
HOLY ONE and the Just," telling them that they
had denied God's Son, their promised Messiah—the
God of their fathers *in flesh.*

In Luke 4:34 we are told that the *demons* recognized Jesus as the Holy One of God. They said, "Let

us alone; what have we to do with thee, thou *Jesus of Nazareth?* art thou come to destroy us? I know thee who thou art; *the HOLY ONE OF GOD.*"

Jesus — "the Lord":

In Malachi 3:1 we read, "Behold, I will send my messenger, and he shall prepare the way before me: *and the Lord, whom ye seek,* shall suddenly come to His temple, even the messenger of the covenant, whom ye delight in: behold, He shall come, saith the *LORD of hosts.*"

In the first part of this verse, *the Lord* is spoken of as the One "whom ye seek" — in other words, One not yet come.   In the last part of the verse, *"the LORD of hosts"* is the One speaking. Luke 2:11 tells us who "the Lord" is: "For unto you is born this day in the city of David *a Saviour, which is CHRIST THE LORD.*" Yes, the One of whom Malachi spoke is the One born in the city of David: *Christ the Lord.*

Acts chapter 9 records the conversion of Saul of Tarsus; and in verse 17 we read, "Ananias went his way, and entered into the house; and putting his hands on him said, *Brother Saul, the LORD, even JESUS, that appeared unto thee in the way as thou camest, hath sent me, that thou mightest receive thy sight, and be filled with the Holy Ghost.*"

In this verse, Ananias clearly identified "the Lord" and Jesus as one and the same Person — and this is true: Jesus *is* the Lord, "Lord of hosts," Jehovah God in flesh.

When others of the disciples told Thomas they had seen the risen Lord, he said, "Except I shall see in His hands the print of the nails, and put my finger into the print of the nails, and thrust my hand into His side, I will not believe." But a week later Jesus again appeared to the disciples when Thomas was present, and said to him, "Reach hither thy finger, and behold my hands; and reach hither thy hand, and thrust it into my side: and be not faithless, but believing." Then Thomas exclaimed, *"My Lord AND MY GOD!"* (John 20:24—28).

"The Lord" is used several hundred times with reference to Jesus. The word translated "lord" is sometimes used in the New Testament in speaking of *men* (as in Acts 25:26), but not in the same way it is used of Christ. He is spoken of as "THE Lord" just as *Jehovah God* is spoken of as *The Lord*. Acts 4:26, 33 tells us, "The kings of the earth stood up, and the rulers were gathered together *against THE LORD, and against HIS CHRIST.* . . . And with great power gave the apostles witness of the resurrection of *THE LORD JESUS:* and great grace was upon them all."

Now note Psalm 2:2, 3: "The kings of the earth set themselves, and the rulers take counsel together, *against THE LORD*, and *against HIS ANOINTED*, saying, Let us break their bands asunder, and cast away their cords from us."

In Psalm 45:6, 7 we read, "Thy throne, O God, is for ever and ever: the sceptre of thy kingdom is a right sceptre. Thou lovest righteousness, and hatest wickedness: therefore God, thy God, hath anointed thee with the oil of gladness above thy fellows."

Compare these verses with the verbally inspired words in Paul's letter to the Hebrew believers: *"But unto the SON He saith,* Thy throne, O God, is for ever and ever: a sceptre of righteousness is the sceptre of thy kingdom. Thou hast loved righteousness, and hated iniquity; therefore God, even thy God, hath anointed thee with the oil of gladness above thy fellows" (Heb. 1:8, 9).

Also compare Psalm 110:1—"The Lord said unto my Lord, Sit thou at my right hand, until I make thine enemies thy footstool"—with the inspired words of the following New Testament passages:

"The Lord said unto my Lord, Sit thou on my right hand, till I make thine enemies thy footstool" (Matt. 22:44).

"For David is not ascended into the heavens: but he saith himself, The Lord said unto my Lord, Sit thou on my right hand, until I make thy foes thy footstool" (Acts 2:34, 35).

"But to which of the angels said He at any time, Sit on my right hand, until I make thine enemies thy footstool?" (Heb. 1:13).

One day *EVERY* tongue will confess that Jesus Christ is Lord "to the glory of God the Father" (Phil. 2:11).

King David *in spirit* called Jesus "Lord": "While the Pharisees were gathered together, Jesus asked them, saying *What think ye of Christ? Whose Son is He?* They say unto Him, *The son of David.* He saith unto them, *How then doth David in spirit call Him LORD,* saying, The LORD said unto *my Lord,* Sit thou on my right hand, till I make thine enemies thy footstool? If David then call Him Lord, how is He his son?" (Matt. 22:41—45).

The Lord Jesus Christ is expressly invested with divine names. In Isaiah 9:6, 7 we are told, "Unto us a child is born, unto us a son is given . . . *and His name shall be called Wonderful, Counsellor, The mighty God, The everlasting Father, The Prince of Peace.* Of the increase of His government and peace there shall be no end, upon the throne of David, and upon His kingdom, to order it, and to establish it with judgment and with justice from henceforth even for ever. *The zeal of THE LORD OF HOSTS will perform this.*"

Who would doubt the identity of "the Mighty God" or "the Everlasting Father"? And certainly *"the Prince of Peace"* was the fulness of the Godhead displayed bodily (Col. 2:9).

The Scriptures in both the Old and New Testaments clearly declare Christ as the Eternal One, from everlasting to everlasting:

"But thou, Bethlehem Ephratah, though thou be little among the thousands of Judah, yet *out of thee shall He come forth unto me that is to be Ruler in Israel; WHOSE GOINGS FORTH HAVE BEEN FROM OF OLD, FROM EVERLASTING"* (Micah 5:2).

Now read Matthew 2:6: "And thou Bethlehem, in the land of Juda, art not the least among the princes of Juda: for out of thee shall come a Governor, that shall rule my people Israel."

And in John 7:42 we read, "Hath not the Scripture said, That Christ cometh of the seed of David, and out of the town of Bethlehem, where David was?"

Jesus — "God with us":

God spoke through the Prophet Isaiah giving the prophecy of the virgin birth of the Saviour. His birth was foretold as the means through which the Eternal God could be "Immanuel" *(God with us):*

"Therefore the Lord Himself shall give you a sign: Behold, a virgin shall conceive, and bear a son, *and shall call His name Immanuel"* (Isa. 7:14).

Now notice Matthew 1:23: "Behold, a virgin shall be with child, and shall bring forth a son, *and they shall call His name Emmanuel, which being interpreted is, GOD WITH US."*

Jesus — "Lord of all":

"The Word which God sent unto the children of Israel, preaching peace by Jesus Christ: (He is Lord of all)" (Acts 10:36).

Jesus — "Lord of glory":

"Which none of the princes of this world knew:

for had they known it, they would not have crucified *the Lord of glory"* (I Cor. 2:8).

Jesus — "King of glory":

"Who is this King of glory? *The LORD* strong and mighty, *the LORD* mighty in battle. Lift up your heads, O ye gates; even lift them up, ye everlasting doors; and the King of glory shall come in. Who is this King of glory? *The Lord of hosts,* He is *the King of glory"* (Psalm 24:8—10).

Jesus — "mighty God, everlasting Father":

". . . His name shall be called Wonderful, Counsellor, THE MIGHTY GOD, THE EVERLASTING FATHER, The Prince of Peace" (Isa. 9:6).

Jesus — "the great God and our Saviour":

"Looking for that blessed hope, and the glorious appearing of *the great God and our Saviour, Jesus Christ"* (Tit. 2:13).

Jesus Himself affirmed His deity on several occasions while He tabernacled among men. We have already discussed His declaration in the Garden of Gethsemane when He identified Himself as the great "I AM" of the Old Testament. But even before that, He had plainly told the Pharisees, *"Before Abraham was, I AM"* (John 8:58), and they took up stones to stone Him because He applied Jehovah's name to Himself.

In John 8:23, 24 He said to them, "Ye are from beneath; *I AM FROM ABOVE:* ye are of this world: *I am NOT of this world.* I said therefore unto you, that ye shall die in your sins: for *if ye believe not that I am He, ye shall die in your sins."*

In John 10:30—33, Jesus declared, *"I and my Father are ONE.* Then the Jews took up stones again to stone Him. Jesus answered them, Many good works have I shewed you from my Father; for which of those works do ye stone me? The Jews answered Him, saying, For a good work we stone thee not; but for blasphemy; *and because that thou, being a man, makest thyself God."* But they could not destroy Him. He came to die on a cross for the sins of the world, not to be stoned for speaking the truth concerning His deity!

In the Great Commission, given to His disciples just before He returned to His heavenly Father, Jesus again identified Himself as being one with God:

"Go ye therefore, and teach all nations, baptizing them in the name of the Father, and of the Son, and of the Holy Ghost: teaching them to observe all things whatsoever I have commanded you: and, lo, I am with you alway, even unto the end of the world" (Matt. 28:19, 20).

In Mark 14:61, 62, Jesus stood before the high priest to be questioned during trial: "But He held His peace, and answered nothing. Again the high priest asked Him . . . *Art thou the Christ, the Son of the Blessed?* And Jesus said, *I AM: and ye shall see the Son of man sitting on the right hand of power, and coming in the clouds of heaven."*

It was then that He was again accused of blasphemy and condemned to death. "And some began to spit on Him, and to cover His face, and to buffet Him, and to say unto Him, Prophesy: and the servants did strike Him with the palms of their hands" (Mark 14:65).

Whosoever refuses to accept the divinity of Christ— Son of God, Divine Saviour—is guilty of a great sin indeed, for by rejecting the deity of Christ he also rejects God and calls Him a liar:

"He that believeth on the Son of God hath the witness in himself: *he that believeth not God hath made Him a liar;* because he believeth not the record that God gave of His Son. And this is the record, that God hath given to us eternal life, and this life is in His Son. He that hath the Son hath life; and he that hath not the Son of God hath not life" (I John 5:10—12).

Christ's Divine Attributes

The Lord Jesus Christ is OMNIPOTENT:

Here on earth, He possessed and demonstrated all the power the Eternal God has ever demonstrated. He had power over all kinds of diseases—He simply spoke the word and lepers were cleansed, the palsied were healed, the lame were made to walk, the deaf were made to hear, and the blind were given sight. He cast out demons, raised the dead, and *even the elements* were subject to Him!

Power over disease:

In Luke 4:38—41 we read that Jesus "arose out of the synagogue, and entered into Simon's house. And Simon's wife's mother was taken with a great fever; and they besought Him for her. And He stood over her, and *rebuked* the fever; *and it left her: and IMMEDIATELY she arose and ministered unto them.*

"Now when the sun was setting, *all they that had any sick with DIVERS DISEASES brought them unto Him; and He laid His hands on every one of them, and healed them.*

"And *DEVILS* also came out of many, crying out, and saying, Thou art Christ the Son of God. And He rebuking them suffered them not to speak: for they knew that He was Christ."

Power over death:

In Luke 7:11—16, Jesus broke up a funeral pro-

cession by restoring life to a poor widow's only son.
As He approached the city of Nain, "behold there was
a dead man carried out, the only son of his mother,
and she was a widow: and much people of the city
was with her.

"And when the Lord saw her, He had compassion
on her, and said unto her, Weep not. And He came
and touched the bier: and they that bare him stood
still. And He said, *Young man, I say unto thee,
ARISE. And he that was dead sat up, and began to
speak. And He delivered him to his mother.* And
there came a fear on all: and they glorified God, saying, That a great prophet is risen up among us; and,
That God hath visited His people."

In Luke 8:49—55 Jesus robbed the grave of a little
maiden. When He heard of the death of the daughter
of Jairus (a ruler of the synagogue), He said, "Fear
not: believe only, and she shall be made whole."
Coming to Jairus' house where people were weeping
and bewailing the little girl's death, *"He put them all
out, and took her by the hand, and called, saying,
Maid, arise. And her spirit came again, and she arose
straightway:* and He commanded to give her meat."

Even *more remarkable* is the account of the raising
of Lazarus—a man who had lain in the grave for four
days and whose body was beginning to deteriorate!
When Lazarus became ill, his sisters Mary and Martha
sent a message to Jesus saying, *"Lord, behold, he
whom thou lovest is sick."* However, Jesus did not
immediately *return* to Bethany, and when He finally
arrived there Lazarus had been dead for four days
and his body had begun to decay. Martha said, "Lord,
by this time he stinketh!"

But that made no difference to Jesus, because God
can raise the dead regardless of how long death has
held them. The hour will come when the trumpet
will sound and *ALL the dead in Christ* shall rise—the

departed saints of all ages will come forth at His call.

He proved His deity as He stood by the tomb of Lazarus. At His instruction "they took away the stone from the place where the dead was laid. And Jesus lifted up His eyes, and said, *Father, I thank thee that thou hast heard me. And I knew that thou hearest me always: but BECAUSE OF THE PEOPLE WHICH STAND BY I said it, that they may believe that thou hast sent me.*"

Then He cried with a loud voice, "*Lazarus, COME FORTH!*" and a man who had been dead for four days came from the grave "bound hand and foot with graveclothes: and his face was bound about with a napkin. *JESUS SAITH UNTO THEM, Loose him, and let him go!*" (John 11:1—44).

Only God can raise the dead—but JESUS WAS GOD in flesh. He personally conquered the world, the flesh, the devil, death, hell, and the grave; and in Revelation 1:18 He declares:

"*I am He that liveth, and was dead; and, behold, I am alive FOR EVERMORE, Amen! and have the KEYS of hell and of DEATH!*"

Power over demons:

Jesus also proved His deity by casting out demons. The people brought unto Him many who were demon-possessed: "When the even was come, they brought unto Him many that were possessed with devils: *and He cast out the spirits with His word . . .*" (Matt. 8:16).

Luke 4:33—37 also tells us that Jesus rebuked demons and delivered people from their power. The people were amazed at this, "and spake among themselves, saying, *What a word is this! for with authority and power He commandeth the unclean spirits, and they come out!*"

In verse 41 of that same chapter we read, "Devils

also came out of many, crying out, and saying, *THOU
ART CHRIST THE SON OF GOD.* And He rebuking
them suffered them not to speak: for *they knew that
He was CHRIST."* Yes, the devil has more respect
for Jesus than do some liberal modern preachers and
professors of religion! There are men in pulpits today
who *deny the deity of Christ,* but the devil has never
made such denial and demons recognized Him when-
ever they came in contact with Him.

Power over the wind and sea:

Not only did Christ prove His omnipotence through
healing all kinds of sickness, raising the dead, and
casting out demons—*He also had power over the elements.* The wind and the sea were subject to His
words. On one occasion, as Jesus and His disciples
were crossing the Sea of Galilee in a fishing boat, a
mighty tempest arose and the stormy waves threatened
to destroy the little ship.

From events recorded just previous to this incident,
we know that our Lord had had a day of intense
activity, undoubtedly He was very tired, and when
the storm arose "He was in the hinder part of the
ship, asleep." The disciples awakened Him and said,
"Master, carest thou not that we perish?"

*"And He arose, and rebuked the wind, and said
unto the sea, PEACE, BE STILL! And the wind
ceased, and there was a great calm."* The disciples
were amazed—"they feared exceedingly, and said one
to another, *What manner of Man is this, THAT EVEN
THE WIND AND THE SEA OBEY HIM!"* (Mark
4:35—41).

As God the Father is omnipotent, *Jesus the Son*
is omnipotent. He is "far above all principality, and
power, and might, and dominion, and every name that
is named, not only in this world, but also in that
which is to come" (Eph. 1:21). God the Father has

given Him "a name which is above every name: that at the name of Jesus every knee should bow, of things in heaven, and things in earth, and things under the earth; and that every tongue should confess that Jesus Christ is Lord, to the glory of God the Father" (Phil. 2:9—11). All power is given unto Him, both in heaven and in earth (Matt. 28:18), and *He upholds all things by the word of His power* (Heb. 1:3).

The Lord Jesus Christ is OMNISCIENT:

He knew men's lives, He knew all about them, even the secrets of their hearts. He "did not commit Himself unto them, because *He knew all men, and needed not that any should testify of man: for He knew what was in man*" (John 2:24, 25).

He knew the heart and mind of man:

In John 4:3—42, when Jesus "left Judaea, and departed again into Galilee," He went through Samaria, and wearied from His journey He stopped to rest at Jacob's well while His disciples went into the city to buy food. It was "about the sixth hour" of the day, and as Jesus sat resting on the well, a woman of Samaria came to draw water.

This was unusual—both from the standpoint of time, and the fact that the woman was alone. According to the time used in that locality in those days, *the sixth hour* would have been high noon. It was the custom for the women to come *early in the morning* to draw water, and they came *in groups*. The unusual hour at which this woman came to the well, and the fact that she came alone, indicated that she had no friends and chose to come to the well when no one else would be there. She was a home-wrecker, a heart-breaker, and no doubt she was ostracized by the other women in the community.

As this poor, sinful woman approached the well, Jesus did not wait for her to open the conversation. He said to her, *"Give me to drink."* The woman was surprised by His request. She asked, "How is it that thou, being a *Jew,* askest drink of *me,* which am a woman of Samaria? *for the Jews have no dealings with the Samaritans."*

Jesus then began His message to her: "If thou knewest the gift of God, and who it is that saith to thee, Give me to drink, thou wouldest have asked of Him, and He would have given thee living water. . . . Whosoever drinketh of the water that I shall give him shall never thirst; but the water that I shall give him shall be in him a well of water springing up into everlasting life."

The woman then said to Him, "Sir, give me this water, that I thirst not, neither come hither to draw." Jesus then said to her, "Go, call thy husband, and come hither."

The woman answered, "I *have* no husband"—and Jesus then proved His omniscience. He replied, "Thou hast well said, I have no husband: for *thou hast had FIVE husbands; and he whom thou now hast is NOT thy husband. In that saidst thou truly!"*

When Jesus made this statement, the woman was amazed. Realizing that she was in the presence of an unusual Man she said, "Sir, I perceive that thou art a prophet." She then began to discuss religious matters—worshipping, and the proper place to worship—but what she really needed was the Saviour. What caused her to really pay attention to the words of Jesus, words which brought saving faith to her heart, was His omniscience—the fact that He told her exactly what she had been, giving the exact facts of her past life! He read her history perfectly, and as He led her step by step she realized that she was standing in the presence of the Messiah. She received the living water and ran into the city with an artesian well bubbling in her soul, and a great revival broke out because of her testimony: *"Come, see a man, which told me all things that ever I did: Is not this THE CHRIST?"*

II Chronicles 6:14—42 records Solomon's prayer of dedication for the temple, and in verse 30 we read, "Hear thou from heaven thy dwelling place, and forgive, and render unto every man according unto all his ways, *whose heart thou knowest: (for THOU ONLY KNOWEST THE HEARTS OF THE CHILDREN OF MEN)."* Solomon here declared that only Jehovah God knows the hearts of men; so *in omniscience* Jesus the Son of God was equal with the Father. He knew the hearts of men when He walked on earth, He knows every man's heart today, He knows every *secret* of every heart.

Jeremiah 17:9, 10 declares, "The heart is deceitful above all things, and desperately wicked: who can know it? *I THE LORD SEARCH THE HEART, I try the reins, even to give every man according to his ways, and according to the fruit of his doings."*

According to these inspired words, only God knows the heart—but *Jesus* knew the hearts of men, and He proved it to them by revealing their thoughts, their past history, and their present condition.

He knew man's future:

Not only did Jesus know the past history and the present thoughts of men—He knew *their future plans as well.* For instance, in John 6:64 He said, "There are some of you that believe not"—then the last part of the verse explains, *"FOR JESUS KNEW FROM THE BEGINNING WHO THEY WERE THAT BELIEVED NOT, AND WHO SHOULD BETRAY HIM!"* The disciples were astounded when Jesus said to them (speaking of Judas), "Have not I chosen you twelve, *and one of you is a devil?"* (John 6:70). In the original Greek, the article "a" does not appear. It simply reads, "one of you is *devil*," thus identifying Judas as the devil incarnate, as Jesus was God incarnate; and as Jesus perfectly carried out God's will and did everything the Father directed Him to do, *Judas was energized by Satan* and was used to carry out the devil's program.

Jesus knew this when He chose Judas as one of the twelve, and many people ask, "Since He *knew* what Judas was, why did He choose him?" The only answer I can give to this question is found in Deuteronomy 29:29: *"The secret things belong unto the Lord our God:* but those things which are revealed belong unto us and to our children for ever, that we may do all the words of this law."

It is not our business to try to learn what God did not see fit to reveal to us. In Romans 9:20, 21 the Apostle Paul wrote, under inspiration:

"Nay but, O man, who art thou that repliest against God? Shall the thing formed say to Him that formed it, Why hast thou made me thus? Hath not the potter power over the clay, of the same lump to make one vessel unto honour, and another unto dishonour?"

In John 1:43—49, Jesus called Philip to follow Him and immediately Philip sought out Nathanael and announced:

"We have found Him of whom Moses in the law, and the prophets, did write, Jesus of Nazareth, the son of Joseph."

Nathanael replied, "Can *any good thing* come out of Nazareth?" and Philip simply invited, "Come and see!"

"Jesus saw Nathanael coming to Him, and saith of him, Behold an Israelite indeed, in whom is no guile! Nathanael saith unto Him, *Whence knowest thou me?* Jesus answered and said unto him, *Before that Philip called thee, when thou wast under the fig tree, I saw thee.* Nathanael answered and saith unto Him, *Rabbi, THOU ART THE SON OF GOD; thou art the King of Israel!"*

Nathanael knew that *only God is omniscient,* and when Jesus displayed omniscience Nathanael recognized Him as the Son of God, very God in flesh.

Jesus knew God's future plans:

Christ not only knew the hearts and thoughts of *men;* He also knew *God's plans* for the future. In Luke 22:7—13 He gave the disciples instructions in preparing for the last Passover. He told Peter and John, "Go and prepare us the passover, that we may eat. And they said unto Him, Where wilt thou that we prepare? And He said unto them, *Behold, when ye are entered into the city, there shall a man meet you, bearing a pitcher of water; follow him into the house where he entereth in. And ye shall say unto the goodman of the house,* The Master saith unto thee, Where is the guest-chamber, where I shall eat the passover with my disciples? *And he shall shew you a large upper room furnished:* there make ready.

"AND THEY WENT, AND FOUND AS HE HAD SAID UNTO THEM: and they made ready the passover."

John 13:1 tells us that Jesus even knew *the exact hour* when He would return to His heavenly Father:

"Now before the feast of the passover, WHEN JESUS KNEW THAT HIS HOUR WAS COME THAT HE SHOULD DEPART OUT OF THIS WORLD UNTO THE FATHER, having loved His own which were in the world, He loved them unto the end."

The secrets of creation were known to Jesus:

Luke 5:1—11 records the account of a most unusual fishing expedition: After a night of toiling at their nets without catching any fish, Peter and his companions left their boats and were washing their nets on the shore when Jesus saw them. He borrowed Peter's boat for a pulpit from which He taught the multitudes, and "when He had left speaking, He said unto Simon, *Launch out into the deep, and let down your nets for a draught.*"

Peter replied, "Master, we have toiled all the night, and have taken nothing: *NEVERTHELESS AT THY WORD I will let down the NET.*" In other words, Peter said, "Master, out of respect to you I will do as you say; but we are experienced fishermen and we have fished *all night* in vain. There is no point in casting the nets again, but at your direction we will let down the net."

Notice—Jesus told Peter to let down *"nets"* (plural); but they had already washed their nets and were ready to pack them away until the next fishing expedition—and washing nets was hard work. So Peter said, "We will let down *one net.*"

"And when they had this done, they inclosed *a great multitude of fishes: and their net brake.* And they beckoned unto their partners, which were in the other ship, that they should come and help them. And they came, *and filled both the ships, so that they began to sink.*

"When Simon Peter saw it, he fell down at Jesus' knees, saying, Depart from me; for I am a sinful man, O Lord. *For he was astonished, and all that were with him, at the draught of the fishes which they had taken:* And so was also James, and John, the sons of Zebedee, which were partners with Simon. And Jesus said unto Simon, Fear not; *from henceforth thou shalt catch men.* And when they had brought their ships to land, *they forsook all, and followed Him.*"

The omniscience of Jesus was plainly revealed in

this experience, and Peter's partial obedience caused him to lose the greater part of the miraculous draught of fishes. Had he obeyed his Lord completely he would have had the greatest number of fish he had ever taken to market!

We find another revelation of Christ's omniscience in Matthew 17:24—27: The tax collectors in Capernaum came to Peter and asked, "Doth not your Master pay tribute?" Peter replied, "Yes." And then we read, "When he was come into the house, Jesus prevented him, saying, What thinkest thou, Simon? Of whom do the kings of the earth take custom or tribute? of their own children, or of strangers?

"Peter saith unto Him, Of strangers. Jesus saith unto him, Then are the children free. *Notwithstanding, lest we should offend them, GO THOU TO THE SEA, AND CAST AN HOOK, AND TAKE UP THE FISH THAT FIRST COMETH UP; and when thou hast opened his mouth, THOU SHALT FIND A PIECE OF MONEY: that take, and give unto them for me and thee!*"

Certainly no one could question omniscience on display here. Jesus knew there was a fish in the Sea of Galilee with a coin in its mouth which would be exactly enough to pay His and Peter's taxes. He told Peter exactly what to do, Peter obeyed, and found exactly as Jesus had said.

Jesus knows ALL things:

In John 21:17 Peter acknowledged the omniscience of Jesus. This time it was *the risen Lord* who appeared to the disciples as they were fishing. Another night had been spent in fruitless toiling at their nets, "but when the morning was now come, Jesus stood on the shore: but the disciples knew not that it was Jesus."

He asked them, "Children, have ye any meat?"

They replied, "No." He then directed them to cast
the net on the right side of the ship, they obeyed,
"and now they were not able to draw it for the multitude of fishes."

It was then that John, "that disciple whom Jesus
loved," recognized the Man on the shore, and he said
to Peter, "It is the Lord!" This so overjoyed Peter
that he "girt his fisher's coat unto him," cast himself
into the sea, and swam ashore while the other disciples
came in the ship bringing the net full of fishes.

As soon as they were come to shore they discovered
that Jesus had breakfast waiting for them—"they saw
a fire of coals there, and fish laid thereon, and bread.
. . . Jesus saith unto them, *Come and dine.* And none
of the disciples durst ask Him, Who art thou? knowing
that it was the Lord."

After breakfast, Jesus turned to Simon Peter and
asked, "Simon, son of Jonas, lovest thou me more
than these?" Peter replied, "Yea, Lord; *thou KNOW-
EST that I love thee.*"

Jesus then asked the second time, "Simon, son of
Jonas, lovest thou me?" Again Peter replied, "Yea,
Lord; *thou KNOWEST that I love thee.*" Then in
verse 17 we read:

"He saith unto him the *third* time, Simon, son of
Jonas, lovest thou me? Peter was grieved because He
said unto him the third time, Lovest thou me? and he
said unto Him, *Lord, thou knowest ALL THINGS;
thou knowest that I love thee.* Jesus saith unto him,
Feed my sheep." (Read John 21:1—17.)

In John chapter 16 Jesus taught His disciples concerning the persecution they were certain to encounter,
and about the coming of the Holy Spirit after His
return to the Father. He then taught them concerning
His death, His resurrection, and His second coming;
and when that tremendous lesson ended the disciples
declared:

"Now are we SURE that thou knowest ALL THINGS, and needest not that any man should ask thee: by this WE BELIEVE THAT THOU CAMEST FORTH FROM GOD" (John 16:30).

Beloved, *whoever* you are, *wherever* you are, whatever you are *doing* at this very moment, *Jesus knows all about it.* He knows everything you have ever done, He knows everything you *will do* in the future.

The Lord Jesus Christ is OMNIPRESENT:

He is everywhere, just as *God* is everywhere. This is shown in His conversation with Nicodemus (recorded in John 3:1—21):

Jesus was in heaven while here on earth:

Nicodemus, the outstanding teacher in Israel, came to Jesus by night and confessed, *"Rabbi, we KNOW that thou art a teacher COME FROM GOD: FOR NO MAN can do these miracles that thou doest, except God be with him."*

Jesus then told this outstanding religious leader that if he would enter the kingdom of God he must be born again, and as He explained the new birth He said, "No man hath ascended up to heaven, but He that came *down* from heaven, even *the Son of man which IS IN heaven"* (v. 13). Notice: Jesus was talking with Nicodemus on earth, yet at the same moment He declared that He was *also in heaven*—and He was. We believe in *ONE GOD manifest in three Persons:* Father, Son, and Holy Ghost.

Jesus had told His disciples that He was going away, He would soon be returning to the Father's house, but in John 14:16—20 He encouraged them with these words:

"I will pray the Father, and He shall give you another Comforter, that He may abide with you for ever; even the Spirit of truth; whom the world cannot receive, because it seeth Him not, neither knoweth Him: but ye know Him; for He dwelleth with you, and shall be in you. I will not leave you comfortless: I will come to you. Yet a little while, and the world seeth me no more; but ye see me: because I live, ye shall live also. At that day ye shall know that *I AM IN MY FATHER, and ye in me, and I in you."*

Standing in the presence of His disciples Jesus said, "I am *in the Father."* The Father was in heaven, and since Jesus was in the Father then *He was also in heaven* even as He stood before His disciples. Do not ask me to explain this, for if I could explain the words of Jesus here I would be *equal* with Him in omniscience! I refer you again to Deuteronomy 29:29: *"The secret things belong unto the Lord . . . ."*

Jesus is in every believer:

Not only was Jesus in the Father at the same time He was standing in the presence of His disciples here on earth, but God's Word clearly teaches that *while the risen Lord sits at the right hand of the Majesty on high, He also dwells in the heart of every born again believer!* He is in every believer, every believer is *in HIM.* The Apostle Paul declares that the mystery of the Church is "Christ in you, the hope of glory" (Col. 1:27); and it was also to the believers in the Colossian Church that he wrote, "For ye are dead, and *your life is hid with Christ in God"* (Col. 3:3).

Then in II Corinthians 13:5 we read, "Examine yourselves, whether ye be in the faith; prove your own selves. *Know ye not your own selves, how that JESUS CHRIST IS IN YOU, except ye be reprobates?"*

Jesus is in the midst of believers gathered in His name:

Jesus promised, "Where two or three are gathered

together in my name, there am I in the midst of them"
(Matt. 18:20). Yes, even though He sits at the right
hand of God in heaven, He is present in every place
on earth where believers gather in His name!

*Jesus is present with everyone who goes forth to
proclaim the Word:*

In Matthew 28:19, 20 Jesus said to His disciples,
"Go ye therefore, and teach all nations, baptizing
them in the name of the Father, and of the Son, and
of the Holy Ghost: teaching them to observe all things
whatsoever I have commanded you: *and, lo, I AM
WITH YOU ALWAY, EVEN UNTO THE END OF
THE WORLD.* Amen." Today Jesus is our great
High Priest, interceding for us before the Father, yet
He is present with His people on earth wherever the
Gospel is being preached in purity and power. No
matter how uneducated one may be, if he goes forth
to win souls, make disciples, and teach men to observe
the things of God, Jesus promised to be present.

Jesus is the Good Shepherd (John 10:11) and a
good shepherd never leaves his sheep:
"The Lord is my Shepherd; I shall not want. He
maketh me to lie down in green pastures: He leadeth
me beside the still waters. He restoreth my soul: He
leadeth me in the paths of righteousness for His name's
sake. Yea, though I walk through the valley of the
shadow of death, I will fear no evil: for thou art with
me; thy rod and thy staff they comfort me. Thou pre-
parest a table before me in the presence of mine enemies: thou anointest my head with oil; my cup run-
neth over. *Surely goodness and mercy shall follow me
ALL THE DAYS OF MY LIFE: and I will dwell in
the house of the Lord FOR EVER"* (Psalm 23).

Jesus "filleth all in ALL":

Ephesians 1:15—23 records one of Paul's prayers

for the believers at Ephesus:

"Wherefore I also, after I heard of your faith in
the Lord Jesus, and love unto all the saints, cease not
to give thanks for you, making mention of you in my
prayers; that the God of our Lord Jesus Christ, the
Father of glory, may give unto you the spirit of wisdom and revelation in the knowledge of Him: the
eyes of your understanding being enlightened; that ye
may know what is the hope of His calling, and what
the riches of the glory of His inheritance in the saints,
and what is the exceeding greatness of His power to
us-ward who believe, according to the working of His
mighty power, which He wrought in Christ, when He
raised Him from the dead, and set Him at His own
right hand in the heavenly places, far above all principality, and power, and might, and dominion, and
every name that is named, not only in this world, but
also in that which is to come: And hath put all things
under His feet, *and gave Him to be the head over all
things to the Church, WHICH IS HIS BODY, THE
FULNESS OF HIM THAT FILLETH ALL IN ALL.*"

The Lord Jesus Christ, our Saviour and soon-coming
King, is indeed omnipresent: *He filleth all in all!*

Christ was in the beginning:

Micah prophesied that Jesus would be *born* in
Bethlehem—but he also declared Him to be *"from
everlasting"*:

"But thou, Bethlehem Ephratah, though thou be
little among the thousands of Judah, yet out of thee
shall He come forth unto me that is to be Ruler in Israel; *whose goings forth have been FROM OF OLD,
FROM EVERLASTING"* (Mic. 5:2).

The Psalmist declared, "Lord, thou hast been our
dwelling place in all generations.   Before the mountains were brought forth, or ever thou hadst formed
the earth and the world, *even from everlasting to ever-*

lasting, THOU ART GOD" (Psalm 90:1, 2).

Then in the New Testament we read, *"In the be-ginning was the WORD, and the Word was WITH God, and the Word WAS God.* The same was in the beginning with God. . . . *And the Word was made FLESH, and dwelt among us,* (and we beheld His glory, the glory as of the only begotten of the Father,) full of grace and truth"* (John 1:1, 2, 14).

Under inspiration, the Apostle Paul penned down the divine fact that Jesus *"is the image of the in-visible God, the firstborn of every creature: for BY HIM were all things created, that are in heaven, and that are in earth, visible and invisible, whether they be thrones, or dominions, or principalities, or powers: ALL THINGS were created BY HIM, and for Him: and HE IS BEFORE ALL THINGS, AND BY HIM ALL THINGS CONSIST"* (Col. 1:15—17).

Isaiah, also under inspiration, testified that the Lord Jesus Christ was *"Wonderful, Counsellor, The mighty God, The everlasting Father, The Prince of Peace"* (Isa. 9:6).

Jesus Himself declared that He was from all eter-nity. In John 8:58 He told the Jews, *"Before Abraham was, I AM."* In John 17:5 He prayed, *"And now, O Father, glorify thou me with thine own self with the glory which I had with thee BEFORE THE WORLD WAS."*

In God's love-letter to His "little children" John the Beloved declared that the message he delivered concerned *Him "which was FROM THE BEGINNING,* which we have heard, which we have seen with our eyes, which we have looked upon, and our hands have handled, of the Word of life"* (I John 1:1). The "Word of Life" was Jesus—the Word Incarnate.

He who was born of the Virgin Mary and named JESUS (meaning *Saviour*) did not *begin* to live; *HE WAS IN THE BEGINNING.* The Son of God was

from all eternity. He is the Alpha and the Omega—
the beginning and the ending, and all there is between.

Not only is Jesus from all eternity; not only is He
omnipotent, omniscient, and omnipresent: *He is also
UNCHANGEABLE.* The Apostle Paul declared, *"Jesus Christ the same yesterday, and to day, and FOR
EVER"* (Heb. 13:8).

In Hebrews 1:10—12 we read, "Thou, Lord, in the
beginning hast laid the foundation of the earth; and
the heavens are the works of thine hands: *They shall
perish; BUT THOU REMAINEST;* and they all shall
wax old as doth a garment; and as a vesture shalt
thou fold them up, *and they shall be changed: BUT
THOU ART THE SAME, AND THY YEARS SHALL
NOT FAIL!"*

Before His incarnation Jesus was in the form of
God: "Let this mind be in you, which was also in
*Christ Jesus: WHO, BEING IN THE FORM OF
GOD, thought it not robbery to be EQUAL WITH
GOD:* But made Himself of no reputation, and took
upon Him the form of a servant, and was made in the
likeness of men: and being found in fashion as a
man, He humbled Himself, and became obedient unto
death, even the death of the cross" (Phil. 2:5—8).

The Greek word here translated "form" means
the form by which a person or thing strikes the vision
—in other words, *the external appearance.* Therefore
Jesus was in the form of God in external appearance
until He was conceived of the Holy Ghost and born
of the Virgin Mary. God gave Him a body of flesh
like unto our body: "For what the law could not do,
in that it was weak through the flesh, God sending
His own Son *in the likeness of sinful flesh,* and for
sin, condemned sin in the flesh: that the righteousness of the law might be fulfilled in us, who walk
not after the flesh, but after the Spirit" (Rom. 8:3, 4).

"Wherefore *in all things* it behoved Him to be

made like unto His brethren, that He might be a merciful and faithful high priest in things pertaining to God, to make reconciliation for the sins of the people" (Heb. 2:17).

The attributes of God are definitely and clearly ascribed to the Lord Jesus Christ, and according to Paul's inspired words to the Colossian believers, *all the fulness of the Godhead* dwells in Him (Col. 2:9).

Christ's Seven Divine Offices Prove His Deity

He is the Creator of all created things:

"In the beginning was the Word, and the Word was with God, and the Word was God. . . . *All things were made by Him; and without Him was not any thing made that was made"* (John 1:1, 3).

"God, who at sundry times and in divers manners spake in time past unto the fathers by the prophets, hath in these last days spoken unto us *by His Son, whom He hath appointed heir of all things, BY WHOM ALSO HE MADE THE WORLDS* . . . Thou, Lord, in the beginning hast laid the foundation of the earth: and the heavens are the works of thine hands" (Heb. 1:1, 2, 10).

In Colossians 1:15, 16 the Apostle Paul declares that Christ is "the image of the invisible God, the firstborn of every creature: For *BY HIM WERE ALL THINGS CREATED, that are in heaven, and that are in earth, visible and invisible, whether they be thrones, or dominions, or principalities, or powers: ALL THINGS were created BY Him, and FOR Him."*

Christ is the Preserver of all things:

He is "the brightness of (God's) glory, and the express image of His person . . . *UPHOLDING ALL THINGS by the word of His power"* (Heb. 1:3).

Christ Jesus the Lord has power to forgive sins:

The Scriptures plainly declare that only God can forgive sins. Therefore the fact that Jesus forgave sins even while He was here on earth is proof of His divinity.

We find one instance of sins forgiven in Luke 7: 36—50. Simon the Pharisee, no doubt an influential religious leader, invited Jesus to his home for a meal. While they were eating, "Behold, a woman in the city, which was a sinner, when she knew that Jesus sat at meat in the Pharisee's house, brought an alabaster box of ointment, and stood at His feet behind Him weeping, and began to wash His feet with tears, and did wipe them with the hairs of her head, and kissed His feet, and anointed them with the ointment."

The Pharisee was quite upset about this. He said to himself, "This Man, if He were a prophet, would have known who and what manner of woman this is that toucheth Him: *for she is a sinner.*"

Jesus knew *exactly* what kind of woman she was— and He also knew what Simon was thinking, even though the Pharisee did not speak his thoughts aloud. Jesus then said to him, "Simon, I have somewhat to say unto thee." Simon replied, "Master, say on."

Jesus then gave him the following parable: "There was a certain creditor which had two debtors: the one owed five hundred pence, and the other fifty. And when they had nothing to pay, he frankly forgave them both. Tell me therefore, which of them will love him most?

"Simon answered and said, I suppose that he to whom he forgave most. And (Jesus) said unto him, Thou hast rightly judged.

"And He turned to the woman and said unto Simon, Seest thou this woman? I entered into thine house, thou gavest me no water for my feet: but she hath washed my feet with tears, and wiped them with the hairs of her head. Thou gavest me no kiss: but this woman since the time I came in hath not ceased to kiss my feet. My head with oil thou didst not anoint: but this woman hath anointed my feet with ointment.

"Wherefore I say unto thee, *Her sins, which are MANY, are forgiven; for she loved much: but to whom little is forgiven, the same loveth little.* And He said unto her, *Thy sins are forgiven.*

"And they that sat at meat with Him began to say within themselves, *WHO IS THIS THAT FORGIV-ETH SINS ALSO?* And He said to the woman, Thy faith hath saved thee; go in peace" (Luke 7:41—50).

Jesus made no apology for boldly declaring that He had forgiven this woman's scarlet sins, even though He knew that those present at the house of Simon the Pharisee were familiar with the fact that *only GOD had the power to forgive sins.*

John 8:1—11 records another instance where Jesus forgave the sins of a fallen woman:

As He taught the early morning Bible class in the temple, the scribes and Pharisees brought a woman whom they declared was taken in the act of adultery, and they "set her in the midst" and said to Jesus, "Master, this woman was taken in adultery, in the very act. Now Moses in the law commanded us, that such should be stoned: *but what sayest thou?"*

These men had probably spent an entire night in search for a victim through whom they could condemn Jesus, for verse 6 plainly declares, *"This they said, TEMPTING HIM, that they might have to accuse Him."* They were not interested in cleaning up the morals of the community, nor did they have a concern for the soul of a fallen woman. They were looking for evidence by which they could accuse and condemn Jesus and they expected His reply to their question to provide that evidence. If He told them to *stone* the woman, they could accuse Him of contradicting His own teaching as to why He had come into the world. On the other hand, if He instructed them *not* to stone her, they could accuse Him of contradicting the law He had come to fulfill!

But Jesus gave them no reply. Instead, He "stooped down, and with His finger wrote on the ground, as though He heard them not." The Scripture does not tell us what He wrote, but *whatever* He wrote was the Word of God.

The enemies of Jesus did not give up easily. They continued asking Him, and He then replied, "He that is *without sin* among you, let *him* first cast a stone at her!" Again He stooped down, and wrote on the ground.

I repeat—whatever Jesus wrote was the Word of God, and *"the Word of God is quick, and powerful, and sharper than any twoedged sword,* piercing even to the dividing asunder of soul and spirit, and of the joints and marrow, *and is a discerner of the thoughts and intents of the heart"* (Heb. 4:12). Therefore what Jesus wrote on the ground had a twofold result: it convicted the men of their own ungodliness, and convinced the woman that she was in the presence of the Saviour.

I do not doubt that one of these men was the other party to the act of adultery; but at any rate, while Jesus was writing on the ground the second time, they slipped out of the temple one by one, leaving Him alone with the woman. She, too, had read what He wrote, and "faith cometh by hearing, and hearing by the Word of God" (Rom. 10:17).

This sinful woman needed to be born again, and sinners are born again *"not of corruptible seed, but of incorruptible, BY THE WORD OF GOD,* which liveth and abideth for ever" (I Pet. 1:23).

"When Jesus had lifted up Himself, and saw none but the woman, He said unto her, Woman, where are those thine accusers? Hath no man condemned thee? She said, No man, Lord. And Jesus said unto her, *Neither do I condemn thee: go, and SIN NO MORE!"* (John 8:10, 11).

Mark 2:1—12 gives an interesting account of sins forgiven the palsied man. Jesus was preaching in Capernaum, and when the news spread about that He was in a certain house, so many people gathered to hear Him that "there was no room to receive them, no, not so much as about the door."

There was a palsied man in the community, and his friends believed that if they could only get him to Jesus, he would be made whole. So they *carried* him on his bed--but when they arrived at the house where Jesus was preaching they could not get through the multitude already crowded inside. They therefore removed some of the tiles from the roof of the house and lowered the man through the roof, thus laying him at the feet of Jesus.

"When Jesus saw their faith, He said unto the sick of the palsy, *SON, THY SINS BE FORGIVEN THEE.* But there were certain of the scribes sitting there, and reasoning in their hearts, *Why doth this Man thus speak blasphemies? Who can forgive sins but GOD ONLY?"*

Jesus knew what they were thinking, and He said to them, "Why reason ye these things in your hearts? Whether is it easier to say to the sick of the palsy, *Thy sins be forgiven thee;* or to say, Arise, and take up thy bed, and walk? *But that ye may KNOW that THE SON OF MAN HATH POWER ON EARTH TO FORGIVE SINS,* (He saith to the sick of the palsy,) I say unto thee, *ARISE, AND TAKE UP THY BED, and go thy way into thine house.*

"AND IMMEDIATELY HE AROSE, TOOK UP

*THE BED, AND WENT FORTH BEFORE THEM
ALL; insomuch that they were all amazed and glorified God, saying, We never saw it on this fashion!"*
This verse plainly tells us that the people *recognized God* in this miracle. Jesus made no attempt to
hide His deity, but rather affirmed it—and proved it
by the miracles He wrought, miracles that no one but
Almighty God could do!

All sin is *against God,* and since Jesus and God
the Father are one, all sin is against Jesus. You will
notice in the account of Simon the Pharisee and the
fallen woman in Luke chapter 7, Jesus declared that
both the Pharisee and the woman were sinners and
debtors to Himself. The prodigal in Luke 15:21 cried
out, "I have sinned against heaven and in thy sight."
After committing a horrible sin David cried, "Have
mercy upon me, O God . . . *against thee, thee only,
have I sinned,* and done this evil in thy sight . . ."
(Psalm 51:1, 4).

Jesus has power to forgive all kinds of sin, and
will forgive all kinds of sin except the sin against the
Holy Ghost (the unpardonable sin) described in Matthew 12:31, 32:

"Wherefore I say unto you, *ALL MANNER OF
SIN and blasphemy shall be forgiven unto men: but
the blasphemy against the Holy Ghost SHALL NOT
BE FORGIVEN UNTO MEN.* And whosoever speak-
eth a word against the Son of man, it shall be for-
given him: but *whosoever speaketh against the Holy
Ghost, it shall NOT be forgiven him, NEITHER IN
THIS WORLD, NEITHER IN THE WORLD TO
COME!"*

Christ Jesus the Lord has power to raise the dead:

Only God could return life to a corpse. I know
there will be objections to that statement. Some of
you will ask, "Did not the Apostle Paul raise a young

man who fell from a window and was killed? (Acts
20:9—12). The answer is *NO—God raised the dead:*
"And *God* wrought special miracles by the hands of
Paul" (Acts 19:11).

Did not Elijah and Elisha raise the dead? No.
When Elijah raised the widow's son, he "cried unto
the Lord, and said, *O Lord my God, I pray thee, let
this child's soul come into him again.* And the Lord
heard the voice of Elijah; and the soul of the child
came into him again, and he revived" (I Kings 17:
21, 22).

When Elisha restored life to the son of the Shu-
nammite woman he went into the room where the
child was, "and shut the door upon them twain, and
prayed unto the Lord" (II Kings 4:32—35).

You will notice, when Jesus prayed at the tomb
of Lazarus, He prayed because of the people around
Him: "And Jesus lifted up His eyes, and said, Father,
I thank thee that thou hast heard me. *And I knew
that thou hearest me ALWAYS: but BECAUSE OF
THE PEOPLE WHICH STAND BY I said it, that
they may believe that thou hast sent me*" (John 11:
41, 42).

In John 5:21 Jesus said, "As *the Father* raiseth up
the dead, and quickeneth them; even so *the Son* quickeneth whom He will," and in verses 28 and 29 of that
same chapter He said, "Marvel not at this: *for the
hour is coming, in the which ALL THAT ARE IN
THE GRAVES shall hear His voice,* and shall come
forth; they that have done good, unto the resurrection
of life; and they that have done evil, unto the resurrection of damnation."

The righteous dead will be raised in the first resurrection, when "the Lord Himself shall descend from
heaven with a shout, with the voice of the archangel,
and with the trump of God: and the dead in Christ
shall rise first: Then we which are alive and remain

shall be caught up together with them in the clouds, to meet the Lord in the air: and so shall we ever be with the Lord" (I Thess. 4:16, 17).

But none of the *wicked dead* will be raised when Jesus comes for His Church in the Rapture. They will be raised a thousand years later, just before the Great White Throne judgment:

"And I saw thrones, and they sat upon them, and judgment was given unto them: and I saw the souls of them that were beheaded for the witness of Jesus, and for the Word of God, and which had not worshipped the beast, neither his image, neither had received his mark upon their foreheads, or in their hands; and *they lived and reigned with Christ a thousand years. BUT THE REST OF THE DEAD LIVED NOT AGAIN UNTIL THE THOUSAND YEARS WERE FINISHED. This is the first resurrection. . . .*

"And I saw a Great White Throne, and Him that sat on it, from whose face the earth and the heaven fled away; and there was found no place for them. And I saw the dead, small and great, stand before God; and the books were opened: and another book was opened, which is the book of life: and the dead were judged out of those things which were written in the books, according to their works.

"And the sea gave up the dead which were in it; and death and hell delivered up the dead which were in them: and they were judged every man according to their works. And death and hell were cast into the lake of fire. This is the second death. And whosoever was not found written in the book of life was cast into the lake of fire" (Rev. 20:4, 5, 11—15).

Jesus is the Master of death—He conquered death, and He has the keys to death and hell (Rev. 1:18).

Christ Jesus the Lord will transform our bodies:

"For our conversation is in heaven; from whence

also we look for the Saviour, *the Lord Jesus Christ: Who shall change our vile body*, that it may be fashioned like unto His glorious body, according to the working whereby He is able even to subdue all things unto Himself" (Phil. 3:20, 21).

He will give us a body like unto His own glorious body: "Beloved, NOW are we the sons of God, and it doth not yet appear what we shall be: but *we know that, when He shall appear, we shall be like Him;* for we shall see Him as He is" (I John 3:2).

This corruptible will put on incorruption. Our bodies will be fashioned anew, never to be tired or sick, never to die: "Behold, I shew you a mystery: We shall not all sleep (die), but we shall all be changed, in a moment, in the twinkling of an eye, at the last trump: for the trumpet shall sound, and the dead shall be raised incorruptible, and we shall be changed. For this corruptible must put on incorruption, and this mortal must put on immortality. So when this corruptible shall have put on incorruption, and this mortal shall have put on immortality, then shall be brought to pass the saying that is written, Death is swallowed up in victory" (I Cor. 15:51—54).

Christ Jesus the Lord will judge all men:

"For the Father judgeth no man, but hath committed ALL JUDGMENT unto the Son" (John 5:22).

No man will be judged after death as to whether he is saved or lost; that is settled in this life. Sins must be forgiven this side of the grave for there is no "second chance" after death. Believers will be judged for their stewardship, and the wicked will be judged according to their wickedness. In Romans 14:9—12 the Apostle Paul declared:

"For to this end Christ both died, and rose, and revived, that He might be Lord both of the dead and living. But why dost thou judge thy brother? or why

116

Bible Truth

dost thou set at nought thy brother? *for we shall ALL stand before the judgment seat of CHRIST.* For it is written, As I live, saith the Lord, every knee shall bow to me, and every tongue shall confess to God. *SO THEN EVERY ONE OF US SHALL GIVE ACCOUNT OF HIMSELF TO GOD."* Yes, everyone will stand before the judgment seat of Christ, not one will escape!

In II Timothy 4:1, 2 we read, "I charge thee therefore before God, and *the Lord Jesus Christ, who shall judge the quick and the dead at His appearing* and His kingdom: Preach the Word; be instant in season, out of season; reprove, rebuke, exhort with all long-suffering and doctrine."

In this charge, Paul declared that Christ Jesus will judge the living and the dead, and it seems needful here to point out the difference between the judgment of the righteous and the judgment of the unrighteous:

I repeat—no one will be judged after death as to whether he is saved or lost. The *wicked* open their eyes in hell immediately after death (Luke 16:23, 24). The *righteous* enter Paradise when they depart this life. (To be absent from the body is to be *present with the Lord*—II Cor. 5:8.) Paul declared, "For to me to live is Christ, and to die is gain. But if I live in the flesh, this is the fruit of my labour: yet what I shall choose I wot not. For I am in a strait betwixt two, having a desire to depart, and to be with Christ; which is far better: Nevertheless to abide in the flesh is more needful for you" (Phil. 1:21—24).

Believers will be judged according to their stewardship and rewarded for all labors of love done in the name of Jesus to the glory of God. This is clearly taught in Paul's letter to the believers in Corinth:

"For other foundation can no man lay than that is laid, which is Jesus Christ. Now if any man build upon this foundation gold, silver, precious stones,

wood, hay, stubble; every man's work shall be made
manifest: for the day shall declare it, because it shall
be revealed by fire; and the fire shall try every man's
work of what sort it is.

"If any man's work abide which he hath built
thereupon, he shall receive a reward. If any man's
work shall be burned, he shall suffer loss: but he
himself shall be saved; yet so as by fire" (I Cor. 3:
11—15).

It is clearly pointed out here that *"every man's
work"* will be tried by fire. This could not be speaking of redemption because *redemption is not MAN'S
WORK.* It is man's *stewardship* that will be tried by
fire, and *the "fire" is the WORD.* "Is not my Word
like as a FIRE? saith the Lord; and like a hammer
that breaketh the rock in pieces?" (Jer. 23:29).

The believer's *stewardship* will be judged—not with
reference to the *size* of the work, but to *the SORT of
work* it is—i. e., its purity. Are we doing what we are
doing *for the glory of God*—or for some other reason?
If we render stewardship for reason other than to bring
glory to God we will *lose our reward.* Paul spelled
this out in words easily understood.

"If any man's work *abide* . . . he shall receive a
reward." Paul said to these same believers in Corinth,
"Whether therefore ye eat, or drink, or *whatsoever ye
do, do all to the glory of God"* (I Cor. 10:31).

"If any man's work shall be *burned,* he shall *suffer
loss* . . . ." This does not speak of the soul, because
the next statement clearly says, *"but HE HIMSELF
shall be SAVED."* The meaning here is that the *soul*
will be saved, but the *reward* will be lost. I do not
know what it will mean to be in heaven without a
reward, but there will be people there who have none.
There will be others with *partial* reward, and still
others will receive a *full* reward.

John the Beloved also warns that it is possible for

a believer to lose his reward. In II John, verses 7—11 we read, "For many deceivers are entered into the world, who confess not that Jesus Christ is come in the flesh. This is a deceiver and an antichrist. *Look to yourselves* (be alert), *that we lose not THOSE THINGS WHICH WE HAVE WROUGHT, but that we receive a FULL reward.*

"Whosoever transgresseth, and abideth not in the doctrine of Christ, hath not God. He that abideth in the doctrine of Christ, he hath both the Father and the Son. *If there come any unto you, and bring not this doctrine, receive him not into your house, neither bid him God speed: FOR HE THAT BIDDETH HIM GOD SPEED IS PARTAKER OF HIS EVIL DEEDS.*"

The "things which we have wrought" have nothing to do with redemption, for salvation is of God. The reference here is to stewardship and rewards. And then John makes it very clear that if we as believers befriend the enemies of Jesus, we thereby become partakers of their evil deeds—and we will lose our reward.

I am glad God's scales do not weigh as man's scales, and that His yardstick does not measure as man measures. Jesus will judge in righteousness, and regardless of whether you are saint or sinner, at God's judgment you will receive exactly what is right!

Revelation 20:11—15 describes the Great White Throne judgment: "And I saw a great white throne, and Him that sat on it, from whose face the earth and the heaven fled away; and there was found no place for them. And I saw the dead, small and great, stand before God; and the books were opened: and another book was opened, which is the book of life: and the dead were judged out of those things which were written in the books, according to their works.

"And the sea gave up the dead which were in it; and death and hell delivered up the dead which were in them: and they were judged every man according

to their works. And death and hell were cast into
the lake of fire. This is the second death. And whosoever was not found written in the book of life was
cast into the lake of fire."

Christians who depart this life are referred to as
"resting" or "sleeping." The *wicked* are declared
"dead." This does not mean that they are unconscious, but rather that they do not possess eternal
life.

Only the wicked will appear at the Great White
Throne judgment; no believers will be there. The
books will be opened and the wicked will be judged
out of the things written there—but notice: they will
be judged out of the *"books."* They will not be judged
from the *"book of life"* because *their names are not
IN the book of life*—and according to Revelation 21:27
only those whose names are in the book of life will
enter heaven: *"And there shall in no wise enter into
it any thing that defileth, neither whatsoever worketh
abomination, or maketh a lie: BUT THEY WHICH
ARE WRITTEN IN THE LAMB'S BOOK OF LIFE."*

Notice, the dead will be judged out of the things
written in the books *"according to their WORKS."*
Hell will be *in intensity* what the wicked make it
through their wickedness on earth. Not all sinners
will suffer the same degree of torment throughout
eternity—God could not be just and righteous if that
were true. But God *is* just and righteous, and every
sinner will receive exactly the hell, damnation, and
torment that is coming to him. None will suffer, in
intensity, any more than is deserved. For instance,
the heathen who has never heard the name of Jesus
will be *lost eternally*—but he will not suffer the same
damnation that will be meted out to people in America
and other enlightened places where the Bible has been
preached freely—and rejected over and over again!
The person who dies without Christ *after having heard*

and rejected the Gospel will suffer much more torment than the person who has never even *heard* a verse of Scripture.

Jesus taught this same truth while He was on earth. In Luke 12:47, 48 He declared, "That servant, which *knew* his Lord's will, and prepared not himself, neither did according to His will, shall be beaten with *many stripes*. But he that *knew not*, and did commit things worthy of stripes, shall be beaten with *few* stripes. *For unto whomsoever much is given, of him shall be much required:* and to whom men have committed much, of him they will ask the more."

Someone may say, "I am lost, I am going to spend eternity in hell anyway, so I will commit all the sin I possibly can!" Friend, even if you plan to spend eternity in hell (and I am sure *no one* actually makes such plans) it would pay you to live a respectable life on earth, because your agony and torment in hell will be according to the truth rejected and your wickedness while you travel through this life! Christ the Righteous Judge will judge *in righteousness.*

Christ Jesus the Lord *gives eternal life:*

These are the words of Jesus: "I am that *bread of life.* Your fathers did eat manna in the wilderness, and are dead. This is the bread which cometh down from heaven, that a man may eat thereof, and not die. I am the *living* bread which came down from heaven: *if any man eat of this bread, he shall LIVE FOR EVER:* and the bread that I will give is my flesh, which I will give for the life of the world.

The Jews therefore strove among themselves, saying, How can this Man give us His flesh to eat? Then Jesus said unto them, Verily, verily, I say unto you, Except ye eat the flesh of the Son of man, and drink His blood, ye have no life in you. Whoso eateth my flesh, and drinketh my blood, hath eternal life; and

I will raise him up at the last day. For my flesh is meat indeed, and my blood is drink indeed. He that eateth my flesh, and drinketh my blood, dwelleth in me, and I in him.

"As the living Father hath sent me, and I live by the Father: so he that eateth me, even he shall live by me. This is that bread which came down from heaven: not as your fathers did eat manna, and are dead: he that eateth of this bread shall live for ever. *These things said He in the synagogue, as He taught in Capernaum*" (John 6:48—59).

In verse 63 of the same chapter Jesus said, "It is the spirit that quickeneth; the flesh profiteth nothing: *the words that I speak unto you, they are spirit, and they are LIFE.*"

In John 5:24 He declared, "Verily, verily, I say unto you, He that heareth *my word,* and believeth on Him that sent me, hath *everlasting life,* and shall not come into condemnation; but is passed from death unto life."

In John 10:27, 28 Jesus said, "My sheep hear my voice, and I know them, and they follow me: And *I give unto them ETERNAL LIFE;* and they shall never perish, neither shall any man pluck them out of my hand."

In John 17:1, 2 He prayed, "Father, the hour is come; glorify thy Son, that thy Son also may glorify thee: As thou hast given Him power over all flesh, *that He should give ETERNAL LIFE to as many as thou hast given Him.*"

Then in I John 5:9—13 we read: "If we receive the witness of men, the witness of God is greater: for this is the witness of God which He hath testified of His Son. He that believeth on the Son of God hath the witness in himself: he that believeth not God hath made Him a liar; because he believeth not the record that God gave of His Son. *And this is the record,*

*that GOD HATH GIVEN TO US ETERNAL LIFE,
AND THIS LIFE IS IN HIS SON.* He that hath
the Son *hath life;* and he that hath *not* the Son of
God *hath not life.* These things have I written unto
you that believe on the name of the Son of God; that
ye may KNOW that ye HAVE ETERNAL LIFE, and
that ye may believe on the name of the Son of God."

I am so thankful that eternal life is the gift of
God, not of works. *God gave Jesus,* and *Jesus gives
eternal life* to all who will believe on His name. It
is not God's will that any should perish; He has no
pleasure in the death of the wicked. The last invitation God gives in His Word emphasizes the fact that
ALL are invited: "The Spirit and the bride say, Come.
And let him that heareth say, Come. And let him
that is athirst come. *And WHOSOEVER WILL, let
him take the water of life freely"* (Rev. 22:17).

Space will not allow me to give the *text* of the
following Scriptures, but *in summary* these are references which will help anyone who desires to know
the truth concerning *the divinity of Christ:*

Divine titles are ascribed to the Lord Jesus Christ:
John 1:1; 20:28; Romans 1:4; 9:5; II Thessalonians 1:12;
Titus 2:13; Hebrews 1:8; I John 5:20.

Divine perfections and divine attributes are ascribed
to Him: Matthew 11:28; 18:20; 28:20; John 1:2; 2:23–
25; 3:13; 5:17; 21:17; Hebrews 1:3, 11, 12; 13:8; Revelation 1:8, 17, 18; 2:23; 11:17; 22:13.

Divine works are ascribed to Him: John 1:3, 10;
Colossians 1:16, 17; Hebrews 1:3.

The New Testament clearly teaches that *worship
should be directed to the Lord Jesus Christ:* Acts
7:59, 60; I Corinthians 1:2; Philippians 2:9, 10; Hebrews
1:6; Revelation 1:5, 6; 5:12, 13.

While He lived on earth, Jesus Himself *allowed,
received, and approved worship* from those who loved
Him: Matthew 14:33; 28:9; John 20:28, 29.

Old Testament and New Testament
Scriptures Compared

There are many statements in the Old Testament which speak specifically of the eternal God, Jehovah. In the New Testament, holy men whom God called and anointed to pen down His Word quoted those same statements with definite reference to the Lord Jesus Christ. We have not space to give all of those Scriptures, but we will look at a few of them:

In Psalm 102:24—27 we read, "I said, O my God, take me not away in the midst of my days: thy years are throughout all generations. Of old hast thou laid the foundation of the earth: and the heavens are the work of thy hands. They shall perish, but thou shalt endure: yea, all of them shall wax old like a garment; as a vesture shalt thou change them, and they shall be changed. But thou art the same, and thy years shall have no end."

Now compare these verses with the words of the Apostle Paul in his letter to the Hebrew Christians:

"Thou, Lord, in the beginning hast laid the foundation of the earth; and the heavens are the works of thine hands: They shall perish; but thou remainest; and they all shall wax old as doth a garment; and as a vesture shalt thou fold them up, and they shall be changed: but thou art the same, and thy years shall not fail" (Heb. 1:10—12).

In these passages, the Psalmist was speaking of *Jehovah God*. Paul was speaking of *Jesus Christ*, God in flesh.

In Isaiah 40:3, 4 we find a statement referring to John the Baptist, forerunner of Jesus:

"The voice of him that crieth in the wilderness, *Prepare ye the way of the LORD*, make straight in the desert a highway *for our GOD*. Every valley shall be exalted, and every mountain and hill shall be made

low: and the crooked shall be made straight, and the
rough places plain."

Two of the Gospel writers quote part of that same
statement, made by Isaiah centuries before John the
Baptist announced the coming of Jesus. In Matthew
3:3 we read, "This is he that was spoken of by the
prophet Esaias, saying, The voice of one crying in the
wilderness, Prepare ye the way of the Lord, make His
paths straight."

The beloved physician Luke wrote, "Blessed be
the Lord God of Israel; for He hath visited and redeemed His people, and hath raised up an horn of
salvation for us in the house of His servant David . . .
And thou, child, shalt be called the prophet of the
Highest: for thou shalt go before the face of the Lord
to prepare His ways" (Luke 1:68, 69, 76).

Isaiah was speaking of Jehovah God. Matthew
and Luke both spoke of the Lord Jesus Christ, for
certainly the Son of God is the Lord before whom the
messenger was to prepare the way.

In Jeremiah 11:20 we read, "O Lord of hosts, that
judgest righteously, that triest the reins and the heart,
let me see thy vengeance on them: for unto thee have
I revealed my cause."

Jeremiah 17:10 declares, "I the Lord search the
heart, I try the reins, *even to give every man according
to his ways,* and according to the fruit of his doings."

In these verses, Jeremiah declared that Jehovah
God judges righteously, that He searches and knows
the heart, and that He rewards every man according
to his ways and according to *the fruit of his doings.*
In Revelation 2:23, John the Beloved speaks of One
who will do exactly the same thing—and *John's reference is to the Lord Jesus Christ:* "And I will kill her
children with death; and all the churches shall know
that *I am He which searcheth the reins and hearts:
and I will give unto every one of you according to*

your works."

In one of the most beloved Psalms we read, *"The LORD is my Shepherd; I shall not want"* (Psalm 23:1). Then in Isaiah 40:10,11 we read, "Behold, *the Lord God* will come with strong hand, and His arm shall rule for Him: behold, His reward is with Him, and His work before Him. *He shall feed His flock like a shepherd: He shall gather the lambs with His arm, and carry them in His bosom,* and shall gently lead those that are with young."

The Psalmist and the Prophet Isaiah were speaking of *Jehovah,* the eternal God. Now hear the words of *Jesus* as He tabernacled among men: *"I AM THE GOOD SHEPHERD: the Good Shepherd giveth His life for the sheep"* (John 10:11).

In the Old Testament, *Jehovah* is the Good Shepherd; in the New Testament, *Jesus* is the Good Shepherd — one God manifested in three Persons: Father, Son, and Holy Ghost, co-equal in deity.

The Prophet Ezekiel wrote of One who would seek out His sheep: "For thus saith *the Lord GOD;* Behold, I, even I, will both search my sheep, and seek them out. As a shepherd seeketh out his flock in the day that he is among his sheep that are scattered; so will I seek out my sheep, and will deliver them out of all places where they have been scattered in the cloudy and dark day" (Ezek. 34:11,12).

Jehovah is the One of whom Ezekiel spoke, but hear the words of the Lord Jesus Christ as He dwelt on earth in His body of humiliation: "For *the SON OF MAN is come to seek and to save that which was lost"* (Luke 19:10).

In the Old Testament, Jehovah God sought the lost. In the New Testament, Jesus seeks and saves the lost.

Isaiah 6:1—10 gives a moving description of that prophet's experience when he saw the glory of God:

"In the year that king Uzziah died I saw also the Lord sitting upon a throne, high and lifted up, and His train filled the temple. Above it stood the seraphims: each one had six wings; with twain he covered his face, and with twain he covered his feet, and with twain he did fly. And one cried unto another, and said, Holy, holy, holy, is the Lord of hosts: the whole earth is full of his glory. And the posts of the door moved at the voice of him that cried, and the house was filled with smoke.

"Then said I, Woe is me! for I am undone; because I am a man of unclean lips, and I dwell in the midst of a people of unclean lips: for mine eyes have seen the King, *the Lord of hosts.* Then flew one of the seraphims unto me, having a live coal in his hand, which he had taken with the tongs from off the altar: and he laid it upon my mouth, and said, Lo, this hath touched thy lips; and thine iniquity is taken away, and thy sin purged. Also I heard the voice of the Lord, saying, Whom shall I send, and who will go for us? Then said I, Here am I; send me.

"And He said, Go, and tell this people, Hear ye indeed, but understand not; and see ye indeed, but perceive not. Make the heart of this people fat, and make their ears heavy, and shut their eyes; lest they see with their eyes, and hear with their ears, and understand with their heart, and convert, and be healed."

Now let us compare this passage from Isaiah with the words of John the Beloved as the Holy Ghost spoke through him and he penned down the message for our instruction. In John 12:37—41 we read:

"Though He (Jesus) had done so many miracles before them, yet they believed not on Him: *that the saying of Esaias the prophet might be fulfilled,* which he spake, Lord, who hath believed our report? and to whom hath the arm of the Lord been revealed? *There-*

*fore they could not believe, because that Esaias said
again, HE HATH BLINDED THEIR EYES, AND
HARDENED THEIR HEART; THAT THEY SHOULD
NOT SEE WITH THEIR EYES, NOR UNDERSTAND
WITH THEIR HEART, AND BE CONVERTED, AND
I SHOULD HEAL THEM. These things said Esaias,
when he saw His glory, and spake of Him."*

Isaiah saw the glory of *Jehovah God.* Certainly
John the Beloved assured us of the deity of Christ
when he quoted the words of Isaiah and declared
that the prophet saw *the glory of Jesus,* our Saviour!

In the Old Testament, *the stone of stumbling* is
Jehovah God. In the New Testament the stone of
stumbling is *Jesus Christ*—Father and Son, *yet one
and the same.* In Isaiah 8:13–15 we read, "Sanctify
the Lord of hosts Himself; and let Him be your fear,
and let Him be your dread. And He shall be for a
sanctuary; but for *a stone of stumbling and for a rock
of offence* to both the houses of Israel, for a gin and
for a snare to the inhabitants of Jerusalem. And many
among them shall stumble, and fall, and be broken,
and be snared, and be taken."

Now read the words Peter penned down as the
Holy Spirit spoke to him: "Wherefore also it is contained in the Scripture, Behold, I lay in Sion *a chief
corner stone, elect, precious:* and he that believeth
on Him shall not be confounded. Unto you therefore
which *believe* He is precious: but *unto them which
be disobedient, the stone which the builders disallowed,
the same is made the head of the corner, and A
STONE OF STUMBLING, AND A ROCK OF OF-
FENCE, even to them which stumble at the word,
being disobedient: WHEREUNTO ALSO THEY WERE
APPOINTED"* (I Pet. 2:6—8).

There are many other statements recorded in the
Old Testament Scriptures which definitely speak of
Jehovah God, the eternal Father, and *quotations* from

those passages are given in the New Testament with
definite application to the Lord Jesus Christ—proof
positive of His deity.

God the Father and Jesus Christ the Son

In the New Testament, the names of Jehovah God
and Jesus Christ are coupled together in passages too
numerous to quote here, but if you will read the following Scriptures you can see beyond any shadow of
doubt that Jesus was the virgin-born Son of God, yea,
GOD IN FLESH. Had He been simply "a good man"
it would have been impossible for the verbally inspired Scriptures to couple His name with that of Jehovah as it is found in these references. Please read
them prayerfully and carefully:
   Matthew 28:19; John 14:1, 23; 17:3; Romans 1:7;
I Corinthians 12:4—6; II Corinthians 13:14; Colossians
2:2; I Thessalonians 3:11; Titus 3:4, 5; James 1:1; II Peter 1:1; Revelation 5:13; 7:10.
   If these Scriptures do not convince you that God
and Jesus are co-equal and that Jesus was "the fulness
of the Godhead bodily" (Col. 2:9), you would not be
convinced if I gave every passage in the Word of God
which couples the names of Jehovah God and Jesus
Christ our Saviour!
   Thanks be unto God for His *saving* grace, for His
keeping grace, and for His *teaching grace:* and unless
one is *willing to be taught* by the grace of God
through the Spirit, he cannot *understand* the things
of God:
   "For *the grace of God that bringeth salvation* hath
appeared to all men, *TEACHING us that, denying un-*
godliness and worldly lusts, we should live soberly,
righteously, and godly, in this present world; looking
for that blessed hope, and the glorious appearing of
the great GOD AND OUR SAVIOUR JESUS CHRIST"

(Tit. 2:11—13).

One glorious day in the not-too-distant future, we who are saved will witness and take part in the glorious second coming of "the great God and our Saviour, Jesus Christ"!

Jesus Worshipped by Men

Either Jesus was the Son of God, virgin-born and all that He claimed to be, or He was the greatest impostor this world has ever known! To teach that He was just "a good man" (thus denying His deity) and then invite men to worship Him, is to advertise inexcusable ignorance; for if Jesus was *not* the Son of God He was a liar, and such a person could not help others.

But praise God, Christ Jesus the Lord was not an impostor! He was the second Person of the Godhead, *God incarnate;* and the Scriptures prove beyond all doubt that He was the virgin-born Son of God. Therefore, He was entitled to all adoration and worship.

In Matthew 4:8—10 the devil tempted Jesus by offering Him all the kingdoms of the world in return for His worship: "Again, the devil taketh Him up into an exceeding high mountain, and sheweth Him all the kingdoms of the world, and the glory of them; and saith unto Him, *All these things will I give thee, if thou wilt fall down and worship me.* Then saith Jesus unto him, Get thee hence, Satan: for it is written, *Thou shalt worship THE LORD THY GOD, and HIM ONLY shalt thou serve!"*

Here, Jesus plainly declared that God alone is worthy of worship—yet He never rebuked any man for worshipping Him when He walked among them in His body of humiliation. We see examples of this in the following Scriptures:

In Matthew 14:31—33, when Jesus "stretched forth His hand" and saved Peter from drowning, "they that were in the ship *came and worshipped Him,* saying, Of a truth thou art the Son of God."

In Matthew 28:9, when the disciples met the risen Lord, "they came and held Him by the feet, *and worshipped Him."*

In Luke 24:51, 52, at the ascension of Jesus, "it came to pass, while He blessed them, He was parted from them, and carried up into heaven. *And they worshipped Him,* and returned to Jerusalem with great joy."

In contrast with these passages, Acts 10:25, 26 tells of *Peter's forbidding* Cornelius to worship *him.* We read, "As Peter was coming in, Cornelius met him, and fell down at his feet, and worshipped him. *But Peter took him up, saying, Stand up; I myself also am a MAN!"*

In Revelation 22:8, 9, John the Beloved testified concerning the angel before whom he fell down to worship:

"And I John saw these things, and heard them. And when I had heard and seen, I fell down to worship before the feet of the angel which shewed me these things. Then saith he unto me, *See thou do it not: for I am thy fellowservant, and of thy brethren the prophets, and of them which keep the sayings of this book: WORSHIP GOD."*

God the Father wants us to worship and honor Christ the Son even as we worship and honor the Father, and "he that *honoureth not* the Son *honoureth not the Father which hath sent Him"* (John 5:23).

The angels of God, as well as men, *worship Jesus:* "And again, when He bringeth in the firstbegotten into the world, He saith, *And let all the angels of God worship Him"* (Heb. 1:6).

Then in Philippians 2:9—11 we read, "Wherefore God also hath highly exalted Him, and given Him a name which is above every name: *that at the name*

*of Jesus EVERY KNEE SHOULD BOW, of things
IN HEAVEN, and things IN EARTH, and things
UNDER the earth; and that every tongue should confess that Jesus Christ is Lord,* to the glory of God
the Father."

Now hear these inspired words from the pen of
John the Beloved as the Holy Spirit moved him to
write:

"And when He had taken the book, the four beasts
and four and twenty elders *fell down before the Lamb,*
having every one of them harps, and golden vials full
of odours, which are the prayers of saints. And they
sung a new song, saying, *Thou art worthy to take the
book, and to open the seals thereof: for thou wast
slain, and hast redeemed us to God by thy blood out
of every kindred, and tongue, and people, and nation . . .*

"And I beheld, and I heard *the voice of many angels* round about the throne and the beasts and the
elders: and the number of them was ten thousand
times ten thousand, and thousands of thousands; saying with a loud voice, *Worthy is the Lamb that was
slain to receive power, and riches, and wisdom, and
strength, and honour, and glory, and blessing.*

"And *every creature* which is in heaven, and on
the earth, and under the earth, and such as are in
the sea, and all that are in them, heard I saying,
*Blessing, and honour, and glory, and power, be unto
Him that sitteth upon the throne, and unto the Lamb
for ever and ever.*

"And the four beasts said, Amen. *And the four
and twenty elders fell down AND WORSHIPPED
HIM THAT LIVETH FOR EVER AND EVER!"* (Rev.
5:8—14).

Not only should we worship Jesus as we worship
God the Father, but we are to pray *to* Him and *in
His name.* In John 14:13, 14 He instructed His dis-

ciples, "Whatsoever ye shall ask *in my name,* that will I do, that the Father may be glorified in the Son. *If ye shall ask any thing IN MY NAME, I will do it.*"

In Acts 7:59, *Stephen* prayed to the Lord Jesus: "And they stoned Stephen, *calling upon God,* and saying, *LORD JESUS, receive my spirit.*"

In I Corinthians 1:2,3 the Apostle Paul wrote, "Unto the church of God which is at Corinth, to them that are sanctified in Christ Jesus, called to be saints, *with all that in every place call upon the name of Jesus Christ our Lord,* both their's and our's: Grace be unto you, and peace, from God our Father, and from the Lord Jesus Christ."

Throughout the Bible, from Genesis through Revelation, we find Scriptures that clearly and unmistakeably declare the deity of Jesus Christ, the Son of God, and to *reject* His deity is an insult to God and to the living Word! If you refuse to confess the divinity of Christ and bow your knees to Him here on earth, I assure you on the basis of God's Word that He will one day *force* you to confess that Jesus is the Christ; but it will be too late then, for you will be standing before the judgment bar of God:

"For it is written, *AS I LIVE, saith the Lord, EVERY KNEE SHALL BOW TO ME, AND EVERY TONGUE SHALL CONFESS TO GOD*" (Rom. 14:11).

All who confess Jesus here on earth and receive Him by faith, He will confess before the heavenly Father; but all who *deny* Him on earth He will deny before the Father. This fact He clearly declared during His earthly ministry:

"Whosoever therefore shall confess me before men, him will I confess also before my Father which is in heaven. But whosoever shall deny me before men, him will I also deny before my Father which is in heaven" (Matt. 10:32,33).

The Apostle Paul emphasizes this in Romans 10:9,

10: "If thou shalt confess with thy mouth the Lord Jesus, and shalt believe in thine heart that God hath raised Him from the dead, thou shalt be saved. For with the heart man believeth unto righteousness; and with the mouth confession is made unto salvation."

If you are not a believer, I urge you to humble your heart *now* and talk to Jesus. Tell Him that you believe He is the Son of God—crucified, buried, and risen according to the Scriptures. Then invite Him to come into your heart and save you. He will do it—and you will know it!

Jesus Was Both Human and Divine

Jesus was the God-man. That He was God we have proved beyond any shadow of doubt—yet He was just as truly man, *made like unto His brethren "in ALL things"* (Heb. 2:17). He is called "the Son of man" more than seventy-five times in the New Testament—not only while He was here on earth, but He was called "Man" and "the Son of man" after He ascended back to the Father. We will look at just a few of these Scriptures:

Luke 19:10 declares, *"The Son of man is come to seek and to save that which was lost."*

The eternal Word was made flesh in the Person of Christ Jesus the Lord: "In the beginning was the Word, and the Word was with God, and the Word was God. . . . And the Word was made flesh, and dwelt among us, (and we beheld His glory, the glory as of the only begotten of the Father,) full of grace and truth. . . . No man hath seen God at any time; the only begotten Son, which is in the bosom of the Father, He hath declared Him" (John 1:1, 14, 18). In other words, *God's CHRIST* was in the beginning. *Man's JESUS* was born of the Virgin Mary about two thousand years ago.

The character of God demanded this in order to provide the atonement, for *GOD cannot die* (Psalm 90:1, 2), nor can He be tempted with evil (James 1:13). But "the wages of sin is death" (Rom. 6:23), and it was necessary that a qualified substitute be provided to die in the sinner's place in order that we might be saved.   It was also necessary that the qualified substitute be tempted in all points as we are—yet without sin—in order that He might know the feeling of our infirmities and become our faithful High Priest (Heb. 2:17).

Even though the law is holy and honorable, the law could not make atonement, could not redeem, because of the weakness of the flesh: "For what the law could not do, in that it was weak through the flesh, God sending His own Son *in the likeness of sinful flesh,* and for sin, condemned sin in the flesh" (Rom. 8:3).

It *had to be* God's Son, for only God *could* provide a qualified substitute for the sinner. Because of God's character and His nature, the substitute must be righteous, holy, sinless, and undefiled—*untouched by evil;* yet He must be flesh as *man* is flesh. Jesus perfectly filled these qualifications. He satisfied God so completely that He, the Man Christ Jesus, is now seated in the highest seat of heaven at the Father's right hand.

The Word—God's Christ who was in the beginning with God—*was made flesh* in order that we might be made acceptable to God in Christ Jesus: "Having predestinated us unto the adoption of children by Jesus Christ to Himself, according to the good pleasure of His will, to the praise of the glory of His grace, *wherein He hath made us ACCEPTED IN THE BELOVED*" (Eph. 1:5, 6).

No man hath seen God the Eternal Spirit (John 1:18), *"but we see JESUS, who was made a little lower than the angels for the suffering of death, crowned with glory and honour; that He by the grace of God should taste death for EVERY MAN"* (Heb. 2:9).

We have not seen God the Eternal Spirit, but John the Beloved penned the message for this day and hour:

"That which was from the beginning, which we have heard, which we have seen with our eyes, which we have looked upon, and our hands have handled, of the Word of life; (For the life was manifested, and we have seen it, and bear witness, and shew unto you that eternal life, which was with the Father, and was manifested unto us;) That which we have seen and heard declare we unto you, that ye also may have fellowship with us: and truly our fellowship is with the Father, and with His Son Jesus Christ. And these things write we unto you, that your joy may be full.

"This then is the message which we have heard of Him, and declare unto you, that God is light, and in Him is no darkness at all. If we say that we have fellowship with Him, and walk in darkness, we lie, and do not the truth: but if we walk in the light, as He is in the light, we have fellowship one with another, and the blood of Jesus Christ His Son cleanseth us from all sin" (I John 1:1—7).

Now let us look more closely at this passage, penned under inspiration by "that disciple whom Jesus loved":

"That which was from the beginning . . . ." (In the beginning was *the WORD*.)

". . . which we have heard . . . ." (John heard Jesus preach and teach. "Faith cometh by hearing, and hearing by the Word of God"—Rom. 10:17.)

". . . which we have seen with our eyes . . . ." (John personally saw Jesus in the flesh.)

". . . which we have looked upon . . . ." (John did not simply see Jesus in a casual way. He walked with Him, talked with Him, and fellowshipped with

Him for three and one-half years.)

"... *and our hands have handled* ...." (John not only saw and heard Jesus in the flesh—he *touched* Him, he knew that He was real. It was John who leaned on the Master's breast at the last Passover— John 13:23.)

"... *of the Word of Life* ...." (The Word that was in the beginning took the form of human life. *The Word IS life*, and *through* the Word God created all things that are created, in heaven and in earth.)

"*For the life was manifested ... that ETERNAL life* ...." (In I John 5:11, 12 John declares, "This is the record, that *God hath given to us ETERNAL LIFE, and this life is in His SON*. He that hath the Son hath life; and he that hath not the Son of God hath not life.")

"That which we have *seen* and *heard* declare we unto you, that ye also may have fellowship with us: and truly *our fellowship is with the Father* (Jehovah God), *and with His Son Jesus Christ*. And these things write we unto you, *that your joy may be FULL*.

"*THIS THEN IS THE MESSAGE which we have heard of Him, and declare unto you, that God is light, and in Him is no darkness at all.* ... *If we walk in the light, as He is in the light, we have fellowship one with another, and the blood of Jesus Christ His Son cleanseth us from all sin.*"

Thus, "*we see JESUS*"—that is, we believe the message God gave *concerning* Jesus, and with the eye of the inner man we see Him by faith. We have never seen Him as John saw Him but we know He is everything John declared, because John *saw* Him, *heard* Him, *touched* Him, and *through inspiration he passed this message on to us, that we might have full joy!*

We KNOW Jesus lived, that He was God in flesh, that He was tempted in all points as we are, yet without sin, and we know that He conquered the world, the flesh, the devil, death, hell, and the grave. We know this because the Word of God declares it and *"through faith we understand"* (Heb. 11:3).

Peter expresses it in these words: "Blessed be the God and Father of our Lord Jesus Christ, which according to His abundant mercy hath begotten us again unto a lively hope by the resurrection of Jesus Christ from the dead, to an inheritance incorruptible, and undefiled, and that fadeth not away, reserved in heaven for you, who are kept by the power of God through faith unto salvation ready to be revealed in the last time. Wherein ye greatly rejoice, though now for a season, if need be, ye are in heaviness through manifold temptations: *That the trial of your faith, being much more precious than of gold that perisheth, though it be tried with fire, might be found unto praise and honour and glory at the appearing of Jesus Christ: WHOM HAVING NOT SEEN, YE LOVE; IN WHOM, THOUGH NOW YE SEE HIM NOT, YET BELIEVING, YE REJOICE WITH JOY UNSPEAKABLE AND FULL OF GLORY"* (I Pet. 1:3—8).

Jesus was "made a little *lower* than the angels." Angels are created spirits, but Jesus was made "like unto *His brethren."* He was made thus to suffer death, and when He came into the world He knew exactly why He was here.

In Hebrews 2:10 we learn that it was a divine necessity that Jesus be made "a little lower than the angels" and suffer death in order to bring *"many sons* unto glory." It was through suffering that "the Captain of (our) salvation" was made perfect, and in verses 14—18 of that same chapter in Hebrews we learn *more* about the *human nature* of Jesus:

"Forasmuch then as the children are *partakers of flesh and blood, He also Himself likewise took part of the same;* that through death He might destroy him

that had the power of death, that is, the devil; and
deliver them who through fear of death were all their
lifetime subject to bondage. For verily He took not
on Him the nature of angels; but He took on Him the
seed of Abraham. Wherefore in all things it behoved
Him to be made like unto His brethren, that He might
be a merciful and faithful high priest in things pertaining to God, to make reconciliation for the sins of
the people. For in that He Himself hath suffered being tempted, He is able to succour them that are
tempted."

Our children are partakers of our flesh and blood—
and Jesus *"took part of the same."* That is, He took
the flesh part of man and was made *like unto* sinful
flesh. Jesus received His flesh from the Virgin Mary;
but the life of the flesh is in the blood (Lev. 17:14),
and *His blood was the blood of God.* The Apostle
Paul instructed the Ephesian elders concerning the
care of *"the Church of God, which He hath purchased
with HIS* (God's) *OWN BLOOD"* (Acts 20:28)—and
certainly the Church was purchased with the blood
of *Jesus* (Eph. 5:25).

The Son of God took a body of flesh in order that
He might die, and in that body of flesh He did what
the law could never have done: He fulfilled every
demand of God's righteousness and God's holiness.
Now God can be just, and yet justify the ungodly:

"But now *the righteousness of God without the
law* is manifested, being witnessed by the law and
the prophets; even the righteousness of God which is
by faith of Jesus Christ unto all and upon all them
that believe: for there is no difference: for all have
sinned, and come short of the glory of God; being
justified freely by His grace through the redemption
that is in Christ Jesus: Whom God hath set forth to
be a propitiation through faith in His blood, to declare His righteousness for the remission of sins that

are past, through the forbearance of God; to declare, I say, at this time *His righteousness: that He might be just, and the Justifier of him which believeth in Jesus.* Where is boasting then? It is excluded. By what law? of works? Nay: but by the law of faith. *Therefore we conclude that a man is justified by faith WITHOUT THE DEEDS OF THE LAW"* (Rom. 3:21—28).

Through Paul's writing to Timothy we are assured that *there is a MAN in heaven:* "For there is one God, and one Mediator between God and men, *THE MAN Christ Jesus"* (I Tim. 2:5).

It is a serious thing indeed to deny the reality of Christ's body of flesh. This is definitely a mark of the spirit of Antichrist:

"Beloved, believe not every spirit, but try the spirits whether they are of God: because many false prophets are gone out into the world. *HEREBY KNOW YE THE SPIRIT OF GOD: Every spirit that confesseth that Jesus Christ is come IN THE FLESH is of God: and every spirit that confesseth not that Jesus Christ is come in the flesh is NOT of God: and this is THAT SPIRIT OF ANTICHRIST, whereof ye have heard that it should come; and even now already is it in the world.* Ye are of God, little children, and have overcome them: because *greater is He* (Christ) *that is in you, than he* (Satan) *that is in the world!"* (I John 4:1—4).

Even after His resurrection, the body of Jesus was a body of *flesh and bones.* He gave His *blood* that we might have life, but in Luke 24:38, 39 the risen Lord said to His terrified disciples, "Why are ye troubled? and why do thoughts arise in your hearts? *Behold my hands and my feet, that it is I myself: handle me, and see; for a spirit hath not FLESH AND BONES, as ye see me have!"*

In His resurrection body our Lord also *ate:* "And

while they (the disciples) yet believed not for joy, and wondered, He said unto them, *Have ye here any meat?* And they gave Him a piece of a broiled fish, and of an honeycomb. *And He took it, AND DID EAT BE-FORE THEM"* (Luke 24:41—43).

Since *our* glorified bodies will be like the glorious body of Jesus, I believe we, too, can eat if we so desire; but I do not believe it will be *necessary* that we eat after we have become like Him.

On occasion, even while Jesus tabernacled in His body of flesh, *the divine glory within* broke through, and some of His disciples *beheld* that glory. Three of the Gospel writers recorded one event, when Jesus took Peter, James, and John "up into an high mountain apart, and was transfigured before them: and His face did shine as the sun, and His raiment was white as the light" (Matt. 17:1, 2). Also read Mark 9:2—8 and Luke 9:28—31.

Stephen saw *the MAN* Christ Jesus standing at God's right hand: "He, being full of the Holy Ghost, looked up stedfastly into heaven, and saw *the glory of God, and Jesus standing on the right hand of God,* and said, Behold, I see the heavens opened, and the Son of man standing on the right hand of God" (Acts 7:55, 56).

In Revelation 5:6, John the Beloved wrote, "And I beheld, and, lo, in the midst of the throne and of the four beasts, and in the midst of the elders, stood *a LAMB as it had been slain . . . ."* John saw the Lamb of God, the Lord Jesus Christ—*THE MAN Christ Jesus*—who is even now at the right hand of God the Father.

Jesus declared to His enemies, *"Hereafter shall ye see THE SON OF MAN sitting on the right hand of power, and coming in the clouds of heaven"* (Matt. 26:64). The Man Christ Jesus—the same Man in the same body—will return to earth in the clouds, just as

He went away; God's Word declares it:

"And when (Jesus) had spoken these things, while they beheld, He was taken up; and *A CLOUD received Him out of their sight*. And while they looked stedfastly toward heaven as He went up, behold, two men stood by them in white apparel; which also said, Ye men of Galilee, why stand ye gazing up into heaven? *This SAME JESUS, which is taken up from you into heaven, shall so come IN LIKE MANNER AS YE HAVE SEEN HIM GO INTO HEAVEN*" (Acts 1:9—11).

Jesus will return in the clouds—yes, the same Man in the same glorified body in which He ascended from the Mount of Olives as His disciples gazed after Him. There is a Man in heaven now—a Man who knows us better than we know ourselves. He is our Mediator, our Intercessor, our Advocate, and our soon-coming King. Praise His name!

The Word of God declares that when Jesus comes in the clouds to call His own to meet Him in the air (I Thess. 4:13—18), He will change our vile bodies and fashion them like unto His own glorious resurrection body:

"For our conversation (citizenship) is in heaven; from whence also we look for the Saviour, *the Lord Jesus Christ: WHO SHALL CHANGE OUR VILE BODY, that it may be fashioned like unto HIS GLORIOUS BODY*, according to the working whereby He is able even to subdue all things unto Himself" (Phil. 3:20, 21).

John the Beloved declares, *"Beloved, NOW are we the sons of God, and it doth not yet appear what we SHALL be: but we know that, when He shall appear, WE SHALL BE LIKE HIM; for we shall see Him as He is"* (I John 3:2), "and as we have borne the image of the earthy, *we shall also bear the image of the heavenly"* (I Cor. 15:49).

The Human Nature of Christ Jesus

I have had much to say and have given many
Scriptures concerning the divinity of Jesus. I would
now point out that the Scriptures just as clearly teach
that Jesus was also *human*. He was flesh and bones
as we are, but His blood was the blood of God. Joseph and Mary did not live together as man and wife
until after Jesus was born. God's Word declares that
Joseph *"knew her NOT till she had brought forth her
firstborn son: and he called His name JESUS"* (Matt.
1:25).

Luke 2:7 tells us that Mary "brought forth her
firstborn son, and wrapped Him in swaddling clothes,
and laid Him in a manger; because there was no room
for them in the inn."

Acts 2:30 speaks of the fact that *David,* "being a
prophet," knew that "God had sworn with an oath
to him, that of the fruit of his loins, *according to the
flesh,* He would raise up Christ to sit on his throne."

Acts 13:22, 23 *also* speaks of David, a man after
God's own heart, of whose seed "God *according to
His promise* raised unto Israel a Saviour, *Jesus."*

In Romans 1:3 we read "concerning (God's) Son
Jesus Christ our Lord, *which was made of the seed
of David ACCORDING TO THE FLESH."*

Galatians 4:4 declares, *"When the fulness of the
time was come, God sent forth His Son, MADE OF
A WOMAN . . . ."*

Then in Hebrews 7:14 we read, "For it is evident
that our Lord sprang out of Juda; of which tribe Moses
spake nothing concerning priesthood."

These Scriptures clearly teach that Jesus was "the
fruit of David's loins," that He was of the seed of
David "according to the flesh," and that He was
"made of a *woman"*—the Virgin Mary. She was as
truly the mother of Jesus as the dear woman who gave

me birth is *my* mother. The difference in human birth and the birth of Jesus is that *He* had a human mother but God Almighty was His Father. The Holy Ghost overshadowed Mary, she conceived, and brought forth the only begotten Son of God. Jesus was of the seed of David, of the tribe of Judah—*very man*, although very *God.*

As the Son of Man,
Jesus Possessed Human Limitations

There are many Scriptures which clearly teach that Jesus was human from the standpoint of hunger, thirst, weariness, and *in every other way that WE are limited because of the flesh.* It is true that He was absolutely sinless, but His flesh was exactly like ours from the standpoint of *physical* limitations.

In the account of Jesus and His meeting with the Samaritan woman at Jacob's well (John 4:6—42), His human limitations are clearly displayed. In verse 6 we read, "Now Jacob's well was there. *Jesus therefore, BEING WEARIED WITH HIS JOURNEY, sat thus on the well . . . .*" But while this passage so clearly shows the *humanity* of Jesus, it reveals *His deity* as well, for the fact that "He must needs go through Samaria" (v. 4) suggests that He knew He would find there a soul who needed salvation. His omniscience is very clearly declared in verses 17 and 18 in that He told the Samaritan woman everything she had ever done. In verse 29 she testified to her acquaintances, *"Come, see a Man which told me all things that ever I did! Is not this THE CHRIST?"*

As GOD, Jesus was never weary; but *as the Son of MAN* He grew tired the same as we do. In Isaiah 40:28 we read, "Hast thou not known? Hast thou not heard, that *the everlasting God, the Lord, the Creator of the ends of the earth, fainteth not, neither is weary?*

There is no searching of His understanding." Psalm
121:3, 4 declares, ". . . *He that keepeth thee will not
slumber. Behold, He that keepeth Israel shall neither
slumber nor sleep."* But the *human limitation* of Jesus
as the Son of man is clearly seen in Matthew 8:23—27
when, after a strenuous day in His ministry, He was
so sound asleep in the ship that the disciples had to
awaken Him in the midst of a storm! Mark tells us
that Jesus "was in the hinder part of the ship *asleep
on a PILLOW"* (Mark 4:38).

As the Son of man, Jesus became hungry (Matt.
21:18); but as God, He was the bread of life (John
6:35, 48).

As the Son of man, He became thirsty (John 4:7;
19:28). As God, He was the living water (John 7:37,38).

As the Son of man He was as capable of knowing
pain as *we* are capable of knowing it. Surely He suffered indescribable agony under the Roman scourge
and as the thorns were pressed into His brow; but
even in the Garden of Gethsemane He *prayed* in such
agonizing intensity that "His sweat was as it were
great drops of blood falling down to the ground!"
(Luke 22:44).

As the *Son of man,* Jesus died—He became the Son
of man *in order to die,* that He might taste death for
us! The Scriptures plainly reveal that He was very
man just as truly as He was very God. He was "made
like unto His brethren" that He might know weariness, hunger, thirst, pain—*and death!* But the physical
limitations of Jesus were definitely in His human nature. *As God* He was omnipotent, omniscient, and
omnipresent.

In Luke 2:52 we are told that Jesus grew as *all*
normal children grow—both intellectually and physically. He "increased in wisdom and stature, and in
favour with God and man." In Mark 13:32 we read
of the Lord's return in glory, "but of that day and

that hour knoweth *no man, no, not the angels which are in heaven, NEITHER THE SON, but the Father."*

However, these Scriptures speak of *the human nature* of Jesus. As God, He was *omniscient—* He knew all things from the beginning to the ending. It was *a divine necessity* that the Son of God become as human as we are, sin apart, in order to take our place, pay the sin-debt, and become the Saviour of all who believe in His shed blood and finished work.

As the Son of man Jesus could feel as we feel. This was necessary since He was to become our Saviour, Mediator, and Intercessor:

"For in that He Himself hath suffered being tempted, He is able to succour them that are tempted" (Heb. 2:18).

"For we have not an High Priest which cannot be touched with the feeling of our infirmities; but was in all points tempted like as we are, yet without sin" (Heb. 4:15).

It has already been pointed out that *Jehovah God cannot be tempted* (James 1:13); but it was necessary that *our Substitute* be tempted, it was necessary that He face everything the sinner faced, if He would take the sinner's place. Therefore, God took a body of flesh; and *in that flesh* as the Man Christ Jesus, God incarnate was tempted! His *divinity* was not tempted, but as the Son of man He was tempted in all points as we are.

Carnality is not an essential part of human nature as God *created* man. Rather, carnality *became* a part of man's nature through the fall. But *Jesus* was not carnal, "for to be carnally minded is death; but to be spiritually minded is life and peace. *Because the carnal mind is enmity against God: for it is not subject to the law of God, neither indeed can be"* (Rom. 8:6, 7). We know that Jesus did always those things that pleased God (John 8:29), and that He *completely fulfilled the law of God* (Matt. 5:17, 18).

As the Son of man, the physical limitations of Jesus were self-imposed—that is, He *voluntarily* took a body of humiliation, *"made Himself* of no reputation, and *took upon Him* the form of a servant, and was made *in the likeness of men:* and being found in fashion as a man, *He humbled Himself,* and became obedient unto death, even the death of the cross" (Phil. 2:7, 8). He voluntarily placed Himself in the position He occupied as the Son of man in order to redeem man and make it possible for poor, lost, hell-deserving sinners to be saved by grace through faith in the shed blood and finished work of the Lamb of God. Yes, Jesus was made like unto us. He was tempted in all points as we are tempted, yet He never sinned. He was *unimpeachable holiness!*

As the Son of man—*but ONLY as the Son of man*—Jesus was limited in power. Even in His body of humiliation He worked miracles that only Almighty God could perform. Being limited in His human nature did not limit His power *as the second Person in the Godhead,* but the Scriptures record twenty-five instances where He *PRAYED for power* for specific work He was to do, and for specific victory. He prayed as other men pray—He obtained what He desired by calling upon God. The Scriptures clearly bear out this truth:

Jesus prayed early in the morning—the very best time to pray: "And in the morning, rising up *a great while before day,* He went out, and departed into a solitary place, and there prayed" (Mark 1:35).

When He was nearing Calvary He prayed—*alone,* withdrawn from even His disciples: "And He was withdrawn from them about a stone's cast, *and kneeled down, and prayed,* saying, Father, if thou be willing, remove this cup from me: nevertheless not my will, but thine, be done.

"And there appeared an angel unto Him from heaven, strengthening Him. And *being in an agony He prayed more earnestly:* and His sweat was as it were great drops of blood falling down to the ground. And when He rose up from prayer, and was come to His disciples, He found them sleeping for sorrow, and said unto them, Why sleep ye? *Rise and PRAY, lest ye enter into temptation"* (Luke 22:41—46).

After the feeding of the five thousand, "straightway Jesus constrained His disciples to get into a ship, and to go before Him unto the other side, while He sent the multitudes away. *And when He had sent the multitudes away, HE WENT UP INTO A MOUNTAIN APART TO PRAY: and when the evening was come, He was there ALONE"* (Matt. 14:22, 23).

Writing to the Hebrew believers, the Apostle Paul declared that Jesus, "in the days of His flesh . . . offered up prayers and supplications *with strong crying and tears"* (Heb. 5:7).

Not only did Jesus pray to God for power and victory on many occasions, He was also *anointed* "with the Holy Ghost and with power" as God has always anointed His ministers. In Acts 10:36—38 Peter tells us, "The word which God sent unto the children of Israel, preaching peace by Jesus Christ: (He is Lord of all:) that word, I say, ye know, which was published throughout all Judaea, and began from Galilee, after the baptism which John preached: *How GOD ANOINTED JESUS OF NAZARETH WITH THE HOLY GHOST AND WITH POWER: who went about doing good, and healing all that were oppressed of the devil; FOR GOD WAS WITH HIM."*

God's Christ, our Saviour, was just as human as *we* are. He was human in all things. When He appeared to Mary as she wept by the empty tomb on the morning of His resurrection, He said, "Touch me not; for I am not yet ascended to my Father: but go to my brethren, and say unto them, I ascend unto *my* Father, and *your* Father; and to *MY GOD,* and *your* God" (John 20:17). Jehovah was just as truly the God of the Son of man as He was the God of Mary Magdalene. Jesus was a real man in every respect, and He *became* man in order that *we* might become sons of God:

"For ye know the grace of our Lord Jesus Christ, that, though He was rich, yet for your sakes He became poor, that ye through His poverty might be rich" (II Cor. 8:9).

Christ Jesus our Saviour, Son of man yet Son of God, took *human* nature that *we* might become partakers of *divine nature:* "Whereby are given unto us exceeding great and precious promises: that by these ye might be *partakers of the divine nature,* having escaped the corruption that is in the world through lust" (II Pet. 1:4).

God's Christ—He who was in the beginning *with* God—became man, that men might become members of *the household of God:* "Now therefore ye are no more strangers and foreigners, but fellowcitizens with the saints, and of *the household of God* . . . in whom ye also are builded together for an habitation of God through the Spirit" (Eph. 2:19, 22).

Christ Jesus took a body of humiliation that *we* might become *members of HIS body:* "For we are members of His body, of His flesh, and of His bones" (Eph. 5:30). "For as the body is one, and hath many members, and all the members of that one body, being many, are one body: *so also is Christ.* For by one Spirit are we all baptized *into one body,* whether we be Jews or Gentiles, whether we be bond or free; and have been all made to drink into one Spirit" (I Cor. 12:12, 13).

I confess I do not understand all of this, but we are not supposed to be able to understand all the deep things of God. We are saved by grace through *faith* (Eph. 2:8), *"the just shall live by faith"* (Rom. 1:17), and *"whatsoever is NOT of faith is sin"* (Rom. 14:23). We are finite, God is *infinite;* and Bible truths that seem to contradict each other *harmonize perfectly* in the infinite wisdom of God. The "secret things" belong unto Him, but there is enough truth revealed that we can plainly understand man's position as a sinner—lost, in need of a Saviour; and we can also clearly understand that Jesus is the Saviour of sinners. One glorious day God will explain all things, and what is now *beyond* our understanding will be made plain.

The Holy Spirit has no fear in putting the *deity* and the *manhood* of Jesus in one short passage—or even in *one verse* of Scripture. For instance, in Matthew 8:23—27 *the Man* Christ Jesus was asleep in the ship when a storm arose; but when the disciples awakened Him, *God's Christ* spoke words of Deity and the wind and waves obeyed!

Also in the following Scriptures we see Christ's deity and His manhood side by side:

"Now when all the people were baptized, it came to pass, that *Jesus also being baptized, and praying,* the heaven was opened, and the Holy Ghost descended in a bodily shape like a dove upon Him, and a voice came from heaven, which said, *Thou art my beloved Son; in thee I am well pleased"* (Luke 3:21, 22).

"And it came to pass about an eight days after these sayings, *He took Peter and John and James, and went up into a mountain to pray.* And as He prayed, *the fashion of His countenance was altered, and His raiment was white and glistering.* . . . And there came a voice out of the cloud, saying, *This is my beloved Son: hear Him"* (Luke 9:28, 29, 35).

". . . when He bringeth in the firstbegotten into the world, He saith, And *let all the angels of God worship Him"* (Heb. 1:6).

"For in that *He Himself hath suffered being tempted,* He is able to succour them that are tempted" (Heb. 2:18).

"Seeing then that *we have a great High Priest,* that is passed into the heavens, *Jesus the Son of God,* let us hold fast our profession. For we have not a High Priest which cannot be touched with the feeling of our infirmities; but was *in all points tempted like as we are, YET WITHOUT SIN"* (Heb. 4:14, 15).

And in Colossians 2:9 we read, *"IN HIM* (Jesus) *dwelleth all the fulness of the Godhead bodily."*

The Subordination of the Son of Man to God the Father

We have dwelt at length on the subject of Christ's deity—the fact that He was in the beginning with God, co-equal with God. Yet Jesus Himself declared, "My Father is *greater* than I" (John 14:28)—which sounds like a direct contradiction to His deity.

However, we must remember that God cannot die (Psalm 90:1, 2), nor can He be tempted with evil (James 1:13). Therefore Jesus was made "a little lower than the angels," He was made to be tempted in all points as we are, He was made to die in our stead, and *AS THE SON OF MAN* He was *subordinate* to God the heavenly Father.

"For unto which of the angels said He at any time, Thou art my SON, *this day have I BEGOTTEN thee?* And again, I will be to Him a Father, and He shall be to me a Son?" (Heb. 1:5).

"And the Word was made flesh, and dwelt among us, (and we beheld His glory, the glory as of *the only BEGOTTEN of the Father,*) full of grace and truth" (John 1:14).

"For God so loved the world, that He gave *His*

only BEGOTTEN Son, that whosoever believeth in Him should not perish, but have everlasting life" (John 3:16).

God the Father begot Jesus the Son: The angel said to Mary, "The Holy Ghost shall come upon thee, and the power of the Highest shall overshadow thee: therefore also that holy thing which shall be born of thee shall be called *the Son of GOD"* (Luke 1:35).

What does the Scripture mean when it declares that Jesus was "begotten of the Father"? Does that statement refer to the origin of *the Eternal Word,* or does it speak of the origin of *God in flesh,* the Man Christ Jesus?

The Eternal Word was *in the beginning* with the Father, in the bosom of the Father. *Jesus* (the child born of the Virgin Mary) was *begotten* of God. He was born in a stable, wrapped in swaddling clothes, and laid in a manger. He grew up in the home of Joseph and Mary, probably helping Joseph in the carpenter's shop. When He was approximately thirty years old He entered into His public ministry and for more than three years He preached the Gospel, healed the sick, raised the dead, cleansed the lepers, and declared God to man. He was crucified, buried, and on the third day He rose from the dead. He appeared to men for a short season of forty days after His resurrection, and then ascended back to the heavenly Father from whence He had come. *And now,* the Man Christ Jesus who sits at the right hand of God is the Personality *begotten* of God through the Holy Ghost and born of the Virgin Mary. True, He is now in His glorified body, but He is still "the MAN, Christ Jesus" (I Tim. 2:5).

It was to God the Father that Jesus gave credit for His life as the Son of Man. As God's Christ, Son of God, *He had no beginning;* but He became *Jesus* (Saviour) when He was conceived of the Holy Ghost and born of the Virgin Mary. *CHRIST* is His *divine* name. *JESUS* is His *earthly* name.

Jesus definitely gave the Father credit for His life as the Son of man. In John 6:57 He said, *"As the living Father hath SENT me, and I LIVE BY THE FATHER,* so he that eateth me, even he shall live by me."

When Jesus healed the impotent man who, for thirty-eight years, had waited for healing by the pool of Bethesda (John 5:1—9), the Jews objected on the ground that this was done on the Sabbath. "But Jesus answered them, *My Father worketh hitherto, and I work.* Therefore the Jews sought the more to kill Him, because He not only had broken the sabbath, but said also that God was His Father, making Himself equal with God."

Jesus then made this memorable declaration: "Verily, verily, I say unto you, *THE SON CAN DO NOTHING OF HIMSELF, but what He seeth the Father do: for what things soever HE doeth, these also doeth the SON likewise"* (John 5:16—19).

Jesus declared that He could do nothing independently of the Father. He was on earth in obedience to a direct command of the Father, and in John 10:17, 18 He said, *"Therefore doth my Father love me,* because I lay down my life, that I might take it again. No man taketh it from me, but I lay it down of myself. I have power to lay it down, and I have power to take it again. *This commandment have I received of my Father."*

This passage makes it clear that Jesus did not die *unwillingly. HE WAS WILLING TO LAY HIS LIFE DOWN.* But He came into the world to do the will of His Father, to glorify the Father, and He did nothing *independently* of the Father. The Jews asked Him, "What shall we do, that we might work the works of God?" He replied, *"This is the work of God, that*

ye believe on Him whom He hath SENT" (John 6:
28, 29).

Jesus made a similar statement in John 8:29: *"He
that SENT me is WITH me:* the Father hath not left
me alone; for I do always those things that please
Him." Then in verse 42 of that same chapter He said
to His enemies, "If God were your Father ye would
love me: *for I proceeded forth and came from God;
NEITHER CAME I OF MYSELF, BUT HE SENT
ME."*

Jesus, Son of man, was *sent* by the Father, He
received commandment from the Father, and in His
body of humiliation He was under the Father's *direc-
tions;* but even before the beginning of the creation
He knew this would be true. He knew who He was,
He knew why He had come into the world, He knew
that He would return to the Father when His mission
on earth was finished. He even knew *the time* of His
departure—the hour "that He should depart out of
this world unto the Father." He knew *"that the Father had given ALL THINGS into His hands, and
that He was come FROM God, and went TO God"*
(John 13:1, 3).

God the Father outlined the works of Jesus, those
things which He should accomplish in His earthly
ministry. In John 5:36 Jesus said, "I have *greater
witness* than that of John: for *the works which the
Father hath GIVEN ME to finish, the same works
that I do, bear witness of me, that the Father hath
sent me."*

In John 14:10, 11 He said to His disciples, "Believ-
est thou not that I am in the Father, and the Father
in me? *The words that I speak unto you I speak NOT
OF MYSELF: but the Father that dwelleth in me,
HE DOETH THE WORKS.* Believe me that I am in
the Father, and the Father in me: or else *believe me
FOR THE VERY WORKS' SAKE."*

Christ Jesus came into this world as a babe in a manger almost two thousand years ago. By-and-by He will *return*—as King of kings and Lord of lords. He said to His disciples, "I appoint you a kingdom, *as my Father hath appointed unto me*" (Luke 22:29).

Writing under inspiration—and for our enlightenment—the Apostle Paul said, "I would have you know, that the head of every man is Christ; and the head of the woman is the man; *and the head of Christ is GOD*" (I Cor. 11:3).

Then in I Corinthians 15:27, 28 Paul wrote, "For He hath put all things under His feet. But when He saith all things are put under Him, it is manifest that He is excepted, which did put all things under Him. And when all things shall be subdued unto Him, then shall the Son also Himself be subject unto Him that put all things under Him, *THAT GOD MAY BE ALL IN ALL.*"

Jesus Is the Way to the Father

The only possible way for man to draw near to God is through God's Christ who became Jesus, Saviour, Mediator. In John 14:6 Jesus Himself declared, "I am the way, the truth, and the life: *NO MAN cometh unto the Father but BY ME.*"

In Hebrews 7:25 we read, "Wherefore He is able also to save them to the uttermost *that come unto God BY HIM*, seeing He ever liveth to make intercession for them."

The Eternal God, Father of our Lord Jesus Christ, is the *source* of Deity. Jesus was *begotten* of Deity through the Holy Spirit; therefore God's Christ who became our Jesus was Deity in its *outflow*—Deity in a body of flesh. He came to declare God, to make known the love of God and the grace of God; and to save all who will draw near to God through faith in His shed blood and finished work.

The Eternal God—*fountain* of Deity; Christ Jesus the Son—the *outflow* of Deity; but the outflow possessed all the perfection of the fountain. In Christ dwelt all the fulness of the Godhead bodily (Col. 2:9). As a spring is the source of cool, bubbling water that becomes a flowing stream as it moves toward the river and the river flows on toward the sea, so God the Eternal Father is the source (the spring) of all glory. *Jesus*—Deity in flesh—was the *shining forth* of God's glory. He was the glory of God on display—"the brightness of His glory and the express image of His person" (Heb. 1:3).

The Scriptures given in this section (the Son of man subordinate to God the Father) have reference to *the Incarnate Christ;* they do not speak of *the pre-existent WORD* who was in the beginning with the Father. *Christ HAD no beginning.* As the Father had life in Himself, the Son had life in Himself; but as *Jesus, Son of man,* He began to live approximately two thousand years ago.

The Character of Jesus

The Word of God uses many expressions and figures to produce an adequate conception of the absolute holiness and moral purity of Jesus. It is almost impossible for man's language to do justice to His holiness, and the only thing in nature with which to *compare* the perfect holiness and moral purity of Christ is light—*blazing* light! Jesus Himself said, "I am the Light of the world" (John 8:12).

I John 1:5 describes God's message to man through Jesus Christ: "This then is the message which we have heard of Him, and declare unto you, that *God is light, and in Him is no darkness at all.*"

On the Mount of Transfiguration, the face of Jesus shone "as the sun, and His raiment was white as the light" (Matt. 17:2). The dazzling white light that glorified the face and raiment of our Lord was nothing more than the outshining of His absolute holiness and unimpeachable moral purity.

There are many, many passages of Scripture that clearly teach the holiness of Jesus. For example:

When He was casting out demons in Capernaum, the demons cried out, "Let us alone! What have we to do with thee, thou Jesus of Nazareth? Art thou come to destroy us? *I know thee who thou art, the HOLY ONE of God"* (Mark 1:24).

In Peter's second sermon he said to the Jews, "Ye denied *the HOLY ONE and the Just,* and desired a murderer to be granted unto you" (Acts 3:14).

When persecution of the early church began and the disciples were forbidden to preach in the name of Jesus, they prayed to God: "Of a truth against *thy HOLY CHILD JESUS,* whom thou hast anointed, both Herod, and Pontius Pilate, with the Gentiles, and the people of Israel, were gathered together, for to do whatsoever thy hand and thy counsel determined before to be done. And now, Lord, behold their threatenings: and grant unto thy servants that with all boldness they may speak thy word, by stretching forth thine hand to heal; and that signs and wonders may be done *by the name of thy HOLY CHILD JESUS"* (Acts 4:27—30).

In I John 2:20 the beloved disciple wrote, "But ye have an unction *from the HOLY ONE,* and ye know all things."

When we say that Jesus was absolutely holy we mean that He was (and *is*) absolutely *pure*—untouched by sin or anything that would defile. He was "in all points *tempted like as we are, YET WITHOUT SIN"* (Heb. 4:15). Hebrews 7:26 declares Him to be *"HOLY, harmless, undefiled,* separate from sinners, and made higher than the heavens."

As our Substitute, Christ *"offered Himself WITH-OUT SPOT* to God" (Heb. 9:14), and II Corinthians 5:21 emphatically declares that *Jesus "KNEW NO SIN,"* but God made Him to be sin *for us,* "that we might be made (become) the righteousness of God in Him."

I John 3:3 tells us, "Every man that hath this hope in him purifieth himself, *even as HE* (Jesus) *IS PURE."*

Jesus proved His holiness. He loved godliness, righteousness, and purity. He hated sin and unrighteousness: *"Thou hast loved righteousness, and hated iniquity;* therefore God, even thy God, hath anointed thee with the oil of gladness above thy fellows" (Heb. 1:9).

Peter testified to the sinlessness of Jesus—"who did no sin, neither was guile found in His mouth" (I Pet. 2:22).

Jesus not only proved His holiness *negatively;* He also proved it *positively* by doing everything God sent Him to do. In John 8:29 He said, "I do *always* those things that please Him."

The holiness of Jesus was manifested in many ways, but its crowning manifestation was His death on the cross. He so loved righteousness and hated sin that He was willing to lay aside His divine glory and be made like unto His brethren in all things. Fashioned as a man, He was willing to die the most shameful death mortal man could die, that sinners might be saved. He was willing to be rejected by both man and God, that others—yes, even you and I—might become partakers of divine nature and share His glory throughout eternity. He bore our sins "in His own body on the tree, that we, being dead to sins, should live unto righteousness . . ." (I Pet. 2:24).

"For Christ also hath once suffered for sins, the Just for the unjust, that He might bring us to God, being put to death in the flesh, but quickened by the Spirit" (I Pet. 3:18).

"Christ hath redeemed us from the curse of the law, being made a curse for us: for it is written, Cursed is every one that hangeth on a tree" (Gal. 3:13).

Today, much is said about the *love of God,* and the love of Jesus for sinners—but in many instances the *deity* of Jesus is denied. Men talk much of *the HOLINESS of God and the LOVE of Jesus;* but the Word of God clearly teaches that Jesus—Son of God, Son of man—is just as holy as Jehovah God is holy, and that God the Father is just as loving as *Jesus* is loving.

Christ Jesus the Lord was God in flesh. Therefore in holiness, in righteousness, in purity, in love—in all things—God the Eternal Father and Jesus the Son are ONE (John 10:30). Until we believe, confess, and fully embrace the *holiness* of Jesus, we cannot possibly have an adequate conception of His *love!*

Even Judas Iscariot confessed that Jesus was holy. He sold the Lord for the price of a slave, but later returned the thirty pieces of silver to the chief priests and elders, saying, *"I have sinned in that I have betrayed the INNOCENT blood!"* (Matt. 27:3, 4).

One of the two thieves who were crucified with Jesus confessed that the Son of God was sinless: "We receive the due reward of our deeds: *but THIS MAN hath done nothing amiss"* (Luke 23:41).

Three times Pontius Pilate confessed that Jesus was without fault—therefore holy: In John 18:38 he said to the Jews, *"I find in Him NO FAULT AT ALL."* In John 19:4 he again said to the multitude, "Behold, I bring Him forth to you, that ye may know that *I FIND NO FAULT in Him."* And in John 19:6, when the Jews continued to demand the crucifixion of Jesus, Pilate said to them, "Take ye Him and crucify Him: for *I FIND NO FAULT in Him!"*

Jesus Himself challenged His enemies, *"Which of you convinceth me of SIN?"* (John 8:46).

God Is Love—Jesus Is Love

The Bible makes it clear that Jesus possessed every attribute of Jehovah God. When Philip said, "Lord, shew us the Father," Jesus replied, "He that hath seen *me* hath seen the *Father"* (John 14:8, 9). Since Jesus was God manifested in flesh, those who saw Him in person *saw God.* Today we who see Jesus *with the eye of faith* see God. To know Christ is to know God, and those who do not know Christ *do not* know God. To know the meaning of God's love in its power, purity, and fulness, we must look at Christ Jesus, God's only begotten Son. He was the love of God on display.

Christ's Love for the Father:

During His entire earthly ministry, Jesus definitely let it be known that His first love was to God the Father. He loved God supremely, and His uppermost desire was to glorify the Father in all that He did and said. He said to His disciples, "Whatsoever ye shall ask in my name, that will I do, *that the Father may be GLORIFIED IN THE SON"* (John 14:13).

Jesus proved His love to the Father in perfect obedience. To His disciples He said, "If ye keep my commandments, ye shall abide in my love; even as I have kept my *Father's commandments,* and abide in *His* love" (John 15:10). Jesus never questioned the will of God. He followed in detail the divine instructions given by the Father. No wonder John the Beloved cried out, *"BEHOLD, WHAT MANNER OF LOVE THE FATHER HATH BESTOWED UPON US!"*

Jesus loved the Father so perfectly that He did not falter at forsaking the glories of heaven in exchange for the shame of earth and a body of humiliation, a body made in the likeness of sinful flesh. He humbled Himself and obeyed His heavenly Father—even unto the death of the cross (Phil. 2:8).

The shame of earth was no surprise to Jesus. The cruelty of the cross did not shock Him. When He left the bosom of the Father He knew full well that in accordance with the agreement within the Godhead His blood would be shed at Calvary. It was for that purpose that He came into the world, and from the time He left heaven until He cried out, "It is finished!" He walked deliberately toward the cross.

When we think of Calvary, when by faith we see the Lamb of God, bruised and bleeding, a crown of thorns piercing His brow, we are led to say, "How He *loved* us! to die such a death that we might live eternally!" But even though Jesus loved sinners so very much, His love for His heavenly Father was the primary reason He endured the shame and the agony of the cross. So as we look at Calvary and consider how the Son of God loved us, we might well exclaim, *"Behold, how He loved His FATHER!"*

Jesus said to His enemies, "If I honour myself, my honour is nothing: it is my Father that honoureth me; of whom ye say, that He is your God: Yet ye have not known Him; *but I know Him:* and if I should say, I know Him not, I shall be a liar like unto you: but *I know Him, AND KEEP HIS SAYING"* (John 8:54, 55).

Jesus kept the Word of God—and that means much more than simply obeying His commandments. He *guarded* God's Word as we might guard a precious treasure. In truth, the Word *IS* the most precious treasure heaven holds, and if the devil could discredit the Word of God he could undermine the very foundation of salvation and we would all be destined to damnation! Jesus *kept* God's Word, and the Psalmist declared, "For ever, O Lord, thy Word is settled in heaven" (Psalm 119:89). All the forces of hell cannot discredit or destroy God's Holy Word!

Jesus proved His love for and complete obedience to the heavenly Father when, at the age of twelve, His anxious parents found Him in the temple, "sitting in the midst of the doctors, both hearing them, and asking them questions." Mary said to Him, "Son, why hast thou thus dealt with us? Behold, thy father and I have sought thee sorrowing." Jesus replied, *"How is it that ye sought me? Wist ye not that I must be about MY FATHER'S BUSINESS?"* (Luke 2:46—49).

We have already discussed the *humanity* of Jesus— the fact that He, like all men, became tired, thirsty, and hungry. But His devotion to His heavenly Father was so great that He sometimes forgot His natural hunger for food that satisfies the physical body. When He talked with the woman of Samaria at Jacob's well, the disciples returned from the city where they had gone to buy meat. They said to Him, "Master, *eat.*" But a needy soul had taken away His physical hunger and He said to them, "I have meat to eat that ye know not of. . . . *MY meat is to do the will of Him that sent me, and to finish His work"* (John 4:30—34).

Jesus was the only person who ever lived on earth who could truthfully say, "I do always those things that are pleasing to God." Such obedience was proof of His love for His Father. The first Adam was self-ish—he wanted to be "as gods" (Gen. 3:5). The last Adam—the Lord Jesus Christ—never manifested selfish-ness in any form; He was completely *unselfish.* He came into the world, not to please Himself or follow His own will, but to do the Father's will—*always and without exception.* In John 5:30 He said, *"I can of*

mine own self do nothing: as I hear, I judge: and
my judgment is just; because *I seek not mine own
will, but the will of the Father which hath sent me.*"

Some men long for treasures of gold, silver, and
precious stones. Some live for pleasure and gratifica-
tion of their own lusts. Still others seek after honor
and fame. But *Jesus* sought *to please His Father* in
every detail of His life and work; and when He came
to the end of His earthly ministry He could look to
God and say *in truth,* "I have finished the work which
thou gavest me to do!" (John 17:4).

The supreme sacrifice Christ made for us finds its
original source in His love for His Father—perfect
love that produced perfect obedience to the Father's
will. Jesus loved the Eternal Father before there was
a sinner to love—yea, before the world was; and it
was His love to God *in the beginning* that brought
Him down to earth to die on the cross. Therefore,
His substitutionary death was in perfect obedience
and complete devotion to God the Father.

Glory to God seemed uppermost in the mind of
God's Son at all times, and as He neared the cross
He said, "Father, the hour is come; glorify thy Son,
that thy Son also may glorify thee . . . I have glorified thee on the earth: I have finished the work which
thou gavest me to do. And now, O Father, glorify
thou me with thine own self with the glory which I
had with thee before the world was" (John 17:1, 4, 5).

A lawyer once asked Jesus, "Master, which is the
great commandment in the law?" Jesus replied, *"Thou
shalt LOVE THE LORD THY GOD with all thy
heart, and with all thy soul, and with all thy mind.
This is the first and great commandment"* (Matt.
22:36—38).

The consuming passion of the earthly life of Jesus
was to glorify His Father. He lived, planned, prayed,
worked, suffered, and died to glorify God, and His life

as He tabernacled among men is the supreme display
of the law which He taught this lawyer.

Christ's love for sinners:

Although Jesus loves the Father supremely and
loves His saints in a very special way, He also loves
the vilest of sinners. He loved Judas Iscariot even
though He knew from the beginning that Judas would
betray Him; and in the Garden of Gethsemane at
the time of His arrest He called Judas "friend" (Matt.
26:50).

Jesus loves all mankind. He loved the men who
nailed Him to the cross, and prayed for them: "Father, forgive them; for they know not what they do"
(Luke 23:34). He loves sinners today, just as He loved
them when He walked among them on earth. He is
not willing that any should perish, but that all should
come to repentance.

Jesus loved His enemies and died for them (Rom.
5:10; Col. 1:21). In Romans 5:6, 8 we read, "When we
were yet without strength, in due time Christ died
for the ungodly. . . . God commendeth His love toward
us, in that, *while we were yet sinners,* Christ died
for us." We were unlovely—yet Jesus loved us. *"We
love HIM because He first loved US"* (I John 4:19).
Had He *not* first loved us, we would *never* have loved
Him.

Jesus loved His own people (according to the flesh)
in a very special way. He came to the Jew first, and
when He sent out the twelve He said to them, "Go
not into the way of the Gentiles, and into any city
of the Samaritans enter ye not: *But go rather to the
lost sheep of the house of Israel"* (Matt. 10:5, 6). The
Apostle Paul declared that the Gospel was *"to the
Jew first"* (Rom. 1:16). Jesus loves *all* people; He
especially loved those of God's chosen nation—but
they rejected Him in spite of His love!

He loved His mother; and even in His last moments of agony on the cross He thought of her: "When Jesus therefore saw His mother, and the disciple standing by, whom He loved, He saith unto His mother, Woman, behold thy son! Then saith He to the disciple, Behold thy mother! And from that hour that disciple took her unto his own home" (John 19:26, 27).

Jesus had a deep love for little children. I am sure their tender hearts and minds could feel His love for them, and they recognized Him as an unusual person. The people "brought young children to Him, that He should touch them: and His disciples rebuked those that brought them. But when Jesus saw it, He was much displeased, and said unto them, Suffer the little children to come unto me, and forbid them not: for of such is the kingdom of God. Verily I say unto you, *Whosoever shall NOT receive the kingdom of God AS A LITTLE CHILD, he shall not enter therein.* And He took them up in His arms, put His hands upon them, and blessed them" (Mark 10:13—16).

The disciples asked Jesus, "Who is the greatest in the kingdom of heaven?" He called a little child to Him, "and set him in the midst of them, and said: Verily I say unto you, *Except ye be converted, and become as little children, ye shall not enter into the kingdom of heaven. . . .* But whoso shall *offend* one of these little ones which believe in me, it were better for him that a millstone were hanged about his neck, and that he were drowned in the depth of the sea. . . . Take heed that ye despise not one of these little ones; for I say unto you, That in heaven their angels do always behold the face of my Father which is in heaven" (Matt. 18:1—10 in part). A person who does not love children does not know the love Jesus possessed— the love He gives to all who trust and believe in Him.

Some of those whom Jesus loved were especially near and dear to Him. John 11:5 tells us that He loved Martha, Mary, and Lazarus—dear friends in whose home He was undoubtedly a frequent and welcome visitor.

John the Beloved seemed a little closer to the Lord than the other disciples. He is mentioned in John 13:23 and 19:26 as *the disciple "whom Jesus loved."*

Jesus Proved His Love

It is not enough to *say* that we love someone. We *prove* our love by doing, giving, and living. It is by works that we prove our love to God and our faith in Christ, for "faith without works is dead" (James 2:20, 26).

Jesus proved His love for all mankind: "For ye know the grace of our Lord Jesus Christ, that, though He was rich, yet for your sakes He became poor, that ye through His poverty might be rich" (II Cor. 8:9). The finite mind of man cannot appreciate the riches of God—yet Jesus turned His back on the riches of heaven and embraced the poverty of earth: He was "in the *form of God,* thought it not robbery to be *equal* with God: but made Himself of no reputation, and took upon Him the form of a servant, and was made in the likeness of men: and being found in fashion as a man, He humbled Himself, and became obedient unto death, even the death of the cross" (Phil. 2:6—8).

From the manger in Bethlehem to the cross on Calvary the life of Jesus was a life of sacrifice. He who *created* the earth and all things therein had no place of His own as He dwelt among men. He said to His disciples, "The foxes have holes, and the birds of the air have nests; but the Son of man hath not where to lay His head" (Matt. 8:20).

It was through Christ's voluntary poverty that we became rich—"children of God, and if children, then

heirs; *heirs of God, and joint-heirs with Christ . . ."*
(Rom. 8:16, 17).

Jesus proved His love for us by giving Himself.
To His disciples He said, "Greater love hath no man
than this, that a man lay down His life for His
friends" (John 15:13), and in I John 3:16 we read,
"Hereby perceive we the love of God, *because He
laid down His life for us . . . ."*

In Ephesians 5:2 we are instructed to "walk in
love, *as Christ also hath loved us, and hath given
Himself for us an offering and a sacrifice to God* for
a sweetsmelling savour."

The Apostle Paul testified, "I am crucified with
Christ: nevertheless I live; yet not I, but Christ liveth
in me: and the life which I now live in the flesh I
live by the faith of the Son of God, *who loved me,
and gave Himself for me"* (Gal. 2:20).

Jesus willingly laid His life down for us, that we
might have life and have it abundantly.   They are
hypocrites and liars who profess to know Him but
do not follow His steps in love:

"For this is the message that ye heard from the
beginning, that we should *love one another.*   Not as
Cain, who was of that wicked one, and slew his brother.   And wherefore slew he him?   Because his own
works were evil, and his brother's righteous.   Marvel
not, my brethren, if the world hate you.   *We know
that we have passed from death unto life, because
WE LOVE THE BRETHREN.   He that loveth not
his brother abideth in death.*

"Whosoever hateth his brother is a murderer: and
ye know that no murderer hath eternal life abiding
in him.   Hereby perceive we the love of God, because
He laid down His life for us: and we ought to lay
down our lives for the brethren.   But whoso hath this
world's good, and seeth his brother have need, and
shutteth up his bowels of compassion from him, *how*

dwelleth the love of God in him?

"My little children, *let us not love in word, neither in tongue; but in deed and in truth.* And hereby we know that we are of the truth, and shall assure our hearts before Him" (I John 3:11—19).

Jesus Loves the Church

He loves the Church with a peculiar, special kind of love because the Church is *the bride of Christ.* The born again man loves everyone, but he loves his wife and family in a singular way. So it is with Christ. He loves everyone—sinner or saint; but He loves the Church with a peculiar, very special love.

Christ loves the Church *as a body,* but He also loves each believer *individually.* We might describe His love as being *in general* for all mankind, and *in particular* for the Church which is His body, His bride. In Ephesians 5:25 Paul declares that a husband should love his wife *"even as Christ also loved the Church, and GAVE HIMSELF for it,"* and in Ephesians 5:1, 2 we are told, "Be ye therefore followers of God, as dear children; *and walk in love, as Christ also hath loved us, and hath GIVEN HIMSELF for us an offering and a sacrifice to God for a sweet-smelling savour."*

Jesus loved as none other has ever loved. His love did not change, it did not vary with His feelings or with the season of the year. He loved His own fervently and with a pure love, and John 13:1 declares, ". . . having loved *His own* which were in the world, He loved them unto the end."

"His own" in this statement refers to each and every believer who makes up the body of Christ. This does not mean, however, that some are elected to make up the body of Christ while others are left out. Jesus made it very clear that everyone belongs to this

"elect" *if they will come to Him.* In John 6:37 He promised, "Him that cometh to me I will in no wise cast out."

To teach that some are elected to be saved while others are elected to be damned is to accuse God of being a respecter of persons, and His Word plainly states that *"there is no respect of persons with God"* (Rom. 2:11). The Scripture also declares that God is "longsuffering to us-ward, not willing that *any* should perish, *but that ALL should come to repentance"* (II Pet. 3:9).

To His own people after the flesh Jesus said that they would die in their sins — not because they were not "elected" to be saved, but because they refused to come to Him (John 5:40). In Luke 13:34, 35 Jesus wept over the holy city: *"O Jerusalem, Jerusalem, which killest the prophets, and stonest them that are sent unto thee; how often would I have gathered thy children together, as a hen doth gather her brood under her wings, AND YE WOULD NOT!* Behold, your house is left unto you desolate: and verily I say unto you, Ye shall not see me, until the time come when ye shall say, Blessed is He that cometh in the name of the Lord!"

Born again believers are recipients of a very special love. Jesus ministers to His own in a very special way. He guards them, supplies their needs, and promises never to leave them nor forsake them. In His prayer of intercession He specifically prayed for believers:

"Holy Father, keep through thine own name those whom thou hast given me, that they may be one, as we are. While I was with them in the world, I kept them in thy name: those that thou gavest me I have kept, and none of them is lost, but the son of perdition; that the Scripture might be fulfilled. . . . Neither pray I for these alone, but for them also which shall believe on me through their word" (John 17:11, 12, 20).

The love of Jesus for His Church is an enduring love. It will last throughout eternity:

"Who shall separate us from the love of Christ? Shall tribulation, or distress, or persecution, or famine, or nakedness, or peril, or sword? . . . Nay, in all these things we are more than conquerors through Him that loved us. *For I am persuaded, that neither death, nor life, nor angels, nor principalities, nor powers, nor things present, nor things to come, nor height, nor depth, NOR ANY OTHER CREATURE, shall be able to separate us from the love of God, which is in Christ Jesus our Lord"* (Rom. 8:35—39 in part).

Precious truth! Jesus manifests Himself in a very special way to those who are His obedient followers, those who obey His commandments and yield themselves unreservedly to Him. He said to His disciples, "As the Father hath loved me, so have I loved you: continue ye in my love. If ye keep my commandments, ye shall abide in my love; even as I have kept my Father's commandments, and abide in His love" (John 15:9, 10). In Mark 3:35 He said, "Whosoever shall do the will of God, the same is my brother, and my sister, and mother."

When Jesus said, "Keep my commandments" He was not speaking of the Law of Moses, but of the *commandments of Jesus.* The New Testament is filled with His commandments, and those who keep them are loved by Him in the same way He is loved by God the Father. Believers are joint-heirs with Christ (Rom. 8:17), *and that includes the love of God.*

I am glad God's love for us is not measured by our behaviour. Sometimes even the most consecrated Christians can, like Peter, deny the Lord—perhaps not *in word* so much as by the company we keep or the spirit we display before the world. But Peter's denial did not change the love of Jesus toward him, and on the morning of His resurrection Peter was given a special invitation to return to the disciple band.   The women at the empty tomb received the instruction, "Go your way, *tell His disciples AND PETER* that He goeth before you into Galilee: there shall ye see Him, as He said unto you" (Mark 16:7).

Thank God for saving grace, for keeping grace, and for teaching grace—grace that is greater than all our sin!   Jesus loves us in spite of our faults and failures, because "He knoweth our frame; *He remembereth that we are dust"* (Psalm 103:14).

Jesus did not cease to love us when He left this earth and returned to God's right hand.   He promised to prepare a place for His own, and at the appointed time He would return for the Church:

To His discouraged disciples He said, "Let not your heart be troubled: ye believe in God, believe also in me.   In my Father's house are many mansions: if it were not so, I would have told you. *I go to prepare a place for you.*   And if I go and prepare a place for you, *I will come again, and receive you UNTO MYSELF;* that where I am, there ye may be also" (John 14:1–3).

How wonderful to know that when we depart this life we who are saved by God's grace will go to heaven!   But even more wonderful is the fact that Jesus is coming to receive us *"unto HIMSELF."*   True believers are pilgrims and strangers on earth, this world is not our home.   Our citizenship is in heaven from whence we look for the Saviour.   We long to see Jesus, and the more dedicated we are, the more lonesome this world becomes.   Face it, beloved: there is not much left in this world in our day for a dedicated Christian to enjoy!

Moving words are these with which the Apostle Paul describes Christ's coming for His own: "The

Lord *Himself* shall descend from heaven with a shout, and with the voice of the archangel, and with the trump of God: and the dead in Christ shall rise first: *Then we which are alive and remain shall be caught up together with them in the clouds, to meet the Lord in the air: and SO SHALL WE EVER BE WITH THE LORD.* Wherefore comfort one another with these words" (I Thess. 4:16—18).

Writing to the church at Corinth, Paul gives these encouraging words: "Behold, I shew you a mystery: We shall not all sleep (die), but *we shall all be changed,* in a moment, in the twinkling of an eye, at the last trump: for the trumpet shall sound, and the dead shall be raised incorruptible, and we shall be changed. For this corruptible must put on incorruption, and this mortal must put on immortality. So when this corruptible shall have put on incorruption, and this mortal shall have put on immortality, then shall be brought to pass the saying that is written, *Death is swallowed up in victory!* O death, where is thy sting? O grave, where is thy victory?" (I Cor. 15:51—55).

We wait and long for that glorious day when Jesus will come to call us up to meet Him in the clouds in the air; but no matter how we may yearn to see Him, *His* longing for *us* is much deeper. The Church is the bride of Christ, and a bridegroom cannot be completely happy while he is separated from his bride. Many believers are already resting with Jesus in Paradise, but there are many, many Christians on earth today, living in this land of sorrow and darkness; and Jesus longs for *all of His own* to be with Him where He is—at the right hand of God the Father.

Christ's love for the Church manifested itself two thousand years ago when He became obedient unto death. He died for the Church. But today He continues His ministry: He lives to sanctify the Church,

to cleanse it with the washing of water by the Word
(Eph. 5:26). And in the sweet by-and-by He will come
for His bride, and the Church will be presented to
Him, "a glorious Church, not having spot, or wrinkle,
or any such thing; but . . . holy and without blemish"
(Eph. 5:27). What a glorious day that will be! with
the marriage of the Lamb and then the marriage supper
in the sky! For believers, the best is just ahead.

The Compassion of Jesus

Over and over again I have emphasized the fact
that Jesus was the God-Man, Deity in flesh; and just
as He *loved* like no one else has ever loved, He also
had *incomparable compassion* for those around Him.
When He saw the multitudes "scattered abroad, as
sheep having no shepherd" He was moved with compassion (Matt. 9:36).

He was moved with compassion when He realized
that those around Him were hungry. He called His
disciples to Him and said, "I have compassion on
the multitude, because they have now been with me
three days, and have nothing to eat: and if I send
them away fasting to their own houses, they will
faint by the way: for divers of them came from far"
(Mark 8:1—3).

Not only did Jesus have compassion on people
because of their spiritual need; He also had compassion on them because of their *physical* needs. Matthew 14:14 tells us, "Jesus went forth, and saw a great
multitude, and was moved with compassion toward
them, *and He healed their sick.*"

The heart of our Lord was moved with compassion
for *individuals*, as well as for the multitudes. A great
crowd followed Him as He was leaving Jericho; but
there were also two blind men sitting by the wayside
and they cried out, "Have mercy on us, O Lord, thou

son of David!" When Jesus asked them, "What will ye that I shall do unto you?" they asked that their eyes be opened. "So Jesus had compassion on them, and touched their eyes: and immediately their eyes received sight, and they followed Him" (Matt. 20: 29—34).

He had compassion on the poor widow who was on her way to bury her only son. He said to the sorrowing mother, "Weep not." Then He touched the funeral bier and said to the young man, "Arise." And the boy sat up and began to speak. Jesus then "delivered him to his mother" (Luke 7:12—15).

In the days when Jesus tabernacled among men there were many lepers in Jerusalem. They were social outcasts, and when they approached those who were not lepers they were compelled to cry out, "Unclean! Unclean!" But Jesus overstepped all the laws of science and society and touched the lepers: "And there came a leper to Him, beseeching Him, and kneeling down to Him, and saying unto Him, If thou wilt, thou canst make me clean. And Jesus, *moved with compassion,* put forth His hand and touched him, and saith unto him, *I will; be thou clean.* And as soon as He had spoken, immediately the leprosy departed from him, and he was cleansed" (Mark 1:40—42).

The tender, compassionate heart of Jesus caused Him to weep with the broken-hearted sisters of Lazarus. Mary came to meet Jesus as He returned to Bethany, and she said, "Lord, if thou hadst been here, my brother had not died." Then we read, "When Jesus therefore saw her weeping, and the Jews also weeping which came with her, *He groaned in the spirit, and was troubled, and said,* Where have ye laid him? They said unto Him, Lord, come and see. *Jesus wept.* Then said the Jews, *Behold how He loved him!*" (John 11:32—36).

But Jesus also had compassion on those who *refused* to follow Him. He loved the rich young ruler who was so in love with his "great possessions" that he turned his back on the Saviour even after Jesus, "beholding him, *LOVED him,* and said unto him, One thing thou lackest: go thy way, sell whatsoever thou hast, and give to the poor, and thou shalt have treasure in heaven: and come, take up the cross, and follow me" (Mark 10:17—22).

Jesus did not go about His earthly ministry from a cold, formal sense of duty. He came into the world because of love—love to God, love for a lost and dying world. He loved *mankind,* and His compassionate heart went out to individuals or multitudes, as the case might be. He had mercy on all who would allow and accept His mercy.

Jesus Was a Man of Prayer

The words "pray" and "prayer" are found at least twenty-five times in the Gospels in connection with the prayer life of Jesus, and undoubtedly there were many *unrecorded* occasions when He prayed. No characteristic of His earthly life is more definitely pointed out than His prayerfulness.

Jesus prayed much at night—sometimes He prayed *all* night. I think I know why He found the night hours a good time for prayer: He could be alone, undisturbed by the multitudes that thronged Him, thus having perfect communion with God the Father.

Jesus prayed before every important step in His life here on earth:

He prayed *before His baptism:* "Now when all the people were baptized, it came to pass, that Jesus also being baptized, *and praying,* the heaven was opened, and the Holy Ghost descended in a bodily shape like a dove upon Him, and a voice came from heaven, which said, Thou art my beloved Son; in thee I am well pleased" (Luke 3:21, 22).

He prayed *before making an evangelistic tour:* "And in the morning, rising up a great while before day, He went out, and departed into a solitary place, *and there prayed.* And Simon and they that were with Him followed after Him. And when they had found Him, they said unto Him, All men seek for thee. And He said unto them, Let us go into the next towns, that I may preach there also: for therefore came I forth. And He preached in their synagogues *throughout all Galilee,* and cast out devils" (Mark 1:35 — 39).

He prayed *before choosing His twelve disciples:* "And it came to pass in those days, that He went out into a mountain to pray, *and continued ALL NIGHT in prayer to God.* And when it was day, He called unto Him His disciples: and of them He chose twelve, whom also He named apostles" (Luke 6:12, 13).

He prayed *before announcing to His disciples that He would be crucified:* "And it came to pass, *as He was alone praying,* His disciples were with Him: and He asked them, saying, Whom say the people that I am? They answering said, John the Baptist; but some say, Elias; and others say, that one of the old prophets is risen again. He said unto them, But whom say ye that I am? Peter answering said, The Christ of God. And He straitly charged them, and commanded them to tell no man that thing; saying, *The Son of man MUST suffer many things,* and be rejected of the elders and chief priests and scribes, *and be slain,* and be raised the third day" (Luke 9:18 — 22).

He always prayed *before He ate:* "He commanded the multitude to sit down on the grass, and took the five loaves, and the two fishes, and *looking up to heaven, He blessed,* and brake, and gave the loaves

to His disciples, and the disciples to the multitude"
(Matt. 14:19).

In Luke 24:30, after talking with the disciples on
the road to Emmaus, "it came to pass, as He sat at
meat with them, *He took bread, and blessed it,* and
brake, and gave to them."

Why was it necessary for Jesus to pray? He was
God in flesh—that is true; but He was also human—
very man, sin apart. He made many strenuous jour-
neys that took toll of His physical strength. He
wrought many miracles, and with each miracle He
expended His power. When the believing woman
simply touched His garment, *"knowing . . . that virtue
had gone out of Him"* He turned and asked, "Who
touched my clothes?" (Mark 5:25—34).

Jesus prayed to guard against temptation. He was
tempted in all points as we are, for He was as truly
man as He was truly God. He warned His disciples
to pray lest they enter into temptation (Luke 22:46).
Prayer is important and profitable to the believer, and
we must meet temptation with the same weapons Jesus
used against the tempter—*the Word of God, and
prayer.*

More and more the fame of Jesus spread abroad.
Great multitudes came to hear Him teach and preach.
Scores of people were healed of their infirmities. What
did Jesus do in the face of such publicity? Did He
boast or brag about His ministry? No. The Word of
God tells us that *"He withdrew Himself into the
wilderness, and PRAYED"* (Luke 5:15, 16).

Many times we are *too busy* to pray, but the busi-
er Jesus was, the more He prayed! There were times
when He did not have time to eat (Mark 3:20, 21);
times when He needed both *rest and food* (Mark 6:31);
but He was never too busy, too hungry, or too tired
to pray! If *Jesus* needed to pray, how much more
do *we* need to pray! There has never been a great

spiritual leader who has not also been a great prayer warrior.

We can pray anywhere, any time; but Jesus had a special place of prayer. All four of the Gospel writers mention His going to the mountain to pray:

In Luke 22:39 we read, "He came out, and went, as He was wont (or as was His custom), to *the Mount of Olives;* and His disciples also followed Him."

In Matthew 14:23, He sent the multitudes away and "went up *into a mountain apart to pray:* and when the evening was come, He was there *alone.*"

In Mark 6:46 He sent the people away and "*departed into a mountain to pray.*"

In Luke 6:12 "He went out *into a mountain to pray, and continued ALL NIGHT* in prayer to God."

In John 6:15, when Jesus knew that the crowd would take Him by force and make Him their king, He again departed "*into a mountain Himself alone,*" undoubtedly to commune with God in prayer.

In Mark 1:35, Jesus rose up *a great while before day* and "departed into a solitary place, and there prayed." We are not told where this "solitary place" was, but the fact that Jesus sought a place of solitude tells us that there are times when we, too, need to be alone with God. There is a time and a place for public prayer, and Christians should assemble together and pray as a group. There is also a time—and an obligation—for *family prayer;* but the Scriptures often mention that Jesus prayed *alone,* and so should we. At some time through the day we should seek our favorite place of prayer, there to commune with God, alone, away from any and all things that would distract us.

In Luke 11:1 we read where Jesus and His disciples were "praying in a certain place," and they said to Him, "*Lord, teach US to pray.*" The prayer He gave them is often referred to as "the Lord's prayer," but

actually *the Lord's prayer* is recorded in the seven-
teenth chapter of John.   Jesus gave the disciples a
model prayer, and its first petition was that God's
name be hallowed.

In Matthew 6:9—13 Jesus said to His disciples,
"After this manner therefore pray ye: Our Father which
art in heaven, Hallowed be thy name. Thy kingdom
come. Thy will be done in earth, as it is in heaven.
Give us this day our daily bread. And forgive us our
debts, as we forgive our debtors.   And lead us not
into temptation, but deliver us from evil: For thine
is the kingdom, and the power, and the glory, for
ever. Amen."

In the Lord's intercessory prayer (John chapter 17)
in verses 9 and 20 we read where Jesus prayed for
believers.   He said, "I pray for them: *I pray NOT
for the world,* but for them which thou hast given
me; for they are thine. . . . Neither pray I for these
alone, *but for them also which shall believe on me
through their word."*

How it touches my heart to know that Jesus prayed
for me!   He prayed for Peter individually (Luke 22:31),
and He still intercedes for us today. You will note
in the passage just quoted from John 17, He said, "I
pray not for *the world."*   Jesus *died* for the world.
He gave His blood, made the supreme sacrifice, and
did all He could possibly do for the world, and it is
true that He prayed for His enemies; but He prays
for His own in a quite different sense.   He ever lives
to make intercession for us.

Thank God for these promises: Because of Christ's
unchangeable priesthood, "He is able also to save
them to the uttermost that come unto God by Him,
seeing *He ever liveth* to make intercession for them"
(Heb. 7:25).   Christ died and rose from the dead, and
"is even at the right hand of God, who also maketh
intercession for us" (Rom. 8:34).

Hear this precious promise from I John 2:1: "My little children, these things write I unto you, that ye sin not. And *IF any man sin, we have an Advocate with the Father, Jesus Christ the righteous.*"

Each and every time Jesus prayed, His uppermost desire and motive was for the glory of the heavenly Father. In John 17:1 He prayed, "Father, the hour is come; glorify thy Son, *that thy Son also may glorify thee.*" In Matthew 26:42 He prayed, "O my Father, if this cup may not pass away from me, except I drink it, *thy will be done!*"

It is most interesting to study the *posture* of Jesus in prayer:

In Luke 22:41, "He was withdrawn from them about a stone's cast, *and KNEELED DOWN, and prayed.*"

In Matthew 26:39 He *"FELL ON HIS FACE, and prayed,* saying, O my Father, if it be possible, let this cup pass from me: nevertheless not as I will, but as thou wilt."

In John 17:1 we are not told whether He was kneeling, standing, or sitting down. The Scripture simply says, "These words spake Jesus, *and LIFTED UP HIS EYES to heaven . . . .*"

It is not unscriptural to pray with our eyes open. When we are praying in a group, or where there are things to distract us, we close our eyes; but we can pray very effectively looking to heaven when we are alone—perhaps in the early morning hours, or walking along the seashore or in the countryside.

Another interesting thing about the prayers of Jesus is that He did not *"say" prayers,* nor did He *read* them. Luke 22:44 tells us that He prayed *earnestly*— so earnestly, in fact, that "His sweat was as it were great drops of blood falling down to the ground."

In Hebrews 5:7 Paul tells us that Jesus prayed *"with strong crying and tears."* The Greek word here translated "crying" is a very strong word, meaning

"with an outcry," and its force is further increased
by the addition of the descriptive word *"strong."*
Therefore Jesus prayed with a strong (or mighty) outcry. His soul was in such agony, so burdened as He
neared the cross to die for the sins of the world, that
He prayed with a strong outcry of anguish.

There are times when we, too, pray under such
heavy burden of soul that we cannot speak words.
It is at such times that the Holy Spirit intercedes for
us: "Likewise the Spirit also helpeth our infirmities:
for we know not what we should pray for as we ought:
but the Spirit itself maketh intercession for us *with
groanings which cannot be uttered.* And He that
searcheth the hearts knoweth what is the mind of the
Spirit, because *He maketh intercession for the saints
according to the will of God"* (Rom. 8:26, 27).

We should be very careful how we judge those
who pray, and we should not criticize *the way in
which they pray.* It may be your manner to pray very
calmly whereas someone else may weep or moan in
an agony of prayer. I am sure there were times when
Jesus communed quietly with His Father, but He also
prayed with strong crying and bitter tears.

Prayer should always be seasoned with thanksgiving. When the stone was removed from the grave
of Lazarus, "Jesus lifted up His eyes, and said, *Father, I THANK THEE that thou hast heard me. And
I knew that thou hearest me always:* but because of
the people which stand by I said it, that they may
believe that thou hast sent me" (John 11:41, 42).

This passage plainly shows that Jesus prayed with
a thankful heart and with a believing heart. He *believed* Lazarus would come forth, and He thanked God
for his resurrection even while Lazarus was still in
the tomb! We, too, should pray in faith, believing
that God will hear and answer. Even though the answer does not come in a moment, or at the time we

think it should, God *will* answer, in His own time and according to His own will.

Several times in this study we have referred to Hebrews 5:7 where Jesus prayed "with strong crying and tears *unto Him that was able to save Him from death, and was heard in that He feared."* What is the meaning of the statement that Jesus prayed to the One who was able to save Him from death, and that His prayer was heard (or answered)? Did Jesus not *die?* Yes, He died *on the cross*—the death He was ordained to die. He was praying to the heavenly Father that He would be delivered from *premature* death —death at the hands of Satan before He *reached* Calvary! Throughout the Old Testament Scriptures it is clearly taught that Jesus would be lifted up on a tree; but Satan did everything in his diabolical power to thwart God's plan and program. From the moment God promised the seed of the woman (Gen. 3:15) until Jesus cried out from the cross, "It is finished!" (John 19:30) the devil caused a river of blood to flow—yes, all the way from Eden to Calvary! But in spite of his untiring efforts he could not touch the Lamb of God because it was foreordained and settled that Jesus would die on a cross. Therefore, when the Son of God tabernacled among men, He prayed to God "with strong crying and tears" that He would be saved from a premature death before He reached the appointed time. *His goal was Calvary.*

The Meekness of Jesus

Meekness is exactly opposite of harshness and contentiousness, and shows itself in gentleness and tenderness in dealing with others—those who do not love us, as well as our loved ones and friends. If we are meek only toward those who love us, we are no better than the hypocrites. Jesus displayed meekness and patient submissiveness under hot fire from the enemy. He endured injustice and injury in a spirit of meekness, and His invitation *to all* is *"Come unto me, all ye that labour and are heavy laden, and I will give you rest.   Take my yoke upon you, and learn of me; for I AM MEEK AND LOWLY IN HEART: and ye shall find rest unto your souls"* (Matt. 11:28, 29).

Zechariah prophesied that the King of Israel would be meek: "Rejoice greatly, O daughter of Zion; shout, O daughter of Jerusalem: behold, thy King cometh unto thee: He is just, and having salvation; *lowly, and riding upon an ass*, and upon a colt the foal of an ass" (Zech. 9:9).   Matthew 21:1–5 records the fulfillment of this prophecy:

"And when they drew nigh unto Jerusalem, and were come to Bethphage, unto the Mount of Olives, then sent Jesus two disciples, saying unto them, Go into the village over against you, and straightway ye shall find an ass tied, and a colt with her: loose them, and bring them unto me.   And if any man say ought unto you, ye shall say, The Lord hath need of them; and straightway he will send them.   *All this was done, that it might be fulfilled which was spoken by the prophet, saying,* Tell ye the daughter of Sion, *Behold, thy King cometh unto thee, meek, and sitting upon an ass, and a colt the foal of an ass."*

In II Corinthians 10:1 the Apostle Paul spoke of *"the meekness and gentleness of Christ,"* and believers should strive to be like Him.   In Galatians 6:1 we are instructed, "Brethren, if a man be overtaken in a fault, ye which are spiritual, *restore such an one in the spirit of MEEKNESS;* considering thyself, lest thou also be tempted."

Paul instructed young Timothy in meekness: "The servant of the Lord must not strive; but be *gentle* unto all men, *apt to teach, patient, in MEEKNESS* instructing those that oppose themselves; if God peradventure will give them repentance to the acknowledging of the truth" (II Tim. 2:24, 25).

Paul also instructed Titus "to speak evil of no man, to be no brawlers, *but gentle, shewing all MEEK-NESS unto all men*" (Tit. 3:2).

In the days of our Lord's earthly ministry the sin of adultery carried a death sentence by stoning; but when the sinful woman came to the house of Simon the Pharisee, bathed the feet of Jesus with her tears and wiped them with the hairs of her head, Jesus did not deal with her according to the harshness of the law. Instead, He treated her kindly, spoke to her in gentleness, and forgave her sins. Read the entire account in Luke 7:36—50.

When the woman who had had an "issue of blood twelve years" pushed her way through the multitudes in order to touch the garments of the Lord, she was instantly healed—and Jesus *knew* instantly that someone had touched Him. Turning to His disciples He asked, "Who touched my clothes?" They replied, "Thou seest the multitude thronging thee, and sayest thou, *Who touched me?*" The dear woman then came, fearful and trembling, and fell down at the feet of Jesus and told Him all that had happened to her. Note His gentleness in dealing with her: He said to her, "Daughter, thy faith hath made thee whole; go in peace, and be whole of thy plague." (Read Mark 5:25—34.)

The Lord rebuked Thomas for his unbelief—but He did it in meekness and love. When the other disciples told Thomas they had seen Jesus after His resurrection, that stubborn disciple vowed he would not believe unless he could *touch* the risen Lord. When Jesus next appeared to the disciple band, Thomas was present. "Then saith He to Thomas, Reach hither thy finger, and behold my hands; and reach hither thy hand, and thrust it into my side: and be not faithless, but believing." Thomas then exclaimed, "My Lord and my God!" Jesus then rebuked him gently, with not a word of harshness. He said, "Thomas, because thou hast *seen* me, thou hast believed: *blessed are they that have NOT seen, and yet have believed*" (John 20:24—29).

Jesus also rebuked Peter—but gently, tenderly, in meekness. After the crucifixion, when Peter should have been near the tomb waiting for that glorious promised resurrection, he took the other disciples fishing! It was after that fishing expedition that Peter and those who were with him ate breakfast with the Lord on the shore of Galilee, and "when they had dined, Jesus saith to Simon Peter, Simon, son of Jonas, lovest thou me more than these? He saith unto Him, Yea, Lord; thou knowest that I love thee. He saith unto him, Feed my lambs.

"He saith to him again the second time, Simon, son of Jonas, lovest thou me? He saith unto him, Yea, Lord; thou knowest that I love thee. He saith unto him, Feed my sheep.

"He saith unto him the third time, Simon, son of Jonas, lovest thou me? Peter was grieved because He said unto him the third time, Lovest thou me? And he said unto Him, Lord, thou knowest all things; thou knowest that I love thee. Jesus saith unto him, Feed my sheep" (John 21:15—17).

Even Judas was dealt with in meekness and gentleness. Jesus knew the hearts of men, and He knew from the beginning that this one of His disciple band would betray Him (John 6:64, 70, 71). Yet in that dark hour when Judas was ready to sell the Lord and betray Him to His enemies, Jesus spoke to him in meekness and kindness. At the passover table, when Jesus announced that one of the disciples would betray Him, they looked at one another in amazement. John then asked, "Lord, who is it?"

"Jesus answered, He it is, to whom I shall give a sop, when I have dipped it. And when He had dipped the sop, He gave it to Judas Iscariot, the son of Simon. And after the sop Satan entered into him. Then said Jesus unto him, *That thou doest, do quickly.*"

So quietly was this done that "no man at the table knew for what intent He spake this unto him. For some of them thought, because Judas had the bag, that Jesus had said unto him, Buy those things that we have need of against the feast; or, that he should give something to the poor" (John 13:21—29).

As He hung on the cross Jesus looked upon the very men who had nailed Him there, and in meekness and love He prayed, "Father, *forgive them;* for they know not what they do!" (Luke 23:34).

Yes, our Lord Jesus was meek and lowly, kind and gentle indeed!

The Humility of Jesus

The humility of Jesus was manifested in His coming into the world—not to be ministered unto, but to minister, to take the place of a servant and give His life a ransom for many. One glorious day He is coming again as the Lion of the tribe of Judah, but He came almost two thousand years ago as the Lamb of God, the Humble One, to lay down His life—THE Sacrifice through which we have the atonement.

Human nature craves praise and recognition, but Jesus avoided notoriety and praise of men. He emphatically declared, *"I seek not mine own glory"* (John 8:50). He was in the world to glorify the Father and to minister to lost souls. Satan "setteth Him on a pinnacle of the temple, and saith unto Him, *IF thou be the Son of God, cast thyself down:* for it is written, He shall give His angels charge concerning thee: and in their hands they shall bear thee up, lest at any time thou dash thy foot against a stone." Jesus replied, *"It is written . . .* Thou shalt not tempt the Lord thy God!" (Read Matthew 4:1—11.)

He could have become famous that day by leaping from the pinnacle of the temple and landing, unhurt, on the ground below; but He did not come into the world to be famous. *He came to be hurt*—soul, spirit, and body. He came to pay the sin-debt, and *sin hurts*.

The Old Testament plainly foretold the humility of Jesus. For example, Isaiah 42:2 plainly declares, *"He shall not cry, nor lift up, nor cause His voice to be heard in the street."* He was the Lowly One. He never sought His own glory. On the contrary, everything He did and said was first to the glory of God the Father, and then to the blessing of humanity. He never wrought a miracle to bring honor, gain, or comfort to Himself, and instead of having an "advance man" or an advertising committee He charged those whom He blessed, healed, and fed that they were not to tell it abroad.

Jesus came to do in flesh what flesh could not do because of the weakness that came upon flesh through the curse. Therefore He sought no praise of man. When He moved into a community He did not seek to be sponsored by civic and religious leaders. No welcoming committee met Him at the edge of town to conduct Him to a pre-arranged lodging place.

He further proved His humility by associating with the outcast, the downcast, and the despised. On more than one occasion the religious leaders declared that He could not possibly be a prophet, for if He *were* a prophet He would not keep company with some of the people with whom He was seen. For instance, in Matthew 9:10—12 we read:

"And it came to pass, as Jesus sat at meat in the house, behold, many publicans and sinners came and sat down with Him and His disciples. And when the

Pharisees saw it, they said unto His disciples, *Why eateth your Master with publicans and sinners?* But when Jesus heard that, He said unto them, *They that be whole need not a physician, but they that are sick."*

In Luke 15:1, 2, as publicans and sinners crowded around Jesus to hear Him, the Pharisees and scribes said, *"This Man receiveth sinners, and eateth with them!"*

Human nature is prone to "fight back." Rare indeed is the saint who has the necessary grace to turn the other cheek! But Jesus proved His humility by patient submission to outrageous, uncalled-for, and inhuman treatment at the hands of those whom He came to save. He healed the sick, fed the hungry, cleansed the leper, raised the dead, blessed those who would allow His blessing; yet He was treated like a criminal of lowest degree.

The Prophet Isaiah wrote of this submissiveness of Jesus. In Isaiah 50:5, 6 we read, "The Lord God hath opened mine ear, and I was not rebellious, neither turned away back. I gave my back to the smiters, and my cheeks to them that plucked off the hair: I hid not my face from shame and spitting."

Writing to the Hebrew believers Paul said, "Wherefore seeing we also are compassed about with so great a cloud of witnesses, let us lay aside every weight, and the sin which doth so easily beset us, and let us run with patience the race that is set before us, looking unto Jesus the author and finisher of our faith; who for the joy that was set before Him endured the cross, despising the shame, and is set down at the right hand of the throne of God. For consider Him that endured such contradiction of sinners against Himself, lest ye be wearied and faint in your minds. Ye have not yet resisted unto blood, striving against sin" (Heb. 12:1—4).

Isaiah 53:7 also foretold the humility of Jesus: "He

was oppressed, and He was afflicted, *yet He opened not His mouth:* He is brought as a lamb to the slaughter, and as a sheep before her shearers is dumb, so *He openeth not His mouth."*

The enemies of Jesus hurled every possible insult at Him—even accusing Him of being a child of fornication (John 8:41). They accused Him of performing miracles by the power of Beelzebub, prince of devils (Matt. 12:24). On more than one occasion they said, "Thou hast a devil" (John 7:20; 8:52). Many of the people said, "He hath a devil, and is mad" (John 10:20). Yet under all these insults Jesus manifested true humility. Even when false witnesses testified against Him at His trial, He held His peace (Matt. 26:60—63). Herod questioned Him "in many words, but He answered him nothing" (Luke 23:9).

Peter declared that Jesus "did no sin, neither was guile found in His mouth: who, when He was reviled, reviled not again; when He suffered, He threatened not; *but committed Himself to Him that judgeth righteously"* (I Pet. 2:22, 23).

Jesus manifested His humility in performing the most lowly services. Even though He was in the form of God He took the place of a servant. After the last passover He left the supper table, "laid aside His garments, and took a towel and girded Himself. After that He poureth water into a bason, and began to wash the disciples' feet, and to wipe them with the towel wherewith He was girded" (John 13:4, 5). People in that day wore *sandals,* and as they traveled the dusty roads their feet became dusty and tired. It was the duty of a servant to wash the feet of those who came to visit in his master's home—one of the most humble tasks any servant was called upon to perform.

Jesus was fashioned as a man, and as a man *"He humbled Himself,* and became obedient unto death, even the death of the cross" (Phil. 2:8). If He had so desired He could have been the most famous and honored personality on earth; but instead, He was the most despised, the most rejected.

As God in flesh, He should have been the most honored guest at the marriage in Cana; but instead, when the refreshments ran out *He served* by turning water into wine (John 2:1—12).

By the pool of Bethesda He healed a man who had been paralyzed for thirty-eight years. Think of the praise and honor that would be bestowed upon any minister today who could stand by the bedside of a helpless invalid, lift him up and make him perfectly healthy and whole! But instead of receiving praise and honor for such a miracle, the Jews persecuted Jesus and "sought to slay Him, because He had done these things on the sabbath day" (John 5:1—16).

In Matthew 20:20—28 Jesus gave His *disciples* a lesson in humility. The mother of James and John, children of Zebedee, came to Him and asked a great favor of Him. She said, "Grant that these my two sons may sit, the one on thy right hand, and the other on the left, in thy kingdom."

Jesus replied, "Ye know not what ye ask. . . . to sit on my right hand, and on my left, is not mine to give, but it shall be given to them for whom it is prepared of my Father."

Now when the other disciples heard this request, "they were moved with indignation against the two brethren"—but not so with Jesus. His reply to the ambitious mother was firm, but kind; and then to His disciples He said, *"Whosoever will be great among you, let him be your minister; and whosoever will be chief among you, let him be your servant: EVEN AS THE SON OF MAN CAME NOT TO BE MINISTERED UNTO, BUT TO MINISTER, AND TO GIVE HIS LIFE A RANSOM FOR MANY."*

When the chief priests and Pharisees sent officers
to arrest Jesus, the officers returned without Him.
His enemies asked, "Why have ye not brought Him?"
The officers replied, *"Never man spake like THIS
MAN!"* (John 7:44—46).

Never man *spake* like this Man.

Never man was *born* like this Man.

Never man *lived* like this Man.

Never man *healed* like this Man.

Never man *died* like this Man.

There has never *been* another man like Jesus. He
was God's Christ in the beginning, but in the fulness
of time—conceived of the Holy Ghost and born of the
Virgin Mary—God's Christ became man's Jesus, *Saviour.* The Scriptures prove beyond all doubt that Jesus
was God in flesh, and those who deny His deity will
be damned. It is impossible to know God apart from
Jesus Christ, and *only through HIM can we enter the
kingdom of God* (John 10:9; 14:6).

The Jews were expecting a powerful, magnificent
king who would deliver them from Roman rule, and
they refused to accept the meek and humble Lamb
of God. They despised and rejected Him. He was
indeed "a Man of sorrows, and acquainted with grief,"
for He bore *our* sorrows and carried *our* grief. He
was "smitten of God, and afflicted . . . He was wounded
for our transgressions . . . bruised for our iniquities:
the chastisement of our peace was upon Him; and
with His stripes we are healed."

Even though "all we like sheep have gone astray,"
God laid on Jesus "the iniquity of us all." He bore
the sin of the world and nailed it to the cross, looking
beyond Calvary to the joy that was set before Him,
the glory He would share at the Father's right hand.
"It pleased the Lord to bruise Him" because He knew
that through His bruising and His grief He would
"make His soul an offering for sin," and through be-

lieving in His shed blood and finished work sinners could be saved!

But one glorious day, Jesus will be King of kings and Lord of lords. "Therefore," God declared, "I will divide Him a portion with the great, and He shall divide the spoil with the strong; because He hath poured out His soul unto death: and He was numbered with the transgressors; and He bare the sin of many, and made intercession for the transgressors."

Every word in the tremendous fifty-third chapter of Isaiah—portions of which we have just quoted—will be literally fulfilled when Jesus sits on the throne of David and the knowledge of the Lord covers the earth as the waters now cover the sea. Romans 8:3 is the fulfillment of Isaiah chapter 53—that is, Jesus did what the law could not do in that it was weak through the flesh.

"As it is written, There is none righteous, no, not one: There is none that understandeth, there is none that seeketh after God. They are all gone out of the way, they are together become unprofitable; there is none that doeth good, no, not one.

"Their throat is an open sepulchre; with their tongues they have used deceit; the poison of asps is under their lips: Whose mouth is full of cursing and bitterness: Their feet are swift to shed blood: Destruction and misery are in their ways: And the way of peace have they not known: There is no fear of God before their eyes.

"Now we know that what things soever the law saith, it saith to them who are under the law: that every mouth may be stopped, and all the world may become guilty before God. Therefore by the deeds of the law there shall no flesh be justified in His sight: for by the law is the knowledge of sin. But now the righteousness of God without the law is manifested, being witnessed by the law and the prophets; even

the righteousness of God which is by faith of Jesus
Christ unto all and upon all them that believe: for
there is no difference: *For ALL HAVE SINNED, and
come short of the glory of God;* being justified freely
by His grace through the redemption that is in Christ
Jesus: whom God hath set forth to be a propitiation
through faith in His blood, to declare His righteousness for the remission of sins that are past, through
the forbearance of God; to declare, I say, at this time
His righteousness: that He might be just, and the
justifier of him which believeth in Jesus.

"Where is boasting then? It is excluded. By what
law? Of works? Nay: but by the law of faith. Therefore we conclude that a man is justified by faith without the deeds of the law" (Rom. 3:10—28).

Chapter Three

BIBLE TRUTH CONCERNING
THE DEATH OF JESUS CHRIST

". . . Christ died for our sins according to the Scriptures" (I Cor. 15:3).

The death of Jesus is mentioned approximately two hundred times in the New Testament, and the Old Testament Scriptures contain many prophetic and typical references to His death, thus pointing out the importance of that subject.

Christ's death on the cross was not simply an "incident" in His life: it was *the supreme purpose* of His coming into the world. His *incarnation* was for the purpose of death.

GOD cannot die (Psalm 90:1, 2). God is an eternal Spirit (John 4:24), and it is impossible for Him to die. In His original state with God the Father, *Christ* could not die; but the Eternal Word was made flesh (John 1:14), God's Christ became the Man Christ Jesus, that He might die as man in order that fallen man might be lifted from the miry clay of sin and have his feet planted on the Solid Rock.

Jesus was lifted up on the cross that we might sit with Him in heavenly places:

"As Moses lifted up the serpent in the wilderness, even so must the Son of man be lifted up: that whosoever believeth in Him should not perish, but have eternal life" (John 3:14, 15).

Jesus declared, "And I, if I be lifted up from the earth, will draw all men unto me" (John 12:32).

In Ephesians 2:5, 6 we are told that God "hath quickened us together with Christ . . . and hath raised us up together, and made us sit together in heavenly places in Christ Jesus."

God's Son — Salvation's Center

It is through His Son that God executes His plans from everlasting to everlasting:

"In the beginning was the Word, and the Word was with God, and the Word was God. The same was in the beginning with God. *All things were made by Him; and without Him was not any thing made that was made*" (John 1:1–3).

"For by Him were all things created, that are in heaven, and that are in earth, visible and invisible, whether they be thrones, or dominions, or principalities, or powers: all things were created by Him, and for Him: And He is before all things, and by Him all things consist" (Col. 1:16, 17).

Christ Jesus our Saviour is the Mediator—the WORD—through whom God speaks, through whom He reveals Himself:

"God, who at sundry times and in divers manners spake in time past unto the fathers by the prophets, hath in these last days spoken unto us by His Son, whom He hath appointed heir of all things, by whom also He made the worlds" (Heb. 1:1, 2).

"No man hath seen God at any time; *the only begotten Son,* which is in the bosom of the Father, *He hath declared Him*" (John 1:18).

Christ Jesus is the personal living Organ in whom God has manifested *Himself*—His nature, His love, His holiness—yea, even the fulness of the Godhead: "For in Him dwelleth all the fulness of the Godhead bodily" (Col. 2:9).

The Lord Jesus Christ is the center of the whole history of God's mighty creation, the sum of all divine revelation. He was appointed Mediator before the foundation of the world, "according to the eternal purpose which (God) purposed in Christ Jesus our Lord" (Eph. 3:11).

God is omniscient. From eternity He foresaw that sin would enter the Garden of Eden, and death by sin. Therefore He appointed His Son to redeem and take away the sin of a world that had not yet been created. Thus was made possible justification for man before there was a man to *need* justification!

It is from eternity—not from two thousand years ago—that we must view the death of Jesus on the cross, for His death was settled in the unknown eternity behind us, before the beginning of years. It was only "in the fulness of the time" that He was born of the virgin, "made like unto His brethren" in all things (Heb. 2:17), lived among men and "was in all points tempted like as we are, yet without sin" (Heb. 4:15). He took away the sin of the world (John 1:29), nailed our sins to the cross (I Pet. 2:24), and willingly laid His life down that we might have life (John 10:11, 15, 17, 18).

Christ Jesus (the center of all divine revelation) and His cross belong eternally together. A Christ without a cross could never have brought salvation. The atonement was a divine necessity, and it was settled before the world was. Christ's willing death on the cross, His offering Himself to God, was "through the Eternal Spirit" (Heb. 9:14). Therefore we know the Spirit was also present in eternity when God the Father and God the Son settled the plan of redemption.

Jesus laid His life down two thousand years ago on Golgotha's rugged hill in Palestine; but though His death was carried out in the midst of time as we

know time, it was determined and settled before ever
time began. Yes, the plan of redemption reaches from
eternity to eternity.

Jesus Became Partaker of Flesh in Order to Die

"But we see Jesus, who was made a little lower
than the angels for the suffering of death, crowned
with glory and honour; *that He by the grace of God
should taste death for every man.* . . . Forasmuch then
as the children are partakers of flesh and blood, He
also Himself likewise took part of the same; that
through death He might destroy Him that had the
power of death, that is, the devil; and deliver them
who through fear of death were all their lifetime subject to bondage. For verily He took not on Him the
nature of angels; but He took on Him the seed of
Abraham" (Heb. 2:9, 14—16).

Jesus was "made a little lower than the angels"
in order that He might die for men, that *men* might
be exalted *above* angels. *God cannot DIE.* Therefore
Jesus laid aside the glory He had with the Father in
the beginning, and took human form in order that He
(God in flesh) might suffer, bleed, and die. This was
the purpose of the Incarnation—that He might taste
death for us, that we might share the glory and honor
with Him throughout all eternity!

Yes, Jesus tasted death *for ALL men.* He suffered
what you and I should have suffered. He came into
the world to take the sinner's place, the Just paying
the penalty for the unjust. God visited mankind in
the Person of His Son, suffered sin's penalty, took
man's place and died in man's stead—but only by
His grace. And that grace becomes ours when we
make it ours *by FAITH.*

The children of men are *"partakers of flesh and
blood"* which they receive from their parents. Jesus

"Himself likewise *took part of the same*"—and the Greek word here rendered "took part" implies *taking part in something outside of one's self.* Jesus received His flesh from the Virgin Mary, but His blood was from Almighty God (Acts 20:28).

It was imperative that He take flesh in order to die. In His original sphere of existence He was incapable of dying, for He was God and God cannot die.

In a body of flesh Jesus personally attacked Satan, the archenemy of man. He won that battle and took from Satan the keys of death. To John the Beloved on the Isle of Patmos, Jesus said, "I am He that liveth, and was dead; and, behold, I am alive for evermore, Amen; *and have the keys of hell and of death*" (Rev. 1:18). Thus, through death, He destroyed him who held sway in the realm of death, rendered him powerless and stripped him of his rule in that realm— *and delivered "them who through fear of death were all their lifetime subject to bondage."* Therefore Christians no longer fear death. "Perfect love casteth out fear" (I John 4:18), and those who are trusting completely in Jesus are not afraid to live, nor are they afraid to die!

The Greatest Bible Conference Ever Held

"And it came to pass about an eight days after these sayings, He took Peter and John and James, and went up into a mountain to pray. And as He prayed, the fashion of His countenance was altered, and His raiment was white and glistering. And, behold, there talked with Him two men, which were Moses and Elias: who appeared in glory, and spake of His decease which He should accomplish at Jerusalem.

"But Peter and they that were with Him were heavy with sleep: and when they were awake, they

saw His glory, and the two men that stood with Him.
And it came to pass, as they departed from Him,
Peter said unto Jesus, Master, it is good for us to be
here: and let us make three tabernacles; one for thee,
and one for Moses, and one for Elias: not knowing
what he said.

"While he thus spake, there came a cloud, and
overshadowed them: and they feared as they entered
into the cloud. And there came a voice out of the
cloud, saying, This is my beloved Son: hear Him.
And when the voice was past, Jesus was found alone.
And they kept it close, and told no man in those days
any of those things which they had seen" (Luke 9:
28—36).

Why do I say this was the greatest Bible Conference ever held? I say it because the speakers on that
day were the greatest who ever spoke on earth, and
because of the subject they discussed.

Earth has known no mortal man greater than Moses
and Elijah. *Moses* is the only man whose funeral
God personally supervised (Deut. 34:6), and when
Elijah had fulfilled the task God gave him on earth,
he was carried to heaven in a chariot of fire (II Kings
2:11). Jesus came to *fulfill* the law and the prophets;
and it was Moses (to whom God *gave* the law) and
Elijah (*chief* of prophets) "who appeared in glory,
and spake of His decease." In other words, in their
glorified bodies they came down upon the mountain
and talked with Jesus concerning His death "which
He should accomplish at Jerusalem."

Jesus Often Spoke of the Death He Would Die

During the last weeks of His life on earth, Jesus
repeatedly taught His disciples that He had come into
the world to die. In Matthew 20:28 He clearly declared that He came, "not to be ministered unto, but

to minister, and to give His life a ransom for many."

He plainly taught them that His blood would be shed for the remission of sins: "He took the cup, and gave thanks, and gave it to them, saying, Drink ye all of it; for this is my blood of the new testament, which is shed for many for the remission of sins" (Matt. 26:27, 28).

Long after His baptism in the river Jordan He spoke of *another* baptism—the baptism of death— which He declared He must experience. In Luke 12:50 we read, "I have a baptism to be baptized with; and how am I straitened till it be accomplished!"

On another occasion Jesus told His disciples (although they did not understand) that He would die in the city He loved. He said, "Nevertheless I must walk to day, and to morrow, and the day following: *for it cannot be that a prophet perish out of Jerusalem"* (Luke 13:33).

When He instituted the Lord's Supper He plainly told them that He would die a sacrificial death: "He took bread, and gave thanks, and brake it, and gave unto them, saying, This is my body which is given for you: this do in remembrance of me. Likewise also the cup after supper, saying, This cup is the new testament in my blood, which is shed for you" (Luke 22:19, 20).

The disciples were familiar with the account of Moses and the serpent of brass. Therefore Jesus explained that *He* must be lifted up in the same manner: "As Moses lifted up the serpent in the wilderness, even so must the Son of man be lifted up: That whosoever believeth in Him should not perish, but have eternal life" (John 3:14, 15).

He also declared that God's love provided the Gift (Himself) that eternal life should be made possible to those who believe: "For God so loved the world, that He gave His only begotten Son, that whosoever believeth in Him should not perish, but have ever-lasting life" (John 3:16).

Jesus also described the *manner* of His death, that men might be drawn to Him and have eternal life: "And I, if I be lifted up from the earth, will draw all men unto me. This He said, signifying what death He should die" (John 12:32, 33).

The disciples were well acquainted with the shepherds in Palestine, and with the shepherd's relationship to his flock. Therefore Jesus said to them, "I am the Good Shepherd: The Good Shepherd giveth His life for the sheep. . . . Therefore doth my Father love me, because I lay down my life, that I might take it again. No man taketh it from me, but I lay it down of myself. I have power to lay it down, and I have power to take it again. This commandment have I received of my Father" (John 10:11, 17, 18).

He also illustrated His death by speaking of a grain of wheat that falls into the ground and dies in order to bring forth life. The disciples were familiar with the process of farming; they knew that the planted grain dies and brings forth *more* grain. Jesus explained, "Except a corn of wheat fall into the ground and die, it abideth alone: but if it die, it bringeth forth much fruit" (John 12:24).

As Jesus drew nearer to Calvary, He spoke of the "hour" that was approaching, the hour He was born to face, the hour when by His death He would pay the ransom for sinners and make it possible for them to be set free. In John 12:27 He said, "Now is my soul troubled; and what shall I say? Father, save me from *this hour:* but for this cause came I unto this hour." Then in John 13:1 we read, "Now before the feast of the Passover, *when Jesus knew that HIS HOUR was come that He should depart out of this world unto the Father,* having loved His own which were in the world, He loved them unto the end."

The disciples were saddened by the Lord's declarations that He would be arrested, condemned, and put to death, but He assured them that they had no reason to be troubled. He would prepare a place for them and would return to receive them unto Himself:

"Let not your heart be troubled: ye believe in God, believe also in me. In my Father's house are many mansions: if it were not so, I would have told you. I go to prepare a place for you. And if I go and prepare a place for you, I will come again, and receive you unto myself; that where I am, there ye may be also" (John 14:1—3).

The disciples did not understand the depth of Christ's teaching concerning His death for sinners. Even after His crucifixion (and with a clear promise that He would rise again the third day) they did not understand and had to be reminded of His teaching.

In Luke 24:6—8 we read, "He is not here, but is risen: *remember* how He spake unto you when He was yet in Galilee, saying, The Son of man must be delivered into the hands of sinful men, and be crucified, *and the third day rise again. AND THEY REMEMBERED HIS WORDS.*"

Then in verses 44 and 45 of that same chapter we read, "And He (Jesus) said unto them, These are the words which I spake unto you, while I was yet with you, that all things must be fulfilled, which were written in the law of Moses, and in the prophets, and in the psalms, concerning me. *Then opened He their understanding, that they might understand the Scriptures.*"

To believers today, it seems strange that the disciples did not clearly understand the words of Jesus, strange that they did not believe. Peter said, "I go fishing," and the other disciples went with him. Instead of staying near the tomb, they went back to their old trade. They thought it was all over. Jesus was dead and buried—and they thought they would never see Him again!

But we should not think too harshly of those men, because there are literally millions on earth today who have heard the Bible account of how Jesus died for sinners, how He rose again the third day and now sits at the right hand of God to make intercession for us. Yet having *heard,* those millions refuse to believe. Many believe intellectually, but that is not the kind of belief God honors. His Word declares, *"With the HEART man believeth unto righteousness . . ."* (Rom. 10:10).

Head-belief does not bring saving faith, but *with the heart* man must believe "that Christ died for our sins according to the Scriptures; and that He was buried, and that He rose again the third day according to the Scriptures" (I Cor. 15:3, 4).

In the death of Jesus, God provided satisfaction to Himself—satisfaction that only He could provide. The death of Jesus satisfied the holiness and righteousness of God and *fulfilled the law* of God. Through the death of Jesus, God provided salvation for mankind—atonement for sin—which brings about a relationship between God and man that makes it possible for God to be just, and yet grant remission of sins.

The death of Jesus was a propitiation for sins. God set Him forth to be a propitiation by His blood. His death was the revelation of the grounds on which a righteous God can remit the penalty of sin (death). *We* live because *HE* lives. We live because He took our place and died on Calvary. But death could not hold Him. He conquered death and the grave, *and through HIM we are more than conquerors* (Rom. 8:37).

The Death of Jesus a Divine Necessity

"Behold, all souls are mine; as the soul of the

father, so also the soul of the son is mine: the soul that sinneth, it shall die" (Ezek. 18:4).

God's law is holy (Rom. 7:12), and in order for God's law to be fulfilled, the death of an innocent, spotless substitute was demanded. Therefore the fulfillment of God's law required the death of the Lamb of God. The wages of sin is death—but not just an ordinary death of an ordinary person. He who paid the sin-debt had to be without sin, and Jesus the Lamb of God was the Sinless One. He was *"delivered for OUR offences,* and was raised again *for OUR justification"* (Rom. 4:25).

In the death of Jesus the wrath of God is met: for "being now justified by His blood, *we shall be SAVED FROM WRATH through Him"* (Rom. 5:9).

By the death of Jesus, the righteousness of God is upheld: "Whom God hath set forth to be a propitiation through faith in His blood, *to declare His righteousness for the remission of sins that are past,* through the forbearance of God; to declare, I say, at this time *HIS RIGHTEOUSNESS: that (God) might be just, and the Justifier of him which believeth in Jesus"* (Rom. 3:25, 26).

Because of the death of Jesus, God can be merciful and extend mercy *to all who repent and believe:* "Thus it is written, and thus it behoved Christ to suffer, and to rise from the dead the third day: and that repentance and remission of sins should be preached in His name among all nations, beginning at Jerusalem" (Luke 24:46, 47).

In the death of Jesus, God's perfect wisdom is displayed and His power is communicated to us: "Unto them which are called, both Jews and Greeks, *Christ the power of God, and the wisdom of God"* (I Cor. 1:24).

By the death of Jesus, God the Eternal Father is glorified: "Be ye therefore followers of God, as dear children; and walk in love, as Christ also hath loved us, and hath given Himself for us *an offering and a sacrifice to God for a sweetsmelling savour*" (Eph. 5:1, 2).

The Prophets

"Of which salvation the prophets have inquired and searched diligently, who prophesied of the grace that should come unto you: searching what, or what manner of time the Spirit of Christ which was in them did signify, when it testified beforehand the sufferings of Christ, and the glory that should follow. Unto whom it was revealed, that not unto themselves, but unto us they did minister the things, which are now reported unto you by them that have preached the Gospel unto you with the Holy Ghost sent down from heaven; which things the angels desire to look into" (I Pet. 1:10—12).

The Old Testament is filled with prophecies pointing to the death of Jesus—a subject of unusual interest to the Old Testament prophets, and about which *even the angels* inquired.

It has already been pointed out that the death of Jesus must be viewed from everlasting to everlasting, because His death is the central theme of the new song that will be sung by the host of heaven in that glorious, victorious morning:

"And when He had taken the book, the four beasts and four and twenty elders fell down before the Lamb, having every one of them harps, and golden vials full of odours, which are the prayers of saints. And they sung a new song, saying, *Thou art worthy to take the book, and to open the seals thereof: FOR THOU WAST SLAIN, AND HAST REDEEMED US TO GOD BY THY BLOOD* out of every kindred, and tongue, and people, and nation; and hast made us unto our God kings and priests: and we shall reign on the earth.

"And I beheld, and I heard the voice of many angels round about the throne and the beasts and the elders: and the number of them was ten thousand times ten thousand, and thousands of thousands; saying with a loud voice, *Worthy is THE LAMB THAT WAS SLAIN to receive power,* and riches, and wisdom, and strength, and honour, and glory, and blessing" (Rev. 5:8—12).

Paul, the apostle to whom God revealed the mystery of this dispensation of His saving grace—the mystery hidden from everlasting—declares that the death of Jesus on the cross is the center, soul, bloodstream, and very life of salvation. *Apart* from His death there is no remission of sin, no salvation from sin's penalty.

In I Corinthians 15:1—4 Paul wrote: "Moreover, brethren, I declare unto you the Gospel which I preached unto you, which also ye have received, and wherein ye stand; by which also ye are saved, if ye keep in memory what I preached unto you, unless ye have believed in vain. For I delivered unto you first of all that which I also received, how that Christ died for our sins according to the Scriptures; and that He was buried, and that He rose again the third day according to the Scriptures."

It was also to the Corinthian church that Paul declared, *"I DETERMINED not to know any thing among you, save JESUS CHRIST, AND HIM CRUCIFIED"* (I Cor. 2:2).

Then in Hebrews 9:22 we read, "And almost all things are by the law purged with blood; *and WITHOUT shedding of blood is NO REMISSION!"*

The Purpose of the Death of Jesus

"Surely He hath borne our griefs, and carried our sorrows: yet we did esteem Him stricken, smitten of

God, and afflicted. But He was wounded for our transgressions, He was bruised for our iniquities: the chastisement of our peace was upon Him; and with His stripes we are healed. *ALL we like sheep have gone astray; we have turned every one to his own way; and the Lord hath laid on Him the iniquity of us ALL.*

"He was oppressed, and He was afflicted, yet He opened not His mouth: He is brought as a lamb to the slaughter, and as a sheep before her shearers is dumb, so He openeth not His mouth. He was taken from prison and from judgment: and who shall declare His generation? For He was cut off out of the land of the living: for the transgression of my people was He stricken. And He made His grave with the wicked, and with the rich in His death; because He had done no violence, neither was any deceit in His mouth.

"Yet it pleased the Lord to bruise Him; He hath put Him to grief: when thou shalt make His soul an offering for sin, He shall see His seed, He shall prolong His days, and the pleasure of the Lord shall prosper in His hand. He shall see of the travail of His soul, and shall be satisfied: by His knowledge shall my righteous Servant justify many; for He shall bear their iniquities. Therefore will I divide Him a portion with the great, and He shall divide the spoil with the strong; because He hath poured out His soul unto death: and He was numbered with the transgressors; and He bare the sin of many, and made intercession for the transgressors" (Isa. 53:4—12).

Centuries before Jesus was born, Isaiah spoke of His death as already accomplished because *the death of Jesus was a settled fact from all eternity!* Sin demanded His death—not *His own sin,* for He had none. He died for the sins of others. His death was vicarious—*the Just* dying for the unjust.

God decreed, *"The soul that sinneth, it shall DIE"* (Ezek. 18:4). To Adam He said, "In the day that thou eatest thereof *thou shalt SURELY* (positively) *die!"* (Gen. 2:17). Since "ALL have sinned and come short of the glory of God" (Rom. 3:23), all deserve to die. Therefore Jesus, the One who deserved to live, died for those who do not deserve to live, that we who deserve hell might inherit eternal life.

"Christ died for *our* sins . . ." (I Cor. 15:3).

He was "delivered for *our* offences . . ." (Rom. 4:25).

He "suffered for *us*, leaving us an example, that (we) should follow His steps: who did no sin, neither was guile found in His mouth: who, when He was reviled, reviled not again; when He suffered, He threatened not; but committed Himself to Him that judgeth righteously: *who His own self bare OUR sins in His own body on the tree, that WE, being dead to sins, should live unto righteousness: by whose stripes (we) were healed"* (I Pet. 2:21—24).

"For Christ also hath once suffered for sins, *the Just for the unjust,* that He might bring us to God, being put to death in the flesh, but quickened by the Spirit" (I Pet. 3:18).

In the Garden of Eden, Satan kidnapped the whole human race when he led Adam to do the one thing God had commanded him *not* to do. It is true that only Adam and Eve were present that day, but they are the parents of the human race, and "as by one man sin entered into the world, and death by sin . . . *so death passed upon ALL men,* for that all have sinned" (Rom. 5:12). There have been many kidnap victims and many ransoms paid, ransoms which involved many thousands of dollars; but no ransom paid by man could ever touch the hem of the garment in comparison with the ransom Jesus paid on Calvary. He gave *His life* "a ransom for many" (Matt. 20:28).

The death of Jesus goes much deeper than His ceasing to breathe, much deeper than the spikes in His hands and feet. The Word of God declares that Jesus *made His SOUL an offering for sin* (Isa. 53:10)— for your sin and mine; and it is on the grounds of His horrible death on the cross that God grants forgiveness of sins:

"For the love of Christ constraineth us; because we thus judge, that if One died for all, then were all dead: and that He died for all, that they which live should not henceforth live unto themselves, but unto Him which died for them, and rose again. . . . And all things are of God, who hath reconciled us to Himself by Jesus Christ, and hath given to us the ministry of reconciliation; to wit, that God was in Christ, reconciling the world unto Himself, not imputing their trespasses unto them; and hath committed unto us the word of reconciliation. . . . For He (God) hath made Him (Jesus) to be sin for us, who (Jesus) knew no sin; that we might be made the righteousness of God in Him" (II Cor. 5:14—21).

Leviticus chapter 6 sets forth, in type, what Jesus accomplished on the cross for us: "And the Lord spake unto Moses, saying: If a soul sin, and commit a trespass against the Lord . . . and he shall bring his trespass-offering unto the Lord, a ram without blemish out of the flock, with thy estimation, for a trespass-offering, unto the priest: and the priest shall make an atonement for him before the Lord: and it shall be forgiven him for any thing of all that he hath done in trespassing therein" (Lev. 6:1, 2, 6, 7).

"Smitten of God"

"He is despised and rejected of men; a man of sorrows, and acquainted with grief: and we hid as it were our faces from Him; He was despised, and we esteemed Him not.   Surely He hath borne our griefs, and carried our sorrows: yet we did esteem Him *stricken, SMITTEN OF GOD, and afflicted"* (Isa. 53:3, 4).

It was God the Father who set Jesus forth to be a propitiation for sin through the shedding of His blood on the cross.   Through His death the wrath of God against sinners is satisfied when sinners place their trust in *the shed blood and finished work* of God's only begotten Son.

The death of Jesus on the cross was God's love on display—and more: In the horrible death Jesus died, God's holiness and hatred of sin were manifested. God loves the sinner but He hates sin; and if sinners were to be redeemed, it was imperative that the wrath of God strike.   He will not acquit the wicked (Nah. 1:3).   Because of His character, God's wrath must strike the sinner—or strike upon a lawful substitute; and Jesus was *the one and only* lawful Substitute.

"ALL we like sheep have gone astray; we have turned every one to his own way; *and the Lord hath laid on Him THE INIQUITY OF US ALL.* . . . He was taken from prison and from judgment: and who shall declare His generation? for He was cut off out of the land of the living: for the transgression of my people was He stricken"* (Isa. 53:6, 8).

Yes, Jesus was "smitten of God."   The blow that fell on Jesus at Calvary should have fallen upon every man, because all have sinned.   But Jesus took our place, and the stroke due us fell on Him.   Now God can be just, and the Justifier of all who believe on Jesus (Rom. 3:26).   Truly, *"herein is love! not that we loved God, but that HE LOVED US, and sent His Son to be the propitiation for our sins"* (I John 4:10).

God thundered out, "The soul that sinneth, it shall die!" (Ezek. 18:4), and He has not changed His mind about sin.   With God, sin and death are **synonymous.**

Jesus died on the cross as our Passover sacrifice. His blood was shed in order for God to remain God—holy, righteous, pure—*and yet pass over* (or spare) *us* on the merit of the blood of the Lamb of God. Paul declared, "For even Christ *our Passover* is sacrificed for us" (I Cor. 5:7b).

In Exodus 12:12—23 we find these words:

"I will pass through the land of Egypt this night, and will smite all the firstborn in the land of Egypt, both man and beast; and against all the gods of Egypt I will execute judgment: I am the Lord. And the blood shall be to you for a token upon the houses where ye are: and when I see the blood, I will pass over you, and the plague shall not be upon you to destroy you, when I smite the land of Egypt.

"And this day shall be unto you for a memorial; and ye shall keep it a feast to the Lord throughout your generations; ye shall keep it a feast by an ordinance for ever. . . .

"Then Moses called for all the elders of Israel, and said unto them, Draw out and take you a lamb according to your families, and kill the passover. And ye shall take a bunch of hyssop, and dip it in the blood that is in the bason, and strike the lintel and the two side posts with the blood that is in the bason; and none of you shall go out at the door of his house until the morning. For the Lord will pass through to smite the Egyptians; and when He seeth the blood upon the lintel, and on the two side posts, the Lord will pass over the door, and will not suffer the destroyer to come in unto your houses to smite you."

Then in Hebrews 9:22 we read, "And almost all things are by the law purged with blood; and without shedding of blood is no remission."

According to Romans 3:20, "by the deeds of the law" no flesh shall be justified before God. Transgression of the law is *sin*, the wages of sin is death, therefore the law demands the death of the sinner. But Jesus died on Calvary to redeem them that were under the law, and His death on the cross serves as grounds upon which *we who believe* are delivered from the claims of God's holy law. Thus we are born into the family of God and receive the adoption of sons:

"When the fulness of the time was come, God sent forth His Son, made of a woman, made under the law, to redeem them that were under the law, that we might receive the adoption of sons" (Gal. 4:4, 5).

The unregenerate man is by nature a child of the devil. He walks "according to the course of this world, according to the prince of the power of the air (the devil), the spirit that worketh in the children of disobedience" (Eph. 2:2, 3). See also John 8:44.

Writing to Titus, Paul describes the unregenerate person as "foolish, disobedient, deceived, serving divers lusts and pleasures, living in malice and envy, hateful, and hating one another" (Tit. 3:3). The Lord Jesus Christ "gave Himself for our sins, that He might *deliver us* from this present evil world, according to the will of God . . ." (Gal. 1:4).

Unbelievers are in bondage—bound by sin and condemned because of sin. Christ's death on the cross delivers us from such bondage when we believe on Him and His finished work. We become citizens of heaven. No longer sons of the devil, we become sons of God—instantaneously: "Beloved, *NOW are we the sons of God,* and it doth not yet appear what we shall be: but we know that, when He shall appear, we shall be like Him; for we shall see Him as He is" (I John 3:2).

"For our conversation (citizenship) is in heaven; from whence also we look for the Saviour, the Lord Jesus Christ" (Phil. 3:20).

"Even so we, when we were children, were in

bondage under the elements of the world: but when
the fulness of the time was come, God sent forth His
Son, made of a woman, made under the law, to redeem them that were under the law, that we might
receive the adoption of sons. . . . Wherefore thou art
no more a servant, but a son; and if a son, then an
heir of God through Christ" (Gal. 4:3—7).

"Stand fast therefore in the liberty wherewith Christ
hath made us free, and be not entangled again with
the yoke of bondage" (Gal. 5:1).

Only through the death of Jesus can we be brought
to God and placed in the right relationship with Him:
"For Christ also hath once suffered for sins, the Just
for the unjust, that He might bring us to God, being
put to death in the flesh, but quickened by the Spirit"
(I Pet. 3:18). When Adam sinned, fellowship between
God and man was broken; and the only way that im-
passable gulf can be spanned is through the shed
blood of the Lamb of God.

There are those who say beautiful things about
Jesus. They declare that He was an *unusual man,*
extraordinary in every way. They credit Him with
having wrought *great miracles.* But they deny His
deity, they refuse to accept Him as God in flesh. Beloved, no one could ever have been saved through the
holy, sinless life of the Man Christ Jesus. His spotless life reveals our own exceeding sinfulness, but it
was through His death that He bought salvation! He
Himself explained this in John 12:24 when He said,
*"Except a corn of wheat fall into the ground and die,
it abideth alone: but if it die, it bringeth forth much
fruit."*

From the death of Jesus on the cross sprang the
new race—*the heavenly race*—children of God in whom
divine nature dwells: "Whereby are given unto us
exceeding great and precious promises: that by these
ye might be *partakers of the divine nature,* having

escaped the corruption that is in the world through lust" (II Pet. 1:4).

Christ Died for All

"All we like sheep have gone astray; we have turned every one to his own way; and the Lord hath laid on Him the iniquity of us all" (Isa. 53:6).

Some people teach that Jesus died for "the elect" — that is, they teach that some are elected to be saved while others are *not* elected; but the Bible teaches no such doctrine. Certainly the Bible teaches the sovereignty of God — He knows all things, from eternity through eternity; but this does not alter the responsibility of the individual. God created man in His own image, breathed into his nostrils the breath of life, and man became a living soul. But God also gave man the right to choose whether he would serve his Creator, or serve the devil. Men who die in sin and open their eyes in hell do so because they choose to reject Jesus. They refuse to come to Him that they might have life (John 5:40).

On one occasion Jesus astonished His disciples with the declaration, "It is easier for a camel to go through the eye of a needle, than for a rich man to enter into the kingdom of God." The disciples then asked among themselves, "Who then can be saved?"

Who CAN be saved? For whom did Jesus die? Ministers do not agree on the answer to this question, religions do not agree, teachers do not agree. The Bible answer to these questions is to be found only in the Word of God; so let the Scripture answer:

John 3:16 declares, "For *God so loved THE WORLD*, that He gave His only begotten Son, that *WHOSOEVER* believeth in Him should not perish, but have everlasting life."

In Romans 8:32 we read, "He that spared not His

own Son, but *delivered Him up FOR US ALL,* how shall He not with Him also freely give us all things?"

In Ephesians 5:2 the Apostle Paul declared that we should "walk in love, as *Christ also hath loved US,* and hath *given Himself for US* an offering and a sacrifice to God for a sweetsmelling savour."

Titus 2:14 tells us that Jesus *"gave Himself FOR US,* that He might *redeem US* from all iniquity, and purify unto Himself a peculiar people, zealous of good works."

I Corinthians 5:7 declares that "Christ *OUR Passover* is sacrificed *for US."*

II Corinthians 5:21 tells us that God made Christ "to be sin *FOR US . . . that WE might be made the righteousness of God in Him."*

Romans 10:13 is very clear: *"For WHOSOEVER shall call upon the name of the Lord shall be saved."*

Finally, in Revelation 22:17 we find this invitation: "The Spirit and the bride say, Come. And let him that heareth say, Come. *And let HIM THAT IS A-THIRST come. And WHOSOEVER WILL, let him take the water of life freely!"*

Yes, Jesus "gave Himself *a ransom for ALL"* (I Tim. 2:6). He died for the whole world, and on the grounds of His death God can deal in mercy with the entire human race. He came to take away the sin of the entire world (John 1:29). "He is the propitiation for our sins: *and not for our's only, but also FOR THE SINS OF THE WHOLE WORLD"* (I John 2:2).

How could it be made plainer? Christ is the propitiation for the sins of the whole world, depending upon the individual's exercise of faith in His shed blood (without which there IS no remission—Heb. 9:22).

"For as in Adam all DIE, even so in Christ shall ALL be made alive" (I Cor. 15:22). Jesus paid the

ransom price for all mankind, and all who will receive Him are ransomed from the penalty of sin. Therefore we preach mercy to *"whosoever will."* Those who *believe* receive remission of sins, but the wrath of God abides upon those who refuse to believe.

"To Him give all the prophets witness, that through His name *WHOSOEVER believeth in Him* shall receive remission of sins" (Acts 10:43).

"He that believeth on the Son hath everlasting life: and he that believeth not the Son shall not see life; *but THE WRATH OF GOD abideth on him"* (John 3:36).

Yes, the blood Jesus shed on Calvary is sufficient to cleanse all mankind from sin, from Adam to the last man born on earth; but only those who *by faith* accept His shed blood are pardoned and saved:

"He was in the world, and the world was made by Him, and the world knew Him not. He came unto His own, and His own received Him not. *But AS MANY AS RECEIVED HIM, to them gave He power to become the sons of God, even to them that believe on His name:* which were born, not of blood, nor of the will of the flesh, nor of the will of man, but of God" (John 1:10—13).

"We see Jesus, who was made a little lower than the angels for the suffering of death, crowned with glory and honour; *that He by the grace of God should taste death FOR EVERY MAN"* (Heb. 2:9). Jesus died for every man—for each individual in every race; and on the grounds of His death, God can deal in mercy with each individual who will come to Him claiming salvation through the finished work of the Lord Jesus Christ, the Lamb of God without blemish and without spot.

Christ Died for the Church

"When Jesus came into the coasts of Caesarea

Philippi, He asked His disciples, saying, Whom do men say that I the Son of man am? And they said, Some say that thou art John the Baptist: some, Elias; and others, Jeremias, or one of the prophets.

"He saith unto them, *But whom say YE that I am?* And Simon Peter answered and said, Thou art *the Christ,* the Son of the living God. And Jesus answered and said unto him, Blessed art thou, Simon Bar-jona: for flesh and blood hath not revealed it unto thee, but my Father which is in heaven. And I say also unto thee, That thou art Peter, and *upon this rock I will build my Church;* and the gates of hell shall not prevail against it" (Matt. 16:13–18).

"For other *foundation* can no man lay than that is laid, which is *Jesus Christ"* (I Cor. 3:11).

"For the husband is the head of the wife, even as Christ is the head of the Church: and He is the Saviour of the body. Therefore as the Church is subject unto Christ, so let the wives be to their own husbands in every thing. Husbands, love your wives, even as Christ also loved the Church, and gave Himself for it; that He might sanctify and cleanse it with the washing of water by the Word, that He might present it to Himself a glorious Church, not having spot, or wrinkle, or any such thing; but that it should be holy and without blemish.

"So ought men to love their wives as their own bodies. He that loveth his wife loveth himself. For no man ever yet hated his own flesh; but nourisheth and cherisheth it, *even as the Lord the Church: For we are members of His body, of His flesh, and of His bones. . . . This is a great mystery: but I speak concerning CHRIST AND THE CHURCH"* (Eph. 5:23–32).

The New Testament Church is the body of Christ. He is the Saviour of that body, He is the head and the foundation of the Church. God has "put all things under His feet, and gave Him to be *the head over all things to the Church, which is HIS BODY*, the fulness of Him that filleth all in all" (Eph. 1:22, 23).

It is true that Jesus died for the Church as a body, He is the Saviour of the Church; but the Church is made up of *individual believers.* The moment one believes in the shed blood and finished work of Jesus, that individual is united to the body of Christ: "For as the body is one, and hath many members, and all the members of that one body, being many, are one body: *so also is Christ.* For by one Spirit are we all baptized into one body, whether we be Jews or Gentiles, whether we be bond or free; and have been all made to drink into one Spirit" (I Cor. 12:12, 13). Therefore Jesus gave Himself for *individuals,* so that every believer can say with Paul, "He loved me, and gave Himself for me" (Gal. 2:20).

As believers, members of the body of Christ, we are not our own. We are bought with a price (I Cor. 6:19, 20), and we are responsible to other believers. Therefore we dare not live selfishly and, by so doing, hurt or hinder others who may not be as strong in the faith as we are. Paul admonished the believers at Rome, "If *thy brother* be grieved with thy meat, *now walkest thou not charitably.* Destroy not him with thy meat, for whom Christ died" (Rom. 14:15).

To the Corinthian Christians he wrote, "If any man see thee which hast knowledge sit at meat in the idol's temple, shall not the conscience of him which is weak be emboldened to eat those things which are offered to idols; and *through thy knowledge shall the weak brother perish,* for whom Christ died? But when ye sin so against the brethren, and wound their weak conscience, ye sin against Christ." And then Paul vowed, *"Wherefore, if meat make my brother to offend, I will eat no flesh while the world standeth, lest I make my brother to offend!"* (I Cor. 8:10—13).

Jesus died for the weak believer just as surely as He died for the believer whose faith is strong. The enlightened, mature Christian has nothing to boast about. We are what we are because of God's grace and through the death of Jesus on the cross. "Not by works of righteousness which we have done, but according to His mercy He saved us, by the washing of regeneration, and renewing of the Holy Ghost; which He shed on us abundantly through Jesus Christ our Saviour" (Tit. 3:5, 6).

True righteousness is imputed. "We are all as an unclean thing, and *all OUR righteousnesses are as filthy rags . . .*" (Isa. 64:6). But when we believe on Jesus, *God imputes HIS righteousness to us.* Some believers grow more rapidly than others, thereby becoming stronger in the faith; and those who are strong are responsible for the weaker brethren for whom Christ died.

Yes, in the body of Christ, the New Testament Church, there are representatives from all nations, every tribe and every tongue. In Revelation 5:8, 9 we read: "When He had taken the book, the four beasts and four and twenty elders fell down before the Lamb, having every one of them harps, and golden vials full of odours, which are the prayers of saints. And they sung a new song, saying, Thou art worthy to take the book, and to open the seals thereof: *for thou wast slain, and hast redeemed us to God by thy blood OUT OF EVERY KINDRED, AND TONGUE, AND PEOPLE, AND NATION!*"

I would also point out here that the Scriptures clearly teach that the death of Jesus was voluntary. He did not die under pressure. All that He accomplished—in His life and in His death—was voluntary. The following questions and answers will show that He gave Himself because of His love—first to His Father, and then to us:

For *what* did Jesus give Himself? He gave Himself *"for OUR SINS"* (Gal. 1:4).

Why did Jesus give Himself? *Because He "LOVED me,* and gave Himself for me" (Gal. 2:20). It humbles my heart to think that Jesus went to Calvary and died there *for ME!* Think of it, beloved—He died *for me* and for *you.*

What did Jesus give? *He gave "His LIFE* a ransom for many" (Matt. 20:28). *He "gave HIMSELF* a ransom for all . . ."* (I Tim. 2:6).

For *what purpose* did Jesus give Himself? He "gave Himself for us, *that He might REDEEM us from all iniquity, and purify unto Himself a peculiar people, zealous of good works"* (Tit. 2:14).

The Results of Christ's Death on the Cross

It would be impossible to give, in this study, full details of all the results of the death of Jesus, but we will note the *outstanding* results, with Scripture for each of them:

1. First of all, the death of Jesus on the cross *assures all men of the love of God toward us,* in spite of our sin and just deserts:

All have sinned (Rom. 3:23), the wages of sin is death (Rom. 6:23), and God made it clear to Adam that disobedience would bring death (Gen. 2:17). God's decree is, "The soul that sinneth, *it shall DIE"* (Ezek. 18:4). Sin and death are synonymous. Therefore Jesus on the cross is God's display of His love toward us, "in that, while we were yet sinners, Christ died for us" (Rom. 5:8). "In this was manifested the love of God toward us, because that God sent His only begotten Son into the world, that we might live through Him" (I John 4:9).

2. The death of Jesus on the cross *made possible re-*

demption from sin:

He paid the necessary penalty for sin, He met the demands of a holy God and made it possible for God to be just and yet justify the sinner, thus freeing him from condemnation that should rightfully come upon him: "For even the Son of man came not to be ministered unto, but to minister, and to give His life a ransom for many" (Mark 10:45). He was delivered for *our* offences (Rom. 4:25). He "redeemed us from the curse of the law, being made a curse for us: for it is written, Cursed is every one that hangeth on a tree" (Gal. 3:13).

"But now the righteousness of God without the law is manifested, being witnessed by the law and the prophets; even the righteousness of God which is by faith of Jesus Christ unto all and upon all them that believe: for there is no difference: For all have sinned, and come short of the glory of God; being justified freely by His grace through the redemption that is in Christ Jesus: whom God hath set forth to be a propitiation through faith in His blood, to declare His righteousness for the remission of sins that are past, through the forbearance of God; to declare, I say, at this time His righteousness: that He might be just, and the Justifier of him which believeth in Jesus.

"Where is boasting then? It is excluded. By what law? of works? Nay: but by the law of faith. Therefore we conclude that a man is justified by faith without the deeds of the law" (Rom. 3:21–28).

"So Christ was *once offered* to bear the sins of many; and unto them that look for Him shall He appear the second time *without sin* unto salvation" (Heb. 9:28).

3. The death of Jesus provided *the ONE OFFERING for sin that satisfied God:*

The animal offerings of the Old Testament could

never take away sin, "for it is not *possible* that the blood of bulls and of goats should take away sins. . . . *but THIS MAN* (Jesus) *after He had offered ONE sacrifice for sins for ever,* sat down on the right hand of God" (Heb. 10:4, 12).

4. The death of Jesus represented *perfect obedience* to God:

Such obedience had never been known until Jesus became obedient unto death. "Being found in fashion as a man, He humbled Himself, and became obedient unto death, *even the death of the cross*" (Phil. 2:8), and "as by one man's disobedience many were made sinners, so *by the OBEDIENCE of One* shall many be made righteous" (Rom. 5:19).

In His perfect obedience to God, Jesus fulfilled every jot and tittle of the law (Matt. 5:17). Therefore *"Christ is the END of the law for righteousness to every one that believeth"* (Rom. 10:4).

5. The death of Jesus on the cross *made possible the reconciliation between God and man:*

Reconciliation results when enmity is taken away. However, the Word of God does not imply that the world's enmity is now *removed*, but rather that the death of Jesus on Calvary so altered *the judicial state* of the world before God that He is said to have reconciled the world unto Himself. In II Corinthians 5:18, 19 we read, "All things are of God, who hath reconciled us to Himself by Jesus Christ, and hath given to us the ministry of reconciliation; to wit, that God was in Christ, reconciling the world unto Himself, not imputing their trespasses unto them; and hath committed unto us the word of reconciliation."

Ephesians 2:14−16 is an interesting passage on reconciliation: "For He (Jesus) is our peace, who hath made both one, and hath broken down the middle wall of partition between us; *having abolished in His*

flesh the enmity, even the law of commandments
contained in ordinances; for to make in Himself of
twain one new man, so making peace; and that He
might reconcile both unto God in one body *by the
cross, having slain the enmity thereby.*"

Colossians 2:20, 22 asks, "Wherefore if ye be *dead
with Christ* from the rudiments of the world, why,
as though living in the world, are ye subject to ordinances . . . after the commandments and doctrines
of men?"

6. The death of Jesus on the cross *removed all moral
hindrances in God's mind concerning the saving of
sinners:*

By the death of Jesus, God is propitiated and
therefore declared to be righteous even though He
(anticipating the value of the sacrifice of Jesus on
the cross) passes over the sins of His people who
lived *before* the cross.   Thus through the death of
Jesus God can remain holy, righteous, and just, and
yet justify the ungodly when sinners believe in the
shed blood and finished work of Jesus (Rom. 3:25, 26).
"And for this cause He is the Mediator of the New
Testament, that by means of death, for the redemption of the transgressions that were under the first
testament, they which are called might receive the
promise of eternal inheritance" (Heb. 9:15).

I would point out here that this aspect of the
death of Jesus is to be distinguished from all other
aspects of His death because of its effect upon the
eternal God.   In the death of Jesus, God's infinite
love and power are released from restraint by the
accomplishment of every judgment which His righteousness and holiness could demand against each
and every sinner.   Therefore, in the death of Jesus,
God is more advantaged than all of the world com-
bined.

The Death of Jesus in Relation to the Believer

The death of Jesus was an eternal fact known to God before the world was:

"Forasmuch as ye know that ye were not redeemed with corruptible things, as silver and gold, from your vain conversation received by tradition from your fathers; but with the precious blood of Christ, as of a lamb without blemish and without spot: *who verily was foreordained BEFORE THE FOUNDATION OF THE WORLD, but was manifest in these last times for you*" (I Pet. 1:18—20).

Jesus came nineteen hundred years ago to take away the sin of the world (John 1:29)—and please notice the Holy Spirit makes it clear that He came to take away *"SIN"* (singular), not *sins* (plural). He died to take away the sin of unbelief that damns the soul. He is coming again—not as a babe in a manger, nor as Christ on the cross—but as King of kings and Lord of lords. He is coming to take away *sins* and put down sin. He died for our *sin*, He *lives* to make intercession for us as our Mediator, our Intercessor:

"For there is one God, and one Mediator between God and men, the Man Christ Jesus" (I Tim. 2:5).

"My little children, these things write I unto you, that ye sin not. And if any man sin, we have an advocate with the Father, Jesus Christ the righteous" (I John 2:1).

In His death Christ became our Substitute, bearing the total penalty for the sin of every sinner:

"And Aaron shall lay both his hands upon the head of the live goat, and confess over him all the iniquities of the children of Israel, and all their transgressions in all their sins, putting them upon the head of the goat, and shall send him away by the hand of a fit man into the wilderness" (Lev. 16:21).

"For I say unto you, that this that is written must

yet be accomplished in me, And He was reckoned among the transgressors: for the things concerning me have an end" (Luke 22:37).

"ALL we like sheep have gone astray; we have turned every one to his own way; and the Lord hath laid on Him the iniquity of us ALL" (Isa. 53:6).

"Christ also hath once suffered for sins, the just for the unjust, that He might bring us to God, being put to death in the flesh, but quickened by the Spirit" (I Pet. 3:18).

The death of Jesus, our Substitute, is the grounds for assurance to all who will come to God for salvation, trusting in the shed blood of God's only begotten Son. It is not enough to believe that Jesus died for the whole wide world. There must be a *personal conviction* that one's own *personal sin* has been perfectly borne by Him. *Each individual* must believe in the shed blood and finished work of Jesus. Salvation is of the Lord. It is He who "borns" us into heaven's family. Salvation, the mighty work of God, is wrought instantly to the individual who believes on Jesus, and he can declare with Paul, *"I know WHOM I have believed, and am persuaded that He is able to keep that which I have committed unto Him against that day"* (II Tim. 1:12).

To the church in Rome the Apostle Paul wrote, "Now the God of hope fill you with all joy and peace in believing, that ye may abound in hope, through the power of the Holy Ghost" (Rom. 15:13).

In Hebrews 9:13—15 we read, "If the blood of bulls and of goats, and the ashes of an heifer sprinkling the unclean, sanctifieth to the purifying of the flesh: how much more shall the blood of Christ, who through the eternal Spirit offered Himself without spot to God, purge your conscience from dead works to serve the living God? And for this cause He is the Mediator of the New Testament, that by means of death, for the redemption of the transgressions that were under the first testament, they which are called might receive the promise of eternal inheritance."

Jesus died for the WORLD—yes, in spite of the teaching of hyper-Calvinists, those who believe and teach limited atonement. He Himself declared this divine truth:

"For God so loved *the world*, that He gave His only begotten Son, that *whosoever* believeth in Him should not perish, but have everlasting life. For God sent not His Son into the world to condemn the world; *but that the WORLD through Him might be saved*" (John 3:16, 17).

In John 12:32 Jesus declared, "And I, if I be lifted up from the earth, *will draw ALL men unto me.*"

In I John 2:2 we read, "And He (Jesus) is the propitiation for our sins; *and not for our's only, but also for the sins of THE WHOLE WORLD.*"

Propitiation for sin avails for all, but propitiation *fully avails* only to the believer: "Therefore we both labour and suffer reproach, because we trust in the living God, *who is the Saviour of ALL men, SPECIALLY OF THOSE THAT BELIEVE*" (I Tim. 4:10).

Jesus died to save the *world*; all who believe are saved, and all who burn in hell will do so because they *refused* to believe: "He that believeth on (Jesus) is not condemned: but *he that BELIEVETH NOT is condemned already*, because he hath not believed in the name of the only begotten Son of God" (John 3:18).

It is on the basis of the death of Jesus that God can deal in mercy with the world. He can and will have mercy on any individual who will come to Him in the name of Jesus, trusting in His shed blood. It is in Jesus' name and for His sake that God saves any and all who will believe: "Neither is there salvation in any other: for there is none other name under heaven given among men, *whereby we MUST be saved"* (Acts 4:12).

In Ephesians 4:32 the Apostle Paul admonishes, "Be ye kind one to another, tenderhearted, forgiving one another, *even as God FOR CHRIST'S SAKE hath forgiven YOU."*

I do not doubt that someone will ask, "How did God deal in mercy with sinners *before* Jesus came into the world and laid His life down?" The answer to that question is found in Revelation 13:8: "And all that dwell upon the earth shall worship him, whose names are not written in the book of life of *THE LAMB SLAIN FROM THE FOUNDATION OF THE WORLD."* The death of Christ was, *in God's sight,* an eternal fact.

Jesus was made a guilt-offering for sin. Through His death He paid *the wages of sin* and made it possible for us to be born into the family of God. Thus He sees His seed (Isa. 53:10) and through His death we are spiritual sons, begotten of God:

"As many as received Him, to them gave He power to become the sons of God, even to them that believe on His name: which were born, not of blood, nor of the will of the flesh, nor of the will of man, *but of GOD"* (John 1:12, 13).

"Being born again, not of corruptible seed, but of incorruptible, BY THE WORD OF GOD, which liveth and abideth for ever" (I Pet. 1:23).

Through the power of Christ's death, burial, and resurrection, believers are new creations in Him: "Therefore if any man be in Christ, he is a new creature: old things are passed away; behold, all things are become new" (II Cor. 5:17).

The new race (the sons of God) springs from Christ's death on the cross. To His disciples He said, "Verily, verily, I say unto you, Except a corn of wheat fall into the ground and die, it abideth alone: but if it die, it bringeth forth much fruit" (John 12:24). In this spiritual progeny He sees of the travail of His soul and is satisfied (Isa. 53:11).

By the death of Jesus, believers are redeemed from the curse of the law. We are not *BEING redeemed;* we are redeemed *already* since we are trusting in His shed blood and finished work. What the law could not do because of the weakness of the flesh, Jesus did *IN the flesh* in a body of humiliation. The penalty of the broken law was satisfied and the law no longer has any claim for satisfaction upon the believer. We are not under the law, *but under grace* (Rom. 6:14).

Through His death on the cross, Jesus *blotted out* "the handwriting of ordinances that was against us, which was contrary to us, and took it out of the way, nailing it to His cross; and having spoiled principalities and powers, He made a shew of them openly, triumphing over them in it" (Col. 2:14,15). Therefore the bond written in ordinances that were against us is satisfied before a holy God, the curse has been removed, and God's holy law has been satisfied. Thus, "Christ is the *end* of the law for righteousness to every one that believeth" (Rom. 10:4).

This does not mean that God has done away with the law, but rather that Jesus perfectly fulfilled the law and it has no further claim on the believer: "But if the ministration of death, written and engraven in stones, was glorious, so that the children of Israel could not stedfastly behold the face of Moses for the glory of his countenance; which glory was to be done away: how shall not the ministration of the spirit be rather glorious? For if the ministration of condemnation be glory, much more doth the ministration of righteousness exceed in glory. For even that which was made glorious had no glory in this respect, by reason of the glory that excelleth. For if that which is done away was glorious, much more that which remaineth is glorious" (II Cor. 3:7—11).

"For He is our peace, who hath made both one, and hath broken down the middle wall of partition between us; having abolished in His flesh the enmity, even the law of commandments contained in ordinances; for to make in Himself of twain one new man, so making peace. And that He might reconcile both unto God in one body by the cross, having slain the enmity thereby" (Eph. 2:14—16).

Many men in pulpits today are trying to mix law and grace in every sermon they preach; but according to the Apostle Paul, salvation is by grace—grace plus nothing. It is impossible to mix law and grace. There is no such thing as being *saved by grace* and then being *kept saved* through the keeping of the law. God's Word clearly declares, "By the deeds of the law there shall no flesh be justified in His sight" (Rom. 3:20). Christ fulfilled the law. Therefore He is the end of the law for righteousness to the believer.

During the Dispensation of Law, the law separated Jews and Gentiles; but in His flesh Jesus abolished this and now in Him "there is neither Jew nor Greek, there is neither bond nor free, there is neither male nor female: for ye are all one in Christ Jesus" (Gal. 3:28).

By the death of Jesus, Jewish believers are redeemed from subjection to the law and receive the adoption of sons: "Even so we, when we were children, were in bondage under the elements of the world: but when the fulness of the time was come, God sent forth His Son, made of a woman, made under the law, to redeem them that were under the law, that we might receive the adoption of sons" (Gal. 4:3—5).

Before Calvary, Gentiles were "aliens from the commonwealth of Israel, and strangers from the covenants of promise, having no hope, and without God in the world: But now in Christ Jesus ye who sometimes were far off are made nigh by the blood of Christ" (Eph. 2:12, 13). Through the death of Jesus, we are now fellow citizens with the saints, of the family and household of God!

Through the death of Jesus on the cross, believers have forgiveness of sins. We do not *beg* for forgiveness, nor is forgiveness something we are to secure at some future time. The blood of Jesus has *already* secured forgiveness for us, and through faith we have *appropriated* that forgiveness.

According to Ephesians 1:7, in Christ "we have redemption through His blood, the forgiveness of sins, according to the riches of His grace." Not only does the blood of Jesus redeem us *from the GUILT* of sin ("the wages of sin," *eternal death*—Rom. 6:23), but the blood of Jesus *"cleanseth us from ALL sin"*—sin that would damn us *before* we believe, and sin that would rob us of joy, victory, and rewards *after* we believe!

In I John 1:4—10 we read: "These things write we unto you, that your joy may be full. This then is the message which we have heard of Him, and declare unto you, that God is light, and in Him is no darkness at all. If we say that we have fellowship with Him, and walk in darkness, we lie, and do not the truth: but if we walk in the light, as He is in the light, we have fellowship one with another, *and the blood of Jesus Christ His Son CLEANSETH US FROM ALL SIN.* If we say that *we HAVE no sin,* we deceive ourselves, and the truth is not in us. If we confess our sins, He is faithful and just to *forgive* us our sins, and to *cleanse us FROM ALL UNRIGHTEOUS-NESS.* If we say that we have not sinned, we make Him a liar, and His Word is not in us."

Now let us consider Scriptures in the Old Testament and in the New which clearly set forth the truth that the blood of Jesus redeems us from *the GUILT*

*of sin—*but does not stop there. His blood cleanses
us day by day, moment by moment, as we travel this
pilgrim journey:

Leviticus 14:19—31: "And the priest shall offer
the sin-offering, and make an atonement for him that
is to be cleansed from his uncleanness; and afterward
he shall kill the burnt-offering: and the priest shall
offer the burnt-offering and the meat-offering upon the
altar: and the priest shall make an atonement for him,
and he shall be clean. . . .

"And the priest shall take the lamb of the trespass-
offering, and the log of oil, and the priest shall wave
them for a wave-offering before the Lord: And he
shall kill the lamb of the trespass-offering, and the
priest shall take some of the blood of the trespass-
offering, and put it upon the tip of the right ear of
him that is to be cleansed. . . .

"And he shall offer the one of the turtledoves, or
of the young pigeons, such as he can get; even such
as he is able to get, the one for a sin-offering, and
the other for a burnt-offering, with the meat-offering:
and the priest shall make an atonement for him that
is to be cleansed before the Lord."

Leviticus 16:30: "For on that day shall the priest
make an atonement for you, to cleanse you, that ye
may be clean from all your sins before the Lord."

Leviticus 17:11: "For the life of the flesh is in
the blood: and I have given it to you upon the altar
to make an atonement for your souls: for it is the
blood that maketh an atonement for the soul."

Jeremiah 33:8: "And I will cleanse them from all
their iniquity, whereby they have sinned against me;
and I will pardon all their iniquities, whereby they
have sinned, and whereby they have transgressed
against me."

Psalm 51:7: "Purge me with hyssop, and I shall be
clean: wash me, and I shall be whiter than snow."

Going over into the New Testament, in *Matthew 26:28* Jesus declared, *"This is MY blood of the NEW testament,* which is shed for many for the remission of sins."

In *Romans 3:24, 25* we read, "Being justified freely by His grace through the redemption that is in Christ Jesus: whom God hath set forth to be a propitiation through faith in His blood, to declare His righteousness for the remission of sins that are past, through the forbearance of God."

Romans 5:9: "Much more then, being now justified by His blood, we shall be saved from wrath through Him."

Ephesians 1:7: "In whom we have redemption through His blood, the forgiveness of sins, according to the riches of His grace."

Hebrews 9:22—24 tells us, "Almost all things are by the law purged with blood; and without shedding of blood is no remission. It was therefore necessary that the patterns of things in the heavens should be purified with these; but the heavenly things themselves with better sacrifices than these. For Christ is not entered into the holy places made with hands, which are the figures of the true; but into heaven itself, now to appear in the presence of God for us."

In *Revelation 1:5,* John the Beloved speaks of "Jesus Christ, who is the faithful witness, and the first begotten of the dead, and the prince of the kings of the earth. . . . Him that loved us, and washed us from our sins in His own blood." Then in *Revelation 7:14* he speaks of those "which came out of great tribulation, *and have washed their robes, and made them white IN THE BLOOD OF THE LAMB."*

I think you will agree that these passages clearly teach that cleansing by the blood of Jesus is *cleansing from the GUILT sin brings* upon the sinner, and through the shed blood of Jesus *believers* who walk in

the light are cleansed *continuously*—every moment of
every day, for as long as we travel this pilgrim journey.

There may still be sin in the believer from the
standpoint of the *flesh,* but "that which is born of
the flesh is flesh; and that which is born of the Spirit
is spirit" (John 3:6). The Man Christ Jesus—living
and seated at the right hand of the Father—continually
makes intercession for Christians who sin. Salvation
does not license believers to commit sin, and certainly
it is not God's *will* that His children sin; but *IF we
sin* "we have an Advocate with the Father, Jesus
Christ the righteous" (I John 2:1).

In I John 3:9 we read, "Whosoever is born of God
doth not commit sin; for His seed remaineth in him:
and he cannot sin, because he is born of God." *But
who IS born of God?* Those who believe in the shed
blood and finished work of Jesus are born of God.
And what is *the new birth?* Is it a flesh-birth? No.
Nicodemus asked the Lord Jesus, "How can a man
be born when he is old? Can he enter the second
time into his mother's womb, and be born?" (John
3:4). Jesus then clearly instructed Nicodemus that the
birth from above is *a SPIRITUAL birth*—"that which
is born of the Spirit is spirit"—and you can rest assured that the spirit born of God does not commit
sin. Believers are partakers of divine nature (II Pet.
1:4). Believers are possessors of the Holy Spirit. We
are *indwelt* by the Spirit, *led* by the Spirit, and the
Spirit bears witness with our spirit that we *are* children
of God (Rom. 8:9, 14, 16); and by the Holy Spirit we are
sealed until the day of redemption (Eph. 4:30).

Through the death of Jesus and by His shed blood,
believers are justified from ALL things:

"Who shall lay anything to the charge of God's
elect? It is God that justifieth. Who is he that con-
demneth? It is Christ that died, yea rather, that is
risen again, who is even at the right hand of God,

who also maketh intercession for us" (Rom. 8:33, 34).

In Jesus we are not only redeemed from sin, we are also saved (Eph. 1:7; Col. 1:14). Someone may ask, "Are not salvation and redemption one and the same? If Jesus is our Saviour, is He not also our Redeemer?"

It is true that when we are redeemed we are saved. Through His blood Jesus redeemed us from the iniquity of sin—but I not only need a Redeemer: *I also need a Saviour.* We can no more *keep ourselves* from the *power* of sin daily than we can *redeem* ourselves from the *penalty* of sin. He lives to save us daily from the power of sin—*redeemed* through His *death,* saved from the pitfalls of the devil day by day *through His LIFE!* Then in the Rapture He will save us from the very *presence* of sin (I Thess. 4:13—18; Col. 3:1—4).

"And they sung a new song, saying, Thou art worthy to take the book, and to open the seals thereof: for thou wast slain, and hast redeemed us to God by thy blood out of every kindred, and tongue, and people, and nation" (Rev. 5:9). Believers are saved by God's marvelous grace because "by the grace of God" Jesus tasted death for every man (Heb. 2:9). We are redeemed through His precious blood, but our Redeemer, our Saviour, ever lives as our Advocate: "For if, when we were enemies, we were reconciled to God by the death of His Son, much more, being reconciled, we shall be *saved by His life*" (Rom. 5:10).

In Hebrews 7:25 we read, "Wherefore He is able also to save them to the uttermost that come unto God by Him, seeing He ever liveth to make intercession for them."

To the church at Rome, the Apostle Paul wrote, "We are saved by hope: but hope that is seen is not hope: for what a man seeth, why doth he yet hope for?" (Rom. 8:24).

John the Beloved declared, "If we say that we have no sin, we deceive ourselves, and the truth is not in us. *If we CONFESS our sins, He is faithful and just to forgive us our sins, and to CLEANSE US from all unrighteousness"* (I John 1:8, 9).

It was a divine necessity that the *death* of Jesus precede His exaltation to the right hand of the Majesty as our great High Priest.   When Jesus entered into the presence of God, He did not enter by the "blood of others"—that is, with the blood of lambs or turtle doves—as did the Old Testament priests.   He entered by (and with) His own blood (Heb. 9:24—28).   And because of His sacrificial death and finished work, God the Father accepted Him as the believer's Representative.   Therefore, He is now our great High Priest: "For when God made promise to Abraham, because He could swear by no greater, He sware by Himself, saying, Surely blessing I will bless thee, and multiplying I will multiply thee.   And so, after he had patiently endured, he obtained the promise.   For men verily swear by the greater: and an oath for confirmation is to them an end of all strife.   Wherein God, willing more abundantly to shew unto the heirs of promise the immutability of His counsel, confirmed it by an oath: that by two immutable things, in which it was impossible for God to lie, we might have a strong consolation, who have fled for refuge to lay hold upon the hope set before us: which hope we have as an anchor of the soul, both sure and stedfast, and which entereth into that within the veil; *whither the FORERUNNER is for us entered, even Jesus, MADE AN HIGH PRIEST FOR EVER after the order of Melchisedec"* (Heb. 6:13—20).

Therefore, believers have "boldness to enter into the holiest *by the blood of Jesus, BY A NEW AND LIVING WAY, which He hath consecrated for us, through the veil, that is to say, HIS FLESH"* (Heb. 10:19, 20).

Jesus is our Saviour, our Redeemer, our Advocate,

our great High Priest. He conquered death, hell, and the grave, *and because HE lives, WE live.* He is our life: *"For ye are dead, and your life is hid WITH CHRIST IN GOD. When Christ, WHO IS OUR LIFE, shall appear, then shall ye also appear with Him in glory"* (Col. 3:3, 4).

John 1:4 declares, *"IN HIM WAS LIFE;* and the life was the light of men." Then in I John 5:11, 12 we read, "And this is the record, that God hath given to us *eternal life, and THIS LIFE IS IN HIS SON. He that hath the Son HATH LIFE;* and he that *hath not* the Son of God *hath not life."*

Apart from Christ *there IS no life.* He said to Thomas, "I am the way, the truth, and *the LIFE: no man cometh unto the Father, but by ME"* (John 14:6).

There are some people who think that because they are *saved,* they have reached the ultimate—but salvation is only the beginning. To be saved is to have *eternal life,* and life moves forward, produces, and grows! Jesus forgives us of all sin when we believe in His finished work—but forgiveness is negative. Therefore He does more than forgive: He *justifies*— and justification is positive. Someone has said, "To be justified is to be just as just as Jesus is just." Through justification we are reckoned positively righteous, and when God the Father looks on us and sees the blood that covers us, He sees the holiness of His sinless Son and we are "accepted in the Beloved" (Eph. 1:6). To the Israelites in Egypt, God said, "When I see the blood, I will pass over you" (Ex. 12:13); and just as surely as blood was necessary on the doorposts that night in Egypt when the death angel passed through, it is necessary today, for God's Word clearly declares, *"Without* shedding of blood is *NO REMISSION!"* (Heb. 9:22).

Because of the death of Jesus on the cross, there

is an interchange of positions between the Son of God
and the believer. On the cross He took our place of
condemnation before God, and when we believe in
His shed blood *we take HIS place of acceptance before God.* Although Jesus was sinless, God made Him
to be sin *for us,* "that we might be made the righteousness of God *in Him"* (II Cor. 5:21).

Because of Christ's death on Calvary, no one can
lay anything to the charge of God's elect—the born
again, blood-washed believers. "There is therefore now
*NO CONDEMNATION to them which are in Christ
Jesus . . .*" (Rom. 8:1). The death of Jesus was absolute—it settled the sin-question once, for all, forever;
and now all who believe in His shed blood are recipients of His saving grace, His redeeming power, and
His keeping power. Thus we stand before God's holiness—not in ourselves, but in the righteousness of
Christ.

Thus "by *one offering* He hath *perfected for ever*
them that are sanctified" (Heb. 10:14). This does not
mean that believers are perfect in our present state
as we tabernacle on earth in a body of flesh, but we
are perfect *in our standing before God.* Through the
death of Jesus, the believer is forever cleansed from
the guilt of breaking God's holy law. His sins are
put away by the one perfect, all-sufficient sacrifice of
the blood of the Lamb of God. "For if the blood of
bulls and of goats, and the ashes of an heifer sprinkling the unclean, sanctifieth to the purifying of the
flesh: *how much MORE shall the blood of Christ,
who through the eternal Spirit offered Himself without
spot to God, purge your conscience from dead works
to serve the living God?*" (Heb. 9:13, 14).

It is the flesh that is sinful. God gave up flesh in
the Garden of Eden and destined it to return to dust.
But we *overcome* in the flesh because greater is He
who is within the believer than he who is in the world

(I John 4:4), and at the Rapture and the first resurrection this corruption will put on incorruption and every believer will receive a glorified body like the glorified resurrection body of Jesus (I John 3:2).

Not only does the blood of Jesus relieve the conscience of the believer from the guilt of sin that would damn the soul, it also delivers from the burden of trying to atone for sin through good works—"*dead works.*" So the believer, with conscience free from guilt and free from the burden of his own imperfect works, enters into the service of the living God in the liberty and power of sonship:

"For as many as are led by the Spirit of God, they are the sons of God. For ye have not received the spirit of bondage again to fear, but ye have received the Spirit of adoption, whereby we cry, Abba, Father. The Spirit Himself beareth witness with our spirit, that we are the children of God: and if children, then heirs; heirs of God, and joint-heirs with Christ; if so be that we suffer with Him, that we may be also glorified together" (Rom. 8:14—17).

There are tens of thousands of church members today who are constantly under the burden of "doing something" in an effort to atone for sins and thus bring peace between themselves and God. It will be a happy day in the lives of those believers when they realize that *JESUS did all that CAN be done.* He laid His life down, and His blood has completely and forever satisfied God. Therefore when we *believe in* the shed blood and finished work of God's dear Son, He forgives us *"for Christ's sake"* (Eph. 4:32) and we become partakers of divine nature, blood-bought children of God.

We notice three groups—three lines of thought— among men today:

First, there are those who never think of their sin, they are never burdened because of their wickedness, they love sin and live in it.

The second group is made up of people who are "religious"—i. e., because of the burden of sin they have "joined" some local church and day by day they seek to rid themselves of their burden by the process of good works, saying prayers, giving money, and doing all the "good" they possibly can. This is what God's Word refers to as *"dead works"* (Heb. 9:14). Peace does not come through man's striving after good works. Our only hope lies in *the work of JESUS*—His death, burial, resurrection, and ascension.

The third group is made up of believers. They have trusted in Christ's atoning blood, they believe God's Word to be truth, and *through* His Word, *by faith,* they have seen sin settled forever because they have accepted the finished work of Jesus. They are cleansed from the guilt of sin and from the futility of dead works. These people are filled with the love of God, the Holy Spirit possesses the "inner man." They serve the living God in liberty, knowing that the blood of Jesus redeems and cleanses from all sin, and they can sing, "Nothing in my hand I bring. Simply to thy cross I cling!"

God is holy, sinners are unholy; but through the shed blood of Jesus *believers* can enter boldly into the holy place—yea, into the very presence of God! Believers are perfected, sanctified forever on the grounds of the eternal sacrifice made by Jesus on the cross. We dare not rush into God's presence except in the blood of His only begotten Son. "Blessed are they that do His commandments, that they may have right to the tree of life, and may enter in through the gates into the city" (Rev. 22:14).

Positionally, the believer died when Christ died. As a believer I should see myself nailed to a cross. Therefore *the person I was* no longer exists. The "old person" was a cursed person, and as a curse was nailed to the cross: "Christ hath redeemed us from the curse of the law, *being made a curse FOR US: for it is written, Cursed is every one that hangeth on a tree*" (Gal. 3:13). Since I am crucified with Christ, I should not try to live as I lived before I believed. I should trust Christ who "liveth in me" (Gal. 2:20).

It is of this that the Apostle Paul speaks in Romans 6:6—11: "Knowing this, that *our old man is crucified with (Christ), that the body of sin might be destroyed*, that henceforth we should not serve sin. For *he that is dead is freed from sin.* Now if we be dead with Christ, we believe that we shall also live with Him: knowing that Christ being raised from the dead *dieth no more; death hath no more dominion over Him.* For in that He died, He died unto sin once: but in that He liveth, He liveth unto God. *LIKEWISE RECKON YE ALSO YOURSELVES TO BE DEAD INDEED UNTO SIN, but alive unto God through Jesus Christ our Lord.*"

To the Galatian believers Paul said, *"God forbid that I should glory, SAVE IN THE CROSS OF OUR LORD JESUS CHRIST, by whom the world is crucified unto me, and I unto the world"* (Gal. 6:14). To realize that as believers we are crucified with Christ (therefore we are dead to the world) is to glory in the cross—never in self or self-achievement; but very few Christians enjoy this spiritual birthright.

The reason there are so many average Christians— and so few *extraordinary* Christians—is that most believers have never realized the fulness of the life we possess in Christ Jesus. We know we are redeemed from the penalty of sin, condemnation is removed, we are possessors of divine nature and we have eternal life; but very few of us enjoy the *fulness* of our spiritual possession because we fail to fully understand our *position* spiritually. Therefore, when we do not surrender soul, spirit, and body to Jesus, the "old

man" still attempts to operate in our daily living—and
in some instances he succeeds! As believers, we must
come to the full realization that we are *dead with
Christ* (and then live accordingly) before we can know
the abundance of His saving grace:

"For the love of Christ constraineth us; because
we thus judge, that if one died for all, then were all
dead" (II Cor. 5:14).

To the Christians at Colosse Paul wrote, "If ye
then be risen with Christ, seek those things which are
above, where Christ sitteth on the right hand of God.
Set your affection on things above, not on things on
the earth. For ye are dead, and your life is hid with
Christ in God" (Col. 3:1—3).

The Death of Jesus in Relation to the Devil

The death of Jesus produced definite results in relation to the devil, his demons, and the powers of
darkness. Satan is still operating, he still walks about
"as a roaring lion . . . seeking whom he may devour"
(I Pet. 5:8). He still transforms himself "into an angel
of light" (II Cor. 11:14). *But he is a defeated foe.*

In Genesis 3:15 God declared enmity between the
seed of the serpent and the seed of the woman. To
Satan He said, "I will put enmity between thee and
the woman, and between thy seed and her seed; it
shall bruise thy head, and thou shalt bruise his heel."
But in spite of the fact that on Calvary Satan bruised
the heel of Jesus, the cross spelled total defeat for
him. Because of the death of Jesus, the devil is a
usurper whose ultimate dethronement and absolute
defeat are assured and guaranteed. Just before He
went to the cross, Jesus declared, *"Now is the judgment of this world: now shall THE PRINCE OF
THIS WORLD be cast out"* (John 12:31).

The death of Jesus was death to Satan's power. In

Hebrews 2:14 we read, "Forasmuch then as the children are partakers of flesh and blood, He also Himself likewise took part of the same; *that through death He might DESTROY him that had the POWER OF DEATH, that is, THE DEVIL.*"

In Ephesians 6:11, 12 the Apostle Paul declares that we should "put on the whole armour of God, that ye may be able to stand against the wiles of the devil. *For we wrestle not against flesh and blood, but against PRINCIPALITIES, AGAINST POWERS, AGAINST THE RULERS OF THE DARKNESS OF THIS WORLD, AGAINST SPIRITUAL WICKEDNESS IN HIGH PLACES.*"

Then in Colossians 2:15 Paul tells us that by His death Jesus *"SPOILED principalities and powers,"* *and triumphed over them.*

The moment when Jesus cried out, "It is finished!" seemed to be Satan's moment of victory. But instead of victory, it was the moment of his total and overwhelming defeat! He is a conquered foe. He will operate only as long as God allows it. Then one day Jesus will personally supervise placing Satan in the lake of fire that burns with brimstone, where he will be tormented along with the doomed throughout eternity. John describes this as it was revealed to him on the Isle of Patmos:

"I saw an Angel come down from heaven, having the key of the bottomless pit and a great chain in His hand. And He laid hold on the dragon, that old serpent, which is the Devil, and Satan, and bound him a thousand years, and cast him into the bottomless pit, and shut him up, and set a seal upon him, that he should deceive the nations no more, till the thousand years should be fulfilled: and after that he must be loosed a little season. . . . And the devil that deceived them was cast into the lake of fire and brimstone, where the beast and the false prophet are, and

shall be tormented day and night for ever and ever"
(Rev. 20:1—3, 10).

The Death of Jesus in Relation to the Earth

In Genesis 1:1 we read, "In the beginning God
created the heaven and the earth." Then in the next
verse we read, "And the earth was without form, and
void; and darkness was upon the face of the deep...."
We do not know how old the earth is—God *created*
the earth "in the *beginning.*" We do know that approximately six thousand years ago He brought order
out of chaos and then created the first man, Adam.

God is perfect; and a perfect Creator could not
create imperfection. Therefore we know God did not
create the earth *without form, void, and engulfed by
darkness.* Most outstanding Bible scholars believe such
a condition was brought about by judgment striking
the earth when God cast Lucifer out of heaven and
he became Satan, the personality known today as the
devil.

I personally believe that in his original state, Satan
was *Lucifer,* one of the archangels—perhaps their chief.
The Scripture mentions two archangels by name: Michael and Gabriel. I believe Lucifer was the *third.*
Isaiah describes him as *"Lucifer, son of the morning,"*
and reveals the sin that caused him to be cast out of
heaven:

"How art thou fallen from heaven, O Lucifer, son
of the morning! how art thou cut down to the ground,
which didst weaken the nations! For thou hast said
in thine heart, *I will ascend into heaven, I will exalt
my throne above the stars of God: I will sit also
upon the mount of the congregation, in the sides of
the north: I will ascend above the heights of the
clouds; I will be like the most High.*

"Yet thou shalt be brought down to hell, to the

sides of the pit. They that see thee shall narrowly look upon thee, and consider thee, saying, Is this the man that made the earth to tremble, that did shake kingdoms; that made the world as a wilderness, and destroyed the cities thereof; that opened not the house of his prisoners?" (Isa. 14:12—17).

In his original state, Lucifer was *perfect*. We find the record in Ezekiel 28:12—17:

"Son of man, take up a lamentation upon the king of Tyrus, and say unto him, Thus saith the Lord God: Thou sealest up the sum, *full of wisdom, and perfect in beauty*. Thou hast been in Eden the garden of God; every precious stone was thy covering, the sardius, topaz, and the diamond, the beryl, the onyx, and the jasper, the sapphire, the emerald, and the carbuncle, and gold: the workmanship of thy tabrets and of thy pipes was prepared in thee in the day that thou wast created. *Thou art the anointed cherub that covereth*; and I have set thee so: *thou wast upon the holy mountain of God*; thou hast walked up and down in the midst of the stones of fire. *Thou wast PERFECT IN THY WAYS from the day that thou wast CREATED, till INIQUITY was found in thee.*

"By the multitude of thy merchandise they have filled the midst of thee with violence, and thou hast sinned: therefore I will cast thee as profane out of the mountain of God: and I will destroy thee, O covering cherub, from the midst of the stones of fire. Thine heart was lifted up because of thy beauty, thou hast corrupted thy wisdom by reason of thy brightness: I will cast thee to the ground, I will lay thee before kings, that they may behold thee."

The person here described by Ezekiel was not a man *as WE are men*. We read twice in this account that he was *"created,"* and we know that God created only Adam and Eve, the mother and father of the human race. All persons *since* Adam and Eve have been born of earthly parents.

We also read that this person was *"perfect"* in all
of his ways. Since there has been only *ONE perfect
Person* since Adam (and that One was the Lord Jesus
Christ), we know this description could not refer to a
literal earthly king.

The passage just quoted from *Isaiah* points out
the *"iniquity"* that was found in Lucifer: *he became
jealous.* He was envious of God, not willing to be
subordinate to the Almighty. Therefore he brainwashed
some of the angels, led them astray, and with their
help attempted to overthrow God and take the throne
of heaven! Thus his angels, too, left their first estate.
II Peter 2:4 tells us that God "spared not the angels
that sinned, but cast them down to hell, and delivered
them into chains of darkness, to be reserved unto
judgment." Jude also describes these fallen angels
as having "left their own habitation," and tells us
that they are "reserved in everlasting chains under
darkness unto the judgment of the great day" (Jude 6).

As I have already pointed out, many Bible scholars
believe that catastrophe struck this earth when Lucifer
and his angels were cast out of heaven.

The whole universe was cursed a second time when
Adam sinned and God drove him from the Garden of
Eden. In Romans 8:18—25 Paul explains that the
whole creation groans and travails until now, awaiting
that glorious day when Jesus will come the second
time to put down sin and Satan and deliver not only
man, but *the entire creation* from the curse of sin!

This universe has fallen from God in connection
with sin (Rom. 8:20; Gen. 3:18)—the earth, man, the
animal kingdom, even the heavens. The devil is "the
prince of the power of the air" (Eph. 2:2), and the
very air above us is filled with demons, "principalities
and powers . . . spiritual wickedness in high places"
(Eph. 6:12).

But hallelujah! through Christ's death on the cross the universe will one day be delivered from the pollution and the curse of sin and iniquity! In the Old Testament era, God's anointed high priest took the blood of the sacrifice into the most holy place, which was a type of heaven. The Lord Jesus Christ, *OUR High Priest*, has taken the blood of the "better" Sacrifice, *His own precious blood*, into heaven itself and cleansed it. Colossians 1:20 plainly declares that Christ made peace through the blood of His cross, by which *He reconciled ALL things unto Himself*, "whether they be things in earth, or things in heaven."

Yes, *ALL things*—in heaven and in earth—will be cleansed and reconciled to God. The entire creation will be delivered from the bondage of corruption and given the liberty of the glory of the children of God. II Peter 3:13 says, "Nevertheless we, *according to His promise*, look for *NEW heavens* and *a NEW earth, wherein dwelleth righteousness!*"

All this is included in Christ's atonement. God is able to do exceeding and abundantly above anything we think or ask; He will do things far above anything we can conceive in our poor, finite minds. The atonement of Christ has an immense sweep that extends far beyond the reach of our imagination. The death of Jesus affects earth and hell, satisfies heaven, and provides ample grace, power, and strength for believers to overcome sin and live victoriously in this present world. What the law could not do because of the weakness of the flesh, what the blood of bulls and goats could not do, the blood of Jesus Christ has done, is doing, and will continue to do.

Chapter Four

BIBLE TRUTH CONCERNING
THE BODILY RESURRECTION OF JESUS

"Now upon the first day of the week, very early in the morning, they came unto the sepulchre, bringing the spices which they had prepared, and certain others with them. And they found the stone rolled away from the sepulchre. And they entered in, and found not the body of the Lord Jesus. And it came to pass, as they were much perplexed thereabout, behold, two men stood by them in shining garments: and as they were afraid, and bowed down their faces to the earth, they said unto them, Why seek ye the living among the dead? He is not here, but is risen: remember how He spake unto you when He was yet in Galilee, saying, The Son of man must be delivered into the hands of sinful men, and be crucified, and the third day rise again. And they remembered His words, and returned from the sepulchre, and told all these things unto the eleven, and to all the rest" (Luke 24:1—9).

The bodily resurrection of Jesus was the greatest bombshell ever to explode in the face of an unbelieving world. To the *Jews*, His resurrection was so completely unexpected that it was destined to have far-reaching repercussions—and *until this day* they believe and teach that His friends stole His body from the tomb!

Thus after the resurrection of Jesus, the Jews were

divided into two factions, and that division has continued down to this present time. The *religious leaders* of the Jewish nation declared that the disciples of Jesus had stolen His body and hidden it away, while the *apostles* declared that He had risen from the dead, and gave testimony that they had seen Him, fellowshipped with Him—even *touched* Him—after His resurrection. Therefore we are compelled to face an issue:

Either the Lord Jesus Christ rose bodily from the grave—or death overcame Him, He remained in the tomb, and His ministry ended in utter defeat! The only place to find the right answer to such a question is in the Word of God, penned down by "holy men of God . . . as they were moved by the Holy Ghost" (II Pet. 1:21).

The Foundation of Christianity

The bodily resurrection of Jesus is unquestionably the foundation fact on which Christianity is built. To destroy the truth of His bodily resurrection would be to undermine the Christian faith: *"If Christ be not raised, your faith is vain; ye are yet in your sins. Then they also which are fallen asleep in Christ are perished"* (I Cor. 15:17, 18). The very proof of the *deity* of Jesus depends upon His bodily resurrection from the dead.

On many occasions, Jesus plainly told His disciples that He would be crucified, buried, and on the third day would rise from the dead.

When the scribes and Pharisees asked Him for a "sign," He replied, "An evil and adulterous generation seeketh after a sign; and there shall no sign be given to it, but the sign of the prophet Jonas: For as Jonas was three days and three nights in the whale's belly; *so shall the Son of man be three days and three nights in the heart of the earth"* (Matt. 12:39, 40).

Just before His triumphal entry into the Holy City, Jesus took the twelve apostles aside and said to them, "Behold, we go up to Jerusalem; and the Son of man shall be betrayed unto the chief priests and unto the scribes, and they shall condemn Him to death, and shall deliver Him to the Gentiles to mock, and to scourge, and *to crucify Him: and the third day He shall rise again"* (Matt. 20:17—19).

Just after the institution of the Lord's Supper Jesus again told His disciples, "All ye shall offended because of me this night: for it is written, I will smite the Shepherd, and the sheep of the flock shall be scattered abroad. But *after I am risen again,* I will go before you into Galilee" (Matt. 26:30—32).

He declared the same truth in Luke 18:31—33: "Then He took unto Him the twelve, and said unto them, Behold, we go up to Jerusalem, and all things that are written by the prophets concerning the Son of man shall be accomplished. For He shall be delivered unto the Gentiles, and shall be mocked, and spitefully entreated, and spitted on: and they shall scourge Him, *and put Him to death: and the third day He shall rise again."*

When He drove the money-changers from the temple, the Jews asked Him, "What sign shewest thou unto us, seeing that thou doest these things?" Jesus replied, "Destroy this temple, and *in three days I will raise it up"* (John 2:18—21). They did not understand that He was speaking of the temple of His body.

In these passages just quoted, we note five instances when the Lord Jesus Christ clearly declared that He would rise from the dead. Had He *not* risen, we would not have known whether or not He was the Son of God. Therefore I repeat: *the proof of His deity* rests upon the fact of His **bodily resurrection**.

In Romans 1:3, 4 the Apostle Paul speaks of "Jesus Christ our Lord, which was made of the seed of David according to the flesh; *and declared to be the Son of God with power,* according to the Spirit of holiness, *BY THE RESURRECTION FROM THE DEAD."*

"The wages of sin is *death"* (Rom. 6:23). The verdict has been reached, the sentence has been passed. Since Jesus came to take the sinner's place it was imperative that He die—but if He had *remained* dead we would not have eternal life. He said, "Because I live, ye shall live also" (John 14:19). It was foreordained that Jesus should die in our stead, that we might have remission of sins through the redemption that is in His precious blood (I Pet. 1:18—20), and if He had not risen from the dead we would not have known whether or not He took our place.

Jesus came into the world with the sentence of death upon Him. In John 10:18 He said, "No man taketh (my life) from me, but I lay it down of myself. I have power to lay it down, and I have power to take it again. *This commandment have I received of my Father."* But death could not hold Him. His sentence was that He should remain in the grave for three days; and when those three days were up, no power on earth or in hell could keep Him in the tomb one minute longer than His appointed time! God raised Him up, "having loosed the pains of death: *because it was not POSSIBLE that He should be holden of it"* (Acts 2:24).

Centuries before Jesus was born, the Psalmist prophesied, *"Thou wilt not leave my soul in hell; neither wilt thou suffer thine HOLY ONE to see corruption"* (Psalm 16:10). The Jews believed that corruption set in the fourth day after a body was laid in the tomb. But Jesus rose again on the *third* day, having *conquered* death. On the Day of Pentecost, when Peter preached to the Jews, he *referred* to the prophecy of Psalm 16:10. He said, "Men and brethren, let me freely speak unto you of the patriarch David, that he is both dead and buried, *and his sepulchre is with us unto this day.* Therefore being a prophet, and knowing that God had sworn with an oath to him, that of the fruit of his loins, according to the flesh, He would raise up Christ to sit on his throne; he seeing this before spake of the resurrection of Christ, that His soul was not left in hell, neither His flesh did see corruption. *This Jesus hath God raised up, WHEREOF WE ALL ARE WITNESSES"* (Acts 2:29—32).

When Jesus appeared to John the Beloved on the Isle of Patmos He declared, "I am He that liveth, and was *dead;* and, behold, *I am ALIVE FOR EVERMORE*, Amen; and have the keys of hell and of death" (Rev. 1:18).

Death did not conquer Christ. He pursued death into its own dominions and came forth conqueror, leading captivity captive and announcing, *"I AM THE RESURRECTION, AND THE LIFE: he that believeth in me, though he were dead, yet shall he live: and whosoever liveth and believeth in me shall never die. . ."* (John 11:25, 26).

To the Ephesian church the Apostle Paul wrote, "Unto every one of us is given grace according to the measure of the gift of Christ. Wherefore He saith, *When He ascended up on high, He led captivity captive*, and gave gifts unto men. (Now that He ascended, what is it but that He also descended first into the lower parts of the earth? He that descended is the same also that ascended up far above all heavens, *that He might fill all things.)"* (Eph. 4:7—10).

When the Lord Jesus Christ rose from the dead He *ABOLISHED DEATH,"* and *"brought life and immortality to light"* (II Tim. 1:10). He removed the sting of death. Through His death, burial, and resur-

rection the Lord Jesus Christ made provision by which
believers shall be freed from the bonds of death by
the resurrection of the body:

"So when this corruptible shall have put on incorruption, and this mortal shall have put on immortality, then shall be brought to pass the saying that
is written, *Death is swallowed up in victory.* O death,
where is thy sting? O grave, where is thy victory?
The sting of death is sin; and the strength of sin is
the law. *But thanks be to God, which giveth us the
victory THROUGH OUR LORD JESUS CHRIST"*
(I Cor. 15:54—57).

Since death could not hold Jesus, it cannot hold
the believer; for "if the Spirit of Him that raised up
Jesus from the dead dwell in you, He that raised up
Christ from the dead *shall also quicken YOUR mortal
bodies* by His Spirit that dwelleth in you" (Rom. 8:11).

Paul told the Colossian believers, "If ye then be
risen with Christ, seek those things which are above,
where Christ sitteth on the right hand of God. Set
your affection on things above, not on things on the
earth. *For ye are DEAD, and your life is hid WITH
CHRIST in God. When Christ, WHO IS OUR LIFE,
shall appear, then shall ye also appear WITH HIM
in glory"* (Col. 3:1—4).

Ultimately there will be no more death: *"And God
shall wipe away all tears from their eyes; and there
shall be NO MORE DEATH,* neither sorrow, nor crying, neither shall there be any more pain: for the
former things are passed away" (Rev. 21:4).

The Fact of the Bodily Resurrection of Jesus

There can be no question of the fact of the *death*
of Jesus on the cross. Matthew, Mark, Luke, and
John all tell us that He "yielded up His spirit":

In Matthew 27:50 we read, "Jesus, when He had

cried again with a loud voice, *yielded up the ghost.*"

Mark 15:37 declares, "Jesus cried with a loud voice, *and gave up the ghost.*"

Luke 23:46 tells us, "When Jesus had cried with a loud voice, He said, *Father, into thy hands I commend my spirit:* and having said thus, *He gave up the ghost.*"

John 19:30 records the mighty proclamation when Jesus cried out, *"IT IS FINISHED!* And He bowed His head, *and gave up the ghost.*"

It is true that the words verbally inspired and penned down by the four Gospel writers differentiate the death of Jesus from all other physical death, because He died by His own volition, literally dismissing His spirit when He could say, "It is finished." Nevertheless, *the fact of His DEATH* is established.

The Roman soldiers also gave testimony of His death when they came to break the legs of the men they had crucified. John 19:33 declares that "when they came to Jesus, *and saw that He was DEAD ALREADY, they brake not His legs.*"

Even supposing He had not been actually dead when He was removed from the cross, supposing He had only swooned, most assuredly He would have been smothered to death by the graveclothes which were bound about His head and body.

Also, the centurion who had stood near the cross of Jesus testified that He was dead. When Joseph of Arimathaea came to Pilate and asked for the body of Jesus in order to prepare Him for burial, Pilate marvelled that He was dead so soon. And "calling unto him the centurion, he asked him whether He had been any while dead. *AND WHEN HE KNEW IT OF THE CENTURION, he gave the body to Joseph*" (Mark 15:43—45).

Then in Matthew 27:62—66 we read that the chief priests and Pharisees "came together unto Pilate, saying, Sir, we remember that that deceiver said, while He was yet alive, *After three days I will rise again.* Command therefore that the sepulchre be made sure until the third day, lest His disciples come by night, and steal Him away, and say unto the people, He is risen from the dead: so the last error shall be worse than the first.

"Pilate said unto them, Ye have a watch: go your way, make it as sure as ye can. So they went, and made the sepulchre sure, sealing the stone, and setting a watch."

Yes, there is plenty of proof positive that Jesus was dead when He was taken down from the cross—and even then His enemies took every possible precaution to see that His body would not be removed from the tomb. He had said He would rise again on the third day, and if His body disappeared from the sepulchre He would be a greater threat to them than when He walked among them. So to make His burial doubly sure, they sealed the tomb with a Roman seal and set over it the best guard Rome could afford!

The Angel of the Lord

But there were other guards present, unseen by human eye. *Angels* kept watch over the resting place of the Lord Jesus:

"In the end of the sabbath, as it began to dawn toward the first day of the week, came Mary Magdalene and the other Mary to see the sepulchre. And, behold, there was a great earthquake: *for THE ANGEL OF THE LORD descended from heaven, and came and rolled back the stone from the door, and sat upon it.* His countenance was like lightning, and his raiment white as snow: *and for fear of him the keepers did shake, and became as dead men*" (Matt. 28:1—4).

The Scripture says *the angel of the Lord* rolled the stone from the door of the sepulchre of Jesus — and I believe it. But he did not roll away the stone *in order to let the Lord come forth.* I believe the angel removed the stone in order for the soldiers and others to see that the body of Jesus was no longer in the tomb. This gave testimony to His promise to rise again, testimony that He had kept His word.

Multitudes witnessed the *death* of Jesus, but *not one mortal* witnessed His resurrection! Certainly the *disciples* did not see Him walk from the tomb. He had told them over and over again that He would rise from the dead — but they did not understand. To them, His death spelled defeat of their hopes, and they did not linger by the tomb.

The *women* who were His devout followers did not see Him come from the tomb. They appeared there on the resurrection morning, but they did not come to see the risen Lord. They were not expecting Him to rise again, and they brought spices to further embalm His body.

The *Roman soldiers* did not witness His resurrection. They were "as dead men," and when they revived and discovered that His body was missing, they went into Jerusalem "and shewed unto the chief priests all the things that were done. And when they were assembled with the elders, and had taken counsel, *they gave large money unto the soldiers*, saying, Say ye, His disciples came by night, and stole Him away while we slept. And if this come to the governor's ears, we will persuade him, and secure you.

"So (the soldiers) took the money, and did as they were taught: and this saying is commonly reported among the Jews until this day" (Matt. 28:11—15).

The devil is THE Lie and the father of lies; but the lie told by the Roman guards was so absurd that no thinking person would have believed it! In the

first place, any Roman soldier who fell asleep on duty
was executed without mercy. In the second place, if
the soldiers were asleep when the body of Jesus disappeared, how could they possibly have known what
happened to it? And if it was stolen, how was that
feat accomplished without being seen by people other
than the soldiers? It was the Passover season and
hundreds of folk were camped in the hillsides around
the city—pilgrims who had come from great distances
to attend the feast. It would have been almost impossible for the body of Jesus to have been carried
away without being seen by at least some of the people who were camped outside the city.

Also, if the Jewish leaders had *really believed* that
the body had been stolen by the disciples they would
have offered a large reward for its return, because to
produce the body of Jesus, *still in the bonds of death,*
would deny His resurrection! But no reward was
offered, no search was made for the body. Instead,
"large money" was paid to the Roman guards by way
of inducing them to spread the false report that the
disciples of Jesus had stolen His body from the tomb.

John's Remarkable Testimony

Perhaps the strongest testimony to the bodily resurrection of Jesus is given by John, the "disciple whom
Jesus loved." When Mary Magdalene came to the
sepulchre in early morning, "when it was yet dark,"
and saw the stone rolled away from the door, she
ran back toward the city until she met Peter and John.
To them she exclaimed, "They have taken away the
Lord out of the sepulchre, and we know not where
they have laid Him!"

Peter and John then ran to the sepulchre and found
it empty—but notice: Simon Peter "went into the
sepulchre, *and seeth the linen clothes lie, and the*

napkin, that was about His head, not lying with the linen clothes, but wrapped together in a place by itself. Then went in also that other disciple . . . and he saw, and believed" (John 20:1—8).

The graveclothes of Jesus were still in the tomb— not lying in a heap as though hurriedly discarded and tossed aside, but like a cocoon, as they had been wrapped around the Lord's body. The napkin which had been wrapped around His head lay by itself in another place, the proper distance from the graveclothes which still bore the shape of His body.

In accordance with Jewish custom in those days, as the body was wrapped for burial the embalming materials and spices were placed in the burial clothes. Thus the clothes *stiffened* around the body. This clearly signifies that when Jesus rose from the dead He simply emerged from the graveclothes as a butterfly emerges from its cocoon, leaving the garments intact, undisturbed, mute testimony that His body had *not* been stolen, but that He had indeed risen.

It would be beyond all reason to suggest that the disciples of Jesus stole His body from the tomb. They had not believed in His resurrection, they had not understood what He meant; and even *after* His resurrection *Thomas* would not believe when the other disciples told him they had *seen* the risen Lord! Their lack of faith in the resurrection is plainly shown by the fact that not one of them lingered near the tomb in expectancy on the morning of the third day; and when they finally *approached* the sepulchre they were amazed to find the stone rolled away. Had the disciples stayed near the tomb throughout the three days and nights of Christ's entombment, their actions might have added suspicion to the charge that they had stolen His body; but their absolute absence during that time is conclusive proof that they had nothing to do with His disappearance from the sepulchre.

Although no one actually witnessed the resurrection of Jesus, many saw Him *after* His resurrection—even on the day He arose. Now if the lie of the devil had been truth, if Jesus had only swooned on the cross instead of dying, He would have been a pitiable spectacle indeed when He revived and came forth after spending three days and nights in the grave! With the wound in His side, nail-wounds in His hands and feet, the scars in His brow still torn from the crown of thorns, He would have been too weak physically to do more than drag Himself about; but such was not the case. When Jesus appeared to the women and to His disciples, He was in perfect health. He was able to walk from Jerusalem to Emmaus—a distance of about twelve miles. Yes, in spite of the abuse heaped upon Him just before His crucifixion, in spite of the wounds that had been inflicted in His side, His hands, and His feet, when our Lord came forth from the tomb He was in perfect health!

The Day of His Resurrection

On the day Jesus rose from the dead He made five recorded appearances:

1. He appeared to Mary Magdalene:

"Mary stood without at the sepulchre weeping: and as she wept, she stooped down, and looked into the sepulchre, and seeth two angels in white sitting, the one at the head, and the other at the feet, where the body of Jesus had lain. And they say unto her, Woman, why weepest thou? She saith unto them, Because they have taken away my Lord, and I know not where they have laid Him.

"And when she had thus said, she turned herself back, and saw Jesus standing, and knew not that it was Jesus. Jesus saith unto her, Woman, why weepest thou? Whom seekest thou?

"She, supposing Him to be the gardener, saith unto Him, *Sir, if thou have borne Him hence, tell me where thou hast laid Him, and I will take Him away.* Jesus saith unto her, *Mary.* She turned herself, and saith unto Him, *Rabboni;* which is to say, *Master.*

"Jesus saith unto her, Touch me not; for I am not yet ascended to my Father: but go to my brethren, and say unto them, I ascend unto my Father, and your Father; and to my God, and your God.

"Mary Magdalene came and told the disciples that she had seen the Lord, and that He had spoken these things unto her" (John 20:11—18).

2. *He appeared to the women:*

"As they went to tell His disciples, behold, *Jesus met them, saying, All hail.* And they came and held Him by the feet, and worshipped Him. Then said Jesus unto them, Be not afraid: go tell my brethren that they go into Galilee, and there shall they see me" (Matt. 28:9, 10).

3. *He appeared to Peter:*

In I Corinthians 15:5 the Apostle Paul declared that Jesus "was seen of Cephas, then of the twelve," and in Luke 24:34 we find the plain statement, "The Lord is risen indeed, and hath appeared to Simon."

4. *Late in the afternoon of that same day He appeared to the two disciples on the road to Emmaus:*

"And, behold, two of them went that same day to a village called Emmaus, which was from Jerusalem about threescore furlongs. And they talked together of all these things which had happened. And it came to pass, that, while they communed together and reasoned, *Jesus Himself drew near, and went with them.* But their eyes were holden that they should not know Him. And He said unto them, What manner of communications are these that ye have one to another, as ye walk, and are sad? . . . And beginning at Moses and all the prophets, He expounded unto them in all the Scriptures the things concerning Himself.

"And they drew nigh unto the village, whither
they went: and He made as though He would have
gone further. But they constrained Him, saying, Abide
with us: for it is toward evening, and the day is far
spent. And He went in to tarry with them. *And it
came to pass, as He sat at meat with them, He took
bread, and blessed it, and brake, and gave to them.
AND THEIR EYES WERE OPENED, AND THEY
KNEW HIM; and He vanished out of their sight"*
(Luke 24:13—31 in part).

5. *On the evening of the same day, the risen Lord
appeared to a number of His disciples who had gathered in the upper room:*

"Then the same day at evening, being the first
day of the week, when the doors were shut where the
disciples were assembled for fear of the Jews, came
Jesus and stood in the midst, and saith unto them,
Peace be unto you" (John 20:19).

Luke records this appearing of Jesus in these words:
"And as they thus spake, Jesus Himself stood in the
midst of them, and saith unto them, Peace be unto
you. *But they were terrified and affrighted, and supposed that they had seen a spirit.*

"And He said unto them, Why are ye troubled?
and why do thoughts arise in your hearts? Behold my
hands and my feet, that it is I myself: handle me,
and see; *for a spirit hath not flesh and bones, as ye
see me have.*

"And when He had thus spoken, He shewed them
His hands and His feet. And while they yet believed
not for joy, and wondered, He said unto them, *Have
ye here any meat?* And they gave Him a piece of a
broiled fish, and of an honeycomb. *And He took it,
and did eat before them.* And He said unto them,
These are the words which I spake unto you, while I
was yet with you, that all things must be fulfilled,

which were written in the law of Moses, and in the prophets, and in the psalms, concerning me.

"Then opened He their understanding, that they might understand the Scriptures" (Luke 24:36—45).

Thomas was not present at the Lord's first appearing to the disciples in the upper room, but eight days later Jesus again appeared to them, and on that occasion Thomas was present. John gives the following account:

"But Thomas, one of the twelve, called Didymus, was not with them when Jesus came. The other disciples therefore said unto him, *We have seen the Lord.* But he said unto them, *Except I shall see in His hands the print of the nails, and put my finger into the print of the nails, and thrust my hand into His side, I will not believe.*

"And after eight days again His disciples were within, and Thomas with them: then came Jesus, the doors being shut, and stood in the midst, and said, *Peace be unto you.* Then saith He to Thomas, Reach hither thy finger, and behold my hands; and reach hither thy hand, and thrust it into my side: and be not faithless, but believing.

"And Thomas answered and said unto Him, *MY LORD AND MY GOD.* Jesus saith unto him, Thomas, because thou hast seen me, thou hast believed: blessed are they that have not seen, and yet have believed" (John 20:24—29).

On a later occasion Jesus appeared to seven of His disciples on the shore of the Sea of Galilee:

"After these things Jesus shewed Himself again to the disciples at the sea of Tiberias; and on this wise shewed He Himself. There were together Simon Peter, and Thomas called Didymus, and Nathanael of Cana in Galilee, and the sons of Zebedee, and two other of His disciples. Simon Peter saith unto them, I go a fishing. They say unto him, We also go with thee.

They went forth, and entered into a ship immediately;
and that night they caught nothing. But when the
morning was now come, Jesus stood on the shore:
but the disciples knew not that it was Jesus.

"Then Jesus saith unto them, Children, have ye
any meat? They answered Him, No. And He said
unto them, Cast the net on the right side of the ship,
and ye shall find. They cast therefore, and now they
were not able to draw it for the multitude of fishes.
Therefore that disciple whom Jesus loved saith unto
Peter, It is the Lord. Now when Simon Peter heard
that it was the Lord, he girt his fisher's coat unto
him, (for he was naked,) and did cast himself into the
sea. And the other disciples came in a little ship;
(for they were not far from land, but as it were two
hundred cubits,) dragging the net with fishes.

"As soon as they were come to land, they saw a
fire of coals there, and fish laid thereon, and bread.
Jesus saith unto them, Bring of the fish which ye have
now caught. Simon Peter went up, and drew the net
to land full of great fishes, an hundred and fifty and
three: and for all there were so many, yet was not
the net broken.

"Jesus saith unto them, Come and dine. And none
of the disciples durst ask Him, Who art thou? knowing
that it was the Lord. Jesus then cometh, and taketh
bread, and giveth them, and fish likewise. *This is
now the third time that Jesus shewed Himself to His
disciples, after that He was risen from the dead"*
(John 21:1—14).

Jesus again appeared to the eleven, and gave them
commission to preach the Gospel to "all nations":

"Then the eleven disciples went away into Galilee,
into a mountain where Jesus had appointed them. . . .
And Jesus came and spake unto them, saying, *All
power is given unto me in heaven and in earth. GO
YE THEREFORE, AND TEACH ALL NATIONS,*

baptizing them in the name of the Father, and of the Son, and of the Holy Ghost: *Teaching them to observe all things whatsoever I have commanded you: and, lo, I AM WITH YOU ALWAY, EVEN UNTO THE END OF THE WORLD.* Amen" (Matt. 28:16—20).

In Mark 16:14—20 we read, "Afterward He appeared unto the eleven as they sat at meat, and upbraided them with their unbelief and hardness of heart, because they believed not them which had seen Him after He was risen. And He said unto them, Go ye into all the world, and preach the Gospel to every creature. He that believeth and is baptized shall be saved; but he that believeth not shall be damned. And these signs shall follow them that believe: In my name shall they cast out devils; they shall speak with new tongues; they shall take up serpents; and if they drink any deadly thing, it shall not hurt them; they shall lay hands on the sick, and they shall recover.

"So then after the Lord had spoken unto them, He was received up into heaven, and sat on the right hand of God. And they went forth, and preached every where, the Lord working with them, and confirming the Word with signs following."

In I Corinthians 15:6 the Apostle Paul tells us that Jesus *"was seen of above five hundred brethren at once"*—and it is absurd to suggest that five hundred people could all be mistaken or deceived! Even though Paul penned his epistle to the Corinthians twenty-seven years after Jesus rose from the dead, he declared that the greater part of those five hundred witnesses were still living at that time.

Jesus then appeared to *James* (I Cor. 15:7), and forty days after His resurrection He ascended to heaven, even while He spoke with His disciples on the Mount of Olives:

"He led them out as far as to Bethany, and He lifted up His hands, and blessed them. *And it came to pass, while He blessed them, He was parted from them, AND CARRIED UP INTO HEAVEN.* And they worshipped Him, and returned to Jerusalem with great joy: and were continually in the temple, praising and blessing God" (Luke 24:50—53).

In Acts 1:1—11, Luke recorded a vivid description of the Lord's last moments with His disciples before He ascended back to the heavenly Father:

"The former treatise have I made, O Theophilus, of all that Jesus began both to do and teach, until the day in which He was taken up, after that He through the Holy Ghost had given commandments unto the apostles whom He had chosen: to whom also *He shewed Himself alive after His passion by MANY INFALLIBLE PROOFS, being seen of them forty days, and speaking of the things pertaining to the kingdom of God:* And, being assembled together with them, commanded them that they should not depart from Jerusalem, but wait for the promise of the Father, which, saith He, ye have heard of me. For John truly baptized with water; but ye shall be baptized with the Holy Ghost not many days hence.

"When they therefore were come together, they asked of Him, saying, Lord, wilt thou at this time restore again the kingdom to Israel? And He said unto them, It is not for you to know the times or the seasons, which the Father hath put in His own power. But ye shall receive power, after that the Holy Ghost is come upon you: and ye shall be witnesses unto me both in Jerusalem, and in all Judaea, and in Samaria, and unto the uttermost part of the earth.

"*And when He had spoken these things, WHILE THEY BEHELD, HE WAS TAKEN UP; AND A CLOUD RECEIVED HIM OUT OF THEIR SIGHT.*

"And while they looked stedfastly toward heaven

as He went up, behold, two men stood by them in white apparel; which also said, *Ye men of Galilee, why stand ye gazing up into heaven? THIS SAME JESUS, which is taken up from you into heaven, shall so come IN LIKE MANNER AS YE HAVE SEEN HIM GO INTO HEAVEN."*

The question is often asked, "Why did the risen Christ not appear to Pilate, or to the chief priests and the unbelieving religious leaders — those who were His enemies?"

The answer is found in the Word of God. Jesus clearly declared to the Jews, "Ye shall not see me henceforth, till ye shall say, Blessed is He that cometh in the name of the Lord" (Matt. 23:39). He was not referring to the Rapture, but to *the revelation stage* of His second coming, the time when He will come "with clouds; *and every eye shall see Him,* and they also which pierced Him: and all kindreds of the earth shall wail because of Him" (Rev. 1:7).

Saul of Tarsus was the only one of His enemies to whom Jesus appeared after the resurrection. Saul (later to become the Apostle Paul) was traveling from Jerusalem to Damascus, with authority to persecute the Christians in that city. This was, of course, after the Lord's ascension; but God parted the sky, Jesus looked down upon the man who, *by his own admission,* was outstanding in his persecution of the Church — and the brightness of His face struck Saul down and blinded him! (Read the account in Acts 9:1–20.) In speaking of this meeting with Christ, Paul said, "Last of all *He was seen of me also, as of one born out of due time.* For I am the least of the apostles, that am not meet to be called an apostle, because I persecuted the Church of God" (I Cor. 15:8, 9).

Approximately sixty-five years after His resurrection, Jesus appeared to John the Beloved on the Isle of Patmos. He appeared for a specific purpose — to

give John the last book in the Bible, *The Revelation,*
which is in itself sufficient proof of the Lord's resurrection.

No Discrepancy

It has been suggested that there is a discrepancy
between John's account of the visit of the women to
the sepulchre on the morning of the resurrection of
Jesus, and the account of that event as given by the
other Gospel writers—but not so. There are no dis-
crepancies in the Word of God when the truth is rightly divided.

In Mark 16:1—7 we learn that Mary Magdalene,
along with two other women, came to the tomb at
dawn.   As they approached, wondering how they
should manage to roll the huge stone away from the
door, they saw the stone *already* rolled away, and the
sepulchre was empty. Mary *left* the other women and
ran back toward the city to tell the disciples that
the body of Jesus was missing from the tomb.

After Mary had gone, the two other women *entered*
the sepulchre and saw a young man in white garments.
He said to them, "Be not affrighted: Ye seek Jesus
of Nazareth, which was crucified: He is risen; He is
not here: behold the place where they laid Him. But
go your way, tell His disciples and Peter that He goeth before you into Galilee: there shall ye see Him,
as He said unto you." The women left the tomb at
once.

In the meantime, Mary Magdalene met Peter and
John and told them, *"They have taken away the Lord
out of the sepulchre, and we know not where they
have laid Him!"* The two disciples ran to the tomb,
saw that it was empty save for the grave clothes, and
"then the disciples went away again unto their own
home" (John 20:1—10).

Mary then *returned* to the tomb, alone—and weeping. She stooped and looked into the tomb, and saw two angels robed in white, one sitting at the head and the other at the foot of the place where the body of Jesus had lain. They asked her, "Woman, why weepest thou? She saith unto them, *Because they have taken away my Lord, and I know not where they have laid Him!"*

It was then that Jesus appeared, but in her grief Mary did not recognize Him. She supposed Him to be the gardener—and then He spoke her name: "Mary!"

"She turned herself, and saith unto Him, *Rabboni;* which is to say, *Master.* Jesus saith unto her, Touch me not; for I am not yet ascended to my Father: but go to my brethren, and say unto them, I ascend unto my Father, and your Father; and to my God, and your God." Jesus then disappeared, and Mary went in search of the disciples, to tell them she had seen the risen Christ (John 20:11—18).

Shortly after this, Jesus met *the other women* on their way to tell His disciples of the empty tomb. He greeted them, saying, "All hail. *And they came AND HELD HIM BY THE FEET, and worshipped Him"* (Matt. 28:9).

This brings up the question of why Jesus said to Mary, "Touch me *not,"* and then a short time later *permitted the other women to touch Him.* The answer is simple: Between the time Jesus forbade Mary to touch Him and the time when He met the other women, *He had ascended to God the Father*—and returned to earth! Certainly if we believe the Word of God we will have no difficulty in believing that Jesus could have made His ascension and return to earth in a split second of time. Personally, I believe He went to the Father, presented His shed blood, then returned and met the group of women as they searched for the disciples to tell them that the body of their Lord was missing from the tomb.

On the Day of Atonement, after God's appointed high priest offered the blood of the atonement on the altar, if anyone *touched* him before he could carry the blood into the holy of holies and make atonement, the offering was of no avail. *Jesus* offered His *own* blood on the cross; and if Mary had touched Him before He ascended to the Father (into the most holy place) to offer His blood, His finished work and His blood sacrifice would have been rendered ineffective. He came, not to destroy the law, but to *fulfill* it, to satisfy every jot and tittle. Therefore He commanded Mary not to touch Him.

The Risen Lord Was Real

Although Jesus rose from the grave in a glorified body, He was nevertheless in a body of flesh and bone, a physical form that could—and did—perform the functions of a human body. True, He had the power to enter a room with all the doors closed, He could appear and disappear at will, and He could remain unrecognized until such time as He desired to reveal His identity. But in spite of His spiritual qualities, the risen Christ was a Man of flesh and bones, not a spirit as the disciples supposed Him to be when they first saw Him after His resurrection (Luke 24:39).

We have already discussed the fact that the women held Him by the feet as they worshipped Him on the day He rose from the dead (Matt. 28:9).

He asked His disciples for food, and ate broiled fish and honeycomb in their presence (Luke 24:41—43).

He walked several miles with two of His disciples on the road from Jerusalem to Emmaus, and "as He sat at meat with them, He took bread, and blessed it, and brake, and gave to them" (Luke 24:13—31).

He invited Thomas to examine the wounds in His

hands and side (John 20:27).

He breakfasted with His disciples on the shore of the Sea of Galilee after the weary men had fished unsuccessfully all night (John 21:9—14).

The Scriptures are filled with proof positive that the Lord's resurrection body was real, and *our own resurrection bodies* will be like *His* glorified body insofar as capabilities and powers are concerned. In I John 3:2 we read, *"Beloved, NOW are we the sons of God, and it doth not yet appear what we SHALL BE: but we know that, when He shall appear, WE SHALL BE LIKE HIM; for we shall see Him as He is!"*

The bodily resurrection of Jesus changed the whole attitude of His disciples and completely revolutionized their lives. Whereas they had been fearful, they became fearless. Whereas they had been powerless, they became powerful. Whereas they had been wavering, unfaithful followers of Jesus, they became faithful servants. His bodily resurrection became the central theme of their preaching, further proof that He was very God in flesh. As very God, He laid down His life for us. As very God, He rose again from the dead. Therefore I ask with the Apostle Paul, "Why should it be thought a thing incredible . . . that God should raise the dead?" (Acts 26:8).

Christ Is Risen

Christ is risen! This is the victorious cry of the Gospel of the grace of God, and the Gospel is *the power of God* unto salvation. The message of Calvary is the message of the resurrection: He died for our sins "according to the Scriptures," He rose again because it was not possible that death should hold Him. He is the fountain of all created life: "In Him was life; and the life was the light of men" (John 1:4). He is "the Prince of life" (Acts 3:15)—and He who is *the Author of LIFE* could not be conquered by death!

Jesus could have returned to heaven *without a body.* He was with the Father in the beginning (John 1:1, 18), He existed *eternally* with the Father—but without a human body. Before the Incarnation He was The Eternal One, and He could have *returned* to the Father as The Eternal One immediately after His death. He could have returned in spiritual nature, as He was before He took a body of humiliation. But in order to carry out the full meaning of redemption it was necessary that He return to the Father in His *resurrection body.* His resurrection was the Redeemer's total victory over death—and that is what He came into the world to accomplish. He came to destroy him who had the power of death:

"We see Jesus, who was made a little lower than the angels for the suffering of death, crowned with glory and honour; that He by the grace of God should taste death for every man. . . . Forasmuch then as the children are partakers of flesh and blood, He also Himself likewise took part of the same; *that through death He might destroy him that had the power of death, that is, the devil;* and deliver them who through fear of death were all their lifetime subject to bondage" (Heb. 2:9, 14, 15).

The bodily resurrection of Jesus proclaimed total victory over physical death, and if He had returned to heaven *without* His resurrection body that victory would not have been displayed. It was prophesied, *"Thou wilt not leave my SOUL in hell; neither wilt thou suffer thine Holy One to see CORRUPTION"* (Psalm 16:10). If Jesus had returned in spiritual nature only, He would have displayed victory over death spiritually and morally *but not physically*, and His victory would not have been complete.

Therefore, since He conquered the world, the flesh,

the devil, death, hell, and the grave, He ascended back to the heavenly Father *bodily*, thereby proclaiming complete victory over spiritual, moral, and physical death! *We* are more than conquerors because *Jesus* conquered, and delivered soul, spirit, and body from death.

Death is not cessation of existence, but dissolution of the human personality; not extinction of being, but the tearing asunder of the connection between spirit, soul, and body. Therefore *victory* over death must be displayed in the restoration of this oneness, the *re-establishing* of this organic connection of soul, spirit, and body. When man dies, the body returns to dust; but the eternal part of man—the soul—returns to God who gave it. Therefore, *because Jesus rose again bodily*, when He comes in the Rapture the *believer's* body will be raised incorruptible and will be reunited with soul and spirit. Then our salvation will be complete, and we will live in a glorified body throughout eternity. The bodily resurrection of Jesus reveals Him as Victor over physical death. Had He not risen *bodily* there would have been no triumphant display of that victory:

"So when this corruptible shall have put on incorruption, and this mortal shall have put on immortality, then shall be brought to pass the saying that is written, *Death is swallowed up in victory.* O death, where *is* thy sting? O grave, where *is* thy victory? The sting of death is sin; and the strength of sin is the law. *But thanks be to God, which giveth us the victory THROUGH OUR LORD JESUS CHRIST!"* (I Cor. 15:54—57).

It is appointed unto men once to die (Heb. 9:27). Whether saint or sinner, *in Adam ALL die* (I Cor. 15:22). Death is the last enemy to be destroyed (I Cor. 15:26), and only by the resurrection of the body can it be shown that that enemy has been wholly conquered.

The sting of death is sin; but thanks be unto God, *Jesus PAID the sin-debt.* He laid His life down for our sins, He rose again for our justification. Now the believer can look death in the face and cry, "O death, where is thy sting? O grave, where is thy victory?" We know that *we* are conquerors *because HE conquered.* The Spirit 'of Him that raised up Jesus from the dead shall also quicken our mortal bodies (Rom. 8:11), and because He lives, we shall live also. *HE is our victory!*

Christ's Bodily Resurrection
the Foundation of Saving Faith

"Now if Christ be preached that He rose from the dead, how say some among you that there is no resurrection of the dead? But if there be no resurrection of the dead, then is Christ not risen: and if Christ be not risen, then is our preaching vain, and your faith is also vain. Yea, and we are found false witnesses of God; because we have testified of God that He raised up Christ: whom He raised not up, if so be that the dead rise not. For if the dead rise not, then is not Christ raised: *AND IF CHRIST BE NOT RAISED, YOUR FAITH IS VAIN; YE ARE YET IN YOUR SINS. Then they also which are fallen asleep in Christ are perished.* If in this life only we have hope in Christ, we are of all men most miserable. *But now IS Christ risen from the dead, AND BECOME THE FIRSTFRUITS of THEM THAT SLEPT"* (I Cor. 15:12—20).

We are saved by God's grace. Grace is unmerited, unearned favor—God's favor toward man. Man *appropriates* grace *by faith*—but how is saving faith exercised? The answer is found in Romans 10:13—17:

"For *whosoever shall call upon the name of the*

Lord shall be saved. How then shall they call on Him in whom they have not *believed?* and how shall they believe in Him of whom they have not *heard?* and how shall they hear *without a preacher?* and how shall they preach, except they be *sent?* As it is written, How beautiful are the feet of them that preach the Gospel of peace, and bring glad tidings of good things! But they have not all obeyed the Gospel. For Esaias saith, Lord, who hath believed our report? *So then FAITH COMETH BY HEARING, and hearing by the Word of God."*

Now let us see, step by step, how we exercise saving faith unto salvation:

I Corinthians 1:21 declares, "After that in the wisdom of God the world by wisdom knew not God, it pleased God *by the foolishness of preaching* to save them that believe." In the passage just quoted from Romans 10, Paul plainly states that *"whosoever* shall call upon the name of the Lord shall be saved"—but it is evident that the unbeliever cannot *call* until he has *believed,* he cannot believe in Him of whom he has never *heard,* and he cannot *hear* unless the Word be *preached.* So, since *"faith cometh by hearing,* and hearing by the Word of God," it pleases God to call men to preach the Word. Sinners *hear* the Word, the Word brings saving faith to the heart, and the unbeliever, hearing and *believing* the Word, exercises faith in the shed blood and finished work of Jesus; and that exercise of faith brings saving grace.

THEREFORE: since faith comes through preaching the Word of God to those who are lost, and since the message of the Word is the death, burial, and resurrection of Jesus "according to the Scriptures," I declare that the bodily resurrection of Jesus is the foundation of saving faith; and if Jesus had not risen there would be no salvation, there would be no message to bring salvation, the preacher would have no

saving message to preach in order to turn the sinner
from his sin!

Individual faith goes back to the faith that was in
the beginning: When an individual believes on Jesus,
that individual believes because of the testimony of
the person who delivered the Gospel message that
caused him to believe. The unbeliever who hears and
believes a preacher's message, believes because the
preacher believed before him; and the *preacher* believed because he heard someone deliver the Gospel
message. Thus saving faith goes back to those who
first exercised faith in the finished work of the Lord
Jesus Christ.

Jesus instructed His disciples to tarry in Jerusalem
until they were endued with power from on high (Luke
24:49). In Acts 1:8, moments before He was taken up
into heaven He said, "Ye shall receive power, after
that the Holy Ghost is come upon you: and ye shall
be witnesses unto me both in Jerusalem, and in all
Judaea, and in Samaria, *and unto the uttermost part
of the earth"* — and that includes US!

The men who waited in the upper room preached
the Gospel, and souls were saved. Those who were
saved also preached the Gospel and *other* souls were
saved. Thus through the Gospel message of the death,
burial, and resurrection of Jesus, *those who believe*
are saved today. Individual faith comes through the
testimony of those who have already believed, and
those who believed before us could not have exercised
faith apart from the message of the men who walked
with Jesus, witnessed His death, and gave personal
testimony to His bodily resurrection. Because *they*
believed and preached the Gospel, *we* have the message that saves today:

"Now therefore ye are no more strangers and foreigners, but fellowcitizens with the saints, and of the
household of God; *and are built upon the foundation*

OF THE APOSTLES AND PROPHETS, JESUS CHRIST HIMSELF BEING THE CHIEF CORNER STONE; in whom all the building fitly framed together groweth unto an holy temple in the Lord: in whom ye also are builded together for an habitation of God through the Spirit" (Eph. 2:19—22).

John the Beloved testified, "That which was from the beginning, *which we have HEARD, which we have SEEN with our eyes, which we have looked upon, AND OUR HANDS HAVE HANDLED,* of the Word of life; (for the life was manifested, and *we have seen it, and bear witness,* and shew unto you that eternal life, which was with the Father, and was manifested unto us;) *That which we have seen and heard declare we unto you,* that ye also may have fellowship with us: and truly our fellowship is with the Father, and with His Son Jesus Christ. And these things write we unto you, that your joy may be full" (I John 1:1—4).

It is true that the faith of the disciples crumbled when Jesus died on the cross, but it was re-established through His bodily resurrection and His appearing to them in His resurrection body. In spite of the fact that Jesus had repeatedly told the disciples that He had come into the world to die, they could not comprehend the meaning of His words. They thought He had come to set up a glorious kingdom, and when He was arrested, tried, condemned, and crucified, their faith crumbled and they fled. They did not believe He would rise again, and had He *not* risen bodily, no reasonable person would ever have believed on the crucified Jesus. The fact that He remained in the tomb would have contradicted His promise to rise again, a promise made on many occasions.

For example, in Matthew 16:21 we read, "From that time forth began Jesus to shew unto His disciples, how that He must go unto Jerusalem, and suffer many things of the elders and chief priests and scribes, and be killed, *and be raised again the third day.*"

In Matthew 17:22, 23, Jesus said to His disciples, "The Son of man shall be betrayed into the hands of men: and they shall kill Him, *and the third day He shall be raised again. . . .*"

In Matthew 20:18, 19 Jesus took the twelve disciples apart from the crowd and told them, "Behold, we go up to Jerusalem; and the Son of man shall be betrayed unto the chief priests and unto the scribes, and they shall condemn Him to death, and shall deliver Him to the Gentiles to mock, and to scourge, and to crucify Him: *and the third day He shall rise again.*"

Even to His enemies Jesus declared, "As Jonas was three days and three nights in the whale's belly; *so shall the Son of man be three days and three nights in the heart of the earth*" (Matt. 12:40).

Also to His enemies He said, speaking of His body, "Destroy this temple, *and in three days I will raise it up*" (John 2:19).

So you see, if Jesus had not risen bodily, certainly no one would have believed in Him as Saviour. But the miracle of the resurrection occurred exactly as He had said it would. He rose the third day, appeared in His resurrection body on many occasions, and *the disciples "remembered HIS WORDS"* (Luke 24:8). Faith comes by hearing, and hearing by the Word. The disciples believed because Jesus rose again bodily as He declared He would, and *WE believe because THEY believed.*

The bodily resurrection of Jesus Christ is God's seal on the Person and work of His only begotten Son: "This Jesus hath God raised up, whereof we all are witnesses. Therefore being by the right hand of God exalted, and having received of the Father the promise of the Holy Ghost, He hath shed forth this, which ye now see and hear" (Acts 2:32, 33).

The bodily resurrection of the Lord Jesus Christ demonstrated that He was the Prophet who would come, He was God's only begotten Son: He was "declared to be the Son of God with power, according to the Spirit of holiness, by the resurrection from the dead" (Rom. 1:4).

The bodily resurrection of Jesus is the seal on the testimony of the Old Testament prophets, for by His resurrection we know they prophesied truth:

The Psalmist prophesied, "Thou wilt not leave my soul in hell; neither wilt thou suffer thine Holy One to see corruption" (Psalm 16:10).

Hosea prophesied, "After two days will He revive us: in the third day He will raise us up, and we shall live in His sight" (Hos. 6:2).

Isaiah prophesied: "He was taken from prison and from judgment: and who shall declare His generation? For He was cut off out of the land of the living: for the transgression of my people was He stricken. And He made His grave with the wicked, and with the rich in His death; because He had done no violence, neither was any deceit in His mouth. Yet it pleased the Lord to bruise Him; He hath put Him to grief: when thou shalt make His soul an offering for sin, He shall see His seed, He shall prolong His days, and the pleasure of the Lord shall prosper in His hand" (Isa. 53:8—10).

The bodily resurrection of Jesus is the seal on His own testimony given to His disciples concerning His suffering, death, and resurrection: "From that time forth began Jesus to shew unto His disciples how that He must go unto Jerusalem, and suffer many things of the elders and chief priests and scribes, and be killed, and be raised again the third day" (Matt. 16:21).

To the Jews Jesus said, "Destroy this temple, and in three days I will raise it up. . . . But He spake of the temple of His body. When therefore He was risen from the dead, *His disciples remembered that He had said this unto them; and they believed the Scripture, and the WORD which Jesus had said"* (John 2:19—22).

The bodily resurrection of the Lord Jesus Christ is the seal on the testimony of His disciples: The Apostle Paul declared, "If Christ be not risen, then is our preaching vain, and your faith is also vain. *Yea, and we are found false witnesses of God;* because we have testified of God that He raised up Christ: whom He raised not up, if so be that the dead rise not" (I Cor. 15:14, 15).

The bodily resurrection of Jesus is the seal on His Sonship: "God hath fulfilled the same unto us their children, in that He hath raised up Jesus again; as it is also written in the second Psalm, *Thou art my Son, this day have I begotten thee"* (Acts 13:33).

The bodily resurrection of Jesus is the seal on His Kingship: "And as concerning that He raised Him up from the dead, now no more to return to corruption, He said on this wise, I will give you the sure mercies of David" (Acts 13:34).

The bodily resurrection of Jesus is the seal on His full authority as the true, universal Judge: "Because (God) hath appointed a day, in the which He will judge the world in righteousness by that Man whom He hath ordained; whereof He hath given assurance unto all men, in that He hath raised Him from the dead" (Acts 17:31).

The bodily resurrection of the Lord Jesus Christ is the seal and full guarantee of the future bodily resurrection of every born again believer:

"But I would not have you to be ignorant, brethren, concerning them which are asleep, that ye sorrow not, even as others which have no hope. *FOR IF WE BELIEVE THAT JESUS DIED AND ROSE A-GAIN, EVEN SO THEM ALSO WHICH SLEEP IN*

JESUS WILL GOD BRING WITH HIM. For this we say unto you by the Word of the Lord, that we which are alive and remain unto the coming of the Lord shall not prevent them which are asleep. *For the Lord Himself shall descend from heaven with a shout, with the voice of the archangel, and with the trump of God: and THE DEAD IN CHRIST SHALL RISE FIRST:* Then we which are alive and remain shall be caught up together with them in the clouds, to meet the Lord in the air: and so shall we ever be with the Lord. Wherefore *comfort one another with these words"* (I Thess. 4:13—18).

The bodily resurrection of the Lord Jesus Christ is a proven fact, the most authentic and best attested event in the history of salvation by grace through faith in the shed blood of the Lamb of God, foreordained before the foundation of the world!

Paul's Testimony Concerning the Bodily Resurrection of Jesus

God called the Apostle Paul to be minister to the Gentiles. In Romans 11:13 Paul himself testified, "I speak to you Gentiles, inasmuch as I am the apostle of the Gentiles, I magnify mine office."

God revealed to Paul the mystery of the New Testament Church, a mystery hidden from eternity:

"For this cause I Paul, the prisoner of Jesus Christ for you Gentiles, if ye have heard of the dispensation of the grace of God which is given me to you-ward: How that by revelation He made known unto me the mystery; (as I wrote afore in few words, whereby, when ye read, ye may understand my knowledge in the mystery of Christ) which in other ages was not made known unto the sons of men, as it is now revealed unto His holy apostles and prophets by the Spirit; that the Gentiles should be fellowheirs, and of the

same body, and partakers of His promise in Christ
by the Gospel: Whereof I was made a minister, according to the gift of the grace of God given unto me
by the effectual working of His power.

"Unto me, who am less than the least of all saints,
is this grace given, that I should preach among the
Gentiles the unsearchable riches of Christ; and to
make all men see what is the fellowship of the mystery, which from the beginning of the world hath been
hid in God, who created all things by Jesus Christ:
to the intent that now unto the principalities and
powers in heavenly places might be known by the
Church the manifold wisdom of God, according to
the eternal purpose which He purposed in Christ Jesus
our Lord: in whom we have boldness and access with
confidence by the faith of Him" (Eph. 3:1–12).

In I Corinthians chapter 15, Paul sets forth four
clearly-stated proofs of the bodily resurrection of the
Lord Jesus Christ:
1. *The experience of salvation as accomplished in
the believers in Corinth:* "Moreover, brethren, I declare unto you the Gospel which I preached unto you,
which also ye have received, and wherein ye stand;
by which also ye are saved, if ye keep in memory
what I preached unto you, unless ye have believed
in vain" (I Cor. 15:1, 2).

Paul here declares that he preached *the Gospel*
to the Corinthians, they received the Gospel, they
were standing in the Gospel, they were saved by the
Gospel—and the next two verses give a clear *definition*
of the Gospel.
2. *Scripture proves that Jesus rose bodily from the
dead:* "For I delivered unto you first of all that which
I also received, how that Christ died for our sins according to the Scriptures; and that He was buried,
and that He rose again the third day according to
the Scriptures" (I Cor. 15:3, 4).

Here we see that the Gospel is *the death, burial, and resurrection of Jesus* "according to the Scriptures" —and the "Scriptures" to which Paul refers are the Old Testament prophecies (such as Isaiah, Zechariah, and many other of the prophets set forth), as well as prophecies made by Jesus Himself while He was on earth.

3. *Many witnesses prove the bodily resurrection of Jesus:* "He was seen of Cephas, then of the twelve: After that, He was seen of above five hundred brethren at once: of whom the greater part remain unto this present, but some are fallen asleep. After that, He was seen of James; then of all the apostles. And last of all He was seen of me also, as of one born out of due time" (I Cor. 15:5—8).

There were many living witnesses in the days of the Corinthian church who could testify that they saw the Lord Jesus after His bodily resurrection. Paul, "as one born out of due time," saw Him on the road to Damascus, after the Lord's resurrection and ascension.

4. *Christ's finished work is proof of His resurrection:* "If there be no resurrection of the dead, then is Christ not risen: and if Christ be not risen, then is our preaching vain, and your faith is also vain. Yea, and we are found false witnesses of God; because we have testified of God that He raised up Christ: whom He raised not up, if so be that the dead rise not. For if the dead rise not, then is not Christ raised: and if Christ be not raised, your faith is vain; ye are yet in your sins. Then they also which are fallen asleep in Christ are perished. If in this life only we have hope in Christ, we are of all men most miserable" (I Cor. 15:13—19).

Salvation comes by faith in the finished work of Jesus, and had He not risen from the grave His work would not have been finished.

We cannot separate the cross and the bodily resurrection of Jesus; they belong together. The cross was a divine imperative; the resurrection was just as surely *a divine MUST*, for had He not risen bodily as He declared He would, the shedding of His blood would have been to no avail. If we could preach only the blood, if we did not have proof of His bodily resurrection, our preaching would be empty and in vain. *Christ crucified* meant Christ *risen*, because the crucified Christ died in order to rise again. His death and resurrection were both necessary that we might be saved. In John 10:17, 18 He declared:

"Therefore doth my Father love me, because I lay down my life, that I might take it again. No man taketh it from me, but I lay it down of myself. I have power to lay it down, and I have power to take it again. This commandment have I received of my Father."

Christ *the Risen One* lives forever as *the Crucified One*. Paul declared, "I determined not to know any thing among you, save *Jesus Christ, and Him crucified*" (I Cor. 2:2). In Revelation 5:6 John the Beloved tells us, "I beheld, and, lo, in the midst of the throne and of the four beasts, and in the midst of the elders, stood *a Lamb as it had been slain*, having seven horns and seven eyes, which are the seven Spirits of God sent forth into all the earth."

Christ's resurrection is eternally connected with His cross. This is plainly seen in John 20:24–29 when Thomas vowed that he would not believe in the risen Lord unless he could see and touch the nailprints in His hands, and thrust his hand into the wound in His side. Jesus gave him the opportunity to do just that. The Scripture does not tell us that Thomas *touched* the scars. He saw the risen Christ, saw the scars in His hands and side, and exclaimed, "My Lord and my God!"

Zechariah tells us that when Jesus returns in the Revelation and every eye shall see Him, the scars will still be visible. All Israel will see Him, "and one shall say unto Him, *What are these wounds in thine hands?* Then He shall answer, *Those with which I was wounded in the house of my friends"* (Zech. 13:6).

There is no doubt in my mind that the marks of Calvary will be with Jesus throughout eternity—yes, even to the thorn-prints in His brow! and this should cause us to love Him more, worship Him more, and glorify His name even more through the endless ages to come.

Redemption of the soul rests upon the saving power of the cross of Jesus and His bodily resurrection. These divine facts *in unison* make redemption possible. We are reconciled to God by faith in Christ's finished work; and His finished work includes all that He did *before* His death, plus His death on the cross, plus His bodily resurrection and all that He did up to the very moment He ascended, bodily, back to the Father's right hand. The reconciliation of the believer is a fact *because* the believer exercises faith in Christ, His cross, and His bodily resurrection:

"For if, when we were enemies, we were reconciled to God by the *death* of His Son, much more, being reconciled, we shall be saved by His *life"* (Rom. 5:10).

Through Christ's cross and His bodily resurrection we have divine assurance concerning the putting away of sin in believers: "For in that He died, He died unto sin once: but in that He liveth, He liveth unto God. Likewise reckon ye also yourselves to be dead indeed unto sin, but alive unto God through Jesus Christ our Lord" (Rom. 6:10, 11).

Through Christ's cross and His bodily resurrection we have divine assurance of fellowship with Him— now and throughout eternity: "For God hath not appointed us to wrath, but to obtain salvation by our

Lord Jesus Christ, who died for us, that, whether we
wake or sleep, we should live together with Him"
(I Thess. 5:9, 10).

Through Christ's cross and His bodily resurrection,
He is Lord of all: "For to this end Christ both died,
and rose, and revived, that He might be Lord both
of the dead and living" (Rom. 14:9).

Through Christ's cross and His bodily resurrection,
He is our great High Priest. As the Man Christ Jesus
He sits at the right hand of God the Father to make
intercession for all believers: "Who is he that con-
demneth? It is Christ that died, yea rather, that is
risen again, who is even at the right hand of God,
who also maketh intercession for us" (Rom. 8:34).

Because of Christ's death on the cross and His
glorious bodily resurrection, *He will come again for
His own* and will be united with His glorified Church,
which is His body:

"For the husband is the head of the wife, *even
as Christ is the head of the Church: and He is the
Saviour of the body.* Therefore as the Church is subject unto Christ, so let the wives be to their own
husbands in every thing. Husbands, love your wives,
even as Christ also loved the Church, and gave Himself for it; that He might sanctify and cleanse it with
the washing of water by the Word, that He might
present it to Himself a glorious Church, not having
spot, or wrinkle, or any such thing; but that it should
be holy and without blemish.

"So ought men to love their wives as their own
bodies. He that loveth his wife loveth himself. For
no man ever yet hated his own flesh; but nourisheth
and cherisheth it, even as the Lord the Church: FOR
WE ARE MEMBERS OF HIS BODY, OF HIS FLESH,
AND OF HIS BONES. . . . This is a great mystery:
but I speak concerning Christ and the Church" (Eph.
5:23 — 32).

Through faith in the death, burial, and bodily resurrection of Christ, *believers possess new life:* "Therefore if any man be in Christ, he is a new creature: old things are passed away; behold, all things are become new" (II Cor. 5:17).

"Therefore we are buried with Him by baptism into death: that like as Christ was raised up from the dead by the glory of the Father, even so we also should walk in newness of life. For if we have been planted together in the likeness of His death, we shall be also in the likeness of His resurrection: Knowing this, that our old man is crucified with Him, that the body of sin might be destroyed, that henceforth we should not serve sin. For he that is dead is freed from sin.

"Now if we be dead with Christ, we believe that we shall also live with Him: knowing that Christ being raised from the dead dieth no more; death hath no more dominion over Him. For in that He died, He died unto sin once: but in that He liveth, He liveth unto God" (Rom. 6:4—10).

Jesus was the sin-offering that satisfied God's holiness, God's righteousness, and God's law concerning sin. No previous offering had brought pleasure or satisfaction to God:

"*In burnt-offerings and sacrifices for sin thou hast had no pleasure. . . .* Sacrifice and offering and burnt-offerings and offering for sin thou wouldest not, *neither hadst pleasure therein;* which are offered by the law. . . . *But THIS MAN, after He had offered ONE sacrifice for sins for ever, sat down on the right hand of God;* from henceforth expecting till His enemies be made His footstool. *For BY ONE OFFERING He hath perfected FOR EVER them that are sanctified*" (Heb. 10:6—14).

Glory to His precious name! Because we have, *through faith in His shed blood,* now received the forgiveness of sin, God can now be just and justify us, thereby making us righteous (Rom. 3:26). We are NOW His children, and *because* we are His children *God has sent forth the Spirit of His Son into our hearts,* crying, "Abba, Father." We are no more servants, but sons, *heirs of God through Christ* (Gal. 4:6,7).

Through faith in the finished work of Christ at Calvary by which we have redemption, reconciliation, and salvation, *we have an organic union with Christ:* "For if we have been planted together in the likeness of His death, we shall be also in the likeness of His resurrection" (Rom. 6:5). The believer can say with Paul, "For I through the law am dead to the law, that I might live unto God. I am crucified with Christ: nevertheless I live; yet not I, but Christ liveth in me: and the life which I now live in the flesh I live by the faith of the Son of God, who loved me, and gave Himself for me" (Gal. 2:19, 20).

Colossians 3:3 tells us, "Ye are dead, and your life is hid with Christ in God." Therefore, the redeemed share in the *death* of the Redeemer, but we also *fellowship with Him IN LIFE.* In His discourse on the bread of life Jesus said to the Jews:

"Verily, verily, I say unto you, Moses gave you not that bread from heaven; but my Father giveth you the true bread from heaven. For the bread of God is He which cometh down from heaven, and giveth life unto the world. . . . I am the bread of life: he that cometh to me shall never hunger; and he that believeth on me shall never thirst. . . . I am that bread of life. Your fathers did eat manna in the wilderness, and are dead. This is the bread which cometh down from heaven, that a man may eat thereof, and not die. I am the living bread which came down from heaven: if any man eat of this bread, he shall live for ever: and the bread that I will give is my flesh, which I will give for the life of the world.

"The Jews therefore strove among themselves, saying, How can this Man give us His flesh to eat? Then Jesus said unto them, Verily, verily, I say unto you, Except ye eat the flesh of the Son of man, and drink His blood, ye have no life in you. Whoso eateth my flesh, and drinketh my blood, hath eternal life; and I will raise him up at the last day. For my flesh is meat indeed, and my blood is drink indeed. He that eateth my flesh, and drinketh my blood, dwelleth in me, and I in him. As the living Father hath sent me, and I live by the Father: so he that eateth me, even he shall live by me. This is that bread which came down from heaven: not as your fathers did eat manna, and are dead: he that eateth of this bread shall live for ever" (John 6:32—58).

In this passage we see that the Lord Jesus Christ was the fulfillment of the passover lamb slain in the land of Egypt the night before the Exodus:

"And the Lord spake unto Moses and Aaron in the land of Egypt, saying, This month shall be unto you the beginning of months: it shall be the first month of the year to you. Speak ye unto all the congregation of Israel, saying, In the tenth day of this month they shall take to them every man a lamb, according to the house of their fathers, a lamb for an house: And if the household be too little for the lamb, let him and his neighbour next unto his house take it according to the number of the souls; every man according to his eating shall make your count for the lamb.

"*Your lamb shall be WITHOUT BLEMISH*, a male of the first year: ye shall take it out from the sheep, or from the goats: and ye shall keep it up until the fourteenth day of the same month: and the whole assembly of the congregation of Israel shall kill it in the evening. *And they shall take of the BLOOD, and strike it on the two side posts and on*

the upper door post of the houses, wherein they shall
eat it.   And they shall eat the flesh in that night,
roast with fire, and unleavened bread; and with bitter
herbs they shall eat it" (Ex. 12:1—8).

Then in I Corinthians 5:7, Paul instructs believers,
"Purge out therefore the old leaven, *that ye may be
A NEW LUMP,* as ye are unleavened. *For even
CHRIST OUR PASSOVER is sacrificed for us.*"

In Hebrews 13:10—14 we read, "We have an altar,
whereof they have no right to eat which serve the
tabernacle.   For the bodies of those beasts, whose
blood is brought into the sanctuary by the high priest
for sin, are burned without the camp. Wherefore Jesus
also, that He might sanctify the people with His own
blood, suffered without the gate.   Let us go forth
therefore unto Him without the camp, bearing His
reproach.   For here have we no continuing city, but
we seek one to come."

Christ actually abides in the heart of each believer
—"Christ in you, the hope of glory" (Col. 1:27).

We are partakers of divine nature (II Pet. 1:4), possessors of the Holy Spirit—the third Person of the
Triune God (Rom. 8:9, 14, 16).

Jesus left the Father's bosom and took a body of
humiliation that He might become our substitute. He
took our place, paid the sin-debt, and fulfilled every
jot and tittle of God's holy law. But the doctrine of
substitution in the Word of God deals with something
much higher and much more noble than the intellectual
process of subtracting our sins and adding the Holy
Spirit through faith in Christ's finished work. Substitution is concerned with *the organic interweaving
of a complete new life-principle*—divine and personal.
We are *now* sons of God, we are *now* possessors of
divine nature, we are *now* seated with Christ in heavenly places, and Christ abides in us *now*. The moment we trusted Jesus as personal Saviour we began

to live eternally. That very moment we became citizens of heaven, "from whence also we look for the Saviour, the Lord Jesus Christ" (Phil. 3:20).

The Lord Jesus Christ is not only our Redeemer, He is also our *redemption:* We are *"in Christ Jesus, who of God is made unto us wisdom, and righteousness, and sanctification, and REDEMPTION:* that, according as it is written, He that glorieth, let him glory in the Lord" (I Cor. 1:30, 31).

To the Ephesian believers Paul wrote, "Blessed be the God and Father of our Lord Jesus Christ, who hath blessed us with all spiritual blessings in heavenly places in Christ: according as He hath chosen us in Him before the foundation of the world, that we should be holy and without blame before Him in love: having predestinated us unto the adoption of children by Jesus Christ to Himself, according to the good pleasure of His will, to the praise of the glory of His grace, wherein He hath made us *accepted IN THE BELOVED, IN WHOM WE HAVE REDEMPTION through His blood,* the forgiveness of sins, according to the riches of His grace" (Eph. 1:3—7).

Saving faith is not an *external* faith, nor is it an *intellectual* faith. Saving faith brings the believer into union with Christ personally—that is, it brings the believer *into* Christ. *"IN CHRIST"* describes the origin and the essence of saving faith—faith that brings redemption, justification, and salvation. Paul uses that expression almost one hundred and seventy times in his epistles. For example, in Romans 8:1 he declares, "There is therefore now no condemnation to them which are *IN Christ Jesus."* In Galatians 3:28 he says, *"Ye are all one IN CHRIST JESUS."*

It is *in Christ* that we become God's righteousness. When we *believe* on the Lord Jesus Christ God *imputes* righteousness:

"For what saith the Scripture? *Abraham believed*

God, and it was counted unto him for righteousness.
Now to him that worketh is the reward not reckoned
of grace, but of debt. But to him that worketh not,
but believeth on Him that justifieth the ungodly, his
faith is counted for righteousness. Even as David
also describeth the blessedness of the man, unto whom
God *imputeth* righteousness without works, saying,
Blessed are they whose iniquities are forgiven, and
whose sins are covered. Blessed is the man to whom
the Lord will not impute sin" (Rom. 4:3—8).

In II Corinthians 5:21 we read, "For He (God)
hath made Him (Jesus) to be sin for us, who knew
no sin; *that we might be made THE RIGHTEOUS-
NESS OF GOD IN HIM."*

The Lord Jesus Christ is not only the Propitiator,
He is also the *propitiation* for our sins: "My little
children, these things write I unto you, that ye sin
not. And if any man sin, we have an Advocate with
the Father, Jesus Christ the righteous: and *He is
THE PROPITIATION for our sins: and not for our's
only, but also for the sins of the whole world"* (I John
2:1, 2).

Jesus is our propitiatory sacrifice. He is not only
the propitiation for our sins, but as fulfillment of the
Old Testament *type* He is the mercy seat, *sprinkled—*
not with the blood of innocent animals slain, *but with
His OWN blood.*

Jesus completely honored and satisfied God's holy
law by enduring its righteous sentence in our stead;
and now God (who ever foresaw the cross) *through*
the cross is vindicated in having passed over sins from
Adam to Moses (Rom. 5:13, 14) and the sins of believers
under the old covenant. *Now,* under the *new covenant*
(through the shed blood of Jesus) God can be *just* and
yet justify the sinner. However, the propitiatory sacrifice of the Lord Jesus Christ can righteously benefit
only those who have exercised *faith* in His shed blood

and finished work, being united to Him through the miracle of the new birth—born of the Spirit, born from above.

I pointed out earlier that the reconciliation Jesus made for us is *an organic union* of the believer and Christ; but this organic union can exist only because Jesus took a body of humiliation and in that body laid His life down. He had a body exactly like our own body, except that He was sinless (Heb. 2:14—17; 4:15). He was crucified, buried, but death could not hold Him. He conquered death and rose again in *a glorified body,* a body without blood, but with flesh and bones; and in that body He walked, talked, and ate with His disciples as He had done before His death.

In that body He ascended back to the Father, to take His place at the Father's right hand. I therefore declare that there is a Man in heaven—Christ Jesus the Lord (I Tim. 2:5), and He will *remain* a man, yes indeed He will, *forever!* Since He is the Man Christ Jesus, seated at the right hand of the Majesty, He *requires eternally* a body of flesh and bones. If He had gone back to heaven in spirit and not in a resurrection body, He would have left the human order altogether and could not have been the finisher and transfigurer of the work of redemption wrought by His incarnation.

Therefore, the bodily resurrection of the Lord Jesus Christ denotes the Redeemer's return to the Father's right hand, His humanity immortalized in transfigured, glorified form! and every moment He sits at God's right hand in that body, He displays complete victory over the world, the flesh, the devil, death, hell, and the grave. Since He is our Mediator, we know we are *MORE than conquerors* through Him.

In a body "made like unto His brethren," Jesus was tempted in all points as we are, yet He was with-

out sin. This divine fact, together with His death,
burial, and resurrection, indicates that He was, beyond
doubt, *the last Adam:*

"Wherefore as by one man sin entered into the
world, and death by sin; and so death passed upon
all men, for that all have sinned: (For until the law
sin was in the world: but sin is not imputed when
there is no law. Nevertheless death reigned from Adam
to Moses, even over them that had not sinned after
the similitude of Adam's transgression, who is *the
figure of Him that was to come.*

"But not as the offence, so also is the free gift.
For if through the offence of one many be dead, much
more the grace of God, and the gift by grace, *which
is by one Man, Jesus Christ,* hath abounded unto
many. And not as it was by one that sinned, so is
the gift: for the judgment was by one to condemnation, but the free gift is of many offences unto justification. *For if by one man's offence death reigned
by one; much more they which receive abundance of
grace and of the gift of righteousness shall reign in
life by one, Jesus Christ.*)

"Therefore as *by the offence of one* judgment came
upon *all men* to condemnation; even so *by the righteousness of One* the free gift came upon all men *unto
justification of life.* For as *by one man's disobedience*
many were made sinners, so *by the obedience of One*
shall many be made righteous. Moreover the law
entered, that the offence might abound. But *where
sin abounded, grace did much more abound:* that as
sin hath reigned unto death, even so might grace reign
through righteousness unto eternal life by Jesus Christ
our Lord" (Rom. 5:12—21).

The bodily resurrection of Jesus not only proves
that He was the last Adam, it also proves that He
is "the second Man" from heaven:

"And so it is written: The first man Adam was

made a living soul; the last Adam was made a quickening spirit. Howbeit that was not first which is spiritual, but that which is natural; and afterward that which is spiritual. The *first* man is of the earth, earthy: *the SECOND Man is the Lord from heaven"* (I Cor. 15:45—47).

Seated now in heaven at the right hand of God the Father, the Man Christ Jesus is *the beginner,* the head, of a redeemed, spiritual mankind: "Ye men of Galilee, why stand ye gazing up into heaven? *This SAME JESUS,* which is taken up from you into heaven, *SHALL SO COME IN LIKE MANNER as ye have seen Him go into heaven"* (Acts 1:11).

The Man Christ Jesus has been highly exalted. He sits at the right hand of God, all things have been put under His feet, and God has given Him "to be the head over all things to the Church" (Eph. 1:22). One day He *will return,* and will "change *our* vile body, that it may be fashioned like unto *His glorious body,* according to the working whereby He is able even to subdue *all things* unto Himself" (Phil. 3:21).

Some people say, "I cannot *understand* these deep spiritual truths." I would encourage you, beloved, for I, too, confess that many truths concerning the God-Man are beyond my comprehension—nor will man ever understand them fully. But I thank God for the words of the Apostle Paul: *"Through FAITH we understand!"* (Heb. 11:3).

I do not understand fully the fact that there is a Man of flesh and bones seated at the right hand of the Majesty on high, making intercession for poor, unworthy creatures such as we; but the Holy Scriptures, verbally inspired, clearly teach the eternal humanity of Jesus. I know God's Word cannot lie—"For ever, O Lord, thy Word is settled in heaven" (Psalm 119:89). Therefore I gladly accept this assuring truth *even though I must understand "BY FAITH."*

The divine *fact* that there is a *Man* in heaven guarantees that He who intercedes for us is very capable of understanding our needs. "For in that He Himself hath suffered being tempted, He is able to succour them that are tempted" (Heb. 2:18). He is *"the firstborn* among many brethren" (Rom. 8:29), and the victory He won over death must include *His endless continuance as the Man Christ Jesus,* seated at the right hand of God, pleading our case.

Paul makes this very clear in Colossians 1:15−22 when he declares Christ to be "the *image* of the *invisible God,* the *firstborn of every creature:* For by Him were all things created, that are in heaven, and that are in earth, visible and invisible, whether they be thrones, or dominions, or principalities, or powers: *ALL things* were created *BY Him, and FOR Him:* And He is *before* all things, and by Him all things consist.

"And He is the head of the body, the Church: who is *the beginning, THE FIRSTBORN FROM THE DEAD; that in ALL things He might have the pre-eminence.* For it pleased the Father that *IN HIM should all fulness dwell;* and, having made peace through the blood of His cross, by Him to reconcile all things unto Himself; by Him, I say, whether they be things in earth, or things in heaven.

"And you, that were sometime alienated and enemies in your mind by wicked works, yet now hath He reconciled IN THE BODY OF HIS FLESH through death, to present you holy and unblameable and unreproveable in His sight."

Since the Lord Jesus Christ conquered the world, the flesh, the devil, death, hell, and the grave, He is truly "the firstborn among many brethren" (Rom. 8:29).

He is "the Captain of our salvation" (Heb. 2:10).

He is "the Author of eternal salvation unto all

them that obey Him" (Heb. 5:9).

By the death and bodily resurrection of Jesus, believers are "begotten again unto a lively hope" (I Pet. 1:3).

We are in Christ, Christ is in us (Col. 1:27; 3:3), we are "members of His body, of His flesh, and of His bones" (Eph. 5:30).

Because the Lord Jesus Christ conquered death and rose again, believers experience "the power of His resurrection" (Phil. 3:10). We "walk in newness of life" because we are risen with Him (Rom. 6:4), and the life we now live in the flesh, we live by the faith of the Son of God, who loved us and gave Himself for us (Gal. 2:20).

We who are believers serve the living God and fellowship with Him because we possess His nature (II Pet. 1:4). We approach Him, entering even *"into the holiest* by the blood of Jesus, by *a new and living way,* which He hath consecrated for us, through the veil, that is to say, *HIS FLESH"* (Heb. 10:19, 20).

In Romans 7:4−6 we read, "Wherefore, my brethren, ye also are become dead to the law by the body of Christ; that ye should be married to another, even to Him who is raised from the dead, that we should bring forth fruit unto God. For when we were in the flesh, the motions of sins, which were by the law, did work in our members to bring forth fruit unto death. *But now we are delivered from the law, that being dead wherein we were held; that we should serve IN NEWNESS OF SPIRIT, and not in the oldness of the letter."*

The bodily resurrection of Jesus was not alone *a work of God the Father wrought on Jesus the Son* as set forth in Acts 2:32, nor was His bodily resurrection only "by *the glory of the Father"* as testified in Romans 6:4. His coming forth bodily went beyond either of these: *it was an indispensable element.* Jesus (raised by the power of God the Father, by the glory of God the Father) was also raised *by His OWN power*—by the voluntary exercise of the power of His own life:

"For as the Father hath life in Himself; so hath He given to the Son to have life in Himself" (John 5:26).

Jesus Himself declared, ". . . I *lay down* my life, that I might take it again. No man taketh it from me, but *I lay it down of myself. I have POWER to lay it down, and I have power to take it again.* This commandment have I received of my Father" (John 10:17, 18).

The Bodily Resurrection of Jesus Guarantees the Transfiguration of All Creation

The bodily resurrection of the Lord Jesus Christ guarantees the resurrection of the body of the believer. His bodily resurrection also guarantees deliverance of the earth from the curse. In that glorious day when the curse is lifted, the kingdom of God's glory will be right here on this earth. This will occur when Jesus comes to set up His kingdom and occupy the throne of David in Jerusalem.

The bodily resurrection of Jesus gives further guarantee of the transfiguration of the whole universe—not only the earth, but all creation. His resurrection ("the firstfruits") is the *basis* for *all resurrection:*

"For as the Father hath life in Himself; so hath He given to the Son to have life in Himself; and hath given Him authority to execute judgment also, because He is the Son of man. Marvel not at this: for the hour is coming, in the which *all that are in the graves shall hear His voice, and shall come forth;* they that have done good, unto the resurrection of life; and they that have done evil, unto the resurrection of damnation" (John 5:26—29).

If death had won the victory over Jesus, *OUR bodies would have been destined to return eternally to dust!* We will rise again bodily because our Redeemer won total victory over physical death and His resurrection guarantees the transfiguration of our mortal bodies:

"Now is Christ risen from the dead, *and become THE FIRSTFRUITS of them that slept.* For since by man came death, by Man came also the resurrection of the dead. For as in Adam all die, even so in Christ shall all be made alive. *BUT EVERY MAN IN HIS OWN ORDER: Christ the firstfruits; afterward they that are Christ's at His coming"* (I Cor. 15:20—23).

At the resurrection of Jesus the bodies of many Old Testament saints—bodies that had been sleeping for many years—came forth from the grave (Matt. 27:53), proving that the way of the resurrection of the body has been opened and divinely guaranteed through Christ's victory over death. Thus His victory assures us that we will rise again, for "if the Spirit of Him that raised up Jesus from the dead dwell in you, He that raised up Christ from the dead shall also quicken your mortal bodies by His Spirit that dwelleth in you" (Rom. 8:11).

To the Thessalonian believers Paul declared, "I would not have you to be ignorant, brethren, concerning them which are asleep, that ye sorrow not, even as others which have no hope. *For if we believe that Jesus died and rose again, even so them also which SLEEP IN JESUS will God bring with Him"* (I Thess. 4:13, 14).

As the risen Lord—*the Man* Christ Jesus—now sits at the right hand of the Father on the throne, His body is the pattern for *our* glorified bodies, and when He comes in the Rapture we will then be like Him: "For our conversation is in heaven; from whence also we look for the Saviour, the Lord Jesus Christ: *who*

*shall change our vile body, that it may be fashioned
like unto His glorious body,* according to the working
whereby He is able even to subdue all things unto
Himself" (Phil. 3:20, 21).

To the Corinthians Paul explained, "As we have
borne the image of the *earthy,* we shall also bear the
image of the *heavenly*" (I Cor. 15:49); and John the
Beloved declares, *"Beloved, NOW are we the sons of
God, and it doth not yet appear what we SHALL be:
but we know that, when He shall appear, we shall
be LIKE HIM; for we shall see Him as He is!"* (I John
3:2).

In John 5:27—29 you will notice that not only will
the *born again* ("those who have done good") be
raised, but the *ungodly* ("those who have done wickedly") will also be raised. So even *the resurrection
of the wicked* is committed unto the Lord Jesus Christ,
the last Adam. As in "the *first* Adam" all *die,* so
in "the *last* Adam" shall all be made alive—but those
who have rejected His shed blood and finished work
will be raised *"unto damnation."*

It is to be understood that the resurrection of the
just will occur at least *one thousand years* before the
resurrection of the *unjust.* This is clearly taught in
Revelation 20:4—6. John the Beloved declared:

"And I saw thrones, and they sat upon them, and
judgment was given unto them: and I saw the souls
of them that were beheaded for the witness of Jesus,
and for the Word of God, and which had not worshipped the beast, neither his image, neither had received his mark upon their foreheads, or in their hands;
and they lived and reigned with Christ a thousand
years. *But the rest of the dead lived not again until
the thousand years were finished. THIS IS THE
FIRST RESURRECTION.* Blessed and holy is he
that hath part in the first resurrection: on such the
second death hath no power, but they shall be priests

of God and of Christ, and shall reign with Him a thousand years."

The Bodily Resurrection of Jesus Guarantees the Millennium

Seven hundred and fifty years before the birth of Jesus, Isaiah wrote, under inspiration, "Unto us a Child is born, unto us a Son is given: and the government shall be upon His shoulder: and His name shall be called Wonderful, Counsellor, The mighty God, The everlasting Father, The Prince of Peace. Of the increase of His government and peace there shall be no end, upon the throne of David, and upon His kingdom, to order it, and to establish it with judgment and with justice from henceforth even for ever. The zeal of the Lord of hosts will perform this" (Isa.9:6, 7).

The Child Jesus was born as prophesied—and He was all Isaiah declared He *would* be. He was "Wonderful," He was "The mighty God," He was "The Prince of Peace." But there has never yet *been* peace on earth, good will toward men. The government has not yet *been* upon His shoulders. This will come to pass in the future, at Christ's second coming, when He will set up His kingdom and reign from the throne of David in Jerusalem as prophesied.

God not only gave Isaiah the prophecy concerning the coming of the King, He also gave him prophecy concerning *the character of the REIGN of the King* and the quality of the kingdom over which He will reign:

"And there shall come forth a rod out of the stem of Jesse, and a Branch shall grow out of his roots: And the Spirit of the Lord shall rest upon Him, the spirit of wisdom and understanding, the spirit of counsel and might, the spirit of knowledge and of the fear

of the Lord; and shall make Him of quick understanding in the fear of the Lord: and He shall not judge
after the sight of His eyes, neither reprove after the
hearing of His ears: But with righteousness shall He
judge the poor, and reprove with equity for the meek
of the earth: and He shall smite the earth with the
rod of His mouth, and with the breath of His lips
shall He slay the wicked. And righteousness shall be
the girdle of His loins, and faithfulness the girdle of
His reins.

"The wolf also shall dwell with the lamb, and
the leopard shall lie down with the kid; and the calf
and the young lion and the fatling together; and a
little child shall lead them. And the cow and the
bear shall feed; their young ones shall lie down together: and the lion shall eat straw like the ox. And
the sucking child shall play on the hole of the asp,
and the weaned child shall put his hand on the cock-
atrice' den. *They shall not hurt nor destroy in all
my holy mountain: for the earth shall be full of the
knowledge of the Lord, as the waters cover the sea.*
And in that day there shall be a root of Jesse, which
shall stand for an ensign of the people; to it shall the
Gentiles seek: and His rest shall be glorious" (Isa.
11:1—10).

The promise God made to Abraham and his seed,
the promise given to David, spoke of *an eternal, transfigured, human kingdom:* "He shall build an house
for my name, and I will establish the throne of His
kingdom for ever" (II Sam. 7:13).

For such a kingdom there must be a King, even
the Son of man who will come the second time to
this earth, "and His feet shall stand in that day upon
the mount of Olives, which is before Jerusalem on
the east, and the mount of Olives shall cleave in the
midst thereof toward the east and toward the west,
and there shall be a very great valley; and half of the

mountain shall remove toward the north, and half of it toward the south" (Zech. 14:4).

The Prophet Daniel describes the promised kingdom: "I saw in the night visions, and, behold, one like the Son of man came with the clouds of heaven, and came to the Ancient of days, and they brought Him near before Him. *And there was given Him dominion, and glory, and a kingdom, that all people, nations, and languages, should serve Him: His dominion is an EVERLASTING dominion, which shall not pass away, and His kingdom that WHICH SHALL NOT BE DESTROYED"* (Dan. 7:13, 14).

When Jesus was arrested and brought before Caiaphas, the high priest said to Him, "I adjure thee by the living God, that thou tell us whether thou be the Christ, the Son of God." Jesus replied, "Thou hast said: nevertheless I say unto you, *Hereafter shall ye see THE SON OF MAN sitting on the right hand of power, and coming in the clouds of heaven"* (Matt. 26:63, 64).

In Revelation 1:12—18, John the Beloved describes the scene that was revealed to him on the Isle of Patmos: "I turned to see the voice that spake with me. And being turned, I saw seven golden candlesticks; *and in the midst of the seven candlesticks ONE LIKE UNTO THE SON OF MAN,* clothed with a garment down to the foot, and girt about the paps with a golden girdle. His head and His hairs were white like wool, as white as snow; and His eyes were as a flame of fire; and His feet like unto fine brass, as if they burned in a furnace; and His voice as the sound of many waters. And He had in His right hand seven stars: and out of His mouth went a sharp twoedged sword: and His countenance was as the sun shineth in His strength. And when I saw Him, I fell at His feet as dead. And He laid His right hand upon me, saying unto me, Fear not; *I am the first and the last:*

I AM HE THAT LIVETH, AND WAS DEAD; and, behold, I AM ALIVE FOR EVERMORE, Amen; and have the keys of hell and of death!"

The bodily resurrection of Jesus is the foundation and divine guarantee for the new birth of the earth, and therefore guarantees the Millennium:

"Then answered Peter and said unto Him, Behold, we have forsaken all, and followed thee; what shall we have therefore? And Jesus said unto them, Verily I say unto you, *That ye which have followed me, in the regeneration when the Son of man shall sit in the throne of His glory, ye also shall sit upon twelve thrones, judging the twelve tribes of Israel. And every one that hath forsaken houses, or brethren, or sisters, or father, or mother, or wife, or children, or lands, for my name's sake, shall receive an hundredfold, and shall inherit everlasting life"* (Matt. 19:27–29).

In verse 28 of this passage, the Greek word translated "regeneration" is *palingenesia*, meaning "re-creation or making new." The same word is used in Titus 3:5 with reference to the new birth, the spiritual birth of the believer; but here in Matthew it speaks of the deliverance of the earth.

In Romans 8:18–23 the Apostle Paul wrote, under inspiration, "I reckon that the sufferings of this present time are not worthy to be compared with the glory which shall be revealed in us. For the earnest expectation of the creature waiteth for the manifestation of the sons of God. For the creature was made subject to vanity, not willingly, but by reason of Him who hath subjected the same in hope. Because *the creature itself also shall be delivered from the bondage of corruption into the glorious liberty of the children of God. For we know that THE WHOLE CREATION GROANETH AND TRAVAILETH IN PAIN TOGETHER UNTIL NOW. And not only they, but ourselves also, which have the firstfruits of the Spirit,*

*even we ourselves groan within ourselves, waiting
for the adoption, to wit, THE REDEMPTION OF
OUR BODY."*

The day will come when the earth *WILL BE delivered* from its groaning, delivered from the curse,
all things made new! (Please study the entire eleventh
chapter of Isaiah.) God will fulfill His promise to
David. In Acts 13:32—34 Paul declared to the Jews,
"We declare unto you glad tidings, *how that the promise which was made unto the fathers, GOD HATH
FULFILLED THE SAME UNTO US THEIR CHILDREN, in that He hath raised up Jesus again;* as
it is also written in the second Psalm, Thou art my
Son, this day have I begotten thee. And as concerning that He raised Him up from the dead, now no
more to return to corruption, He said on this wise,
I will give you THE SURE MERCIES OF DAVID."

In verse 34 of this passage, the Greek reads, "I
will give you *the inviolable blessings promised to
David."* Paul was speaking of the prophecy given to
Isaiah: "Incline your ear, and come unto me: hear,
and your soul shall live; and I will make *an everlasting
covenant with you, even THE SURE MERCIES OF
DAVID"* (Isa. 55:3).

On the Day of Pentecost, Peter preached to a congregation gathered from every nation at that time,
and he, too, declared that the seed of David would
be king as promised: "For David speaketh concerning
Him, I foresaw the Lord always before my face, for
He is on my right hand, that I should not be moved:
Therefore did my heart rejoice, and my tongue was
glad; moreover also my flesh shall rest in hope: Because thou wilt not leave my soul in hell, neither wilt
thou suffer thine Holy One to see corruption. Thou
hast made known to me the ways of life; thou shalt
make me full of joy with thy countenance.

"Men and brethren, let me freely speak unto you

of the patriarch David, that he is both dead and buried, and his sepulchre is with us unto this day. Therefore being a prophet, and knowing that God had sworn with an oath to him, that of the fruit of his loins, according to the flesh, He would raise up Christ to sit on his throne: he seeing this before spake of the resurrection of Christ, that His soul was not left in hell, neither His flesh did see corruption" (Acts 2:25—31).

The Spiritual Resurrection of Israel

Some people teach that God has finished with the Jews, that He has cast the nation Israel aside. They declare that the English-speaking people are now Israel, and that God has given to the Church the promises He made to Abraham. This is false doctrine, and those who teach it are nothing short of spiritual thieves and robbers. God will deal with them in the day of judgment.

God *has NOT* turned His back on Israel, He has not ceased to love that nation. Paul makes this very clear in Romans chapter 11:

"I say then, *HATH God cast away His people?* God forbid! For I also am an Israelite, of the seed of Abraham, of the tribe of Benjamin. *God hath NOT cast away His people which He foreknew.* Wot ye not what the Scripture saith of Elias? how he maketh intercession to God against Israel, saying, Lord, they have killed thy prophets, and digged down thine altars; and I am left alone, and they seek my life. *But what saith the answer of God unto him?* I have reserved to myself seven thousand men, who have not bowed the knee to the image of Baal. *Even so then at this present time also THERE IS A REMNANT ACCORDING TO THE ELECTION OF GRACE....*

"What then? Israel hath not obtained that which he seeketh for; but the election hath obtained it, *and the rest were blinded* (according as it is written, God hath given them the spirit of slumber, eyes that they should not see, and ears that they should not hear;) *unto this day. . . .* I say then, Have they stumbled that they should fall? God forbid! But rather *through their fall* salvation is come unto the Gentiles, for to provoke them to jealousy. Now if the *fall* of them be the riches of the world, and the *diminishing* of them the riches of the Gentiles; *how much more their FUL-NESS?* . . . For if the casting away of them be the reconciling of the world, what shall the receiving of them be, but life from the dead? . . .

"*And so all Israel shall be saved: AS IT IS WRIT-TEN, There shall come out of Sion the Deliverer, and shall turn away ungodliness from Jacob: For this is my covenant unto them, when I shall take away their sins. . . . FOR THE GIFTS AND CALLING OF GOD ARE WITHOUT REPENTANCE.*" (We have quoted exerpts from Romans 11:1—29, but it would be well if you would read and study the entire chapter.)

The nation Israel will be resurrected spiritually, a nation will be born and will recognize their Messiah. They will then love and serve Him as their God and King. Ezekiel describes that day in his vision of the valley of dry bones:

"The hand of the Lord was upon me, and carried me out in the Spirit of the Lord, and set me down in the midst of the valley which was full of bones . . .

"And He said unto me, Son of man, can these bones live? And I answered, O Lord God, thou knowest. . . .

"Thus saith the Lord God unto these bones: *Behold, I will cause breath to enter into you, and ye shall live: and I will lay sinews upon you, and will bring up flesh upon you, and cover you with skin, and put breath in you, and ye shall live; AND YE*

SHALL KNOW THAT I AM THE LORD. . . .

"So I prophesied as He commanded me, and the breath came into them, and they lived, and stood up upon their feet, an exceeding great army. Then He said unto me, Son of man, *these bones are the whole house of Israel:* behold, they say, Our bones are dried, and our hope is lost: we are cut off for our parts. Therefore prophesy and say unto them, *Thus saith the Lord God:* Behold, O my people, I will open your graves, and cause you to come up out of your graves, and bring you into the land of Israel. And ye shall know that I am the Lord, when I have opened your graves, O my people, and brought you up out of your graves, *and shall put my Spirit in you, and ye shall live, and I shall place you in your own land: then shall ye know that I the Lord have SPOKEN IT, AND PERFORMED IT,* saith the Lord" (Ezek. 37:1—14).

The most glorious days for Israel are yet ahead! God will fulfill every promise He made to Abraham and to his seed. To the Prophet Isaiah God revealed the eternal blessing of Israel which will be right here on earth when the earth is created new:

"For, behold, I create new heavens and a new earth: and the former shall not be remembered, nor come into mind. But be ye glad and rejoice for ever in that which I create: for, behold, I create Jerusalem a rejoicing, and her people a joy. . . .

"And it shall come to pass, that before they call, I will answer; and while they are yet speaking, I will hear. The wolf and the lamb shall feed together, and the lion shall eat straw like the bullock: and dust shall be the serpent's meat. They shall not hurt nor destroy in all my holy mountain, saith the Lord" (Isa. 65:17—25).

Please study Isaiah chapter 66 and Revelation chapter 22 in connection with the passages quoted here; you will find them very enlightening.

The Spiritual New Birth of the Nations

"His foundation is in the holy mountains. The Lord loveth the gates of Zion more than all the dwellings of Jacob. Glorious things are spoken of thee, O city of God.

"I will make mention of Rahab and Babylon to them that know me: behold Philistia, and Tyre, with Ethiopia; this man was born there. And of Zion it shall be said, This and that man was born in her: and the highest Himself shall establish her. The Lord shall count, when He writeth up the people, that this man was born there. As well the singers as the players on instruments shall be there: all my springs are in thee" (Psalm 87).

As was pointed out in Romans 8:22, *the whole creation* is groaning and travailing in pain, all the inhabitants of the earth are under the curse. The only peace in this world is the peace of God which dwells in the heart of the believer. We live in an earth that is cursed because of Adam's sin. But one day *the earth and the nations* will be delivered from the curse.

James declared this truth before the council at Jerusalem. He said, "Men and brethren, hearken unto me: Simeon hath declared how God at the first did visit the Gentiles, to take out of them a people for His name. And to this agree the words of the prophets; as it is written, After this I will return, and will build again the tabernacle of David, which is fallen down; and I will build again the ruins thereof, and I will set it up: that the residue of men might seek after the Lord, and all the Gentiles, upon whom my name is called, saith the Lord, who doeth all these things. Known unto God are all His works from the beginning of the world" (Acts 15:13—18).

As nations, Egypt and Assyria have never been God's people. They have never been at peace with

God, but Isaiah prophesied:

"The Lord shall be known to Egypt, and the Egyptians shall know the Lord in that day, and shall do sacrifice and oblation; yea, they shall vow a vow unto the Lord, and perform it. And the Lord shall smite Egypt: He shall smite and heal it: and they shall return even to the Lord, and He shall be intreated of them, and shall heal them.

"In that day shall there be a highway out of Egypt to Assyria, and the Assyrian shall come into Egypt, and the Egyptians into Assyria, and the Egyptians shall serve with the Assyrians.

"In that day shall Israel be the third with Egypt and with Assyria, even a blessing in the midst of the land: whom the Lord of hosts shall bless, saying, Blessed be Egypt my people, and Assyria the work of my hands, and Israel mine inheritance" (Isa. 19: 21—25).

Also in Isaiah 25:7, 8 we read this prophecy: "And He will destroy in this mountain the face of the covering cast over all people, and the vail that is spread over all nations. He will swallow up death in victory; and the Lord God will wipe away tears from off all faces; and the rebuke of His people shall He take away from off all the earth: for the Lord hath spoken it."

All Nature Will Experience a New Birth

Again I point out that the whole creation—man, the earth, the solar systems, the animal kingdom, *all things created*—is groaning and travailing even until this present moment because of Adam's sin; but one day there will be *a re-birth of ALL NATURE.*

The animals will no longer be destructive, killing and being killed: "The wolf also shall dwell with the lamb, and the leopard shall lie down with the kid; and the calf and the young lion and the fatling together; and a little child shall lead them. And the cow and the bear shall feed; their young ones shall lie down together: and the lion shall eat straw like the ox" (Isa. 11:6, 7).

Men will again live to be hundreds of years old: "There shall be no more thence an infant of days, nor an old man that hath not filled his days: for the child shall die an hundred years old; but the sinner being an hundred years old shall be accursed. And they shall build houses, and inhabit them; and they shall plant vineyards, and eat the fruit of them. They shall not build, and another inhabit; they shall not plant, and another eat: for as the days of a tree are the days of my people, and mine elect shall long enjoy the work of their hands" (Isa. 65:20—22).

These glorious things are divinely guaranteed and assured because of the victory Jesus won at Calvary. He rose bodily from the dead, and as "the Man Christ Jesus" He now sits at the right hand of God, where He will remain until that glorious moment when the trumpet of God sounds and Jesus returns to catch away His bride, the New Testament Church. Then, in due time, a time appointed by and known only to God, He will return to this earth to deliver it from the curse. Satan will be placed in the bottomless pit with the beast, the false prophet, and all the wicked. The knowledge of the Lord will cover the earth as the waters cover the sea. There will be peace on earth, good will toward men. *All things* will be made *new,* and there will be no more sorrow, no more dying, no more pain, but *one eternal day* of peace and glory *with Him!*

The New Heaven and the New Earth

"And I saw a new heaven and a new earth: for the first heaven and the first earth were passed away; and there was no more sea. And I John saw the holy

city, new Jerusalem, coming down from God out of
heaven, prepared as a bride adorned for her husband.

"And I heard a great voice out of heaven saying,
Behold, the tabernacle of God is with men, and He
will dwell with them, and they shall be His people,
and God Himself shall be with them, and be their
God.   And God shall wipe away all tears from their
eyes; and there shall be no more death, neither sorrow, nor crying, neither shall there be any more pain:
for the former things are passed away.

"And He that sat upon the throne said, BEHOLD,
I MAKE ALL THINGS NEW.   And He said unto
me, Write; FOR THESE WORDS ARE TRUE AND
FAITHFUL. . . .

"And there came unto me one of the seven angels
which had the seven vials full of the seven last
plagues, and talked with me, saying, Come hither, I
will shew thee the bride, the Lamb's wife. And he
carried me away in the spirit to a great and high
mountain, and shewed me that great city, the holy
Jerusalem, descending out of heaven from God, having
the glory of God . . .

"And I saw no temple therein: for the Lord God
Almighty and the Lamb are the temple of it.   And
the city had no need of the sun, neither of the moon,
to shine in it: for the glory of God did lighten it,
and the Lamb is the light thereof.   And the nations
of them which are saved shall walk in the light of
it: and the kings of the earth do bring their glory
and honour into it.   And the gates of it shall not be
shut at all by day: for there shall be no night there.
And they shall bring the glory and honour of the nations into it.   And there shall in no wise enter into it
any thing that defileth, neither whatsoever worketh
abonimation, or maketh a lie: but they which are
written in the Lamb's book of life. . . .

"*AND THERE SHALL BE NO MORE CURSE:*

but the throne of God and of the Lamb shall be in it; and His servants shall serve Him: and they shall see His face; and His name shall be in their foreheads. And there shall be no night there; and they need no candle, neither light of the sun; for the Lord God giveth them light: and they shall reign for ever and ever.

"And He said unto me . . . BEHOLD, I COME QUICKLY: blessed is he that keepeth the sayings of the prophecy of this book" (Rev. 21:1 through 22:7).

The Millennium will be one thousand years of glorious peace on earth and good will toward men, when King Jesus will sit on the throne of David and the knowledge of the Lord will cover the earth as the waters cover the sea; but glorious though the millennial kingdom will be, it is only *the introduction* to "all things made new"!

At the close of the thousand years of peace on earth, the battle of Gog and Magog will be fought:

"And when the thousand years are expired, Satan shall be loosed out of his prison, and shall go out to deceive the nations which are in the four quarters of the earth, Gog and Magog, to gather them together to battle: the number of whom is as the sand of the sea. And they went up on the breadth of the earth, and compassed the camp of the saints about, and the beloved city: and fire came down from God out of heaven, and devoured them" (Rev. 20:7—9).

The devil will be cast into the lake of fire, never to be loosed again: "And the devil that deceived them was cast into the lake of fire and brimstone, where the beast and the false prophet are, and shall be tormented day and night for ever and ever" (Rev. 20:10).

The unbelieving dead will be called to judgment at the Great White Throne: "And I saw a great white throne, and Him that sat on it, from whose face the earth and the heaven fled away; and there was found

no place for them.   And I saw the dead, small and
great, stand before God; and the books were opened:
and another book was opened, which is the book of
life: and the dead were judged out of those things
which were written in the books, according to their
works.   And the sea gave up the dead which were
in it; and death and hell delivered up the dead which
were in them: and they were judged every man according to their works.   And death and hell were
cast into the lake of fire.   This is the second death.
And whosoever was not found written in the book of
life was cast into the lake of fire" (Rev. 20:11—15).

Then the eternity of eternities will begin: There
will be a new heaven, a new earth, and the Pearly
White City.   Then will soul and spirit be glorified,
the redeemed will have bodies like the Lord's glorious
resurrection body, nature and all matter will be *completely transfigured*, created new.   Heaven and earth
will bear no trace of sin or the curse, and the city
where the bride of Christ will dwell will be filled
with glories beyond adequate description in man's
language.   We can appreciate them fully only when
we see Jesus in that glorious eternity of eternities.

The bodily resurrection of Jesus is the *guarantee*
that all things will be created new.   It was when
He came forth from the tomb that matter was, for
the first time, transfigured.   To the ten disciples the
risen Lord said, "Behold my hands and my feet, that
it is I myself: handle me, and see; for a spirit hath
not flesh and bones, as ye see me have.   And when
He had thus spoken, He shewed them His hands and
His feet.   And while they yet believed not for joy,
and wondered, He said unto them, Have ye here any
meat?   And they gave Him a piece of a broiled fish,
and of an honeycomb.   And He took it, and did eat
before them" (Luke 24:39—43).

"Then saith He to Thomas, Reach hither thy finger,

and behold my hands; and reach hither thy hand, and thrust it into my side: and be not faithless, but believing" (John 20:27).

Thus the bodily resurrection of Jesus proves beyond any doubt that matter is *capable* of transfiguration, and guarantees that matter *will be* transfigured in the fulness of time, as appointed by the Godhead. Jesus is not only the *firstfruits* of them that *sleep;* He is also the firstfruits of *all things created new,* all things transfigured. (Study I Corinthians 15:20— 23.)

Our bodily resurrection, the transfiguration of heaven and earth and all things created new, depend entirely on the bodily resurrection of the Lord Jesus Christ. He died to redeem that which Adam lost in the fall, He finished that which He came to do. And because of His finished work we have a divine guarantee that believers, too, will be raised incorruptible, and there will be a new heaven and a new earth, completely free from the curse.

In that new creation Jesus will reign supremely. Therefore the final results of His bodily resurrection are declared: *"BEHOLD, I CREATE NEW HEAVENS AND A NEW EARTH: AND THE FORMER SHALL NOT BE REMEMBERED, NOR COME INTO MIND"* (Isa. 65:17). II Peter 3:13 declares that believers *"according to His promise,* look for new heavens and a new earth, wherein dwelleth righteousness!"

In Closing

Resurrection is the substance of all the promises of God from Adam through the transfiguration of all things.

Jesus in His resurrection body is the fulfillment of God's promise to the fathers, the fulfillment of all of God's promises from Genesis 3:15 until the creation

of all things new.   The bodily resurrection of Jesus
is God's guarantee of the fulfillment of all of His
promises to all people, from Adam until the eternity
of eternities.

Jesus endorsed the promises of God (Luke 24:44).
His bodily resurrection declares Him to be the only
begotten Son of God with power and assures us that
the promises of the Bible are the sure words of Almighty God who cannot lie (Heb. 6:18; Tit. 1:2).

The bodily resurrection of Jesus reveals God's ability to *keep* His promises, and reveals His mighty power to us-ward.   The God who kept His Word concerning the raising of His only begotten Son will surely
fulfill all of His promises to His children: "Be it
known unto you therefore, men and brethren, that
through this Man is preached unto you the forgiveness
of sins: and *by Him* all that believe are justified
from all things, from which ye could not be justified
by the law of Moses" (Acts 13:38, 39).

I close this chapter by declaring again the statement with which I *opened* the chapter: The greatest
bombshell ever to explode in the face of an unbelieving world was the bodily resurrection of the Lord Jesus
Christ!   And I add: *the bodily resurrection of the
Lord Jesus Christ is the visible display of the EX-
CEEDING GREATNESS of God's power to us-ward—
yea, to ALL who believe!*

"Yet a little while, and the world seeth me no
more; but ye see me: *BECAUSE I LIVE, ye shall
live also"* (John 14:19).

"And if Christ be in you, *the body is dead* because
of sin; but *the Spirit is life* because of righteousness"
(Rom. 8:10).

"If thou shalt confess with thy mouth the Lord
Jesus, and shalt believe in thine heart that God hath
raised Him from the dead, thou shalt be saved.   For
with the heart man believeth unto righteousness; **and**

with the mouth confession is made unto salvation"
(Rom. 10:9, 10).

Chapter Five

BIBLE TRUTH CONCERNING
CHRIST'S ASCENSION AND EXALTATION

"The former treatise have I made, O Theophilus, of all that Jesus began both to do and teach, until the day in which He was taken up, after that He through the Holy Ghost had given commandments unto the apostles whom He had chosen: to whom also He shewed Himself alive after His passion by many infallible proofs, being seen of them forty days, and speaking of the things pertaining to the kingdom of God: and, being assembled together with them, commanded them that they should not depart from Jerusalem, but wait for the promise of the Father, which, saith He, ye have heard of me. For John truly baptized with water; but ye shall be baptized with the Holy Ghost not many days hence.

"When they therefore were come together, they asked of Him, saying, Lord, wilt thou at this time restore again the kingdom to Israel? And He said unto them, It is not for you to know the times or the seasons, which the Father hath put in His own power. But ye shall receive power, after that the Holy Ghost is come upon you: and ye shall be witnesses unto me both in Jerusalem, and in all Judaea, and in Samaria, and unto the uttermost part of the earth. And when He had spoken these things, while they beheld, He was taken up; and a cloud received

Him out of their sight.

"And while they looked stedfastly toward heaven as He went up, behold, two men stood by them in white apparel; which also said, Ye men of Galilee, why stand ye gazing up into heaven? This same Jesus, which is taken up from you into heaven, shall so come in like manner as ye have seen Him go into heaven" (Acts 1:1—11).

After His resurrection Jesus tabernacled among men for forty days, teaching His disciples "of the things pertaining to the kingdom of God." He commanded them to tarry in Jerusalem until they received "the promise of the Father," the baptism of the Holy Ghost. And even while He was speaking to them "He was taken up, and a cloud received Him out of their sight."

Yes, the disciples witnessed the ascension of the risen Lord, and after He disappeared from sight they still stood gazing after Him. Then two heavenly messengers appeared and declared that *"this SAME Jesus"* will return in the same manner as they had seen Him go.

The Man Christ Jesus assuredly ascended back to the heavenly Father, and His ascension and exaltation are spoken of between thirty-five and forty times in the New Testament.

Stephen, the first martyr from the New Testament Church, was stoned to death for his testimony. As he died he *"looked up stedfastly into heaven, and saw the glory of God, AND JESUS STANDING ON THE RIGHT HAND OF GOD. . . .* And they stoned Stephen, calling upon God, and saying, *Lord Jesus, receive my spirit.* And he kneeled down, and cried with a loud voice, Lord, lay not this sin to their charge. And when he had said this, he fell asleep" (Acts 7:54—60).

To the Hebrew believers, Paul testified in these words concerning the ascension and exaltation of the

Lord Jesus Christ: "God, who at sundry times and in divers manners spake in time past unto the fathers by the prophets, hath in these last days spoken unto us *by His Son, whom He hath appointed heir of all things*, by whom also He made the worlds; who being the brightness of His glory, and the express image of His person, and upholding all things by the word of His power, *when He had by Himself purged our sins, SAT DOWN ON THE RIGHT HAND OF THE MAJESTY ON HIGH*" (Heb. 1:1—3).

Hebrews chapter 10 plainly tells us that Jesus did *in reality* what the *types* of the Old Testament economy foreshadowed. It was not possible for the blood of bulls and goats to take away sins. Therefore God gave Jesus a body, and *in that body of humiliation* He did what the law *could not* do, what the blood of *animal sacrifices* could not do. Then, after "this Man" Christ Jesus had fulfilled every jot and tittle of the law, after He had satisfied God's holiness and righteousness, after He had offered the one sacrifice that settled the sin-debt eternally, He "*SAT DOWN on the right hand of God;* from henceforth expecting till His enemies be made His footstool" (Heb. 10:12, 13).

Does this Scripture contradict the passage in Acts when Stephen saw Jesus *standing* at the right hand of God? No, it does not. I personally believe Jesus stood *to receive the spirit of Stephen;* but since His ascension He has been *seated* because He finished the work He came into the world to do as *the Man* Christ Jesus; and now in His resurrection body, a body of flesh and bones, He sits in the highest seat of heaven, at the right hand of the Majesty. To young Timothy Paul declared, "For there is one God, and one Mediator between God and men, *the Man Christ Jesus*" (I Tim. 2:5).

There is no mistaking the fact that the Apostle Paul believed and taught that Jesus was *crucified*

bodily, and that He *arose* bodily from the grave, and
that He *ascended bodily into heaven.* In Ephesians
4:8−10 Paul wrote, "Wherefore He saith, When He
ascended up on high, *He led captivity captive,* and
gave gifts unto men. (Now that He *ascended,* what
is it but that *He also DESCENDED first into the
lower parts of the earth?* He that descended *is the
same also that ascended* up far above all heavens,
that He might fill all things.)"

Jesus "led captivity captive" in that when He died
He descended into the lower parts of the earth, and
when He rose again He brought the spirits of the
righteous out of the Paradise which, in the Old Testament economy and up to the resurrection of Jesus,
was in the center of the earth. There are no spirits
of the righteous in the center of the earth now; only
the spirits of the wicked are there.

Previous to the death and resurrection of Jesus,
there were two compartments in hell, with a great
gulf fixed between the spirits of the righteous and
the spirits of the wicked. Luke 16:19−31 gives the
account of the beggar who died ("and was carried by
the angels into Abraham's bosom") and the rich man
who died (and was buried, and lifted up his eyes in
hell). Seeing the beggar Lazarus resting in Abraham's
bosom, the rich man begged Abraham to send Lazarus
to him with a drop of water to cool his parching
tongue; "For," said he, "I am tormented in this
flame!" But Abraham replied, "Son, remember that
thou in thy lifetime receivedst thy good things, and
likewise Lazarus evil things: but now he is comforted,
and thou art tormented. *And beside all this, between
us and you THERE IS A GREAT GULF FIXED:*
so that they which would pass from hence to you
cannot; neither can they pass to us, that would come
from thence."

It was into the Paradise side of hell that Jesus

descended, where the spirits of the righteous were; and He led them out of the lower parts of the earth, ascending up *far above all heavens,* and now the spirits of departed saints rest with Him.

The New Testament clearly points out *three heavens:*

The *first* heaven is the region of the clouds, the atmosphere above us.

The *second* heaven is the region of the stars and planets.

The *third* heaven is God's house—Paradise; and it was into this heaven of heavens, the abode of God, that Jesus ascended.

In II Corinthians 12:1—4 the Apostle Paul gives testimony concerning the third heaven: "It is not expedient for me doubtless to glory. I will come to visions and revelations of the Lord. *I knew a man in Christ above fourteen years ago,* (whether in the body, I cannot tell; or whether out of the body, I cannot tell: God knoweth;) *such an one caught up to THE THIRD HEAVEN.* And I knew such a man, (whether in the body, or out of the body, I cannot tell: God knoweth;) *How that He was caught up into PARADISE, and heard unspeakable words, which it is not lawful for a man to utter!"*

Many Bible scholars believe that this man was Paul himself—probably when he was stoned at Lystra, dragged outside the city, and left for dead (Acts 14:19). Be that as it may, the Scripture definitely declares the existence of *a THIRD heaven*—and since there is a *third* heaven, there must of necessity be a *first* and *second* heaven! And since Jesus "ascended up *far above ALL heavens,"* it is evident that He was taken up into the third heaven, God's house. But He is no longer "in the *bosom* of the Father" (John 1:18), but *seated at the right hand of the Father,* His rightful position by merit of His finished work in His body of humiliation.

The Manner of the Ascension of Jesus Christ

". . . Thus it is written, and thus it behoved Christ to suffer, and to rise from the dead the third day: and that repentance and remission of sins should be preached in His name among all nations, beginning at Jerusalem. And ye are witnesses of these things.

"And, behold, I send the promise of my Father upon you: but tarry ye in the city of Jerusalem, until ye be endued with power from on high. And He led them out as far as to Bethany, and He lifted up His hands, and blessed them. *And it came to pass, while He blessed them, HE WAS PARTED FROM THEM, AND CARRIED UP INTO HEAVEN.* And they worshipped Him, and returned to Jerusalem with great joy: and were continually in the temple, praising and blessing God" (Luke 24:46—53).

The *manner* of the Lord's ascension is clearly set forth in the Scripture, and if we want the truth we can see it in the Word of God. Many people spiritualize His ascension, just as they spiritualize His resurrection and His second coming. They teach that He did not *rise* bodily, that He did not *ascend* bodily to heaven, and that He will not *come again* bodily. But the Word of God is crystal clear in declaring that the Lord Jesus Christ rose again bodily, ascended bodily, and that *the same Jesus* will come again exactly as He went away:

Acts 1:9: "And when He had spoken these things, *while they beheld, HE WAS TAKEN UP; AND A CLOUD RECEIVED HIM OUT OF THEIR SIGHT.*"

Luke 24:51: "And it came to pass, *while He blessed them, HE WAS PARTED FROM THEM, AND CARRIED UP INTO HEAVEN.*"

Can it be made plainer? The same Jesus who

appeared to the disciples in the upper room, the same Jesus who ate broiled fish and honeycomb in their presence, *was taken up into heaven BODILY while they were looking at Him,* and they watched Him until a cloud received Him out of their sight. Then *immediately,* as they gazed after Him in bewilderment, *the heavenly messengers appeared* and assured the disciples that Jesus would return *in exactly the same manner* as they had seen Him ascend.

In John 17:4, 5, just before He went to Calvary, Jesus prayed, "I have glorified thee on the earth: I have finished the work which thou gavest me to do. And now, O Father, *glorify thou me with thine own self WITH THE GLORY WHICH I HAD WITH THEE BEFORE THE WORLD WAS.*"

Jesus was the eternal Word; He was with the Father in the beginning (John 1:1, 2).

The Word was made flesh and dwelt among men (John 1:14).

He came from the bosom of the Father to declare God to man (John 1:18).

He declared to Philip, "He that hath seen *me* hath seen *the Father*" (John 14:9).

And now, because of His total victory, because of the work accomplished in His body of humiliation, He *does* share the glory with the Father—the glory He had with Him before the world was; but He shares that glory *in a body,* not in spiritual form. Today He sits at the right hand of God, sharing all the glory heaven affords!

The Purpose of the Ascension and Exaltation of Christ

"These words spake Jesus, and lifted up His eyes to heaven, and said, Father, the hour is come; glorify thy Son, that thy Son also may glorify thee" (John 17:1).

Jesus was in the beginning *with* the Father, He
shared the glory and the power of the Father, He was
co-equal with the Father. Yet His every word and
deed were carefully guarded, that everything He said
and everything He did might be *to the honor and
glory* of the Father. In the darkest hours of His earthly life He prayed, "Not as I will, but as thou wilt."
On several occasions He said, "The words I speak are
the words of Him who sent me. The works I do are
the works given to me by Him who sent me." He
made it clear to friends and enemies alike that He
proceeded from God, that He was in the world to do
God's will and to finsh the work God had given Him
to do; and when He had *finished* that work He ascended back to the right hand of the Majesty on high.
Jesus was glorified *in order that He might glorify the
heavenly Father.*

Exalted that He might forgive sins:

The risen, ascended, exalted One now sits at the
right hand of God, making intercession for believers
and granting salvation to any and all who will confess their sins and believe in His shed blood. It is
only for the sake of His Son that God forgives the
sinner. This is clearly stated in Paul's letter to the
believers in Ephesus:

"God, who is rich in mercy, for His great love
wherewith He loved us, even when we were dead in
sins, hath quickened us together with Christ, (by
grace ye are saved;) and hath raised us up together,
and made us sit together in heavenly places in Christ
Jesus: *That in the ages to come He might shew the
exceeding riches of His grace in His kindness toward
us THROUGH CHRIST JESUS*" (Eph. 2:4—7).

Exalted as a Forerunner for us:

In John chapter 13 Jesus spoke very plainly with

His disciples, repeating what He had told them on many other occasions—the fact that He would be arrested, tried, condemned, and crucified. This saddened them greatly, but He encouraged them with this promise:

"Let not your heart be troubled: ye believe in God, believe also in me. In my Father's house are many mansions: if it were not so, I would have told you. *I go to prepare a place for you.* And if I go and prepare a place for you, *I WILL COME AGAIN, and receive you unto myself; that where I am, there ye may be also*" (John 14:1—3).

Since His ascension, Jesus has been preparing a place for His bride, the New Testament Church. In His *resurrection* He became "the firstfruits of them that slept" (I Cor. 15:20). In His *ascension* He just as truly became *the forerunner* for us. He has entered heaven, He has gone on before us, into that place He is preparing where we will dwell eternally with Him: "Which hope we have as an anchor of the soul, both sure and stedfast, and which entereth *into that within the veil; whither THE FORERUNNER is for us entered, even Jesus,* made an High Priest for ever after the order of Melchisedec" (Heb. 6:19, 20).

The "how" of this is clearly stated in Paul's letter to the Hebrew believers, chapter 9, verses 19 through 24:

"For when Moses had spoken every precept to all the people according to the law, he took the blood of calves and of goats, with water, and scarlet wool, and hyssop, and sprinkled both the book, and all the people, saying, This is the blood of the testament which God hath enjoined unto you. Moreover he sprinkled with blood both the tabernacle, and all the vessels of the ministry. And almost all things are by the law purged with blood; *and without shedding of blood is no remission.*

"It was therefore necessary that the *patterns* of things in the heavens should be purified with these; *BUT THE HEAVENLY THINGS THEMSELVES WITH BETTER SACRIFICES THAN THESE. For Christ is not entered into the holy places made with hands, which are the figures of the true; but INTO HEAVEN ITSELF, now to appear in the presence of God FOR US.*"

The Man Christ Jesus entered into heaven; He is there as our great High Priest, ministering on our behalf. He entered the holy of holies—the Father's abode—with His own blood. He presented *(and IS presenting)* the blood of atonement for us:

"Having therefore, brethren, *boldness* to enter into the holiest by the blood of Jesus, by *a new and living way, which He hath consecrated for us,* through the veil, that is to say, His flesh" (Heb. 10:19, 20). The work of Jesus now for sinning saints is acceptable to God through His shed blood; and because of the eternal efficacy of His blood He restores us to fellowship when we sin. God does not want His saints to sin, and most assuredly *grace does not issue a licence* for believers to sin; but if we *do* sin, "we have an Advocate with the Father, Jesus Christ the righteous" (I John 2:1).

The Psalmist wrote, "The Lord said unto my Lord, *Sit thou at my right hand, until I make thine enemies thy footstool*" (Psalm 110:1).

In Hebrews 10:12, 13 the Apostle Paul declared, "*THIS MAN,* after He had offered one sacrifice for sins for ever, *SAT DOWN on the right hand of God; from henceforth expecting till His enemies be made His footstool.*"

In his sermon at Pentecost, Peter cried out, "David is not ascended into the heavens: but he saith himself, *The Lord said unto my Lord, SIT THOU ON MY RIGHT HAND, UNTIL I MAKE THY FOES*

THY FOOTSTOOL. Therefore let all the house of Israel know assuredly, that *God hath made that same Jesus, whom ye have crucified, BOTH LORD AND CHRIST"* (Acts 2:34—36).

Then in Acts 3:19—21 Peter said to the people, "Repent ye therefore, and be converted, that your sins may be blotted out, when the times of refreshing shall come from the presence of the Lord; *and He shall send Jesus Christ,* which before was preached unto you: *whom the heaven must receive until the times of restitution of all things,* which God hath spoken by the mouth of all His holy prophets since the world began."

He who by men was nailed to a cross and lifted up as prophesied has ascended into glory and is now awaiting the complete subjection of His enemies and the restitution of all things. At the appointed time— and that time *will come—*this same Jesus will come forth the second time and will destroy His enemies. All opposition will be completely subdued and the knowledge of the Lord will cover the earth as the waters cover the sea: "Now that He ascended, what is it but that He also descended first into the lower parts of the earth? He that descended is the same also that ascended up far above all heavens, *THAT HE MIGHT FILL ALL THINGS"* (Eph. 4:9, 10).

The Results of the Ascension and Exaltation of Jesus as Having to Do with Believers

The Apostle Paul declared, "I am crucified with Christ! Nevertheless I live; yet not I, but Christ liveth in me: and the life which I now live in the flesh I live by the faith of the Son of God, who loved me, and gave Himself for me" (Gal. 2:20).

Glorious truth! Because of His ascension and exaltation, believers share in all that Jesus accomplished.

It is through His cross that the world is crucified unto us, and we are dead to the world (Gal. 6:14). Positionally, we are seated in heaven even now—we "sit together in heavenly places *in Christ Jesus*" (Eph. 2:6).

Since He is our great High Priest, we obtain mercy and find rest through Him: "For we have not an high priest which cannot be touched with the feeling of our infirmities; but was in all points tempted like as we are, yet without sin. Let us therefore come boldly unto the throne of grace, that we may obtain mercy, and find grace to help in time of need" (Heb. 4:15, 16).

In Colossians 3:1—4 believers are instructed, "If ye then be *risen with Christ,* seek those things which are above, where Christ sitteth on the right hand of God. Set your affection on things above, not on things on the earth. For *ye are dead, and your life is hid WITH CHRIST IN GOD.* When Christ, who is our life, shall appear, then shall ye also appear with Him in glory."

What glorious consolation to know that we are crucified with Christ; we are raised with Him; we walk in newness of life because we have become partakers of divine nature; we are possessors of the Holy Spirit; our citizenship is in heaven; we are hid with Christ in God and sealed until the day of redemption; and when Christ who is our life shall appear, we shall appear with Him in glory. We know the Lord will descend from heaven "with a shout, with the voice of the archangel, and with the trump of God." The saints who have died will be raised, the spirit will unite with the glorified body, and believers who are living will be changed "in the twinkling of an eye." Then we will be caught up together to meet the Lord in the clouds in the air—*and so shall we ever be with our Lord* (I Thess. 4:16—18; I Cor. 15:51—53). Believers have this assurance because of *Christ's victory over death* and His acceptance by God the Father upon the merit of His accomplishment and finished work on earth.

Jesus not only assured the disciples that He would prepare a place for them and then return to call them unto Himself; He also gave them the promise of the Holy Spirit, which would be their gain. As long as He remained with them in body He was limited to one place at a time—i. e., He could not be in Jerusalem and in Nazareth simultaneously. Therefore He would lay His life down, take it up again, and ascend back to the Father to continue His ministry on their behalf; but He would not leave them comfortless. After His ascension and exaltation He would send *the Holy Spirit,* who would be forever *with them and IN them.* Thus they would be equipped in a much better way after He departed than while He was with them bodily.

John chapter 14 records the promise of the Spirit. Jesus said to His disciples, "I will pray the Father, and *He shall give you another Comforter, that He may abide with you for ever; even the Spirit of truth;* whom the world cannot receive, because it seeth Him not, neither knoweth Him: but ye know Him; for *He dwelleth WITH you and shall be IN you.* I will not leave you comfortless: I will come to you.

"Yet a little while, and the world seeth me no more; but ye see me: because I live, ye shall live also. At that day ye shall know that *I am in my Father, AND YE IN ME, and I IN YOU. . . .* If a man love me, he will keep my words: and my Father will love him, *and we will come unto him, AND MAKE OUR ABODE WITH HIM. . . .*

"*These things have I spoken unto you, BEING YET PRESENT WITH YOU. But the Comforter, which is the Holy Ghost, whom the Father will send*

*in my name, He shall teach you ALL things, and
bring all things to your remembrance, whatsoever I
have said unto you"* (John 14:16—26 in part).

We are not only *born* of the Spirit, but *every born
again believer today* is indwelt by the Spirit, and "if
any man *have not* the Spirit of Christ, he is none of
His" (Rom. 8:9).

Every believer is *led* by the Spirit: "For as many
as are led by the Spirit of God, they are the sons of
God" (Rom. 8:14).

Every believer is *assured* by the Spirit: "The Spirit
Himself beareth witness with our spirit, that we are
the children of God" (Rom. 8:16).

The Holy Spirit leads believers into paths of righteousness, paths of right living (Psalm 23:3) and into
the path of victory. To the believers in the Galatian
church Paul said, *"Walk in the Spirit, and ye shall
not fulfil the lust of the flesh. . . .* But the fruit of
the Spirit is love, joy, peace, longsuffering, gentleness,
goodness, faith, meekness, temperance: against such
there is no law. And they that are Christ's have crucified the flesh with the affections and lusts. *If we
LIVE in the Spirit, let us also WALK in the Spirit"*
(Gal. 5:16, 22—25).

The believer is *sealed* by the Holy Spirit "unto the
day of redemption" (Eph. 4:30).

All who are willing to surrender fully to the will
and direction of God are *filled* with the Spirit: "Be
not drunk with wine, wherein is excess; *but BE
FILLED WITH THE SPIRIT;* speaking to yourselves
in psalms and hymns and spiritual songs, singing and
making melody in your heart to the Lord; giving thanks
always for all things unto God and the Father in the
name of our Lord Jesus Christ; submitting yourselves
one to another in the fear of God" (Eph. 5:18—21).

To the believer the Holy Spirit makes known all
truth. Jesus clearly told His disciples that there was

more truth to be revealed to them, truth which the Holy Spirit would make known:

"I have yet many things to say unto you, but ye cannot bear them now. Howbeit when He, the Spirit of truth, is come, He will guide you into ALL truth: for He shall not speak of Himself; but whatsoever He shall hear, that shall He speak: *and He will shew you things to come.* He shall glorify me: for He shall receive of mine, and shall shew it unto you. All things that the Father hath are mine: therefore said I, that He shall take of mine, and shall shew it unto you" (John 16:12—15).

Not only would this additional *revelation* be given, but there would be *new prophecies*—"He will shew you *THINGS TO COME.*" We who are believers today know that the Holy Spirit *did* give much truth and many prophecies to the New Testament writers. We now have "the perfect law of liberty" (James 1:25), the complete Word of God, *"all truth."* "That which is perfect is come" (I Cor. 13:10). While Jesus tabernacled among men "the perfect law of liberty" had *not* come. We did not have the Scriptures in their fulness and completeness until almost a hundred years after the birth of Christ. But through the centuries God has protected His Word, and only men *called of Him and inspired of the Holy Ghost* penned down these sacred words of soberness and truth, words for man to *live by*, and *die* by!

Peter gave testimony to the verbal inspiration of the Scriptures. In II Peter 1:16—21 he declared, "We have not followed cunningly devised fables, when we made known unto you the power and coming of our Lord Jesus Christ, but were eyewitnesses of His majesty. For He received from God the Father honour and glory, when there came such a voice to Him from the excellent glory, This is my beloved Son, in whom I am well pleased. *And this voice which came from heaven WE HEARD,* when we were with Him in the holy mount.

"We have also a more sure word of prophecy; whereunto ye do well that ye take heed, as unto a light that shineth in a dark place, until the day dawn, and the day star arise in your hearts: knowing this first, that *no prophecy of the Scripture is of any private interpretation. FOR THE PROPHECY CAME NOT IN OLD TIME BY THE WILL OF MAN: BUT HOLY MEN OF GOD SPAKE AS THEY WERE MOVED BY THE HOLY GHOST.*"

The Apostle Paul instructed young Timothy, "*ALL Scripture is given by inspiration of God,* and is profitable for doctrine, for reproof, for correction, for instruction in righteousness: that the man of God may be perfect, throughly furnished unto all good works" (II Tim. 3:16, 17).

The coming of the Holy Spirit was made *possible* by the ascension and exaltation of the Lord Jesus Christ. He explained to His disciples, "It is *expedient for YOU* that I go away: for *if I go NOT away, the Comforter will not come unto you; but IF I DEPART, I will send Him unto you*" (John 16:7).

Jesus ascended—and the Holy Spirit came as promised. Believers are now indwelt by the Author of the Scriptures, therefore we now have within us the *Teacher* of the Scriptures. In God's love letter to His "little children" we read, "*Ye have an unction from the Holy One, and ye know ALL things. . . .* The anointing which ye have received of Him abideth in you, *and ye need not that any man teach you:* but as the same anointing *teacheth you of all things, and is truth,* and is no lie, and even as it hath taught you, ye shall abide in Him" (I John 2:20, 27).

In Ephesians 1:17—20 Paul speaks of "the Spirit of wisdom and revelation in the knowledge of Him: *the eyes of your understanding being enlightened;* that ye may know what is the hope of His calling, and what the riches of the glory of His inheritance in the saints, and what is the exceeding greatness of His power to us-ward who believe, according to the working of His mighty power, which He wrought in Christ, *when He raised Him from the dead, and set Him at His own right hand in the heavenly places."*

Read the Scriptural account of the actions and activities of the apostles before Pentecost, and then *study their lives AFTER Pentecost*—and note the marked contrast. Truly, the eyes of their understanding *were* opened, they *were* enlightened, they *did* believe the things Jesus told them before His crucifixion, and they were transformed from spineless weaklings to spiritual giants! After the arrest of Jesus, the men who had walked with Him were so terrified for their lives that they ran and hid; but *after Pentecost* those same men stood before the religious leaders and men in high places and declared, *"WE OUGHT TO OBEY GOD RATHER THAN MEN!"* (Acts 5:29). Certainly the ascension and exaltation of the Lord Jesus Christ produced tremendous results in the lives of the apostles —and in the lives of *all* believers—through the coming of the Comforter, the Holy Spirit.

While Jesus was on earth, He taught the multitudes; but after His ascension and exaltation the Holy Spirit came, made known *all truth,* and holy men penned it down. Now believers have the truth complete, and are indwelt by *the Author and Teacher* of all truth. Glorious results of our Lord's ascension and exaltation. Hallelujah!

"Seeing then that we have a great High Priest, that is passed into the heavens, Jesus the Son of God, let us hold fast our profession. For we have not an High Priest which cannot be touched with the feeling of our infirmities; but was in all points tempted like as we are, yet without sin. *Let us therefore come*

BOLDLY unto the throne of grace, that we may OB-
TAIN MERCY, and find GRACE TO HELP IN TIME
OF NEED" (Heb. 4:14—16).

Through the death, resurrection, ascension, and
exaltation of Jesus our High Priest we can draw near
to God in boldness; and as we approach the throne
of grace, if we hesitate or tremble at the thought of
God's majesty, holiness, and power, all we need do
is remember that He who loved us and died for us now
sits *at the right hand of God* and makes intercession
for us: "Now of the things which we have spoken
this is the sum: *WE HAVE SUCH AN HIGH PRIEST,*
WHO IS SET ON THE RIGHT HAND OF THE
THRONE OF THE MAJESTY IN THE HEAVENS"
(Heb. 8:1).

In John 7:37—39 Jesus prophesied concerning the
coming of the Holy Spirit: "In the last day, that
great day of the feast, Jesus stood and cried, saying,
If any man thirst, let him come unto me, and drink.
He that believeth on me, as the Scripture hath said,
out of his belly shall flow rivers of living water. (But
this spake He of *the Spirit,* which they that believe
on Him should receive: for *the Holy Ghost was not*
yet given; BECAUSE THAT JESUS WAS NOT YET
GLORIFIED.)"

It was necessary that Jesus be glorified before the
Holy Spirit could be poured out as promised. Jesus
declared, "John truly baptized with water; but ye
shall be baptized with the Holy Ghost not many days
hence" (Acts 1:5). Then in Acts 2:1—4 we read, "And
when the Day of Pentecost was fully come, they were
all with one accord in one place. And suddenly there
came a sound from heaven as of a rushing mighty
wind, and it filled all the house where they were sitting. And there appeared unto them cloven tongues
like as of fire, and it sat upon each of them. *AND*
THEY WERE ALL FILLED WITH THE HOLY

GHOST, and began to speak with other tongues, *as THE SPIRIT gave them utterance!"*

In Peter's sermon on that same day he declared, "Therefore being by the right hand of God exalted, and having received of the Father the promise of the Holy Ghost, *He hath shed forth this, which ye now see and hear"* (Acts 2:33).

Today all who believe on Jesus receive the Holy Spirit, and by the Holy Spirit we are baptized into the body of Christ: "For by one Spirit are we all baptized into one body, whether we be Jews or Gentiles, whether we be bond or free; and have been all made to drink into one Spirit" (I Cor. 12:13).

To His disciples Jesus prophesied, "Verily, verily, I say unto you, *He that believeth on me, the works that I do shall he do also; and GREATER works than these shall he do;* because I go unto my Father" (John 14:12). We find the fulfillment of this prophecy recorded in Acts chapter 2, when Peter preached on the Day of Pentecost and "they that gladly received his word were baptized: *and the same day there were added unto them about THREE THOUSAND SOULS"* (Acts 2:41).

The Results of the Ascension and Exaltation as Pertaining to Jesus

I have repeatedly pointed out that Jesus was in the beginning with the Father, co-equal with the Father in every respect (John 1:1, 3, 18).

In the fulness of time He was born of woman (Gal. 4:4, 5). He took a body of humiliation, "made Himself of no reputation, and took upon Him the form of a servant, and was made in the likeness of men: and being found in fashion as a man, He humbled Himself, and became obedient unto death, even the death of the cross" (Phil. 2:6—8).

He was "made a little lower than the angels for the suffering of death." He was given a body in which He could lay His life down, "that He by the grace of God should taste death for every man" (Heb. 2:9). He died, but death could not hold Him. He rose again, He ascended, and today He sits at the right hand of the Father, clothed in the glory of God, and all the honor of heaven has been bestowed upon Him. He has been "made *so much better* than the angels, as He hath by inheritance obtained a more excellent name than they" (Heb. 1:4).

In His body of humiliation, the Son of God was obedient unto death, even the death of the cross; "wherefore God also hath highly exalted Him, and given Him a name which is above every name: that at the name of Jesus every knee should bow, of things in heaven, and things in earth, and things under the earth; and that every tongue should confess that Jesus Christ is Lord, to the glory of God the Father" (Phil. 2:9—11).

Peter declares that Jesus "is gone into heaven, and is on the right hand of God; angels and authorities and powers being made subject unto Him" (I Pet. 3:22).

Because of His complete submission to the will of His heavenly Father, because He satisfied the holiness, righteousness, and law of God, because He finished the work the Father sent Him to do, God granted His only begotten Son the highest seat of heaven; and in the fulness of time every knee *will* bow and every tongue *will* confess that Jesus Christ is Lord to the glory of God the Eternal Father!

Chapter Six

BIBLE TRUTH CONCERNING
CHRIST'S SECOND COMING

"Let not your heart be troubled: ye believe in God, believe also in me. In my Father's house are many mansions: if it were not so, I would have told you. I go to prepare a place for you. And if I go and prepare a place for you, I will come again, and receive you unto myself; that where I am, there ye may be also" (John 14:1—3).

"And when He had spoken these things, while they beheld, He was taken up; and a cloud received Him out of their sight. And while they looked stedfastly toward heaven as He went up, behold, two men stood by them in white apparel; which also said, Ye men of Galilee, why stand ye gazing up into heaven? This same Jesus, which is taken up from you into heaven, shall so come in like manner as ye have seen Him go into heaven" (Acts 1:9—11).

The *first* coming of the Lord Jesus Christ is intimately associated with His *second* coming. In fact, a careful study of the Scriptures, rightly dividing the Word of Truth, will reveal that His first coming *demands* His second coming, and just as surely as He came the first time He will come *again* at the appointed time.

He appeared the first time a tiny "star" in the east, seen by the wise men; He is coming the second

337

time "the bright and morning star." He came the
first time a babe in a manger; He is coming the second
time King of kings and Lord of lords. He came the
first time the lowly Nazarene; He is coming the second
time the Lion of the Tribe of Judah. He came the
first time to lay His life down; He is coming the second time to reign eternally supreme.

It would be impossible to here discuss all of the
Scriptures which clearly set forth the first and second
comings of Christ, but we will consider as many of
them as space permits.

Christ's Decease and Glory

". . . Jesus Christ: whom having not seen, ye
love; in whom, though now ye see Him not, yet believing, ye rejoice with joy unspeakable and full of
glory: receiving the end of your faith, even the salvation of your souls. Of which salvation the prophets
have inquired and searched diligently, who prophesied
of the grace that should come unto you: searching
what, or what manner of time the Spirit of Christ
which was in them did signify, when He testified beforehand the sufferings of Christ, and the glory that
should follow. Unto whom it was revealed, that not
unto themselves, but unto us they did minister the
things, which are now reported unto you by them that
have preached the Gospel unto you with the Holy
Ghost sent down from heaven; which things the angels
desire to look into" (I Pet. 1:8—12).

The Old Testament prophets prophesied of Christ's
sufferings and His glory, but they did not understand
the meaning of the message given to them by the Holy
Spirit, to be penned down for us.

In II Peter 1:16—18 we read, "We have not followed cunningly devised fables, when we made known
unto you *the power and coming* of our Lord Jesus

Christ, but were *eyewitnesses of HIS MAJESTY.* For He received from God the Father honour and glory, when there came such a voice to Him from the excellent glory, This is my beloved Son, in whom I am well pleased. *And this voice which came from heaven we heard, when we were with Him in the holy mount."*

In these verses Peter spoke of his experience when he, with James and John, was with Jesus on the Mount of Transfiguration where they were *eyewitnesses of His MAJESTY.* Luke 9:28—36 records a detailed account of that great Bible conference, and in that account we see the combination of Christ's atonement and His second coming:

"And it came to pass . . . He took Peter and John and James, and went up into a mountain to pray. *And as He prayed, the fashion of His countenance was altered, and His raiment was white and glistering.* And, behold, there talked with Him two men, which were *Moses and Elias:* who appeared in glory, and spake of His *decease* which He should accomplish at Jerusalem.

"But Peter and they that were with Him were heavy with sleep: and when they were awake, they saw His glory, and the two men that stood with Him. And it came to pass, as they departed from Him, Peter said unto Jesus, Master, it is good for us to be here: and let us make three tabernacles; one for thee, and one for Moses, and one for Elias: not knowing what he said.

"While he thus spake, there came a cloud, and overshadowed them: and they feared as they entered into the cloud. *And there came a voice out of the cloud, saying, This is my beloved Son: hear Him.* And when the voice was past, Jesus was found alone. And they kept it close, and told no man in those days any of those things which they had seen."

Moses and Elijah in their glorified bodies appeared
to Jesus on the mount, and the theme of their conversation was "His decease," His death on Calvary.
His death was a divine imperative, for had He not
died, the glory could never have been. It was for the
glory, "the joy that was set before Him," that He
"endured the cross, despising the shame, and is set
down at the right hand of the throne of God" (Heb.
12:2). Had there never been a crown of *thorns* there
could not have been a crown of *glory*. The sin-debt
had to be paid in full before the glory of God could
be displayed, because *the source* of the glory of God
is Jesus Christ—crucified, buried, risen, ascended.

When Jesus cried out, "It is finished!" *two eternities met.* That which was foreordained before the
foundation of the world was now accomplished. Jesus
came into the world knowing exactly why He came.
He did not come in darkness or ignorance. Before
there was dust from which God created Adam, before
there was a sinner to need salvation, the members of
the Godhead discussed and fully settled the fact that
Jesus the Lamb would die on the cross for the sins
of the world; and had He *not* laid His life down as
divinely designed, all the blood shed from Eden to
Calvary would have been in vain!

The blood of the Old Testament sacrifices did not
take away sin (Heb. 10:4). Those sacrifices were only
shadows pointing to the Lamb of God crucified. Therefore all who are saved—from the beginning until the
end of time—will be saved through the blood shed
by Christ on Calvary. When He said, "It is finished,"
with His left hand He reached *all the way back to
the Garden of Eden* and with His right hand He
reached all the way *forward* to the day when eternity
begins, and with His arms He gathered all of His
children unto Himself—but remember, that gathering
includes only those who are *willing* to be gathered,

those who hear and answer His call.

God is sovereign, knowing the end in the beginning; and thanks be unto Him, all hell cannot stop the foreordained, settled program of His eternal love! Christ's announcement "It is finished" revealed to the world the fulfilled and accomplished counsel of Almighty God. *Jesus,* through His blood, *purchased and secured* the redemption and glory of His people. *Christ crucified* is the center, soul, and life-stream of redemption and glory. Apart from His death on the cross there could have been no redemption, therefore there could be no glory. The Rock was smitten at Calvary, and from that smitten Rock flows the living water of salvation and the divine assurance that glory will follow.

Yes, the glorification of the saints of God is so sure, so eternally settled, that Moses and Elijah were already in their glorified bodies when they visited this earth even *before* the death of Jesus. *"For ever, O Lord, thy Word is settled in heaven"* (Psalm 119:89).

The Lord's Supper and the Coming Kingdom

"And as they were eating, Jesus took bread, and blessed it, and brake it, and gave it to the disciples, and said, Take, eat; this is my body. And He took the cup, and gave thanks, and gave it to them, saying, Drink ye all of it; for this is my blood of the new testament, which is shed for many for the remission of sins. But I say unto you, I will not drink henceforth of this fruit of the vine, until that day when I drink it new with you in my Father's kingdom" (Matt. 26:26—29).

Notice the two phrases Jesus used here: "This is my blood . . . this fruit of the vine." These two statements definitely speak of the cross and the kingdom to come. His blood spoke of *His atoning death—*

"Without shedding of blood is no remission" (Heb. 9:22). The fruit of the vine spoke of *the outcome* of His death.

In the Garden of Eden, God rejected the fig-leaf covering designed by Adam and Eve, and Himself provided a covering through the blood sacrifice of innocent animals. He wrapped the shame of Adam and Eve in coats of skins provided at the expense of the blood of innocent substitutes. "By faith *Abel* offered unto God a more excellent sacrifice than Cain" (Heb. 11:4). Abel offered a blood sacrifice. Cain offered the product of his own labors.

"The fruit of the vine" was a familiar term to the disciples. There were acres and acres of vineyards in Palestine, and the ripe grapes were taken from the vine and placed in a huge vat where they were trampled and crushed in order to obtain the juice, or wine. Thus was Jesus telling His disciples that He would be crushed in the winepress of God's wrath before they could benefit from or through His first coming into the world. As long as He remained with them in His body of humiliation, even though He was God in flesh His services to them were limited. He had not come into the world to remain here in a mortal body. He was given that body that it might be crushed, *"that He by the grace of God should taste death for every man"* (Heb. 2:9).

The disciples, like the prophets of old, could not understand that Jesus must suffer, the corn of wheat must fall into the ground and die. In instituting the Lord's Supper He was teaching them the absolute necessity that His blood be poured out for the remission of sins. (In the Greek language, "remission" signifies not only guilt taken away, but the *removing of the sins* which *brought* guilt upon the individual.)

The Lord's Supper has not only a commemorative meaning, but a prophetic meaning as well, and in partaking of the bread and the fruit of the vine, believers not only show forth His death on Calvary, but also testify to the time when He will come again to set up His kingdom, when He will sit on the throne of David and reign in righteousness. Jesus declared, "I will not drink henceforth of this fruit of the vine *until that day* when I drink it new with you in my Father's kingdom."

Tens of thousands of church members today receive the Lord's Supper without any idea of the significance of what they are doing when they take the unleavened bread and the fruit of the vine. The Apostle Paul instructed the Corinthian believers concerning this, and his instructions to them are also for *our* admonition:

"For I have received of the Lord that which also I delivered unto you, That the Lord Jesus the same night in which He was betrayed took bread: and when He had given thanks, He brake it, and said, Take, eat: this is my body, which is broken for you: this do in remembrance of me.

"After the same manner also He took the cup, when He had supped, saying, This cup is the new testament in my blood: this do ye, as oft as ye drink it, in remembrance of me. *For as often as ye eat this bread, and drink this cup, YE DO SHEW THE LORD'S DEATH TILL HE COME*" (I Cor. 11:23—26).

True believers who observe the Lord's Supper in the spirit in which God intended it to be observed experience a foretaste of the great marriage supper of the Lamb which will be celebrated at His second coming. This is described in Revelation chapter 19. After the horrible judgments are poured out upon the harlot Babylon, and upon apostate Christendom, John the Beloved declares, "I heard as it were the voice of a great multitude, and as the voice of many waters, and as the voice of mighty thunderings, saying, *AL-*

LELUIA! *for the Lord God omnipotent reigneth! Let us be glad and rejoice, and give honour to Him: FOR THE MARRIAGE OF THE LAMB IS COME,* and His wife hath made herself ready. And to her was granted that she should be arrayed in fine linen, clean and white: for *the fine linen is THE RIGHTEOUS-NESS OF SAINTS.* And he saith unto me, Write, *Blessed are they which are called UNTO THE MAR-RIAGE SUPPER OF THE LAMB.* And he saith unto me, These are the true sayings of God" (Rev. 19:6—9).

So we see that the Lord's Supper shows forth Christ's death *until He comes again.*

Hebrews Chapter Ten

"For the law having a shadow of good things to come, and not the very image of the things, can never with those sacrifices which they offered year by year continually make the comers thereunto perfect. For then would they not have ceased to be offered? because that the worshippers once purged should have had no more conscience of sins. But in those sacri-fices there is a remembrance again made of sins every year.

"For it is not possible that the blood of bulls and of goats should take away sins. Wherefore when He cometh into the world, He saith, Sacrifice and offering thou wouldest not, but a body hast thou prepared me: In burnt-offerings and sacrifices for sin thou hast had no pleasure. Then said I, Lo, I come (in the volume of the book it is written of me,) to do thy will, O God. Above when He said, Sacrifice and offering and burnt-offerings and offering for sin thou wouldest not, neither hadst pleasure therein; which are offered by the law; then said He, Lo, I come to do thy will, O God. He taketh away the first, that He may establish the second. By the which will we are sanctified through the offering of the body of Jesus Christ once for all. And every priest standeth daily ministering and offering oftentimes the same sacrifices, which can never take away sins: *But THIS MAN, after He had offered one sacrifice for sins for ever, sat down on the right hand of God; from henceforth expecting till His enemies be made His footstool. For BY ONE OFFERING He hath perfected FOR EVER them that are sanctified"* (Heb. 10:1—14).

Here we have the expiation and expectation concerning the atoning death of Jesus. He offered *one* sacrifice for sins forever, a sacrifice that so thoroughly satisfied God that it will never again be necessary for a sacrifice to be offered; and having offered the perfect sacrifice, He ascended back to heaven and sat down on the right hand of God.

Expiation means "to give satisfaction for evil committed." Through faith in the shed blood of Jesus the sin of the sinner is expiated (atoned for), and *apart from the shed blood of Jesus there IS no expiation or atonement for sin.*

There are no words to describe the infinite value of Christ's death on Calvary. He left the glories of heaven, took a body of humiliation, and in that body He finished the work the Father sent Him to do. He willingly, lovingly laid His life down, through His eternal spirit He offered Himself without spot to God, and through this offering of Himself brought eternal life and benefit to all who believe in His shed blood and finished work. Surely, we have no words in our language to describe value such as this!

Jesus offered one sacrifice for sins and then *sat down* at the right hand of God; *the work of atonement was finished.* He will never rise to make another offering—there is *no need* for another offering for sin, for His one offering of His own blood satisfied God *completely and eternally.* Therefore, faith in the one perfect offering of Christ places the believer into the perfect state, *perfected forever* because the offering is eternal. The sin-question is settled, sins are remitted on the ground of the perfect offering, and *"where remission of these is, there is NO MORE OFFERING FOR SIN"* (Heb. 10:18).

The virtue of Christ's finished work remains eternally available as the need of man exists. He will never repeat His atoning work, but *He will return to earth* to set up His kingdom. He came the first time to settle the sin-question from the standpoint of *penalty;* He ever lives at the right hand of the Father to keep us from the *power* of sin. (We are overcomers because *He overcame.*) He will come again to put all enemies under His feet and destroy every trace of sin. Isaiah declares, "They shall not hurt nor destroy in all my holy mountain: *for the earth shall be full of the knowledge of the Lord, as the waters cover the sea"* (Isa. 11:9).

"THIS MAN, after He had offered one sacrifice for sins for ever, SAT DOWN on the right hand of God; FROM HENCEFORTH EXPECTING TILL HIS ENEMIES BE MADE HIS FOOTSTOOL" (Heb. 10: 12, 13). The Greek word here translated "expecting" is used only of someone waiting for another, and is also rendered "wait for . . . tarry for . . . look for." The same Greek word is used in John 5:3 where at the pool of Bethesda the impotent folk were *"waiting for* the moving of the water."

The same word is used in Acts 17:16 where Paul, at Athens, *"waited for"* Timothy and Silas to join him there.

It is used again in I Corinthians 16:11 where Paul, speaking of Timothy, said, "I *look for* him with the brethren."

The same Greek word is used in I Corinthians 11:33 where Paul admonished the Corinthian believers to "*tarry* one for another" in partaking of the Lord's Supper.

We find the same word again in Hebrews 11:10, where Abraham "*looked for* a city which hath foundations, whose builder and maker is God."

James uses the same word in James 5:7: ". . . Behold, the husbandman *waiteth for* the precious fruit of the earth . . . ," and in I Peter 3:20 the word is used with reference to the longsuffering of God who "*waited* in the days of Noah, while the ark was a preparing . . . ."

Just so, *CHRIST IS WAITING* "*till His enemies be made His footstool.*" When the bride of Christ is complete the Church will be caught up to meet the Lord, the marriage supper of the Lamb will be celebrated, believers will be rewarded for faithful stewardship. We will then return with the Lord, and at that time He will destroy His enemies. They will be trampled under His mighty feet. John the Beloved describes this in Revelation 19:11—21:

"I saw heaven opened, and behold a white horse; and He that sat upon him was called Faithful and True, and in righteousness He doth judge and make war. His eyes were as a flame of fire, and on His head were many crowns; and He had a name written, that no man knew, but He Himself. And He was clothed with a vesture dipped in blood: and His name is called The Word of God. And the armies which were in heaven followed Him upon white horses, clothed in fine linen, white and clean. And out of His mouth goeth a sharp sword, that with it He should smite the nations: and He shall rule them with a rod of iron: and He treadeth the winepress of the fierceness and wrath of Almighty God. And He hath on His vesture and on His thigh a name written, KING OF KINGS, AND LORD OF LORDS.

"And I saw an angel standing in the sun; and he

cried with a loud voice, saying to all the fowls that
fly in the midst of heaven, Come and gather yourselves
together unto the supper of the great God; that ye
may eat the flesh of kings, and the flesh of captains,
and the flesh of mighty men, and the flesh of horses,
and of them that sit on them, and the flesh of all
men, both free and bond, both small and great.

"And I saw the beast, and the kings of the earth,
and their armies, gathered together to make war against
Him that sat on the horse, and against His army.
And the beast was taken, and with him the false
prophet that wrought miracles before him, with which
he deceived them that had received the mark of the
beast, and them that worshipped his image. These
both were cast alive into a lake of fire burning with
brimstone. And the remnant were slain with the sword
of Him that sat upon the horse, which sword proceeded out of His mouth: and all the fowls were filled
with their flesh."

Yes, the Babe of Luke 2:12, "wrapped in swaddling
clothes, lying in a manger," in Revelation becomes
the Lion of the Tribe of Judah, King of kings and Lord
of lords. The Lamb without spot who in the Gospels
willingly submitted to His enemies and laid His life
down, in Revelation becomes the Warrior, the Conquering One. He will conquer the dragon (Satan),
and will personally put him into the lake of fire. He
will conquer the seven-headed, ten-horned beast of
the mighty Satanic empire. With the brightness of
His coming He will conquer and destroy the false
prophet of Antichrist. He will cause the harlot—the
corrupt woman of Christendom, drunk on the blood
of saints—to be slaughtered by the people who worshipped her. He will completely destroy the corrupt,
sin-riddled, demon-possessed city of Babylon. The
nations which have opposed Him He will crush with
the rod of His power—the sharp sword (the Word)

which will proceed out of His mouth. He will destroy all who have defied Him. He will set up His kingdom and will rule from the throne of David in Jerusalem.

He who because of man's sin was trodden in the winepress of God's wrath will tread underfoot all who have fought against Him and rejected Him, and blood will flow from "the winepress of the wrath of God" until the valley of Jehoshaphat will be *filled with blood:*

"And I looked, and behold a white cloud, and upon the cloud One sat like unto the Son of man, having on His head a golden crown, and in His hand a sharp sickle. And another angel came out of the temple, crying with a loud voice to Him that sat on the cloud, Thrust in thy sickle, and reap: for the time is come for thee to reap; for the harvest of the earth is ripe. And He that sat on the cloud thrust in His sickle on the earth; and the earth was reaped.

"And another angel came out of the temple which is in heaven, he also having a sharp sickle. And another angel came out from the altar, which had power over fire; and cried with a loud cry to him that had the sharp sickle, saying, Thrust in thy sharp sickle, and gather the clusters of the vine of the earth; for her grapes are fully ripe. And the angel thrust in his sickle into the earth, and gathered the vine of the earth, *and cast it into the great winepress of the wrath of God. And the winepress was trodden without the city, AND BLOOD CAME OUT OF THE WINE-PRESS, EVEN UNTO THE HORSE BRIDLES, BY THE SPACE OF A THOUSAND AND SIX HUN-DRED FURLONGS*" (Rev. 14:14—20).

Christ's Suffering and Glory

The prophets prophesied of "the sufferings of Christ, and the glory that should follow" (I Pet. 1:10,11). This

is the theme of the Scriptures from Genesis through
Revelation.   The Old Testament prophets did not
understand what they were prophesying when they
spoke of the sufferings of their King, they did not
understand the period between His suffering and His
glorification.   They did not see the Church Age nor
the things that have occurred, and *will occur* up to
the Rapture.   But the Holy Spirit revealed to them
that Messiah *would* suffer and would later be glorified.

For example, *Isaiah* declared that the Saviour would
be a man of sorrows, acquainted with grief, wounded,
bruised, bearing the iniquity of us all (Isa. 53); but he
also prophesied concerning the glorious kingdom which
will be right here on earth, and that Jesus would reign
from the throne of David (Isa.11).

Not only did the *prophets* prophesy concerning
Christ's sufferings and the glory that should follow,
but He Himself discussed that topic and clearly explained to His troubled disciples that events *must
take place as recorded* by the prophets.   On the day
of His resurrection, when He joined the two disciples
as they walked from Jerusalem to Emmaus, He asked
them, "What manner of communications are these that
ye have one to another, as ye walk, and are sad?"
(Luke 24:17).   Since "their eyes were holden that they
should not know Him" (v. 16), they assumed Him to
be a stranger in Jerusalem and therefore they recounted
to Him the events of the past few days—of how He
whom they had trusted would prove to be their Messiah had been arrested, tried, condemned, and put to
death.   They told of how the women had gone to the
sepulchre early that morning and brought news of the
resurrection, "But," said they, *"Him they saw not."*

Jesus then said to them, "O fools, and slow of
heart to believe *all that the PROPHETS have spoken!
Ought not Christ to have suffered these things, and*

to enter into His GLORY? And beginning at Moses and all the prophets, HE EXPOUNDED UNTO THEM IN ALL THE SCRIPTURES THE THINGS CONCERNING HIMSELF" (vv. 25—27). In other words, He explained to them that Messiah would first suffer and be crowned with thorns as prophesied by the prophets—Isaiah, Jeremiah, Ezekiel, Zechariah, and others including all prophecies from Genesis through Malachi. Then after the crown of thorns, after the suffering, would come the crown of glory and His exaltation. "And it came to pass, as He sat at meat with them, He took bread, and blessed it, and brake, and gave to them. And their eyes were opened, and they knew Him; and He vanished out of their sight. And they said one to another, Did not our heart burn within us... *while He opened to us the Scriptures?"* (Luke 24:13—32 in part). Please read all of Luke chapter 24.

The first and second advents of Christ are intimately connected one to the other, but there is just as definitely a *contrast* between the two. His first coming was in humiliation—a Lamb slain. His second coming will be in glory—King of kings.

The Word of God makes it clear that Jesus knew exactly why He came into the world the first time. He came to declare God to man (John 1:18). He came to take away the sin of the world (John 1:29). He came to lay His life down (John 10:17). He came—not to destroy the law, but to fulfill it (Matt. 5:17). He came to do what the law could not do because of the weakness of the flesh (Rom. 8:3).

Jesus Himself declared that He came into the world to call sinners to repentance (Matt. 9:13). He also declared the authority by which He had come into the world and under which He worked and taught (John 5:36—43). He declared that He had come to give life and light to all who would believe on His name (John 5:26; 12:46).

His first coming was that salvation might be provided for the world: "For God sent not His Son into
the world to condemn the world; but that the world
through Him might be saved" (John 3:17). He will
come the second time to fulfill the covenant God made
with Abraham concerning Israel and the land of Palestine, and to fulfill the covenant God made with
David concerning his throne. In short, His second
coming will be to fulfill all that has to do with the
times of restitution spoken of by all the prophets
throughout the Old Testament. Therefore, in his sermon recorded in Acts 3:12—26 Peter preached both
the *first and second* comings of Jesus:

"Ye men of Israel . . . those things, *which God
before had shewed by the mouth of all His prophets,*
that Christ should suffer, *He hath so fulfilled.* Repent
ye therefore, and be converted, that your sins may be
blotted out, when the times of refreshing shall come
from the presence of the Lord; and He shall send Jesus
Christ, which before was preached unto you: *whom
the heaven must receive until the times of restitution
of all things,* which God hath spoken by the mouth
of all His holy prophets since the world began. . . .
Ye are the children of the prophets, and of the covenant which God made with our fathers, saying unto
Abraham, And in thy seed shall all the kindreds of
the earth be blessed. Unto you first God, having
raised up His Son Jesus, sent Him to bless you, in
turning away every one of you from his iniquities"
(Acts 3:12—26 in part).

In Matthew 20:28 Jesus said of His first coming,
"The Son of man came not to be ministered unto, but
to minister, and to give His life a ransom for many."
He died instead of "many" dying; and were it not for
His vicarious death *we would all be destined to eternal
death and damnation!* When He left the Father's
bosom to come into the world, He knew perfectly well

that Calvary would be the climax of His earthly life. There was no compulsion upon Him; He willingly gave His life to ransom us from sin.

A *ransom* denotes payment equivalent to a life destroyed. In Exodus 21:30 we read that a man shall give for the ransom of his life whatsoever sum of money shall be laid upon him.

A ransom denotes the price required to redeem a slave. In Exodus 21:26 we read, "If a man smite the eye of his servant, or the eye of his maid, that it perish; he shall let him go free for his eye's sake."

A ransom denotes propitiation for sin. In Job 33:24 we read, "Then he is gracious unto him, and saith, Deliver him from going down to the pit: I have found a ransom."

Jesus willingly and voluntarily *gave His LIFE,* a ransom for many—*for ALL who will believe in His finished work and shed blood.* So it was at His *first* advent—but hear this most glorious promise made by Him concerning His *second* coming as related to those servants whom He finds faithfully watching for Him—dressed, fully prepared, with their lamps trimmed and burning:

"Let your loins be girded about, and your lights burning; and ye yourselves like unto men that wait for their lord, when he will return from the wedding; that when he cometh and knocketh, they may open unto him immediately.

"Blessed are those servants, whom the Lord when He cometh shall find watching: verily I say unto you, that *He shall gird Himself, and make them to sit down to meat, and will come forth and serve them.* And if He shall come in the second watch, or come in the third watch, and find them so, blessed are those servants. . . . Be ye therefore ready also: for the Son of man cometh at an hour when ye think not" (Luke 12:35—40).

I am sure that *we who are redeemed* feel as Mary Magdalene did when Jesus spoke her name and she recognized Him at the empty sepulchre on the morning of His resurrection. Overcome with joy, she would have cast herself at His feet in humble adoration and worship—and certainly *we* would be willing to do the same; but fellow believers, Jesus has plainly declared that *He* is coming forth *to serve US.* This is too wonderful for me! I bow my head in humble thanksgiving that He who laid His life down for me that I might enjoy this glorious peace, hope, and assurance which I now possess, is coming again one glorious day to serve His faithful servants! *"Unto them that LOOK FOR HIM shall He appear the second time without sin unto salvation"* (Heb. 9:28).

Precious words! Jesus is the Door (John 10:9). He is the Way, the Truth, and the Life (John 14:6). He is the Author of eternal salvation (Heb. 5:9). He is the Author and Finisher of our faith (Heb. 12:2).

All who have received Him are sons of God NOW (John 1:12, 13; I John 3:2). But hear the words of Paul as he wrote to the Colossian believers—and to you and me:

"If ye then be risen with Christ, seek those things which are above, where Christ sitteth on the right hand of God. Set your affection on things above, not on things on the earth. For ye are dead, and your life is hid with Christ in God. *When Christ, WHO IS OUR LIFE, shall appear, THEN SHALL YE ALSO APPEAR WITH HIM IN GLORY"* (Col. 3:1—4).

Think of it, beloved! He who said, "I give unto them eternal life" will come and receive us unto Himself, that where He is, there we may be with Him throughout eternity! He is our life, and when He appears the second time, believers will appear *with* Him—*"IN GLORY."*

The first epistle of John is God's love letter to His

"little children," and we find the key to that epistle in chapter 1, verse 4: *"These things write we unto you, THAT YOUR JOY MAY BE FULL."*

Also in his first epistle John states the *fact* of Christ's manifestation in the flesh: "That which was from the beginning, which we have *heard,* which we have *seen* with our eyes, which we have *looked upon,* and our hands have *handled,* of the Word of life; (for *the life was manifested,* and we have *seen* it, and bear witness, and shew unto you that eternal life, which was with the Father, and was *manifested unto us.*) That which we have *seen and heard* declare we unto you, that ye also may have fellowship with us: and truly our fellowship is with the Father, and with His Son Jesus Christ" (I John 1:1—3).

John not only states the *fact* of the manifestation of the Son of God, but gives the *reason* for that manifestation. In I John 3:8 we read: "He that committeth sin is of the devil; for the devil sinneth from the beginning. *FOR THIS PURPOSE THE SON OF GOD WAS MANIFESTED, THAT HE MIGHT DESTROY THE WORKS OF THE DEVIL."*

John also declares that Jesus will be manifested in the *future:* "And now, little children, abide in Him; that, *when He shall appear,* we may have confidence, and not be ashamed before Him at His coming" (I John 2:28). He was manifested the *first* time "that He might destroy the works of the devil." He will be manifested the *second* time to make His children like unto Himself: "Beloved, *now* are we the sons of God, and it doth not yet appear what we *shall be:* but we know that, *when He shall appear, WE SHALL BE LIKE HIM; for we shall see Him as He is"* (I John 3:2).

I do not hesitate to say that the first coming of Jesus *demands* His second coming, for without the second, the first would not be complete. His glorious

appearing in the Rapture will be the compliment of
His past coming.

Christ Appeared Once — He Will Appear Again

". . . ONCE in the end of the world (in the end
of the ages) HATH HE APPEARED to put away sin
by the sacrifice of Himself" (Heb. 9:26b).

Jesus appeared as a Babe in a manger "because
there was no room for them in the inn" (Luke 2:7).

He "grew, and waxed strong in spirit, filled with
wisdom: and the grace of God was upon Him" (Luke
2:40).

He "increased in wisdom and stature, and in favour
with God and man" (Luke 2:52).

When the time came for Him to enter His public
ministry He appeared where John the Baptist was
baptizing in Jordan, and God then and there placed
His seal of approval upon His Son and upon His Son's
ministry: "And Jesus, when He was baptized, went
up straightway out of the water: and, lo, the heavens
were opened unto Him, and he saw the Spirit of God
descending like a dove, and lighting upon Him: *and
lo a voice from heaven, saying, THIS IS MY BE-
LOVED SON, IN WHOM I AM WELL PLEASED"*
(Matt. 3:16, 17).

From that day forward, Jesus walked with His
eye singled on Calvary. He knew why He had come
into the world and He was determined to march on
to that moment when His work should be accomplished
and He could give His cry of victory: "It is finished!"
(John 19:30).

He *did* appear in the end of the ages—these present
days are the end of time. When this marvelous Day
of Grace comes to a close and God's program concerning Israel and the nations is completed, the eternity
of eternities will begin. Jesus appeared and offered

one sacrifice for sins, the sacrifice that satisfied God completely; and that sacrifice will never be offered again—nor will any other. Just as surely as He appeared the first time to put away sin, so will He "appear *the second time* without sin unto salvation" (Heb. 9:28). That is, He will come again *without a sin-offering*—not for the redemption of the soul, but for *the salvation of the BODY*. Believers who have died will be raised incorruptible and living believers will be translated.

The Greek word rendered "appear" in Hebrews 9:28 denotes *the object seen* rather than the act of seeing. The same word is translated "seen" with reference to Christ's having been seen by various persons after His resurrection. The proper meaning in the Greek is "to look into the face of another."

The same Greek word is used in the New Testament on many occasions in speaking of the revelation of Jesus when every eye shall see Him. It is used in Matthew 24:30; Mark 13:26, 14:62; Luke 21:27; John 16:16, 17, 19, 22; I John 3:2; Revelation 1:7 and 22:4.

When Jesus comes the second time He will be "seen unto salvation," and *salvation* includes not only what we are saved *from*, but what we are saved *to*. We are *redeemed* through His precious blood; we are *saved* through His *life*. Redemption is instantaneous and complete—i. e., the instant we *believe* we are as redeemed as we will ever be. But *salvation is continuous* until that glorious day when Jesus comes and we experience the glory of *full* salvation:

"For if, when we were enemies, we were reconciled to God by the DEATH of His Son, much MORE, being reconciled, we shall be SAVED BY HIS LIFE" (Rom. 5:10).

The Importance of the Doctrine of the Second Coming

There can be no question of the vital importance

of the doctrine of the second coming of the Lord Jesus
Christ.   The prophecies of the Old Testament speak
of His *second* coming many more times than His *first*
coming is mentioned.   In the New Testament, His
second coming is mentioned approximately three hundred and twenty times.   Since there are only two hundred and sixty chapters in the entire New Testament,
the Lord's second coming is spoken of more than once
per chapter—as a matter of fact, it is mentioned once
in every twenty-five verses, from the Gospel of Matthew
through Revelation!

There are always some folk who ask, "Why are you
so sure that His second coming will be a personal,
bodily return?   Why are premillennialists so dogmatic
in this teaching?"   There are those who teach that the
second coming of Jesus is *the death of a born again
believer.*   Others teach that His second coming took
place *at Pentecost* when the Holy Spirit came.   There
are some who teach that His second coming occurred
at the destruction of Jerusalem in 70 A. D. when Titus
the Roman led his armies into that city and completely
destroyed it.   Still others teach that *the conversion of a
sinner* is the second coming of Christ.   But a careful
look at these suggestions will show that they are vain
and entirely without foundation:

*Is THE DEATH OF A BORN AGAIN BELIEVER
the second coming of Christ?*   Let us first consider
what the Scripture says concerning His coming.

In John 14:2, 3 Jesus promised His disciples, "I go
to prepare a place for you. . . . *I will come again,
and receive you unto myself.*"

In I Thessalonians 4:16, 17 the Apostle Paul tells
us, "The Lord Himself shall descend from heaven
*with a shout, with the voice of the archangel, and
with the trump of God: and the dead in Christ shall
rise first: Then we which are alive and remain shall
be caught up together with them in the clouds, to*

meet the Lord in the air: and so shall we ever be with the Lord."

We know that when a believer dies, Jesus does not personally come to the bedside and receive the spirit of that believer. I believe angels are there, and just as truly as they carried Lazarus to Abraham's bosom (Luke 16:22), I believe they receive the spirit of a believer at death. But Jesus does not come *in person* when a believer dies, He does not descend from heaven with a shout, with the voice of the archangel, and with the trump of God as Paul describes in the passage just given from I Thessalonians.

The promise of Jesus, *"I will come again,"* is equivalent to Paul's declaration, "The Lord Himself shall descend from heaven . . . ," and the words of Jesus, "I will . . . *receive you unto myself"* equal the explanation of Paul that we will be "caught up together . . . to meet the Lord in the air." When a believer dies, the Lord Jesus does not come personally for the spirit, He does not descend from heaven with a shout and the plainly stated signs of His second coming, nor are the dead in Christ raised at that time. And in addition to these given proofs, we have the promise that when Jesus comes the second time, *that SAME Jesus will come IN LIKE MANNER* as the disciples saw Him go into heaven (Acts 1:11). Therefore, *the death of a believer CANNOT be the second coming of Christ!*

Was PENTECOST His second coming? No, that could not be true. Pentecost was very real, very important; but it was not the second coming of Christ as such. It was, rather, the fulfillment of His promise to His disciples given in John 14:16—18. He said, "I will pray the Father, and He shall give you another Comforter, that He may abide with you for ever; even the Spirit of truth; whom the world cannot receive, because it seeth Him not, neither knoweth Him: but ye know Him; for He dwelleth with you, and shall be in you. I will not leave you comfortless: I will come to you."

In a sense, Jesus *did* come at Pentecost—but He came in the Person of the Holy Spirit, and it was *not* the *Holy Spirit* of whom He spoke in John 14:2, 3 when He said, *"I go . . . I will come again."* The Holy Spirit, third Person of the Triune Godhead, was not the *"same Jesus"* whom the heavenly messengers promised would return (Acts 1:11).

We believe in one God manifested in three Persons —Father, Son, and Holy Spirit. It is the second Person of the Trinity who will come again to receive His own unto Himself—the Man Christ Jesus who now sits at the right hand of God the Father; and He will so come as He went away—*BODILY*, in the clouds.

We must also consider that all the promises in the epistles concerning the second coming of Jesus were made *AFTER Pentecost.* On the Day of Pentecost *the Holy Spirit came to be with US;* but when *Jesus* comes the second time *WE will be caught up to be with HIM.* The Holy Spirit came to abide with us and in us, and every born again believer is indwelt by the Spirit (Rom. 8:9; Eph. 4:30); but when *Jesus* comes the second time He will take *us* to be *with Him,* He will fashion anew these bodies of humiliation (Phil. 3:21), this corruption will put on incorruption, this mortal will put on immortality (I Cor. 15:53), and we will be made exactly *like HIM* (I John 3:2).

When the Holy Spirit came on the Day of Pentecost there was no trumpet of God, no voice of the archangel, no shout heralding the Lord's return; the bodies of the saints were not raised and no living saints were caught up to meet Jesus in the air. Pentecost is a matter of record, an historical event that occurred fifty days after the resurrection of the Lord Jesus Christ; but it was not His second coming. That day is yet in the future.

Was THE DESTRUCTION OF JERUSALEM in 70 A. D. the second coming of Christ? History records the fact that every stone was thrown down, the city was completely destroyed, and approximately a million Jews were slaughtered; but again there was no shout from heaven, no voice of the archangel, no trump of God, the dead in Christ did not rise, and living saints were not translated.

Also, according to Bible authorities, the Gospel of John was written about 85 A. D., which would have been about fifteen years after Titus the Roman destroyed the city of Jerusalem. Yet in John's Gospel the beloved disciple recorded the words of Jesus when He said to Peter, "If I will that (John) tarry *till I come,* what is that to thee? Follow thou me" (John 21:22). Even on the Isle of Patmos, many, many years after the destruction of Jerusalem, John still looked toward the return of the Lord: "He which testifieth these things saith, *Surely I come quickly. Amen. EVEN SO, COME, LORD JESUS!"* (Rev. 22:20).

Therefore I declare it to be absurd to even *suggest* that the destruction of Jerusalem was the event of which Jesus spoke when He said, "I go ... *I will come again!"*

Is THE CONVERSION OF A SINNER the second coming of Christ? This, too, is absurd, as any thinking person will see as he studies the Word of God and allows the Holy Spirit to teach him. When a sinner is converted there is no shout from heaven, no voice of the archangel, no trumpet of God. The dead in Christ are not raised and living saints are not caught up. The sinner receives Jesus by faith and then, *in the Person of the Holy Spirit,* Christ takes up His abode in the heart of the new convert. But when Jesus comes the second time He will return bodily, just as He went away; and this does not take place when a sinner believes unto salvation!

Beloved, the second coming of Jesus Christ is the hope of the Church, and His return for His own is yet future. "Of that day and hour knoweth no man, no, not the angels of heaven." Only the heavenly Father knows the exact time of Christ's return (Matt. 24:36). But we do know that He will keep His promise, and one glorious day *the Lord Himself—yes, THAT SAME JESUS—"shall descend from heaven* with a shout, with the voice of the archangel, and with the trump of God: and the dead in Christ shall rise first: Then we which are alive and remain shall be caught up together with them in the clouds, to meet the Lord in the air: and so shall we ever be with the Lord. *Wherefore comfort one another with these words"* (I Thess. 4:16—18).

The Apostle Paul declared, "Behold, I shew you a mystery: We shall not all sleep"—that is, we shall not all *die*—"but we shall all be changed, in a moment, in the twinkling of an eye, at the last trump: for the trumpet shall sound, and the dead shall be raised incorruptible, and we shall be changed. For this corruptible must put on incorruption, and this mortal must put on immortality. So when this corruptible shall have put on incorruption, and this mortal shall have put on immortality, then shall be brought to pass the saying that is written, *Death is swallowed up in victory!"* (I Cor. 15:51—54).

All Born Again Christians Believe in the Second Coming of Christ

The Bible is clear on the subject of how to be saved. Writing to the believers in Ephesus Paul clearly explained, *"By GRACE are ye saved through faith; and that not of yourselves: IT IS THE GIFT OF GOD:* not of works, lest any man should boast. For we are His workmanship, created in Christ Jesus unto good works, which God hath before ordained that we should walk in them" (Eph. 2:8—10).

Salvation, then, is *the gift of God* by His grace—His unmerited, unearned favor to a hell-deserving sinner. All saved people are recipients of God's grace through faith, and there *is* no salvation *apart* from grace. But the grace of God not only saves us, it also *teaches* us. To Titus, his son in the ministry, the Apostle Paul wrote, "The grace of God that bringeth salvation hath appeared to all men, *TEACHING us that, denying ungodliness and worldly lusts, we should live soberly, righteously, and godly, in this present world; LOOKING FOR THAT BLESSED HOPE, and the glorious appearing of the great God and our Saviour Jesus Christ;* who gave Himself for us, that He might redeem us from all iniquity, and purify unto Himself a peculiar people, zealous of good works" (Tit. 2:11—14).

Several facts are clearly stated in these verses:

First of all, the grace of God brings salvation—but it does not stop there. It also teaches us to deny ungodly practices and worldly lusts and live righteously in this present, sinful world. How much confidence could be placed in the testimony of a person who claimed to be saved and yet committed all kinds of ungodly acts, participated in all kinds of worldly lusts, and lived a life of general intemperance in all things? Therefore the *grace* of God teaches the Christian to live a life befitting the born again *child* of God.

The grace of God also teaches us to look for *"that blessed hope,"* the hope of man, the hope of the Church, the hope of all creation: *"the glorious appearing of the great God and our Saviour JESUS CHRIST"—the SAME JESUS* who gave Himself on the cross to redeem us from all iniquity. And He *will* come *"in like manner" as He went away.*

All who are recipients of God's grace believe in and look for the second coming of Jesus, and according to the Scripture *those who deny His second coming are not saved:*

"So Christ was once offered to bear the sins of many; *and unto them that LOOK for Him shall He appear THE SECOND TIME* without sin unto salvation" (Heb. 9:28).

John the Beloved was exiled to Patmos "for the Word of God, and for the testimony of Jesus Christ" (Rev. 1:9). He was "in the Spirit on the Lord's day," and he heard "a great voice, as of a trumpet." The voice said, "I am Alpha and Omega, the first and the last." Certainly we know that this is none other than the Lord Jesus Christ. Then the voice said, "What thou seest, write in a book"—and after penning down twenty-two chapters John heard again the same voice he had heard at the beginning of his writing; and the voice said: *"He which testifieth these things* (the Alpha and Omega) *saith, SURELY I COME QUICKLY. AMEN!"* And John replied, "Even so, COME, LORD JESUS!"

How interesting that our Bible closes with the announcement from the Son of God Himself, declaring that He will *come quickly;* and in answer to that announcement the last *prayer* in the Bible pleads for His coming! This is the eager desire of every born again, blood-washed believer.

To the Christian, the second coming of Jesus is a *"blessed* hope" (Tit. 2:13), a *comforting* hope (I Thess. 4:18), and a *purifying* hope (I John 3:3). The hope of His second coming causes us to live a life of watchfulness, fidelity, activity, self-restraint, prayer, and consecration.

Jesus warned His disciples, *"Therefore be ye also ready: for in such an hour as ye think not the Son of man cometh"* (Matt. 24:44). In Luke 21:34—36 He warned, "Take heed to yourselves, lest at any time your hearts be overcharged with surfeiting, and drunkenness, and cares of this life, and so that day come upon you unawares. For as a snare shall it come on all them that dwell on the face of the whole earth. *Watch ye therefore, and pray always, that ye may be accounted worthy to escape all these things that shall come to pass, and to stand before the Son of man.*"

Believers anxiously expect the Lord's return, knowing that no man knows the day or the hour; therefore it could be *any* day, *any* hour, and a special *blessing* is assured all who are eagerly awaiting His return: "Blessed are those servants, whom the Lord when He cometh shall find watching: verily I say unto you, that He shall gird Himself, and make them to sit down to meat, and will come forth and serve them. And if He shall come in the second watch, or come in the third watch, and find them so, blessed are those servants. . . . Be ye therefore ready also: for the Son of man cometh at an hour when ye think not" (Luke 12:37—40).

Those who are found watching for His coming will receive a special *reward:* a crown of righteousness. In Paul's last testimony he wrote to young Timothy, "I am now ready to be offered, and the time of my departure is at hand. I have fought a good fight, I have finished my course, I have kept the faith: Henceforth there is laid up for me *a crown of righteousness, which the Lord, the righteous Judge, shall give me at that day: and not to me only, BUT UNTO ALL THEM ALSO THAT LOVE HIS APPEARING*" (II Tim. 4:6—8).

Truly born again believers look for the Lord's soon return; but the doctrine of His second coming is hated and ridiculed by the world and by worldly-minded, unregenerate church members. They naturally do not long for the coming of Jesus because they are walking after their own lusts, they are not ready for His appearing. Peter describes these mocking church members. He declares that *"in the last days"*—these days in which we live—there will come *"scoffers, walking after their own lusts,* and saying, Where is the promise of His coming? for since the fathers fell asleep, all things continue as they were from the beginning of the creation. For this they willingly are ignorant of, that by the Word of God the heavens were of old, and the earth standing out of the water and in the water: whereby the world that then was, being overflowed with water, perished: but the heavens and the earth, which are now, by the same Word are kept in store, reserved unto fire against the day of judgment and perdition of ungodly men" (II Pet. 3:3—7).

The Two Stages of the Second Coming of Christ:
The Rapture — The Revelation

"I would not have you to be ignorant, brethren, concerning them which are asleep, that ye sorrow not, even as others which have no hope. For if we believe that Jesus died and rose again, even so them also which sleep in Jesus will God bring with Him. For this we say unto you by the Word of the Lord, that we which are alive and remain unto the coming of the Lord shall not prevent them which are asleep. For the Lord Himself shall descend from heaven with a shout, with the voice of the archangel, and with the trump of God: and the dead in Christ shall rise first: Then we which are alive and remain shall be caught up together with them in the clouds, to meet the Lord in the air: and so shall we ever be with the Lord. Wherefore comfort one another with these words.

"But of the times and the seasons, brethren, ye have no need that I write unto you. For yourselves know perfectly that the day of the Lord so cometh as a thief in the night. For when they shall say, Peace and safety; then sudden destruction cometh upon them, as travail upon a woman with child; and they shall not escape. But ye, brethren, are not in darkness, that that day should overtake you as a thief. Ye are all the children of light, and the children of the day: we are not of the night, nor of darkness. Therefore let us not sleep, as do others; but let us watch and be sober" (I Thess. 4:13 through 5:6).

"Behold, I shew you a mystery: We shall not all sleep, but we shall all be changed, in a moment, in the twinkling of an eye, at the last trump: for the trumpet shall sound, and the dead shall be raised incorruptible, and we shall be changed. For this corruptible must put on incorruption, and this mortal must put on immortality. So when this corruptible shall have put on incorruption, and this mortal shall have put on immortality, then shall be brought to pass the saying that is written, Death is swallowed up in victory. O death, where is thy sting? O grave, where is thy victory? The sting of death is sin; and the strength of sin is the law. But thanks be to God, which giveth us the victory through our Lord Jesus Christ. Therefore, my beloved brethren, be ye stedfast, unmoveable, always abounding in the work of the Lord, forasmuch as ye know that your labour is not in vain in the Lord" (I Cor. 15:51—58).

"I tell you, in that night there shall be two men in one bed; the one shall be taken, and the other shall be left. Two women shall be grinding together; the one shall be taken, and the other left. Two men shall be in the field; the one shall be taken, and the other left" (Luke 17:34—36).

These passages just quoted have reference to the Rapture, the first stage of the second coming of Jesus—the time when He will come for His saints. Now let

us look at some passages which refer to the Revelation,
the second stage of His second coming:

"Behold, the day of the Lord cometh, and thy
spoil shall be divided in the midst of thee. For I
will gather all nations against Jerusalem to battle; and
the city shall be taken, and the houses rifled, and the
women ravished; and half of the city shall go forth
into captivity, and the residue of the people shall not
be cut off from the city.

"Then shall the Lord go forth, and fight against
those nations, as when He fought in the day of battle.
And His feet shall stand in that day upon the Mount
of Olives, which is before Jerusalem on the east, and
the Mount of Olives shall cleave in the midst thereof
toward the east and toward the west, and there shall
be a very great valley; and half of the mountain shall
remove toward the north, and half of it toward the
south.   And ye shall flee to the valley of the mountains; for the valley of the mountains shall reach unto
Azal: yea, ye shall flee, like as ye fled from before
the earthquake in the days of Uzziah king of Judah:
and the Lord my God shall come, and all the saints
with thee" (Zech. 14:1—5).

"The day of the Lord will come as a thief in the
night; in the which the heavens shall pass away with
a great noise, and the elements shall melt with fervent
heat, the earth also and the works that are therein
shall be burned up.   Seeing then that all these things
shall be dissolved, what manner of persons ought ye
to be in all holy conversation and godliness, looking
for and hasting unto the coming of the day of God,
wherein the heavens being on fire shall be dissolved,
and the elements shall melt with fervent heat?

"Nevertheless we, according to His promise, look
for new heavens and a new earth, wherein dwelleth
righteousness.   Wherefore, beloved, seeing that ye look
for such things, be diligent that ye may be found of

Him in peace, without spot, and blameless" (II Pet. 3:10—14).

"Behold, He cometh with clouds; and every eye shall see Him, and they also which pierced Him: and all kindreds of the earth shall wail because of Him. Even so, Amen" (Rev. 1:7).

"And I saw heaven opened, and behold a white horse; and He that sat upon him was called Faithful and True, and in righteousness He doth judge and make war. His eyes were as a flame of fire, and on His head were many crowns; and He had a name written, that no man knew, but He Himself. And He was clothed with a vesture dipped in blood: and His name is called The Word of God.

"And the armies which were in heaven followed Him upon white horses, clothed in fine linen, white and clean. And out of His mouth goeth a sharp sword, that with it He should smite the nations: and He shall rule them with a rod of iron: and He treadeth the winepress of the fierceness and wrath of Almighty God. And He hath on His vesture and on His thigh a name written, KING OF KINGS, AND LORD OF LORDS" (Rev. 19:11—16).

Now if we allow the Holy Spirit to lead in the study of these verses, by comparing Scripture with Scripture we can readily see that the two *groups* of Scripture quoted here do not relate to the same event. It is evident that the second coming of Jesus is definitely in two stages—the Rapture, and the Revelation. We will discuss the Rapture—the time when He comes *for His saints;* and then we will study those Scriptures which pertain to the Revelation—the time when He returns to earth *WITH His saints.*

The Rapture

In the passage from I Thessalonians, the Holy

Spirit clearly points out several things concerning the
first stage of the second coming. Some of the believers
in the Thessalonian church were troubled about their
loved ones who had departed this life, and Paul wanted them to have wisdom and understanding on that
subject. He wanted them to know that the spirits of
departed saints were resting with Jesus, and therefore
they should not be sorrowful as were unbelievers who
had no hope.

"If we believe that Jesus died and rose again...."
In Paul's day, as in these days in which we live,
there were people who did not believe in the bodily
resurrection of Jesus. The Pharisees believed that
the dead would rise again, the Sadducees *did not*
believe in resurrection. But faith in the bodily resurrection of Jesus is essential to salvation, for "if Christ
be not risen, then is our preaching vain, and your
faith is also vain. . . . And if Christ be not raised,
your faith is vain; ye are yet in your sins. Then they
also which are fallen asleep in Christ are perished"
(I Cor. 15:14—18).

There is no salvation apart from the bodily resurrection of Jesus, but *"them also which sleep IN JESUS
will God bring with Him."* The spirits of the redeemed are immediately present with the Lord at
death. Paul explained to the Corinthian believers,
"Therefore we are always confident, knowing that,
whilst we are *at home in the body,* we are *absent from
the Lord* . . . We are confident, I say, and willing
rather to be *absent* from the *body,* and to be *present*
with the *Lord"* (II Cor. 5:6, 8).

The Apostle Paul believed and taught that at the
death of a believer the spirit goes to be with God in
Paradise. To the Philippians he testified, "I am in a
strait betwixt two, having *a desire to depart, and to
be with Christ; which is far better:* nevertheless to
abide in the flesh is more needful for you" (Phil.

1:23, 24).

So when Jesus comes the second time, in the first stage of His coming (the Rapture) He will bring with Him the spirits of the righteous who have departed this world, and at that time their bodies will be raised, incorruptible. However, He will not at that time descend to the earth. He will come *in the clouds in the air* and will call the saints up to meet Him there.

"This we say unto you by the word of the Lord." Paul wanted it clearly understood that he had divine authority for his teaching. *"We which are alive and remain unto the coming of the Lord shall not prevent* (or hinder or precede) *them which are asleep"*—(those whose bodies are lying in the grave).

"For the Lord HIMSELF shall descend from heaven," God will not send an angel, He will not send the cherubim, seraphim, the Old Testament prophets, nor any other heavenly creature. *Jesus HIMSELF* will descend from heaven. When the Bible speaks of *heaven* (singular) we know it is referring to the Father's house because Jesus is now seated there at God's right hand. He will descend from His seat on the throne in heaven "with a shout, with the voice of the archangel, and with the trump of God—*and the dead in Christ shall rise . . . ."*

Please notice that *ONLY the dead in Christ* will be raised when the Rapture occurs. Their bodies, from which the spirit is now separated, will be raised and glorified. Then those saints who are *living* will be changed (corruption will put on incorruption, mortal will put on immortality), and together with the risen saints will be caught up to meet Jesus in the air—*and so shall we ever be in His blessed presence!*

All of this will take place "in the twinkling of an eye"—that is, in the way man measures time, *in one split second.*

We have already pointed out that only God the

Father knows when the Rapture will take place; but He has given enough information in His Word that we *can* know *how* it will take place and how to be ready for it. Therefore Paul continues:

"Of the times and the seasons, ye have no *need* that I write unto you."* Paul had taught these people well; they were rooted and grounded in the truth concerning the second coming of the Lord Jesus Christ. They knew "perfectly" that He *would come,* and now Paul reminds them of the *way* in which He will come — *"as a THIEF in the night."*

When *Jesus* preached on earth He spoke in language easily understood, words so simple that even a child could not miss His meaning. He spoke of the lilies of the field; the sparrows; the sower and the seed; light; bread; salt; a mother hen and her little chickens. Who could not understand such terms as these? So it is with the teaching of the Holy Spirit as He spoke through Paul in this passage. If you will study the characteristics of a thief's coming, you can understand what will take place in the Rapture.

A thief comes silently, unannounced. So it will be when Jesus comes for His Church. His coming will not be publicly announced; it will be completely unexpected insofar as the masses are concerned. Only the saints will hear the trumpet.

A thief does not tarry. He takes what he came for and hastily departs. Jesus will catch away His jewels "in a moment, in the twinkling of an eye"—but like the thief, He will leave much more than He takes.

"When they shall say, PEACE AND SAFETY . . . ." Not only will Christ's coming "as a thief" be *sudden,* it will also be at a time when people on earth are talking "Peace," and carrying out safety programs.

"Then sudden destruction cometh upon them . . . and they shall not escape." Unbelievers (people who

will be left on earth when the Rapture occurs) are those upon whom this "sudden destruction" will come —such destruction as this world has never known! Every born again believer will be instantly and simultaneously caught out of the world. Christians who are driving automobiles will be taken from behind the steering wheel. (Imagine the sudden slaughter which will take place on the world's highways!) Christian pilots will be taken from their planes, and born again engineers will be caught out from the cabs of locomotives. Christian bus drivers will be taken from behind the steering wheel of their vehicles, and every born again policeman will be caught away from his place of duty. Picture, if you can, the "sudden destruction" that will come upon this earth when every born again believer is instantaneously removed!

In spite of the fact that much is being said about "peace" today, and in spite of the latest inventions and gadgets designed to provide "safety," this is the most dangerous, deadly time man has known since God created Adam and placed him in the Garden of Eden. Yes, men are saying, *"Peace and safety."* But at any moment sudden destruction can strike this earth—and it will not necessarily have to come through nuclear warfare. At any moment Jesus can call His Church up to meet Him in the clouds in the air; and when that time comes *every believer* will be taken. Then will come such destruction as the mind of man cannot imagine! Beloved, *will YOU be taken*—or will you be one of those who will be left when the Lord of glory comes to catch away His bride?

To the Corinthian believers Paul said, *"Behold, I shew you a mystery."* A mystery revealed is a mystery no longer. Therefore, since Paul taught the Thessalonians the same doctrine taught in the Corinthian church concerning the Rapture, the same doctrine Jesus taught when He tabernacled on earth, he gave them this warning:

"Ye, brethren, are not IN DARKNESS that that day should overtake you as a thief. Ye are all the children of LIGHT and the children of the day . . . Therefore let us not sleep, as do others; but let us WATCH and be sober (alert)."

In the beginning of this section of our study I quoted from Luke 17:34—36 where Jesus taught His disciples concerning the Rapture. He explained clearly, "In that night there shall be two men in one bed; the one shall be taken, and the other shall be left. Two women shall be grinding together; the one shall be taken, and the other left. Two men shall be in the field; the one shall be taken, and the other left." Now let us examine this passage more closely.

First of all, this Scripture tells us that the Rapture will be world-wide. We know that when it is nighttime in America it is early morning, or noon, or late afternoon in other parts of the world. Jesus said "in that *night*" when He comes, two will be sleeping in one bed. The believer will be taken, the unbeliever will be left. "Two women shall be *grinding* together." In Palestine the women do the grinding of the grain, and they do it in the morning hours. If one of the women is a believer and the other an unbeliever, the believer will be taken, the unbeliever will be left. Then He said, "Two men shall be *in the field,"* denoting a later time of day, perhaps mid-afternoon. The believer will be taken, the unbeliever will be left.

When the Rapture occurs, every born again believer will be taken, supernaturally snatched away in a split second, so quickly that unbelievers will not know what has taken place until suddenly they miss their fellow-workers and members of their family. Babies will be taken, as will innocent children who have not reached the age of accountability. Wives and mothers will be taken, husbands and fathers left. In other instances husbands and fathers will be taken, unbelieving wives and mothers will be left.

For the *Christian*, the Rapture will be a time of glory beyond compare. It is the "blessed hope," the comforting hope, the assuring hope of the Church. But for *unbelievers* it will be a time of destruction, tragedy, misery, and woe such as this world has never known!

The Nature of the Rapture

We have repeatedly stated that at the appointed time Jesus Himself will descend from heaven, with a shout, with the voice of the archangel and the trump of God, and the dead in Christ will be raised. Then living believers will be translated, and together with the resurrected saints will be caught away. Blessed day, when we will shout the victory!

In I Thessalonians 4:17 the Greek word translated "caught up" is *harpazo*, and the literal meaning is "to sieze hastily, to take with violence, to draw one to one's self swiftly, suddenly." The same Greek word is used in Acts 23:10 where Paul was taken from the mob *"by force,"* literally torn away by the Roman soldiers. He was taken by violence, *snatched away* lest the mob tear him to bits: "When there arose a great dissension, the chief captain, fearing lest Paul should have been *pulled in pieces* of them, commanded the soldiers to go down, and to *take him BY FORCE from among them*, and to bring him into the castle."

When the Rapture occurs, believers will suddenly be caught up, *snatched away* from all distress of spirit, soul, and body: "For in this we groan, earnestly desiring to be clothed upon with our house which is from heaven: if so be that being clothed we shall not be found naked. For we that are in this tabernacle do groan, being burdened: not for that we would be unclothed, but clothed upon, that mortality might be

swallowed up of life" (II Cor. 5:2—4). Jesus will
"change our vile body, that it may be *fashioned like
unto HIS glorious body,* according to the working
whereby He is able even to subdue all things unto
Himself" (Phil. 3:21).

When the Rapture occurs, believers will instantly
be delivered from all persecution and oppression by
the enemies of Christ, the demons, and even Satan
himself. We will be caught out of the sphere of sin,
snatched away from the very *presence* of sin: "Knowing this, that our old man is crucified with Him, that
the body of sin might be destroyed, that henceforth
we should not serve sin. For he that is dead is freed
from sin" (Rom. 6:6, 7).

When the Rapture occurs, *rest* will come to all
saints—rest that only Jesus can bestow: "And to you
who are troubled rest with us, when the Lord Jesus
shall be revealed from heaven with His mighty angels"
(II Thess. 1:7).

Believers are redeemed from the *penalty* of sin
now; we are saved from the *power* of sin moment by
moment as we are kept in His love; but when Jesus
comes for His Church we will experience the fulness
of divine grace—"the grace that is to be brought unto
(us) *at the revelation of Jesus Christ"* (I Pet. 1:13).

Believers are recipients of divine mercy now—God
extended His mercy when He redeemed us from the
penalty of sin; but when Jesus comes in the Rapture
we will experience divine mercy such as we could
never know apart from His personal return for His
own: "Keep yourselves in the love of God, *looking
for THE MERCY OF OUR LORD JESUS CHRIST*
unto eternal life" (Jude 21).

The Rapture of the Church will be an act of divine
omnipotence which will change this corruptible to
incorruption, bring immortality to this mortal, and
transfigure us into conformity with the Lord Jesus

Christ, thus elevating us to a glorious spiritual body exactly like the resurrection body of Jesus. When the Rapture occurs, the power of God which now moves the entire universe, holds the planets in their courses, and sustains all creation will act upon our mortal bodies, transforming and fashioning them like unto His glorious resurrection body (Phil. 3:21).

In I Thessalonians 1:10 where Paul speaks of the Rapture as deliverance from "the wrath to come," he uses the Greek word *rhuo,* meaning "to rescue with power." In II Timothy 4:17 he used the same Greek word to describe *the preservation of his life* as being "delivered out of the mouth of the lion." Thus did the Holy Spirit, through the pen of Paul, describe the Rapture of the Church as a swift, powerful event—and indeed it will be!

Not only will we be suddenly caught up to be united with the Lord Jesus Christ, but at that time He will present the Church to Himself—a pure Church, *"a glorious Church, not having spot, or wrinkle, or any such thing; but that it should be holy and without blemish. . . .* For we are members of His body, of His flesh, and of His bones" (Eph. 5:27, 30).

"For as the body is one, and hath many members, and all the members of that one body, being many, are one body: so also is Christ. For by one Spirit are we all baptized into one body, whether we be Jews or Gentiles, whether we be bond or free; and have been all made to drink into one Spirit" (I Cor. 12: 12, 13).

Yes, when Jesus comes in the Rapture, all members of the Church will be united *literally.* We are united *spiritually* now because all believers are united to the body of Christ by the miracle of the baptism of the Holy Spirit; but when the Rapture occurs the saints who have departed this life and the saints who will be living at that time will be *literally united* and

caught up together to meet Jesus, the head of the New
Testament Church; and for the first time since the
Church was born, all members the world over—including those who are now resting in Paradise—will
unite in one happy, glorious family, and will gather
at the marriage supper in the sky:

"Let us be glad and rejoice, and give honour to
Him: for the marriage of the Lamb is come, and His
wife hath made herself ready. And to her was granted
that she should be arrayed in fine linen, clean and
white: for the fine linen is the righteousness of saints.

"And he saith unto me, Write, Blessed are they
which are called unto the marriage supper of the
Lamb.   And he saith unto me, These are the true
sayings of God" (Rev. 19:7—9).

Will All Believers Be Taken in the Rapture?

Some people teach that the Church will pass
through the tribulation period. Others teach that the
Church will go through only *half* of the tribulation
and will be raptured in the middle of that period.
Still others teach that all believers will be caught out
before the tribulation *begins.* But the Word of God
is very clear on the subject of the Rapture as pertaining to who will be taken and who will be left.

According to I Corinthians 12:12,13, all born again
believers are members of the body of Christ, baptized
into that body by the Holy Spirit the split second we
believe; and that same Scripture also makes it plain
that the body of Christ is *ONE body.* When Jesus
comes in the Rapture He is coming for His Church,
His body—and certainly that body will not be divided,
part of it taken and part of it left! He will take the
Church in its entirety. Not one child of God will
be left behind.

The Bible proves beyond any shadow of doubt that

the Church will not enter or go through any part of the Great Tribulation. In I Thessalonians 5:9 we read, *"For God hath not appointed us to WRATH, but to obtain salvation by our Lord Jesus Christ."* In this verse, "wrath" speaks of the Great Tribulation.

Revelation 3:10 also assures us that believers will not enter the tribulation period: "Because thou hast kept the word of my patience, I also will keep thee from the hour of temptation, which shall come upon all the world, to try them that dwell upon the earth." Here, *"the hour of temptation"* speaks of the tribulation.

After Revelation chapter 4 the Church is not seen *on earth* any more until chapter 19 when the saints appear with Jesus coming from heaven. The time *between* those two chapters in Revelation has to do with the Great Tribulation period, the reign of Antichrist, and the battle of Armageddon.

If believers who want to know the truth about the second coming of Christ would allow the Holy Spirit to *rightly divide the truth,* if they would distinguish between the Lord's coming *for* His saints and His coming *with* His saints, they would understand that the Rapture will take place many, many years before Jesus comes in the Revelation to put down the Antichrist and set up His kingdom on earth.

Our Spiritual Bodies

Many times during the years of my ministry I have been asked, "Why should there be a *bodily* resurrection? Why not simply pure spirit-body?" The answer is clear to all who will accept unadulterated scriptural truth:

The human body is not *a prison for the soul and spirit,* but belongs to the essence of man. Man was created body, soul, and spirit; and *without* a body

man is naked, unclothed. In II Corinthians 5:1—3 the
Apostle Paul said, "We know that if our earthly house
of this tabernacle were dissolved, we have a building
of God, an house not made with hands, eternal in the
heavens.   For in this we groan, earnestly desiring to
be clothed upon with our house which is from heaven:
*If so be that being clothed WE SHALL NOT BE
FOUND NAKED."*

Here on earth, believers are the temple of the Holy
Spirit of God: "If the Spirit of Him that raised up
Jesus from the dead dwell in you, He that raised up
Christ from the dead shall also quicken your mortal
bodies *by His Spirit that dwelleth in you*" (Rom. 8:11).

In I Corinthians 3:16 Paul asks, "Know ye not that
ye are the temple of God, and that the Spirit of God
dwelleth in you?"

Then in I Corinthians 6:19,20 we read, "What?
*Know ye not that your body is the temple of the Holy
Ghost which is in you,* which ye have of God, and
ye are not your own? For ye are bought with a price:
therefore glorify God in your body, and in your spirit,
which are God's."

This fact is clear: The separation of spirit and
soul from the body was brought about through sin.
If Adam had not sinned, man would never have died.
God plainly said to Adam, "Of the tree of the knowledge of good and evil, thou shalt not eat of it: for
in the day that thou eatest thereof *thou shalt SURELY
die*" (Gen. 2:17).   In the deeper sense, of course, this
meant spiritual death; but it included *eventual physical death* as well.   Therefore, since physical death is
the direct result of sin, were there no *bodily* resurrection then something of *the effects of sin* would remain
in the redeemed.   In other words, as a result of sin,
man would be stripped of one-third of his essence.

Man is a trinity—soul, spirit, and body. If in eternity he should be only soul and spirit—or pure spirit—

without a body, sin would have won a partial victory. But Jesus completely satisfied the sin-debt, He paid the full penalty for sin and came forth victorious over the world, the flesh, the devil, death, hell, and the grave. Therefore our salvation is *complete*—soul, spirit, and body. Jesus died on the cross to redeem us from sin. Soul and spirit are redeemed now, and when He comes the second time He will redeem the body!

Our God does not abandon the works of His mighty hands. This earth and all creation will one day be delivered from the curse. The bodily resurrection of Jesus guarantees all things created new—and certainly His redeemed children will not be allowed to suffer eternally the consequences of sin, even *in part.* God Almighty will not permit redemption apart from the body because Jesus our Redeemer purchased *full* redemption. Therefore we *will be* glorified, death *will be* swallowed up in victory: "O death, where is thy sting? O grave, where is thy victory? The sting of death is sin; and the strength of sin is the law. *But thanks be to God, which giveth us the victory THROUGH OUR LORD JESUS CHRIST"* (I Cor. 15:55—57).

Yes, death will be swallowed up in victory, "and the Lord God will wipe away tears from off all faces; and the rebuke of His people shall He take away from off all the earth: *for the Lord hath spoken it"* (Isa. 25:8).

In Hosea 13:14 Jehovah God declared, "I will ransom them from the power of the grave; I will redeem them from death: O death, I will be thy plagues; O grave, I will be thy destruction: repentance shall be hid from mine eyes."

What proof do we have that our resurrection bodies will be *tangible* bodies of flesh and bone, a body in which we can walk, talk, and fellowship as we do in this present tabernacle cursed by sin? Proof positive

is found in the resurrection body of our Lord and Saviour Jesus Christ.   He is the living resurrection (John
11:25), and *His body* was plainly visible.   To the ten
in the upper room He said, *"Behold my hands and
my feet,* that it is I myself: handle me, and see; for
a spirit hath not flesh and bones, as ye see me have.
And when He had thus spoken, *He shewed them His
hands and His feet"* (Luke 24:39, 40).   To Thomas He
said, "Reach hither thy finger, and behold my hands;
and reach hither thy hand, and thrust it into my side:
and be not faithless, but believing" (John 20:27).

In His resurrection body the Lord Jesus Christ ate
broiled fish and honeycomb: "And while they yet
believed not for joy, and wondered, He said unto them,
Have ye here any meat?   And they gave Him a piece
of a broiled fish, and of an honeycomb.   And He took
it, *and did eat before them"* (Luke 24:41 — 43).

The Greek word *ostea,* translated "bones" in Luke
24:39, is also used in John 19:36—"A *bone* of Him shall
not be broken" — and in Hebrews 11:22 where we read,
"By faith Joseph, when he died, made mention of the
departing of the children of Israel; and gave commandment concerning his *bones."*   Therefore it is pure falsehood to teach that the risen Lord had no actual body
and that His nature was pure spirit, not flesh and
bone as we know them literally.

There is yet another teaching, also false, to the
effect that Jesus came back from the grave in a body
of flesh and bone, presented Himself to His disciples,
and then, *when He ascended,* laid that body aside.
Certainly this could not be true, because *Stephen*
testified that He *saw* Jesus standing on the right hand
of God (Acts 7:55, 56).

Not only do the Scriptures assure us that the Man
Christ Jesus, in a body of flesh and bone, sits today
at the right hand of God, but we are further assured
that *our* glorified body will be *exactly like HIS glorious*

resurrection body:

"Beloved, *NOW are we the sons of God,* and it doth not yet appear what we shall be: but we know that, when He shall appear, *we shall be LIKE HIM;* for we shall see Him as He is" (I John 3:2).

"For whom He did foreknow, He also did predestinate to be *conformed to the image of His Son,* that He might be the firstborn among many brethren" (Rom. 8:29).

Philippians 3:21 also assures us that when Jesus comes for His Church He will re-fashion these vile bodies, that we may be "fashioned like unto His glorious body, according to the working whereby He is able even to subdue all things unto Himself." Then, "as we have borne the image of the earthy, we shall also bear the image of the heavenly" (I Cor. 15:49).

It is true that in I Corinthians 15:50 Paul declares, *"flesh and blood cannot inherit the kingdom of God"*— but we are not speaking of *flesh and BLOOD.* Jesus shed His blood for the remission of sin. It was *with His blood* that He paid the sin-debt. When He ascended, He presented His blood to the Father, and now He sits at the Father's right hand as our great High Priest, making intercession for us. Therefore, our glorified body will be spiritual—but it will also be flesh and bones, like the resurrection body of Jesus.

The Scripture teaches that *this body* will be raised from the grave: ". . . the hour is coming, in the which all that are in the graves shall hear His voice, and shall come forth . . ." (John 5:28, 29).

The Scripture also teaches that it is *this body* that will be glorified—this corruptible will put on incorruption, this mortal will put on immortality (I Cor. 15:54).

This body will be changed, "fashioned like unto His glorious body" (Phil. 3:21).

This body will be made alive: "If the Spirit of

Him that raised up Jesus from the dead dwell in you,
He that raised up Christ from the dead shall also
quicken your *mortal bodies* by His Spirit that dwelleth
in you" (Rom. 8:11).

The Apostle Paul clearly taught that *this mortal
body* sown in corruption will be raised incorruptible
and immortal:

"There is one glory of the sun, and another glory
of the moon, and another glory of the stars: for one
star differeth from another star in glory. So also is
the resurrection of the dead. It is sown in corruption;
it is raised in incorruption: it is sown in dishonour;
it is raised in glory: it is sown in weakness; it is
raised in power: it is sown a natural body; it is raised
a spiritual body. There is a natural body, and there
is a spiritual body. . . . This corruptible must put on
incorruption, and this mortal must put on immortality.
So when this corruptible shall have put on incorruption, and this mortal shall have put on immortality,
then shall be brought to pass the saying that is written, Death is swallowed up in victory" (I Cor. 15:
41—54).

If there is no direct relation between the spiritual
body and our present mortal body, why does the Scripture clearly declare that the graves will be opened and
bodies will *come forth FROM the grave?* If there is
no connection between this body of humiliation and
the glorified body we will receive in the resurrection,
they why the resurrection *at all?*

The believer's resurrection body will be glorious
beyond the description of man's language:

We shall "shine forth as the sun" in the Father's
kingdom (Matt. 13:43).

In our glorified bodies we will shine as the dazzling
white snowflakes (Mark 9:3).

"He that winneth souls is *wise*" (Prov. 11:30), and
soul winners are born again Christians. "They that

be *wise* shall shine as the brightness of the firmament; and they that turn many to righteousness as the stars for ever and ever" (Dan. 12:3). Think of it! In our glorified bodies we shall shine as the brightness of the *firmament* — as the brightness of the sun, the planets, the stars, the constellations.

On the Mount of Transfiguration, the face of Jesus "did shine as the sun, and His raiment was white as the light" (Matt. 17:2). In our glorified bodies we will display such splendor and glory as the Lord Jesus Himself displayed in *His* glory: "We all, with open face beholding as in a glass the glory of the Lord, are changed into the same image from glory to glory, even as by the Spirit of the Lord" (II Cor. 3:18). Splendor, glory, majesty, and beauty beyond man's description — and all because Jesus took our place, took a body of humiliation and in that body conquered all the forces of evil. Now He sits at the right hand of the Majesty on high, making intercession for us until the time when He will return for us — and we shall be *like Him!*

In our glorified bodies we will be free from the restrictions of distance; we will be able to pass through space at will. There will be a new heaven, a new earth, and the New Jerusalem — a complete new creation; and we will have access to all of it. We will not be restricted to the laws of time and space as we are in this mortal body. You will remember that when Mary recognized Jesus the morning of His resurrection, He said to her, "Touch me not; for I am not yet ascended to my Father" (John 20:17). A bit later He met the women returning from the empty tomb, "and they came *and held Him by the feet,* and worshipped Him" (Matt. 28:9). During the time between His meeting with Mary Magdalene when He said, "Touch me not," and His appearance to those whom He *permitted* to touch Him, He had ascended to the heavenly Father, presented His blood, and returned to earth in

His glorified body. True, when He spoke to Mary He
was in the form of man, in a body; but not in the
same body in which He returned to earth and walked
the road to Emmaus, appeared to the disciples in the
upper room, and invited them to touch Him for assurance that He was not a spirit, but flesh and bones.
He forbade Mary to touch Him because He had not
at that time completed His work—He had not presented His blood to the Father. When He had fully
accomplished this He returned to earth to walk and
talk with men as He had before His crucifixion. He
was not limited by the laws of space—He ascended
to God the Father, and immediately returned to earth.
He was not limited by matter—He entered the upper
room when the doors and windows were closed, He
appeared and disappeared at will.

The most glorious of all truths is that *the redeemed
will be conformed to Christ!* He is "the firstborn
among many brethren" and we shall be conformed to
His image (Rom. 8:29). The first man, Adam, was of
the earth, created from dust. The second Man, the
Lord Jesus Christ, is of heaven. And just as surely
as we have borne the image of the first Adam, believers will bear the image of the *last* Adam, the One
from heaven. God's Word declares:

"The first man Adam was made a living soul; the
last Adam (the Lord Jesus Christ) was made a quickening spirit. Howbeit that was not first which is
spiritual, but that which is natural; and afterward
that which is spiritual. The first man is of the earth,
earthy: the second Man is the Lord from heaven. As
is the earthy, such are they also that are earthy: and
as is the heavenly, such are they also that are heavenly. And as we have borne the image of the earthy,
we shall also bear the image of the heavenly" (I Cor.
15:45—49).

Yes, praise God! *"We shall be like Him . . . fash-*

ioned like unto His glorious body" (I John 3:2; Phil. 3:21).

Believers Will Be Judged

At the second coming of Jesus, Christians will not be judged as to whether they are saved or lost; that is determined in this life. *Today* is the day of salvation, *now* is the accepted time (II Cor. 6:2), and there is no "second chance" after death. But in spite of the fact that the second coming of Jesus is *"that blessed hope"* for the Christian (Tit. 2:13), at the judgment seat of Christ some believers will suffer loss—not loss of the soul, but loss of reward.

I fear that ministers today—including myself—do not preach often enough on the subject of the judgment seat of Christ. All too many Christians fail to understand that they must give an account for their stewardship. The Word of God teaches no such thing as a "general" judgment, a time when *all* of mankind—the wicked and righteous together—will be gathered into one great courtroom, some to be consigned to hell and others to be invited into the Pearly White City. The Bible speaks of *the judgment seat of Christ* before which all believers must appear, and *the Great White Throne judgment* when only the wicked will be present.

The judgment seat of Christ will be just after the Rapture, just after all believers have been caught up to meet Jesus. We will sit at the marriage supper in the sky, at which time we will be judged and rewarded for our labors here on earth: "For we must all appear before the judgment seat of Christ; that every one may receive the things done in his body, according to that he hath done, whether it be good or bad" (II Cor. 5:10). In the Scriptures this is spoken of as "the day of our Lord Jesus Christ" (I Cor. 1:8), "the day of the Lord Jesus" (I Cor. 5:5; II Cor. 1:14), "the day of Jesus Christ" (Phil. 1:6), and "the day of Christ" (Phil. 1:10;

2:16).

The judgment for believers will be before the Millennium, before the visible kingdom of glory is set up here on earth, and *ONLY believers* will be present. This is also to be distinguished from the judgment of the nations described in Matthew 25:31—46, which will occur at the beginning of the millennial kingdom and will have to do with the nations living on earth when Jesus comes with His Church after the battle of Armageddon. The Great White Throne judgment (where *only the wicked* will appear) is described in Revelation 20:11—15, but it will not take place until one thousand years after the first resurrection (Rev. 20:4—6).

The Scripture does not leave us to wonder who the Judge will be. Under inspiration of the Holy Spirit the Apostle Paul declared, "Henceforth there is laid up for me a crown of righteousness, *which THE LORD, THE RIGHTEOUS JUDGE, shall give me at that day:* and not to me only, but unto all them also that love His appearing" (II Tim. 4:8). Jesus Himself declared, "The Father judgeth no man, *but hath committed ALL JUDGMENT unto the Son*" (John 5:22).

To the believers in Rome the Apostle Paul declared, *"We shall all stand before the judgment seat of Christ.* For it is written, As I live, saith the Lord, every knee shall bow to me, and every tongue shall confess to God. *So then EVERY ONE OF US SHALL GIVE ACCOUNT OF HIMSELF TO GOD"* (Rom. 14:10b—12).

I repeat—this has nothing to do with redemption of the soul. The Word of God guarantees that those who have heard the Word and believed on Jesus will never come into condemnation. In John 5:24 Jesus promised, "He that *heareth my WORD*, and believeth on Him that sent me, *HATH everlasting life,* and

SHALL NOT come into condemnation; but IS PASSED from death unto life." By His one offering Jesus has *"perfected for ever* them that are sanctified" (Heb. 10:14), and Romans 8:1 plainly declares, *"There is therefore now NO CONDEMNATION to them which are in Christ Jesus."*

At the judgment seat for believers the question will be *faithfulness,* not salvation. Paul instructed the Corinthian believers, "Let a man so account of us, as of the ministers of Christ, and stewards of the mysteries of God. *Moreover it is required in stewards, that a man be found FAITHFUL.* But with me it is a very small thing that I should be judged of you, or of man's judgment: yea, I judge not mine own self. For I know nothing by myself; yet am I not hereby justified: but *He that judgeth me is the LORD.* Therefore judge nothing before the time, until the Lord come, who both will bring to light the hidden things of darkness, and will make manifest the counsels of the hearts: and then shall every man have praise of God" (I Cor. 4:1—5).

This judgment will determine the reward of each believer. Some will receive a *full* reward, some will receive a *partial* reward, and some will suffer *total loss* of reward—i. e., their works will be burned, they will be stripped of all eternal reward, but their spirit will be saved "yet so as by fire." I must confess that I have no idea what it will be like to be in heaven and have no reward, but according to the Word of God there will be saved people whose works will be burned and they will stand before the Righteous Judge *without reward:*

"For other foundation can no man lay than that is laid, which is Jesus Christ. Now if any man build upon this foundation gold, silver, precious stones, wood, hay, stubble; every man's work shall be made manifest: for the day shall declare it, because it shall be revealed by fire; and the fire shall try every man's work of what sort it is. If any man's work abide which he hath built thereupon, he shall receive a reward. *If any man's work shall be burned, he shall suffer loss: BUT HE HIMSELF SHALL BE SAVED; yet so as by fire"* (I Cor. 3:11−15).

I wonder how many of us have really thought this through? Do we fully realize how serious a matter it is to have our stewardship *"made manifest"* before the judgment seat of Christ? We will face not only our deeds, but our possibilities—not the number, *but the weight* of our works, and we will either receive a reward or see our works burned.

We are commanded, "Whether therefore ye eat, or drink, or *whatsoever ye do, DO ALL TO THE GLO-RY OF GOD"* (I Cor. 10:31).

Paul admonished the Philippian believers, "Wherefore, my beloved, as ye have always obeyed, not as in my presence only, but now much more in my absence, *work out your own salvation WITH FEAR AND TREMBLING"* (Phil. 2:12).

The Lord will judge His people (Heb. 10:30), and in II Corinthians 5:11 Paul warns of "the terror of the Lord." II John 8 warns believers, "Look to yourselves, that we *lose not those things which we have WROUGHT*, but that we receive *a FULL reward,"* and in I John 2:28 the beloved disciple penned this admonition: "And now, little children, *abide in Him;* that, when He shall appear, we may have confidence, *and not be ashamed before Him at His coming!"*

Yes, according to the Scriptures just given on these pages, it is entirely possible for a believer to be saved as "a brand plucked out of the fire" (Zech. 3:2; I Cor. 3:15), or as a person escapes a burning building with only his life, minus all personal possessions. If you will read Genesis 19:16−29 you will see that Lot is an example of this.

II Corinthians 5:10 declares that at the judgment seat of Christ we will receive according to our *good* works, and also according to our *bad* works—and again I would remind you that this is speaking of *believers,* not unsaved people. In Colossians 3:23—25 we are instructed, *"Whatsoever* ye do, do it heartily, as to the Lord, and not unto men; knowing that of the Lord ye shall receive the reward of the inheritance: for ye serve the Lord Christ. But he that doeth wrong shall receive for the wrong which he hath done: *and there is no respect of persons!"* (Also please study Luke 12:45—48, and 19:11—27.)

The standard by which believers will be judged will not be *how much* they did, how *big* the work was, but the spirit in which it was done—"of what sort it is" (I Cor. 3:13). Do we serve faithfully to the glory and honor of God—or to glorify self? Do we take advantage of our opportunities and develop them to the fullest, *buying up* opportunities for service—or do we meet them with indifference and neglect? It is the sin of *omission* more than sins of *commission* that will rob us of a full reward. God's Word plainly states, *"To him that KNOWETH to do good, and DOETH IT NOT, to him it is SIN"* (James 4:17).

Therefore the important thing will be—not the bigness of the *work,* but the faithfulness of the *worker;* not the number of deeds done, but in whose honor they were performed: "Talk no more so exceeding proudly; let not arrogancy come out of your mouth: for the Lord is a God of knowledge, *and by Him actions are weighed"* (I Sam. 2:3).

We may never attain that for which we strive; but if we faithfully *strive TO attain,* we will receive a full reward. Dedicated service, sacrifices made to the glory of God, unselfish devotion to God and our fellowman, giving from a free and open heart—all of these things faithfully performed will *add to* our reward, or if left undone they will *take away* from our reward.

You can rest assured that the day we stand before the judgment seat of Christ will be a day of great surprise, and the results will be varied. The Lord cannot judge unrighteously or unjustly. Even with His own children He is "the Righteous Judge" (II Tim. 4:8). Every believer will be treated right. Those who have been careless and have built "wood, hay, and stubble" will see their works burned. Those who are faithful stewards will build "gold, silver, and precious stones." Their work will stand the fire-test and they will be rewarded.

What is the "fire" by which our works will be tested? The fire is the Word of God: *"Is not my Word like as a FIRE? saith the Lord;* and like a hammer that breaketh the rock in pieces?" (Jer. 23:29).

Jesus declared, "If any man *hear my WORDS*, and believe not, I judge him not: for I came not to judge the world, but to save the world. He that rejecteth me, and receiveth not *my WORDS*, hath One that judgeth him: *THE WORD THAT I HAVE SPOKEN, THE SAME SHALL JUDGE HIM IN THE LAST DAY"* (John 12:47, 48).

Since we will be judged by the Word, consider these passages *from* the Word which should help us to be found faithful:

The faithful will be great in the kingdom of heaven (Matt. 5:19; 25:21; Luke 19:17); but those who have sown to the flesh will reap corruption (Gal. 6:7, 8).

The pure and blameless will win the prize (I Cor. 1:8; Phil. 3:14); those who have been carnal will be disapproved (I Cor. 9:27; II Tim. 2:5).

The poor in heart, the faithful servant, will have boldness in that day of judgment (I John 4:17); but others will be ashamed (I John 2:28).

Each believer will receive his due and just reward

(Heb. 6:10; I Cor. 4:5; II Tim. 4:8)—and you may rest assured that God has no respect of persons (I Pet. 1:17; II Cor. 5:10; Col. 3:24, 25).

Redemption is the gift of God, not of works. There is nothing man can do to earn salvation (Eph. 2:8, 9). *Rewards* are the results of faithful works; rewards are earned. Jesus came and died on the cross to redeem us; He is coming again to reward us. He promises, "Behold, I come quickly; *and my reward is with me, to give every man ACCORDING AS HIS WORK SHALL BE*" (Rev. 22:12).

All of the redeemed will dwell in the Pearly White City throughout eternity; all will have glorified bodies; all will *shine* in that celestial city—but in different degrees of glory and splendor. (Please study I Corinthians 15:40—42.) In that eternal day there will be *great* vessels, and there will be *small* vessels; but *all* vessels will be *filled*. The great vessel will be full, the small vessel will be full. There will be different degrees of glory but no difference in happiness. All will be completely happy in that land that is fairer than day. (Study Matthew 20:1—16.)

All the redeemed will see His face and will walk in the light of His glory. In that day the servants and the services will be many—but there will be *only ONE Lord!*

The Scripture speaks of various crowns which can be won through faithful stewardship:

The crown of righteousness: This will be given to the victorious soldier. The Apostle Paul wrote to young Timothy, "I have fought a good fight, I have finished my course, I have kept the faith: *Henceforth there is laid up for me a CROWN OF RIGHTEOUSNESS,* which the Lord, the righteous judge, shall give me at that day: and not to me only, but unto all them also that love His appearing" (II Tim. 4:7, 8).

The incorruptible crown: This crown will be given

to the stedfast runner. Again we quote from the inspired writings of Paul: "Every man that striveth for the mastery is temperate in all things. Now they do it to obtain a corruptible crown; *but we an INCORRUPTIBLE.* I therefore so run, not as uncertainly; so fight I, not as one that beateth the air: but I keep under my body, and bring it into subjection: lest that by any means, when I have preached to others, I myself should be a castaway" (I Cor. 9:25–27).

The crown of life: This will be given to the martyr, the Christian who is faithful unto death: "Fear none of those things which thou shalt suffer: behold, the devil shall cast some of you into prison, that ye may be tried; and ye shall have tribulation ten days: be thou faithful unto death, *and I will give thee a CROWN OF LIFE"* (Rev. 2:10). See also James 1:12.

The crown of rejoicing: This is a special crown for the unselfish steward. "For what is our hope, or joy, *or CROWN OF REJOICING?* Are not even ye in the presence of our Lord Jesus Christ at His coming?" (I Thess. 2:19). In Philippians 4:1 Paul wrote, "Therefore, my brethren dearly beloved and longed for, *MY JOY AND CROWN,* so stand fast in the Lord, my dearly beloved."

The crown of glory: This crown will be given to the shepherd who is the right example to his flock: "Feed the flock of God which is among you, taking the oversight thereof, not by constraint, but willingly; not for filthy lucre, but of a ready mind; neither as being lords over God's heritage, but being ensamples to the flock. *And when the Chief Shepherd shall appear, ye shall receive a CROWN OF GLORY that fadeth not away"* (I Pet. 5:2–4).

After the marriage supper of the Lamb and after the saints are judged and rewarded, Jesus will return in glory *with* His saints to exercise judgment upon this earth and upon Antichrist. It is then that He will set up His glorious kingdom: "And I heard as it were the voice of a great multitude, and as the voice of many waters, and as the voice of mighty thunderings, saying, *Alleluia: for the Lord God omnipotent reigneth*" (Rev. 19:6).

Yes, that will indeed be a glorious day for the Church, the redeemed; but it will be a day of great judgment upon the peoples of earth, the wicked kings and their subjects:

"*And it shall come to pass in that day, that the Lord shall punish the host of the high ones that are on high, and the kings of the earth upon the earth.* And they shall be gathered together, as prisoners are gathered in the pit, and shall be shut up in the prison, and after many days shall they be visited. Then the moon shall be confounded, and the sun ashamed, when the Lord of hosts shall reign in Mount Zion, and in Jerusalem, and before His ancients gloriously" (Isa. 24:21–23).

That will be the glorious day when the promise of Luke 12:32 will be fulfilled: "Fear not, little flock; for it is your Father's good pleasure to *give you the kingdom.*"

John the Beloved also spoke of the time when the kingdom, power, and glory will be given to the saints: "And I saw thrones, and they sat upon them, *and judgment was given unto them:* and I saw the souls of them that were beheaded for the witness of Jesus, and for the Word of God, and which had not worshipped the beast, neither his image, neither had received his mark upon their foreheads, or in their hands; *and they lived and reigned with Christ a thousand years*" (Rev. 20:4).

The Prophet Daniel also foresaw that day when the saints of God will receive the kingdom:

"*The saints of the most High shall take the king-*

*dom, and possess the kingdom for ever, even for ever
and ever.* Then I would know the truth of the fourth
beast, which was diverse from all the others, exceeding
dreadful, whose teeth were of iron, and his nails of
brass; which devoured, brake in pieces, and stamped
the residue with his feet; and of the ten horns that
were in his head, and of the other which came up,
and before whom three fell; even of that horn that
had eyes, and a mouth that spake very great things,
whose look was more stout than his fellows. I beheld,
and the same horn made war with the saints, and
prevailed against them; *until THE ANCIENT OF
DAYS CAME, and judgment was given to the saints
of the most High; and the time came that the saints
possessed the kingdom"* (Dan. 7:18—22).

Those who have been faithful stewards—faithful
over even a *few* things—will be made ruler over many
things (Luke 19:17; Matt. 25:21). However, God is one
God, there is but one Lord, and believers are *one body.*
Therefore there will be no individual glory over another
individual glory. There will be the glory of *the one
body, the Church,* and the individual will have only
a portion therein. Believers are "partakers of the inheritance of the saints in light" (Col. 1:12), we are
"a royal priesthood" (I Pet. 2:9), we are "kings and
priests unto God" (Rev. 1:6), and as kings and priests
we will reign with Him on the earth (Rev. 5:10); *but
we will reign as ONE BODY,* not as proud individuals.
The royal realm of glory is comprised of the *oneness*
of Father, Son, and God's people. There is no place
for *pride* in God's economy, in His great eternal government as described in Isaiah 9:6,7. The whole body
of believers is superior to the *individual* believer; the
individual cannot be perfected apart from all other
members of God's eternal family. Each believer will
be perfected in connection with God's perfect community when all things are created new.

Thus believers who now sleep in Christ wait for the perfecting of future believers at the consummation of all things. This is clearly declared in Paul's letter to the Hebrews. Speaking of the Old Testament saints he said, "These all, having obtained a good report through faith, *received not the promise:* God having provided some better thing for us, *that they WITHOUT US should not be made perfect"* (Heb. 11:39, 40).

This truth is also declared in Revelation 6:9—11: "And when he had opened the fifth seal, I saw under the altar the souls of them that were slain for the Word of God, and for the testimony which they held: and they cried with a loud voice, saying, How long, O Lord, holy and true, dost thou not judge and avenge our blood on them that dwell on the earth? And white robes were given unto every one of them; and it was said unto them, that *they should rest yet for a little season, until their fellowservants also and their brethren, that should be killed as they were, should be FULFILLED."*

When the dead in Christ are raised and "clothed upon with our house which is from heaven" (II Cor. 5:1—4), living believers will (at the same time) be changed and glorified (I Thess. 4:15—17; I Cor. 15: 51—55). Then not only will the *individual* be redeemed and glorified, but the body as a whole, the entire New Testament Church of which Jesus is the head and the foundation, will be redeemed and glorified. Then will be not only *individual* glory and blessedness, but the kingdom of God will be right here on earth as Matthew 6:10 teaches: "Thy kingdom come. Thy will be done *in earth,* as it is in heaven."

The devil is the god of this age in which we live (II Cor. 4:4). He is "the prince of the power of the air" (Eph. 2:2), "and the whole world lieth in wickedness (or *in the Wicked One)"* (I John 5:19). But when Jesus comes, the forces of evil will be put down, the universe will be delivered from the curse, the air will be renovated by fire, and the glorified saints of God will reign as kings and priests with Christ over all of God's new creation:

"And there shall be no night there; and they need no candle, neither light of the sun; for the Lord God giveth them light: *and they shall reign for ever and ever*" (Rev. 22:5).

"Do ye not know that the saints shall judge the world? and if the world shall be judged by you, are ye unworthy to judge the smallest matters? Know ye not that we shall judge angels? How much more things that pertain to this life?" (I Cor. 6:2, 3).

"For unto the angels hath He not put in subjection the world to come, whereof we speak" (Heb. 2:5).

Jesus promises, "To him that overcometh will I grant to sit with me in my throne, even as I also overcame, and am set down with my Father in His throne" (Rev. 3:21).

To His disciples Jesus promised, "Blessed are those servants, whom the Lord when He cometh shall find watching: Verily I say unto you, that He shall gird Himself, and make them to sit down to meat, and will come forth and serve them" (Luke 12:37).

When the last promise in the Bible was given, *"Surely I come quickly,"* is it any wonder John the Beloved replied, *"EVEN SO, COME, LORD JESUS"*? (Rev. 22:20).

The Coming of Antichrist

"I am come in my Father's name, and ye receive me not: if another shall come in his own name, him ye will receive" (John 5:43).

What will occur on earth immediately after the rapture of the saints and also during the approximately seven years following the Rapture? The Bible clearly answers this question.

Immediately following the Rapture, after every born again believer is removed from this earth, there will be a time of chaos such as the world has never known! It is then that Antichrist will appear and offer peace to the troubled world—and for the next three and one-half years there will *be* peace. However, at the end of that time the Antichrist will break every promise he has made, he will break his covenant with Israel, and for the duration of his reign the peoples of earth will receive such a blood-bath as man has never known.

In Revelation 6:2 we read, "And I saw, and behold a white horse: and he that sat on him had a *bow;* and a crown was given unto him: and he went forth conquering, and to conquer." This rider is none other than Antichrist. (It is true that the Lord Jesus Christ will also ride out on a white horse, but He does not appear until Revelation 19:11.) The rider of the first white horse is not *Christ,* but Antichrist.

He comes with an offer of peace. You will notice he carries a *bow,* but no arrows—and it is not with a bow that men are killed. But after three and one-half years of peace, the red horse of war will come forth: "And there went out another horse that was red: and power was given to him that sat thereon *to take peace from the earth,* and that they should kill one another: and there was given unto him *a great sword*" (Rev. 6:4).

Following the red horse of war will be the black horse of famine (Rev. 6:5, 6), and after *famine,* "behold a pale horse: and his name that sat on him was *Death,* and Hell followed with him. And power was given unto them over the fourth part of the earth, to kill with sword, and with hunger, and with death, and with the beasts of the earth" (Rev. 6:8).

Yes, the rider of the white horse in Revelation 6:2 is definitely the Antichrist; and during the time the

Church is in the air with Jesus at the marriage supper
of the Lamb, and while believers are being judged
and rewarded for their stewardship, Antichrist will be
reigning here on earth. The seventieth week of Daniel's seventy prophetic weeks will then run its course:

"And whiles I was speaking, and praying, and
confessing my sin and the sin of my people Israel,
and presenting my supplication before the Lord my
God for the holy mountain of my God; Yea, whiles I
was speaking in prayer, even the man Gabriel, whom
I had seen in the vision at the beginning, being caused
to fly swiftly, touched me about the time of the evening oblation.   And he informed me, and talked with
me, and said, O Daniel, I am now come forth to give
thee skill and understanding. At the beginning of thy
supplications the commandment came forth, and I am
come to shew thee; for thou art greatly beloved: therefore understand the matter, and consider the vision.

"Seventy weeks are determined upon thy people
and upon thy holy city, to finish the transgression,
and to make an end of sins, and to make reconciliation for iniquity, and to bring in everlasting righteousness, and to seal up the vision and prophecy, and to
anoint the most Holy. Know therefore and understand,
that from the going forth of the commandment to
restore and to build Jerusalem unto the Messiah the
Prince shall be seven weeks, and threescore and two
weeks: the street shall be built again, and the wall,
even in troublous times.

"And after threescore and two weeks shall Messiah
be cut off, but not for Himself: and the people of the
prince that shall come shall destroy the city and the
sanctuary; and the end thereof shall be with a flood,
and unto the end of the war desolations are determined. And he shall confirm the covenant with many
for one week: and in the midst of the week he shall
cause the sacrifice and the oblation to cease, and for

the overspreading of abominations he shall make it desolate, even until the consummation, and that determined shall be poured upon the desolate" (Dan. 9:20—27).

The "weeks" spoken of here are *weeks of years*— seventy weeks of seven years each. Within these weeks of years the national chastisement of Israel will be ended and God's chosen people will be re-established in everlasting righteousness (v. 24).

These seventy weeks of years are divided as follows: *Seven* weeks of years (or 49 years), plus "threescore and two weeks" (*sixty-two* weeks or 434 years). This makes a total of sixty-nine weeks of years, with only *one week* remaining.

We are also clearly told that during the forty-nine years Jerusalem would be rebuilt and the time of the rebuilding would be *"troublous times."* This was literally fulfilled, as recorded by Ezra and Nehemiah.

Sixty-two weeks (434 years) thereafter, Messiah was to come (v. 25). This, too, was fulfilled in the birth of Jesus and is recorded by the New Testament writers. So only *one week* of years remains—seven years, obviously an intermediate period.

The exact date of the crucifixion of Jesus is not fixed. We read, *"AFTER threescore and two weeks shall Messiah be cut off,"* but we are not told *how long* after the sixty-two weeks He would be crucified. However, His crucifixion was the *first* fulfillment of prophetic events mentioned in Daniel 9:26, and the *second* prophecy in that verse was fulfilled in 70 A. D. when Titus the Roman destroyed Jerusalem and had more than a million Jews killed.

Then *"unto the end"* (v. 26) is also a period not fixed, the number of years is not named; but this period has lasted almost two thousand years up to now. God revealed to Daniel that wars and desolations would continue, and in Matthew 24:6—14 *Jesus* declared that "wars and rumours of wars" will continue, and that these events are definitely a sign of the end.

In the New Testament we find many mysteries *revealed* which were hidden from the Old Testament prophets. This is evident in the words of Jesus in Matthew 13:11—17 and in Paul's letter to the Ephesians, chapter 3, verses 1 through 11. (Please study these passages in detail.)

During the period that has lasted from the crucifixion of Jesus until this present day, the New Testament Church has been established (Matt. 16:18), and it was revealed to the Apostle Paul that the Church Age would run its course during this period of time that is not definitely marked off but has already lasted almost two thousand years. It will continue until the Rapture, and that is the time when the last "week of years" will begin. However, this date is not revealed in the Scripture, and no man knows the day or the hour when the saints of God will be raptured, caught up to meet Jesus in the air.

It is the last "week of years" with which Daniel 9:27 has to do. The personality "he" in that verse is the Antichrist, "the prince that shall come" in verse 26, the "little horn" of Daniel chapter 7, verse 8. He will make a covenant with the Jews, allowing them to restore their temple worship and sacrifices for a time; but in the midst of that period he will *break* his covenant, "he shall cause the sacrifice and the oblation to cease" and Daniel 12:11 will be fulfilled: "And from the time that the daily sacrifice shall be taken away, and the abomination that maketh desolate set up, there shall be a thousand two hundred and ninety days."

Paul speaks of this in II Thessalonians 2:3, 4: "Let no man deceive you by any means: for that day shall not come, except there come a falling away first, *and that man of sin be revealed, the son of perdition;* who opposeth and exalteth himself above all that is called God, or that is worshipped; so that he as God sitteth in the temple of God, shewing himself that he is God."

Between the sixty-ninth week (after which Messiah was cut off) and the seventieth week (when the "little horn" of Daniel 7 will run his earthly reign) we find the Church Age, and Daniel 9:27 deals with the last three and one-half years of this seventieth week. That will be the Great Tribulation described in Matthew 24:15—28, the time known as "a time of trouble, such as never was since there was a nation . . ." (Dan. 12:1).

In Revelation 3:10 John the Beloved speaks of the tribulation period as "the hour of temptation, which shall come upon all the world, to try them that dwell upon the earth." This will be the reign of Antichrist, the last world dictator, and his power will extend through almost seven years.

In accordance with prophecy revealed and fulfilled in God's Word, I declare without hesitation that *the world is ready* for the appearing of Antichrist—but he will not appear until *after* the Rapture of the Church. Believers are looking for THE Christ, not Antichrist. We are praying, *"Come quickly, LORD JESUS!"*

The Church will not convert the world. The purpose of the Church is not to convert the world, but to make disciples. There is no Scripture to substantiate the doctrine that righteousness will eventually prevail, the Church will convert the world and set up the kingdom. On the contrary, God's Word tells us that lawlessness will increase, "and because iniquity shall abound, the love of many shall wax cold" (Matt. 24:12). In Luke 18:8 Jesus asked, "When the Son of man cometh, shall He find faith on the earth?" And in II Timothy 3:13 the Word declares, *"Evil men and seducers shall wax worse and worse,* deceiving, and being deceived."

According to the Bible, the world will not become more righteous or more Christianized, but more unbelieving and more ungodly:

II Timothy 3:1—4: "This know also, that *in the last days* perilous times shall come. For men shall be lovers of their own selves, covetous, boasters, proud, blasphemers, disobedient to parents, unthankful, unholy, without natural affection, trucebreakers, false accusers, incontinent, fierce, despisers of those that are good, traitors, heady, highminded, lovers of pleasures more than lovers of God."

II Timothy 4:3,4: "For the time will come when they will not endure sound doctrine; but after their own lusts shall they heap to themselves teachers, having itching ears; and they shall turn away their ears from the truth, and shall be turned unto fables."

II Peter 3:3: ". . . there shall come *in the last days* scoffers, walking after their own lusts."

I Timothy 4:1—3: "Now the Spirit speaketh expressly, that *in the latter times* some shall depart from the faith, giving heed to seducing spirits, and doctrines of devils; speaking lies in hypocrisy; having their conscience seared with a hot iron; forbidding to marry, and commanding to abstain from meats, which God hath created to be received with thanksgiving of them which believe and know the truth."

Paul admonishes us not to be deceived concerning the return of our Lord. We are not to allow ourselves to be deceived by man's teaching, but rather by studying and rightly dividing the Word, we are to stand firm on the Word of the living God:

"Now we beseech you, brethren, by the coming of our Lord Jesus Christ, and by our gathering together unto Him, that ye be not soon shaken in mind, or be troubled, neither by spirit, nor by word, nor by letter as from us, as that the day of Christ is at hand. *Let no man deceive you BY ANY MEANS:* for that day shall not come, except there come a falling away first, and that man of sin be revealed, the son of perdition . . . And then shall that Wicked be revealed, whom the Lord shall consume with the spirit of His mouth, and shall destroy with the brightness of His coming" (II Thess. 2:1—3, 8).

The battle between the Seed of the woman and the seed of the serpent began shortly after Eden when Cain murdered Abel, and the conflict will intensify until the end. There will be no agreement between God and civilization. He will not finally overlook man's failures, but as lawlessness and evil grow worse and worse God will destroy the kingdom of men by the shattering, destructive blow of the Stone cut out of the mountain without hands.

Daniel and John the Beloved each give an account of the manner in which the Lord Jesus Christ will triumph victoriously over the devil and the forces of evil. In Daniel 2:34, 35 we read, "Thou sawest till that *a Stone was cut out without hands,* which smote the image upon his feet that were of iron and clay, and brake them to pieces. Then was the iron, the clay, the brass, the silver, and the gold, broken to pieces together, and became like the chaff of the summer threshingfloors; and the wind carried them away, that no place was found for them: and the Stone that smote the image became a great mountain, and filled the whole earth."

In Revelation 19:11—21 John the Beloved wrote, under inspiration: "I saw heaven opened, and behold a white horse; *and He that sat upon him was called Faithful and True, and in righteousness He doth judge and make war.* His eyes were as a flame of fire, and on His head were many crowns; and He had a name written, that no man knew, but He Himself. And He was clothed with a vesture dipped in blood: *and His name is called The Word of God.*

"And the armies which were in heaven followed Him upon white horses, clothed in fine linen, white and clean.   And out of His mouth goeth a sharp sword, that with it He should smite the nations: and He shall rule them with a rod of iron: and He treadeth the winepress of the fierceness and wrath of Almighty God.   And He hath on His vesture and on His thigh a name written, KING OF KINGS, AND LORD OF LORDS.

"And I saw an angel standing in the sun; and he cried with a loud voice, saying to all the fowls that fly in the midst of heaven, Come and gather yourselves together unto the supper of the great God; that ye may eat the flesh of kings, and the flesh of captains, and the flesh of mighty men, and the flesh of horses, and of them that sit on them, and the flesh of all men, both free and bond, both small and great.

"And I saw the beast, and the kings of the earth, and their armies, gathered together to make war against Him that sat on the horse, and against His army. And the beast was taken, and with him the false prophet that wrought miracles before him, with which he deceived them that had received the mark of the beast, and them that worshipped his image.   These both were cast alive into a lake of fire burning with brimstone.   And the remnant were slain with the sword of Him that sat upon the horse, which sword proceeded out of His mouth: and all the fowls were filled with their flesh."

Yes, the time is coming when there will be peace on earth and good will among men, but it will not come through the evolution of man nor through man's "world program."

For centuries man has sought to bring about Utopia, that glorious day of peace and prosperity; and when Antichrist first comes on the scene it will seem that Utopia has finally arrived! According to prophecy, the first part of his reign will see systems of civilization reach the highest degree since the creation of man. The Antichrist will be a mighty genius, a man of great power (Rev. chapter 13). He will perform miracles second to none save those wrought by the Lord Jesus Christ. He will be the *counterfeit* Christ and he will do his utmost to *perfectly* counterfeit the Son of God.   During his reign as the supreme leader of men he will create a false sense of *security and rest* henceforth unknown on earth. He will sit in the temple in Jerusalem and announce that He is God (II Thess. 2:4). He will be *worshipped* as God (Rev. 13:8); and through flatteries and the promise of world peace, the first years of his reign will be glorious. But in spite of his power, his miracles, and his almost universal following, Jesus will destroy him "with the spirit of His mouth" and "with the brightness of His coming" (II Thess. 2:8).

In Contrast

The Antichrist will be the counterfeit of God's Christ. He will be the "son of perdition" (the son of Satan), and he will appear in a body just as Jesus, *God's* Son, appeared in a body. I personally believe that just as the Holy Ghost overshadowed the Virgin Mary and she brought forth *God's* only begotten Son, the Antichrist will be conceived of the devil and born of a harlot.

God's Christ came from above. He was in the bosom of the Father in the beginning. He came down from heaven to tabernacle among men (John 1:1, 14, 18; 6:38).

Antichrist will ascend from the bottomless pit. Just as the Spirit of God overshadowed Mary and she brought forth God's Son, the spirit of the devil will proceed from the bottomless pit and Antichrist will come into the world in a body, definitely a personality (Rev. 11:7).

Christ came in His Father's name and the world rejected Him (John 5:43a).

Antichrist will come in his own name and the world will receive him (John 5:43b).

Christ "humbled Himself, and became obedient unto death, even the death of the cross" (Phil. 2:8).

Antichrist will be the proud one. He will exalt himself and demand that the people worship him (II Thess. 2:4).

Christ was "despised and rejected of men" (Isa. 53:3; Luke 23:18).

Antichrist will be admired, and men will build a great image in his honor (Rev. 13:14, 15).

Christ obeyed God the Father in all things, He finished the work the Father gave Him to do, and He is now exalted and given a name that is above every name (Phil. 2:9).

Antichrist will exalt himself but he will be cast down to hell (Isa. 14:14, 15).

Christ came into the world to do the will of God (John 6:38).

Antichrist will not be in subjection to another. He will do that which he *himself* wills to do (Dan. 11:36).

Christ came into the world "to seek and to save that which was lost" (Luke 19:10).

Antichrist will come to destroy, and during the last half of his reign there will be a time of bloodshed such as this world has never known (Dan. 8:24; Rev. 6:1—8).

Christ is the Good Shepherd (John 10:14).

Antichrist will be the wicked shepherd (Zech. 11:16).

Christ is "the true vine" (John 15:1).

Antichrist will be "the vine of the earth" (Rev.

14:18).

Christ is the Truth (John 1:14; 14:6).

Antichrist will be the Lie. He is a liar and the father of lies (II Thess. 2:11; John 8:44).

Christ is the Holy One. He was God in flesh—spotless, without sin (Mark 1:24; II Cor. 5:19).

Antichrist will be the lawless one (II Thess. 2:8).

Christ was "the Man of sorrows, and acquainted with grief" (Isa. 53:3).

Antichrist will *bring* sorrow such as the mind of man cannot imagine (Matt. 24:21, 22).

Christ is the Son of God, the only begotten of the Father (Matt. 3:17; 17:5; Luke 1:35).

Antichrist will be the son of perdition (John 17:12; II Thess. 2:3).

Christ is "the mystery of godliness"—God manifested in flesh (I Tim. 3:16; II Cor. 5:19).

Antichrist will be "the mystery of iniquity"—Satan manifested in flesh (II Thess. 2:7).

The Name "Antichrist"

John the Beloved uses the name *"Antichrist"* five times in his epistles:

I John 2:18: "Little children, it is the last time: and as ye have heard that *antichrist* shall come, even now are there many *antichrists* (plural); whereby we know that it is the last time."

I John 2:22: "Who is a liar but he that denieth that Jesus is the Christ? He is *antichrist*, that denieth the Father and the Son."

I John 4:3: "Every spirit that confesseth not that Jesus Christ is come in the flesh is not of God: and this is that spirit of *antichrist*, whereof ye have heard that it should come; and even now already is it in the world."

II John 7: "For many deceivers are entered into

the world, who confess not that Jesus Christ is come in the flesh. This is a deceiver and an *antichrist.*"

There is no doubt that "Antichrist" of I John 2:18 is the same person to whom Paul refers as "the Man of Sin . . . the son of perdition . . . that Wicked (or lawless)" (II Thess. 2:3—8). He is the "beast" who will appear out of the sea in Revelation 13:1—10, the "little horn" who will rise up out of the fourth world empire (Dan. chapter 7).

According to the Scriptures, the Antichrist will be *a real person,* but he will also be a *system.* As a *person* he will head up a system of lawlessness and ungodliness heretofore unknown. As an *inspiration* he is always present, as declared in the passages just quoted from I and II John. In II Thessalonians 2:7 we read that "the mystery of iniquity" (the *spirit* of Antichrist) was already in the world when the Apostle Paul and John the Beloved penned their epistles, and he will remain here until the appearing of the *personal* Antichrist who will be revealed after the Rapture of the Church.

Jesus said to the Jews, "I am come in my Father's name . . . another shall come in his own name" (John 5:43). *"Another"* here refers to the Man of Sin, and proves that he will be *a person,* an individual, just as surely as *the Man Christ Jesus* was an individual.

In Matthew 24:15 Jesus spoke of "the abomination of desolation" who would stand "in the holy place" as prophesied by Daniel. The "abomination of desolation" is clearly connected with the reign of Antichrist, and as a *definite personality* he will stand in "the holy place." In II Thessalonians 2:4 Paul tells us that the Man of Sin will sit *in the temple of God* and announce that he *is* God. (See also Daniel 12:11.)

Just as the Lord Jesus Christ, an individual, *a real Person,* tabernacled among men and wrought miracles such as had not been seen "since the world began"

(John 9:32), *Antichrist* (an individual, a real person) will tabernacle among men and perform great miracles. He will call down fire from heaven and will cause the giant image to speak (Rev. 13:13, 15).

God's kingdom is a kingdom of righteousness. The kingdom of *Antichrist* will be a kingdom of lawlessness (Rev. chapter 13). The Man of Sin will head up a human system which will be directly at enmity with God and righteousness.

Our God is a *Triune God*—one God manifested in three Persons: Father, Son, and Holy Spirit; and just as surely as there is a *Holy* Trinity there is a *Satanic* trinity: the Dragon, the Beast, and the False Prophet. His reign will have to do with three cities: Jerusalem, Babylon, and Rome—and he will be concerned with politics, economics, and religion.

The Satanic Trinity

"And I saw three unclean spirits like frogs come out of the mouth of the *dragon,* and out of the mouth of the *beast,* and out of the mouth of the *false prophet*" (Rev. 16:13).

"And the devil that deceived them was cast into the lake of fire and brimstone, where the beast and the false prophet are, and shall be tormented day and night for ever and ever" (Rev. 20:10).

Three persons make up the diabolical system of Antichrist:

The Dragon (the anti-God): "And there appeared another wonder in heaven; and behold a great red dragon, having seven heads and ten horns, and seven crowns upon his heads. . . . And there was war in heaven: Michael and his angels fought against the dragon; and the dragon fought and his angels, and prevailed not; neither was their place found any more in heaven. And the great dragon was cast out, that old serpent, called the Devil, and Satan, which deceiveth the whole world: he was cast out into the earth, and his angels were cast out with him" (Rev. 12:3—9).

The Beast (the anti-Son): "And I stood upon the sand of the sea, and saw a beast rise up out of the sea, having seven heads and ten horns, and upon his horns ten crowns, and upon his heads the name of blasphemy. And the beast which I saw was like unto a leopard, and his feet were as the feet of a bear, and his mouth as the mouth of a lion: and the dragon gave him his power, and his seat, and great authority.

"And I saw one of his heads as it were wounded to death; and his deadly wound was healed: and all the world wondered after the beast. And they worshipped the dragon which gave power unto the beast: and they worshipped the beast, saying, Who is like unto the beast? Who is able to make war with him?

"And there was given unto him a mouth speaking great things and blasphemies; and power was given unto him to continue forty and two months. And he opened his mouth in blasphemy against God, to blaspheme His name, and His tabernacle, and them that dwell in heaven. And it was given unto him to make war with the saints, and to overcome them: and power was given him over all kindreds, and tongues, and nations. And all that dwell upon the earth shall worship him, whose names are not written in the book of life of the Lamb slain from the foundation of the world" (Rev. 13:1—8).

The False Prophet (the anti-Spirit): "And I beheld another beast coming up out of the earth; and he had two horns like a lamb, and he spake as a dragon. And he exerciseth all the power of the first beast before him, and causeth the earth and them which dwell therein to worship the first beast, whose deadly wound was healed. And he doeth great wonders, so that he maketh fire come down from heaven on the earth in the sight of men, and deceiveth them that dwell on the earth by the means of those miracles which he had power to do in the sight of the beast; saying to them that dwell on the earth, that they should make an image to the beast, which had the wound by a sword, and did live.

"And he had power to give life unto the image of the beast, that the image of the beast should both speak, and cause that as many as would not worship the image of the beast should be killed. And he causeth all, both small and great, rich and poor, free and bond, to receive a mark in their right hand, or in their foreheads: and that no man might buy or sell, save he that had the mark, or the name of the beast, or the number of his name. Here is wisdom. Let him that hath understanding count the number of the beast: for it is the number of a man; and *his number is Six hundred three score and six*" (Rev. 13:11—18).

Now let us discuss these personalities individually:

The anti-God: The dragon, the first person in the Satanic trinity, is the counterpart of the true God, the Father of our Lord and Saviour Jesus Christ. He is the head of the Satanic system, he is "that old serpent, called the Devil, and Satan" (Rev. 12:9). The dragon stands in relationship to the beast as God the Father stands in relationship to Christ Jesus the Son. God sent His Son into the world (John 6:57), and the dragon, Satan, will send *his* son, "the son of perdition," into the world (John 17:12).

God the Father has given all authority to Christ Jesus the Son. In Matthew 28:18 Jesus Himself declared, *"ALL POWER is given unto me in heaven and in earth."* (See also John 17:2.)

In the same manner the dragon will give *his power and his throne* to the *beast:* ". . . and the dragon gave him his power, and his seat, and great authority"

(Rev. 13:2).

The anti-Son: The beast, second person in the Satanic trinity, will be "the opposer" of II Thessalonians 2:4, "who opposeth and exalteth himself above all that is called God, or that is worshipped; so that he as God sitteth in the temple of God, shewing himself that he is God."

As already pointed out in the contrasts given earlier in this study, the beast, "the son of perdition," will be exactly the opposite of Jesus, the "only begotten Son of God."   As Jesus was in the likeness of God (John 1:18; 14:9; Heb. 1:3), the second person in the Satanic trinity will be in the exact likeness of the dragon. You will notice in Revelation 12:3 the dragon (Satan) has seven heads and ten horns. Then in Revelation 13:1 the beast (son of Satan) has seven heads and ten horns.

The Lord Jesus Christ is the head of the New Testament Church, His bride (Eph. 5:23—32; Rev. 21:9). The second person of the Satanic trinity will have a *counterfeit* church—the harlot of Revelation 17:1—16. *Christ's* Church is a *living organism* (Eph. 1:22, 23; 4:12—16; 5:23—32). The church of Antichrist will not be an organism, but an *organization* (Rev. 13:16—18).

All who come to Jesus will receive eternal life and they shall never perish (John 3:16, 36; chapter 10); but Antichrist will lead his followers into destruction and everlasting damnation.   They will be sent "strong delusion, that they should believe a lie: that they all might be damned who believed not the truth, but had pleasure in unrighteousness" (II Thess. 2:11, 12). Please study Revelation 20:10—15.

The anti-Spirit: The third person of the Satanic trinity (the beast of Revelation 13:11) is the false prophet, counterfeit of the *Holy Spirit* who is the living energy of all *true* prophecy (II Pet. 1:21).

The Holy Spirit came into the world to glorify

the Christ. In John 16:14 Jesus declared, "He shall glorify me: for He shall receive of mine, and shall shew it unto you." Just so, *the false prophet* will magnify *Antichrist* (Rev. 13:12—16).

The Holy Spirit gives life to all who believe (John 6:63; Rom. 8:11). Jesus made it plain that unless we are *born* of the Spirit we cannot enter into the kingdom of God (John 3:5). The counterfeit spirit will "give life unto the image of the beast, that the image of the beast should both speak, and cause that as many as would not worship the image of the beast should be killed" (Rev. 13:15).

The Holy Spirit of God seals all true believers "unto the day of redemption"—the time of the first resurrection when our bodies will be redeemed (Eph. 1:13; 4:30; II Cor. 1:21, 22). The *counterfeit* spirit will cause all men to be sealed with "a mark in their right hand, or in their foreheads: and that no man might buy or sell, save he that hath the mark, or the name of the beast, or the number of his name" (Rev. 13: 16, 17).

Thus from our study of the Holy Scriptures we know that the Satanic trinity will be powerful; but thanks be unto God, *the HOLY Trinity is ALL powerful!* Our God is sovereign and will win complete victory over all the forces of evil. Therefore the "infernal" trinity—the devil, the beast, and the false prophet—will be cast into the lake that burns with fire and brimstone and will be tormented forever and ever:

"And *the beast* was taken, and with him *the false prophet* that wrought miracles before him, with which he deceived them that had received the mark of the beast, and them that worshipped his image. *These both were cast alive into a lake of fire burning with brimstone"* (Rev. 19:20).

"And *the devil* that deceived them was cast into

the lake of fire and brimstone, where the beast and
the false prophet are, and shall be tormented day and
night for ever and ever" (Rev. 20:10).

The end of Satan's reign of terror is linked with
his beginning. Satan *is* Satan—"that old serpent, the
devil"—because of his desire to be above God; and
during the time when he will reign on earth, the years
between the Rapture and the Revelation, he will put
into operation the most blasphemous exhibition of
Satanic power ever to be exhibited since God created
the world!

In his original state, the devil was "the anointed
cherub that covereth." He was "full of wisdom and
perfect in beauty." He was "upon the holy mountain
of God" and was perfect in his ways from the day he
was created until iniquity was found in him. (Study
Ezekiel 28:11−15.)

Isaiah declares that Satan was *Lucifer, the shining
one:* "How art thou fallen from heaven, O Lucifer,
son of the morning! How art thou cut down to the
ground, which didst weaken the nations! For thou
hast said in thine heart, *I will* ascend into heaven,
I will exalt my throne above the stars of God: *I will*
sit also upon the mount of the congregation, in the
sides of the north: *I will* ascend above the heights
of the clouds; *I will* be like the most High. *Yet thou
shalt be brought down to hell, to the sides of the pit"*
(Isa. 14:12−15).

These two passages tell of the origin of Satan.
But in spite of his perfection, his beauty, and his exalted position in God's creation, he was unwilling to
be subordinate to the Creator. He decided to overthrow God and take His throne. He brainwashed
some of the angels and led them against God. Lucifer
was therefore cast out of heaven, and the fallen angels
are "reserved in everlasting chains under darkness
unto the judgment of the great day" (Jude 6).

Because Satan's desire was to be *above God* he has led the whole creation in rebellion against the Creator. Down *through the ages* he has continued his efforts to overthrow God, and his last all-out attempt will be in the battle of Gog and Magog when his armies will be destroyed and Satan himself will be cast into the lake of fire that burns forever and ever. He is a defeated power, and he knows it; but this has not caused him to let up in his vast program of destruction and blasphemy against God. He will continue his diabolical schemes and display his power until the final battle when God will destroy the armies of Gog and Magog:

"And when the thousand years are expired, Satan shall be loosed out of his prison, and shall go out to deceive the nations which are in the four quarters of the earth, Gog and Magog, to gather them together in battle: the number of whom is as the sand of the sea. *And they went up on the breadth of the earth, and compassed the camp of the saints about, and the beloved city: AND FIRE CAME DOWN FROM GOD OUT OF HEAVEN, AND DEVOURED THEM! And the devil that deceived them was cast into the lake of fire and brimstone, where the beast and the false prophet are, and shall be tormented day and night for ever and ever*" (Rev. 20:7—10).

Universal Union Under One Ruler

Bible prophecy foretells a great universal system of civilization, a religious, political, and commercial union under one ruler. This will be the fulfillment of the desire of men down through the ages beginning with Nimrod (Genesis chapters 10 and 11) when the whole world was "of one language, and of one speech."

Is there scriptural teaching for this union? Yes, indeed there is:

Religiously speaking, "all that dwell upon the earth" shall worship the beast, and those who refuse to worship him will be killed (Rev. 13:8, 15).

Politically speaking, "all—both small and great, rich and poor, free and bond"—will receive a mark in their right hand or in their forehead (Rev. 13:16).

Commercially, Revelation 13:17 plainly declares that *NO MAN can buy or sell* unless he bears the mark, the name, or the number of the beast!

Therefore in these verses we see a system which will embrace *everyone*—religiously, politically, economically. It will be so thoroughly organized and so perfectly carried out that each individual must obey and adhere to the commands of the beast—*or be annihilated.* (Study Revelation 11:7; 13:10—17; and 17:6.)

In Daniel 7:2—8 we read of four beast-empires: Babylonian, Persian, Grecian, and Roman:

"Daniel spake and said, I saw in my vision by night, and, behold, the four winds of the heaven strove upon the great sea. And four great beasts came up from the sea, diverse one from another. The first was like *a lion*, and had eagle's wings: I beheld till the wings thereof were plucked, and it was lifted up from the earth, and made stand upon the feet as a man, and a man's heart was given to it.

"And behold another beast, a second, like to *a bear*, and it raised up itself on one side, and it had three ribs in the mouth of it between the teeth of it: and they said thus unto it, Arise, devour much flesh.

"After this I beheld, and lo another, like *a leopard*, which had upon the back of it four wings of a fowl; the beast had also four heads; and dominion was given to it.

"And after this I saw in the night visions, and behold *a fourth beast, dreadful and terrible, and strong exceedingly;* and it had great iron teeth: it devoured and brake in pieces, and stamped the residue with the feet of it: and it was diverse from all the beasts that were before it; and it had ten horns. I considered the horns, and, behold, there came up among them another little horn, before whom there were three of the first horns plucked up by the roots: and, behold, in this horn were eyes like the eyes of man, and a mouth speaking great things."

The system of Antichrist will be *all of these at once.* Notice the beast seen by John in Revelation 13:2: "And the beast which I saw was *like unto a LEOPARD,* and his feet were *as the feet of a BEAR,* and his mouth *as the mouth of a LION."*

The beast in Revelation 13:1, 2 is all of the beasts of Daniel's vision from still *another* aspect: In Daniel, the *lion* had *one head,* the *bear* had one head, the *leopard* had *four* heads, and the *dreadful, terrible beast* had one head, making a total of seven heads in the combination of the four beasts seen by Daniel. But notice: the *ONE beast* in Revelation 13:1 will have *seven heads!*

The same is true concerning the horns. The first three beasts in Daniel's prophecy had no horns, but *the "dreadful and terrible" beast had TEN horns.* The beast in Revelation 13:1 will have ten horns. So inasmuch as this is an exact reproduction of the dragon, the devil, which also has SEVEN HEADS AND TEN HORNS (Rev. 12:3), it becomes plain that the entire development will be *energized by the dragon,* the devil himself.

The program of sin which began in the Garden of Eden has been energized and master-minded by Satan from that time until this present day and will continue so until Jesus personally puts down the dragon and places him in the lake of fire. According to the Word of God, the devil is "the prince of this world" (John 12:31), he is "the prince of the power of the air" (Eph. 2:2), he is "the god of this age" (II Cor. 4:4); and the whole system of human affairs as willed by man and carried out by man is under the leadership and power of Satan himself. John declares, "We know that we are of God, and *the whole world lieth in wickedness*" (I John 5:19). The Greek in this last phrase reads, "The whole world lieth in *the Wicked One*"—Satan.

In I John 2:15—17 we read, "Love not the world, neither the things that are in the world. If any man love the world, the love of the Father is not in him. For all that is in the world, the lust of the flesh, and the lust of the eyes, and the pride of life, is not of the Father, but is of the world. And the world passeth away, and the lust thereof: but he that doeth the will of God abideth for ever."

I repeat—from the Garden of Eden until now the development of man's system has ignored God, and will continue to do so until the consummation of all things. In the person of Antichrist the devil will put on the greatest exhibition of power ever to be exhibited since the beginning of time; but he will be destroyed in *a much greater* display of power which will completely erase from all creation every trace of sin and Satan. The dragon, the beast, and the false prophet will be cast into hell, into the lake that burns with fire and brimstone, and there will be *no memory of former things.*

The Stage Is Set

When Antichrist comes on the scene he will not extend his reign over all the earth instantaneously. He will conquer the world through false peace, flatteries, and vain promises, increasing in power little by little until he brings all the world under his control—religiously, politically, and commercially. As the devil in flesh he will be the most powerful personality the world has ever known aside from the Lord Jesus Christ. He will solve the social problems, he will bring about world peace for a season—and then he will step out in his true character to suppress and destroy all religions, demanding that he alone be worshipped (II Thess. 2:4; Rev. 13:4, 15). By the time he reaches the summit of his power he will completely dominate and control all phases of activity—in religion, in politics, in commerce. He will control the *individual*, both his outward life and his inward (or religious) life: "It was given unto him to make war with the saints, and to overcome them: and power was given him over all kindreds, and tongues, and nations" (Rev. 13:7).

Today the stage is set for the appearing of Antichrist. Already we see signs of prophecy fulfilled. There is much talk about a "United States of the World"—*one world* with a world church, a world bank, a common market, and many other world-wide endeavors. According to Revelation 13:17, at the height of the reign of Antichrist *no one* will be able to buy or sell unless he bears the insignia of the beast—his name, his number, or his mark. Commerce as well as individuals will be forced to buy and sell under the rules and laws of the world dictator, the Antichrist. His dictatorship will include every individual on earth, and those who *refuse* to receive his mark will be killed. Some may find it possible to hide for a season, feeding from the streams and forests, but eventually they will be found—and executed! In connection with this please study Revelation 13:17; 17:6; 18:24 and 20:4.

Everything done by the Satanic trinity is prompted by one ambition and desire: *to overthrow God and destroy Christianity.* But thanks be unto God, Christ's cry of victory at Calvary spelled doom for Satan, for all of his followers, and for all of his systems. He is still operating, and will continue until the time appointed for his destruction; but he was defeated at Calvary when Jesus said, "It is finished."

The World Church

The world church is growing rapidly today but it does not yet include *all* churches and *all peoples*. The Antichrist will not eliminate religion from the earth, but under his reign there will be *one church* which will include all people. Please study Revelation 13: 8–12; 14:9–11; and 16:2.

The religion of Antichrist will be in direct contrast to the religion of Christ—*Christianity*. He will establish a state religion, a religion of Satanic wisdom, Satanic power, and energized by Satan and his demons.

Just as the devil can transform himself into "an angel of light" (II Cor. 11:14) so Antichrist (the devil in flesh) will appear as an emissary of peace and will offer a solution to all world-problems. He will be greatly admired, and in the course of time as his power increases he will be worshipped world-wide (Rev. 13:8). People will become so fanatical in their worship that they will cry out, "Who is like unto the beast? Who is able to make war with him?" (Rev. 13:4). He will exalt himself, he will announce that he is God, he will walk into the temple in Jerusalem and present himself to the people as God, and demand that they worship him as God (II Thess. 2:4). The worship of Antichrist will be universal during the last half of his bloody reign, and all who *resist* him will forfeit their life. He will be a powerful, glamorous, dynamic personality, a genius in science, in art, in religion. He will be the powers of the underworld in flesh—"even him, whose coming is after the working of Satan with all power and signs and lying wonders" (II Thess. 2:9).

The Great Tribulation—Judgment Upon Antichrist

Jesus said, "As the days of Noe were, so shall also the coming of the Son of man be. For as in the days that were before the flood they were eating and drinking, marrying and giving in marriage, until the day that Noe entered into the ark, and knew not until the flood came, and took them all away; so shall also the coming of the Son of man be" (Matt. 24:37—39).

In Luke 17:26—30 He said, "As it was in the days of Noe, so shall it be also in the days of the Son of man. They did eat, they drank, they married wives, they were given in marriage, until the day that Noe entered into the ark, and the flood came, and destroyed them all. Likewise also as it was in the days of Lot; they did eat, they drank, they bought, they sold, they planted, they builded; but the same day that Lot went out of Sodom it rained fire and brimstone from heaven, and destroyed them all. Even thus shall it be in the day when the Son of man is revealed."

In the days of Noah just before the flood there were giants in the land, "men of renown" (Gen. 6:4). The same is true today. We have *intellectual* giants, giants in industry, in science, in astronomy, in economics, and in many other fields. Knowledge has increased, as prophesied in Daniel 12:4. Man is rushing madly to a brilliant intellectual summit—but the moment he *reaches* that summit *a turning point* will rapidly plunge him into disaster such as the world has not yet known.

Gentile world dominion *began* with a great image: "Thou, O king, sawest, and behold *a great image.* This great image, whose brightness was excellent, stood before thee; and the form thereof was terrible" (Dan. 2:31).

Gentile world dominion *will end* with a great image: "And I beheld another beast coming up out of the earth . . . and he doeth great wonders . . . and deceiveth them that dwell on the earth by the means of those miracles which he had power to do in the sight of the beast; saying to them that dwell on the earth, that they should make an image to the beast,

which had the wound by a sword, and did live. And
he had power to give life unto the image of the beast,
that the image of the beast should both speak, and
cause that as many as would not worship the image
of the beast should be killed" (Rev. 13:11—15 in part).

The "times of the Gentiles" began with Nebuchad-
nezzar's capture of Judah.   (Study II Chronicles 36:
1—21.)   Since then the Gentiles have been the ruling
power, and will continue so until "the times of the
Gentiles" be fulfilled. At the appointed time for Gentile world rule to come to an end, the Stone cut out
of the mountain without hands (the Lord Jesus Christ)
will bring swift destruction which will lead to total
collapse of Gentile dominion:

"Thou sawest till that a Stone was cut out without
hands, which smote the image upon his feet that were
of iron and clay, and brake them to pieces. Then was
the iron, the clay, the brass, the silver, and the gold,
broken to pieces together, and became like the chaff
of the summer threshingfloors; and the wind carried
them away, that no place was found for them: and
the Stone that smote the image became a great mountain, and filled the whole earth" (Dan. 2:34, 35).

The seven years of Daniel's seventieth week of
prophecy will be divided into two parts. When Antichrist first comes into power he will bring peace to
the earth (Rev. 6:2). He will make a covenant with
the nation Israel and will allow them to again worship
in their temple and offer their sacrifices. But after
three and one-half years of peace and prosperity he
will *break* his covenant with the Jews and this earth
will become a literal hell! In Daniel 9:27 we read,
"He (Antichrist) shall confirm the covenant with many
for one week: *and in the midst of the week he shall
cause the sacrifice and the oblation to cease,* and for
the overspreading of abominations *he shall make it
desolate, even until the consummation,* and that de-

termined shall be poured upon the desolate."

When Antichrist breaks his covenant with the Jews, the red horse of Revelation 6:4 will appear, followed by the black horse of famine (Rev. 6:5) and the pale horse of death and hell (Rev. 6:8). So great will be the slaughter that "except those days should be shortened, there should no flesh be saved: but for the elect's sake those days shall be shortened" (Matt. 24:22).

We often refer to the seven year period of Daniel's seventieth week of prophecy as "the Great Tribulation period"—and in a sense this is true. But it will be in the *last half* of those seven years that the blood-bath will take place. The reign of terror will begin in the land of Judaea, and from there it will advance to every square foot of this earth:

"When ye therefore shall see the abomination of desolation, spoken of by Daniel the prophet, stand in the holy place, (whoso readeth, let him understand:) *Then let them which be IN JUDAEA flee into the mountains*" (Matt. 24:15, 16).

"And when ye shall see Jerusalem compassed with armies, then know that the desolation thereof is nigh. *Then let them which are IN JUDAEA flee to the mountains; and let them which are in the midst of it depart out; and let not them that are in the countries enter thereinto*" (Luke 21:20, 21).

Please study Matthew 24:15—29—verses which have to do with the "Great Tribulation, such as was not since the beginning of the world to this time, no, nor ever shall be" (v. 21). Then in verse 30 we read, "And then shall appear the sign of the Son of man in heaven . . . ." This will be at the close of the tribulation just before the end of the seven years, when Jesus will return with His saints to set up His kingdom.

There is not time and space in this study for us to discuss fully the things that will occur during the last half of Daniel's seventieth week of prophecy, but I will give you an outline and I trust you will study these Scriptures carefully:

In Revelation 1:19 John was instructed, "Write the things which thou *hast seen,* and the things which *are,* and the things which *shall be* hereafter."

In the first 18 verses of Revelation chapter 1 John recorded what he had seen. In chapters 2 and 3 he recorded the things that were taking place in his day and gave an account of the seven churches which represent the Church throughout this Church Age.

In chapter 3, verses 14 through 21, he described the condition of the church just before the Rapture as being "lukewarm."

But the Philadelphian church (Rev. 3:7–13) was the church of brotherly love and representative of *the true Church.* We know that the true Church will not pass through any part of the tribulation period, because in Revelation 3:10 we read, "Because thou hast kept the word of my patience, I also will keep thee from *the hour of temptation,* which shall come upon all the world, to try them that dwell upon the earth." (The "hour of temptation" is the Great Tribulation.)

Revelation 3:14–19 contains the message to the Laodicean church, and in verses 15 and 16 we read, "I know thy works, that thou art neither cold nor hot: I would thou wert cold or hot. So then because thou art lukewarm, and neither cold nor hot, *I will spue thee out of my mouth!*" The *true* Church will be *caught* out, the false church—those who profess but do not possess—will be *spewed* out.

In Revelation 4:1–3 John experienced *in spirit* what will take place literally in the Rapture. Then in Revelation 4:4 through chapter 5 we read of the elders around the throne, the four living creatures worshipping God, the seven-sealed book which contains

the redemption terms of the earth, and the declaration
that Jesus is worthy to be King over all the earth.

In the beginning of Revelation chapter 6 the Antichrist will appear with a bow and will offer peace to
the world. He will *conquer* the world with flatteries
and false promises, and for the first half of his reign
there will be peace. Then he will break his covenants
and promises, and the last half of his reign will be
filled with such tribulation and bloodshed as has never
been known on earth.

Revelation chapter 6 records the breaking of the
first six seals on the seven-sealed book. Then in chapters 8 through 11 we find the opening of the seventh
seal, the sounding of the seven trumpets, and the
message of the seven thunders.

Chapter 16 records the pouring out of the seven
vials of the wrath of Almighty God, an event which
will bring incredible destruction, misery, woe and
anguish upon the earth. Grievous sores will come upon
those who have the mark of the beast and upon those
who worship his image. The sea will become as the
blood of a dead man. Rivers and fountains of waters
will turn to blood. The sun will move so close to
the earth that men will be scorched and burned with
great heat—but instead of repenting of their sins they
will curse God!

Then the fifth vial of God's wrath will be poured
out and darkness will engulf the seat of the beast,
his entire kingdom will be filled with darkness, men
will gnaw their tongues for pain and blaspheme God
because of their pain. But there will be no repentance
for their evil deeds.

When the sixth vial is poured out, the great river
Euphrates will be dried up, "that the way of the kings
of the east might be prepared"—in other words, to
make a super-highway for the kings of the east; and
we know that today the fanatical system of godless

Communism exists in the east.

Then John saw "three unclean spirits like frogs come out of the mouth of the dragon, and out of the mouth of the beast, and out of the mouth of the false prophet." These evil spirits will go forth to the kings and rulers of earth and will gather them together to fight against God. The armies of earth will gather in the valley of Armageddon, and shortly thereafter the great battle will take place, the battle of Armageddon, as described by John in Revelation 14:14–20, when blood will flow to the horses' bridles for approximately two hundred miles!

Then the seventh vial will be poured out and voices will be heard from heaven, from the throne of God. The cry will be made, "It is done!" (Rev. 16:17). Then will come "voices, and thunders, and lightnings . . . a great earthquake, such as was not since men were upon the earth." The great city Jerusalem will be divided, the cities of the nations will fall, and every island will flee away. The mountains will crumble, and great hailstones will fall from heaven, each stone being "about the weight of a talent." Now a talent varies in weight from one hundred to three hundred pounds, so you can choose your own weight for these hailstones — a chunk of ice weighing from one hundred to three hundred pounds. And in the last part of Revelation 16:21 we read, "for the plague thereof was *exceeding great!*"

How I do thank God that I will not be here in that sad hour — and dear reader, *you* do not have to be here, either. If you are saved, you will be caught out of the earth in the Rapture. If you are *not* saved, give your heart to Jesus, and you, too, will be caught away when He comes for His saints.

The Revelation

"Then shall appear the sign of the Son of man in

heaven: and then shall all the tribes of the earth mourn, *and they shall see the Son of man coming in the clouds of heaven with power and great glory"* (Matt. 24:30).

"Behold, He cometh with clouds; *and every eye shall see Him,* and they also which pierced Him: and all kindreds of the earth shall wail because of Him. Even so, Amen" (Rev. 1:7).

It has already been pointed out that when Jesus comes in the Rapture, when He comes to catch away His bride, He will come "as a thief in the night" and it will all be over "in the twinkling of an eye." But when He comes *in the REVELATION*, He will come "in the clouds of heaven with power and great glory" and *"every eye shall SEE Him."* This will occur at the climax of the Satanic trinity's reign of terror.

"And I saw heaven opened, and behold a white horse; and He that sat upon him was called Faithful and True, and in righteousness He doth judge and make war. His eyes were as a flame of fire, and on His head were many crowns; and He had a name written, that no man knew, but He himself. And He was clothed with a vesture dipped in blood: and His name is called The Word of God.

"And the armies which were in heaven followed Him upon white horses, clothed in fine linen, white and clean. And out of His mouth goeth a sharp sword, that with it He should smite the nations: and He shall rule them with a rod of iron: and He treadeth the winepress of the fierceness and wrath of Almighty God. And He hath on His vesture and on His thigh a name written, KING OF KINGS, AND LORD OF LORDS" (Rev. 19:11—16).

There is no mistaking the identity of this Rider. His name is *"Faithful and True . . . The Word of God."* Certainly this could be none other than the

Lord Jesus Christ. *"In righteousness"* He will judge
and make war. (Here is "the Righteous Judge" of
whom Paul wrote in II Timothy 4:8.) His eyes are
"as a flame of fire" (the description John gave of Jesus
in Revelation 1:14). On His head He wears "many
crowns." (At this time we will have crowned Him
King of kings and Lord of lords.)

His clothing is "dipped in blood." This will be
the blood of His enemies, "for He must reign till He
hath put all enemies under His feet" (I Cor. 15:25).
"Out of His mouth goeth *a sharp sword* . . . ." In
Hebrews 4:12 we read, *"The Word of God is . . . sharper
than any twoedged sword,* piercing even to the dividing asunder of soul and spirit, and of the joints and
marrow, and is a discerner of the thoughts and intents
of the heart." With the word of His mouth He will
smite the nations, He will "rule them with a rod of
iron," He will tread "the winepress of the fierceness
and wrath of Almighty God!"

This is truly King of kings and Lord of lords. This
is the Revelation of Jesus, the time when He will come
*"with ten thousands of His saints, to execute judg-
ment"* (Jude 14, 15). This is the day of vengeance of
which Isaiah wrote:

"Who is this that cometh from Edom, with dyed
garments from Bozrah? this that is glorious in His
apparel, travelling in the greatness of His strength? I
that speak in righteousness, mighty to save. Wherefore art thou red in thine apparel, and thy garments
like him that treadeth the winefat? I have trodden
the winepress alone; and of the people there was none
with me: for I will tread them in mine anger, and
trample them in my fury; and their blood shall be
sprinkled upon my garments, and I will stain all my
raiment.

*"For the DAY OF VENGEANCE is in mine heart,
and the year of my redeemed is come.* And I looked,

and there was none to help; and I wondered that there was none to uphold: therefore mine own arm brought salvation unto me; and my fury, it upheld me. *And I will tread down the people in mine anger, and make them drunk in my fury, and I will bring down their strength to the earth"* (Isa. 63:1—6).

In that day when Jesus appears in the sky He will come as the lightning flashes from the east to the west: "For as the lightning cometh out of the east, and shineth even unto the west; so shall also the coming of the Son of man be" (Matt. 24:27).

His voice will be as the voice of a roaring lion. He will *"roar out of Zion,* and utter His voice from Jerusalem; and the heavens and the earth shall shake . . ." (Joel 3:16).

This will be *the Day of the Lord:* "Alas for the day! For the day of the Lord is at hand, and as a destruction from the Almighty shall it come" (Joel 1:15).

The Day of the Lord will be "a day of darkness and of gloominess, a day of clouds and of thick darkness, as the morning spread upon the mountains . . ." (Joel 2:2). "Shall not the day of the Lord be darkness, and not light? even very dark, and no brightness in it?" (Amos 5:20).

The Day of the Lord will be *a "great and dreadful day"* (Mal. 4:5).

The Day of the Lord will be *the day of His fierce anger:* "Therefore I will shake the heavens, and the earth shall remove out of her place, in the wrath of the Lord of hosts, and in the day of His fierce anger" (Isa. 13:13).

That will be a day of terror such as earth has never known. When Jesus comes in the Revelation "all the tribes of the earth will mourn" (Matt. 24:30) and "all kindreds of the earth shall wail because of Him" (Rev. 1:7).

He will thrust in the sickle of divine judgment and reap (Joel 3:13; Rev. 14:14–19).

In that day, "the kings of the earth, and the great men, and the rich men, and the chief captains, and the mighty men, and every bondman, and every free man" will hide in the ravines and in the rocks of the mountains and beg God to cover them with the rocks and debris, to hide them "from the face of Him that sitteth on the throne, and from the wrath of the Lamb" (Rev. 6:15,16). Isaiah 2:19 declares, "They shall go into the holes of the rocks, and into the caves of the earth, for fear of the Lord, and for the glory of His majesty, when He ariseth to shake terribly the earth!"

In that day of vengeance, men will beg the mountains to fall on them and hide them (Luke 23:30). They will "seek death and shall not find it; and shall desire to die, and death shall flee from them" (Rev. 9:6). There will be no way of escape—how shall *anyone* escape who neglects "so great salvation"? (Heb. 2:3).

In that day, bloodshed will be on every hand and many will be slain (Isa. 66:15,16; Psalm 110:6).

The Apostle Paul describes the Revelation as the day "when the Lord Jesus shall be revealed from heaven with His mighty angels, *IN FLAMING FIRE taking vengeance on them that know not God,* and that obey not the Gospel of our Lord Jesus Christ" (II Thess. 1:7, 8).

Malachi described the day of vengeance as a day "that shall burn as an oven; and all the proud, yea, and all that do wickedly, shall be stubble: and the day that cometh shall burn them up . . . that it shall leave them neither root nor branch" (Mal. 4:1).

Matthew also spoke of that day of fire: "The Son of man shall send forth His angels, and they shall gather out of His kingdom *all things that offend, and them which do iniquity; and shall cast them into a furnace of fire:* there shall be wailing and gnashing of teeth" (Matt. 13:41, 42).

In that day of vengeance, sudden destruction will fall upon this earth (I Thess. 5:3) as in the days of Noah when the judgment waters of the flood came (Matt. 24:38, 39). Fiery judgment will engulf the world in a firebath such as Sodom and Gomorrah experienced (Luke 17:28—30).

Then it is that the King of kings and Lord of lords will take over the reins of earth's government and will sit on the throne of David in Jerusalem. It is then that men will "beat their swords into plowshares, and their spears into pruninghooks" (Mic. 4:3; Isa. 2:4). *Then there will be "on earth PEACE, good will toward men"* (Luke 2:14).

The Doom of the Satanic Trinity

"Then shall that Wicked be revealed, whom the Lord shall consume with the spirit of His mouth, and shall destroy with the brightness of His coming" (II Thess. 2:8).

"But with righteousness shall He judge the poor, and reprove with equity for the meek of the earth: and He shall smite the earth with the rod of His mouth, and with the breath of His lips shall He slay the wicked" (Isa. 11:4).

"He shall judge among the heathen, He shall fill the places with the dead bodies; He shall wound the heads over many countries" (Psalm 110:6).

He will take the beast and the false prophet alive, and will personally cast them into the lake of fire that burns with brimstone (Rev. 19:20). He will take "the dragon, that old serpent, which is the Devil, and Satan," and will bind him, cast him into the bottomless pit, and seal him there for one thousand years (Rev. 20:1—3).

Thus will the Satanic trinity be broken, and one by one they will be consigned to their eternal damnation. The devil will be bound with a chain and placed in the pit for one thousand years. The second and third persons of the Satanic trinity will be cast into the lake of fire and will be tormented forever. God's Christ, when He comes as the Lion of the Tribe of Judah, will triumph over the dragon, the son of the dragon, the spirit of the dragon, and the false church (the bride of Antichrist).

After the collapse of man's efforts to overthrow God and build his own world after his own will, and after God's arch-enemy the devil is placed in the pit for one thousand years and the beast and false prophet are in the lake of fire, the earth will then be ready and the way will be open for the appearing of the kingdom of heaven on earth. Jesus taught His disciples to pray, "Thy kingdom come. Thy will be done in earth, as it is in heaven" (Matt. 6:10) — and this *will be* in the one thousand glorious years of Christ's reign on earth.

The Judgment of the Nations

"When the Son of man shall come in His glory, and all the holy angels with Him, then shall He sit upon the throne of His glory: and before Him shall be gathered all nations: and He shall separate them one from another, as a shepherd divideth his sheep from the goats: And He shall set the sheep on His right hand, but the goats on the left. Then shall the King say unto them on His right hand, Come, ye blessed of my Father, inherit the kingdom prepared for you from the foundation of the world . . . Then shall He say also unto them on the left hand, Depart from me, ye cursed, into everlasting fire, prepared for the devil and his angels" (Matt. 25:31 — 41 in part).

(In connection with this please study Matthew 25:31—46, Daniel 7:9—14, and Revelation 20:4—6.)

The judgment of the nations will take place at the beginning of the millennial reign of Jesus, and it is not *the final judgment* which will come at the consummation of all things when the wicked will be gathered before the Great White Throne (Rev. 20:11—15). The *judgment of the nations* will take place right here on earth, in the valley of Jehoshaphat (Joel 3:12)—and you will notice in the passage quoted from Matthew 25 there is no resurrection of the dead. At the *Great White Throne judgment* the wicked dead will be raised. In Revelation 20:12,13 John said, *"I saw the DEAD, small and great, stand before God;* and the books were opened: and another book was opened, which is the book of life: and *the DEAD were judged* out of those things which were written in the books, according to their works. *And the sea gave up the dead* which were in it; and *death and hell delivered up the dead* which were in them: and they were judged every man according to their works."

There will be a resurrection for the judgment before the Great White Throne, but these are *living nations* which have survived the horrible judgments to be poured out on the earth during the tribulation period.

These nations will be judged according to their treatment of the Jews—the Jewish remnant who will preach the Gospel of the Kingdom during the tribulation. Jesus calls them His "brethren" (Matt. 25:40). In Matthew 24:14 He said, *"This Gospel of the Kingdom shall be preached in all the world for a witness unto ALL NATIONS; and then shall the END come."*

The preachers of the Gospel of the Kingdom are named in Revelation 7:1—8. Study these verses carefully and you will see that there will be 144,000 missionaries—12,000 from each of the twelve tribes of Israel—who will preach the Gospel during the tribula-

tion period.   Like the one hundred and twenty on
the Day of Pentecost, these will undoubtedly have
the gift of tongues and will speak every language on
earth.   They will fulfill the words of Jesus in Matthew
24:14, they will preach the Gospel of the Kingdom to
every nation on earth, and there will be people *saved*—
"a great multitude, which no man could number, of
all nations, and kindreds, and people, and tongues"
(Rev. 7:9).

"Known unto God are all His works from the beginning of the world" (Acts 15:18).   The kingdom of
heaven on earth was planned from the beginning (Matt.
25:34), and all the forces of hell cannot prevent the
completion of that plan.   Jesus founded the kingdom
of heaven; He will rule over it when He sits on the
throne of David in Jerusalem (Luke 1:32, 33).

The kingdom of heaven has always been expected
by believers (Acts 1:6, 7; Rom. 8:19).

The kingdom of heaven will be here on earth (Rev.
11:15; 19:6) and will be set up immediately after the
final catastrophe which will destroy Antichrist and
eliminate all traces of sin and the curse (Rev. 20:7—15).

The kingdom of heaven on earth is the last stage
toward the perfecting of all things, and will run into
the *eternal* kingdom when all things will be made
new (Rev. chapters 21 and 22).

The Millennium—the kingdom of heaven on earth—
is that glorious period which God promised to Abraham, and He will fulfill that promise *literally*.

The kingdom of God's glory which will display
the paramount brightness of the Lamb of God lies
beyond the Millennium.   That will be the eternity of
eternities, the kingdom of Christ and of God (Eph. 5:5).
"And he shewed me a pure river of water of life, clear
as crystal, proceeding out of the throne of *God and
of the Lamb*" (Rev. 22:1).

We must remember, however, that the kingdom of

heaven which will be set up on earth will not come by *gradual process*. The Church will not convert the world and bring in the kingdom. The kingdom of heaven is not of earthly creation; it is of divine and heavenly creation (Luke 19:12; Dan. 7:13,14), and it will come to this earth when the forces of evil are crushed by the Stone cut out of the mountain without hands, the Stone that will smite the image upon his feet and break them to pieces (Dan. 2:34).

Then in verses 44 and 45 of Daniel chapter 2 we read: "And in the days of these kings shall the God of heaven set up a kingdom, which shall never be destroyed: and the kingdom shall not be left to other people, but it shall break in pieces and consume all these kingdoms, and it shall stand for ever. Forasmuch as thou sawest that the Stone was cut out of the mountain without hands, and that it brake in pieces the iron, the brass, the clay, the silver, and the gold; the great God hath made known to the king what shall come to pass hereafter: and the dream is certain, and the interpretation thereof sure."

The kingdom of heaven on earth will not come as the result of human effort, human progress, or human merit; it is the gift of God, made possible through the crucifixion of the Lamb of God.

The kingdom of heaven will display the complete victory of the Lord Jesus Christ (Matt. 26:64).

The kingdom of heaven will be divine revelation of the glory of the Lamb of God (I Pet. 4:13).

When Jesus returns to set up the kingdom on earth, *angels* will accompany Him (Matt. 25:31; II Thess. 1:7).

When He comes to set up the kingdom on earth, the *redeemed* will be with Him (I Thess. 3:13; Jude 14).

When the kingdom of heaven is established, Jesus will be admired by all of His saints (II Thess. 1:10).

All the world will admire and serve Him in worship and honor (Isa. 60:1–3).

He will reign supremely and without opposition because the devil will be chained in the pit (Rev. 12:10; 20:1−3).

He will reign as King of kings and Lord of lords— glory to His name! (Rev. 19:16).

God's Guarantee of the Visible Kingdom on Earth

Since God is God, He cannot break His promise, He cannot lie (Tit. 1:2; Heb. 6:18). The promise that Christ will rule from the throne of David is as clearly stated in the Word of God as the promise of the birth of the Saviour, and will be as surely fulfilled. This is the final goal of the victory Jesus won at Calvary. Not only will He reign on earth for one thousand glorious years, but Father, Son, and Holy Ghost will reign *eternally:*

"And when all things shall be subdued unto Him, then shall the Son also Himself be subject unto Him that put all things under Him, *that God may be ALL IN ALL*" (I Cor. 15:28).

In Romans 11:29 the Apostle Paul declared, "The gifts and calling of God are *without repentance.*" God cannot change His mind *because* He is God. To the natural descendants of Abraham He made promises and gave the land. (Study Genesis 15:4−18.) Those promises did not begin with Moses, but with *Abraham.* In Genesis 12:1−3 God told Abraham to leave his native country, leave his kindred and his father's house, and go to a land as yet unknown to him but which God would show unto him. God also promised to make of Abraham a great nation, and declared, *"IN THEE shall all families of the earth be blessed."* It was through the seed of Abraham that Jesus came, as having to do with the flesh. Please study Genesis 12:1−3, and chapters 13 through 15 in connection with this.

Since God made the promise to Abraham, it was not *law* but *promise,* for the law had not been given at that time: "For the promise, that he should be the heir of the world, was not to Abraham, or to his seed, *through the LAW, but through the righteousness of FAITH.* For if they which are of the law be heirs, *faith is made void, and the promise made of none effect"* (Rom. 4:13, 14).

Because God is God, the promise He made to Abraham cannot be annulled because of Israel's failure. The promise remains unchanged—not for the sake of Israel, but for the sake of God's honor: "Thus saith the Lord God: *I do not this for YOUR sakes, O house of Israel, but for mine holy name's sake,* which ye have profaned among the heathen, whither ye went. And I will sanctify my great name, which was profaned among the heathen, which ye have profaned in the midst of them; and the heathen shall know that I am the Lord, saith the Lord God, when I shall be sanctified in you before their eyes" (Ezek. 36:22, 23).

In Romans 15:8 Paul declared, "I say that Jesus Christ was a minister of the circumcision for the truth of God, *TO CONFIRM the promises made unto the fathers."*

The promise God made to Abraham was confirmed to Isaac. In Genesis 26:1—5 we read that there was a famine in the land, and the Lord appeared to Isaac and said, *"Go not down into Egypt;* dwell in the land which I shall tell thee of: Sojourn in this land, and I will be with thee, and will bless thee; for unto thee, and unto thy seed, I will give all these countries, and I will perform the oath which I sware unto Abraham thy father; and I will make thy seed to multiply as the stars of heaven, and will give unto thy seed all these countries; *and in thy seed shall all the nations of the earth be blessed;* because that Abraham obeyed my voice, and kept my charge, my commandments, my statutes, and my laws."

In Leviticus 26:42 God said, "Then will I remember my covenant with *Jacob,* and also my covenant with *Isaac,* and also my covenant with *Abraham* will I remember; and I will remember the land."

The Word of our God is forever settled in heaven (Psalm 119:89). As sure as the order of nature, as sure as night follows day, as sure as the sun rises in the east and sets in the west, God will keep every promise He has ever made. (Study Isaiah 54:9; Jeremiah 31:35, 36; 33:20—26; Psalm 89:36, 37; and Isaiah 66:22.)

To spiritualize these promises and give them to the Church is nothing short of spiritual robbery, yet there are some people who spiritualize the kingdom on earth and say that there will be no *visible* kingdom. I would remind you that the promises of the Lord's first coming were literally fulfilled as prophesied in the Old Testament. The promises and prophecies concerning His second coming will *also* be *literally fulfilled.*

For example, in Luke 1:30—33 the Scripture declares that the Son of God would be born of a virgin, He would be great, He would be called "the Son of the Highest"—and in the very same breath the Holy Spirit declared, *"and the Lord God shall give unto Him THE THRONE OF HIS FATHER DAVID: and He shall reign over the house of Jacob for ever; and of His kingdom there shall be no end!"*

Now if we are to spiritualize the throne of David, if we are to spiritualize the literal earthly, visible reign of Christ, then we must also spiritualize His birth and all of the other declarations having to do with His first coming. But that cannot be, for the Lord Jesus Christ *was* born of a virgin. He *did* come out of the little village of Bethlehem as prophesied in Micah 5:2, and He *did* ride into Jerusalem on an ass as prophesied in Zechariah 9:9.

Zechariah 11:12 declared that the Lord would be sold for thirty pieces of silver, and this was literally fulfilled when Judas bargained with the chief priests in Matthew 26:15.

In Psalm 22:16 the Psalmist prophesied that His hands and feet would be pierced.

Psalm 34:20 promised that not one of His bones would be broken.

Zechariah 12:10 prophesied that His side would be pierced.

Isaiah 53:5—12 declared that He would be wounded, bruised, oppressed, buried in a rich man's tomb.

Psalm 16:10 prophesied that He would rise again, and Hosea 6:2 declared that He would rise on *the third day.*

Therefore I ask you—if Jesus was literally *born* as prophesied, if He came out of Bethlehem and rode into Jerusalem as prophesied, if He was sold for thirty pieces of silver as prophesied, if every prophecy concerning His death and resurrection was fulfilled literally, *then why should we not expect Him to return literally as King of kings and Lord of lords to reign from a literal throne in the city of Jerusalem as prophesied?*

The visible kingdom of heaven on earth is the only explanation of the words of Jesus in Matthew 23:37—39 when He pronounced judgment upon the nation Israel:

"O Jerusalem, Jerusalem, thou that killest the prophets, and stonest them which are sent unto thee, how often would I have gathered thy children together, even as a hen gathereth her chickens under her wings, and ye would not! *Behold, your house is left unto you desolate.* For I say unto you, *Ye shall not see me henceforth, till ye shall say, Blessed is He that cometh in the name of the Lord.*"

In other words, Jesus said to Israel, "You will be

desolate—*but not everlastingly so.*" The day will
come when Jesus will stand on the Mount of Olives,
Israel will recognize Him as Messiah, the people of
Israel will receive Him and crown Him King.

When the disciples asked Jesus, "Lord, wilt thou
at this time restore again the kingdom to Israel?" you
will notice He did not rebuke them for their question,
nor did He deny that He would one day restore the
kingdom. He answered them, "It is not for you to
know the times or the seasons, which the Father hath
put in His own power" (Acts 1:6, 7).

In Matthew 8:11 Jesus told His disciples, "Many
shall come from the east and west, and shall sit down
with Abraham, and Isaac, and Jacob, *in the kingdom
of heaven.*"

When He instituted the Lord's Supper He said to
the disciples, "I will not drink henceforth of this fruit
of the vine, until that day when I drink it new with
you *in my Father's kingdom*" (Matt. 26:29).

In the book of Revelation, John the Beloved not
only testified under inspiration that the kingdom of
heaven will be a literal kingdom on earth; he also
gave the *duration* of the kingdom: "Blessed and holy
is he that hath part in the first resurrection: on such
the second death hath no power, but they shall be
priests of God and of Christ, *and shall reign with
Him a THOUSAND YEARS*" (Rev. 20:6). Please study
Revelation 20:1—7.

The Divine Purpose
of the Visible Kingdom on Earth

Why did God *promise* such a kingdom? What does
the visible kingdom on earth have to do with redemption and salvation?

God's Word declares, "*The Lord is King* for ever
and ever" (Psalm 10:16).

When the wise men appeared in Bethlehem of Judaea in search of Jesus they inquired, "Where is He that is *born King of the Jews?"* (Matt. 2:2).

When Jesus was brought before Pilate for trial, Pilate asked Him, "Art thou the King of the Jews?" Jesus answered, *"My kingdom is not of this world: if my kingdom were of this* world, then would my servants fight, that I should not be delivered to the Jews: but now is my kingdom not from hence."

Pilate then asked, "Art thou a king then?" And Jesus answered, "Thou sayest that I am a king. *TO THIS END WAS I BORN, AND FOR THIS CAUSE CAME I INTO THE WORLD, that I should bear witness unto the truth"* (John 18:33—37).

You will notice Jesus said, "My kingdom is *not OF this world."* He did not say, "My kingdom is not *FOR this world,"* and He taught His disciples to *pray* for the coming of the kingdom on earth. He was born *THE King of the Jews.* Therefore Jehovah is under divine obligation to give to His anointed King the kingdom promised Him before the world was. Since God is God, He is divinely obligated to see to it that Jesus reigns from the throne promised Him.

Almost two thousand years ago, the Son of God came to earth as a Babe in a manger—but *born* "King of the Jews." He was "despised and rejected of men" (Isa. 53:3); but the same earth which rejected Him will one day see His glory and be filled with the knowledge of the Lord as the waters cover the sea.

I humbly declare that God's righteousness demands a visible kingdom with a visible throne, and Jesus will sit on that throne. Since Adam fell, this earth has been the property of Satan from the standpoint of his being the god of this age; but this earth where Satan has ruled in the hearts of the majority of men will one day witness the crowning of the Lord Jesus

Christ in the city of Jerusalem in the temple on Mount Moriah!

"In the beginning God created the heaven and the earth" (Gen. 1:1)—and since God is holy, righteous, and perfect, any product of His creative power would, of divine necessity, be *perfect.* Therefore He could not have created *an imperfect earth.* But judgment struck the earth and chaos resulted. Peter tells us that "by the Word of God the heavens were of old, and the earth standing out of the water and in the water: *whereby the world that then was, being OVER-FLOWED WITH WATER, perished. But the heavens and the earth, which are NOW, by the same Word are kept in store, RESERVED UNTO FIRE AGAINST THE DAY OF JUDGMENT AND PERDITION OF UNGODLY MEN"* (II Pet. 3:5—7).

This poor world has been under the curse since the day Satan entered the Garden of Eden and caused Adam to sin. God did not create the earth to be empty and laid waste, He created it to be inhabited to His glory; but thus far earth has never known the happiness, glory, contentment, and rest of a people completely controlled by the Spirit of God. In fact, mortal man does not know how happy, peaceful, and glorious life on this earth *could be* if the Person of Jesus dwelt among us and reigned over us in right-eousness!

Such a time will come when Jesus sits on the throne of David and rules over His promised kingdom. He will wipe away all tears and there will be no more sickness, no more sorrow, no more war, no more blood-shed during that glorious period. Through the glory of His kingdom on earth God will prove that men were created to live in peace and joy. The bloodshed, sorrow, misery, and woe known today are the result of man's own disobedience to God, through which disobedience *sin entered the world,* and corruption and death by sin. But there *will be* one thousand years of glory and peace on earth, years in which the Church will reign with Christ over Israel and the saved nations.

However, the end of the kingdom on earth will show just how hopeless man is by nature. (I am not speaking of the Church, but of those on earth over whom Jesus and the Church will reign.) Notice: *AF-TER ONE THOUSAND YEARS of perfect government under the auspices of Almighty God and the leadership of the King of kings, WHAT DOES MAN DO?* The sad commentary is recorded by John the beloved disciple in Revelation 20:7—9:

"And *when the thousand years are expired, Satan shall be loosed out of his prison, and shall go out to deceive the nations which are in the four quarters of the earth,* Gog and Magog, to gather them together to battle: the number of whom is as the sand of the sea. And they went up on the breadth of the earth, and compassed the camp of the saints about, and the beloved city: and fire came down from God out of heaven, and devoured them."

At the close of the Millennium, Satan will be loosed out of his prison for a little season. There will be millions of people living who will be born during the millennial reign of Christ, and these people will have known no temptation because with Satan chained in the abyss there will be no devil to tempt them. Therefore he will be loosed for a little season—and events which will then occur will prove the total depravity of man apart from the miracle of God's saving grace!

Proceeding out of the most ideal political and economic conditions, after one thousand years of the most abundant proofs of God's grace, the nations will have learned so very little! When Satan is released from his prison he will go forth to deceive them, and he will seduce *multitudes* who will band together to form the most fearful human army ever assembled on earth. They will declare war on God Almighty and the saints.

Thus will the climax of the Millennium provide tragic proof of the totally depraved, helpless and hopeless condition of man in his unregenerate state! Not only is man unable to *create* ideal conditions, but even when he exists for a thousand years of the most brilliant period human history can know, he will not improve. Man cannot improve *himself,* and events at the close of the Millennium will prove God's wisdom and righteousness in providing redemption entirely exclusive of anything man can do.

What God demanded to redeem sinners, only God could provide. He could not allow man to touch redemption in any way because man has corrupted everything he has ever touched; and the Scripture plainly declares that we are not redeemed with *corruptible* things, "but with *the precious blood of Christ,* as of a lamb without blemish and without spot" (I Pet. 1:18, 19).

There was only one way to lead man to peace and rest, and that way was by the gift of God's grace through the sufferings of Jesus and His death on the cross at Calvary. Thus was made possible the redemption of the sinner, the redemption of all creation— and *as time moves into eternity ALL THINGS will be created NEW* (Rev. 21:5).

The New Heaven and the New Earth

"The day of the Lord will come as a thief in the night; in the which the heavens shall pass away with a great noise, and the elements shall melt with fervent heat, the earth also and the works that are therein shall be burned up. Seeing then that all these things shall be dissolved, what manner of persons ought ye to be in all holy conversation and godliness, looking for and hasting unto the coming of the day of God, wherein the heavens being on fire shall be dissolved, and the elements shall melt with fervent heat?

"Nevertheless we, according to His promise, look for NEW HEAVENS AND A NEW EARTH, wherein dwelleth righteousness. Wherefore, beloved, seeing that ye look for such things, be diligent that ye may be found of Him in peace, without spot, and blameless" (II Pet. 3:10—14).

"And I saw *a new heaven and a new earth:* for the first heaven and the first earth were passed away; and there was no more sea. And I John saw the holy city, new Jerusalem, coming down from God out of heaven, prepared as a bride adorned for her husband.

"And I heard a great voice out of heaven saying, Behold, the tabernacle of God is with men, and He will dwell with them, and they shall be His people, and God Himself shall be with them, and be their God. And God shall wipe away all tears from their eyes; and there shall be no more death, neither sorrow, nor crying, neither shall there be any more pain: for the former things are passed away. And He that sat upon the throne said, Behold, I make all things new. And He said unto me, Write: for these words are true and faithful. . . .

"And there came unto me one of the seven angels which had the seven vials full of the seven last plagues, and talked with me, saying, Come hither, I will shew thee the bride, the Lamb's wife. And he carried me away in the spirit to a great and high mountain, and shewed me that great city, the holy Jerusalem, descending out of heaven from God, having the glory of God . . ." (Rev. 21:1—11).

"And there shall be no more curse: but the throne of God and of the Lamb shall be in it; and His servants shall serve Him: and they shall see His face;

and His name shall be in their foreheads. And there shall be no night there; and they need no candle, neither light of the sun; for the Lord God giveth them light: and they shall reign for ever and ever.

"And he said unto me, These sayings are faithful and true: and the Lord God of the holy prophets sent His angel to shew unto His servants the things which must shortly be done. Behold, I come quickly: blessed is he that keepeth the sayings of the prophecy of this book" (Rev. 22:3—7).

Universal destruction will occur just before the appearing of the new heaven, the new earth, and the holy city, the new Jerusalem. This earth will go up in flames, the stars will be destroyed, the heavens will be shattered. (Study Haggai 2:6 and Hebrews 12:26—28.)

Isaiah 51:6 tells us, ". . . the heavens shall vanish away like smoke, and the earth shall wax old like a garment."

In the process of world judgment and fiery destruction, the godless will be burned up as in the days of Sodom and Gomorrah (Mal. 4:1).

This earth will break in pieces and dissolve (Isa. 24:19).

The stars will melt and the heavens will roll together as a scroll (Isa. 34:4).

The earth and the heavens will perish, they will "wax old like a garment" (Psalm 102:26).

The elements will be turned to liquid fire and the earth will explode with a great noise (II Pet. 3:7, 10).

This powerful destruction of the elements of the universe is God's answer to the devil's hellish revolt *against* His universe. The fiery display of judgment will be God's revelation of His righteous indignation and wrath against sin—on earth and in the heavens above us. But out of this fire-baptism will emerge a new and glorious earth, a new heaven, and the Pearly

White City, the eternal abode of the saints.

This does not mean *annihilation,* but transformation; not *desolation,* but transfiguration (Psalm 102:26; Heb. 1:12; 12:25—29). This universe will be dissolved, but God will bring about a new creation. When this earth passes away, out of its passing will come a new earth. Out of the passing of the heaven just above us will come a transformation under the divine government of Almighty God, a transition which will give both "new heavens and a new earth, *wherein dwelleth righteousness"* (II Pet. 3:13).

In Isaiah 65:17 God declares, "Behold, I create new heavens and a new earth: *and the former shall not be remembered, nor come into mind."* A new earth will emerge from the flames of the old, and in place of this fragile earth of dust there will be a new creation formed of *heavenly* matter. In place of this earth of sin, a super-earth of divine perfection will come into being—not *another* earth, but a *new* earth.

The Bible clearly teaches that this earth will never be annihilated. In Psalm 104:5 we are told that God laid the foundations of the earth *"that it should not be removed for ever."* God will not reject His creation; He will redeem it (Rom. 8:18—23), set it in order, create anew, transfigure. This earth will then be one great Garden of Eden, more complete and more beautiful than the *original* Garden.

The heavens, too, will share in this glorious transfiguration. The redemption Jesus purchased at Calvary embraces not only man, but all of God's creation, and "heavenly things" will be cleansed through the blood He shed at Calvary (Heb. 9:23).

The cleansing of heavenly places is necessary because the atmosphere just above us is the dwelling place of demons and fallen spirits. Satan himself is the prince of the power of the air (Eph. 2:2).

The Scriptures clearly teach that down through

the ages the devil has had access to the heavenly regions:

In Job 1:6 we read, "Now there was a day when the sons of God came to present themselves before the Lord, and Satan came also among them."

Also in Job 2:1 we read, "Again there was a day when the sons of God came to present themselves before the Lord, and Satan came also among them to present himself before the Lord."

In I Kings 22:19—23 we learn that Satan has access to heavenly regions, and Revelation 12:7—10 is further proof of this fact, declaring that he accuses the saints before God "day and night."

In Daniel 10:1—14 we learn that the forces of evil hindered the answer to Daniel's prayer for twenty-one days!

Therefore the whole creation groans and travails in pain, waiting for the day when creation will be redeemed from the presence of sin and created anew (Rom. 8:23).

"The earth is the Lord's, and the fulness thereof; the world, and they that dwell therein" (Psalm 24:1). The humanity of Jesus is the fundamental principle of salvation, and apart from His humanity there could have been no salvation. It was imperative that Christ take a body of humiliation and in that body accomplish what the law could *not* accomplish because of the weakness of the flesh (Rom. 8:3). Therefore the humanity of the Son of God (God in Christ) is the fundamental of salvation—on earth, in heaven, and in all eternity.

The earth is the Lord's. Man was created from *the dust of the earth,* therefore this earth is the dwelling place of man. But the earth *redeemed* will become the dwelling place of God. At this hour the throne of God is in heaven (Psalm 103:19); but one day this earth which is now God's footstool will become the place where His throne will be set up, the capital of His new creation.

The Pearly White City

Jesus said, "I go to prepare a place for you. . . . I will come again, and receive you unto myself" (John 14:2, 3). This glorious city, the heavenly Jerusalem which Jesus has gone to prepare, will descend from God out of heaven, and it will be the eternal home of the bride of Christ, the New Testament Church. I personally believe the Scripture indicates that the city will be suspended just above the new earth, and its glory will furnish light for all of God's new creation. It is in the Pearly White City that God, in the ages to come, will display "the exceeding riches of His grace in His kindness toward us through Christ Jesus" (Eph. 2:7).

In Revelation 21:10 John tells us, "He (the angel) carried me away in the Spirit to a great and high mountain, and shewed me that great city, the holy Jerusalem, descending out of heaven from God." The remaining verses in the chapter describe the city in its glory—its jeweled foundations, its walls of jasper, its gates of pearls, its inhabitants, its municipal life, the incredible size of it.

This will be a city of perfection and splendor. It will be built of and decorated with the most precious things known to man—gold, precious stones, pearls, all kinds of priceless materials. If gold and jewels are beautiful *now*, think what magnificence they will possess when the curse is lifted! With a street of transparent gold, twelve gates, each gate one gigantic pearl; jasper walls, and foundations garnished with precious stones, the eternal home of the Church will shine like a palace of crystal, and a crystal river will flow out from the throne of God.

The *complete transfiguration of all things* is the ultimate goal of the redemption Jesus purchased through His shed blood at Calvary. *All* things will be made new. There will be a holy, transfigured people—believers in glorified bodies—living in the Pearly White City. The earth transfigured will be illuminated with the brightness of Shekinah glory from the city suspended just *above* the earth. In Revelation 21:23—25 we read:

"The city had no need of the sun, neither of the moon, to shine in it: for the glory of God did lighten it, and the Lamb is the light thereof. And the nations of them which are saved shall walk in the light of it: and the kings of the earth do bring their glory and honour into it. And the gates of it shall not be shut at all by day: for there shall be no night there."

The Lamb of God is mentioned seven times in chapters 21 and 22 of Revelation:

In chapter 21 verse 9, John was caught up to see "the bride, the *Lamb's* wife."

In chapter 21 verse 14 we read that the twelve foundations of the city bore "the names of the twelve apostles of *the Lamb*."

In chapter 21 verse 22 we are told that John "saw no temple therein: for the Lord God Almighty and *the Lamb* are the temple of it."

In chapter 21 verse 23 we read, "*the Lamb* is the light thereof."

In chapter 21 verse 27 we are told that only those whose names are "written in *the Lamb's* book of life" can enter the holy city.

In chapter 22 verse 1 we read of the river of the water of life which flows "out of the throne of God and of *the Lamb*."

In chapter 22 verse 3 we read that "the throne of God and of *the Lamb*" will be in that city.

According to Revelation 21:17, the wall of the city

will be approximately two hundred and fifty feet high.
According to the measurements given in verse 16, the
city is 12,000 furlongs on each side, making a total of
48,000 furlongs around the wall. One furlong can be
figured as approximately 582 feet. If we multiply
12,000 furlongs by 582 feet and divide by 5,280 (the
number of feet in a mile) we will find that the city
is 1,500 miles long, 1,500 miles wide, and 1,500 miles
high — 6,000 miles in circumference, a total of more
than 3,000,000,000 cubic miles!

In verse 18 we are told that the wall of the city
is of *jasper,* which Bible scholars define as being the
same stone as our diamonds. Imagine a diamond
6,000 miles long, two hundred and fifty feet high, and
of corresponding thickness. (The Scripture does not
give the thickness of the wall.) What glory and splendor! What brightness such a wall will shed forth — a
brilliance so great that the city becomes a giant sun
to the rest of God's new creation and the peoples of
the new earth will walk in the light of it! Is it any
wonder the Apostle Paul cried out that the sufferings
of this present time are not worthy to be compared
with the glory which shall be revealed in us — *and TO
us?* (Study Romans 8:18 — 23.)

In Revelation 21:21 we are told that the twelve
gates of the city are each of one great pearl, and verse
25 declares that the gates will never be shut. This
is in interesting contrast to the entrance to the Garden
of Eden, for when man sinned and God drove him out
of the garden He placed cherubim at the gate, "and a
flaming sword which turned every way, to keep the
way of the tree of life" (Gen. 3:24). *SIN closed the
gate* to Paradise in the beginning of man's sojourn on
earth, *but God's marvelous grace OPENED the gates
of pearl into the Pearly White City, gates that will
never* be closed!

Who will live in the Pearly White City? First and

foremost, *the Lord God Almighty and the Lamb* will
dwell there (Rev. 22:1—3), together with myriads of
angels (Heb. 12:22—24).

The born again, blood-washed believers will dwell
there, for that city is the home of the Church (Gal.
4:26; Heb. 12:22,23; 13:14; Rev. 3:12,13).

The remnant of Israel—the remnant "according to
the election of grace"—will dwell there (Rom. 11:5).

The redeemed of the Old Testament era will have
access to the new Jerusalem, for "they without us
should not be made perfect" (Heb. 11:40). They, too,
were pilgrims and strangers on earth. They "all *died
in faith,* not having received the promises, but having
seen them afar off, and were persuaded of them, and
embraced them, and confessed that they were strangers
and pilgrims on the earth" (Heb. 11:13).

The saved nations will have *access* to the Pearly
White City.   This will be the "sheep" nations of
Matthew 25:33—40, those nations which will befriend
Israel during the blood-bath of the Great Tribulation.
"The nations of them which are saved shall walk in
the light of it: and the kings of the earth do bring
their glory and honour into it" (Rev. 21:24).

The question is sometimes asked, "How will there
be *room* in that city for the great hosts of saints who
will dwell there, as well as those who will have free
access into it?"   In the measurements given in Revelation 21:16 we found that the city will embrace approximately 3,000,000,000 cubic miles.   It is said that if
we could gather every building on earth, from every
city, every village, and from the countryside and group
them all together, they would occupy only *three hundred* cubic miles.   According to Bible history, only
two hundred generations have lived and died since
God created Adam; so the God who spoke this world
into existence is very capable of preparing a city for
His people where there will be room for hundreds of

thousands of generations.

Although this beautiful city will be the eternal home of the New Testament Church, the angels and all of the redeemed of all ages will have access to it. The Church is the pearl of great price to God, and He will display "the exceeding riches of His grace" in that city as it is suspended between God's house and the new earth. All creation will gaze upon its splendor, glory, and majesty throughout the endless ages of eternity (Eph. 2:4—7).

In I Peter 1:3—5 we read, "Blessed be the God and Father of our Lord Jesus Christ, which according to His abundant mercy hath begotten us again unto a lively hope by the resurrection of Jesus Christ from the dead, *to AN INHERITANCE INCORRUPTIBLE, AND UNDEFILED, AND THAT FADETH NOT A-WAY, reserved in heaven for you, who are kept by the power of God through faith unto salvation ready to be revealed in the last time."*

The New Paradise
and the River of the Water of Life

The beginning and the end of history belong to-gether. The first chapter of Genesis and the last chap-ter of Revelation correspond.

The Word of God *begins* in Paradise, in the garden God planted in Eden (Gen. 2:8—10), and *closes* with the new Paradise (Rev. 22:1—7)—but the heavenly and eternal Paradise outshines the Garden of Eden. *Danger* existed in *Eden*, and God solemnly warned Adam, "Of every tree of the garden thou mayest freely eat: *but of the tree of the knowledge of good and evil, thou SHALT NOT eat of it: for in the day that thou eatest thereof THOU SHALT SURELY DIE"* (Gen. 2:16, 17).

But *security* reigns in the glorified Paradise of

Revelation 22.   There is no danger, "there shall be
no more curse" (Rev. 22:3).

Satan entered the *first* Paradise and suggested to
Eve that God had been unfair in forbidding her to
eat of the tree of the knowledge of good and evil.
This was the devil's first lie to man—and how costly
it was! He said to Eve, "Ye *shall not* surely die: for
God doth know that in the day ye eat thereof, then
your eyes shall be opened, and ye shall be as gods,
knowing good and evil" (Gen. 3:4, 5).

But in the eternal Paradise described in Revelation
chapter 22 where the redeemed will dwell with God,
"His name shall be in their foreheads" (Rev. 22:4),
which means that God's nature will be in all who
dwell there.   Satan will be in the lake of fire to be
tormented forever; nothing that defiles will ever enter
the holy city. It will be divinely secure.

In the glorified Paradise there will be no tree of
the knowledge of good and evil. The *tree of life* will
be there, and it will bear twelve kinds of fruit, yielding a harvest every month—and the *leaves of the tree*
will be "for the healing of the nations" (Rev. 22:2).
There will be no forbidden fruit there. We will have
the mind of Christ, we will see His face, and we will
be like Him. *Unlike Eve,* we will have no desire for
more knowledge because we will have *perfect* knowledge!

The Paradise God planted in Eden came to a tragic end. God drove Adam and Eve from the garden
and placed cherubim at the entrance to see that they
did not re-enter the garden and partake of the tree of
life (Gen. 3:24). But there will be no tragedy in the
eternal Paradise described in the last chapter of our
Bible. An angel will stand by each gate (Rev. 21:12),
but those gates will never be closed and there will
be no guards.

In the Paradise where Adam was placed, there was

a river that flowed *out* of Eden (Gen. 2:10—14); but in the new creation, in the Holy City, there will be only the river of life proceeding out of God's throne (Rev. 22:1).

Adam walked in the light of the *created* sun; but in the new Paradise, God and the Lamb will be the light and we will walk in their presence in Shekinah glory forever and ever (Rev. 22:5).

From his place of exile on the Isle of Patmos, John the Beloved saw seven new things: (1) a new heaven; (2) a new earth; (3) new peoples; (4) the new Jerusalem; (5) a new temple; (6) the new light; (7) the new Paradise and the river of the water of life.

In Revelation 21:5 John declared, "And He that sat upon the throne said, *Behold, I make ALL things new.* And He said unto me, *Write: for these words are true and faithful.*" All things, from eternity to eternity, are to the glory of God. He is the *Creator* of all things, all things were created for His glory, and eventually all things—in heaven and in earth—*will* glorify God.

"Lord, thou hast been our dwelling place in all generations. Before the mountains were brought forth, or ever thou hadst formed the earth and the world, even *from everlasting to everlasting, THOU ART GOD*" (Psalm 90:1, 2). God Himself is King of the ages—"King eternal, immortal, invisible, the only wise God" (I Tim. 1:17). He spoke this world into existence, He is the Architect for the Pearly White City just described in this part of our study, and He is very capable of creating and preparing worlds as He pleases. The God of all ages will do as He *wills* to do *if* He wills to do, and throughout the endless ages His creatures will worship and praise Him:

"And every creature which is in heaven, and on the earth, and under the earth, and such as are in the sea, and all that are in them, heard I saying,

*Blessing, and honour, and glory, and power, be unto
Him that sitteth upon the throne, and unto the Lamb
for ever and ever.* And the four beasts said, *Amen.*
And the four and twenty elders fell down *and worshipped Him that liveth for ever and ever"* (Rev.
5:13, 14).

When we study the Scriptures which clearly tell
us of the glorious things that lie ahead for believers,
we ask, "Why did God love us so?" We were dead
in sins, we walked according to the course of this
world, we were followers of the prince of the power
of the air, we were by nature the children of the devil—not following Jesus but fulfilling the desires of the
flesh and of the mind. Why, then, did God love us
so much? The answer is found in Paul's letter to the
Ephesian believers:

"But God, who is rich in mercy, for His great love
wherewith He loved us, even when we were dead in
sins, hath quickened us together with Christ, (by grace
ye are saved;) and hath raised us up together, and
made us sit together in heavenly places in Christ Jesus:
*that in the ages to come He might shew the exceeding
riches of His grace in His kindness toward us through
Christ Jesus.* For by grace are ye saved through faith;
and that not of yourselves: it is the gift of God: not
of works, lest any man should boast" (Eph. 2:4—9).

Never forget—*it is FOR CHRIST'S SAKE that
God has forgiven our sins* (Eph. 4:32).

Chapter Summary

It is extremely important that we understand the
facts pertaining to the second coming of the Lord Jesus
Christ. To the Thessalonian believers the Apostle
Paul wrote, *"I would not have you to be IGNORANT,*
brethren, concerning them which are asleep, that ye
sorrow not, even as others which have no hope"—and

then in the verses that follow, he explained the occurrence of the Rapture. (Please read I Thessalonians 4:13—18.)

The Word of God clearly declares that Jesus will return to this earth in exactly the same manner as He went away, and that His return will be *personal.* To His disciples Jesus promised, "I go to prepare a place for you. And if I go and prepare a place for you, *I will come again, and receive you unto myself; that where I am, there ye may be also"* (John 14:2, 3).

After His crucifixion and resurrection, after His forty post-resurrection days on earth, they stood with Him on the Mount of Olives and "while they beheld, He was taken up: and a cloud received Him out of their sight. And while they looked stedfastly toward heaven as He went up, behold, two men stood by them in white apparel; which also said, *Ye men of Galilee, why stand ye gazing up into heaven? THIS SAME JESUS, which is taken up from you into heaven, shall so come IN LIKE MANNER as ye have seen Him go into heaven"* (Acts 1:9—11).

The apostles also testified to the second coming of Jesus. Paul said to the Philippians, "Our conversation (citizenship) is in heaven; from whence also *we look for the Saviour, the Lord Jesus Christ"* (Phil. 3:20). To Titus he explained that the same grace that saves us also teaches us to live godly lives in this present world, *"looking for that blessed hope, and the glorious appearing of the great God and our Saviour Jesus Christ"* (Tit. 2:11—13).

In Hebrews 9:28 Paul said, under inspiration of the Holy Spirit, "So Christ was once offered to bear the sins of many; and *UNTO THEM THAT LOOK FOR HIM SHALL HE APPEAR THE SECOND TIME without sin unto salvation."*

James believed in and declared the fact of the Lord's personal return. He said, *"Be patient therefore,*

brethren, UNTO THE COMING OF THE LORD"
(James 5:7).

Peter made it very clear that *he* believed in the
second coming of Jesus. He said, "We have not followed cunningly devised fables, when we made known
unto you the power and coming of our Lord Jesus
Christ, but were *eyewitnesses of HIS MAJESTY"* (II
Pet. 1:16). Peter was speaking here of the transfiguration as recorded in Matthew 17:1—6, which was *a type*
of Christ's second coming. *Moses and Elijah appeared
with Him* on the mount—Moses as a type of the resurrection saints, Elijah as a type of living saints who
will be translated when Jesus comes in the Rapture.
Peter, James, and John (who were on the Mount of
Transfiguration with Jesus) were a type of the Jewish
remnant who will be on earth and will see Him at
His coming. The remaining disciples at the foot of
the mountain, powerless to cast a demon out of a boy
(Matt. 17:14—21), were a type of those professed followers of Jesus who will be left behind when He comes
in the Rapture—powerless in that hour because they
have not been born of the Spirit and washed in the
blood!

According to Jude 14, 15, *Enoch,* "the seventh man
from Adam," also prophesied of the second coming of
Jesus: "Behold, the Lord cometh with ten thousands
of His saints, to execute judgment upon all, and to
convince all that are ungodly among them of all their
ungodly deeds which they have ungodly committed,
and of all their hard speeches which ungodly sinners
have spoken against Him."

Certainly John the Beloved believed in and taught
the second coming of Jesus. In I John 2:28 we read,
"And now, little children, *abide in Him; that, WHEN
HE SHALL APPEAR, we may have confidence, and
not be ashamed before Him at His coming."* Then
in Revelation 1:7 he boldly declared, *"Behold, He*

cometh with clouds; and EVERY EYE SHALL SEE HIM, and they also which pierced Him: and all kindreds of the earth shall wail because of Him . . . ."

The Lord's Supper testifies of His coming again. Paul said, "As often as ye eat this bread, and drink this cup, *ye do shew the Lord's death TILL HE COME"* (I Cor. 11:26).

In the epistles God has given us through the inspired pen of the Apostle Paul, *baptism* is mentioned thirteen times while the Lord's return is mentioned *fifty* times—in fact, one verse out of every twenty-five verses in *the New Testament* refers to the second coming of the Lord Jesus Christ.

In the Old Testament we find many, many more references concerning the Lord's *second* coming than concerning His *first* coming—*and since He came the FIRST time, you can rest assured He will come the SECOND time as prophesied and promised!*

The second coming of Jesus is yet future, and no man knows the day or the hour when His coming may be (Mark 13:32). Jesus said to His disciples, "It is not for you to know the times or the seasons, which the Father hath put in His own power" (Acts 1:7).

The manner of His coming will be after the manner of His ascension—bodily and visibly (Acts 1:11).

The second coming of Jesus will be in two stages: He will first come into the region of the atmosphere and call His saints up to meet Him (I Thess. 4:13—18; I Cor. 15:51—55). In the second stage of His coming, after the reign of Antichrist and the battle of Armageddon, He will stand on the Mount of Olives and every eye shall see Him (Matt. 16:27; Rev. 1:7; Zech. 14:4).

The Rapture—the first phase of Christ's second coming—will be a surprise—He will come "as a thief in the night" (I Thess. 5:2). It will also be a day of great separation, separating wives from husbands, parents from children, friends from friends. In other words, it will separate saints from sinners, for the saints will be caught up to meet Jesus and the sinners will be left on earth to go through the Great Tribulation.

Jesus said, "In that night there shall be two men in one bed; the one shall be taken, and the other shall be left. Two women shall be grinding together; the one shall be taken, and the other left. Two men shall be in the field; the one shall be taken, and the other left" (Luke 17:34—36). This tells us that the Rapture will be world-wide, occurring all over the world at the same time. When it is morning here, it will be noonday or night in other parts of the world.

Although the Rapture will separate saints from sinners, it will *unite* all members of the Church *literally*. We are united *spiritually now,* because all believers are baptized into the body of Christ by the miracle of the Holy Spirit (I Cor. 12:12, 13); but when the Rapture takes place, the saints who have departed this life and those who will be living at that time will be united and caught up together to meet Jesus, the head of the New Testament Church. Then, for the first time since the Church was born, all members the world over will unite in one happy, glorious family and will gather at the marriage supper in the sky (Rev. 19:7—9).

The second stage of the Lord's return to earth will be *the Revelation,* when He will return *with His saints* (Jude 14; Rev. 19:14); *every eye shall see Him "AND ALL KINDREDS OF THE EARTH SHALL WAIL BECAUSE OF HIM"* (Rev. 1:7). He will put down Antichrist and set up the millennial kingdom, and the saints will live and reign with Him for one thousand glorious years, right here on earth (Isa. 11; Rev. 20:4,6).

The time *between* the Rapture and the Revelation, a period of approximately seven years, will constitute the reign of Antichrist. He will come with an offer of peace, the first half of his reign will *see* peace and prosperity—and then will come such destruction and bloodshed as this earth has never dreamed of! So terrible will those days be that unless the time be shortened there should no flesh be left on earth. But "for the elect's sake" (for the sake of Israel) *God will shorten those days* (Matt. 24:22).

This present Dispensation of Grace is the time when the Holy Spirit here on earth glorifies the Lord Jesus during His *absence* from earth. Just before the close of His ministry here, Jesus said to His disciples:

"Nevertheless I tell you the truth: It is expedient for you that I go away: for if I go not away, the Comforter will not come unto you; but if I depart, I will send Him unto you. And when He is come, He will reprove the world of sin, and of righteousness, and of judgment: of sin, because they believe not on me; of righteousness, because I go to my Father, and ye see me no more; of judgment, because the prince of this world is judged.

"I have yet many things to say unto you, but ye cannot bear them now. Howbeit when He, the Spirit of truth, is come, He will guide you into all truth: for *He shall not speak of Himself; but whatsoever He shall hear, that shall He speak: and He will shew you things to come. HE SHALL GLORIFY ME: FOR HE SHALL RECEIVE OF MINE, AND SHALL SHEW IT UNTO YOU. All things that the Father hath are mine: therefore said I, that He shall take of mine, and shall shew it unto you*" (John 16:7—15).

(In connection with this, please read I Corinthians 12:3—13.) It is during this age that the Holy Spirit is calling out a Gentile bride for the Lord Jesus Christ, and it is at the end of this Church Age (and at the close of the reign of Antichrist) that Jesus will return to set up His visible kingdom on earth.

During His reign on earth, Jesus will occupy the throne of David in the holy city of Jerusalem, and for the first time since the battle of the ages began (through which Satan has consistently sought to destroy the Seed of the woman), there will be peace on earth, good will among men. Then at the appointed time the kingdom on earth will move into the eternal kingdom of God the Father, when the Son will give over His kingdom to the Father:

"Then cometh the end, when He shall have delivered up the kingdom to God, even the Father; when He shall have put down all rule and all authority and power. For He must reign, till He hath put all enemies under His feet. . . . And when all things shall be subdued unto Him, then shall the Son also Himself be subject unto Him that put all things under Him, that God may be all in all" (I Cor. 15:24—28).

The millennial kingdom will be the divine means by which human history, under the leadership and rule of the Son of God, will be carried forward into the eternal kingdom of God the Father, *where the righteous will shine "as the sun!"* (Matt. 13:43).

Chapter Seven

BIBLE TRUTH CONCERNING
THE HOLY SPIRIT

"I will pray the Father, and He shall give you another Comforter, that He may abide with you for ever; even the Spirit of truth; whom the world cannot receive, because it seeth Him not, neither knoweth Him: but ye know Him; for He dwelleth with you, and shall be in you. I will not leave you comfortless: I will come to you" (John 14:16—18).

On the Day of Pentecost the Holy Spirit, third Person of the Godhead, took up residence on earth and will remain here until the Church is caught up to meet Jesus in the clouds in the air. This is one of the great fundamental and far-reaching truths of Christianity.

The Holy Spirit came at the appointed time, as Jesus promised His disciples just before He ascended back to the heavenly Father: He taught them "of the things pertaining to the kingdom of God: and, being assembled together with them, commanded them that they should not depart from Jerusalem, but wait for the promise of the Father, which, saith He, ye have heard of me. For John truly baptized with water; *but ye shall be baptized with the Holy Ghost not many days hence"* (Acts 1:3—5).

The disciples did as Jesus instructed them to do. They remained in Jerusalem, they went to the upper

465

room—and waited:

"And when the Day of Pentecost was fully come, they were all with one accord in one place. And suddenly there came a sound from heaven as of a rushing mighty wind, and it filled all the house where they were sitting. And there appeared unto them cloven tongues like as of fire, and it sat upon each of them. And they were all filled with the Holy Ghost, and began to speak with other tongues, as the Spirit gave them utterance" (Acts 2:1—4).

In this present dispensation, the Person and work of the Holy Spirit are perhaps the most misunderstood and badly abused doctrines of Christianity. Therefore we will use the Word of God as our textbook and call upon the Holy Spirit to guide us into all truth (John 16:13). We will compare spiritual things with spiritual (I Cor. 2:13) and leave man's ideas out of our study.

The Holy Spirit is the divine Representative of the Godhead on earth today. He is here to represent *Christ,* to carry on *His* work and look after *His* interests in His absence. He is the Comforter of whom Jesus spoke in our opening Scripture, promising that God, in Christ's name, would send "the Spirit of truth" to abide *with* them and *in* them.

This promise was fulfilled on the Day of Pentecost —the Holy Spirit came, but He did not come to bear witness of Himself. He came as the divine Representative of the Triune God, and His ministry in this Dispensation of Grace is not to attract men to Himself, but to draw men to Jesus Christ. In John 6:44 Jesus said, "No man can come to me, except the Father which hath sent me draw him: and I will raise him up at the last day." The Holy Spirit is the One *through whom* God draws men to Jesus.

In John 16:8—11 Jesus said, "When He (the Holy Spirit) is come, He will reprove the world of sin, and

of righteousness, and of judgment: Of sin, because
they believe not on me; of righteousness, because I
go to my Father, and ye see me no more; of judgment,
because the prince of this world is judged."

The Holy Spirit *convicts* men of sin, *draws* them
to Jesus, *"borns"* them into the family of God, *indwells* and *leads* the believer, *fills* all who will allow
Him to fill them, *seals* the believer until the day of
redemption—and in that glorious resurrection morning
He will *quicken the bodies* of departed believers and
raise them from the grave. Living believers will then
be changed, this corruptible will put on incorruption,
and we will be caught up to meet Jesus in the glorious
Rapture of the Church.

The Holy Spirit is in the world to attract men to
Christ, all He has to *offer* is Christ, and *Christ is
sufficient*—"for in Him dwelleth all the fulness of the
Godhead bodily," and we are "complete in Him,
which is the head of all principality and power" (Col.
2:9, 10).

The Personality of the Holy Spirit

Is the Holy Spirit a Person? Or is He simply an
"influence" emanating from God the Father and God
the Son? Or is He a *power* which God imparts to all
who believe in the finished work of Jesus? From the
standpoint of worship it is extremely important that
we understand the truth of this matter, because if the
Holy Spirit is a Person as surely as God the Father
and God the Son are Persons, we commit spiritual
robbery when we worship Father and Son and do not
acknowledge the Holy Spirit as part of the Godhead.

The third Person of the Triune God indeed *IS a
Person* and not simply an influence or a power bestowed upon us through the Father and the Son. This
fact is clearly set forth in the Word of God, as we
will see in this study. Just as surely as there was a

divine Representative of the Godhead here on earth
when Jesus tabernacled among men, there is a divine
Person dwelling on earth today.   When the *second*
Person of the Godhead came to earth He was given
a *body* (Heb. 10:5), but the third Person of the Holy
Trinity did not become incarnate: *He dwells in the
hearts of all born again believers.*   Paul reminded the
Corinthian believers, "What?   Know ye not that your
body is the temple of the Holy Ghost which is in
you, which ye have of God, and ye are not your own?
For ye are bought with a price: Therefore glorify God
in your body, and in your spirit, which are God's"
(I Cor. 6:19, 20).

   The Lord Jesus was definitely a Person when He
dwelt among men.   He took a body, and in that body
of humiliation He made God visible to men—He was
the God-man (II Cor. 5:19).   To Philip He said, "He
that hath seen *me* hath seen *the Father*" (John 14:9).
Then after His work on earth was finished, the work
the Father had sent Him to do, He ascended back
to God (Acts 1:9) and is now seated at the right hand
of the Majesty on high (Heb. 1:3).   But the Holy Spirit, third Person of the Godhead, is on earth today as
Christ's Representative; and He is just as truly a Person as Christ is a Person.   We cannot see Him, but
His personality and His presence with us are true
Bible facts.   Now let us look at some Scriptures which
will prove this:

   In John 16:13, 14 Jesus said to His disciples, "Howbeit when *He, the Spirit of Truth,* is come, *He* will
guide you into all truth: for *He* shall not speak of
Himself; but whatsoever *He* shall hear, that shall *He*
speak: and *He* will shew you things to come.   *He*
shall glorify me: for *He* shall receive of mine, and
shall shew it unto you."

   These two verses should be enough to prove to
anyone seeking the truth that the Holy Spirit is not

an influence or a power, *but a PERSON.* Notice the personal pronouns: *HE will come, HE will guide, HE will speak, HE will hear, HE will show things to come, HE will glorify Christ, HE will receive from Christ and will show those things to the Christian.* Here are seven things the Holy Spirit is said to be capable of doing, and while it might be possible to attribute some of those things to an influence or a power, certainly they cannot *all* be thus accounted for. Can a power or an influence *speak,* or *hear,* or *receive?* Of course not! These are things that only *a person* could do.

Ephesians 4:30 also very definitely declares the Holy Spirit to be a Person: *"Grieve not the Holy Spirit of God,* whereby ye are sealed unto the day of redemption." Can an influence or a power be *"grieved"?*

The Word of God ascribes *personal characteristics* to the Holy Spirit, characteristics which could not be ascribed to a power or an influence. For instance, the Spirit has *knowledge.* (Personally I believe He is omniscient, equal to the Father and the Son in knowledge.) Paul wrote to the Corinthian believers, "Eye hath not seen, nor ear heard, neither have entered into the heart of man, the things which God hath prepared for them that love Him. *But God hath revealed them unto us BY HIS SPIRIT: for the Spirit searcheth all things, yea, the deep things of God.* For what man knoweth the things of a man, save the spirit of man which is in him? Even so *the things of God knoweth no man, but THE SPIRIT OF GOD"* (I Cor. 2:9—11).

I John 2:20, 27 tell us, "Ye have an unction from the Holy One, and ye know all things. . . . But *the anointing which ye have received of Him abideth in you,* and ye need not that any man teach you: but as *the same anointing teacheth you of all things,* and is truth, and is no lie, and even as it hath taught you, ye shall abide in Him."

In Romans 8:26, 27 we read, "Likewise the Spirit also *helpeth our infirmities:* for we know not what we should pray for as we ought: but *the Spirit (Himself) maketh intercession for us* with groanings which cannot be uttered. And He that searcheth the hearts knoweth what is the mind of the Spirit, because *He maketh intercession for the saints according to the will of God.*"

Jesus prayed, "Thy will be done." We often pray that prayer, and we want God's will in our lives; but sometimes we are so burdened and broken that it is impossible to know how to pray and to know the will of God IN praying. It is then that the Holy Spirit helps us. He knows God's will, and if we are abiding, yielded children of God the Spirit prays *for* us.

You will notice in verse 27, "He (God) that searcheth the hearts *knoweth what is the MIND of the Spirit.*" The Greek word here translated "mind" is a deep and comprehensive word including the idea of thinking, thought, feeling, and purpose. For instance, in Romans 8:7−9 we read, ". . . *the carnal mind* is enmity against God: for it is not subject to the law of God, neither indeed can be. So then they that are in the flesh cannot please God. *But ye are not in the flesh, but in the SPIRIT,* if so be that the Spirit of God dwell in you. Now if any man have *not* the Spirit of Christ, *he is none of His.*"

The natural man cannot please God, the carnal mind is enmity against God; but when we are *born of the Spirit* we are also *indwelt* by the Spirit. God knows *the mind of the Spirit,* the Spirit knows *the will of God.* Therefore when we are so burdened we do not know how to pray in the will of God, the Spirit makes intercession *for* us "according to the will of God."

The Apostle Paul wrote to the Roman believers, "I beseech you, brethren, for the Lord Jesus Christ's sake, and *for the love of the SPIRIT*, that ye strive together with me in your prayers to God for me" (Rom. 15:30).

Jesus said to His disciples, "I will pray the Father, and He *shall give* you another Comforter" (John 14:16), and in verse 26 of chapter 15 He said, "When the Comforter *IS come*, whom I *WILL send* unto you . . ," thus denoting that the Spirit had not come at that moment but would come at some future date. He was pointing to this Dispensation of Grace when the Holy Spirit would reside on earth and abide in the hearts of believers.

It is true that the Spirit came upon men in the Old Testament era and they performed works and wrought miracles as He imparted power to them; but Jesus was speaking of something entirely different and altogether new. He was teaching His disciples of this Day of Grace when the Holy Spirit would abide with us and in us until that glorious day when we see Jesus face to face. Throughout the Old Testament we read of the Spirit coming upon some chosen vessel —men like David, Gideon, and others—for a specific purpose, ministry, or mission; but He did not come to *abide* in the hearts of men until He came at Pentecost as promised by the Lord Jesus Christ just before the end of His earthly ministry.

It is also true that in the Old Testament era the Holy Spirit came upon *evil* men on given occasions, men like Balaam, who was an evil prophet. However, we find no place in either the Old or the New Testaments where the Holy Spirit *indwelt* evil men. Only the born again, blood-washed, redeemed children of God are possessors of the Holy Spirit, and Jesus made sure that His disciples understood this. He declared that the world—evil men, unbelievers—cannot receive the Holy Spirit, "because it seeth Him not, neither knoweth Him." But *believers* know Him, and He will be *with* us and *in* us (John 14:17).

Jesus came into the world to declare God (John 1:14, 18). The Holy Spirit is here to testify of Christ (John 15:26). Therefore *the PERSON of the Holy Spirit* goes forth today on the mission for which He was sent into the world. He attracts and draws men to Christ, He calls men to work in the vineyard of the Lord, He appoints men to specific offices and directs them into specific ministries.

We read of this in Acts 13:2: "As they ministered to the Lord, and fasted, *THE HOLY GHOST SAID, Separate me Barnabas and Saul for the work whereunto I have called them.*"

The Apostle Paul said to the Ephesian elders, "Take heed therefore unto yourselves, and to all the flock, over the which the Holy Ghost hath made you overseers, to feed the Church of God, which He hath purchased with His own blood" (Acts 20:28).

Not only does the Holy Spirit call and direct men in what they *should* do, He also *forbids* them. In Acts 16:6, 7 we read of Paul and Silas: "Now when they had gone throughout Phrygia and the region of Galatia, *and were FORBIDDEN OF THE HOLY GHOST to preach the Word in Asia, after they were come to Mysia, they assayed to go into Bithynia: BUT THE SPIRIT SUFFERED THEM NOT.*"

The Holy Spirit also *teaches* believers. Jesus said, *"He shall teach you ALL things, and bring all things to your remembrance,* whatsoever I have said unto you" (John 14:26).

Jesus explained to His disciples, "I have yet many things to say unto you, but ye cannot bear them now. Howbeit when He, the Spirit of truth, is come, He will guide you into ALL truth . . ." (John 16:12, 13). Since Jesus is truth (John 1:14; 14:6), He is the subject of the Holy Spirit's teaching.

All of these things are attributes which could not possibly be considered as belonging to an influence or a power. They could be possessed only by a person. We do not think of an influence or power speaking—and Revelation 2:7 tells us *specifically* that the Holy Ghost *speaks:* "He that hath an ear, *let him hear what the SPIRIT SAITH* unto the churches...."

Paul spoke of the marvelous things which God has revealed to us *"by His SPIRIT: for THE SPIRIT searcheth all things,* yea, the deep things of God" (I Cor. 2:10). The Greek word here translated "Spirit" means *wind* or *breath,* and when applied to the Holy Spirit it suggests both wind *and* breath.

When Jesus appeared in the upper room after His resurrection He said to His disciples, "As my Father hath sent me, even so send I you. And when He had said this, *HE BREATHED ON THEM, and saith unto them, Receive ye the Holy Ghost"* (John 20:21,22).

In Genesis 2:7 we are told, "The Lord God formed man of the dust of the ground, *AND BREATHED INTO HIS NOSTRILS THE BREATH OF LIFE; and man became a living soul."*

Job declared, *"The SPIRIT of God hath made me, and THE BREATH OF THE ALMIGHTY hath given me life"* (Job 33:4).

These Scriptures suggest that the Holy Spirit is the breath of Christ and of God—but this does not deny the fact that He is *also a PERSON. Jesus* was in the beginning with the Father, in the bosom of the Father (John 1:1,18); but He is also the *second PERSON* of the Godhead. The fact that *God* breathed on Adam and he became a living soul, and *Christ* breathed on the disciples and said, "Receive ye the Holy Ghost" does not lessen the Bible truth that the Holy Spirit is the third Person of the Triune God!

When Nicodemus asked Jesus to explain the miracle

of being born of the Spirit, Jesus replied, *"The wind*
bloweth where it listeth, and thou hearest the sound
thereof, but canst not tell whence it cometh, and
whither it goeth: so is every one that is born of the
Spirit" (John 3:8).

I readily confess that the depth of this statement
is beyond my ability to understand. Nicodemus had
asked Jesus about a *flesh* birth, and Jesus was at-
tempting to lead him into the knowledge of the "how"
of the *spiritual* birth, comparing the working of the
Spirit with the wind.

John 1:12, 13 declares, "As many as received (Jesus),
to them gave He power to become the sons of God,
even to them that believe on His name: which were
born—not of blood, nor of the will of the flesh, nor
of the will of man—*but of GOD."* Yet Jesus declared
that we must be *born of the SPIRIT* (John 3:3, 5, 6).

Therefore we see that *God* does the "borning,"
the Holy Spirit is the *power* through which He brings
the new birth. It could be, then, that Jesus was saying, "When one is born of the Spirit, the inner man
of that individual receives *the inmost life of God!"*
Certainly we know that when we are born again we
become "partakers of divine nature" (II Pet. 1:4). The
Holy Spirit is the life of God, the nature of God, coming into our inner man when we receive Jesus by faith,
and thus are we quickened, made alive, *born of the
Spirit.*

In His conversation with Nicodemus, Jesus likened
the Holy Spirit to the wind:

The Holy Spirit is *sovereign*—omnipotent, co-equal
with God the Father and God the Son. The *wind* is
sovereign—it "bloweth where it listeth" (John 3:8).

The Holy Spirit is *invisible.* Jesus declared that
the world cannot receive the Holy Spirit "because it
seeth Him not" (John 14:17). The *wind* is invisible—
"Thou hearest the *sound* thereof." We can hear the

sound of the wind, we can see the effects of it as it blows across the grass and through the trees, or as it blows the clouds across the sky or leaves wreckage in the path of a storm; but the wind itself cannot be seen.

The Holy Spirit is like the wind in that He is *inscrutable*—He works, He moves, He ministers, He abides in the bosom of every believer. He is in heaven, IIe is on the earth, He is everywhere. So it is with the *wind*—we hear the sound of it, we see the movement of the trees, but we know not "whence it cometh, and whither it goeth." No one can say, "The wind originated at *this* spot and is going to *that definite location.*" We do not know where it came from nor when it will cease to blow.

The Holy Spirit is *indispensable*. Jesus said to Nicodemus, "Verily, verily, I say unto thee, *Except a man be born again,* he cannot see the kingdom of God. . . . *Except a man be born of water AND OF THE SPIRIT*, he cannot enter into the kingdom of God" (John 3:3, 5). The wind, too, is indispensable. Just as the Holy Spirit is essential to spiritual life, so the wind is essential to physical life. If there were no wind, no air, life could not continue. Wc would all suffocate and die if the wind should cease to be.

The Prophet Ezekiel recorded an interesting account of his vision of the valley of dry bones which represented the nation Israel. In Ezekiel 37:8—10 we read, "And when I beheld, lo, the sinews and the flesh came up upon them, and the skin covered them above: but *there was no BREATH in them.* Then said He unto me, *Prophesy unto the WIND*, prophesy, son of man, and *say to the WIND,* Thus saith the Lord God: *Come from THE FOUR WINDS, O BREATH, and BREATHE upon these slain, that they may live.* So I prophesied as He commanded me, and *the BREATH came into them,* and they lived, and stood up upon their feet, an exceeding great army."

Consider the men who waited for the coming of the Spirit, as Jesus had commanded them to do (Luke 24:49; Acts 1:8). Before Pentecost they were weaklings, cowards; but at Pentecost *they were endued with power from on high.* God gave them power the world could not resist, and like the wind they reached into every corner of the known earth, preaching the Gospel according to the commission Jesus had given them!

Writing to the Corinthian believers, the Apostle Paul names many different operations and manifestations of the Spirit, but stresses the fact that all are of *"one and the selfsame Spirit":*

"Now there are diversities of gifts, *but the same SPIRIT.* . . . But the *manifestation* of the Spirit is given to every man to profit withal. For to one is given by the Spirit the word of *wisdom;* to another the word of *knowledge* by the same Spirit; to another *faith* by the same Spirit; to another the gifts of *healing* by the same Spirit; to another the working of *miracles;* to another *prophecy;* to another *discerning of spirits;* to another *divers kinds of tongues;* to another the *interpretation* of tongues: *But all these worketh that ONE AND THE SELFSAME SPIRIT, dividing to every man severally AS HE WILL"* (I Cor. 12:4—11 in part).

Men *filled* with the Holy Spirit, *led* by the Holy Spirit, and *energized* by the Holy Spirit are like the wind, like cyclones and hurricanes. Things move when such men move into a community! We read that *Stephen,* "full of faith and power, did great wonders and miracles among the people. . . . And they were not able to resist the wisdom and the SPIRIT by which he spake" (Acts 6:8, 10).

When the disciples moved into Thessalonica preaching the Gospel, their enemies declared, *"These that have TURNED THE WORLD UPSIDE DOWN are come hither also!"* (Acts 17:6).

The Office of the Holy Spirit

Jesus said to His disciples, "I will pray the Father, and He shall give you another Comforter, that He may abide with you for ever; even the Spirit of truth; whom the world cannot receive, because it seeth Him not, neither knoweth Him: but ye know Him; for He dwelleth with you, and shall be in you" (John 14:16, 17).

Again I call your attention to the personal pronouns in these two verses. Is it possible that Jesus would have spoken thus of an "influence" or a "power"? The Holy Spirit is that "other Comforter" of whom the Lord spoke, and in this Dispensation of Grace He is filling the office filled by Jesus while He was on earth.

In Matthew 12:31, 32 Jesus again spoke of the Holy Spirit when answering His critics who had accused Him of casting out demons by Beelzebub, prince of demons. He said, "Wherefore I say unto you, *All manner* of sin and blasphemy shall be forgiven unto men: *but the blasphemy against the Holy Ghost SHALL NOT BE FORGIVEN unto men.* And whosoever speaketh a word against the Son of man, it shall be forgiven him: but *whosoever speaketh against the Holy Ghost, it shall NOT be forgiven him, neither in this world, neither in the world to come!"*

The enemies of Jesus had blasphemed the third Person of the Trinity by crediting to Beelzebub the work wrought by the Holy Spirit. It is impossible to blaspheme an influence or a power. The sin of blasphemy is committed against *a person*, and blasphemy against the Holy Spirit is the sin for which there is no forgiveness—in this present world, nor in the world to come.

When Peter questioned Ananias and Sapphira concerning their deception in the offering they brought, he asked, "Why hath Satan filled thine heart to lie to the Holy Ghost, and to keep back part of the price of the land? . . . How is it that ye have agreed together to tempt the Spirit of the Lord?" (Acts 5:3, 9). As a result of their lying to the Holy Spirit, Ananias and Sapphira both dropped dead at the altar and were buried without even the formality of a funeral service! Read the entire account in Acts 5:1—11.

Now I ask you—would it be possible to lie to an impersonal influence, or to a power emanating from another? One can lie *only to a person*. Ananias and Sapphira lied to the third Person of the Holy Trinity and it cost them their lives.

There are some people who believe, theoretically, that the Holy Spirit is a Person, but they do not treat Him as though they believed Him to be real as Jesus is real. The third Person of the Trinity is a *real* Person—loving, kind, strong, wise, worthy of our love, worship, confidence. He came on the Day of Pentecost, He has been here ever since, and His office is to be to each and every believer what Christ was to His disciples when He walked with them in personal fellowship. Am I, are you, fully surrendered to the leadership of the Holy Spirit? Do we know the communion and fellowship we *should* know with Him?

The Deity of the Holy Spirit

Peter said to Ananias, "Why hath Satan filled thine heart to lie *to the Holy Ghost* . . . Thou hast not lied unto men, but *unto God*" (Acts 5:3, 4). This clearly points out the deity of the Holy Spirit. He is as much a Person in the Godhead as the Father and Son are Persons. The Word of God ascribes divine attributes to the Holy Spirit. Divine operations are also ascribed to Him, and His name is used in connection with the name of Jehovah in a way which could not possibly be used in associating a finite being with the infinite God.

The Holy Spirit is *eternal*—from everlasting to everlasting, in the beginning with God: "For if the blood of bulls and of goats, and the ashes of an heifer sprinkling the unclean, sanctifieth to the purifying of the flesh, how much more shall *the blood of Christ, who through THE ETERNAL SPIRIT offered Himself without spot to God,* purge your conscience from dead works to serve the living God?" (Heb. 9:13,14).

God the Eternal Spirit planned our redemption *before the world was.* In the everlasting ages behind us it was foreordained by the Godhead that Jesus, second Person of the Trinity, would shed His blood for the remission of sins. This is clearly taught in I Peter 1:18—20:

"Forasmuch as ye know that ye were not redeemed with corruptible things, as silver and gold, from your vain conversation received by tradition from your fathers; but with the precious blood of Christ, as of a lamb without blemish and without spot: *who verily was foreordained before the foundation of the world,* but was manifest in these last times for you."

The Holy Spirit is *omnipresent,* just as God the Father and God the Son are omnipresent. The Psalmist cried out, "Whither shall I go from thy SPIRIT? or whither shall I flee from thy presence? If I ascend up into heaven, thou art there: if I make my bed in hell, behold, thou art there. If I take the wings of the morning, and dwell in the uttermost parts of the sea; even there shall thy hand lead me, and thy right hand shall hold me" (Psalm 139:7—10).

The Holy Spirit is *omnipotent*—all powerful. In the annunciation the angel said to Mary, *"The Holy Ghost shall come upon thee, and the POWER OF*

THE HIGHEST shall overshadow thee: therefore also that holy thing which shall be born of thee shall be called the Son of God" (Luke 1:35). Jesus was conceived of the Holy Spirit—"the power of the Highest," the power of Jehovah God.

Jesus said of the Holy Spirit, *"He shall teach you ALL things,* and bring all things to your remembrance, whatsoever I have said unto you" (John 14:26). Since the Holy Spirit is capable of *teaching* all things, there is certainly nothing He does not know or understand. As God the Father and God the Son are omniscient, so is the third Person of the Godhead. He knows all; nothing is hidden from Him.

The closing verse in Paul's second letter to the Corinthian church also declares the deity of the Holy Spirit. In II Corinthians 13:14 we read: "The grace of *the Lord Jesus Christ,* and the love of *God,* and the communion of *the Holy Ghost,* be with you all. Amen." Here we see the Holy Trinity—the three names coupled together, denoting equality—one God, three Persons.

Divine Works Are Attributed to the Holy Spirit

"In the beginning God created the heaven and the earth" (Gen. 1:1).

"In the beginning was the Word, and the Word was with God, and the Word was God. The same was in the beginning with God. All things were made by Him; and without Him was not any thing made that was made" (John 1:1—3).

"God, who at sundry times and in divers manners spake in time past unto the fathers by the prophets, hath in these last days spoken unto us by His Son, whom He hath appointed heir of all things, by whom also He made the worlds" (Heb. 1:1, 2).

"And God said, Let us make man in our image, after our likeness: and let them have dominion over the fish of the sea, and over the fowl of the air, and over the cattle, and over all the earth, and over every creeping thing that creepeth upon the earth. So God created man in His own image, in the image of God created He him; male and female created He them" (Gen. 1:26, 27).

It has been said that the *New* Testament is the best commentary on the *Old* Testament. Certainly the only way to understand the Bible is to compare Scripture with Scripture, spiritual things with spiritual (I Cor. 2:13). In the Scriptures just given, we are told that "in the beginning *GOD created* the heaven and the earth." Then John and Paul both tell us that all things were created by the Son who was with the Father in the beginning. So we see that Father and Son created co-equally.

Now hear the words of the Psalmist: *"Thou sendest forth thy SPIRIT, they are CREATED:* and thou renewest the face of the earth" (Psalm 104:30). According to these inspired words, *God sent forth the Spirit* and "they (the earth, the planets) are *created,* and thou (Jehovah, the Holy Spirit) renewest the face of the earth." So we see that *in the beginning GOD—* God the Father, God the Son, God the Holy Spirit— *created all things.*

"And the earth was without form, and void; and darkness was upon the face of the deep. And THE SPIRIT OF GOD moved upon the face of the waters. And God said, Let there be light: *and there was light"* (Gen. 1:2, 3).

We do not have time and space here to discuss *why* the earth was "without form, and void," but approximately six thousand years ago *GOD*—Father, Son, and Holy Spirit—*brought order out of chaos.* The *Spirit* of God moved upon the face of the waters, the waters divided, the darkness disappeared, and dry land appeared.

Job said, *"The SPIRIT OF GOD hath made me,*
and *the breath of the Almighty* hath given me life"
(Job 33:4). God said, "Let US make man in OUR
image, after OUR likeness . . ." (Gen. 1:26). So God
the Father, God the Son, and God the Holy Spirit
created man, God breathed into his nostrils, and man
became a living soul. The fact that creation is ascribed to the third Person of the Trinity is proof positive that the Holy Spirit is not only *a Person,* He is
DEITY as well.

The Holy Spirit imparts life—physical and spiritual.
God is the Author of life, the devil is the author of
death. In John's Gospel chapter 6 we find the discourse on the bread of life. Jesus declared, "I am that
bread of life. . . . Except ye eat the flesh of the Son
of man, and drink His blood, ye have no life in you.
Whoso eateth my flesh, and drinketh my blood, hath
eternal life; and *I will raise him up at the last day"*
(John 6:48—54 in part).

Then in verse 63 of that chapter He declared, *"It
is the SPIRIT that quickeneth;* the flesh profiteth nothing: the words that I speak unto you, *they are SPIR-
IT, and they are LIFE."* Adam was a dust-man until
Almighty God breathed life into him. All men are
spiritually dead until the Spirit quickens the soul of
the inner man through the spiritual birth: Except a
man be *born OF THE SPIRIT* he cannot hope to enter
heaven (John 3:5).

Paul said to the Roman believers, "If *the Spirit of
Him that raised up Jesus from the dead* dwell in you,
He that raised up Christ from the dead shall also
quicken your mortal bodies BY HIS SPIRIT that dwelleth in you" (Rom. 8:11). In Ephesians 2:1 we read,
"And you hath He *quickened,* who were *DEAD in
trespasses and sins,"* and I Timothy 5:6 declares, "She
that liveth in pleasure is *dead while she liveth!"* And
so were we all until the Spirit of God "quickened us

together with Christ" through the miracle of the new birth (Eph. 2:1—7).

Not only is *creation* ascribed to the Holy Spirit, not only does He impart *life*, He is also *the Author of the Word of God.* This is declared in both the Old and New Testaments. In II Samuel 23:2, 3 David, "the sweet psalmist of Israel," said: *"THE SPIRIT OF THE LORD spake by me, and His Word was in my tongue.* The God of Israel said, the Rock of Israel spake to me, He that ruleth over men must be just, ruling in the fear of God." Here we see again the Trinity: The *Spirit* of the Lord spoke, the God of Israel *(Jehovah)* spoke, and "the Rock of Israel" *(the Lord Jesus Christ)* spoke. The Godhead—Father, Son, and Holy Spirit, one as truly as the other—gave the living Word of God.

In the New Testament, Peter warns that "no prophecy of the Scripture is of any private interpretation. For the prophecy came not in old time by the will of man: but *holy men of God spake as they were moved BY THE HOLY GHOST"* (II Pet. 1:20, 21).

Writing to Timothy, his son in the ministry, Paul said, "All Scripture is given *by inspiration of God,* and is profitable for doctrine, for reproof, for correction, for instruction in righteousness: that the man of God may be perfect, throughly furnished unto all good works" (II Tim. 3:16, 17).

The words of our Bible were penned down by holy men, called and ordained of God, men who penned down the words given to them by the third Person of the Godhead, the Holy Spirit. *Every word IN God's Word is God-breathed as the Holy Spirit spoke through holy men.*

Further proof of the deity of the Holy Spirit is found in Scriptures which in the *Old* Testament definitely refer to *Jehovah,* and in the *New* Testament are just as definitely applied to *the Holy Spirit.* It would be impossible to give all such Scriptures here, but the following passages will suffice:

Moved by the Holy Spirit, Isaiah penned these words: "In the year that king Uzziah died I saw also the Lord sitting upon a throne, high and lifted up, and His train filled the temple. . . . Also I heard the voice of the Lord, saying, Whom shall I send, and who will go for us? Then said I, Here am I; send me. And He said, Go, and tell this people, Hear ye indeed, but understand not; and see ye indeed, but perceive not. Make the heart of this people fat, and make their ears heavy, and shut their eyes; lest they see with their eyes, and hear with their ears, and understand with heart, and convert, and be healed" (Isa. 6:1, 8—10).

Now hear the words of the Apostle Paul as penned down by Luke in Acts 28:25—27: *"Well spake THE HOLY GHOST by Esaias the prophet unto our fathers,* saying: Go unto this people, and say, Hearing ye shall hear, and shall not understand; and seeing ye shall see, and not perceive: For the heart of this people is waxed gross, and their ears are dull of hearing, and their eyes have they closed; lest they should see with their eyes, and hear with their ears, and understand with their heart, and should be converted, and I should heal them."

Isaiah declared that it was *"the voice of the LORD"* speaking to him. Paul quoted Isaiah's prophecy and said, "Well spake *THE HOLY GHOST by the prophet Isaiah."* Therefore the voice of Jehovah and the voice of the Holy Ghost are co-equal in speaking in the Word of God.

In Exodus chapter 16 where we read of the murmurings of the children of Israel in the wilderness, Moses wrote, "And in the morning, then ye shall see *the glory of the LORD;* for that He heareth your murmurings *against THE LORD:* and what are we, that ye murmur against us?" (Ex. 16:7).

Under inspiration, the Apostle Paul wrote of this to the Hebrew believers and declared, *"Wherefore as THE HOLY GHOST saith . . .* When your fathers *tempted ME, proved ME,* and saw *MY works* forty years. Wherefore *I* was grieved with that generation, and said, They do alway err in their heart; and they have not known *MY ways.* So *I* sware in *MY wrath,* They shall not enter into *MY rest"* (Heb. 3:7–11).

In Matthew 28:18–20 Jesus instructed His disciples in their commission to carry the Gospel to all people. He said, "All power is given unto me in heaven and in earth. Go ye therefore, and teach all nations, baptizing them *in the name of the Father, and of the Son, and of the Holy Ghost:* Teaching them to observe all things whatsoever I have commanded you: and, lo, I am with you alway, even unto the end of the world. Amen."

The truth declared here *by Him who IS Truth* is that *God is ONE*—not three Gods, but ONE God manifested in three Persons. It has been so since "the beginning"—FATHER, SON, AND HOLY SPIRIT—as having to do with our redemption: God the Father loved us, God the Son died for us, God the Spirit "borns" us into the family of God.

Does the Bible Teach the Doctrine of the Trinity?

Some teachers declare that the doctrine of the Trinity is a man-made doctrine and is not to be found in the Word of God. Those who hold to such teaching are "willingly ignorant" (II Pet. 3:5).

When Jesus was baptized of John the Baptist in the river Jordan, Matthew tells us: "And *Jesus,* when He was baptized, went up straightway out of the water: and, lo, the heavens were opened unto Him, and *he saw THE SPIRIT OF GOD* descending like a dove, and lighting upon Him: and lo *A VOICE FROM HEAVEN*, saying, *This is my beloved SON*, in whom I am well pleased" (Matt. 3:16, 17).

In Luke 3:21, 22 we find the same record: "Now when all the people were baptized, it came to pass, that Jesus also being baptized, and praying, the heaven was opened, and *THE HOLY GHOST descended* in a bodily shape like a dove upon Him, and *A VOICE CAME FROM HEAVEN*, which said, Thou art *my beloved SON*; in thee I am well pleased."

Anyone who is not "willingly ignorant," anyone who is not defending a religion or denomination, can see the truth concerning the Trinity in these passages: *Jesus the SON* standing in the water, *the HOLY SPIRIT in a bodily shape like a dove* descending upon Jesus, and at that same moment *GOD the Eternal Father* speaking from heaven.

In Peter's sermon on the Day of Pentecost he declared, "This Jesus hath God raised up, whereof we all are witnesses. Therefore being by the right hand of God exalted, and having received of the Father the promise of the Holy Ghost, He hath shed forth this, which ye now see and hear" (Acts 2:32, 33). Here Peter draws a clear distinction between *the Son* (at that moment exalted and seated at the right hand of the Father in heaven) and *the Father Himself* (at whose right hand the Man Christ Jesus is now seated). An equally clear distinction is drawn between *the Son exalted*, and *the Holy Ghost* whom the Son received from the Father and shed upon the one hundred and twenty believers in the upper room. There is no mistaking Peter's clear preaching of the Holy Trinity: the Father in heaven, the Son seated at the Father's right hand, the Holy Ghost descending into the upper room, sitting on each of the believers as cloven tongues of fire. Thus was the New Testament Church born, and those present were all *baptized OF THE HOLY*

GHOST into one body:

"For as the body is one, and hath many members, and all the members of that one body, being many, are one body: so also is Christ. For *by ONE SPIRIT are we all baptized into one body,* whether we be Jews or Gentiles, whether we be bond or free; and have been all made to drink into one Spirit" (I Cor. 12: 12, 13).

Over and over again the Word of God draws the clearest possible distinction between Father, Son, and Holy Spirit—one God, yet three separate personalities. They have mutual relations one to the other, they are one in love, one in power, one as having to do with our redemption and our eternal reward.

Names of the Holy Spirit

The Spirit of God:

The third Person of the Holy Trinity is mentioned very early in the Bible. Genesis 1:1 declares, "In the beginning God created the heaven and the earth." Then in verse 2 we read, ". . . the *Spirit of God* moved upon the face of the waters."

In I Corinthians 3:16 Paul wrote to the Corinthian Christians, "Know ye not that ye are the temple of God, and that *the Spirit of God* dwelleth in you?" These verses emphasize the divine origin, the deity, character, and power of the Holy Spirit.

The Spirit of the Lord:

In Isaiah's prophecy concerning the coming Messiah we read, "The *Spirit of the Lord* shall rest upon Him, the spirit of wisdom and understanding, the spirit of counsel and might, the spirit of knowledge and of the fear of the Lord" (Isa. 11:2).

Isaiah also said, "As a beast goeth down into the valley, the *Spirit of the Lord* caused him to rest: so didst thou lead thy people, to make thyself a glorious name" (Isa. 63:14).

The Spirit of the Lord God:

Again in Isaiah we read, "The *Spirit of the Lord God* is upon me; because the Lord hath anointed me to preach good tidings unto the meek; He hath sent me to bind up the brokenhearted, to proclaim liberty to the captives, and the opening of the prison to them that are bound" (Isa. 61:1).

There is no difference between "the Spirit of the Lord" in Isaiah 11:2 and 63:14 and "the Spirit of the Lord God" as used here, except that the latter puts stronger emphasis on the *deity* of the Holy Spirit.

The Spirit of the Living God:

To the believers in Corinth Paul said, "Ye are our epistle written in our hearts, known and read of all men: forasmuch as ye are manifestly declared to be the epistle of Christ ministered by us, written not with ink, but with *the Spirit of the living God;* not in tables of stone, but in the fleshy tables of the heart" (II Cor. 3:2, 3).

The Corinthian Christians were *living epistles*— not written in ink or carved on tables of stone, but living testimonies made alive by and through the Spirit of the living God. They were born of the Spirit, indwelt by the Spirit, living examples of God's saving grace.

The Spirit of Christ:

Writing to the Christians in Rome, Paul said: "So then they that are in the flesh cannot please God. But ye are not in the flesh, but in the Spirit, if so be that the Spirit of God dwell in you. Now if any man have not *the Spirit of Christ*, he is none of His" (Rom. 8:8, 9). Here again we see the Trinity. These verses clearly bring out the relationship of the Holy Spirit to Christ the Son, as well as the Spirit's relationship to God the Father.

The Spirit of His Son:

"Because ye are sons, God hath sent forth *the Spirit of His Son* into your hearts, crying, Abba, Father. Wherefore thou art no more a servant, but a son; and if a son, then an heir of God through Christ" (Gal. 4:6, 7). Here we see that the Holy Spirit actualizes the believer's sonship. We are actually members of the *body of Christ,* vitally united to Him through the mighty miracle of the new birth and the baptism of the Holy Spirit (I Cor. 12:12, 13).

In Colossians 1:27 we read, ". . . *Christ in YOU,* the hope of glory."

In Colossians 3:3 Paul tells us, "Ye are dead, and your life is hid *with Christ in God.*"

In Ephesians 2:6 Paul tells us that God "hath raised us up together, and made us sit together in heavenly places *IN Christ Jesus.*"

The Spirit of Jesus Christ:

In John 14:16—18 Jesus promised His disciples that even though He was going away He would not leave them comfortless: "I will pray the Father, and He shall give you *another Comforter,* that He may abide with you for ever . . . I will not leave you comfortless: *I will come to you.*" He would abide *with them and IN them* in the Person of the Holy Spirit.

From prison Paul wrote to the Philippians, "I know that this shall turn to my salvation through your prayer, and the supply of *the Spirit of Jesus Christ*" (Phil. 1:19).

The Holy Spirit:

Jesus said, "If ye then, being evil, know how to

give good gifts unto your children: how much more
shall your heavenly Father give *the Holy Spirit* to
them that ask Him?" (Luke 11:13). "Holy" denotes
the *character* of the Spirit. He is holy as God the
Father and God the Son are holy—and there are many,
many Scriptures in both the Old and the New Testaments which declare the holiness of God and of Christ.
The Holy Spirit *imparts* holiness when He comes into
the heart of the believer. We are sanctified "according
to *the foreknowledge of God the Father, through sanctification of the Spirit,* unto obedience and sprinkling
of *the blood of Jesus Christ*" (I Pet. 1:2). All born
again believers possess the Holy Spirit, and as possessors of the Holy Spirit we are possessors of sanctification and holiness.

The Spirit of Holiness:

To the Christians in Rome the Apostle Paul wrote
concerning God's Son, "Jesus Christ our Lord, which
was made of the seed of David according to the flesh;
and declared to be the Son of God with power, according to *the Spirit of holiness,* by the resurrection from
the dead" (Rom. 1:3, 4).

To be born of the Spirit and indwelt by the Spirit
is to possess the holiness of God because *the Holy
Spirit IS God.* Holiness is the *nature* of God, and
when we possess the Holy Spirit we possess that divine nature.

The Holy Spirit of Promise:

Paul explained to the Ephesians that believers are
"sealed with *that Holy Spirit of promise,* which is the
earnest of our inheritance until the redemption of the
purchased possession, unto the praise of His glory"
(Eph. 1:13, 14). The Holy Spirit is the seal by which
the believer is sealed "unto the day of redemption"
(Eph. 4:30)—that is, the redemption of the body. The

spirit is redeemed the moment one trusts Jesus for salvation; the body will be redeemed in the first resurrection, and the Holy Spirit is the seal, the guarantee, that protects our eternal inheritance "until the redemption of the purchased possession." He is our Protector until we receive our eternal reward.

The Spirit of Truth:

Jesus promised the disciples that after His departure they would receive "another Comforter . . . even *the Spirit of truth;* whom the world cannot receive, because it seeth Him not, neither knoweth Him: but ye know Him; for He dwelleth with you, and shall be in you" (John 14:16, 17).

In John 15:26 He said, "When the Comforter is come . . . even *the Spirit of truth,* which proceedeth from the Father, He shall testify of me."

Then in John 16:13 Jesus said, "Howbeit when He, *the Spirit of truth,* is come, He will guide you into *all* truth: for He shall not speak of Himself; but whatsoever He shall hear, that shall He speak: and He will shew you things to come." Jesus is truth (John 1:14; 8:32; 14:6; 17:17). The work of the Holy Spirit is to communicate truth; therefore the ministry of the Holy Spirit is to make Christ known. Jesus said of the Spirit, "He shall glorify me: for He shall receive of mine, and shall shew it unto you" (John 16:14).

I John 5:6 tells us, ". . . it is the Spirit that beareth witness, because *the Spirit is truth.*" The very essence of the Spirit is truth, all truth is from Him, and He makes known the deep truths of God.

The Spirit of life:

"Ye are not in the flesh, but in the Spirit, if so be that the Spirit of God dwell in you. Now if any man have not the Spirit of Christ, he is none of His. And if Christ be in you, the body is dead because of sin; but *the Spirit is life* because of righteousness. But if the Spirit of Him that raised up Jesus from the dead dwell in you, He that raised up Christ from the dead shall also quicken your mortal bodies *by His Spirit that dwelleth in you"* (Rom. 8:9—11).

The Holy Spirit not only resurrects the spiritual nature and imparts spiritual life, but in the first resurrection He will also quicken (make alive) our mortal bodies. We will be raised incorruptible, immortal, in glorified bodies like unto the resurrection body of our Lord Jesus Christ.

The Spirit of Grace:

Paul declares that in this Dispensation of Grace sacrifices for sin can no longer be offered. The animal sacrifices under the Jewish economy have lost their efficacy. There is no power in any sacrifice except *the ONE sacrifice Jesus offered—the sacrifice of Himself;* and if a person goes on sinning *wilfully* after he knows the truth concerning the blood offering made by Jesus, then *for that person there IS no more sacrifice for sins.* It is either *Christ's* sacrifice, or no sacrifice at all. Paul pointed out this truth to the Hebrew believers:

"For if we sin wilfully after that we have received the knowledge of the truth, *there remaineth NO MORE SACRIFICE FOR SINS, but a certain fearful looking for of judgment and fiery indignation,* which shall devour the adversaries. He that despised Moses' law died without mercy under two or three witnesses: *Of how much sorer punishment, suppose ye, shall he be thought worthy, who hath trodden under foot the Son of God, and hath counted the blood of the covenant, wherewith he was sanctified, an unholy thing, and hath done despite unto the SPIRIT OF GRACE?"* (Heb. 10:26—29).

It is by *grace* that we are saved through faith—and

that not of ourselves: *"It is THE GIFT OF GOD—* not of works, lest any man should boast" (Eph. 2:8, 9).

The Spirit of Glory:

"If ye be reproached for the name of Christ, happy are ye; *for THE SPIRIT OF GLORY and of God resteth upon you:* on their part He is evil spoken of, but on your part He is glorified" (I Pet. 4:14).

Here we learn that the third Person of the Trinity is not only glorious *Himself,* but He also imparts the glory of God to believers. We are made partakers of divine nature (II Pet. 1:4), and *believing,* we rejoice "with joy unspeakable and full of glory" (I Pet. 1:8). Christians should count it all joy when persecuted for righteousness' sake. It is a joy to suffer for someone we love, and if we are truly born again *we love JE-SUS.* Therefore we rejoice in that He has allowed us to be partakers with Him in suffering:

"But rejoice, inasmuch as ye are partakers of Christ's *sufferings;* that, when His *glory* shall be revealed, ye may be glad also with exceeding joy" (I Pet. 4:13).

"The Spirit Himself beareth witness with our spirit, that we are the children of God: and if children, then heirs; heirs of God, and joint-heirs with Christ; *if so be that we SUFFER with Him, that we may be also GLORIFIED together"* (Rom. 8:16, 17).

The Holy Spirit is the Administrator of saving grace that culminates in joy unspeakable and full of glory. In Paul's prayer for the Ephesian believers he said, ". . . I bow my knees unto the Father of our Lord Jesus Christ, of whom the whole family in heaven and earth is named, that He would grant you, according to the riches of His glory, to be strengthened with might by His Spirit in the inner man; that Christ may dwell in your hearts by faith; that ye, being rooted and grounded in love, may be able to comprehend

with all saints what is the breadth, and length, and
depth, and height; and to know the love of Christ,
which passeth knowledge, that ye might be filled with
all the fulness of God" (Eph. 3:14—19).

The Eternal Spirit:

Not only are God the Father and Christ the Son
from everlasting to everlasting, but *the third Person
of the Trinity is also eternal:*
"For if the blood of bulls and of goats, and the
ashes of an heifer sprinkling the unclean, sanctifieth
to the purifying of the flesh: how much more shall
*the blood of Christ, who through THE ETERNAL
SPIRIT offered Himself without spot to God,* purge
your conscience from dead works to serve the living
God?" (Heb. 9:13, 14).

The Spirit of Burning:

Isaiah saw a vision of the future kingdom on earth,
the glorious kingdom God promised to Abraham; and
he wrote, "When the Lord shall have washed away
the filth of the daughters of Zion, and shall have
purged the blood of Jerusalem from the midst thereof
*by the SPIRIT OF JUDGMENT, and by the SPIRIT
OF BURNING"* (Isa. 4:4).
The name here applied to the Holy Spirit signifies
His searching power, and His refining, dross-consum-
ing, illuminating, energizing power.

The Comforter:

"I will pray the Father and He shall give you
another Comforter, that He may abide with you for
ever" (John 14:16). (The word here translated "Comforter" is rendered "Advocate" in I John 2:1—"We
have an *Advocate* with the Father, Jesus Christ the
righteous.")
The Greek word for Comforter means far more than

our corresponding English word. It means *"one called to another's side."* Jesus said, *"Take my yoke upon you,* and learn of me; for I am meek and lowly in heart: and ye shall find rest unto your souls. For my yoke is easy, and my burden is light"* (Matt. 11: 29, 30). When we think of *a yoke of oxen* we do not think of them as *following* each other, but as walking side-by-side. Therefore Jesus invited, "Take my yoke upon you—get in the yoke with me and walk beside me."

The Holy Spirit is always by our side as well as within our hearts, and when we need One to take our part and help us in our battles, He is our Advocate with God the Father *through Jesus Christ the Righteous One!* And He will never leave us. He will go with us all the way, until we are safe in the Paradise of our God.

The Promise of His Coming; The Fulfillment of the Promise

Before the Holy Spirit could take up residence on earth it was a divine necessity that the second Person of the Godhead—the only begotten Son of God—be crucified, buried, risen, and ascended to the right hand of the Majesty on high. The third Person of the Trinity could not come to dwell with men until Jesus was glorified:

"In the last day, that great day of the feast, Jesus stood and cried, saying, If any man thirst, let him come unto me, and drink. He that believeth on me, as the Scripture hath said, out of his belly shall flow rivers of living water. *(But this spake He of the Spirit, which they that believe on Him should receive: for the Holy Ghost was not yet given; BECAUSE THAT JESUS WAS NOT YET GLORIFIED.)"* (John 7:37—39).

In these verses is contained the great prophecy of the coming of the Holy Spirit to empower the servants of God and change weak, spineless men into spiritual giants for Jesus; but it was necessary that the exaltation and glorification of the Lord Jesus Christ become a reality before the Spirit could come to take up residence here on earth in the new and wonderful way promised while Christ was dwelling among men. Jesus said to His disciples, "If I go not away, the Comforter will not come unto you; but if I depart, I will send Him unto you" (John 16:7). Had Jesus not returned to the heavenly Father, the Holy Spirit would not have come to dwell on earth.

At the appointed time Jesus was arrested, tried, condemned, crucified and buried—and early on the first day of the week He rose from the grave, just as He had promised to do. He showed Himself alive for forty days after His resurrection, and just before His ascension He commanded the disciples "that they should not depart from Jerusalem, but wait for the promise of the Father, which, saith He, ye have heard of me. For John truly baptized with water; but ye shall be baptized with the Holy Ghost not many days hence. . . . Ye shall receive power, after that the Holy Ghost is come upon you: and ye shall be witnesses unto me both in Jerusalem, and in all Judaea, and in Samaria, and unto the uttermost part of the earth" (Acts 1:4—8 in part).

Ten days later, the fiftieth day after His resurrection, the promise was fulfilled: the Holy Spirit came to take up His residence on earth in the hearts of believers:

"When the Day of Pentecost was fully come, they were all with one accord in one place. And suddenly there came a sound from heaven as of a rushing mighty wind, and it filled all the house where they were sitting. And there appeared unto them cloven tongues like as of fire, and it sat upon each of them. And they were all filled with the Holy Ghost, and began to speak with other tongues, as the Spirit gave them utterance" (Acts 2:1—4).

It is absolutely unscriptural for believers to pray, "Come, Holy Spirit," for the Holy Spirit is already here! We should pray to be *led* by the Spirit into paths of righteousness, we should pray to be kept by the power of God, we should pray that we not grieve or quench the Spirit. We should pray that we be *strengthened* by the Spirit in the inner man, and we have a direct command to be *"filled* with the Spirit" (Eph. 5:18). We should pray that rivers of living water flow out of our inner man, making us channels of blessing to others. But all of these are quite different from praying and pleading for God to give us the Holy Spirit! We should be thanking Him for the gift of the Spirit already given. He came at Pentecost, He filled all who were in the upper room. He baptizes every believer into the body of Christ, He abides in the heart of every believer, and He will abide with us and in us until the Church is caught up to meet Jesus in the clouds in the air.

Do All Believers Have the Holy Spirit?

"Verily, verily, I say unto thee, *Except a man be BORN AGAIN*, he cannot see the kingdom of God. . . . *Except a man be born of water and OF THE SPIRIT*, He cannot enter into the kingdom of God. . . . Marvel not that I said unto thee, *YE MUST BE BORN AGAIN"* (John 3:3, 5, 7).

According to these words spoken by the Lamb of God, all who are born again are *born of the SPIRIT;* therefore all born again persons *possess* the Spirit. The Apostle Paul emphatically declared, *"If any man HAVE NOT the Spirit of Christ, he is none of His"*

(Rom. 8:9).

Peter and the apostles declared that God gives the Holy Spirit to all who obey the Gospel: "And we are His witnesses of these things; and so is also *the Holy Ghost, whom God hath given to them that obey Him*" (Acts 5:32). Notice God *"HATH given"* (present tense), not *"will give."* Paul tells us that God *"hath also sealed us,* and given the earnest (the guarantee) of the Spirit in our hearts" (II Cor. 1:22) — and again it is *"HATH given,"* not *"will give"* at some future time.

To the believers in Galatia Paul declared, *"God hath* (already) *sent forth the Spirit of His Son"* into the hearts of believers, "crying, Abba, Father" (Gal. 4:6).

In I Thessalonians 4:8 we read, "He therefore that despiseth, despiseth not man, but God, *who HATH also given unto us HIS HOLY SPIRIT."*

John the Beloved tells us, ". . . hereby we know that He abideth in us, by the Spirit which He HATH given us" (I John 3:24).

Notice that these Scriptures do not say that God will give the Holy Spirit at some future time, but that He has *already* given the Spirit to all who believe. Therefore, instead of praying and begging *for* the Spirit, we should rejoice that He already dwells in our hearts. The Holy Spirit is the gift of God as surely as *redemption* is the gift of God, for the redemption that is in Christ Jesus also gives the Holy Spirit: "Then Peter said unto them, Repent, and be baptized every one of you in the name of Jesus Christ for the remission of sins, *and ye shall receive THE GIFT OF THE HOLY GHOST"* (Acts 2:38).

The Holy Scriptures give no record where anyone prayed for the coming of the Holy Spirit after Pentecost. Believers are exhorted to pray "with all prayer and supplication *IN the Spirit"* (Eph. 6:18). In Jude

20 we read, "But ye, beloved, building up yourselves on your most holy faith, *praying IN the Holy Ghost* . . . ."

We can readily see the difference between praying *FOR the Spirit* and praying *IN the Spirit*. To pray *for* the Spirit means that we do not possess Him. To pray *in* the Spirit means that He is leading us in our praying—and He does just that (Rom. 8:26, 27).

Bought by the Blood — Born of the Spirit

The unregenerate person need not pray to receive the Holy Spirit because God will not grant the Spirit to those who are unsaved. In John 14:17 Jesus emphatically declared that the world *cannot receive* the Spirit of truth. In I Corinthians 2:14 the Apostle Paul declared, "The natural man receiveth not the things of the Spirit of God: for they are foolishness unto him: neither can he know them, because they are spiritually discerned."

It is nothing more than vain repetition for an unsaved person to pray for the gift of the Holy Spirit: "Now we know that God heareth not sinners: but if any man be a worshipper of God, and doeth His will, him He heareth" (John 9:31).

We find a beautiful type of this in the Old Testament concerning the cleansing of lepers. When a leper went to the priest for cleansing, the priest applied the *blood* of the sacrificial lamb—first to the ear of the leper, then to his thumb and his great toe. He then put *oil* on the leper's ear, on his thumb, and on his great toe—first the blood, then the oil (Lev. 14:14—17). In the Old Testament era, leprosy is a type of a sin. The *blood of the sacrifice* pointed to the blood of Jesus, and *oil* is an emblem of the Holy Spirit. Thus we see that even the Old Testament plainly teaches that the Holy Spirit cannot dwell in a vessel which has not been cleansed by the blood. This does not mean, however, that the blood is applied and then the Holy Spirit comes in some time later. The Spirit comes into the heart the instant one believes in the shed blood and finished work of Jesus, but *before* the unbeliever can receive the Holy Spirit he must first be cleansed by the blood of the Lamb of God:

"Almost all things are by the law purged with blood; and *without shedding of blood is no remission*" (Heb. 9:22).

"But if we walk in the light, as He is in the light, we have fellowship one with another, and *the blood of Jesus Christ His Son cleanseth us from ALL sin*" (I John 1:7).

They err who teach that only surrendered, seasoned believers are ready for the mighty baptism and infilling of the Holy Spirit. *All* who receive the Gospel and trust in the shed blood of Jesus are indwelt by the Spirit. When the blood is applied and the heart is *cleansed* by the blood, the Holy Spirit takes up His abode in the heart—but *only* in a heart cleansed by the blood of the Lamb.

It has been said that Leviticus is the Hebrews of the Old Testament, and Hebrews is the Leviticus of the New Testament—and it is certainly true that many tremendous lessons are taught in the book of Leviticus. In chapter 22, verses 10 and 11, for instance, we learn that certain people had neither part nor lot in the hallowed, holy things of Jehovah God:

"There shall no *stranger* eat of the holy thing: a *sojourner* of the priest, or an *hired servant,* shall not eat of the holy thing. But if the priest *buy* any soul with his money, he shall eat of it, and he that is *born* in his house: they shall eat of his meat."

So we see that the stranger, the sojourner, and the hired servant could not partake of holy things. Only one who had been bought by the priest or born in his house was counted worthy to eat of the meat. Believers have been bought with the blood of Jesus (I Cor. 6:19, 20), born of God (John 1:12, 13), and are therefore eligible for the fulness of the Godhead. We have Christ, "in Him dwelleth all the fulness of the Godhead bodily," and we are complete in Him (Col. 2:9, 10). Paul admonished the Corinthian believers, *"YE ARE BOUGHT WITH A PRICE;* be not ye the servants of men" (I Cor. 7:23).

How Are We Born?

Nicodemus asked Jesus, "How can a man be born when he is old? Can he enter the second time into his mother's womb, and be born?" That is a good question, and Jesus answered it for Nicodemus by explaining, "Except a man be born of water and of the Spirit, he cannot enter into the kingdom of God. That which is born of the flesh is flesh; and that which is born of the Spirit is spirit" (John 3:4—6).

It is plain that in the new birth we are born "of water and of the Spirit"—but the *precise manner* of the operation of God in the new birth cannot be put into the language of man. It is God's miracle and is beyond the comprehension of man's finite mind; therefore it must be accepted by faith. In John 3:8, continuing His conversation with Nicodemus, Jesus likens the work of the Holy Spirit in the new birth to the wind which blows where it pleases. We hear it, we see the results of its blowing, but whence it comes and where it goes no man can tell.

I dare not leave this discussion without making a statement about the *water* in John 3:5. Jesus said, "Except a man be born *of water* and of the Spirit . . . ." What does this "water" signify? Does it refer to water baptism, baptism by immersion?

Does the Scripture tell us what Jesus meant when

He spoke of our being born of water and of the Spirit?
Yes, indeed! God's Word clearly explains the "water"
in John 3:5, as can be seen in the following verses:

In John 15:3 Jesus told His disciples, "Now ye are
clean through *the WORD* which I have spoken unto
you."

In Ephesians 5:25, 26 the Apostle Paul explained
how Christ "loved the Church, and gave Himself for
it; that He might *sanctify and cleanse it with the
washing of water by THE WORD.*"

James 1:18 tells us that *God begat us "with THE
WORD of truth,* that we should be a kind of firstfruits
of His creatures."

In I Peter 1:23 we read, "Being *born again,* not of
corruptible seed, but of incorruptible, *BY THE WORD
OF GOD, which liveth and abideth for ever.*"

These Scriptures tell us that Jesus meant, "Except
a man be born of the cleansing and quickening power
of the Holy Spirit *and of the WORD OF GOD,* he
cannot see the kingdom of heaven."

When Jesus spoke with the Samaritan woman at
Jacob's well He asked her for a drink of water. In
the course of their conversation He said to her, "The
water from this well does not satisfy; but the water
which I give shall be in you a well of water springing
up into everlasting life, and whosoever drinketh of
this living water will never thirst again." The woman
then asked Him for the water of which He spoke, and
as their conversation continued she said to Jesus, "I
know that when Messiah cometh He will tell us all
things." Jesus replied, *"I that speak unto thee am
He"*—only seven words, but when Jesus spoke them
the woman asked no further questions. She immediately left her waterpot and ran into the city to declare
that she had met the Christ. The entire account of
this woman's marvelous conversion is given in John
4:6—29.

What did Jesus give her? He gave her living water—*He gave her His WORD, the Word of God.* She believed the Word (the "incorruptible seed" that brings eternal life), and the Holy Spirit "borned" her into God's family when she accepted the Word!

Psalm 119 is rich in references to God's Word and its cleansing, strengthening power. Consider the following verses from that Psalm:

Verse 9: "Wherewithal shall a young man *cleanse* his way? By taking heed thereto *according to thy WORD.*"

Verse 11: "*Thy WORD* have I hid in mine heart, *that I might not sin* against thee!"

Verse 17: "Deal bountifully with thy servant, that I may *live, and keep thy WORD.*"

Verse 25: "My soul cleaveth unto the dust: *quicken thou me according to thy WORD.*"

Verse 28: "My soul melteth for heaviness: *strengthen* thou me according unto *thy WORD.*"

Verses 41 and 42: "Let thy mercies come also unto me, O Lord, even thy salvation, *according to thy WORD.* So shall I have wherewith to answer him that reproacheth me: for *I trust in thy WORD.*"

Verse 49: "Remember *the WORD* unto thy servant, upon which thou hast caused me to hope."

Verses 57 and 58: "Thou art my portion, O Lord: I have said that *I would keep thy WORDS.* I intreated thy favour with my whole heart: be merciful unto me *according to thy WORD.*"

Verse 65: "Thou hast dealt well with thy servant, O Lord, according unto *thy WORD.*"

Verse 67: "Before I was afflicted I went astray: *but now have I kept thy WORD.*"

Verse 81: "My soul fainteth for thy salvation: but *I hope in thy WORD.*"

Verse 89: "*For ever, O Lord, THY WORD IS SETTLED IN HEAVEN.*"

Verse 105: "*Thy WORD* is a lamp unto my feet, and a light unto my path."

Verse 107: "I am afflicted very much: *quicken me*, O Lord, *according unto thy WORD.*"

Verse 114: "Thou art my hiding place and my shield: I hope in *thy WORD.*"

Verse 140: "*Thy WORD is very pure:* therefore thy servant loveth it."

Verse 154: "Plead my cause, and deliver me: quicken me according to *thy WORD.*"

Verse 160: "*Thy WORD is true from the beginning:* and every one of thy righteous judgments endureth for ever."

Verses 169 and 170: "Let my cry come near before thee, O Lord: *give me understanding according to thy WORD.* Let my supplication come before thee: deliver me according to *thy WORD.*"

Verse 172: "My tongue shall speak of *thy WORD:* for all thy commandments are righteousness."

In John 5:24 Jesus said: "Verily, verily, I say unto you, *He that heareth MY WORD, and believeth on Him that sent me, hath everlasting life, and shall not come into condemnation; but is passed from death unto life.*"

We are raised from spiritual deadness by hearing and receiving the Word of God. The entrance of the Word brings light, God is light and life. When the Word comes in, *light* comes in; and when light comes in, *LIFE is imparted*—yea, even divine nature (II Pet. 1:4). We are born of God, begotten with the Word of truth, and the engrafted Word saves the soul.

We are cleansed—not by the water in a baptistry, but *by the mighty power of the WORD OF GOD*, and except a man be born of the living water, the Word, he cannot enter the kingdom of heaven. Except a man be born of the Holy Spirit he cannot enter into the kingdom of heaven, for "if any man have not the

Spirit of Christ" he does not belong to God! (Rom. 8:9).

The Third Person of the Trinity — The Seal

"Now He which stablisheth us with you in Christ, and hath anointed us, is God; *who hath also SEALED US, and given the earnest of the Spirit in our hearts*" (II Cor. 1:21, 22).

Three times in the New Testament we are told that believers are sealed with the Holy Spirit. It is not that the Holy Spirit *seals* the believer, but that *the Holy Spirit Himself IS the seal* by which we are marked as the property of the Lord Jesus Christ. God seals us as His purchased possession the very moment we believe on His only begotten Son.

Christians are not branded with some *visible* mark of identification in the forehead or on the hand as the followers of Antichrist will be marked during the tribulation period, nor are believers identified by wearing peculiar garments or little gold crosses hung around the neck or fastened in a coat lapel. *We are marked BY THE INDWELLING OF THE HOLY SPIRIT.*

We must not confuse being *born* of the Spirit and being *sealed* by the Spirit. By being born of the Spirit we become children of God, members of the family of heaven; and having become children of God, we are *sealed* with the Spirit *because we ARE children of God.* For example, cattlemen brand their cattle—not to *make them the property* of the ranch owner, but because they already *belong to him.* As believers, we are sealed by the Holy Spirit because we are *God's purchased possession* (I Cor. 6:19, 20), and He seals us by "that Holy Spirit of promise, which is the earnest of our inheritance until the redemption of the purchased possession, unto the praise of His glory" (Eph. 1:13, 14).

When the Lord Jesus Christ became flesh and

tabernacled among men, He was sealed by the Father
(John 6:27) on the grounds of His own righteousness,
holiness, and unquestionable perfection. It is different
with believers. The Holy Spirit is not given to us
because of *our* righteousness, holiness, or perfection.
We are not sealed by the Spirit because of our own
progress or maturity, nor because of anything we do,
give, or live. Believers are sealed with the Holy Spirit
simply because we are *redeemed with the precious
blood of the Lamb of God* and we stand in the abiding efficacy of the one sacrifice Jesus offered—once,
for all, forever—the sacrifice of Himself; and this one
sacrifice so pleased the Father that the Son is now
exalted to the right hand of the Majesty on high. It
is because of His accomplishment—His finished work
and the efficacy of His blood—that we are possessors
of the Holy Spirit. When we exercise faith in Christ's
finished work, believe in His shed blood, God "borns"
us of the Spirit, washes us in the blood, and seals us
with the Spirit of promise. What glorious truth! What
unshakeable assurance! We are sealed by the Holy
Spirit of God *"unto the day of redemption"* (Eph.
4:30). Our Seal is secure, absolute—as secure as God
Himself because our Seal *is* the third Person of the
Godhead.

When Do We Receive the Holy Spirit?

There are some people who teach that the unbeliever *believes and is saved,* and then at some later
time—a week, a month, a year or more—that person
receives the Holy Spirit providing he or she meets the
conditions and prays sincerely enough. To prove this
point they use Ephesians 1:13 where Paul said, ". . .
AFTER that ye believed, ye were sealed with that
Holy Spirit of promise." Actually, the Greek here
reads, *"ON BELIEVING ye were sealed."* The sequence here is not a chronological one.

Suppose we say that salvation is a wheel made up of spokes. We name the different spokes: redemption, justification, sanctification, adoption, righteousness, holiness, etc. However many spokes the wheel of salvation may have, when one spoke starts in motion *every spoke* moves at the same second—not one after another, but all together. By this illustration we see that when we receive *Jesus*, according to the Word of God we possess the fulness of the Godhead—Father, Son, and Holy Ghost (Col. 2:9, 10).

In Colossians 1:26, 27 we read of *"the mystery which hath been hid from ages and from generations, but now is made manifest to His saints: to whom God would make known what is the riches of the glory of this mystery among the Gentiles; which is CHRIST IN YOU, the hope of glory."* When one believes on the Lord Jesus Christ, that very split second Christ comes into the heart, into the inner man; and when Christ comes in, the fulness of the Godhead comes in. Therefore when we *believe*, we are redeemed, saved, sanctified, made righteous and holy, adopted into the family of God, justified and sealed until the day of redemption.

God does not save in sequence. When He works the work of grace in the heart of a believer, that work is as perfect as *God* is perfect. Salvation is of the Lord. Christ in you is salvation, and Christ is complete and perfect. Therefore when we receive Jesus, we receive the seal of the Holy Spirit. I am well aware that there are Scriptures in Acts which deal with certain groups who received the Holy Spirit *subsequent* to believing, but we will discuss those passages a little later as we continue our study.

Pentecost

"Behold, I send the promise of my Father upon

you: but tarry ye in the city of Jerusalem, until ye
be endued with power from on high" (Luke 24:49).

"And when the Day of Pentecost was fully come,
they were all with one accord in one place.   And suddenly there came a sound from heaven as of a rushing
mighty wind, and it filled all the house where they
were sitting.   And there appeared unto them cloven
tongues like as of fire, and it sat upon each of them.
And they were all filled with the Holy Ghost, and
began to speak with other tongues, as the Spirit gave
them utterance.   And there were dwelling at Jerusalem
Jews, devout men, out of every nation under heaven.

"Now when this was noised abroad, the multitude
came together, and were confounded, because that
every man heard them speak in his own language.
And they were all amazed and marvelled, saying one
to another, Behold, are not all these which speak Galilaeans?   And how hear we every man in our own
tongue, wherein we were born? Parthians, and Medes,
and Elamites, and the dwellers in Mesopotamia, and
in Judaea, and Cappadocia, in Pontus, and Asia,
Phrygia, and Pamphylia, in Egypt, and in the parts
of Libya about Cyrene, and strangers of Rome, Jews
and proselytes, Cretes and Arabians, we do hear them
speak in our tongues the wonderful works of God"
(Acts 2:1—11).

Jesus instructed His disciples not to begin their
ministry until they were "endued with power from on
high"—in other words, until they were equipped for
the ministry they would carry on in His absence.   They
obeyed His words and tarried in Jerusalem as He had
told them to do.   In the upper room they waited and
prayed until "the Day of Pentecost was fully come."

"Pentecost" simply means *fifty.*   Jesus appeared
to His disciples for forty days after His resurrection
(Acts 1:3).   He ascended into heaven (Acts 1:9), and
ten days later—on the *fiftieth* day after His resurrection

—the Holy Spirit came. In Leviticus 23:15, 16 we learn concerning the feast of Jehovah, "And ye shall count unto you from the morrow after the sabbath, from the day that ye brought the sheaf of the wave-offering; seven sabbaths shall be complete: even unto the morrow after the seventh sabbath shall *ye number fifty days;* and ye shall offer a new meat-offering unto the Lord."

The Israelites were to count forty-nine days from the wave-offering until the new meat-offering, and the meat-offering was to be made on the fiftieth day after the wave-offering. The wave-*loaves* were offered exactly fifty days after the wave-*sheaf.* This was exactly the number of days between the bodily resurrection of Jesus and the coming of the Holy Spirit on the Day of Pentecost.

There was no leaven in the wave-sheaf because leaven is a type of sin, the wave-sheaf was a type of Christ, and Christ was sinless. However, the wave-*loaves* typified the Church on earth and was baked with leaven. The visible Church is not yet spotless and without wrinkle, as the true Church *will be* in its perfection, when Jesus calls believers unto Himself (Eph. 5:26, 27). The wave-*sheaf* was made up of separate stalks of grain bound loosely together; but the wave-*loaves* signified union—one body united, as the Holy Spirit united the believers into one body on the Day of Pentecost, exactly as foreordained of God and set forth *in type* in the Old Testament feasts.

Those who pray for "another Pentecost" are praying in spiritual ignorance. Just as surely as Jesus was born "in the fulness of the time" (or *at the appointed time*) as described in Galatians 4:4, 5, the *Holy Spirit also came* at the appointed time. Jesus *"offered one sacrifice for sins forever"* (Heb. 10:11—14), never to be repeated. The Holy Spirit came on the Day of Pentecost beginning a new dispensation, "a new thing"

upon this earth, and took up residence in the heart
of each and every believer.

Pentecost was the birthday of the Church, and
the Holy Spirit has taken up residence in the New
Testament Church, dwelling in the believers who make
up that body. Some teachers claim that the Church
was born when Jesus said to Peter, "Upon this rock
I will build my Church; and the gates of hell shall
not prevail against it" (Matt. 16:18); but notice Jesus
said, *"I WILL* (future tense) build my Church." He
did not say, "I *have built* my Church," nor did He
say, *"I am BUILDING* my Church." The chief corner-
stone of the New Testament Church was laid when
Jesus died on the cross, shed His blood for the remission of sins and rose again for our justification;
but the Church was not born until Pentecost.

On that day, one hundred and twenty individuals
went into the upper room, but *only ONE came down*
because the Holy Spirit descended on each of them,
filled each of them, and *united them into one organism:* "For as the body is one, and hath many members, and all the members of that one body, being
many, are one body: so also is Christ. For by one
Spirit are we all baptized into one body, whether we
be Jews or Gentiles, whether we be bond or free; and
have been all made to drink into one Spirit. For the
body is not one member, but many" (I Cor. 12:12—14).
Thus the Apostle Paul illustrates by using the human
body to show us exactly what the Church is.

The Church of the living God is the body of Christ,
made up of all blood-washed, born again believers:
"For the husband is the head of the wife, even as
Christ is the head of the Church: and He is the Saviour of the body. . . . For we are members of His
body, of His flesh, and of His bones. . . . This is a
great mystery: but I speak concerning Christ and the
Church" (Eph. 5:23, 30, 32).

The Church is a living organism, not an organization. An *organization* is governed by its president, secretary, treasurer, and various other officers and committees. The Church is governed by Christ, its head. The infant Church was made up of only one hundred and twenty members who became *one body* on the Day of Pentecost; but that same day, under the preaching of the Word in every language known at that time, three thousand other souls were added to the Church.

Then in Acts 2:46, 47 we read, "And they, continuing daily with one accord in the temple, and breaking bread from house to house, did eat their meat with gladness and singleness of heart, praising God, and having favour with all the people. *And the LORD added to the Church daily such as should be saved.*" A little later (Acts 4:4) about five thousand others were added, and throughout the book of Acts we read of additions to the Church as the apostles and early Christians preached the Gospel in mighty power. Since the Day of Pentecost, every blood-washed, born again believer, when he exercises faith in the finished work of the Lamb of God, has been united to the body of Christ through the baptism of the Holy Spirit.

Power for Service

"Ye shall receive power, after that the Holy Ghost is come upon you: and *ye shall be witnesses unto me both in Jerusalem, and in all Judaea, and in Samaria, and UNTO THE UTTERMOST PART OF THE EARTH*" (Acts 1:8).

The men to whom Jesus spoke these words were weaklings and spiritual cowards; but after the Holy Ghost came upon them as promised they were truly endued with power from on high and they became spiritual giants, examples in the faith, and leaders in the New Testament Church. So bold and mighty were

they in their preaching that the religious leaders of
that day—the same crowd who had crucified Jesus—
called them to account and *"commanded them not to
speak at all nor teach in the name of Jesus.*

"But Peter and John answered and said unto them,
Whether it be right in the sight of God to hearken
unto you more than unto God, judge ye. *FOR WE
CANNOT BUT SPEAK THE THINGS WHICH WE
HAVE SEEN AND HEARD.*

"So when they had further threatened them, they
let them go, finding nothing how they might punish
them, because of the people: for all men glorified God
for that which was done" (Acts 4:18—21).

Later, the religious leaders not only called the
apostles before the council for preaching the Gospel;
they also had them brutally beaten:

"And when they had called the apostles, and beat-
en them, they commanded that they should not speak
in the name of Jesus, and let them go. *And they departed from the presence of the council, REJOICING
that they were counted WORTHY TO SUFFER
SHAME FOR HIS NAME. And daily in the temple,
and in every house, they ceased not to teach and
preach Jesus Christ"* (Acts 5:40—42).

A short time later, the Church entered a period of
severe persecution under the leadership of Saul of
Tarsus. Stephen was stoned to death (Acts chapter 7),
"and Saul was consenting unto his death. And at
that time there was a great persecution against the
Church which was at Jerusalem; and they were all
scattered abroad throughout the regions of Judaea and
Samaria, except the apostles. And devout men carried
Stephen to his burial, and made great lamentation
over him. *As for Saul, he made havock of the Church,
entering into every house, and haling men and women
committed them to prison. THEREFORE THEY
THAT WERE SCATTERED ABROAD WENT EV-*

ERY WHERE PREACHING THE WORD" (Acts 8: 1—4).

And so it was! These men were soon known as "these that have turned the world upside down" (Acts 17:6).

In the New Testament we find seven principal words used in connection with the ministry of the Holy Spirit in this Dispensation of Grace:

1. BORN: In John 3:3—6 Jesus taught Nicodemus that it is a divine imperative that men be born of the Spirit if they expect to enter the kingdom of heaven.

2. INDWELT: In Romans 8:9 we read, "If any man have not the Spirit of Christ, he is none of His." In verse 11 of that same chapter we read, "But if the Spirit of Him that raised up Jesus from the dead *dwell in you,* He that raised up Christ from the dead shall also quicken your mortal bodies by His Spirit that *dwelleth in you."* We find the same word in II Timothy 1:14.

3. SEALED: II Corinthians 1:22 tells us that God has *"sealed us,* and given the earnest of the Spirit in our hearts." Ephesians 1:13 declares that we are *"sealed* with that Holy Spirit of promise," and in Ephesians 4:30 we read, "Grieve not the Holy Spirit of God, whereby ye are *sealed* unto the day of redemption."

4. EARNEST: In II Corinthians 1:22 we are told that God has given "the *earnest* of the Spirit in our hearts," and Ephesians 1:14 tells us that the Holy Spirit of promise is "the *earnest* of our inheritance until the redemption of the purchased possession."

5. ANOINTED: "Now He which stablisheth us with you in Christ, and hath *anointed* us, is God" (II Cor. 1:21). All believers have the anointing of the Holy Spirit: "But the *anointing* which ye have received of Him abideth in you, and ye need not that any man teach you: but as the same *anointing* teacheth you of all things, and is truth, and is no lie, and even as it hath taught you, ye shall abide in Him" (I John 2:27).

6. *FILLED:* "Then Peter, *filled* with the Holy Ghost, said unto them, Ye rulers of the people, and elders of Israel . . . And when they had prayed, the place was shaken where they were assembled together; and they were all *filled* with the Holy Ghost, and they spake the Word of God with boldness" (Acts 4:8, 31). In Ephesians 5:18 we are commanded, "Be not drunk with wine, wherein is excess; but be *filled* with the Spirit."

7. *BAPTIZED:*   John the Baptist declared, "I indeed baptize you with water unto repentance: but He that cometh after me is mightier than I, whose shoes I am not worthy to bear: He shall *baptize* you with the Holy Ghost, and with fire" (Matt. 3:11). Jesus told His disciples, "John truly baptized with water; but ye shall be *baptized* with the Holy Ghost not many days hence" (Acts 1:5). Then in I Corinthians 12:13 we read, "For by one Spirit are we all *baptized* into one body, whether we be Jews or Gentiles, whether we be bond or free; and have been all made to drink into one Spirit."

A careful study of these seven words will reveal that they are by no means interchangeable. No two of them mean exactly the same thing. Each word has its own definite and singular significance. The Holy Spirit gave these words to the different writers, and they penned them down as He dictated them.

The Baptism of the Holy Spirit

There is much confusion concerning the baptism of the Holy Spirit—what it is, when it occurs, and how it is evidenced. The truth about the baptism of the Spirit is found in God's Word, not in denominational books of doctrine—nor can we learn the truth by listening to different ministers and teachers, because they do not agree. We must allow the Holy Spirit to lead us into the truth concerning Himself.

The first time the baptism of the Holy Spirit is mentioned in the Bible is in Matthew 3:11. John the Baptist preached, "I indeed baptize you with water unto repentance: but He that cometh after me is mightier than I, whose shoes I am not worthy to bear: *He shall baptize you WITH THE HOLY GHOST, and with fire.*" We find the same statement with but little variation in Mark 1:8 and in Luke 3:16.

John 1:33 also indicates that the Lord Jesus Christ is the One who baptizes with the Holy Spirit. John the Baptist said of Jesus, "I knew Him not: but He that sent me to baptize with water, the same said unto me, Upon whom thou shalt see the Spirit descending, and remaining on Him, the same is He which *baptizeth with the Holy Ghost.*"

These passages are prophetic. The words were spoken *before Pentecost,* but pointed to the day when the Holy Spirit would be resident upon earth in the New Testament Church. After His resurrection the Lord Jesus reminded His disciples of this promise yet to be fulfilled, telling them that the baptism of the Spirit would soon occur: "For John truly baptized with water; but *ye shall be baptized with the Holy Ghost not many days hence*" (Acts 1:5).

The passages referred to in the Gospels cover a period of approximately three and one-half years, during which time the promise of the coming of the Spirit was not fulfilled; yet during that period (from the first mention of the baptism of the Spirit until Jesus ascended back to heaven) the disciples achieved remarkable results in their ministry. They preached the Gospel, people were saved, they performed miracles and healed the sick everywhere they went. In Luke 9:6

we are told that they "went through the towns, preaching the Gospel, and healing every where."

In Luke 10:17 we read, "And the seventy returned again with joy, saying, *Lord, EVEN THE DEVILS are subject unto us through thy name!*"

Mark 6:13 tells us, "And they cast out *many devils*, and anointed with oil many that were sick, and *healed* them."

All of these mighty works occurred *before Pentecost*, before the baptism of the Holy Spirit.

Now notice the passage in Matthew 17:14—21: When Jesus came down from the Mount of Transfiguration a multitude met Him, and one certain man knelt before Him and said, "Lord, have mercy on my son: for he is lunatick, and sore vexed: and ofttimes he falleth into the fire, and oft into the water. *And I brought him to thy disciples, AND THEY COULD NOT CURE HIM. . . .*

"And Jesus rebuked the devil; and he departed out of him: and the child was cured from that very hour. Then came the disciples to Jesus apart, and said, *Why could not WE cast him out?*

"And Jesus said unto them, *Because of your UNBELIEF!* For verily I say unto you, If ye have faith as a grain of mustard seed, ye shall say unto this mountain, Remove hence to yonder place; and it shall remove; and nothing shall be impossible unto you. Howbeit this kind goeth not out but by prayer and fasting."

You will notice Jesus did not tell the disciples they could not cast out the demon *because they had not received the baptism of the Holy Spirit.* He said, "You could not cast out this demon *BECAUSE OF YOUR UNBELIEF.*" You see, while Jesus was here on earth the baptism of the Spirit was not necessary in order that these men do mighty miracles in His name. The baptism of the Spirit was not needed for preaching the Gospel with great results. That baptism came to pass at the appointed time—the birthday of a new dispensation; and it occurred *after* Jesus had returned to the Father in heaven.

The coming of the Holy Spirit at Pentecost and the baptism of the one hundred and twenty believers marked the inauguration of a new era, an era which has continued for almost two thousand years and *will* continue until the New Testament Church is completed. When that time comes, the Church, the body and bride of Christ, will be caught up to meet Jesus in the clouds in the air, and the Holy Spirit will be taken out with the Church.

The Baptism of Fire

In Matthew 3:11, John the Baptist declared that Jesus would baptize "with the Holy Ghost—*and with FIRE*." All who heard John speak would either be baptized with the Holy Ghost, or they would be baptized with fire. But what is the meaning of the declaration concerning the baptism with fire?

In Matthew 3:10—12 "fire" is mentioned three times—once in each of the three verses: "And now also the axe is laid unto the root of the trees: therefore every tree which bringeth not forth good fruit is hewn down, *and cast into the FIRE*. I indeed baptize you with water unto repentance: but He that cometh after me is mightier than I, whose shoes I am not worthy to bear: He shall baptize you with the Holy Ghost, *and with FIRE:* Whose fan is in His hand, and He will throughly purge His floor, and gather His wheat into the garner; but *He will BURN UP the chaff with unquenchable FIRE.*"

Now if we study and rightly divide the Word of truth, if we honestly compare spiritual things with spiritual, can we say that the "fire" means one thing

in one of these verses—and means something entirely
different in the other two? We know that the "wheat"
in verse 12 represents the born again, the righteous;
and the "chaff" represents the wicked. Therefore is
it not clear that in all three of these verses, *"fire"*
signifies judgment upon the wicked?

We must also consider another very significant
fact here as we divide the Word: John the Baptist
was preaching, *"Repent!* for the kingdom of heaven
is at hand!" In Matthew 3:5, 6 we read, "Then went
out to him Jerusalem, and all Judaea, and all the
region round about Jordan, *and were baptized of him
in Jordan, CONFESSING THEIR SINS."*

Then came the Pharisees and the Sadducees re-
questing baptism—but John knew they came with un-
repentant hearts, and he refused to baptize them. Instead, he said to them, "O *generation of vipers,* who
hath warned *you* to flee from the wrath to come?
Bring forth therefore fruits meet for repentance: and
think not to say within yourselves, We have Abraham
to our father: for I say unto you, that God is able
of these stones to raise up children unto Abraham!"
(vv. 7—9).

John the Baptist was speaking here to a mixed
multitude. Many people sincerely confessed their sins,
received all the light given them, and John baptized
them in good faith; but when the Pharisees and Sadducees came, John knew they came with self-righteous,
sinful hearts and he *refused* to baptize them. Therefore his message to this mixed crowd was, "Some of
you will be baptized with the Holy Ghost. Others
will be baptized with fire."

All who heard John's message and repented of
their sins (and later heard the message of Jesus and
believed on Him as Saviour) were baptized with the
Holy Ghost. Those who rejected John's message and
rejected Jesus were headed for the baptism of fire—in

hell where the fire shall never be quenched (Mark 9:42—48).

Paul sheds light on this in Hebrews 10:26, 27: "For if we sin wilfully after that we have received the knowledge of the truth, there remaineth no more sacrifice for sins, but a certain fearful looking for of *judgment and fiery indignation, which shall devour the adversaries.*"

The question may well be asked, "Why is the baptism of fire mentioned in Matthew 3:11 and in Luke 3:16, while Mark 1:8 makes *no mention* of fire?" The reason for this is very clear when we carefully compare these accounts:

Mark's account tells of people who *sincerely repented,* confessing their sins. They were not self-righteous hypocrites, they did not come for baptism declaring that they were the descendants of Abraham and therefore were not in bondage to sin. There were no "vipers" among them, therefore no reason for Mark 1:8 to prophesy the baptism of fire. John the Baptist simply said to these people, "I indeed have baptized you with water: *but HE shall baptize you with THE HOLY GHOST.*" And about three and one-half years later, those who sincerely repented under the preaching of John and accepted Jesus as Messiah truly *were baptized* with the Holy Ghost and became members of the infant Church!

Those who rejected John's message and to whom he promised a baptism of fire *will be* baptized with fire "when the Lord Jesus shall be revealed from heaven with His mighty angels, *in flaming fire taking vengeance* on them that know not God, and that obey not the Gospel of our Lord Jesus Christ" (II Thess. 1:7, 8).

John the Beloved tells us of this in his vision of the Great White Throne judgment: "And I saw a great white throne, and Him that sat on it, from whose face the earth and the heaven fled away; and there was found no place for them. And I saw the dead, small and great, stand before God; and the books were opened: and another book was opened, which is the book of life: and the dead were judged out of those things which were written in the books, according to their works. And the sea gave up the dead which were in it; and death and hell delivered up the dead which were in them: and they were judged every man according to their works. And death and hell were cast into the lake of fire. This is the second death. *And whosoever was not found written in the book of life was cast into THE LAKE OF FIRE"* (Rev. 20:11—15).

All Believers Baptized into One Body

"For as the body is one, and hath many members, and all the members of that one body, being many, are one body: so also is Christ. For by one Spirit are we all baptized into one body, whether we be Jews or Gentiles, whether we be bond or free; and have been all made to drink into one Spirit" (I Cor. 12:12,13).

This is a very important passage on the baptism of the Spirit. It is enlightening and easily understood if we will allow the Word of God to speak and we keep silent.

First of all, how many of the Corinthian believers were baptized into one body? The Scripture plainly tells us, "by one Spirit are we *ALL baptized* into one body." Therefore, *all* of the Corinthian believers were baptized into the body of Christ. Suppose we look into the Word of God and allow it to show us some things about these Corinthian Christians:

In I Corinthians 1:2,3 Paul wrote "unto the church of God which is at Corinth, to them that are sanctified in Christ Jesus, called to be saints, with all that in every place call upon the name of Jesus Christ our Lord, both their's and our's: Grace be unto you, and peace, from God our Father, and from the Lord Jesus Christ."

These words could be spoken only of people who are born again—yet some of the Corinthian believers were far from being separated, consecrated Christians! Some of them were sectarian in spirit, contentious, arguing among themselves (I Cor. 1:10—17). Some of them were carnal, with envyings and divisions among them, walking "as men" (I Cor. 3:1—3).

Some of the Corinthian believers were even going to law against each other before unbelievers (I Cor. 6:6); and above all they were behaving in a disorderly manner at the Lord's table, drinking and eating in excess—some of them even becoming drunken (I Cor. 11:18—22).

The Apostle Paul sternly rebuked these Christians for their carnal ways—but at the same time made it clear that they had truly believed the Gospel, they were truly children of God, washed in the blood, sanctified and justified; and they had shared in the baptism of the Holy Spirit which had made them one in Christ! In I Corinthians 6:9—11 Paul said to these people:

"Know ye not that the unrighteous shall not inherit the kingdom of God? Be not deceived: neither fornicators, nor idolaters, nor adulterers, nor effeminate, nor abusers of themselves with mankind, nor thieves, nor covetous, nor drunkards, nor revilers, nor extortioners, shall inherit the kingdom of God. *AND SUCH WERE SOME OF YOU! But ye are WASHED, but ye are SANCTIFIED, but ye are JUSTIFIED in the name of the Lord Jesus, and by the Spirit of our God.*"

Yes, in spite of their carnality these Corinthian

believers were baptized by the Holy Spirit into one
body. *Why?* Certainly it was not that they might
speak with other tongues. They did not receive the
baptism in order to enjoy a superior spiritual experience. *They were baptized into one body that they
might be ONE UNITED, LIVING ORGANISM — the
New Testament Church, the body of Christ.*

Unity did not exist between God's people in the
Old Testament as it does in this Dispensation of Grace.
The baptism of the Holy Spirit brought about the
formation of the body of Christ, of which all believers
are members — "for we are members of His body, of
His flesh, and of His bones" (Eph. 5:30).

The Holy Spirit uses the human body as an illustration of the body of Christ. The human body is
not an *organization*, but an organism made up of many
members, each with its own function but with the
same life existing in every member and the whole body
governed by the head. Paul explains the functions
of and the necessity for the different members of the
body and then declares, *"God hath tempered the body
together . . .* that there should be no schism in the
body; but that the members should have the same
care one for another. And whether one member suffer,
all the members suffer with it; or one member be hon-
oured, all the members rejoice with it" (I Cor. 12:
24—26). (Please read the first 23 verses of this chapter.)

As with the human body, so it is with the New
Testament Church, the body of Christ. Christ is the
head of the Church, and Paul explains that as different
members of the human body have different functions,
so "God hath set some in the Church—first apostles,
secondarily prophets, thirdly teachers, after that miracles, then gifts of healings, helps, governments, diversities of tongues. Are all apostles? Are all prophets? Are all teachers? Are all workers of miracles?

tongues? Do all interpret? But covet earnestly the best gifts: and yet shew I unto you a more excellent way" (I Cor. 12:28—31).

Is the Baptism of the Spirit
Evidenced by Speaking in Tongues?

There is no place in the New Testament where one person, apart from other individuals, is ever said to have received the mighty baptism of the Spirit with evidence of speaking in other tongues. In the book of Acts, the baptism of the Spirit always occurred where there was a *group* of people. Four such groups are named:

1. The Jewish Christians at Pentecost (Acts 2:1—11).
2. The Samaritan Christians (Acts 8:14—17).
3. The Gentiles in the house of Cornelius (Acts 10: 34—48).
4. The disciples of John the Baptist at Ephesus (Acts 19:1—7).

In discussing these four groups we will see just what happened in each case and how the groups compare—or differ—as having to do with the baptism of the Spirit and the evidence of having received that baptism.

The Jewish Christians at Pentecost:

There were no Gentiles baptized in the Holy Spirit on the Day of Pentecost; they were all Galilaeans (Acts 2:7).

We read that on the Day of Pentecost (the fiftieth day after the resurrection of Jesus) there came a sound from heaven "as of a rushing mighty wind," and it filled the house where the one hundred and twenty believers were assembled. Then there appeared cloven tongues—not *"tongues OF fire,"* but "tongues *LIKE*

AS OF FIRE," and sat upon each of them. I personally believe this is the baptism of which Jesus spoke in Acts 1:5.

The record declares, "They were all filled with the Holy Ghost, and began to speak with other tongues, as the Spirit gave them utterance." They spoke as the Holy Spirit spoke *through* them, and they spoke in other languages—not in their native tongue. Those who *heard* these Jewish Christians represented every known nation in that day, yet each one heard the Gospel in his own tongue: "And they were all amazed and marvelled, saying one to another, Behold, are not all these which speak Galilaeans? And how hear we every man in our own tongue, wherein we were born?" (Acts 2:7, 8).

There was no *"unknown"* tongue on the Day of Pentecost. Every language spoken was understood by someone present. Notice in verses 9—11:

"Parthians, and *Medes,* and *Elamites,* and the dwellers in *Mesopotamia,* and in *Judaea,* and *Cappadocia,* in *Pontus,* and *Asia, Phrygia,* and *Pamphylia,* in *Egypt,* and in the *parts of Libya about Cyrene,* and strangers of *Rome, Jews and proselytes, Cretes* and *Arabians—WE DO HEAR THEM SPEAK IN OUR TONGUES the wonderful works of God!"*

These men who were from every known nation in the world at that time heard the Gospel in their own tongue, and when they returned to their own communities they carried with them the message they had heard on the Day of Pentecost. This was a sign from Almighty God that a new era had begun, a "new thing" had occurred. The Holy Spirit had come as promised in the prophecy of Joel; and as a result of Pentecost the Gospel spread to communities throughout the world within the next few days and weeks.

The Samaritan Christians:

Immediately after the stoning of Stephen, great

persecution broke out against the Church and the Christians were scattered abroad. And in Acts 8:4 we read, "Therefore they that were scattered abroad *went every where preaching the Word."*

Philip went down into Samaria "and preached Christ unto them. And the people with one accord gave heed unto those things which Philip spake, hearing and seeing the miracles which he did. . . . And there was great joy in that city" (Acts 8:5—8).

When the apostles who were still in the city of Jerusalem heard that the Samaritans had received the Word of God with gladness, they sent Peter and John to Samaria; and when Peter and John arrived, they prayed for the Samaritan Christians "that they might receive the Holy Ghost: (for as yet He was fallen upon none of them: only they were baptized in the name of the Lord Jesus.)"

Philip had preached to these people and had given them all the light he had. (He did not know the teaching of the Dispensation of Grace.) The people received his message and he had baptized them in the name of the Lord Jesus. So Peter and John prayed for them, and laid their hands on them, *"and they received the Holy Ghost"* (Acts 8:15—17).

Now compare this baptism with that of Pentecost. Here was no mighty, rushing wind, no sound, no cloven tongues "like as of fire," and the record does not even mention tongues.

You will notice the Samaritans were not invited to pray for the Holy Ghost. Rather, *Peter and John prayed,* laid their hands on the Samaritan believers, and they received the Holy Spirit. As were the Jews at Pentecost, so now the Samaritan Christians were added to the body of Christ. Jesus broke down "the middle wall of partition" (Eph. 2:14), and now "there is neither Jew nor Greek, there is neither bond nor free, there is neither male nor female: *for (we) are all ONE IN CHRIST JESUS"* (Gal. 3:27, 28).

I suppose such hatred has existed nowhere else to compare with the hatred between the Jews and Samaritans. Bible antiquity tells us that a Jew prayed each morning that God would deliver him from seeing the face of a Samaritan that day! But now, in this glorious Dispensation of Grace, both Jew and Samaritan belong to the body of Christ through the mighty miracle of the baptism of the Holy Ghost.

Gentiles in the house of Cornelius:

In Acts chapter 10 we read the moving account of the conversion of Cornelius and the household of this outstanding man.

First of all, we read that Cornelius lived in Caesarea, he was a centurion of the Italian band, "a devout man, and one that feared God with all his house, which gave much alms to the people, and prayed to God alway" (Acts 10:1, 2). But Cornelius did not know the Gospel of the grace of God—salvation by grace through faith in the finished work of Jesus.

God sent him a vision wherein He told Cornelius to send to Joppa and ask for Simon Peter. He obeyed the vision—and in the meantime God revealed to *Peter* that he should go with the servants of Cornelius when they came for him.

In due time Peter arrived at the house of Cornelius where a goodly number of friends and relatives had been called together to hear this first message on the grace of God to be preached to Gentiles. The sermon Peter preached that day is recorded in Acts 10:34—43. Please read the entire passage; we have time and space here to touch only on the highlights.

The first point in Peter's sermon is found in verse 34: *"God is no respecter of persons."* The Gospel was "to the Jew first" (Rom. 1:16). Cornelius was a Gentile, but God loved him.

The second point in Peter's sermon was *the crucifixion* (v. 39). God sent Jesus into the world, He went about doing good, the disciples were "witnesses of all things which He did . . . *whom they slew and hanged on a tree.*"

Peter's third point in his message was *the bodily resurrection of Jesus* (v. 40): *"Him God raised up* the third day, and shewed Him openly." We must believe in the resurrection if we are to be saved, for if there *is* no resurrection our faith is vain, we are still in our sins, and all who have died are eternally lost (I Cor. 15:12—19).

Then Peter moved on to the last point in his sermon: *"To Him give all the prophets witness, that through His name WHOSOEVER BELIEVETH IN HIM SHALL RECEIVE REMISSION OF SINS"* (v. 43).

Notice what happened here: *"While Peter yet spake these words, THE HOLY GHOST FELL ON ALL THEM WHICH HEARD THE WORD.* And they of the circumcision which believed were astonished, as many as came with Peter, because that on the Gentiles also was poured out the gift of the Holy Ghost. *For they heard them speak with tongues,* and magnify God. Then answered Peter, Can any man forbid water, that these should not be baptized, *which have received the Holy Ghost as well as we?* And he commanded them to be baptized in the name of the Lord . . ." (Acts 10:44—48).

Now let us compare this with the baptism of the Holy Spirit at Pentecost and also with the baptism of the Spirit in the community of the Samaritans:

Peter had been preaching salvation through the death, burial, and resurrection of the Lord Jesus, and *while he was still preaching* the Holy Ghost fell on the Gentiles which heard the Word. These people were not seeking, they were not praying, they were simply listening to the Word of God; and as Peter preached the Word, they *believed and received* the Word, the Holy Ghost came upon them, and they spoke with tongues and magnified God.

On the Day of Pentecost the Jews spoke with other tongues, when the Gentiles received the Holy Ghost they spoke with tongues; but when the Holy Ghost fell on the Samaritans there was no mention of tongues.

The disciples of John the Baptist at Ephesus:

"And it came to pass, that, while Apollos was at Corinth, Paul having passed through the upper coasts came to Ephesus: and finding certain disciples, He said unto them, Have ye received the Holy Ghost since ye believed? And they said unto him, We have not so much as heard whether there be any Holy Ghost. And he said unto them, Unto what then were ye baptized? And they said, Unto John's baptism.

"Then said Paul, John verily baptized with the baptism of repentance, saying unto the people, that they should believe on Him which should come after him, that is, on Christ Jesus. When they heard this, they were baptized in the name of the Lord Jesus. And when Paul had laid his hands upon them, the Holy Ghost came on them; and they spake with tongues, and prophesied. And all the men were about twelve" (Acts 19:1—7).

Those who teach that we receive the baptism of the Holy Spirit some time *after* we are born again major on the words in verse 2 in this passage: *"Have ye received the Holy Ghost SINCE ye believed?"* However, in the original Greek the word is not "since," but *"when."* Therefore the question should read, *"Did ye receive the Holy Ghost WHEN ye believed?"*

Now notice the reply these Ephesians gave: *"We*

have not so much as heard whether there BE any Holy Ghost." Dearly beloved, how *could* these disciples of John have received the baptism of the Holy Ghost when they had not even *heard* of the third Person of the Trinity until Paul revealed to them the baptism of the Spirit?

When he asked, "Unto what then were ye baptized?" they answered, "Unto *John's* baptism." Paul reminded these men that John the Baptist had preached the baptism of repentance, pointed the people to Jesus, telling them that they should *believe on Jesus* when He came; and when these disciples of John heard Paul's message they believed on Jesus and were baptized in His name. Then Paul laid his hands on them, the Holy Ghost came upon them, "and they spake with tongues, and prophesied."

Now shall we compare this baptism of the Spirit with the other three groups we have studied? These disciples of John were not asked to pray, they were not asked to seek the baptism of the Spirit, nor were they instructed to tarry for the baptism. In fact, until Paul spoke to them they knew absolutely nothing *about* the Holy Spirit. But when they learned the truth they received it, they were baptized in the name of Jesus, and when Paul laid his hands on them they received the baptism of the Holy Spirit and they spoke with tongues *and prophesied.* (This is the first mention of believers' prophesying when they received the Holy Spirit.)

In this instance, however, there was no sound as of a rushing, mighty wind and no cloven tongues "like as of fire," as there had been at Pentecost. These disciples of John *did* speak with tongues.

In these four groups we have learned that the Jews at Pentecost spoke with tongues, the Gentiles in the house of Cornelius spoke with tongues, John's disciples spoke with tongues and prophesied, but the

Samaritan believers did not speak with tongues. Beyond our study of the Ephesian Christians, the disciples of John the Baptist, we do not read of any individual or group receiving the baptism of the Holy Ghost in any of the remaining chapters of Acts or in any of the epistles except I Corinthians 12:12, 13, where we are told that the Holy Spirit baptizes all believers into the body of Christ. Therefore since the disciples of John the Baptist received the baptism of the Holy Ghost at Ephesus, all believers have been baptized into the body of Christ the moment they believed—not subsequent to salvation, but simultaneously—and *sealed* with the Spirit until the day of redemption.

During the first few years of Christianity—*the transition period*—mighty miracles were wrought by the disciples, and many of the first believers spoke with other tongues. Why? The Word of God tells us:

"Therefore we ought to give the more earnest heed to the things which we have heard, lest at any time we should let them slip. For if the Word spoken by angels was stedfast, and every transgression and disobedience received a just recompence of reward; how shall we escape, if we neglect so great salvation; which *at the first began to be spoken by THE LORD, and was confirmed unto us by them that heard Him; GOD ALSO BEARING THEM WITNESS, BOTH WITH SIGNS AND WONDERS, AND WITH DIVERS MIRACLES, AND GIFTS OF THE HOLY GHOST, according to His own will?*" (Heb. 2:1—4).

In I Corinthians 13:8—10 the Apostle Paul declared: "Charity never faileth: but whether there be prophecies, they shall fail; *whether there be TONGUES, they shall cease;* whether there be knowledge, it shall vanish away. For we know in part, and we prophesy in part. *BUT WHEN THAT WHICH IS PERFECT IS COME, then that which is in part shall be done away."* In this Dispensation of Grace, "that which is perfect" has come. All Scripture has been given and the Word of God is complete.

In I Corinthians 14:1—22 you will find Paul's discussion on speaking in tongues. In verse 22 he tells us, "Wherefore *tongues are for a SIGN,* not to them that *believe,* but to them that *believe not:* but prophesying serveth not for them that believe not, but for them which believe." Tongues are not a sign to the believer that he has been baptized in the Holy Ghost. *"Prophesying"*—teaching and telling out the good news that God loves us and Jesus died for us—this is for the believer, giving out the invitation that "whosoever will" may come, and drink of the water of life freely!

In these verses where Paul deals with speaking in tongues, mention is made of "an *unknown* tongue." Certainly this is not the same as *"other* tongues" spoken at Pentecost, and in the house of Cornelius, and by John's disciples in Acts 19. There were no *"unknown"* tongues at Pentecost, but rather, every man present that day heard the Gospel *in his own tongue.* Every language spoken at Pentecost was understood by those from the various nations represented there. The *"unknown tongue"* of which Paul wrote to the Corinthian believers is not mentioned in any other book in the New Testament, and Paul himself declared, "I thank my God, I speak with tongues more than ye all: Yet in the church *I had rather speak FIVE words with my understanding,* that by my voice I might teach others also, *than ten thousand words in an UNKNOWN tongue"* (I Cor. 14:18, 19).

There are sincere, well-meaning people today who earnestly desire and seek the baptism of the Holy Ghost evidenced by speaking in tongues. (I am not interested in discussing those who claim to have *had* such an experience. That is between them and God.) Many desire this mighty baptism in order to receive

power for effective service, or that they may be able
to perform remarkable miracles in the sight of men;
but even such power—under the control of the Holy
Spirit—does not necessarily imply real communion
with God or whole-hearted dedication to God.

I would be a fool to make that statement if I did
not have Scripture to prove it—but there IS scriptural
proof:

In Numbers 24:2 we read, "Balaam lifted up his
eyes, and he saw Israel abiding in his tents according
to their tribes; *and the Spirit of God came upon him.*"

All Bible students are acquainted with Balaam.
He was an evil man, a greedy man. Jude declared
that Balaam was a lover of gain (Jude 11). Peter spoke
of those who went astray, "following the way of Balaam . . . who loved *the wages of unrighteousness*"
(II Pet. 2:15). He was a corrupt man and he corrupted
others. In Revelation 2:14 we read of "the doctrine
of Balaam, who taught Balac to cast a stumblingblock
before the children of Israel, to eat things sacrificed
unto idols, and to commit fornication." But in spite
of the fact that Balaam was evil and corrupt, *"the
Spirit of God came upon him"* and he was forced to
speak true and wonderful things!

Certainly in the instance of Balaam, sign-gifts did
not prove holiness or devotion to God. Tongues and
other marvelous signs which accompanied the coming
of the Holy Spirit at Pentecost and lingered in the
Church during part of the transition period were of
extreme importance in that they gave divine proof of
the ushering in of the new era, the Dispensation of
Grace.

Mighty signs and wonders accompanied the birth
of Israel as a nation, and their deliverance from Gentile slavery was also marked by great miracles:

"He sent Moses His servant; and Aaron whom He
had chosen. They shewed His signs among them, and

wonders in the land of Ham. He sent darkness, and made it dark; and they rebelled not against His Word. He turned their waters into blood, and slew their fish. Their land brought forth frogs in abundance, in the chambers of their kings. He spake, and there came divers sorts of flies, and lice in all their coasts. He gave them hail for rain, and flaming fire in their land.

"He smote their vines also and their fig trees; and brake the trees of their coasts. He spake, and the locusts came, and caterpillars, and that without number, and did eat up all the herbs in their land, and devoured the fruit of their ground. He smote also all the firstborn in their land, the chief of all their strength.

"He brought them forth also with silver and gold: and there was not one feeble person among their tribes. Egypt was glad when they departed: for the fear of them fell upon them. He spread a cloud for a covering; and fire to give light in the night.

"The people asked, and He brought quails, and satisfied them with the bread of heaven. He opened the rock, and the waters gushed out; they ran in the dry places like a river. For He remembered His holy promise, and Abraham His servant. And He brought forth His people with joy, and His chosen with gladness: and gave them the lands of the heathen: and they inherited the labour of the people; that they might observe His statutes, and keep His laws. Praise ye the Lord" (Psalm 105:26—45).

There is a day coming when God will again show mighty signs and wonders. When this dispensation ends, the millennial age will be ushered in by a great outpouring of the Spirit accompanied by mighty miracles:

"And it shall come to pass afterward (in the last days), that I will pour out my Spirit upon all flesh;

and your sons and your daughters shall prophesy,
your old men shall dream dreams, your young men
shall see visions: and also upon the servants and
upon the handmaids in those days will I pour out
my Spirit.

"And I will shew wonders in the heavens and in
the earth, blood, and fire, and pillars of smoke. The
sun shall be turned into darkness, and the moon into
blood, before the great and the terrible day of the
Lord come. And it shall come to pass, that whosoever
shall call on the name of the Lord shall be delivered:
for in mount Zion and in Jerusalem shall be deliverance, as the Lord hath said, and in the remnant whom
the Lord shall call" (Joel 2:28—32).

The first part of Joel's prophecy was fulfilled on
the Day of Pentecost, but verses 30—32 are yet to be
fulfilled. At Pentecost there were no "wonders in the
heavens and in the earth," there was no "blood, and
fire, and pillars of smoke." The sun was not "turned
into darkness," the moon was not turned "into blood."
But these signs *will occur* when Jesus returns in judgment against the Antichrist.

The book of Acts—especially chapters 1 through
12—deals primarily with the transition period which
was marked with signs, wonders, miracles, speaking
in tongues; but these signs did not continue indefinite-
ly.   God called Paul and anointed him the minister
to the Gentiles.   It was to Paul that God revealed the
mystery of the Church and made known the marvelous
message of saving grace. Yet we search Paul's writings
in vain for any record or suggestion of a baptism of
the Holy Spirit, accompanied by speaking with other
tongues as on the Day of Pentecost, or as in the house
of Cornelius, or among the disciples of John the Baptist as recorded in Acts 19.

The Apostle Paul was jealous for the Gospel of the
Lord Jesus Christ and zealous in his preaching of the

Gospel of the grace of God; but nowhere in his instructions to the churches over which he watched so prayerfully did he invite believers to seek the baptism of the Spirit with the evidence of speaking in other tongues! Nor did Paul ever preach that some believers experienced the baptism of the Spirit while others did not. If this baptism continued during the ministry of the Apostle Paul, it is strange indeed that he who was specially anointed for the ministry to the Church did not proclaim the baptism of the Spirit subsequent to the new birth, especially if that baptism is to be sought by believers today.

The simple truth is—the Apostle Paul preached *salvation by grace through faith!* He emphatically declared, "If any man *have NOT* the Spirit of Christ, he is none of His" (Rom. 8:9). He further declared that all believers are baptized by one Spirit into one body—through the baptism of the Holy Spirit we become members of the body of Christ (I Cor. 12:12, 13). And finally, in his letter to the Ephesian church, Paul wrote that believers are SEALED BY THE SPIRIT "unto the day of redemption" (Eph. 4:30).

Jesus said, *"Ye shall know the TRUTH, and the truth shall make you FREE"* (John 8:32). To misunderstand the truth concerning the Holy Spirit and His ministry and mission on earth during this Church Age will cause much anxiety, unrest, frustration, and grief. On the other hand, to *understand* the ministry and mission of the Holy Spirit will set us *free* from those perplexities, anxieties, and fears.

How miserable are those dear souls who seek what is known as "the mighty baptism of the Holy Ghost" (with evidence of speaking with other tongues) and are unable to accomplish or realize the expected blessing! Yet there are thousands upon thousands of sincere people who have begged, prayed, and agonized *in vain* for such baptism. To these precious souls I declare with Paul, *"There is no RESPECT OF PERSONS with God"* (Rom. 2:11). When one *believes on the name of Jesus,* places his faith in the *finished work* of Jesus, and receives Christ into his heart by faith, that individual possesses the fulness of the Godhead! This fact the Word of God declares: "Beware lest any man spoil you through philosophy and vain deceit, after the tradition of men, after the rudiments of the world, and not after Christ. *For IN HIM dwelleth all the fulness of the Godhead bodily. AND YE ARE COMPLETE IN HIM, which is the head of all principality and power"* (Col. 2:8—10).

Filled with the Spirit

"Be not drunk with wine, wherein is excess; but be filled with the Spirit; speaking to yourselves in psalms and hymns and spiritual songs, singing and making melody in your heart to the Lord; giving thanks always for all things unto God and the Father in the name of our Lord Jesus Christ; submitting yourselves one to another in the fear of God" (Eph. 5:18—21).

There is only one "baptism" of the Holy Spirit but there are many "fillings." Peter was *baptized and filled* with the Holy Ghost on the Day of Pentecost, but in Acts 4:8 we read that he was *filled* with the Holy Spirit. Then in Acts 4:31 we read that when the disciples had prayed, "the place was shaken where they were assembled together; and *they were ALL filled* with the Holy Ghost." Since Peter was in this group, he was filled again.

In Acts 9:17 Ananias went to the house where Paul was staying "and putting his hands on him said, Brother Saul, the Lord, even Jesus, that appeared unto thee in the way as thou camest, hath sent me, that thou mightest receive thy sight, *and be FILLED with the Holy Ghost."* Then in Acts 13:9 we read that Paul was "filled with the Holy Ghost."

A believer can be filled with the Holy Ghost many times. As a minister I never enter the pulpit, speak on the radio, or conduct a prayer meeting without first praying for God to fill me afresh with the Holy Spirit.

Nowhere in Paul's writings are we admonished to be *baptized* with the Holy Spirit, but we do find him pleading with the believers in Rome to present their bodies "a living sacrifice, holy, acceptable unto God," and this, he declares, is our *"reasonable service"* (Rom. 12:1).

In Romans 6:13 he admonishes that believers should not yield their members "as instruments of unrighteousness unto sin," but that we should *yield ourselves* "unto God, as those that are alive* from the dead, and (our) members as *instruments of righteousness unto God.*"

We find that Paul reminded the Corinthian believers that the body is the temple of the Holy Ghost and is not to be defiled. In I Corinthians 3:16,17 we read, "Know ye not that ye are the temple of God, and that the Spirit of God dwelleth in you? If any man defile the temple of God, him shall God destroy; for the temple of God is holy, which temple ye are." Then in I Corinthians 6:19,20 Paul admonishes, "What? Know ye not that your body is the temple of the Holy Ghost which is in you, which ye have of God, and ye are not your own? For ye are bought with a price: therefore glorify God in your body, and in your spirit, which are God's."

Then in our text in Ephesians 5:18 he commands, *"Be FILLED with the Spirit."* He does not invite people to be *sealed* with the Spirit, because He seals us when we are born into the family of God.

To be filled with the Spirit we must keep in mind that a vessel cannot be filled until it is first emptied.

If a bowl has an apple in it and we finish filling the
bowl with water without first removing the apple, we
cannot say that it is filled with *water* because actually
it contains *water plus an apple.* The same is true of
the filling of the Spirit: He cannot fill the believer
until the believer is emptied of self and of the cares
of this life.

Do not misunderstand me: This does not mean
sinless perfection. It simply means presenting our
bodies a living sacrifice, presenting our members as
instruments of righteousness unto God, yielding to
God all that we are, all that we have, all that we
hope to have or become. It means praying, "Lord,
empty me of any and all things that would hinder
my being filled with the Holy Spirit"—and I would
remind you that the Spirit fills *from within,* not from
without!

We might illustrate in this way: Suppose I came
to stay in your home; and while you allowed me in
the livingroom, you refused to allow me in the dining-
room, kitchen, or den. I think I would be a bit saddened, a bit grieved, by such treatment. *But*—suppose,
on the other hand, you invited me not only into your
livingroom, but allowed me the use of the entire house
as well, giving me liberty to take advantage of all
the comforts of the home as though it were my own.
How different that arrangement would be! What we
need to do as Christians is simply say to the Holy
Spirit, "Here is the key to my heart, my soul, my
body, my entire being! Fill me, possess me, lead me,
and whatsoever I do, may it be done to the glory of
God." The Holy Spirit is in the world today to glorify God the Father and Christ the Son.

Please note that there is a tremendous difference
between the Christian's possessing the Holy Spirit
and the Holy Spirit's possessing the Christian. We
need not pray for God to give us *"more* of the Spirit"

because the Spirit is a Person and we do not receive Him in portions, parts, or by measure. We need to pray for God to possess *more of* US through the Spirit. I repeat—the Holy Spirit fills from within; and as we surrender to Him He takes possession, fills, and controls. To yield to the control of the Spirit is to have Him take charge of our lives.

For example, perhaps someone who is truly born again, truly saved by God's grace, has a beautiful voice and has been invited to sing in the church choir or in special singing of some kind. But to yield this talent to God's use under the control of the Spirit would mean time spent at choir practice, pleasures missed, other activities curtailed or adjusted, and so the believer refuses to surrender the God-given talent to Jesus. Such a person can never be filled with the Spirit—and the same is true of other talents and abilities. You may say, "I *have* no talent"—but is that really true? Perhaps you cannot sing as well as some other Christians can, perhaps you lack the talent to stand before a group and speak fluently as a minister, missionary, or Sunday school teacher; but what about visiting the sick? What about carrying the Gospel by way of service rendered to those who need your encouragement and prayers? Surely there is *something* every Christian can do to the glory of God—and remember, it is not the *amount* of what we do, but the spirit in which it is done that counts with Him. A Spirit-filled believer is a Christ-occupied believer, and a Christ-occupied believer is an asset to any church. When the Holy Spirit possesses us He directs our eyes, our thoughts, and our endeavors to Christ and we will no longer be occupied with ourselves and our own selfish desires.

I assure you that the Holy Spirit cannot fill a person who is selfish, covetous, impure in thought; and the only way these things can be cast out is to allow the Holy Spirit to *crowd* them out by filling the life with fruits of the Spirit. According to the Word of God, "the fruit of the Spirit is love, joy, peace, long-suffering, gentleness, goodness, faith, meekness, temperance: against such there is no law" (Gal. 5:22, 23). When we sincerely invite the Holy Spirit to fill us, when we are truly *willing to BE filled*, He *will* fill us; and as He possesses the life these things that *hinder* His filling will automatically move out.

All born again believers *possess* the Holy Spirit, all believers are *sealed* by the Spirit; but I am afraid that not many believers allow themselves to be *filled* with the Spirit. *This should not be!* Since God loved us so much that He gave Jesus to die for us, and since Jesus gave His life to redeem us, certainly we should be willing to give *our all,* surrender unreservedly, and pray for Christ to have the pre-eminence in our lives, that the Holy Spirit be enabled to use us to the glory of God. We should seek to be constantly filled with the Spirit in order to glorify Christ.

We should keep in mind the difference in the activity of the Holy Spirit in the Old Testament economy and His activities in this Day of Grace. Under the Mosaic economy the Spirit came upon certain men for specific missions, miracles, and works which God called upon them to do. For instance, in Judges 6:34 we read that the Spirit of the Lord came upon *Gideon* — and the expression used in the original Hebrew language means that *God clothed Gideon, took complete possession of him,* until he had worked the works and accomplished the purpose for which God possessed him.

Such cases in the Old Testament were not the normal rule. There were men who were chosen instruments of God. The Holy Spirit came upon them, filled, empowered, and used them. Such was true even of John the Baptist, Elisabeth his mother, and

Zacharias his father, as recorded in the New Testament:

In Luke 1:15 we read of John the Baptist, "He shall be great in the sight of the Lord, and shall drink neither wine nor strong drink; and *he shall be FILLED with the Holy Ghost, EVEN FROM HIS MOTHER'S WOMB.*"

In Luke 1:41 we read of Elisabeth, "It came to pass, that, when Elisabeth heard the salutation of Mary, *the babe leaped in her womb; and Elisabeth was FILLED with the Holy Ghost.*"

In Luke 1:67, 68 we read of Zacharias, "And *his father Zacharias was FILLED with the Holy Ghost, and prophesied,* saying, Blessed be the Lord God of Israel; for He hath visited and redeemed His people."

In this dispensation there are many instances recorded in the Bible where the filling of the Holy Spirit was normal, continual, and men were characterized by being full of the Spirit:

In Acts 6:1—6 we read of the appointing of the first deacons in the New Testament Church. There were seven of them, and they were *all* full of the Holy Spirit: "Wherefore, brethren, look ye out among you *seven men of honest report, FULL OF THE HOLY GHOST* and wisdom, whom we may appoint over this business. . . . And they chose Stephen, a man full of faith and of the Holy Ghost, and Philip, and Prochorus, and Nicanor, and Timon, and Parmenas, and Nicolas a proselyte of Antioch: whom they set before the apostles: and when they had prayed, they laid their hands on them."

In Acts 11:22—24 we read of *Barnabas, "a good man, and FULL OF THE HOLY GHOST and of faith."*

In Acts 13:52 we read that *"the disciples were filled with joy, AND WITH THE HOLY GHOST"*—and this in the face of severe opposition and persecution!

From Ephesians 5:18 we know that it is God's
will for each and every believer to be filled with the
Holy Spirit. It is normal in this Dispensation of
Grace for Christians to be filled with the Spirit—and
certainly if we are to enjoy our spiritual birthright
we *must* be filled with the Spirit. Anything less is
not God's will for His children.

There is nothing *mysterious* about the filling of
the Spirit. We simply yield our all to God, and the
Spirit fills us—but notice: The evidence of being filled
with the Spirit is not speaking with other tongues or
in an "unknown" tongue. It is "speaking to yourselves in psalms and hymns and spiritual songs, singing and making melody in your heart to the Lord;
giving thanks always for ALL things unto God and
the Father in the name of our Lord Jesus Christ"
(Eph. 5:19, 20).

My beloved fellow believer, *noise* does not signify
spirituality. Speaking *words* does not necessarily signify spirituality. The Holy Spirit fills and controls
from within, and when a believer is completely filled
with the Spirit, that believer speaks in psalms, spiritual
songs, and makes melody in his heart to the Lord.
"To God be the praise and the glory!" is the cry of
his heart.

"Giving thanks always for all things unto God."
Always, under all circumstances, for all things, a Spirit-filled believer gives thanks. How can this be? Romans 8:28 answers for the believer: *"We know that
ALL THINGS work together FOR GOOD to them
that love God, to them who are the called according
to His purpose!"* Whatever happens, the Spirit-filled
believer knows that he is being molded, shaped, conformed to the image of God's dear Son. The believer
who is truly filled with the Spirit will have a happy
heart—but he will not be found boasting of the fact
that he is filled with the Spirit. His words and his

conduct will not call attention to himself, but to the Lord Jesus Christ, pointing others to Him.

A Spirit-filled believer increasingly realizes that *he is nothing* and *Christ is EVERYTHING.* He increasingly confesses that Jesus spoke truth when He said to His disciples, "Without me ye can do nothing" (John 15:5). And even though a Spirit-filled Christian does not boast of his spirituality, there is something about him that attracts men to Christ. The actions, words, and life of such a believer will remind others of Jesus and draw them to Him.

In I Samuel 3:19 we read, "And Samuel grew, and *the Lord was with him, and did let none of his words fall to the ground!*" The same is true of the Spirit-filled believer. His words, actions, and motives will not "fall to the ground." They will accomplish that whereunto he is called and sent—i. e., bringing glory to God and to the Lord Jesus Christ. Yet the person who is possessed and controlled by the Holy Spirit is always small and insignificant in his own eyes. "God resisteth the proud, but giveth grace unto the humble" (James 4:6).

Various Ways in Which the Holy Spirit Is Hindered in His Work

The Scripture mentions some of the ways by which we can oppose and hinder the Holy Spirit in His work. We can *resist* the Spirit, we can *grieve* the Spirit, we can *quench* the Spirit.

Resisting the Spirit:

In the sermon Stephen preached to the Jews (recorded in Acts chapter 7) he declared, "Ye stiffnecked and uncircumcised in heart and ears, *ye do always RESIST the Holy Ghost:* as your fathers did, so do ye" (Acts 7:51).

John the Baptist came on the scene preaching, "Repent ye! For the kingdom of heaven is at hand" (Matt. 3:1, 2).

When Jesus began His ministry on earth He preached, "Repent! For the kingdom of heaven is at hand" (Matt. 4:17).

The message was to the Jew first. Jesus instructed His disciples, "Go not into the way of the Gentiles, and into any city of the Samaritans enter ye not: But go rather to the lost sheep of the house of Israel" (Matt. 10:5, 6). To the Syrophenician woman He said, "I am not sent but unto the lost sheep of the house of Israel" (Matt. 15:24).

The Apostle Paul said to the Romans, "I am not ashamed of the Gospel of Christ: for *it is the power of God unto salvation to every one that believeth; TO THE JEW FIRST, and also to the Greek*" (Rom. 1:16).

But the Jews *rejected* the message, and it was then delivered to the Gentiles.

It was after the crucifixion, resurrection, and ascension of Jesus, during the early days of the Church, that Stephen preached his stern but moving sermon to Israel — the sermon for which he was stoned to death! The subject of his message was *"the unbelief of Israel."* He reminded the Jews of God's promise and blessings to Abraham. He traced the history of the Jewish people — down into Egypt, their unbearable slavery under the Egyptians, the call of Moses, and the miraculous delivery of the Israelites from their bondage under Pharaoh. He then told them that in spite of these great miracles and God's care for them, they had rebelled against Him.

It would be well for you to read the entire seventh chapter of Acts in connection with this part of our study — read the entire text of Stephen's sermon. We have room here to quote only a few verses:

"Ye stiffnecked and uncircumcised in heart and ears, ye do always resist the Holy Ghost: as your fathers did, so do ye. Which of the prophets have not your fathers persecuted? And they have slain them which shewed before of the coming of the Just One; of whom ye have been now the betrayers and murderers: who have received the law by the disposition of angels, and have not kept it.

"When they heard these things, they were cut to the heart, and they gnashed on him with their teeth. ... Then they cried out with a loud voice, and stopped their ears, and ran upon him with one accord, and cast him out of the city, and stoned him . . ." (Acts 7:51—58).

What the Holy Spirit was doing in the case of the Jews (the elect nation of God) He is doing today with individuals. In that day He was striving with a nation; today He strives with men as individuals, calling them, seeking to lead them to the Saviour in true repentance and saving faith. Jesus declared, "No man can come to me, except the Father which hath sent me draw him" (John 6:44)—and in John 16:8—11 He explained *how* we are drawn to God:

"When He (the Holy Spirit) is come, He will reprove the world of sin, and of righteousness, and of judgment: Of sin, because they believe not on me; of righteousness, because I go to my Father, and ye see me no more; of judgment, because the prince of this world is judged."

The Holy Spirit reproves and convicts men of sin, convinces them that they should live righteously, and draws them to Christ. It is dangerous to resist the drawing power of the Holy Spirit because no man can come to God *except* the Spirit draw him. The Jews heard the Gospel, they saw the mighty miracles of Jesus, they heard His wonderful words of life. They even confessed that He taught "as one having author-

ity, and not as the scribes" (Matt. 7:29; Mark 1:22).
When He cast out demons in the city of Capernaum,
the people were all amazed, "insomuch that they
questioned among themselves, saying, What thing is
this? What new doctrine is this? For *with authority*
commandeth He even the unclean spirits, and they do
obey Him" (Mark 1:27).

Yet in the face of all the evidence of Christ's true
identity, the nation of Israel rejected Him—and literally *millions of Gentiles* are walking in their footsteps
today! They hear the Gospel, they see what it has accomplished in the lives of others, but they reject the
Christ. They attend church services and hear good
sermons, they read Gospel tracts, and they are dis-
turbed by an uneasy feeling in their heart; but they
hurry back to their old friends and old activities and
drive away the convicting power of the Holy Spirit.
They have *resisted the Holy Spirit.*

Someone may ask, "Is this the *'unpardonable sin'?*"
No, this is *not* the unpardonable sin—but it is dangerous to resist the Spirit because "now is the accepted
time . . . now is the day of salvation" (II Cor. 6:2),
and there is nothing in the Scriptures to suggest how
many times one may resist the Holy Spirit and drive
Him away—and still expect Him to return to convict
again.

God said, in the Old Testament economy, "*Ephraim is joined to idols: LET HIM ALONE*" (Hosea
4:17). Solomon warned, "Boast not thyself of *to morrow;* for thou knowest not what a day may bring forth"
(Prov. 27:1). Sinner friend, each time you resist the
Holy Spirit you have one less opportunity to become a
child of God—*and that is all the devil wants!* He
will never ask you to sign a contract to go to hell—he
just wants you to put off salvation *one day at a time.*
If the Holy Spirit convicts and calls you today, the
devil urges you to put Him off until tomorrow—and

so it goes until finally you will wake up in hell.

The Holy Spirit pleads, "To day if ye will hear His voice, harden not your heart" (Psalm 95:7, 8), and Proverbs 29:1 warns, "He, that being often reproved hardeneth his neck, shall suddenly be destroyed, and that without remedy!"

In the days of Noah, God declared, "My Spirit shall not always strive with man, for that he also is flesh: yet *his days shall be an hundred and twenty years*" (Gen. 6:3). The only reasonable explanation of this statement is that God was designating one hundred and twenty years from that time until the flood. His Spirit did not always strive with the people in Noah's day: they had one hundred and twenty years in which to repent before Noah finished the ark; but when the ark was finished and Noah and his family were safe inside, "the Lord shut him in" (Gen. 7:16) *and then the flood came!* Genesis 7:21—23 tells us, "All flesh died that moved upon the earth, both of fowl, and of cattle, and of beast, and of every creeping thing that creepeth upon the earth, *and every man: All in whose nostrils was the breath of life, of all that was in the dry land, died. And every living substance was destroyed* which was upon the face of the ground, both man, and cattle, and the creeping things, and the fowl of the heaven; and they were destroyed from the earth: *AND NOAH ONLY REMAINED ALIVE, and they that were with him in the ark.*" Noah was saved because he believed God—he found grace in the eyes of the Lord by faith (Gen. 6:8; Heb. 11:7).

The most dangerous thing an unsaved person will ever do is resist the Spirit of God. So if you hear the call of the Holy Spirit, if you feel impressed to become a Christian, just pray the simple prayer the publican prayed in the temple: "God be merciful to me, a sinner." Obey Romans 10:9, 10 and God will save you now: "If thou shalt confess with thy mouth the Lord Jesus, and shalt believe in thine heart that God hath raised Him from the dead, *thou shalt be saved.* For with the heart man believeth unto righteousness; and with the mouth confession is made unto salvation."

Grieving the Spirit:

"Grieve not the Holy Spirit of God, whereby ye are sealed unto the day of redemption" (Eph. 4:30).

What does it mean to grieve the Holy Spirit? Does it mean that He will depart from us? Indeed not! If I were living in your home it would be entirely possible for me to be grieved—and still remain in your home. We can say or do things that may *grieve* another member of our family but not necessarily drive them from our home.

In the verse just quoted we read that we are sealed by the Holy Spirit *"until the day of redemption"*—and this redemption speaks of the body, not of the spirit. If we were not redeemed, the Holy Spirit would not be in our hearts in the first place, and therefore could not be grieved. If *anything* is clear in the New Testament, it is certainly clear that no person is a Christian unless he possesses the Holy Spirit (John 3:5; Rom. 8:9).

A born again believer is *a child of God NOW* (I John 3:2).

Born again believers are *ALREADY "bought with a price"* (I Cor. 6:19, 20).

Our citizenship is in heaven (Phil. 3:20), we are but pilgrims and strangers here, and one glorious day Jesus will descend in the clouds and call us up to meet Him in the air. We will then be delivered from these bodies of weakness, sorrow, pain, and disappointment, for we will receive a glorified body. Corruption will put on incorruption, mortality will put on immortality.

Soul, spirit, and body will then be redeemed and our salvation will be perfected! *Until* that glorious moment, believers are *"SEALED with that Holy Spirit of promise,* which is the earnest of our inheritance until the redemption of the purchased possession..." (Eph. 1:13,14).

Jesus promised that the Holy Spirit would abide with believers forever (John 14:16), and until Jesus comes again to receive His own, the Spirit is our Comforter, our Helper, our Shield, our Guide. Thus we are more than conquerors, because the Holy Spirit leads us into paths of righteousness for the name's sake of Jesus.

There are many ways in which a believer may grieve the Holy Spirit. Needless to say, if a Christian should commit such sins as lying, swearing, stealing, or any other wicked thing, it would greatly grieve the Holy Spirit.

To the believers in Galatia, the Apostle Paul wrote: "This I say then, Walk in the Spirit, and ye shall not fulfil the lust of the flesh. For the flesh lusteth against the Spirit, and the Spirit against the flesh: and these are contrary the one to the other: so that ye cannot do the things that ye would. But if ye be led of the Spirit, ye are not under the law" (Gal. 5:16—18).

The Holy Spirit is necessarily grieved by anything unholy; but He can also be grieved by sins of *omission,* as well as sins of commission. Therefore He may be grieved by one whose *outward conduct* is above reproach. The Holy Spirit is in the world to bring glory and honor to the Lord Jesus Christ, and certainly He wants to lead us into the paths of righteousness, purity, and holiness in order that we may glorify HIM. The Spirit will lead us to be generous toward the Lord in our giving, with our service, and with our talents. James declares, "Therefore to him that knoweth to do good, and doeth it not, to him it is SIN" (James 4:17).

The Spirit will be grieved if we are inattentive and occupied with things of the world instead of listening to Him as He tries to lead us to the glory of God. He wants all that we say and all that we do to be to the glory of God the Father and the Lord Jesus Christ.

Quenching the Spirit:

The Apostle Paul instructed the Thessalonian believers, "Quench not the Spirit" (I Thess. 5:19).

Later, John the Beloved warned, "Beloved, believe not every spirit, *but try the spirits whether they are of God:* because many false prophets are gone out into the world" (I John 4:1). When the Holy Spirit leads us to witness, testify, or pray, we should obey His leading, but we must be sure that the One we follow is the Holy Spirit.

The primary purpose of the Holy Spirit's residence on earth is to glorify the Lord Jesus Christ by the formation of the New Testament Church which is the body and bride of Christ. He also works to gather believers into local assemblies, and if the born again Christian will pray and let the Spirit lead, he will certainly not be led to unite with the wrong church, but with an assembly that magnifies Christ, a church that stands as a lampstand in the community, giving forth the light of the Gospel.

In the first days of Christianity, all of the believers in the community assembled in one place. We find such record again and again in the New Testament. On the birthday of the Church, the believers "were all with one accord in one place" (Acts 2:1).

In Acts 20:7 we read that the disciples "came together to break bread," and in I Corinthians 14:23 Paul mentions the whole church coming "together into one place."

These scriptural references show us that the believers in the early Church acknowledged their unity by coming together for prayer, breaking of bread, thanksgiving, edification, and comfort; and in those days *almost every believer took part* in the worship, praise, and prayer service in the church. I fear that human arrangements have taken the place of divine order today. Men are "appointed" to officiate, rather than being led by the Spirit. I realize the need for organization and order, but modern religion has just about "organized" the Holy Spirit out of the local assembly—and certainly He finds little to do in the average church service.

I think you will agree that in most churches today a small minority of the members carry on the work while the majority of the members sit in the pews, put a little envelope in the offering plate once a week, and take the attitude that attending the Sunday service and contributing to the support of the pastor is all that is required of them! I am sure this is not the order the Holy Spirit would follow if He were in full charge today.

It is tragic for the unbeliever to *resist* the Holy Spirit, reject His call and refuse to be drawn to the door of salvation.

It is tragic for a believer to *grieve* the Spirit by disobedience and refusal to allow Him full sway in the Christian life.

It is equally tragic for local churches to *quench* the Spirit by refusing to allow Him to lead in the affairs of the assembly as well as in the life of individual members of the assembly.

Some People Lie to the Holy Spirit

"But a certain man named Ananias, with Sapphira his wife, sold a possession, and kept back part of the price, his wife also being privy to it, and brought a certain part, and laid it at the apostles' feet. But Peter said, Ananias, why hath Satan filled thine heart to lie to the Holy Ghost, and to keep back part of the price of the land? Whiles it remained, was it not thine own? and after it was sold, was it not in thine own power? Why hast thou conceived this thing in thine heart? Thou hast not lied unto men, but unto God.

"And Ananias hearing these words fell down, and gave up the Ghost: and great fear came on all them that heard these things. And the young men arose, wound him up, and carried him out, and buried him.

"And it was about the space of three hours after, when his wife, not knowing what was done, came in. And Peter answered unto her, Tell me whether ye sold the land for so much? And she said, Yea, for so much. Then Peter said unto her, How is it that ye have agreed together to tempt the Spirit of the Lord? Behold, the feet of them which have buried thy husband are at the door, and shall carry thee out.

"Then fell she down straightway at his feet, and yielded up the ghost: and the young men came in, and found her dead, and, carrying her forth, buried her by her husband. And great fear came upon all the Church, and upon as many as heard these things" (Acts 5:1—11).

First of all, the sin of lying to the Holy Spirit must not be confused with the sin of blasphemy against the Spirit. Ananias and Sapphira did not commit the unpardonable sin as such; nor should their sin be confused with resisting, grieving, or quenching the Spirit.

This is a sad commentary on the first people to lie to the Holy Spirit. Others have lied to Him in the same way since that time, but did not always meet with immediate destruction. Wherein, then, lay the peculiar awfulness of the sin that caused Peter to ask Ananias, "Why hath Satan filled thine heart to lie to the Holy Ghost?" What was this sin so deadly? Why did sudden destruction come upon Ananias and his wife?

These were the first days of the Church, a time of tremendous revival, spiritual power, and miracles. Many of the new Christians were sacrificing everything they owned in order to spread the good news of the grace of God. Houses and lands were secondary to this marvelous new faith they had come to know, and they were selling their property, giving the proceeds to the church, surrendering everything to be used to the glory of God, who had sent Jesus to die for their sins. To have anything to do with the new movement was to have to do with the Spirit of God because the movement was HIS. To introduce a deceitful element into such an atmosphere as existed at that time was a most serious thing.

In times of spiritual revival we have seen sin in the life of a prominent churchman take on added seriousness. Sin which hinders revival or someone who has a prominent part in that revival, has often been dealt with and frequently the transgressor has been cut off.

The Scripture does not tell us why Ananias and Sapphira decided to sell their property and give only part of their money—it was not compulsory that they give *any* of it. No one was asked to dispose of property; the Holy Spirit simply led them to do it. Ananias and Sapphira no doubt thought that their lie would not be detected, they would get away with their scheme, and they would have the praise of men.

But the Holy Spirit is omniscient—all-discerning, all-powerful, knowing all, seeing all, and revealing all. The sin of this man and his wife was revealed immediately and they both met instant destruction. It

is a terrible thing to plan and scheme to defraud God
and lie to the Holy Spirit! God forbid that anyone
reading these lines should ever be guilty of that sin.

The Earnest of Our Inheritance

"In (Christ) ye also trusted, after that ye heard
the word of truth, the Gospel of your salvation: in
whom also after that ye believed, ye were sealed with
that Holy Spirit of promise, which is the earnest of
our inheritance until the redemption of the purchased
possession, unto the praise of His glory" (Eph. 1:13,14).

Paul is here speaking of the glorious future which
awaits believers, and he tells us that God the Father
wrought this future for us, *saved* us *for* this future,
and has given us the earnest of the Spirit: "Now He
that hath wrought us for the selfsame thing is God,
who also hath given unto us the earnest of the Spirit"
(II Cor. 5:5).

The Holy Spirit as the seal upon the believer is
given on God's behalf, to denote that we are His purchased possession. We are not our own, we are bought
with a price (I Cor. 6:20). We are redeemed unto
God, and He has "sealed us, and given the earnest
of the Spirit in our hearts" (II Cor. 1:22). This He
has done that we might have comfort, assurance, and
stedfastness of heart.

As the earnest of our inheritance the Holy Spirit
gives us a keen spiritual vision concerning things that
are prepared for us in that land that is fairer than
day. He enables us to enjoy our spiritual birthright
and get a glimpse of heaven with the eye of understanding given to us in the inner man. We are citizens of heaven; and the Spirit is training us to *think
heavenly* and to long for the day when we shall reach
that glorious place which Jesus has gone to prepare
for His own.

Inspired of the Holy Ghost, the Apostle Paul penned these words for all believers: "As it is written, Eye hath not seen, nor ear heard, neither have entered into the heart of man, the things which God hath prepared for them that love Him. But God hath revealed them unto us by His Spirit: for the Spirit searcheth all things, yea, the deep things of God" (I Cor. 2:9, 10). Mortal eye has never seen, mortal ear has never heard—nor can the heart of man comprehend—the things God has prepared for His children! But these things have been revealed to us by the Holy Spirit who *"searcheth ALL things,"* even the deep things of God. Therefore true believers breathe heaven's atmosphere and have joy unspeakable and full of glory because we have "the earnest of the Spirit."

Peter, inspired of the Holy Spirit, penned *these* words of comfort and assurance:

"Blessed be the God and Father of our Lord Jesus Christ, which according to His abundant mercy hath begotten us again unto a lively hope by the resurrection of Jesus Christ from the dead, to an inheritance incorruptible, and undefiled, and that fadeth not away, reserved in heaven for you, who are kept by the power of God through faith unto salvation ready to be revealed in the last time. Wherein ye greatly rejoice, though now for a season, if need be, ye are in heaviness through manifold temptations: that the trial of your faith, being much more precious than of gold that perisheth, though it be tried with fire, might be found unto praise and honour and glory at the appearing of Jesus Christ: Whom having not seen, ye love; in whom, though now ye see Him not, yet believing, ye rejoice with joy unspeakable and full of glory: receiving the end of your faith, even the salvation of your souls" (I Pet. 1:3—9).

The Holy Spirit abiding in the heart of every born again believer is the *pledge* that we shall one day receive that inheritance which is reserved in heaven for us!

The Unpardonable Sin:
Blasphemy Against the Holy Ghost

"Then was brought unto Him one possessed with a devil, blind, and dumb: and He healed him, insomuch that the blind and dumb both spake and saw. And all the people were amazed, and said, Is not this the son of David? But when the Pharisees heard it, they said, This fellow doth not cast out devils, but by Beelzebub the prince of the devils.

"And Jesus knew their thoughts, and said unto them, Every kingdom divided against itself is brought to desolation; and every city or house divided against itself shall not stand: and if Satan cast out Satan, he is divided against himself; how shall then his kingdom stand? And if I by Beelzebub cast out devils, by whom do your children cast them out? Therefore they shall be your judges.

"But if I cast out devils by the Spirit of God, then the kingdom of God is come unto you. Or else how can one enter into a strong man's house, and spoil his goods, except he first bind the strong man? and then he will spoil his house. He that is not with me is against me; and he that gathereth not with me scattereth abroad. Wherefore I say unto you, All manner of sin and blasphemy shall be forgiven unto men: but the blasphemy against the Holy Ghost shall not be forgiven unto men. And whosoever speaketh a word against the Son of man, it shall be forgiven him: but whosoever speaketh against the Holy Ghost, it shall not be forgiven him, neither in this world, neither in the world to come" (Matt. 12:22—32).

Therefore we see that blasphemy against the Holy Spirit cannot and will not be forgiven—in time or eternity!

The definition of *"blaspheme"* is "to speak impiously or irreverently of God or things sacred; in general to speak evil of; to utter impious words or speak profanely against."

Blasphemy has always been a terrible sin in the sight of God. In the Old Testament economy there was no sacrifice to atone for it and the blasphemer was condemned to be stoned to death:

"He that blasphemeth the name of the Lord, he shall surely be put to death, and all the congregation shall certainly stone him: as well the stranger, as he that is born in the land, when he blasphemeth the name of the Lord, shall be put to death" (Lev. 24:16).

Thank God, it is different in this marvelous day of grace! In Mark 3:28, 29 Jesus said, "Verily I say unto you, ALL sins shall be forgiven unto the sons of men, and blasphemies wherewith soever they shall blaspheme: *but he that shall blaspheme AGAINST THE HOLY GHOST hath never forgiveness, but is in danger of eternal damnation."*

Before Paul was born again he was a blasphemer, and he compelled others to blaspheme the name of the Lord. In Acts 26:9—11 he testified, "I verily thought with myself, that I ought to do many things contrary to the name of Jesus of Nazareth. Which thing I also did in Jerusalem: and many of the saints did I shut up in prison, having received authority from the chief priests; and when they were put to death, I gave my voice against them. *And I punished them oft in every synagogue, AND COMPELLED THEM TO BLASPHEME;* and being exceedingly mad against them, I persecuted them even unto strange cities."

In I Timothy 1:12, 13 Paul testified, "I thank Christ Jesus our Lord, who hath enabled me, for that He counted me faithful, putting me into the ministry; *WHO WAS BEFORE A BLASPHEMER, AND A PER-*

*SECUTOR, and injurious: but I obtained mercy,
because I did it ignorantly in unbelief."*

Grace provides forgiveness for taking the Lord's
name in vain and blaspheming God the Father or Jesus the Son; but to blaspheme the Holy Ghost means
eternal damnation.

There are some sincere, well-meaning people who
fear that they have committed the unpardonable sin.
They confess that they have sinned against the light,
they have rejected the Gospel, resisted the call of the
Holy Spirit, and have gone deeper and deeper into sin
until their hearts have grown hard and calloused. Ad-
mittedly this is a serious condition, a terrible sin.   It
is dangerous beyond exaggeration to trifle with the
Word of God and continue in sin after being convinced
of the need to turn to God; but this is not *the unpardonable sin* which goes beyond rejecting Jesus and
turning away the Holy Spirit when He knocks at the
heart's door.   Even Ananias and Sapphira did not
commit the unpardonable sin of blasphemy against
the Holy Ghost.

In our text quoted from Matthew at the beginning
of this discussion, Jesus healed a boy who was blind,
deaf, and dumb.   Matthew tells us that the boy was
"possessed with a devil," and when Jesus healed him
the Pharisees declared, "This fellow (Jesus) doth not
cast out devils but *by Beelzebub the PRINCE of the
devils!"*   In Mark's account of the same occurrence
we read, "And the scribes which came down from
Jerusalem said, He hath Beelzebub, and by the prince
of the devils casteth He out devils" (Mark 3:22).

The statement is clear: Jesus performed a marvelous miracle, and the religious leaders *attributed that
miracle to Beelzebub,* prince of demons, and declared
that Jesus had "an unclean spirit" (Mark 3:30), which
means that they accused Him of being possessed of
demons.   Therefore, they committed the unpardonable

sin: Jesus cast out the demons and healed the boy *by the power of the Holy Spirit* (Matt. 12:28), and the scribes and Pharisees declared that the miracle was wrought by the power of *Beelzebub,* prince of demons. It was then that they sealed their doom, and they are burning in hell today!

We can sum up this part of our study by asking— and answering—four simple questions:

1. What *is* the unpardonable sin and can it be committed today?
2. *Who* can commit the unpardonable sin?
3. Who *will not* commit the unpardonable sin?
4. How can one know if *he has committed* the unpardonable sin?

The first question has already been answered in our previous study: The unpardonable sin is blasphemy against the Holy Spirit—i. e., attributing the works of the Holy Spirit to the spirit of Satan.

Can this sin be committed today? *Indeed it can!* This is the Dispensation of the Holy Spirit, who came into the world at Pentecost and will remain here until the Church is taken out. This has been fully discussed in earlier portions of this chapter. Men certainly can blaspheme the Holy Ghost today—and I am sure there are many who have done exactly that.

Who can commit the unpardonable sin? Any *unbeliever* is a candidate to commit this awful sin. Peter warns, "Be sober, be vigilant; because your adversary the devil, as a roaring lion, walketh about, seeking whom he may devour" (I Pet. 5:8). The uppermost desire of the devil is to damn the souls of men; and if he can cause a person to blaspheme the Holy Spirit he knows that person is *his property,* sealed and waiting to be delivered to the pits of hell! Therefore I say to every unbeliever reading these lines: If you have the faintest desire to become a Christian, fall on your knees this moment, repent of your sins, and

ask God to save you for Jesus' sake. He will save
you and will come to dwell in your heart.

Who will NOT commit the unpardonable sin? Born
again, blood-washed believers will never be guilty of
this sin:

Believers are *born* of the Spirit (John 3:5, 6).

Believers are *indwelt* by the Spirit (Rom. 8:9).

Believers are *led* by the Spirit (Rom. 8:14).

Believers are *assured* by the Spirit (Rom. 8:16).

Believers are *sealed* by the Spirit (Eph. 4:30).

The Holy Spirit draws us to God, "borns" us into
the family of God, indwells us, assures us of our salvation, seals us until the day of redemption and *leads
us* through our earthly pilgrimage; and He certainly
will not lead us to blaspheme His name! Therefore,
beloved, if you are a born again, blood-washed child
of God—saved by God's grace and kept by His power—
you may rest assured that you will never blaspheme
the Holy Spirit! You may *grieve* Him, you may be
guilty of *quenching* the Spirit, but you will never
blaspheme the third Person of the Godhead.

How can one *know* whether or not he has committed the unpardonable sin? Jesus declared that no
man can come to the Father except he be drawn by
the Holy Spirit (John 6:44). He also declared that
when the Holy Spirit came into the world He would
"reprove the world of sin, and of righteousness, and
of judgment" (John 16:7—11). Therefore the Holy
Spirit reproves and convicts men of sin and convinces
them that they should be saved and live righteously
in view of the fact that *all men* must face God's judgment and give an account of themselves before Him.
So if you have the desire to become a Christian—even
a slight desire—you may rest assured that you have
not committed the unpardonable sin.

Any person who is guilty of this terrible sin will
have a heart as hard as stone and as dead as wood.

There will be no desire to seek salvation by grace through faith in the shed blood of Jesus. The desire to become a Christian is planted in the heart through the operation of the Holy Spirit when a sinner hears the Word of God, and no one will seek God in sincerity unless he be *drawn by the Spirit.* If you are concerned about becoming a Christian, if you are aware in your heart that you should repent of your sins and be saved, you may know that you have not committed the unpardonable sin. *So get on your knees NOW* and ask God to save you! Today is the day of salvation, now is the accepted time; and if you put it off until tomorrow, even though you have not committed the unpardonable sin, you may be dead and in hell before you have another opportunity to be saved!

I firmly believe there are some people walking this earth today who are just as sure for hell as if they were already there! They have blasphemed the Holy Spirit and He will never again call or convict them, He will never again trouble them in any way.

The men who accused Jesus of casting out demons by the power of Beelzebub grew worse and worse, their hearts grew harder and harder, until at last they saw Jesus nailed to a cross on Calvary—and even then they mocked and jeered while He died! They had no desire to repent, they had no desire to receive Jesus as their promised Messiah and Saviour. So it will be with the person today who commits the unpardonable sin. He will grow more and more wicked as time goes on until finally the devil claims him completely and he opens his eyes in hell.

Access by One Spirit

Ephesians 2:18 is one of the verses in the New Testament where the three Persons of the Godhead are named in the same verse:

"For through Him *(Christ)* we both (Jew and Gentile) have access by one Spirit *(the Holy Spirit)* unto the Father *(Jehovah)*."

This verse is one of the many reasons why I know the Bible is God-breathed and verbally inspired. To the natural man it would seem sufficient to say, "Through *Christ* we have access unto the Father" — but the Holy Spirit is mentioned *in connection with* our access to God. The reason for this is found in the deeper meaning of the Greek word here translated *"access."* It means much more than our corresponding English word, more than having an entrance or an open door, or the right to enter. It means *"going through"* the door—and we know that Christ is the door (John 10:9), and through His shed blood the door to heaven is opened to all. The invitation is *"Whosoever WILL,* let him enter."

There are many, many people who unite with a local church, they are immersed in water, they give testimony to their church membership and to the goodness of God—*but they never pass THROUGH THE DOOR.* They have everything "religious" but they have never experienced the miracle of the new birth by faith through the operation of the Holy Spirit.

Through the shedding of His blood on the cross, Christ made access to God the Father possible for all who will come to God *by Him,* and the Holy Spirit is the One who leads us to *avail ourselves* of that open door. When the unbeliever hears the Word of God, the Holy Spirit *convicts* the unbeliever, takes him by the hand, as it were, and leads him through the open door of salvation.

How long has it been since you bowed on your knees and sincerely thanked God for loving you while you were yet without strength, dead in trespasses and sins? For even while we were in such despicable condition, God gave Jesus to die for us in order to open the door to salvation—and now nothing stands between us and the very presence of God! When we hear and answer the call of the Holy Spirit and enter the open door of salvation, we have access into the holy of holies through the precious blood of the Lord Jesus Christ:

"Having therefore, brethren, boldness to enter into the holiest by the blood of Jesus, by a new and living way, which He hath consecrated for us, through the veil, that is to say, His flesh" (Heb. 10:19, 20).

Through the Holy Spirit
the Believer is an Habitation of God

"For through Him we both have access by one Spirit unto the Father. Now therefore ye are no more strangers and foreigners, but fellowcitizens with the saints, and of the household of God; and are built upon the foundation of the apostles and prophets, Jesus Christ Himself being the chief corner stone; in whom all the building fitly framed together groweth unto an holy temple in the Lord: in whom ye also are builded together *for an habitation of God through the Spirit"* (Eph. 2:18—22).

"No man hath seen God at any time. If we love one another, *God dwelleth in us, and His love is perfected in us.* . . . And we have known and believed the love that God hath to us. God is love; and he that dwelleth in love dwelleth in God, *AND GOD IN HIM"* (I John 4:12, 16).

Tremendous truth! How it should humble our hearts to know that we are an habitation of God through the third Person of the Trinity! We who were poor, miserable sinners—Gentiles, aliens from the commonwealth of Israel, "strangers from the covenants of promise, having no hope, and without God in the world" (Eph. 2:11—13)—are builded together that God might live in us, that He might find in us the home of His great love.

Christ died for us and made possible the open door of salvation; and as we obey the call of the Spirit we are led through that door into the ark of safety in Christ in God (Col. 3:3). God's love abides in us, and we are His dwelling place.

In Revelation 21:3 we read, "Behold, the tabernacle of God is with men, and He will dwell with them, and they shall be His people, and God Himself shall be with them, and be their God." In that glorious new era when all things are made new, God will dwell with His people and bless them forever in His unveiled presence. Think of it! Dwelling in God, God dwelling in us—and He *does* dwell in the bosom of every believer.

Believers are *builded together* by the Holy Spirit, and by the Spirit God has taken possession of His purchased property. He has taken His redeemed ones for His habitation and He dwells in us and wills the things that please Him. "And we know that all things work together for good to them that love God, to them who are the called according to His purpose" (Rom. 8:28).

Since God is for us, who can be against us? The more we think on this glorious truth the more amazed we become. We stand in awe as the truth fully dawns upon us that through the indwelling of the Holy Spirit we are "an habitation of God"!

By the Holy Spirit
the Believer Is Strengthened in the Inner Man

To the Ephesian Christians the Apostle Paul wrote: ". . . I bow my knees unto the Father of our Lord Jesus Christ . . . That He would grant you, according to the riches of His glory, to be strengthened with might by His Spirit in the inner man; that Christ may dwell in your hearts by faith; that ye, being rooted and grounded in love, may be able to comprehend with all saints what is the breadth, and length, and depth, and height; and to know the love of Christ, which passeth knowledge, that ye might be filled with all the fulness of God. Now unto Him that is able to do exceeding abundantly above all that we ask or think, according to the power that worketh in us, unto Him be glory in the church by Christ Jesus throughout all ages, world without end. Amen" (Eph. 3:14–21).

Every true believer is keenly aware of his own weakness. We can do all things through Christ who strengthens us (Phil. 4:13), but *without* Him we can do *nothing* (John 15:5).

Why did Paul pray that the Ephesian believers would be "strengthened with might" by the Holy Spirit in the inner man? Did he want them to have this strength that they might demonstrate spiritual power and vigor in service? Was it that they might endure hardness and bear up under severe persecution and suffering for Christ's sake? Certainly Christians need spiritual strength in these days, but Paul's desire went much deeper than this: What he prayed for was that the Ephesians—and *all* believers—might be strengthened in the inner man; not only that Christ dwell in our hearts by faith, but that we might also comprehend the breadth, length, depth, and height of the love of Christ *"which passeth knowledge,"* and that we might be "filled with all the fulness of God." The desire of the true believer is to glorify Christ in every word and deed; and the only way this can be done is for the believer to be *strengthened BY THE HOLY SPIRIT in the inner man.*

Jesus told His disciples that when the Holy Spirit came, He would guide them into all truth: "For He shall not speak of Himself; but whatsoever He shall hear, that shall He speak: and He will shew you things to come. *HE SHALL GLORIFY ME: for He shall receive of mine, and shall shew it unto you.* All things that the Father hath are mine: therefore said I, that He shall take of mine, and shall shew it unto you" (John 16:13—15).

The Holy Spirit is in the world to bring glory and honor to the Lord Jesus Christ; and since He abides in our hearts He wants to give us strength and power— not that we may have glory and honor, not that our ministry and service may have praise of men, but that Christ may be glorified.

Hear these wonderful words of the Psalmist: "Many, O Lord my God, are thy wonderful works which thou hast done, and thy thoughts which are to us-ward: they cannot be reckoned up in order unto thee: if I would declare and speak of them, they are more than can be numbered!" (Psalm 40:5).

Then in Psalm 139:17, 18 we read, "How precious also are thy thoughts unto me, O God! how great is the sum of them! If I should count them, they are more in number than the sand: when I awake, I am still with thee."

Truly, the works of our God are numerous and wonderful! His thoughts to usward cannot "be reckoned up in order" for it is impossible for the finite mind to understand God's thoughts concerning His children. It is impossible for these human lips to pray in words that will adequately praise God for His wonderful works, His wonderful thoughts, and His wonderful provisions for us.

Notice in the last part of Ephesians 3:19 Paul prayed that the Ephesians might be *"filled with ALL the fulness of God."* Then in Colossians 2:9, 10 he declares that *IN CHRIST "dwelleth all the fulness of the Godhead bodily,"* and believers are *"complete*

IN HIM.'' Christ is the sum and substance of God's thoughts, purposes, and love; and Christ dwells in the heart of every believer, in the Person of the Holy Spirit. Thus are we made to understand, at least in some measure, the thoughts and wonderful works and immeasurable love of God that abides in our hearts. May God grant that each believer who reads these lines be strengthened with might by the Holy Spirit in the inner man, that honor and glory may be brought to the name of Christ.

Consider Daniel's unique experience, as recorded in chapter 10 of the book that bears his name: Through visions God revealed deep and wonderful things to Daniel; and after the revelations from God, the prophet was left without strength. In Daniel 10:8—19 (in part) we read:

"Therefore I was left alone, and saw this great vision, *and there remained no strength in me:* for my comeliness was turned in me into corruption, *and I retained no strength. . . .* And, behold, one like the similitude of the sons of men touched my lips: then I opened my mouth, and spake, and said unto him that stood before me, O my lord, by the vision my sorrows are turned upon me, and *I have retained no strength.* For how can the servant of this my lord talk with this my lord? for as for me, straightway there remained no strength in me, neither is there breath left in me.

"Then there came again and touched me one like the appearance of a man, and he strengthened me, and said, O man greatly beloved, fear not: peace be unto thee, be strong, yea, be strong. And when he had spoken unto me, I was strengthened, and said, *Let my lord speak;* for thou hast strengthened me.''

Notice when Daniel received strength, the uppermost desire of his heart was to hear more of the wonderful words of God; and so it is in the heart of the believer. Being strengthened in the inner man, we can truthfully declare:

> *More about Jesus would I know,*
> *More of His grace to others show;*
> *More of His saving fullness see,*
> *More of His love who died for me!*

The Fruit of the Spirit

"The fruit of the Spirit is love, joy, peace, long-suffering, gentleness, goodness, faith, meekness, temperance: against such there is no law" (Gal. 5:22, 23).

In John 15:1—8 Jesus said, *"I am the true vine,"* and then explained to the disciples that every branch connected to the vine bears fruit. He declared that God the Father is the husbandman, and He purges the fruit-bearing branch *"that it may bring forth MORE fruit."* He admonished His disciples, "Abide in me, and I in you. As the branch cannot bear fruit of itself, except it abide in the vine; no more can ye, except ye abide in me." Then in verse 8 He makes it very clear that God the Father is glorified when the Christian bears *"MUCH fruit."*

In this passage we notice "fruit . . . *more* fruit . . . and *MUCH fruit"*—and it is *quite possible* for a consecrated believer to bear "much fruit." The fully surrendered, Spirit-filled believer can bear all of the nine graces mentioned in our text from Galatians 5:22, 23. *True Christianity* produces Christian *character*—not just moral or legal correctness, but Christ reproduced in our daily living by the indwelling Holy Spirit.

Paul testified, "To me *to live* is Christ" (Phil. 1:21). In Galatians 2:20 he said, *"I am crucified with Christ: nevertheless I live; yet not I, but Christ liveth in me:* and the life which I now live in the flesh I live by the faith of the Son of God, who loved me, and gave Himself for me."

The truth of these verses should be the testimony of every born again, blood-bought believer! The Christian who is thus yielded to the will of God, completely mastered and controlled by the Holy Spirit, will manifest the graces belonging to the fruit of the Spirit and will be a living example of the Christ as He tabernacled among men.

It is *Christ* "who of God is made unto us wisdom, and righteousness, and sanctification, and redemption: that, according as it is written, He that glorieth, let him glory in the Lord" (I Cor. 1:30,31). *Apart* from Christ it is impossible to bear the fruits of righteousness because *He IS righteousness* and therefore He is *the source* of the fruits of righteousness. He produced and displayed righteousness as He tabernacled among men. Not even His enemies could convince Him of one unrighteous act! In this Dispensation of Grace, the believer is indwelt by the Spirit—and the work of the Spirit is to reproduce Christ in us. To the Philippian believers Paul wrote:

"This I pray: that your love may abound yet more and more in knowledge and in all judgment; that ye may approve things that are excellent; that ye may be sincere and without offence till the day of Christ; *being FILLED with the fruits of righteousness,* which are by Jesus Christ, unto the glory and praise of God" (Phil. 1:9—11).

When God looks at us He sees Jesus, and thus we are "accepted in the Beloved" (Eph. 1:6).

No man can possibly meet God in peace *apart* from Jesus. His declaration to Thomas was very clear: He said, "I am the way, the truth, and the life: *no man cometh unto the Father, BUT BY ME*" (John 14:6).

It is only as we completely yield to the Holy Spirit and set our affections on things above that we can display the fruit of the Spirit—love, joy, peace, longsuffering, gentleness, goodness, faith, meekness, temperance.

Emblems of the Holy Spirit

The dove:

The first mention of any doctrine or type in the Bible is always important. We first read of the *dove* in Genesis 8:6—12 in connection with the flood:

"And it came to pass at the end of forty days, that Noah opened the window of the ark which he had made: And he sent forth a raven, which went forth to and fro, until the waters were dried up from off the earth. Also he sent forth a *dove* from him, to see if the waters were abated from off the face of the ground; but the dove found no rest for the sole of her foot, and she returned unto him into the ark, for the waters were on the face of the whole earth: then he put forth his hand, and took her, and pulled her in unto him into the ark.

"And he stayed yet other seven days; and again he sent forth the dove out of the ark; and the dove came in to him in the evening; and, lo, in her mouth was an olive leaf pluckt off: so Noah knew that the waters were abated from off the earth.

"And he stayed yet other seven days; and sent forth the dove; which returned not again unto him any more."

Notice in verse 7 Noah sent out a *raven,* but the raven did not return to the ark. In Scripture, the raven is a type of the flesh—the natural man, the evil principle born in the heart of the natural man. All men are born in sin and shapen in iniquity. The unregenerated heart is deceitful and desperately wicked. The flood was the scene of judgment and death. Can you imagine the *untold numbers of dead bodies* after the flood—not only the bodies of people, but of animals as well? This was congenial to the *nature* of the raven; therefore he did not return to the ark.

Noah then sent out a dove—but the scene that met the eyes of the dove was unattractive to her and she "found no rest for the sole of her foot." In other words, she found nothing inviting outside the ark, nothing that would entice her to remain; therefore she returned to the ark.

The condition encountered by the dove when Noah first sent her out represents the condition of the world before the Lord Jesus Christ came to pay the sin-debt. In Matthew 3:16, 17 we are told that when Jesus was baptized "the heavens were opened unto him (John), and he saw the Spirit of God descending *like a dove, and lighting upon Him.*" Before Jesus came into the world there was not a man upon whom the Holy Spirit *could "rest."* He came upon certain men for specific ministries, empowered them for special services, and departed from them; but until Jesus came there was no person on earth upon whom He could *rest.*

After seven days, Noah sent forth the dove *a second time*—which is representative of this present age. When the dove went out the second time she found at least one tree that had risen above the judgment waters, and when she returned to the ark this time, she carried an olive leaf. In this day of God's grace there is One who emerged from under the horrible judgment of Almighty God, One who bore our sins and nailed them to His cross. The Lord Jesus Christ suffered the penalty of the law and all that sin demands. He purchased our liberty and set us free (John 8:32, 36).

On the Day of Pentecost, the Holy Spirit came down from heaven and took up residence on earth. He brought the olive branch of peace, and He abides in the heart of every born again believer. When the dove brought the olive leaf to Noah, he knew that the flood waters were subsiding and dry land was appearing. Jesus said, "I must depart—but I will send the Comforter, and He will testify of me."

When the dove went out from the ark the *third* time, the renewed earth, delivered from the flood, was congenial to her and she returned no more to the ark. The regenerated heart is a congenial home for the Holy Spirit, and He abides there—in the heart of every true believer! In that glorious kingdom that is to be, the Holy Spirit will be poured out on all flesh.

In that glorious day, Jehovah will take away the shame and the reproach of His elect nation, Israel: "Yea, the Lord will answer and say unto His people, Behold, I will send you corn, and wine, and oil, and ye shall be satisfied therewith: and I will no more make you a reproach among the heathen" (Joel 2:19).

At that time the prosperity of Jerusalem and Palestine will be abundantly restored: "Be glad then, ye children of Zion, and rejoice in the Lord your God: for He hath given you the former rain moderately, and He will cause to come down for you the rain, the former rain, and the latter rain in the first month. And the floors shall be full of wheat, and the fats shall overflow with wine and oil. And I will restore to you the years that the locust hath eaten, the cankerworm, and the caterpiller, and the palmerworm, my great army which I sent among you" (Joel 2:23—25).

The nation Israel will then be satisfied in their land: "And ye shall eat in plenty, and be satisfied, and praise the name of the Lord your God, that hath dealt wondrously with you: and my people shall never be ashamed" (Joel 2:26). Then it is that the Lord God will pour out His Spirit upon all flesh, and the whole earth will be congenial to the Holy Spirit in that glorious day.

The dew:

In the Old Testament economy, while Israel was in the wilderness, *dew* was an emblem of the Holy

Spirit. In Exodus 16:13—15 we read, "And it came to pass, that at even the quails came up, and covered the camp: and in the morning *the dew lay round about the host.* And when the dew that lay was gone up, behold, upon the face of the wilderness there lay a small round thing, as small as the hoar frost on the ground. And when the children of Israel saw it, they said one to another, It is manna: for they wist not what it was. And Moses said unto them, This is the bread which the Lord hath given you to eat."

Then in Numbers 11:9 we read, "And *when the dew fell* upon the camp in the night, *the manna fell upon it.*"

The *manna* is a type of Christ in His earthly life and ministry, and there are several ways in which comparisons may be made:

The manna was said to be *"small."* Jesus came the first time as a babe, a Lamb, as a tender plant out of dry ground. He made Himself of no reputation and took upon Himself the form of a servant.

Manna was also *"round"*—denoting no unevenness. This was true of the character of Jesus. There was no unevenness in His character or in His earthly life.

Manna was *"white"*—a type of the purity and perfection of Jesus. He was untouched by sin, there was no guile in Him.

Manna was sweet, "like wafers made with honey" (Ex. 16:31). Jesus was the sweetness of God's eternal love, wrapped up in flesh!

John 6:22—59 records our Lord's discourse on the bread of life. In verse 31 those who questioned Jesus spoke of the manna as "bread from heaven." In verse 33 Jesus referred to *Himself* as "the bread of God . . . which cometh down from heaven, and giveth life unto the world," and in verse 48 He plainly stated: *"I AM that bread of life."*

Now notice: The manna was given *only when the DEW lay on the ground* in the stillness of the desert night. If we keep in mind that the dew is a type of the Holy Spirit, then we know that *the appearing of the manna* depended upon *the dew.* Just so, it is impossible for man to know the sweetness of the grace of God and the purity of life in Christ *apart from the Holy Spirit.* "The *natural* man receiveth not the things of the Spirit of God: for they are foolishness unto him: neither can he know them, because they are spiritually discerned" (I Cor. 2:14).

It is impossible for the natural man to know communion with Christ. Such communion comes only when one is born again through the miracle of the new birth by the operation of the Holy Spirit. Jesus declared, "It is the Spirit that quickeneth; the flesh profiteth nothing: the words that I speak unto you, they are spirit, and they are life" (John 6:63). The Holy Spirit attracts and draws us to Jesus, we receive Him, and the Spirit takes up His abode in our hearts and glorifies Christ in our lives as we yield to Him. The more fully yielded we are, the sweeter our communion with Christ.

There is another extremely interesting thing about the manna God gave the Israelites in the wilderness: *It was not appreciated for very long.* They soon tired of it. They complained to Moses, "Our soul is dried away: there is nothing at all, beside this manna, before our eyes" (Num. 11:6). There are plenty of people today who attend church—*but they are tired of Jesus.* If you invite them out to hear a man of God who truly preaches the Word, or a fundamental evangelist who declares, "Thus saith the Lord," they say, "We would *like* to attend your church—but all you people do is talk about Jesus, sing about Jesus, pray to Jesus; and we like a religion with a little less 'Jesus' and a little more entertainment. We want something to make us *laugh.*"

These are the words of unregenerate people. They do not like to sing of "the old rugged cross," nor of the "happy day" when Jesus washed their sins away. They do not like to sing, "Amazing grace—how sweet the sound that saved a wretch like me!" They are tired of these songs, and they have written new ones which by-pass Jesus, the blood, and heaven.

But thank God, in our churches today we still find that precious nucleus on whom the *dew* has fallen! They enjoy Christ, and the more you sing about Him and talk about Him, *the more they enjoy Him.* They feed on the "manna"—the Bread of Life. They appropriate His Word with joy, and their happiest moments are when they are in God's house or with a group of saints of like faith, singing, praying, and praising the wonderful name of Jesus.

The oil:

Throughout the Old Testament economy, *oil* is an emblem of the Holy Spirit. It was used in connection with the meat-offering which is a type of the holy humanity of Christ.

In the ritual of the meat-offering, oil was used in a twofold way:

First: The fine flour which constituted the offering was mingled with oil and the offering was anointed with oil (Lev. 2:5, 6).

Second: The offering contained no leaven (Lev. 2:5, 11). Leaven is a symbol of evil; therefore leaven in the meat-offering would certainly spoil that offering as a type of Christ, the Holy One who was untouched by sin. (In connection with this part of our study, please read the entire second chapter of Leviticus.)

The fact that this offering was mingled with *oil* sets forth the virgin birth of Jesus—conceived of the Holy Ghost: The angel of the Lord appeared to Joseph in a dream, saying, "Joseph, thou son of David, fear not to take unto thee Mary thy wife: *for that which is conceived in her is of THE HOLY GHOST"* (Matt. 1:20). In Luke 1:35 we are told that the angel said to Mary, *"The HOLY GHOST shall come upon thee, and the power of the Highest shall overshadow thee: therefore also that holy thing which shall be born of thee shall be called the Son of God."*

Jesus was born of a human mother but God Almighty was His Father. Therefore He was "that holy thing . . . the Son of God." The fact and manner of His birth proved that there was in His substance that which answered to the mingling with oil which made Him, even in His humanity, infinitely more than any other man ever born of woman.

The Seven Spirits of God

"John to the seven churches which are in Asia: Grace be unto you, and peace, from Him which is, and which was, and which is to come; *and from the seven Spirits which are before His throne"* (Rev. 1:4).

The seven Spirits of God is a perplexing statement to many Bible readers. Immediately someone will ask, "Is there more than one Holy Spirit?" Certainly not. The Word of God answers, "There is *ONE body,* and *ONE Spirit,* even as ye are called in one hope of your calling; *ONE Lord, ONE faith, ONE baptism, ONE God* and Father of all, who is above all, and through all, and in you all" (Eph. 4:4—6). We are all baptized into one body by one Spirit, and have all been made to drink into one Spirit—the third Person of the Godhead.

The book of Revelation itself (in which the words "seven Spirits" occur) teaches *ONE Spirit* (Rev. 1:10; 22:17); but the phrase "seven Spirits" is used to assure us of the completeness, the fulness, and the diversified actions and ministries of *the ONE Holy Spirit.*

Isaiah 11:2 enlightens us: "And the Spirit of the Lord shall rest upon Him, the Spirit of wisdom and understanding, the Spirit of counsel and might, the Spirit of knowledge and of the fear of the Lord."

1. The Spirit of Jehovah
2. The Spirit of wisdom
3. The Spirit of understanding
4. The Spirit of counsel
5. The Spirit of might
6. The Spirit of knowledge
7. The Spirit of the fear of Jehovah

The fulness of the Spirit is in Christ; and we can rest assured that whatever state the church may be in—it may have left its first love, it may be corrupt, it may be dead—but there is in Him who is in the midst of the golden candlesticks adequate spiritual power to meet every need, regardless of what that need may be.

The Holy Spirit as the Teacher

Several remarkable truths are declared in I Corinthians chapter 2 concerning the Holy Spirit. We have not space to include the entire chapter, but we will consider several outstanding verses:

Verse 4: "And my speech and my preaching was not with enticing words of man's wisdom, but in demonstration of the Spirit and of power."

The Holy Spirit gives the message to God's minister to declare to the listeners, and He clothes that message with the power of God. Thus does the minister demonstrate the power of the Holy Spirit—and a man who does *not* preach under the Spirit's power is simply beating the air. His message is empty and lifeless.

Verses 9 and 10: "But as it is written, Eye hath

not seen, nor ear heard, neither have entered into the heart of man, the things which God hath prepared for them that love Him. *But God hath revealed them unto us BY HIS SPIRIT: for the Spirit searcheth all things, yea, the deep things of God."* The Holy Spirit is co-equal with God the Father and God the Son and He knows all things. As Father and Son are omniscient, so is the Spirit omniscient. He knows and understands the deep things of God, He searches all things, and He makes known to us the wonderful things God has prepared—and is preparing—for us in eternity.

Verse 11: "For what man knoweth the things of a man, save the spirit of man which is in him? Even so the things of God knoweth no man, but the Spirit of God." Since the third Person of the Trinity is co-equal with Father and Son in all things, He knows the things of God in the same way *our* spirit knows the things of man.

Verse 12: "Now we have received, not the spirit of the world, but the Spirit which is of God; that we might know the things that are freely given to us of God."

All born again believers have received "the Spirit which is of God"—the Holy Spirit; therefore we do not have the spirit of the world. We cannot even feel *at home* in this world because *our citizenship is in heaven.* We sit together in heavenly places in Christ Jesus, we are hid with Christ in God. The Christian is at home in the things of God, not in the things of this world. We are *in* the world, but we are no longer *of* the world. We are pilgrims traveling to that land that is fairer than day, and as we travel, the Holy Spirit abides in the inner man to lead us and direct us.

Verse 13: "Which things also we speak, not in the words which man's wisdom teacheth, but which the

Holy Ghost teacheth; comparing spiritual things with spiritual."

The most capable teacher of any book is the author of that book. The Holy Spirit is the Author of the Bible and certainly He is the most efficient Teacher of the truths of God. As the Holy Spirit moved upon holy men of old, they penned down the words He gave them. Today He teaches us in our study of the Word—and that is the only possible way to understand the Scriptures. The New Testament is infolded in the Old, and the Old Testament is unfolded in the New; and unless we allow the Word itself (taught us by the Holy Spirit) to be the final commentary we will never understand the Scriptures.

Verse 14: "But the natural man receiveth not the things of the Spirit of God: for they are foolishness unto him: neither can he know them, because they are spiritually discerned."

This verse tells us *why* no one can understand the things of God apart from the Holy Spirit. The natural man cannot receive the things of God because those "things of the Spirit of God" are spiritual and man is carnal. Certainly spirituality and carnality cannot commune. Therefore one must be born of the Spirit before he can understand or accept the truths of God.

The Holy Spirit and the Unbeliever

"I will pray the Father, and He shall give you another Comforter, that He may abide with you for ever; even the Spirit of truth; *whom the world cannot receive, because it seeth Him not, neither knoweth Him:* but ye know Him; for He dwelleth with you, and shall be in you" (John 14:16, 17).

"Nevertheless I tell you the truth: It is expedient for you that I go away: for if I go not away, the Comforter will not come unto you; but if I depart, I

will send Him unto you. And when He is come, He
will reprove the world of sin, and of righteousness, and
of judgment: Of sin, because they believe not on me;
Of righteousness, because I go to my Father, and ye
see me no more; Of judgment, because the prince of
this world is judged" (John 16:7—11).

The unbeliever cannot receive the Holy Spirit until
he has *heard and believed* the Word of God. It is
when the unbeliever hears the Gospel and places his
faith in the finished work of the Lord Jesus Christ
that the Holy Spirit "borns" that one into the family
of God and baptizes him into the body of Christ. The
Spirit then takes up residence in the heart of that
individual and remains there, sealing him until the
day of redemption (Eph. 4:30).

The First and Last Mention
of the Holy Spirit in the Bible

"And the earth was without form, and void; and
darkness was upon the face of the deep. *And THE
SPIRIT OF GOD moved upon the face of the waters*"
(Gen. 1:2). We have already discussed this first mention of the Spirit as He moved with divine energy and
power, giving effect to the Word by which all things
were created and brought into existence.

As God the Father and God the Son are omniscient,
omnipotent, and omnipresent, so is the Holy Spirit.
Therefore with omniscient foresight He moved in divine power and wrought in the earth the great arena
where, in centuries to come, the program of God would
be carried out; and where, eventually, the Lamb of
God would suffer and die for the sin of mankind. The
Holy Spirit is the mighty power by which God the
Father worked in creation, the power by which He
would work in the world throughout the generations
that would *follow* creation. It is by the power of the

Holy Spirit that God will bring about His own gracious, eternal designs—not for man alone, but for the entire creation.

The Holy Spirit was present with the Father and Son in the beginning, He was present at the creation of all things, He has operated on behalf of the souls of men to the glory of God through all the ages past, and He will continue to work until the consummation of all things; and then, Father, Son, and Holy Spirit will abide with God's people through the endless ages of eternity.

So in the first mention of the Holy Spirit, we see His divine power and energy in creation to the honor and glory of God—and in that eternal kingdom, all things will glorify God the Father, and all worship, adoration, and praise will be directed to Him.

The last mention of the Holy Spirit is in Revelation 22:17: *"The SPIRIT and the bride say, COME. And let him that heareth say, Come. And let him that is athirst come. And whosoever will, let him take the water of life freely."*

Here we are approaching the end of God's dealings with man—and with the earth as we know it. John the Beloved was exiled to Patmos for his testimony concerning Christ, and in Revelation 17:3 he was carried away "in the Spirit" into the wilderness to view the terrible judgment that will bring destruction upon the counterfeit bride, the great whore: "And I saw a woman sit upon a scarlet coloured beast, full of names of blasphemy, having seven heads and ten horns."

After John saw the destruction of the counterfeit bride, he was again caught away by the Spirit "to a great and high mountain," where he saw the *true* bride, the New Jerusalem, "descending out of heaven from God, having the glory of God: and her light was like unto a stone most precious, even like a jasper stone, clear as crystal" (Rev. 21:10, 11). This magnificent place will be the home of the bride, the New Testament Church. We will dwell there with the Bridegroom, the Lord Jesus Christ; and we will have access to all of God's new creation. There will be no more trace of sin and sorrow, and all the saved nations will walk in the light of that glorious city!

But that glorious era cannot come until Jesus comes to receive His bride unto Himself. In the closing verses of the last chapter of Revelation He presents Himself as the coming One, the Bright and Morning Star, and in Revelation 22:20 we read:

"He which testifieth these things saith, Surely I come quickly. Amen." And John the Beloved answers, *"Even so, COME, LORD JESUS!"* In other words, "Come *quickly*, Jesus. We are pilgrims and strangers. Our citizenship is in heaven. Come quickly and take us to our heavenly home!" This should be the prayer and the heart-cry of every truly born again Christian.

As I bring this chapter to a close, my sincere prayer is that this study has enlightened your heart and strengthened you in the inner man. Rejoice! because the Holy Spirit of God dwells in the heart of every born again believer. He leads us into paths of right living, He bears witness with our spirit that we are the children of God, and He seals us until the day of redemption. We also have the assurance that the Spirit who raised up Jesus from the dead will also raise our mortal bodies, this corruption will put on incorruption and this mortal will put on immortality.

Chapter Eight

BIBLE TRUTH CONCERNING MAN

"All Scripture is given by inspiration of God, and is profitable for doctrine, for reproof, for correction, for instruction in righteousness: that the man of God may be perfect, throughly furnished unto all good works" (II Tim. 3:16, 17).

"We have also a more sure word of prophecy; whereunto ye do well that ye take heed, as unto a light that shineth in a dark place, until the day dawn, and the day star arise in your hearts: Knowing this first, that no prophecy of the Scripture is of any private interpretation. For the prophecy came not in old time by the will of man: but holy men of God spake as they were moved by the Holy Ghost" (II Pet. 1:19—21).

"Study to shew thyself approved unto God, a workman that needeth not to be ashamed, rightly dividing the word of truth" (II Tim. 2:15).

". . . Let God be true, but every man a liar . . ." (Rom. 3:4).

The Bible is God-breathed. Both the Old and the New Testaments are the Word of the living God, the revelation of God to man. The Bible does not record man's quest for God, but rather God's revelation of Himself in His quest for man whom He created in His own image.

The Origin of Man

I am persuaded that the Bible is the verbally inspired, infallible Word of Jehovah God, in whom I trust and to whom I am responsible. With this firm conviction, I turn to the pages of His Word to see what it tells me about myself. From whence came I? Where did I originate? Did man, over a period of millions of years, *evolve upward* from a lower form of life, perhaps from a one-cell amoeba? *Or—as the* Bible teaches—*was man CREATED by an immediate and direct act of Almighty God?* The only place to find the right answer is in the Word of God:

In Genesis 1:26, 27 we read, "And God said, Let us make man in our image, after our likeness: and let them have dominion over the fish of the sea, and over the fowl of the air, and over the cattle, and over all the earth, and over every creeping thing that creepeth upon the earth. *So God created man in His own image, in the image of God created He him; male and female created He them."*

In Genesis 2:7 we find this additional truth: *"And the Lord God formed man of the dust of the ground, AND BREATHED INTO HIS NOSTRILS THE BREATH OF LIFE; and man became a living soul!"*

We are told that *barah* is the Hebrew word here translated "create," and this Hebrew word occurs more than fifty times in the Old Testament. When it appears in the active voice, *Almighty God is the subject* because He alone can perform the act expressed by *barah.* It is this Hebrew word which is used in the first verse of our Bible in speaking of the creation of this universe.

There was a time in the everlasting ages behind us when *only GOD existed* and only He could put forth the creative act which resulted in this universe being brought into existence. But the earth suffered disaster and was reduced to desolation, darkness, and waste. It became "without form, and void; and darkness was upon the face of the deep" (Gen. 1:2). No one knows how many thousands, millions, or perhaps *billions* of years elapsed between the time of the original creation of the universe and the time when God brought order out of chaos; but *at some time* following the terrible judgment that struck the earth, God repaired the damage wrought and in six days remodeled the wrecked, twisted earth in order that it might receive man, whom God created on the sixth day of that period of reconstruction.

God is omniscient, knowing the end in the beginning. It was no secret to Him that man would be created. In the everlasting ages behind us, the Holy Trinity—Father, Son, and Holy Spirit—held a conference where they planned and decreed that man would be created in the image of God and after His likeness. This was the crowning work of God's six days of reconstruction, and the Hebrew word *barah* indicates that in the creation of man the Godhead brought forth a new type of life that had never existed since the beginning—something different from anything that had been created up to that time. (*Barah* means to bring into existence that which up to its being brought into existence did not exist in any form or substance.) Adam was thus patterned after the likeness and in the image of his Creator.

God formed man's body from the dust of the earth, and up to that point Adam was only a dust-man— without movement, without ability to think, reason, love, or hate. Then God "breathed into his nostrils the breath of life *and man became a living soul*" (Gen. 2:7). Thus did God create that which had never existed up to that moment.

What is meant by the statement that God created man *in His image and after His likeness?* To what do the image and the likeness of God refer? In John 4:24 Jesus said to the woman of Samaria, *"God is a SPIRIT:* and they that worship Him must worship Him in spirit and in truth." I believe the Scriptures declare that man was created in the image and likeness of God in His *spirit-nature.*

In Ephesians 4:23, 24 Paul urges believers to "be renewed in the *spirit of your mind;* and that ye put on the new man, which *after God is created in righteousness and true holiness."*

In Romans 8:29 we are told that those whom God foreknew "He also did predestinate to be conformed to the image of His Son, that He might be the firstborn among many brethren."

In II Corinthians 3:18 Paul wrote, "But we all, with open face beholding as in a glass the glory of the Lord, are changed into the same image from glory to glory, even as by the Spirit of the Lord."

In Colossians 1:15 we are told that Christ "is the image of the invisible God, the firstborn of every creature," and in Colossians 2:9, 10 we read, "In HIM dwelleth all the fulness of the Godhead bodily. And ye are complete in Him, which is the head of all principality and power."

From these Scriptures we clearly see that the image and likeness of God (in which image and likeness man was created) here refers to the intellectual, moral, and spirit-nature of man; but the following passages certainly suggest that God also created man in the *visible* likeness of Himself. Yes, even though God is Spirit, He manifests Himself to the eye:

The Psalmist declared, "As for me, I will behold thy face in righteousness: I shall be satisfied, when I awake, with thy likeness" (Psalm 17:15).

Isaiah testified, "In the year that King Uzziah died I saw also the Lord sitting upon a throne, high and lifted up, and His train filled the temple" (Isa. 6:1).

Stephen declared, as the stones cast by his enemies beat the life from his body, "I see the heavens opened, and the Son of man standing on the right hand of God" (Acts 7:56).

In Philippians 2:6 the Apostle Paul explains that Jesus was "in the form of God," and "thought it not robbery to be equal with God."

Also, in Genesis 5:1—3 we read, "This is the book of the generations of Adam. In the day that God created man, *in the likeness of God* made He him; male and female created He them; and blessed them, and called their name Adam, in the day when they were created. And Adam lived an hundred and thirty years, *and begat a son IN HIS OWN LIKENESS, AFTER HIS IMAGE*; and called his name Seth."

We do not know how much of God's physical likeness Adam lost in the fall, nor do we know to what extent Adam was created in the visible image of God; but we do know he paid a tremendous price for his act of disobedience! How precious and assuring to our hearts is the divine truth that when we are regenerated through faith in the shed blood of Jesus Christ, God creates within us a *new* man:

"If so be that ye have heard Him, and have been taught by Him, as the truth is in Jesus: that ye put off concerning the former conversation the old man, which is corrupt according to the deceitful lusts; and be renewed in the spirit of your mind; and that ye *PUT ON THE NEW MAN, which after God is created in righteousness and true holiness*" (Eph. 4:21—24).

Thus does fallen man *"put on the NEW man, which is renewed in knowledge after the image of Him that created Him"* (Col. 3:10).

"Whereby are given unto us exceeding great and precious promises: that by these ye might be *partakers of the DIVINE NATURE,* having escaped the corruption that is in the world through lust" (II Pet. 1:4).

"Therefore if any man be in Christ, he is a new creature: old things are passed away; behold, *ALL things are become NEW*" (II Cor. 5:17).

Yes, even now, in these bodies of humiliation, we are created anew in Christ Jesus; and when He comes in the Rapture and in the first resurrection, our regeneration will be complete in our *visible* likeness to Him. We possess His spiritual likeness now through the miracle of the new birth, but "we know that, *when He shall appear, we shall be LIKE Him;* for we shall see Him as He is" (I John 3:2).

"For our conversation (citizenship) is in heaven; from whence also we look for the Saviour, *the Lord Jesus Christ: who shall change our vile body, that it may be fashioned LIKE UNTO HIS GLORIOUS BODY*, according to the working whereby He is able even to subdue all things unto Himself" (Phil. 3:20,21).

In John 17:5 Jesus prayed, "And now, O Father, glorify thou me with thine own self with the glory which I had with thee before the world was." Philippians 2:6 also tells us that Christ was in the form of God. Since in that resurrection morning all believers will be in the form of Christ, and Christ was in the form of God, we know that we will also be like unto the Father. Glorious truth! Praise His name!

Numbers chapter 16 records God's terrible judgment upon Korah. In verses 20—22 of that chapter we read, "And the Lord spake unto Moses and unto Aaron, saying, Separate yourselves from among this congregation, that I may consume them in a moment. And (Moses and Aaron) fell upon their faces, and said, *O God, the God of the spirits of all flesh,* shall one man sin, and wilt thou be wroth with all the congregation?"

In Hebrews 12:9 Paul speaks of God as "*the Father of spirits.*" From these Scriptures (and there are many others like them) we see that not only is *God* Spirit,

He is also *the Father of the spirits of men.* Therefore we must conclude that man is the direct creation of Almighty God—and from the standpoint of *creation* all men *are* sons of God. NOTICE: I said from the standpoint of *creation,* not from the standpoint of *redemption.* Only those who are *believers* are sons of God by redemption.

Man is not the product of evolution, but of God's mighty creative hand—and Adam was the first man. There is not one word of Scripture to suggest that such a person as Adam ever existed upon the original earth. Certainly a righteous, holy, and perfect God could not create a universe without form, engulfed in darkness. God is light, and in its original state this earth was perfect, a magnificent Paradise—and I personally believe it was inhabited by angels, cherubim, seraphim, spirit beings, although I have no Scripture to prove this. But *man* did not exist in the original creation. It was after God's reconstruction, on the sixth day of His creative work, that He made man—and He made him in His own image and after His own likeness.

The evolutionists speak of "the missing link"—a form of animal life which they maintain existed in the evolutionary process intermediate between man and the lower animals. They continue their search for this "missing link," suggesting that only a narrow chasm lies between man and the higher species of the animal kingdom. However, *facts prove* that *not* a narrow chasm, but *a great gulf* separates man (created in the image of Almighty God) from the brute beast. I have studied extensively on this subject using books written by scholars, and I offer here, in brief, what I have discovered in my studies of books by these learned men.

There are many outstanding ways in which man differs from animals:

The beast of the field is conscious, but he is not *self*-conscious—i. e., a cow cannot say, "I am a cow," a horse cannot say, "I am a horse." The cow and the horse do not differentiate between themselves and their sensations. The horse, for instance, *perceives things,* but he is unlike man in that he does not have *apperception*—that is, he does not have perception characterized by clearness and by the relating of what is now presented to knowledge previously acquired.

The animal has percepts—he sees (and in a limited way understands) what comes before him; but he does not have *concepts.* He does not have the power of mind to form ideas or to devise schemes or designs, as in works of art. For example, a dog does not have the ability to plan or prepare a blueprint for the building of a doghouse; but when his master plans and constructs a doghouse, the dog knows what it is for, and on a cold, stormy night he is conscious of the fact that he will be warm and dry inside the house whereas he would be cold and miserable if he stayed *outside.*

Beasts do not have a language in the strict sense of the word. Language is the vehicle of thought by which man expresses himself and makes known his thoughts, desires, and plans. Animals do not have this ability. Beasts are unable to interpret words, therefore they are incapable of language. It is true that they communicate, but not by language in the true definition of the term. We might ask, "What about the *parrot?*" A parrot is able to learn words and short sentences, but this in no wise can be considered as possessing *language.* Words are symbols of ideas or concepts; therefore where there is no concept there is no language. A parrot does not have the ability to think, reason, plan, and make known its thoughts and plans through words. Man's language, consisting of words which are the symbol of his ideas, makes man superior to the beast.

Only man has the capacity to associate ideas of similar nature, only man is capable of expressing judgment. For instance, if a dog comes to a busy highway where cars are rushing to and fro, the dog does not have the ability to judge the distance between himself and a car which is approaching at high speed. He cannot, through reason, decide whether or not he has time to cross the road before the car strikes him. In most instances the dog will attempt to beat the speed of the car by dashing across the road as fast as he can run. Sometimes the animal wins, but most of the time the automobile wins; and as we travel the highways we see the bodies of animals that have been killed by cars—mute testimony to the fact that the beast lacks the ability to reason and make proper judgment.

Animals know nothing about the law of causation— the relation between antecedents and consequences. Only man, created in the image of God, possesses this capability. Great men have given their lives to the study of the nature and habits of beasts, and in their studies and research it has been proved that animals perform various acts *by instinct*. Also, *by repetition* they can be trained to do wonderful things—but *only* by repetition; and the animal is always rewarded in some way—perhaps with a tasty morsel of some food of which he is particularly fond, something man would call "dessert." Without the repetitious training and the dessert, the animal would not perform, for he acts only by instinct and by continual repetition.

Animals have no general idea of time, substance, or space. They have no conception of right or wrong. A dog has no conviction that it is wrong for him to kill another dog—but it is born in the heart of man that murder is wrong and that he is not to kill his fellowman. The baby, as he grows into childhood, even before he is old enough to attend school, knows it is wrong for him to take another child's toy; and if a child steals a toy, he will immediately attempt to hide it! If a mother tells the small child not to take candy or cookies and the child disobeys her, he will make every effort to conceal what he has done. By contrast, the animal kingdom does not attempt to hide *anything*—killing, stealing, or any other overt act— because animals do not have the gift God planted in the heart of man.

Animals cannot reason from the specific to the general; therefore they make no progress or advancement. The sparrow builds its nest today in exactly the same way sparrows built their nests when Jesus walked on earth—but men do not build the same type houses today as were built in the days of Christ's earthly ministry. They build better houses today because of man's ability to advance.

We might also note that the sparrow builds its *first* nest as perfectly as it builds its last—there is no progress, it is always the same. This can also be said of the beaver, the fox, the rabbit. They follow the same order of life they have followed down through the centuries. Nor has the honey bee improved on the honeycomb! But this is not true of man, the highest creation of Almighty God. He alone has the ability to form judgments, make generalizations, recognize and profit by the law of causation. Man alone has the ability to make certain combinations of abstract or general ideas. God gave this gift to man—He did not give it to the lower animals.

Any person—regardless of educational degrees— who suggests that man evolved from a one-cell amoeba and progressed through the animal kingdom up to his present state, is simply advertising his own incredible ignorance. If man *is* the product of evolution, then evolution is in reverse—downward, not upward; because in the spiritual sense man is further from God today than he was a thousand years ago *and the judgment of Almighty God hangs heavier over this earth today than it did a thousand years ago!*

Man, created in the image of God, has the ability to plan and move toward a desirable objective. Animals lack this ability. The brute beast is the victim of heredity and environment.

Another fact that is clearly evident is that animals do not have a conscience, or religious nature. When a dog bites a human being, that dog gives no evidence of repentance in that he is sorry for his act of violence. In the face of danger, animals tremble with fear—but they never behave in a way that shows reverence for Almighty God. They never manifest the kind of fear that brings repentance for an act they have committed against a person or against another animal.

Man is incurably religious. Even the most pagan members of the human race worship some kind of god. It is born in man to worship. He may devise his own religious rites and ceremonies, he may make his gods of wood or stone, or worship some "unknown god"; but in one way or another, man will worship. This is not true of the beasts of the field—and this fact alone is enough to convince any thinking person that there is not just a "missing link" between man and the animal kingdom. There is, indeed, a tremendous, eternal gulf—established by Almighty God when He created man from the dust of the earth and breathed into his nostrils the breath of life!

I was reared on the farm, and from my own observation I realize that animal life *parallels* human life in many ways; but it is in another plane. I admit that animals are *guided* by something—but it is not by *thought,* as man is guided. Something *restrains* the animal—but it is not judgment such as God gave to man. Any sincere seeker of truth will admit that

man possesses *a spiritual and intellectual nature* which
is absent from the animal creation.   The beast has
capacity only for things pertaining to the fleshly nature, while man has a capacity for *spiritual* things, a
yearning for God, his Creator.   Man is God's *special
and highest* creation, and in the sense of creation man
is God's child.   These clear, unmistakeable facts differentiate between man and the animals of the field.

In spite of the fact that Adam sinned and man is
therefore depraved and fallen in nature, he still occupies a place of dignity in the economy of God.   We
need to recognize the great honor the Creator has bestowed upon man—but God forbid that we arrive at
the false conclusion that in the breast of every man
lives a spark of divinity!   There is *no divinity* in the
breast of *any* man until that man is born again through
the miracle wrought by the Holy Spirit and based on
faith in the finished work of the Lord Jesus Christ.
Only then does man become partaker of divine nature.
God is GOD, and beside Him there is *no other God!*
He is the self-existing One.   He is omnipotent, omniscient, omnipresent.   It is in Him that we live and
move and have our being, and without Him we could
not live.

But God is a God of grace; and it is through His
mercy and longsuffering that we are permitted to live
upon this earth and enjoy the blessings that come to
us daily: "Every good gift and every perfect gift is
from above, and cometh down from the Father of
lights, with whom is no variableness, neither shadow
of turning" (James 1:17).

The First Couple to Dwell on Earth

"And God said, Let us make man in our image,
after our likeness: and let them have dominion over
the fish of the sea, and over the fowl of the air, and

over the cattle, and over all the earth, and over every creeping thing that creepeth upon the earth.

"So God created man in His own image, in the image of God created He him; male and female created He them. And God blessed them, and God said unto them, Be fruitful, and multiply, and replenish the earth, and subdue it: and have dominion over the fish of the sea, and over the fowl of the air, and over every living thing that moveth upon the earth. And God said, Behold, I have given you every herb bearing seed, which is upon the face of all the earth, and every tree, in the which is the fruit of a tree yielding seed; to you it shall be for meat. And to every beast of the earth, and to every fowl of the air, and to every thing that creepeth upon the earth, wherein there is life, I have given every green herb for meat: and it was so. And God saw every thing that He had made, and, behold, it was very good. And the evening and the morning were the sixth day" (Gen. 1:26—31).

"And the Lord God formed man of the dust of the ground, and breathed into his nostrils the breath of life; and man became a living soul. . . . And the Lord God caused a deep sleep to fall upon Adam, and he slept: and He took one of his ribs, and closed up the flesh instead thereof; and the rib, which the Lord God had taken from man, made He a woman, and brought her unto the man" (Gen. 2:7, 21, 22).

Thus does the holy Scripture declare that God created Adam, then removed a rib from Adam's side, created Eve, and gave her to Adam to be his wife. So on the authority of God's Word we know that these were the first two people to dwell on this earth. Then (Gen. 1:28) God blessed them and said, *"Be fruitful, and multiply, and replenish the earth."* Here we learn that the human family sprang from Adam and Eve.

The Apostle Paul bears this out when he traces the sinfulness of the human race back to Adam in the Garden of Eden. In Romans 5:12—21 Paul wrote:

"Wherefore, as by one man (Adam) sin entered into the world, and death by sin; and so death passed upon all men, for that all have sinned: (For until the law sin was in the world: but sin is not imputed when there is no law. Nevertheless death reigned from Adam to Moses, even over them that had not sinned after the similitude of Adam's transgression, who is the figure of Him that was to come.

"But not as the offence, so also is the free gift. For if through the offence of one many be dead, much more the grace of God, and the gift by grace, which is by one Man, Jesus Christ, hath abounded unto many. And not as it was by one that sinned, so is the gift: for the judgment was by one to condemnation, but the free gift is of many offences unto justification. For if by one man's offence death reigned by one; much more they which receive abundance of grace and of the gift of righteousness shall reign in life by One, Jesus Christ.)

"Therefore as by the offence of one judgment came upon all men to condemnation; even so by the righteousness of One the free gift came upon all men unto justification of life. For as by one man's disobedience many were made sinners, so by the obedience of One shall many be made righteous.

"Moreover the law entered, that the offence might abound. But where sin abounded, grace did much more abound: That as sin hath reigned unto death, even so might grace reign through righteousness unto eternal life by Jesus Christ our Lord."

In the light of these Scriptures, anyone seeking truth concerning the human race must acknowledge Adam and Eve as the father and mother of all humanity.

The Nature of Man's Being: Man Is a Trinity

*"And the very God of peace sanctify you WHOL-
LY; and I pray God your whole SPIRIT and SOUL
and BODY be preserved blameless unto the coming
of our Lord Jesus Christ"* (I Thess. 5:23).

In this inspired passage, penned down by the Apostle Paul as the Holy Spirit gave him the message, we
clearly see that man possesses spirit, soul, and body.
Therefore man is *a trinity*.

The soul and spirit of man are not identical. This
is unquestionably proved by the fact that they are
divisible: "For the Word of God is quick, and powerful, and sharper than any twoedged sword, piercing
even to *the dividing asunder of SOUL and SPIRIT*,
and of the joints and marrow, and is a discerner of
the thoughts and intents of the heart" (Heb. 4:12).

The soul and spirit are also clearly distinguished
in the burial and resurrection of the body. Paul explained to the Corinthian believers, "There are also
celestial bodies, and bodies terrestrial: but the glory
of the celestial is one, and the glory of the terrestrial
is another. There is one glory of the sun, and another
glory of the moon, and another glory of the stars: for
one star differeth from another star in glory.

"So also is the resurrection of the dead. It is sown
in corruption; it is raised in incorruption: It is sown
in dishonour; it is raised in glory: it is sown in weakness; it is raised in power: it is sown a natural body;
it is raised a spiritual body. There is a natural body,
and there is a spiritual body. And so it is written,
*The first man Adam was made a living soul; the last
Adam* (the Lord Jesus Christ) *was made a quickening
spirit"* (I Cor. 15:40—45).

To say that there is no difference between the soul
and the spirit of man is to say that there is no difference between the mortal body in which we now live

and the resurrection body which we will possess when Jesus comes in the Rapture and the first resurrection. Paul plainly declares that the Lord Jesus Christ "shall *change our vile body, that it may be fashioned like unto HIS GLORIOUS BODY,* according to the working whereby He is able even to subdue all things unto Himself" (Phil. 3:21), and John the Beloved tells us that when Jesus appears *"we shall be LIKE Him;* for we shall see Him as He is" (I John 3:2).

In the Word of God, the distinction between man's spirit and man's soul is clearly set forth. The spirit of man is the mind—that part of man which thinks, reasons, and "knows": *"For what man knoweth the things of a man, save the SPIRIT of man which is in him?* Even so the things of God knoweth no man, but the Spirit of God" (I Cor. 2:11).

When Jesus wept at the tomb of Lazarus He *"groaned in His SPIRIT, and was troubled"* (John 11:33); but when He prayed in the Garden of Gethsemane just before facing the cross, He said, *"My SOUL is exceeding sorrowful, even unto death"* (Matt. 26:38). At the tomb of Lazarus He was thinking and sorrowing with Mary and Martha; but in the Garden of Gethsemane He was facing the cup that contained the bitter dregs of all the sins of all the world through all ages, and His soul was feeling the burden of redemption.

Because man possesses soul and spirit he is capable of *God*-consciousness; and because of this he is capable of *communing* with God:

In Job 32:8 we read, "There is a spirit in man: and the inspiration of the Almighty giveth them understanding."

The Psalmist declared, "Thou wilt light my candle: the Lord my God will enlighten my darkness" (Psalm 18:28).

Then in Proverbs 20:27 we read, "The spirit of man

is the candle of the Lord, searching all the inward parts of the belly."

This body in which we live is but the tabernacle which houses the real man—the soul and spirit; and the body *without* the spirit is *dead* (James 2:26).

Paul made it clear to the Corinthian Christians that the body is only the house in which the soul and spirit dwell.

"For we know that if our earthly house of this tabernacle were dissolved, we have a building of God, an house not made with hands, eternal in the heavens. For in this we groan, earnestly desiring to be clothed upon with our house which is from heaven: if so be that being clothed we shall not be found naked. For we that are in this tabernacle do groan, being burdened: not for that we would be unclothed, but clothed upon, that mortality might be swallowed up of life.

"Now He that hath wrought us for the selfsame thing is God, who also hath given unto us the earnest of the Spirit. Therefore we are always confident, knowing that, whilst we are at home in the body, we are absent from the Lord: (For we walk by faith, not by sight:) We are confident, I say, and willing rather to be absent from the body, and to be present with the Lord" (II Cor. 5:1—8).

Now notice Paul's testimony in Philippians 1:21—24: "For to me to live is Christ, and to die is gain. But if I live *in the flesh*, this is the fruit of my labour: yet what I shall choose I wot not. For I am in a strait betwixt two, having a desire to depart, and to be with Christ; which is far better: Nevertheless *to abide in the flesh* is more needful for you."

Notice Paul said, "I live *in the flesh*." In other words, he was saying, "The flesh is not the *real man*. The flesh is but *the house* in which I, Paul, live." The real man is the spirit and soul—that part of man

which is eternal and will never cease to exist. Man
is an eternal creature, and a hundred trillion years
from now you who read these lines will be living—you
will be either rejoicing in the presence of God, or living in unspeakable torment in the flames of hell.

The Original Intellectual
and Moral Condition of Man

Was Adam created an ignoramus or a savage? Or
was he created an intellectual being with lofty intellectual powers?

There is no truth in the doctrine of evolution,
whether it be within the limits of the animal world
or as having to do with man. The theory of evolution
contradicts the Word of God, and it contradicts the
known facts of history. There is absolutely not one
fact to *sustain* the doctrine of evolution, and the very
first record of man declares that in his original state
man was both intellectual and moral:

In Genesis 1:28, God blessed the first man and
woman, told them to multiply and replenish the earth—
"and *subdue* it: and have *dominion* over the fish of
the sea, and over the fowl of the air, *and over every
living thing* that moveth upon the earth!"

Certainly Adam must have been an intellectual
being for God to make him sole ruler over the earth—
a position for which many men have fought and died
(but never attained) down through the annals of history. Time after time wars have been fought in an
effort to make *one man* ruler of this earth; but no man
save Adam has ever yet ruled every square inch of
the known earth at one time. Adam had dominion
over the earth and everything that lived on the land
or in the sea. Yes, God created the first man with
a powerful intellect which gave him the ability to
rule the entire earth.

In Genesis 2:19 we read, "And out of the ground the Lord God formed every beast of the field, and every fowl of the air; and brought them unto Adam to see what he would call them: *and whatsoever Adam called every living creature, that was the name thereof.*" Not only did God commit rulership of earth to Adam, He also gave him the privilege of naming all the beasts of the field and the fowls of the air and the creatures of the sea. Consider the living creatures on this earth! Adam named them all. Surely it is evident that he possessed lofty intellectual powers.

Just as Adam was not created an ignoramus or a savage, neither was he created a sinner. When God breathed into his nostrils the breath of life, Adam became *a living soul*—but not a sinner. It was of his own choice and volition that he sinned, for God gave him the right to choose. Adam was not God's puppet, he was a free moral being with the privilege of choosing whom he would obey and serve. God was more than fair. He not only told Adam what he could do and what he could not do without penalty; He also clearly *spelled out* the penalty for disobeying His command:

"And the Lord God planted a garden eastward in Eden; and there He put the man whom He had formed. And out of the ground made the Lord God to grow every tree that is pleasant to the sight, and good for food; the tree of life also in the midst of the garden, and the tree of knowledge of good and evil. . . . And the Lord God commanded the man, saying, Of every tree of the garden thou mayest freely eat: but *of the tree of the knowledge of good and evil, thou shalt not eat of it: for in the day that thou eatest thereof THOU SHALT SURELY DIE!*" (Gen. 2:8—17 in part).

Adam could eat as *often* as he wanted to eat, as *much* as he wanted to eat, and only the fruit of the

tree of knowledge of good and evil was forbidden to
him.   God explained to him exactly what was forbidden, and just as clearly explained what the results
of disobedience would be; and there was no reason
for a man with Adam's intellectual ability to misunderstand God's instructions.

The Temptation of Eve — The Fall of Man

"Now the serpent was more subtil than any beast
of the field which the Lord God had made.   And he
said unto the woman, *Yea, HATH God said, Ye shall
not eat of every tree of the garden?*   And the woman
said unto the serpent, We may eat of the fruit of the
trees of the garden: but of the fruit of the tree which
is in the midst of the garden, God hath said, Ye shall
not eat of it, *neither shall ye TOUCH it,* lest ye die.

"And the serpent said unto the woman, Ye shall
not surely die: for God doth know that in the day
ye eat thereof, then your eyes shall be opened, and
ye shall be as gods, knowing good and evil.

"And when the woman saw that the tree was good
for food, and that it was pleasant to the eyes, and
a tree to be desired to make one wise, she took of
the fruit thereof, and did eat, and gave also unto her
husband with her; and he did eat.   And the eyes of
them both were opened, and they knew that they
were naked; and they sewed fig leaves together, and
made themselves aprons" (Gen. 3:1—7).

The Scripture does not tell us how long Adam and
Eve lived in their Paradise home before the serpent
entered the garden to tempt Eve.   It could have been
quite a long while, or it could have been a very short
time.   Be that as it may, they lived in innocence,
clothed in Shekinah glory, unaware that they were
naked (Gen. 2:25).

God provided a perfect home for them, He gave

them a perfect diet, and all He required of them was that Adam keep the garden. To make a perfect situation even more sublime, God visited this first couple every evening, in the cool of the day. What man could desire more? And yet it was in this perfect Paradise home that man fell into sin, and through his fall *the entire human family fell* and death moved upon all men!

"Now the serpent was more subtil than any beast of the field . . . ." The "serpent" who entered the Garden of Eden was not a loathesome reptile such as the snakes we know today. From Genesis 3:14 it would seem that he was a creature who walked upright and had the ability to speak—and the Bible tells us that the serpent asked the first question man was called upon to answer. In II Corinthians 11:13, 14 the Apostle Paul speaks of false apostles and deceitful workers who transform themselves into the apostles of Christ, "and no marvel; *for Satan himself is transformed into an angel of light."* It was as "an angel of light" that he entered the garden home of Adam and Eve; and the question he asked seemed harmless enough on the surface, yet it was the method he used to get an audience with Eve, and by which he began a conversation that ended in her downfall.

Satan asked Eve, *"HATH God said,* Ye shall not eat of every tree of the garden?" How did he *know* God had said anything about their eating of the various trees? Insofar as the Bible tells us, only Adam, Eve, God, and Satan had access to the garden, and I personally believe Satan overheard God giving Adam instructions concerning the forbidden fruit of the tree of the knowledge of good and evil. At any rate, he gained his purpose. He asked Eve if God had limited their diet and outlawed one of the trees—and his scheme worked perfectly. Instead of *resisting* Satan, Eve talked with him.

Somehow the devil always manages to do business on his own terms, and the only way to deal with him is to resist him (James 4:7). But Eve became engaged in conversation with him. She said it was true that God had given commandment concerning the trees of the garden:

"We may eat of the fruit of the trees of the garden: but of the fruit of the tree which is *in the midst of the garden,* God hath said, Ye shall not eat of it, *neither shall ye touch it,* lest ye die."

Eve indicated that she was quoting God—but she did not quote Him accurately. God had told them that they could eat freely of every tree in the garden with the exception of one specific tree—but it was not the tree "in *the midst* of the garden." Genesis 2:9 designates *the tree of life* as being in the midst of the garden, and it was not that tree of which God commanded Adam not to eat. He commanded him not to eat of the tree of *the knowledge of good and evil.* So Eve misquoted God in mentioning the wrong tree.

Then she *added to* God's command by saying, "God hath said, *Ye shall not eat of it, NEITHER SHALL YE TOUCH IT.*" God said nothing about touching the tree. He commanded that they should not eat of it, but He did not command them not to touch it. It is extremely dangerous to add to the Word of God.

Next, Eve *took away from* the Word of God. She quoted Him as saying, *"LEST ye die."* God had thundered out, "In the day that thou eatest thereof *thou shalt SURELY DIE!"*

The devil is using that same scheme to damn souls today! By wrongly dividing the Word, adding to or taking away from the Word, by modifying and softening the Word, he continues to lead men away from God.

The Bible clearly warns against tampering with the Scriptures. Paul thundered out, *"Let GOD be true,* but every man a liar!" (Rom. 3:4). Jesus Himself warned that men will be *judged* by the Word:

"If any man hear *my WORDS,* and believe not, I judge him not: for I came not to judge the world, but to save the world. He that rejecteth me, and receiveth not *my WORDS,* hath one that judgeth him: *the WORD that I have spoken, the same shall JUDGE him in the last day"* (John 12:47, 48).

It is impossible for man to fully comprehend just how valuable the Word of God really is. The last warning in the Bible is for those who would tamper with the Word. At the close of the Revelation, God's last written testimony to man, John the Beloved wrote:

"I testify unto every man that heareth *the WORDS of the prophecy of this book,* If any man shall *add unto* these things, God shall add unto him the plagues that are written in this book: and if any man shall *take away from* the words of the book of this prophecy, God shall take away his part out of the book of life, and out of the holy city, and from the things which are written in this book" (Rev. 22:18, 19).

You will notice the serpent started out by simply asking Eve a seemingly harmless question; but when Eve named the wrong tree, added to the Word of God, took away from the Word of God, and softened the judgment God had spelled out, the serpent then brazenly called God a liar. God had said, "In the day that thou eatest thereof *thou shalt surely DIE."* Satan said to Eve, *"Ye shall NOT surely die!"*

He then went on to explain *why* God had commanded Adam and Eve not to eat of the forbidden fruit: "For God doth know that in the day ye eat thereof, then *your eyes shall be opened, and ye shall be as gods,* knowing good and evil." In other words, Satan suggested to Eve that God knew something she did not know, and that He was "holding out" on her because He knew that if she and Adam ate the fruit it would make them wise—they would become "as gods."

The woman listened attentively; then she looked at the tree. It was pleasant to the eye, she saw that the fruit was good for food—and certainly she wanted to be *wise!* So she took of the fruit and ate it, she gave to Adam and he ate, and suddenly *"the eyes of them both were opened, and they knew that they were naked."*

There is no way of knowing—nor words to explain— the feelings of Adam and Eve when they realized what had happened as they ate the forbidden fruit. She-kinah glory departed from their bodies and they saw their nakedness. But they were "as gods" now, they *"knew,"* so they no longer needed God. They did not call for help. They did not cry out, "O God! Have mercy on us!" Instead, they immediately began to exercise their newly acquired knowledge and figured out a way to cover their sin—so they thought; but *"without shedding of blood"* there IS *no covering for sin* (Heb. 9:22).

Adam and Eve decided that *fig leaves* would meet their need, so they sewed fig leaves together and made aprons, which no doubt made a satisfactory covering for the nakedness of their *bodies.* Then everything was lovely—*until "they heard the voice of the Lord God* walking in the garden in the cool of the day."

Up to this time, Adam and Eve had welcomed the daily visit of their Creator and Friend; but now they were *frightened* by His voice. The fig-leaf covering satisfied *them,* but they knew it would never satisfy God; so they *"hid themselves* from the presence of the Lord God amongst the trees of the garden." But their hiding place was not sufficient. *There is no escape from the presence of God* (Psalm 139:7—10), and the only hiding place is in Jesus (Col. 1:27; 3:3).

God called, "Adam, where art thou?" and Adam and Eve came forth from their hiding place to meet Him—but they came making *excuses* for what they had done. The man said, "The *woman* whom thou gavest to be with me, *she* gave me of the tree, and I did eat." The woman said, "The *serpent* beguiled me, and I did eat." So Adam blamed Eve, and Eve blamed the serpent—but God accepted neither their covering nor their excuses! In Genesis 3:14—19 we read:

"And the Lord God said unto *the serpent,* Because thou hast done this, thou art cursed above all cattle, and above every beast of the field; upon thy belly shalt thou go, and dust shalt thou eat all the days of thy life: and I will put enmity between thee and the woman, and between thy seed and her seed; it shall bruise thy head, and thou shalt bruise His heel.

"Unto *the woman* He said, I will greatly multiply thy sorrow and thy conception; in sorrow thou shalt bring forth children; and thy desire shall be to thy husband, and he shall rule over thee.

"And *unto Adam* He said, Because thou hast hearkened unto the voice of thy wife, and hast eaten of the tree, of which I commanded thee, saying, Thou shalt not eat of it: cursed is the ground for thy sake; in sorrow shalt thou eat of it all the days of thy life; thorns also and thistles shall it bring forth to thee; and thou shalt eat the herb of the field; in the sweat of thy face shalt thou eat bread, till thou return unto the ground; for out of it wast thou taken: for dust thou art, and unto dust shalt thou return."

It was in verse 15 of this passage that God promised a Deliverer—the Seed of the woman—to crush the serpent's head. This promise was fulfilled "in the fulness of the time" (Gal. 4:4, 5).

Man is still trying to cover up his sins—but notice

it was *God* who prepared a covering for Adam and
Eve, a covering provided at the expense of innocent
animals.   He made coats of skins and clothed Adam
and Eve (Gen. 3:21).   The only thing He required of
them was that they yield to Him and allow Him to
clothe them—and that is all anyone can do today.
We can submit to God and allow Him to clothe us
with the blood-covering provided by the Lamb of God,
the Seed of the woman promised in Genesis 3:15.

However, God had not yet finished with Adam
and Eve.   They were still in the Garden of Eden, and
they must not be allowed to remain there.   They were
in a fallen nature, and should they then eat of the
tree of life they would live forever in a body that was
destined to a life of pain and sorrow because of sin.
Therefore God drove them from the garden "and He
placed at the east of the garden of Eden Cherubims,
and a flaming sword which turned every way, to keep
the way of the tree of life" (Gen. 3:24).

The Result of the Fall of Adam

"Wherefore, as by one man sin entered into the
world, and death by sin; and so death passed upon
all men, for that all have sinned: (For until the law
sin was in the world: but sin is not imputed when
there is no law.   Nevertheless death reigned from
Adam to Moses, even over them that had not sinned
after the similitude of Adam's transgression, who is
the figure of Him that was to come.

"But not as the offence, so also is the free gift.
For if through the offence of one many be dead, much
more the grace of God, and the gift by grace, which
is by one Man, Jesus Christ, hath abounded unto
many.   And not as it was by one that sinned, so is
the gift: for the judgment was by one to condemnation, but the free gift is of many offences unto justi-

fication. For if by one man's offence death reigned by one; much more they which receive abundance of grace and of the gift of righteousness shall reign in life by One, Jesus Christ.)

"Therefore as by the offence of one judgment came upon all men to condemnation; even so by the righteousness of One the free gift came upon all men unto justification of life. For as by one man's disobedience many were made sinners, so by the obedience of One shall many be made righteous. Moreover the law entered, that the offence might abound. But where sin abounded, grace did much more abound: that as sin hath reigned unto death, even so might grace reign through righteousness unto eternal life by Jesus Christ our Lord" (Rom. 5:12—21).

The first man stood as representative of the human race, he was the father of the human race, therefore all coming generations were in Adam. (For comparison, read Hebrews 7:9, 10.)

When Adam fell, the human race fell: "There is none righteous, NO, NOT ONE: There is none that understandeth, there is none that seeketh after God. They are all gone out of the way, they are together become unprofitable; there is NONE that doeth good, no, not one" (Rom. 3:10—12).

You may say, "I do not think it is right that I should have to suffer for Adam's sin." Beloved, *you will not suffer for Adam's sin*, but for your own sins. It is true that Adam fell, and *IN Adam all men fell*; but if you or I had been Adam we would have fallen *just as HE fell*. Through Adam's sin we became sinners; but thanks be unto God, the *last* Adam—the Lord Jesus Christ—obeyed God's every command, fulfilled every jot and tittle of God's holy law, and through HIM we can be justified and made righteous. Christ offered one sacrifice—the sacrifice of Himself. He tasted death for every man that we might live

through His sacrifice. Now God can be just, "and
the Justifier of him which believeth in Jesus" (Rom.
3:26). When we believe in the shed blood of Jesus,
God saves us for Jesus' sake (Eph. 4:32).

God is sovereign. I cannot explain His sovereignty
but the Bible teaches it. God had no beginning, He
will have no ending. He has always been, He always
will be. He is omniscient, He knew the end in the
beginning. Therefore, before He created the universe,
before He created Adam, He knew everything that
would happen in the centuries ahead and He made
provision for us. Jesus, the last Adam, did for man
what man could never have done for himself, and
sad but so, He did what man *would not* have done
for himself *if he could have!* Therefore we can say
with Paul, "Thanks be unto God for His unspeakable
gift" (II Cor. 9:15).

Jesus made for us every provision God required,
that we might become children of God, that we might
inherit the kingdom of God and dwell with Him forever in the celestial city Jesus has gone to prepare
for us! So my dear friend, if you suffer for sin it will
be for your own sin, not Adam's. Jesus settled the
sin question, He paid the sin-debt, He bore our sins
in His own body and nailed them to the tree; and
the Bible clearly tells us, *"If we confess our sins, He
is faithful and just to forgive us our sins, and to
cleanse us from all unrighteousness"* (I John 1:9).

The Present Standing and Condition
of Men Outside of Christ

Some teachers maintain that all men possess a
spark of divinity, and therefore the only need of man
is to fan that spark to flame through right environment, culture, education, and living by "the golden
rule." Such doctrine is completely foreign to the Word

of God and there is not an iota of truth in it. Man *does not* possess "a spark of divinity." Even though he was created in the image of God, through Adam's fall all men are born in sin and shapen in iniquity (Psalm 51:5; Eccl. 7:20).

The Psalmist declared, "The Lord looked down from heaven upon the children of men, to see if there were any that did understand, and seek God. They are all gone aside, they are all together become filthy: there is none that doeth good, no, not one" (Psalm 14:2, 3).

The Prophet Isaiah wrote, *"ALL we like sheep have gone astray; we have turned every one to his own way, and the Lord hath laid on HIM (Jesus) the iniquity of us ALL"* (Isa. 53:6).

Recorded in Paul's letter to the Christians at Rome we find a clear and complete description of man apart from the redemption that is in Christ Jesus:

Paul declares that *"both Jews and Gentiles"* are all *under sin:* "As it is written, There is none righteous, no, not one: There is none that understandeth, there is none that seeketh after God. They are all gone out of the way, they are together become unprofitable; there is none that doeth good, no, not one.

"Their throat is an open sepulchre; with their tongues they have used deceit; the poison of asps is under their lips: whose mouth is full of cursing and bitterness: Their feet are swift to shed blood: destruction and misery are in their ways: and the way of peace have they not known: There is no fear of God before their eyes.

"Now we know that what things soever the law saith, it saith to them who are under the law: that every mouth may be stopped, and *ALL THE WORLD may become guilty before God"* (Rom. 3:9—19).

The Word of God clearly teaches that man, outside the redemption that is in Christ Jesus, is hopelessly lost—not possessing "a spark of divinity" but rather possessing a nature destined to damn the soul because the natural man cannot receive the things of the Spirit of God (I Cor. 2:14).

The natural man follows after the things of the world, transient things that will soon pass away. We are commanded, "Love not the world, neither the things that are in the world. *If any man love the world, the love of the Father is not in him.* For all that is in the world, the lust of the flesh, and the lust of the eyes, and the pride of life, is not of the Father, but is of the world. *And the world passeth away, and the lust thereof: but he that doeth the will of God abideth for ever"* (I John 2:15—17).

Yes, *"all have sinned,* and come short of the glory of God" (Rom. 3:23); but Christ the Righteous One is the propitiation for our sins, "and not for our's only, but also for the sins of the whole world" (I John 2:2).

Regardless of what men teach or preach, the Word of God stops every mouth and declares the whole world guilty before God and under His condemnation (Rom. 3:19). The Psalmist asked, *"If thou, Lord, shouldest mark iniquities, O Lord, WHO SHALL STAND?"* (Psalm 130:3). Then in Psalm 143:1, 2 we read these words of David: "Hear my prayer, O Lord, give ear to my supplications: in thy faithfulness answer me, and in thy righteousness. *And enter not into judgment with thy servant: FOR IN THY SIGHT SHALL NO MAN LIVING BE JUSTIFIED!"*

Jesus, by the grace of God, tasted death for every man (Heb. 2:9). All men *outside* the grace of God in Jesus Christ are under a curse, and those who refuse to accept God's grace must face that curse which, in the end, will bring them to eternal damnation:

"For as many as have sinned without law shall also perish without law: and as many as have sinned in the law shall be judged by the law" (Rom. 2:12).

"For as many as are of the works of the law are under the curse: for it is written, Cursed is every one that continueth not in all things which are written in the book of the law to do them. But that no man is justified by the law in the sight of God, it is evident: for, The just shall live by faith. And the law is not of faith: but, The man that doeth them shall live in them.

"Christ hath redeemed us from the curse of the law, being made a curse for us: for it is written, Cursed is every one that hangeth on a tree: that the blessing of Abraham might come on the Gentiles through Jesus Christ; that we might receive the promise of the Spirit through faith" (Gal. 3:10—14).

There are only two classes of people on this earth: sons of God, and sons of the devil. To *believers* John the Beloved wrote: *"Beloved, NOW ARE WE THE SONS OF GOD, and it doth not yet appear what we shall be: but we know that, when He shall appear, we shall be like Him; for we shall see Him as He is"* (I John 3:2).

All who have not been born of the Spirit and washed in the blood are children of the devil. Jesus said to His enemies, *"Ye are of YOUR FATHER, THE DEVIL, and the lusts of your father ye will do. He was a murderer from the beginning, and abode not in the truth, because there is no truth in him. When he speaketh a lie, he speaketh of his own: for he is a liar, and the father of it"* (John 8:44).

I John 3:8—10 tells us very clearly, *"He that committeth sin IS OF THE DEVIL;* for the devil sinneth from the beginning. For this purpose the Son of God was manifested, that He might destroy the works of the devil. *Whosoever is born of God doth NOT commit sin;* for His seed remaineth in him: and he cannot sin, because he is born of God. In this the children of God are manifest, and the children of the devil:

whosoever doeth not righteousness is not of God, neither he that loveth not his brother."

Some people say, "I am *neutral*. I am neither sinner nor saint. I am not *for* Christ, nor am I *against* Him." Beloved, this cannot be! The Bible clearly states that we stand *with* Christ, or we stand *against* Him. There is no neutral ground. Jesus Himself made this plain when He said, "He that is not with me is against me; and he that gathereth not with me scattereth abroad" (Matt. 12:30).

All men are God's offspring (Acts 17:28). Therefore all men are His in the sense of being His creatures. But only those who have trusted in the shed blood of Jesus Christ are children of God in the spiritual sense. Jesus "came unto His own, and His own received Him not. *BUT AS MANY AS RECEIVED HIM, to them gave He power to become the sons of God,* even to them that believe on His name: which were born . . . of God" (John 1:11—13).

In Galatians 3:26 the Apostle Paul tells us, "*Ye are all the children of God BY FAITH IN CHRIST JESUS.*"

The Scripture employs many terms to describe and declare the total depravity of man and the hopelessness of his condition apart from the redemption that is in Christ Jesus:

In II Corinthians 4:3, 4 Paul declares that unbelievers are *blind:* "If our Gospel be hid, it is hid to them that are lost: in whom *the god of this world hath BLINDED the minds of them which believe not,* lest the light of the glorious Gospel of Christ, who is the image of God, should shine unto them."

In Ephesians 2:1—3 Paul speaks of unbelievers as being "*DEAD in trespasses and sins,*" walking "according to the course of this world, according to the prince of the power of the air, the spirit that now worketh in *the children of disobedience:* among whom also we all had our conversation in times past in the lusts of our flesh, fulfilling the desires of the flesh and of the mind; and were by nature the children of wrath, even as others."

Also to the believers at Ephesus Paul wrote, "This I say therefore, and testify in the Lord, that ye henceforth walk not as other Gentiles walk, in the vanity of their mind, having the understanding darkened, being alienated from the life of God through the ignorance that is in them, because of the blindness of their heart: who being past feeling have given themselves over unto lasciviousness, to work all uncleanness with greediness" (Eph. 4:17—19).

In I Timothy 5:6 Paul emphatically declared, *"She that liveth in pleasure IS DEAD WHILE SHE LIVETH!"*

The natural man possesses a nature which craves the things of the flesh, and until God works a miracle in the *heart* of man he cannot long after nor understand the things of the Spirit of God. It is natural for the unregenerate man to follow after sin and lust, for he is sinful by nature. It is only when God redeems us through the shed blood of Jesus that we become partakers of *divine* nature (II Pet. 1:4).

Proverbs 4:23 warns, "Keep thy heart with all diligence; for *out of it are the issues of life."* The heart is the seat of life, and the Scriptures do not leave us in ignorance concerning the possibilities of the heart from the spiritual standpoint:

Jeremiah 17:9 tells us, *"The heart is deceitful above all things, AND DESPERATELY WICKED:* who can know it?"

Jesus agreed with Jeremiah. In Mark 7:21—23 He declared: *"From within, OUT OF THE HEART OF MEN, proceed evil thoughts, adulteries, fornications, murders, thefts, covetousness, wickedness, deceit, lasciviousness, an evil eye, blasphemy, pride, foolishness:*

all these evil things come from within, and defile the man."

The only way to control the heart is to let Jesus occupy it by faith, and He will lead us into paths of right living.   Apart from Him, it is impossible for man to *know* his own heart.

In Genesis 6:5—12 we read that man had not been upon this earth a great many hundreds of years, before God looked down and "saw that the *wickedness* of man was great in the earth, and that *EVERY IMAG-INATION OF THE THOUGHTS OF HIS HEART was only evil continually.*   And it repented the Lord that He had made man on the earth, and it grieved Him at His heart.   And the Lord said, I will destroy man whom I have created from the face of the earth; both man, and beast, and the creeping thing, and the fowls of the air; for it repenteth me that I have made them. . . . The earth also was corrupt before God, and the earth was filled with violence.   And God looked upon the earth, and, behold, it was corrupt; for *all flesh had corrupted his way upon the earth.*"

In Genesis 8:21 we read, "And the Lord smelled a sweet savour; and the Lord said in His heart, *I will not again curse the ground any more for man's sake; for THE IMAGINATION OF MAN'S HEART IS EVIL FROM HIS YOUTH;* neither will I again smite any more every thing living, as I have done."

The Psalmist declared, *"The Lord knoweth the THOUGHTS of man, that they are VANITY"* (Psalm 94:11).

So we see that according to the Word of God—not according to the opinion of some fanatical preacher— the entire moral and intellectual nature of the unregenerated man is corrupt, wicked, vile, selfish, and hateful.   Men who are not born of the Spirit and washed in the blood are slaves of the devil—helpless, hopeless, captive to a sinful nature and slowly moving toward eternal damnation.

To the Christians at Rome, Paul wrote: "But God commendeth His love toward us, in that, *while we were yet sinners, CHRIST DIED FOR US.* Much more then, being now justified by His blood, we shall be saved from wrath through Him. For if, when we were enemies, we were reconciled to God by the death of His Son, much more, being reconciled, we shall be saved by His life" (Rom. 5:8—10).

Again to the Romans Paul wrote: "For when we were in the flesh, the motions of sins, which were by the law, did work in our members to bring forth fruit unto death. . . . Sin, taking occasion by the commandment, wrought in me all manner of concupiscence. For without the law sin was dead. . . . For we know that the law is spiritual: but I am carnal, sold under sin. For that which I do I allow not: for what I would, that do I not; but what I hate, that do I. . . . For the good that I would I do not: but the evil which I would not, that I do. Now if I do that I would not, it is no more I that do it, but sin that dwelleth in me. I find then a law, that, when I would do good, evil is present with me. For I delight in the law of God after the inward man: but I see another law in my members, warring against the law of my mind, and bringing me into captivity to the law of sin which is in my members. O wretched man that I am! Who shall deliver me from the body of this death?" (Rom. 7:5—24 in part).

Then in Romans 8:7, 8 Paul explained, "The carnal mind is enmity against God: for it is not subject to the law of God, neither indeed can be. So then *they that are in the flesh cannot please God.*"

The Character of the Unregenerate Man

The *heart* of the unregenerate man is evil: "The

heart is deceitful above all things, and desperately wicked: who can know it?" (Jer. 17:9).

The *mind* of the unregenerate man is carnal: "The carnal mind is enmity against God: for it is not subject to the law of God, neither indeed can be" (Rom. 8:7).

The *reason* of the unregenerate man is gone: "This is an evil among all things that are done under the sun, that there is one event unto all: yea, also the heart of the sons of men is full of evil, and *madness is in their heart while they live,* and after that they go to the dead" (Eccl. 9:3).

The *way* of the unregenerate man is corrupt: "And God looked upon the earth, and, behold, it was corrupt; for all flesh had corrupted his way upon the earth" (Gen. 6:12).

The *understanding* of the unregenerate man is darkened: "Having the understanding darkened, being alienated from the life of God through the ignorance that is in them, because of the blindness of their heart" (Eph. 4:18).

The *tongue* of the unregenerate man is poisonous: "The tongue can no man tame; it is an unruly evil, full of deadly poison" (James 3:8).

The *hands* of the unregenerate man are violent hands: "Their webs shall not become garments, neither shall they cover themselves with their works: their works are works of iniquity, and the act of violence is in their hands" (Isa. 59:6).

The *eyes* of the unregenerate man are blind to spiritual things: "In whom the god of this world hath blinded the minds of them which believe not, lest the light of the glorious Gospel of Christ, who is the image of God, should shine unto them" (II Cor. 4:4).

The *ears* of the unregenerate man are deaf to the voice of God: "They shall turn away their ears from the truth, and shall be turned unto fables" (II Tim. 4:4).

The *entire nature* of the unregenerate man—from the top of his head to the soles of his feet—is diseased, sinful, and full of iniquity: "Why should ye be stricken any more? Ye will revolt more and more: *the whole head is sick, and the whole heart faint. From the sole of the foot even unto the head there is no soundness in it*; but wounds, and bruises, and putrifying sores: they have not been closed, neither bound up, neither mollified with ointment" (Isa. 1:5,6).

Because his eyes are blinded by sin and his understanding darkened, the unbeliever cannot see himself as he is, he cannot see the evil and the deadliness of sin. But hear the testimony of these men of God:

Job said, *"Behold, I AM VILE!"* (Job 40:4).

Isaiah exclaimed, *"Woe is me! for I AM UNDONE"* (Isa. 6:5).

David, a man after God's own heart, confessed: *"I AM POOR AND NEEDY!"* (Psalm 40:17).

Peter declared, *"I am A SINFUL MAN, O Lord"* (Luke 5:8).

The Apostle Paul confessed, *"I am CARNAL"* (Rom. 7:14).

The Lord Jesus Christ said of Himself, "I AM A WORM" (Psalm 22:6).

In the Word of God, the sinner is compared to many things. We will let the Scripture speak for itself, without comment. The sinner is compared to:

The uncleanliness of the *dog* (Prov. 26:11).

The fierceness of the *leopard* (Dan. 7:6).

The subtlety of the *serpent* (Matt. 23:33).

The fierceness of the *lion* (Psalm 22:13).

The stupidity of the *sheep* (Isa. 53:6).

The cunning of the *fox* (Luke 13:32).

The cruelty of the mountain *bear* (Dan. 7:5).

The *sow* that wallows in the mire (II Pet. 2:22).

The *wolf* (John 10:12).
The stubborn *ass* (Job 11:12).

Anyone who will study the Word of God and allow the Holy Spirit to speak to his heart will readily see that man *does not* contain a spark of divinity. On the contrary, he is by nature a child of the devil and it is natural for him to follow after sin. A miracle must be wrought in his heart before he hungers and thirsts after righteousness. But thanks be unto God, this miracle *can* be wrought by faith in the shed blood of the Lord Jesus Christ who took our place and paid the sin-debt. *Through His one sacrifice* eternal life was made possible for all who will believe on Him and trust Him as personal Saviour.

The Destiny of Unregenerated Man

There are people who teach that man is no more than an animal and that when he departs this life he is destined to return to dust—and that will be the end of him. According to the Word of God, that teaching is false.

Others teach that both the righteous and the unrighteous will rest in the grave from death until the resurrection morning, at which time the righteous will be raised to life eternal while the wicked will be raised and destroyed in the burning inferno of the last great judgment. This is only *partially* true.

So let us see what the Bible teaches concerning man's eternal destiny—believer, and unbeliever. The question is asked, "Would a loving God send His created children to hell? The answer is simple: *GOD does not SEND people to hell! they go there of their own accord.* It is not God's will that any should perish, "but that all should come to repentance" (II Pet. 3:9).

"For God sent not His Son into the world to

condemn the world; *but that the world through Him might be saved"* (John 3:17).

However, those who refuse to receive Jesus are *already* lost and facing an eternal destiny in the lake of fire: "He that believeth on Him is not condemned: but *he that believeth NOT is condemned already,* because he hath not believed in the name of the only begotten Son of God. . . . He that believeth on the Son hath everlasting life: and *he that believeth NOT the Son SHALL NOT SEE LIFE; BUT THE WRATH OF GOD ABIDETH ON HIM"* (John 3:18, 36).

Jesus made it very clear that those who die in sin cannot spend eternity with Him. In John 8:21—24 He said to His enemies, "I go my way, and ye shall seek me, and shall die in your sins: whither I go, ye cannot come.

"Then said the Jews, Will He kill Himself? because He saith, Whither I go, ye cannot come. And He said unto them, Ye are from beneath; I am from above: ye are of this world; I am not of this world. I said therefore unto you, that ye shall die in your sins: for if ye believe not that I am He, ye shall die in your sins."

In John 5:28, 29 Jesus said, "Marvel not at this: for the hour is coming, in the which *all that are in the graves shall hear His voice, and shall come forth;* they that have done good, unto the resurrection of *life;* and they that have done evil, unto the resurrection of *damnation."*

Yes, there is a resurrection day coming, and there will also be a day of judgment. *ALL men will be raised from the dead—*those who trust Jesus as Saviour will be raised unto life eternal; those who refuse to trust Him will be raised unto judgment and eternal damnation. The dead in Christ will be raised at His coming in the Rapture. The wicked dead will be raised at the close of the Millennium and will appear

before the Great White Throne judgment as described
in Revelation 20:11—15.

In Romans 2:5—9 the Apostle Paul wrote, inspired
of the Holy Spirit: "But after thy hardness and im-
penitent heart treasurest up unto thyself wrath against
the day of wrath and revelation of the righteous judgment of God; who will render to every man according
to his deeds: To them who by patient continuance
in well doing seek for glory and honour and immortality, eternal life: *But unto them that are contentious,
and do not obey the truth, but obey unrighteousness,
INDIGNATION AND WRATH, TRIBULATION AND
ANGUISH, UPON EVERY SOUL OF MAN THAT
DOETH EVIL,* of the Jew first, and also of the Gentile."

In II Thessalonians 1:7—9 Paul wrote, "To you
who are troubled rest with us, when the Lord Jesus
shall be revealed from heaven with His mighty angels,
*IN FLAMING FIRE TAKING VENGEANCE ON
THEM THAT KNOW NOT GOD, AND THAT OBEY
NOT THE GOSPEL OF OUR LORD JESUS CHRIST:
who shall be punished with EVERLASTING DE-
STRUCTION from the presence of the Lord, and from
the glory of His power."*

All who know not God and who obey not the
Gospel shall die in sin and suffer eternal punishment,
eternal destruction from the face of the Lord Jesus
Christ and from the glory of God. This will occur at
the consummation of all things when time will give
way to eternity. The wicked will be tormented day
and night forever and ever in the lake of fire.

It was never God's will that men should perish
and spend eternity in hell. In the beginning *there
was no hell.* Genesis 1:1 declared, "In the beginning
God created the HEAVEN and the EARTH." Nothing
is said of His creating hell. God does not create that
which is not needed. He creates for His own honor

and glory.

The Word of God does not tell us *when* hell came into being, but it does tell us *why* hell was prepared. In Matthew 25:41 Jesus declared that hell was "prepared *for the devil and his angels.*" In the beginning there was no hell, there was no devil, and therefore no sin and no need for hell. Sin was born in the heart of Lucifer, and God cast him out of heaven along with the angels whom he had led astray. So hell was prepared "for the devil and his angels," and men who choose to follow the devil in this life must spend eternity with him in the lake of fire that burns with brimstone forever—and rest assured, the devil, the Satanic trinity, will *be* there throughout the endless ages! God's Word declares it:

"And *the beast* was taken, and with him *the false prophet* that wrought miracles before him, with which he deceived them that had received the mark of the beast, and them that worshipped his image. These both were cast alive into a lake of fire burning with brimstone. . . . *And THE DEVIL that deceived them was cast into the lake of fire and brimstone, where the beast and the false prophet are, and shall be tormented day and night for ever and ever"* (Rev. 19:20; 20:10).

There are many reasons why I thank God that I will not spend eternity in hell, and one of the outstanding reasons is because of the neighbors I would have throughout eternity. Any thinking person, when purchasing a home, will investigate the kind of people who live in the community where that home is located. Most people want neighbors who are respectable; but those who are so unfortunate as to spend eternity in hell will certainly have some undesirable neighbors! The Word of God lists them as "fearful, and unbelieving, and the abominable, and murderers, and whoremongers, and sorcerers, and idolaters, and all liars" (Rev. 21:8).

Is the Fire in Hell Literal Fire?

Many people ask, "Is hell a lake of *literal* fire as we know fire?" I would answer that it is either literal fire, or something *worse in torment and intensity* than the fire we know!

"Hell" is a Bible term, and the Bible speaks of hell as a place that burns with fire and brimstone—*burning sulphur,* if you please. Suppose we compare Scripture with Scripture and see if we can justifiably believe that the fire in hell is *literal fire:*

Jesus was the first person to use the term "hell fire" in the Bible. In Matthew 5:22 He said, "Whosoever is angry with his brother without a cause shall be in danger of the judgment: and whosoever shall say to his brother, Raca, shall be in danger of the council: but whosoever shall say, Thou fool, shall be *in danger of hell fire."*

The hottest sermon ever preached on hell was preached—not by some fanatical preacher or evangelist, but by the tender, compassionate, loving Lamb of God! In Mark 9:43−48 we read His words:

"If thy hand offend thee, cut it off: it is better for thee to enter into life maimed, than having two hands to go into hell, into the *fire* that never shall be quenched: where their worm dieth not, and the *fire* is not quenched.

"And if thy foot offend thee, cut it off: it is better for thee to enter halt into life, than having two feet to be cast into hell, into the *fire* that never shall be quenched: where their worm dieth not, and the *fire* is not quenched.

"And if thine eye offend thee, pluck it out: it is better for thee to enter into the kingdom of God with one eye, than having two eyes to be cast into *hell fire:*

where their worm dieth not, and the *fire* is not quenched!"

In these verses, Jesus mentioned *fire* six times, and five times declared that the fire would never be quenched. It will burn forever and ever.

In Matthew 7:19 Jesus also said, "Every tree that bringeth not forth good fruit is hewn down, *and cast into the FIRE.*"

In John 15:6 He said, "If a man abide not in me, he is cast forth as a branch, and is withered; and men gather them, *and cast them into the FIRE, and they are burned.*"

In Matthew chapter 13 Jesus gave His disciples several parables, among them the parable of the tares and the wheat. In verse 30 of that chapter He said, "Let both (the tares and the wheat) grow together until the harvest: and in the time of harvest I will say to the reapers, *Gather ye together first the tares, and bind them in bundles TO BURN them:* but gather the wheat into my barn."

In verses 40—42 of that same chapter Jesus said, "As therefore the tares are gathered and *burned in the FIRE;* so shall it be in the end of this world. The Son of man shall send forth His angels, and they shall gather out of His kingdom all things that offend, and them which do iniquity; *and shall cast them into a furnace of FIRE:* there shall be wailing and gnashing of teeth!"

Wherever Jesus spoke, and whatever His subject, He always used words easily understood, illustrations with which His hearers were familiar. In these passages He spoke of FIRE—and illustrated His meaning in words that even a child could understand. The tree that brought forth no fruit was cut down and *"cast into the FIRE."* The branch that withered was *"cast into the FIRE."* The tares were gathered from among the wheat and *burned.* Do we not do these same things today? Certainly in this life we gather wood and branches—*and burn them in LITERAL FIRE.* I see no reason to believe that Jesus was speaking of anything but fire as we know fire.

In Hebrews 6:8 the Apostle Paul used practically the same illustration: "That which beareth thorns and briers is rejected, and is nigh unto cursing; *whose end is to be BURNED."*

Revelation 20:15 warns, "Whosoever was not found written in the book of life was *cast into the lake of FIRE,"* and Revelation 21:8 speaks of the various wicked who "shall have their part in *the lake which burneth with FIRE and brimstone:* which is the second death."

These Scriptures unquestionably reveal that the "fire" in hell is real. Read these passages, let the Bible speak and man keep silent, and hear what the Word of God has to say about "hell fire"!

The Second Death

If hell is a place of literal, everlasting fire—*and it IS*—then why does the Bible speak of the wicked dying "the second death"?

In the Word of God, "death" is a term applied to *unbelievers* who are still living *physically.* They have *life* in the sense of existing here on earth; but the life they have is not true life as God intended it to be. Jesus said, *"THIS is life eternal:* that they might know thee the only true God, and Jesus Christ, whom thou hast sent" (John 17:3).

In I John 1:2 we read, "The life was manifested, and we have seen it, and bear witness, and shew unto you *that eternal life, which was with the Father, and was manifested unto us."*

In the true sense of the word, men do not begin to live until they are in the right relationship with

God through the redemption that is in Christ Jesus who said, "I am come that they might have life, and that they might have it more abundantly" (John 10:10).

Thus we see that "life" in the Word of God is not merely *existing,* but *existing in the right relationship with GOD.* And "death" is not annihilation, but *existing in a state in which God never intended man to exist.*

Writing to the Ephesian believers Paul said, "You hath He quickened (made alive), who were *dead in trespasses and sins*" (Eph. 2:1). These people were living—yet they were *dead.* They were living *physically,* but they were dead *spiritually.* To all outward appearances they were living normal lives; but while they walked about, keeping their homes, carrying on their affairs of business, they were *dead,* spiritually speaking.

To Timothy Paul wrote, "She that liveth in pleasure is *DEAD while she LIVETH*" (I Tim. 5:6). Alive —yet dead.

Let us believe God, prepare to meet Him, and let Him handle His eternal program of dealing with men. Hell *is* a place of fire and brimstone, hell is everlasting, and the wicked *(already dead spiritually)* will die *eternally* in hell! They will die but they will never cease to exist, they will never cease to be conscious. They will not be burned up, they will be tormented day and night throughout the ceaseless ages of God's eternity:

"The same shall drink of *the wine of the wrath of God,* which is poured out *without mixture* into the cup of His indignation; and he shall be *tormented with fire and brimstone* in the presence of the holy angels, and in the presence of the Lamb: and *the smoke of their torment ascendeth up for ever and ever: and they have no rest day nor night . . .*" (Rev.

14:10, 11).

The Destiny of Believers

"And I heard a Voice from heaven saying unto me, Write, *Blessed are the dead which die in the Lord from henceforth:* Yea, saith the Spirit, *that they may REST from their labours;* and their works do follow them" (Rev. 14:13).

Thank God for these comforting, assuring words penned by John the Beloved under inspiration of God! When a born again believer departs this life he goes immediately to be with the Lord. There is no unconscious state between death and resurrection. To be absent from the body is to be immediately present with the Lord:

"For we know that if our earthly house of this tabernacle were dissolved, we have a building of God, an house not made with hands, eternal in the heavens. For in this we groan, earnestly desiring to be clothed upon with our house which is from heaven: If so be that being clothed we shall not be found naked. For we that are in this tabernacle do groan, being burdened: not for that we would be unclothed, but clothed upon, that mortality might be swallowed up of life.

"Now He that hath wrought us for the selfsame thing is God, who also hath given unto us the earnest of the Spirit. Therefore we are always confident, knowing that, whilst we are at home in the body, we are absent from the Lord: (For we walk by faith, not by sight:) We are confident, I say, and willing rather *to be absent from the body, and to be present with the Lord"* (II Cor. 5:1—8).

To the Philippian Christians Paul wrote, "For to me to live is Christ, and to die is gain. But if I live in the flesh, this is the fruit of my labour: yet what I shall choose I wot not. For I am in a strait betwixt

two, *having a desire to depart, and to be with Christ;*
which is far better: Nevertheless to abide in the flesh
is more needful for you" (Phil. 1:21—24).

The Apostle Paul definitely believed and taught
that the moment a Christian leaves this life he is at
once in the presence of God, with Jesus.

The Word of God records two most interesting
testimonies—one from a man who was burning in hell,
the other from a believer who was permitted to visit
the third heaven—Paradise.

In Luke 16:19—31 we read this testimony of a man
in hell: "There was a certain rich man, which was
clothed in purple and fine linen, and fared sumptuously
every day: and there was a certain beggar named
Lazarus, which was laid at his gate, full of sores,
and desiring to be fed with the crumbs which fell
from the rich man's table: moreover the dogs came
and licked his sores.

"And it came to pass, that the beggar died, and
was carried by the angels into Abraham's bosom:
*the rich man also died, and was buried; AND IN
HELL HE LIFT UP HIS EYES, BEING IN TOR-
MENTS, and seeth Abraham afar off, and Lazarus
in his bosom.*   And he cried and said, Father Abraham, have mercy on me, and send Lazarus, that he
may dip the tip of his finger in water, and cool my
tongue; *FOR I AM TORMENTED IN THIS FLAME!*

"But Abraham said, Son, *remember* that thou in
thy lifetime receivedst thy good things, and likewise
Lazarus evil things: but now he is comforted, *and
thou art TORMENTED.*   And beside all this, between
us and you there is a great gulf fixed: so that they
which would pass from hence to you cannot; neither
can they pass to us, that would come from thence.

"Then he said, I pray thee therefore, father, that
thou wouldest send him to my father's house: for I
have five brethren; that he may testify unto them,

lest they also come into this place of torment. Abraham saith unto him, They have Moses and the prophets; let them hear them. And he said, Nay, father Abraham: but if one went unto them from the dead, they will repent. And he said unto him, If they hear not Moses and the prophets, neither will they be persuaded, though one rose from the dead."

This testimony speaks for itself. This is not a parable, but the literal testimony of a man who died— and waked up in hell! I am sure he would agree that the fire in hell is literal fire!

Now hear the testimony of a man who visited Paradise. Many scholars believe that this was the Apostle Paul himself, and that this experience occurred when Paul was stoned at Lystra, and dragged outside the city to be left for dead. Be that as it may, this is the inspired record:

"It is not expedient for me doubtless to glory. I will come to visions and revelations of the Lord. I knew a man in Christ above fourteen years ago, (whether in the body, I cannot tell; or whether out of the body, I cannot tell: God knoweth;) such an one caught up to the third heaven. And I knew such a man, (whether in the body, or out of the body, I cannot tell: God knoweth;) How that he was caught up into Paradise, and heard unspeakable words, which it is not lawful for a man to utter. Of such an one will I glory: yet of myself I will not glory, but in mine infirmities.

"For though I would desire to glory, I shall not be a fool; for I will say the truth: but now I forbear, lest any man should think of me above that which he seeth me to be, or that he heareth of me. And lest I should be exalted above measure through the abundance of the revelations, there was given to me a thorn in the flesh, the messenger of Satan to buffet me, lest I should be exalted above measure.

"For this thing I besought the Lord thrice, that it might depart from me. And He said unto me, My grace is sufficient for thee: for my strength is made perfect in weakness. Most gladly therefore will I rather glory in my infirmities, that the power of Christ may rest upon me. Therefore I take pleasure in infirmities, in reproaches, in necessities, in persecutions, in distresses for Christ's sake: for when I am weak, then am I strong" (II Cor. 12:1—10).

My sincere hope is that each and every person who reads this book will be blessed in a peculiar and definite way.

In closing, I pray the words of the Apostle Paul, used at the close of his second letter to the believers in Corinth:

"The grace of the Lord Jesus Christ, and the love of God, and the communion of the Holy Ghost, be with you all. Amen" (II Cor. 13:14).

have I become like   June 17, 76
   the rose on the bush
✝ ~~Birds in the tree~~
✝ flowers in the tree
Birds on the thrush
                    June 18